||||||

AMERICAN INDIAN MYTHS AND LEGENDS

||||||

AMERICAN INDIAN

MYTHS AND LEGENDS

SELECTED AND EDITED BY
RICHARD ERDOES
AND ALFONSO ORTIZ

PANTHEON BOOKS
NEW YORK

Library of Congress Cataloging in Publication Data
Main entry under title:

American Indian myths and legends.
(Pantheon fairy tale & folklore library)
Bibliography: p.
Includes index.
1. Indians of North America—Legends.   2. Indians
of North America—Religion and mythology.   I. Erdoes,
Richard.   II. Ortiz, Alfonso, 1939–   .   III. Series.
E98.F6A47   1984   389.2'08997   84–42669
ISBN 0–394–50796–7

Grateful acknowledgment is made to the following for permission to reprint or adapt from previously published material. In the case of adaptation, the authors may have retitled the tales.

"Origin of the Gnawing Beaver" and "The Flood," adapted from *Haïda Myths Illustrated in Argillite Carvings*, edited by Marius Barbeau, Bulletin no. 127, Anthropological Series no. 32 (Ottawa, 1953), pp. 52–56 and 184–185. By permission of the National Museum of Man, National Museums of Canada.

"How Coyote Got His Cunning" and "The Coming of Thunder" from *California Indian Nights Entertainments* by E. W. Gifford. Copyright © 1930 by the Arthur H. Clark Company. By permission of the Arthur H. Clark Company.

"Coyote Fights a Lump of Pitch," "Coyote Gets Rich Off the White Men," "Coyote Steals Sun's Tobacco," and "Turkey Makes the Corn and Coyote Plants It" from "Tales of the White Mountain Apache" by Grenville Goodwin in *Memoirs of the American Folklore Society*, vol. 33. Copyright © 1939 by the American Folklore Society. By permission of the American Folklore Society.

"Always-Living-at-the-Coast," "Coyote and the Mallard Ducks," and "Coyote Takes Water from the Frog People" from *Giving Birth to Thunder, Sleeping with His Daughter* by Barry Holstun Lopez. Copyright © 1977 by Barry Holstun Lopez. By permission of the author and Andrews & McMeel, Inc., Fairway, Kansas.

"Apache Chief Punishes His Wife" from "Taos Tales" by Elsie Clews Parsons in *Memoirs of the American Folklore Society*, vol. 34. Copyright © 1940 by the American Folklore Society. By permission of the American Folklore Society.

"A Legend of Multnomah Falls," "Creation of the Animal People," "Creation of the Yakima World," "People Brought in a Basket," "Kulshan and His Two Wives," "When Grizzlies Walked Upright," "Pushing Up the Sky," "The Elk Spirit of Lost Lake," and "Playing a Trick on the Moon" from *Indian Legends of the Pacific Northwest* by Ella E. Clark. Copyright © 1953 by the Regents of the University of California. By permission of the University of California Press.

"The Buffalo Go" from *American Indian Mythology* by Alice Marriott and Carol K. Rachlin (Thomas Y. Crowell Co.). Copyright © 1968 by Alice Marriott and Carol K. Rachlin. By permission of Harper & Row, Publishers, Inc.

Typography and binding design by Susan Mitchell

Manufactured in the United States of America
24689753

C O N T E N T S

INTRODUCTION   xi

■ PART ONE ■

RABBIT BOY KICKED THAT BLOOD CLOT AROUND:
TALES OF HUMAN CREATION   1

RABBIT BOY (WHITE RIVER SIOUX)   5

BLOOD CLOT (SOUTHERN UTE)   8

CORN MOTHER (PENOBSCOT)   11

CREATION OF THE ANIMAL PEOPLE (OKANOGAN)   14

STONE BOY (BRULE SIOUX)   15

THE POWERFUL BOY (SENECA)   20

GLOOSCAP AND THE BABY (ALGONQUIAN)   25

THE OLD WOMAN OF THE SPRING (CHEYENNE)   26

ARROW BOY (CHEYENNE)   29

THE GREAT MEDICINE DANCE (CHEYENNE)   33

THE ORIGIN OF CURING CEREMONIES
(WHITE MOUNTAIN APACHE)   37

CREATION OF FIRST MAN AND
FIRST WOMAN (NAVAJO)   39

HOW MEN AND WOMEN GOT TOGETHER
(BLOOD-PIEGAN)   41

THE WELL-BAKED MAN (PIMA)   46

THE WHITE BUFFALO WOMAN (BRULE SIOUX)   47

THE ORPHAN BOY AND THE ELK DOG (BLACKFOOT)   53

SALT WOMAN IS REFUSED FOOD (COCHITI)   61

THE SACRED WEED (BLACKFOOT)   62

HOW GRANDFATHER PEYOTE CAME TO THE
INDIAN PEOPLE (BRULE SIOUX)   65

THE VISION QUEST (BRULE SIOUX)   69

■ **PART TWO** ■

THE PLACE OF EMERGENCE:
TALES OF WORLD CREATION   73

THE GOOD TWIN AND THE EVIL TWIN (YUMA)   77

THE JICARILLA GENESIS (JICARILLA APACHE)   83

WHEN GRIZZLIES WALKED UPRIGHT (MODOC)   85

OLD MAN COYOTE MAKES THE WORLD (CROW)   88

HOW THE SIOUX CAME TO BE (BRULE SIOUX)   93

PUSHING UP THE SKY (SNOHOMISH)   95

EMERGING INTO THE UPPER WORLD (ACOMA)   97

EARTH MAKING (CHEROKEE)   105

THE EARTH DRAGON (NORTHERN CALIFORNIA COAST)   107

PEOPLE BROUGHT IN A BASKET (MODOC)   109

GREAT MEDICINE MAKES A
BEAUTIFUL COUNTRY (CHEYENNE)   111

THE WHITE DAWN OF THE HOPI (HOPI)   115

CREATION OF THE YAKIMA WORLD (YAKIMA)   117

CHILDREN OF THE SUN (OSAGE)   119

THE VOICE, THE FLOOD, AND THE TURTLE (CADDO)   120

A TALE OF ELDER BROTHER (PIMA)   122

■ **PART THREE** ■

THE EYE OF THE GREAT SPIRIT:
TALES OF THE SUN, MOON, AND STARS   125

SUN CREATION (BRULE SIOUX)   129

WALKS-ALL-OVER-THE-SKY (TSIMSHIAN)   136

THREE-LEGGED RABBIT FIGHTS THE SUN
(WESTERN ROCKIES)   139

COYOTE STEALS THE SUN AND MOON (ZUNI)   140

KEEPING WARMTH IN A BAG (SLAVEY)   143

THE HOPI BOY AND THE SUN (HOPI)   145

A GUST OF WIND (OJIBWAY)   150

DAUGHTER OF THE SUN (CHEROKEE)   152

GRANDMOTHER SPIDER STEALS THE SUN (CHEROKEE)   154

THE STORY OF THE CREATION (DIEGUEÑOS)   156

THE FOOLISH GIRLS (OJIBWAY)   158

MOON RAPES HIS SISTER SUN (INUIT)   161

SUN TEACHES VEEHO A LESSON (CHEYENNE)   162

LITTLE BROTHER SNARES THE SUN (WINNEBAGO)   164

THE SCABBY ONE LIGHTS THE SKY (TOLTEC)   166

PLAYING A TRICK ON THE MOON (SNOQUALMIE)   168

THE THEFT OF LIGHT (TSIMSHIAN)   169

COYOTE PLACES THE STARS (WASCO)   171
DEER HUNTER AND WHITE CORN MAIDEN (TEWA)   173

■ PART FOUR ■

ORDEALS OF THE HERO:
MONSTERS AND MONSTER SLAYERS   177

GLOOSCAP FIGHTS THE WATER MONSTER
(PASSAMAQUODDY, MICMAC, AND MALISEET)   181

LITTLE-MAN-WITH-HAIR-ALL-OVER (MÉTIS)   185

HOW MOSQUITOES CAME TO BE (TLINGIT)   192

HIAWATHA THE UNIFIER (IROQUOIS)   193

THE LIFE AND DEATH OF SWEET MEDICINE
(NORTHERN CHEYENNE)   199

THE QUILLWORK GIRL AND
HER SEVEN STAR BROTHERS (CHEYENNE)   205

ROLLING HEAD (WINTU)   209

SON OF LIGHT KILLS THE MONSTER (HOPI)   211

THE COMING OF THUNDER (MIWOK)   216

WAKINYAN TANKA, THE GREAT THUNDERBIRD
(BRULE SIOUX)   218

COYOTE KILLS THE GIANT (FLATHEAD)   223

A LEGEND OF DEVIL'S TOWER (SIOUX)   225

THE FLYING HEAD (IROQUOIS)   227

THE FIRST SHIP (CHINOOK)   229

CHASE OF THE SEVERED HEAD (CHEYENNE)   230

UNCEGILA'S SEVENTH SPOT (BRULE SIOUX)   237

■ PART FIVE ■

COUNTING COUP: WAR AND THE WARRIOR CODE   243

LITTLE MOUSE COUNTING COUP (BRULE SIOUX)   247

TWO BULLETS AND TWO ARROWS (BRULE SIOUX)   248

A CHEYENNE BLANKET (PAWNEE)   251

THE WARRIOR MAIDEN (ONEIDA)   252

THE SIEGE OF COURTHOUSE ROCK
(WHITE RIVER SIOUX)   254

CHIEF ROMAN NOSE LOSES HIS MEDICINE
(WHITE RIVER SIOUX)   256

BRAVE WOMAN COUNTS COUP (WHITE RIVER SIOUX)   258

SPOTTED EAGLE AND BLACK CROW
(WHITE RIVER SIOUX)   260

WHERE THE GIRL SAVED HER BROTHER (CHEYENNE)   264

TATANKA IYOTAKE'S DANCING HORSE (BRULE SIOUX)   267

■ PART SIX ■
THE SOUND OF FLUTES:
TALES OF LOVE AND LUST   271

THE LEGEND OF THE FLUTE (BRULE SIOUX)   275

TEACHING THE MUDHEADS
HOW TO COPULATE (ZUNI)   279

THE FIGHT FOR A WIFE (ALEUT)   281

TEETH IN THE WRONG PLACES (PONCA-OTOE)   283

THE STOLEN WIFE (TEWA)   285

TOLOWIM WOMAN AND BUTTERFLY MAN (MAIDU)   290

APACHE CHIEF PUNISHES HIS WIFE (TIWA)   291

THE HUSBAND'S PROMISE (TEWA)   295

THE MAN WHO MARRIED THE MOON
(ISLETA PUEBLO)   298

WHY MOLE LIVES UNDERGROUND (CHEROKEE)   305

A LEGEND OF MULTNOMAH FALLS (MULTNOMAH)   306

THE INDUSTRIOUS DAUGHTER WHO
WOULD NOT MARRY (COCHITI)   308

THE WOMAN WHO MARRIED A MERMAN (COOS)   312

COYOTE'S STRAWBERRY (CROW)   314

THE FAITHFUL WIFE AND
THE WOMAN WARRIOR (TIWA)   315

COYOTE AND THE MALLARD DUCKS (NEZ PERCÉ)   318

THE GREEDY FATHER (KAROK)   320

KULSHAN AND HIS TWO WIVES (LUMNI)   321

MEN AND WOMEN TRY LIVING APART (SIA)   324

A CONTEST FOR WIVES (COCHITI)   326

THE SERPENT OF THE SEA (ZUNI)   327

■ PART SEVEN ■
COYOTE LAUGHS AND CRIES: TRICKSTER TALES   333

COYOTE, IKTOME, AND THE ROCK
(WHITE RIVER SIOUX)   337

WHAT'S THIS? MY BALLS FOR YOUR DINNER?
(WHITE RIVER SIOUX)   339

COYOTE AND WASICHU (BRULE SIOUX)   342

HOW BEAVER STOLE FIRE FROM THE PINES
(NEZ PERCÉ)   343

THE RAVEN (ATHAPASCAN)   344

THE BLUEBIRD AND COYOTE (PIMA)   346

ADVENTURES OF GREAT RABBIT (ALGONQUIAN)   347

TURKEY MAKES THE CORN AND COYOTE PLANTS IT
(WHITE MOUNTAIN APACHE)   352

COYOTE TAKES WATER FROM THE
FROG PEOPLE (KALAPUYA) 355

HOW THE PEOPLE GOT ARROWHEADS (SHASTA) 356

IKTOME AND THE IGNORANT GIRL (BRULE SIOUX) 358

COYOTE FIGHTS A LUMP OF PITCH
(WHITE MOUNTAIN APACHE) 359

ALWAYS-LIVING-AT-THE-COAST (KWAKIUTL) 362

GLOOSCAP GRANTS THREE WISHES (ALGONQUIAN) 365

COYOTE'S RABBIT CHASE (TEWA) 368

COYOTE GETS RICH OFF THE WHITE MEN
(WHITE MOUNTAIN APACHE) 369

IKTOME SLEEPS WITH HIS WIFE BY MISTAKE
(BRULE SIOUX) 372

HOW TO SCARE A BEAR (TEWA) 375

COYOTE STEALS SUN'S TOBACCO
(WHITE MOUNTAIN APACHE) 377

DOING A TRICK WITH EYEBALLS
(NORTHERN CHEYENNE) 379

IKTOME HAS A BAD DREAM (BRULE SIOUX) 381

HOW COYOTE GOT HIS CUNNING (KAROK) 382

COYOTE AND THE TWO FROG WOMEN (ALSEA) 384

COYOTE DANCES WITH A STAR (CHEYENNE) 385

■ PART EIGHT ■

FOUR LEGS, TWO LEGS, AND NO LEGS: STORIES OF ANIMALS AND OTHER PEOPLE 387

THE GREAT RACE (CHEYENNE) 390

ORIGIN OF THE GNAWING BEAVER (HAIDA) 392

HOW THE CROW CAME TO BE BLACK (BRULE SIOUX) 395

THE GIRL WHO MARRIED RATTLESNAKE (POMO) 397

WHY THE OWL HAS BIG EYES (IROQUOIS) 398

THE OWL HUSBAND (PASSAMAQUODDY) 399

THE DOGS HOLD AN ELECTION (BRULE SIOUX) 403

THE SNAKE BROTHERS (BRULE SIOUX) 404

BUTTERFLIES (PAPAGO) 407

THE REVENGE OF BLUE CORN EAR MAIDEN (HOPI) 409

THE MEETING OF THE WILD ANIMALS (TSIMSHIAN) 413

A FISH STORY (TEWA) 415

THE NEGLECTFUL MOTHER (COCHITI) 417

THE BEAR AND HIS INDIAN WIFE (HAIDA) 419

WAKIASH AND THE FIRST TOTEM POLE (KWAKIUTL) 423

■ PART NINE ■

SOMETHING WHISTLING IN THE NIGHT: GHOSTS AND THE SPIRIT WORLD   427

TWO GHOSTLY LOVERS (BRULE SIOUX)   432

THE MAN WHO WAS AFRAID OF NOTHING (BRULE SIOUX)   435

✓ THE LAND OF THE DEAD (SERRANO)   438

THE DOUBLE-FACED GHOST (CHEYENNE)   439

A JOURNEY TO THE SKELETON HOUSE (HOPI)   442

THE SKELETON WHO FELL DOWN PIECE BY PIECE (ISLETA PUEBLO)   446

THE SPIRIT WIFE (ZUNI)   447

THE TRANSFORMED GRANDMOTHER (PIMA-PAPAGO)   451

BIG EATER'S WIFE (PEQUOD)   453

THE ORIGIN OF THE HOPI SNAKE DANCE (TEWA)   455

BLUE JAY VISITS GHOST TOWN (CHINOOK)   457

THE GHOST WIFE (BRULE SIOUX)   462

■ PART TEN ■

ONLY THE ROCKS AND MOUNTAINS LAST FOREVER: VISIONS OF THE END   465

WOMAN CHOOSES DEATH (BLACKFOOT)   469

COYOTE AND THE ORIGIN OF DEATH (CADDO)   470

THE FLOOD (HAIDA)   472

THE SEER WHO WOULD NOT SEE (PIMA)   473

THE ELK SPIRIT OF LOST LAKE (WASCO)   475

THE DEATH OF HEAD CHIEF AND YOUNG MULE (NORTHERN CHEYENNE)   477

THE GHOST DANCE AT WOUNDED KNEE (BRULE SIOUX)   481

THE GNAWING (CHEYENNE)   484

THE END OF THE WORLD (WHITE RIVER SIOUX)   485

MONTEZUMA AND THE GREAT FLOOD (PAPAGO)   487

THE BUFFALO GO (KIOWA)   490

THE COMING OF WASICHU (BRULE SIOUX)   491

REMAKING THE WORLD (BRULE SIOUX)   496

APPENDIX   500

BIBLIOGRAPHY   522

INDEX OF TALES   526

INTRODUCTION

The 166 legends recorded here come from the heart and soul of the native people of North America. Some have been told for thousands of years, and they are still being told and retold, reshaped and refitted to meet their audience's changing needs, even created anew out of a contemporary man's or woman's vision. They arise out of the earth—the plants, herbs, and animals which are integral parts of the human realm. They are imbedded in the ancient languages and flow according to the rhythms of the natural world—a different pace indeed from that of a technological, man-made environment. Most industrialized people, eyes ever on the clock, fragmented by the pressing problems of a split-second, microchip society, have little time or inclination, it seems, to speculate on the communal nature of the universe. Mutually shared and supportive legends about the beginning and end of the world (and what happens in between) seem hopelessly beyond their vision.

The native American, following the pace of "Indian time," still lives connected to the nurturing womb of mythology. Mysterious but real power dwells in nature—in mountains, rivers, rocks, even pebbles. White people may consider them inanimate objects, but to the Indian, they are enmeshed in the web of the universe, pulsating with life and potent with medicine. As Ernst Cassirer has written, "The mythical world is at a much more fluid and fluctuating stage than our theoretical world . . . The world of myth is a dramatical world—a world of actions, of forces, of conflicting powers. In every phenomenon of nature it sees the collision of these powers. Mythical perception is always impregnated with these emotional qualities."*

The world of the Pueblo Indians is bounded mythically and geographically by four sacred mountains, where holy men still go on pilgrimages

---

* *An Essay on Man: An Introduction to a Philosophy of Human Culture.* Yale University Press, New Haven, 1962.

to pray for rain and to gather medicines. The associations between geography and mythic events are strong; the mountains of the Northwest, for example, were believed by the native inhabitants to have once been people who fought, schemed, loved, and were eventually given the form they now have by the all-powerful One, mostly as punishment for making trouble. The firmament is filled with stars and planets who were once on earth, human lovers fated to chase each other across the evening sky into eternity. Such roles are not fixed, either; the sun, moon, and morning star seem free to take human form and roam the earth, seeking love and other adventures.

The links between the historic past and the present through myth are strong. Archeologists' evidence shows that the Iroquois of the Northeast have possessed a viable material culture continuously for several thousand years, a chain reflected in an extant body of folklore which has survived despite the attempts of many generations of white society to eradicate (or negatively stereotype) Indian history and culture. The effects of white culture on many other regions, with the notable exceptions of the Southwest and the Plains, and to a degree the Northwest, have been devastating, with whole bodies of Indian literature erased, or warped beyond recognition in their contemporary representations.

Where legends endure, they do so fiercely. Tunka, the stone god, is the Sioux's oldest god, and men still carry oddly shaped pebbles, bits of flint, or lumps of fossil agate in their medicine bundles. They still pray to special sacred rocks and tell legends about them. Rivers, lakes, waterfalls, and mountains are the abodes of spirits and often appear as living characters in stories. Even today a Sioux or Cheyenne might say, "I felt the sacred pipe move in my hands. It was alive. Power flowed from it." Or, "When I touched the sacred sun dance pole, I felt that it was flesh, warm flesh." The ancient tokens and symbols still exist and are carefully preserved. Modern equipment is no match. When the Sioux medicine man Lame Deer first traveled on a modern jet, he immediately related his Boeing 707 to the Wakinyan, the Thunderbirds, whose awesome power ignites the lightning. The airplane suffered greatly by comparison.

To those used to the patterns of European fairy tales and folktales, Indian legends often seem chaotic, inconsistent, or incomplete. Plots seem to travel at their own speed, defying convention and at times doing away completely with recognizable beginnings and endings. Coyote is a powerful creator one moment, a sniveling coward the next. Infants display alarming talents or powers; births and deaths alternate as fast as night and day. To try to apply conventional (Western) logic is not only impossible but unnecessary; spinning out a single image or episode may be the salient feature of—indeed, the whole reason for—telling a tale, and stories are often told in chains, one word, character, or idea bringing to mind a related one, prompting another storyteller to offer a contribution. The howling wind, the bubbling brook, the shrieking magpie all suggest, in their vital immediacy, stories, out of which legends are created. Stories are told for adults and children alike, as elements in solemn ceremonies and as spontaneous creations. Rather then being self-contained units, they are often incomplete episodes in a progression that goes back deep into a tribe's traditions.

Long ago Hubert Howe Bancroft wrote, "Language is thought incarnate; mythology soul incarnate. The one is the instrument of thought, the other the essence of thought. In mythology, language assumes personality and independence. Often the significance of the words becomes the essential idea."* Thus the word for "sun" becomes the name of the sun god, the word for "moon" the name of the moon goddess. The words themselves take on potency, as the Sioux medicine man Leonard Crow Dog explains:

Our modern Sioux language has been white-manized. There's no power in it. I get my knowledge of the old tales of my people out of a drum, or the sound of a flute, out of my visions and out of our sacred herb *pejuta*, but above all out of the ancient words from way back, the words of the grandfathers, the language that was there at the beginning of time, the language given to We-Ota-Wichasha, Blood Clot Boy. If that language, these words, should ever die, then our legends will die too.

In this volume we offer titles and categories for different tales, but these are, in the end, arbitrary appendages for a reader's convenience. No child will ask her grandfather to tell the story of the first arrival of winter, but will clamor instead, "Tell me again about Iktome getting caught when he steals food," or "Tell us about where the girl saved her brother." The tales can be divided in infinite ways, and we hope the chapters we have selected show both the common elements that run through stories told at opposite ends of the continent and the rich diversity of detail.

Legends, of course, vary according to a people's way of life, the geography and the climate in which they live, the food they eat and the way they obtain it. The nomadic buffalo hunters of the Plains tell stories very different from those of Eastern forest dwellers. To the Southwestern

---

* "The Native Races," *Myths and Languages*, vol. 3, A. L. Bancroft & Co., San Francisco, 1883, p. 305.

planters and harvesters, the coming of corn and the changing of seasons are of primal concern, while people of the Northwest who make their living from the sea fill their tales with ocean monsters, swift harpooners, and powerful boatbuilders. All tribes have spun narratives as well for the features of their landscape: how this river came to be, when these mountains were formed, how our coastline was carved.

Legends as well as cultures overlap and influence each other, not only when people of different tribes live in adjacent territory, but even when they encounter each other through migration or trade over long distances. Excavations of a pre-Columbian Hohokam site in Arizona uncovered a Mayan-style ball court, a hard rubber ball, copper bells, and exotic parrot feathers, all of which had to have come from central Mexico, more than a thousand miles away. An Aztec-like image of the male face of the sun, surrounded by rays, is found painted and chipped into rock walls of the Southwestern United States as well as in contemporary Pueblo art. Nao'tsiti, the lost White Sister, and Bahana, the White Brother of Hopi prophecy, may embody memories of the Mayan Kukulcan or the Aztec Quetzalcoatl, the white Plumed Serpent god who comes from the east across the Great Water. Images and tokens were carried to faraway peoples along with trade goods; white seashells and abalone shells are mentioned several times in ancient myths as ritual objects in areas five hundred to a thousand miles from the Pacific Coast.

Yet with all their regional images and variations, a common theme binds these tales together—a universal concern with fundamental issues about the world in which humans live. We encounter again and again, in a fantastic spectrum of forms, North and South, East and West, the story of the children of the sun, of the twin brothers who bring culture, of the sacred four directions, of worlds piled on top of each other, of primordial waters, of perpetual destruction and re-creation, of powerful heroes and tricksters—Veeho, Rabbit, Coyote, and Spider Man.

History enters the mythic world obliquely, but leaves its definite mark in characters and incidents. Many tales and cycles embody the collective experience of a particular tribe, perhaps compacting into a single dramatic myth migrations, natural disasters, and other major events that occurred over generations and centuries, with mythically transformed references to "historical" episodes—the creation and fall from power of the Iroquois League; first sightings and later encounters with Europeans and other whites, beginning with missionaries and traders, later with armed soldiers; the suppression of religion by the Spanish and the Pueblo uprisings of 1680; the arrival in and displacement from traditional homelands and the accompanying deaths or devastations; the dramatic watershed encounters at Fort Stanwix and at Rosebud, Little Bighorn, and

Wounded Knee. By moving often cataclysmic events into the realm of myth or folklore, the storyteller can at once celebrate, mourn, and honor the past—and look ahead to a time when the great heroes may return to their people, bearing powerful medicine to restore former glory.

But these legends do not merely confront cosmic questions about the world as a whole. They are also magic lenses through which we can glimpse social orders and daily life: how families were organized, how political structures operated, how men caught fish, how religious ceremonies felt to the people who took part, how power was divided between men and women, how food was prepared, how honor in war was celebrated. The images that transmit certain timeless concerns are resonant: in one account of the conflict between the sexes, men and women decide to live in separate camps, divided not only by anger and a brooding sense of injustice, but by a mighty river as well. Anthropological accounts seem pale in comparison.

In the end, however, these legends are not told merely for enjoyment, or for education, or for amusement: they are believed. They are emblems of a living religion, giving concrete form to a set of beliefs and traditions that link people living today to ancestors from centuries and millennia past. As Bronislaw Malinowski said, "Myth in its living, primitive form is not merely a story told but a reality lived."

A Note on How These Stories Were Selected

Many of the stories were collected by the authors themselves over a period of twenty-five years. Some of these have never appeared in print before; others which have been circulating for years appear here in a new form as narrated by today's storytellers, freshly translated into English where necessary. Some of the Plains Indian tales were jotted down at powwows, around campfires, even inside a moving car. Most of them were taped, and a few have been edited so that they are understandable in this form.

A second group of tales are classic accounts, which appear here in their original form. A third group come from nineteenth-century sources which, while containing the nuggets of the original tales, were also embellished in the somewhat artificial style typical of the period. The authors have retold these tales to restore them to a more authentic and less stilted form.

PART ONE

RABBIT BOY KICKED THAT BLOOD CLOT AROUND

TALES OF

HUMAN CREATION

Creation myths deal with both how the physical world as we know it came to be and how the many features of specific cultures originated. While the tales in Parts Two and Three will deal with the first theme, the stories here grapple with those permanently vexing questions about the human condition. How and when did gods and humans become separated? Where did Indians get certain important elements in their daily life—foodstuffs like salt or corn, animals like the buffalo or horse, religious artifacts and ceremonies? Why are men and women different, and when did the separation take place? Where did the different races come from? How did evil enter the world? What is death and how does it move in and out of life?

These legends of human creation and the bringing of culture reflect in myriad ways a common belief that people are living part of a natural world, brother and sister to the grain and the trees, the buffalo and the bear. Some Great Lakes tribes recount how they were originally made by the Great Sun or (with the Ojibway) Great Mystery. According to numerous others, the first woman was impregnated by (in the Southwest) a sunbeam, (in the Northwest) a salmon, or as the Iroquois say, by the west wind, giving birth to twin heroes who perform famous deeds. The creation myth of the Great Lakes Algonquians focuses on the wanderings of the god Glooscap, who tames the winds, obtains food and water for the people, and fashions various features of the landscape. He eventually goes off to the west to live in another world, where he makes arrows in preparation for the battle of the last day.

The first human child is often endowed with supernatural powers; it outshines and outwits adults, grows up overnight, or performs great magic like a full-fledged medicine man. His mischief does good, too; disregarding his parents, he wanders away from the camp, perhaps meets and slays a monster or two, receives a token of magic or power, and often encounters an old woman (perhaps his nurse) who puts an ogre in his path to rid herself of his powerful presence. The results of these adventures are significant watermarks in the creation of a culture; before Stone Boy was born, the Sioux had no sacred ceremonies or prayers to guide them. Their spiritual development began when a pile of rocks instructed Stone Boy to build a sweat lodge for purification, for life, for *wichosani*, health.

On the other hand, the Brule Sioux say it was an old woman who was chosen to show her people the way to Grandfather Peyote, the sacred medicine that bestows health and power. Another heroine, White Buffalo Woman, was a spirit who took the form of a beautiful maiden in shining white buckskin. She gave the tribes great herds of buffalo and taught them how to worship, how to marry, and how to cook. Her task completed, she walked away, stopped and rolled over, and turned into a black buffalo, a brown one, a red one, and finally into the sacred white buffalo calf.

Other culture heroines include Changing Woman of the Navajo, Turquoise Woman, White Shell Woman, and the Cheyenne's Little Sister, who calls the buffalo and feeds the people. The attributes of these heroines are often associated with fertility, conception, pregnancy, and birth. Corn maidens bring the all-nourishing maize and the knowledge of planting. They also invent pottery and basketry, as their association with seeds and grains is also with containers and storage. Women are often in charge of the flint which sparks the first cooking fire.

The origins of the grand medicine lodge is a prominent part of the creation myth of the Great Lakes region, which features (like many others) a central set of twins, children of the west wind. When Wolf Brother is drowned by evil manitous as he crosses an icy lake, he is brought back to life by the lamentations of Manabozho, White Rabbit, which become the foundation of the lodge. This particular myth has an important characteristic in common with creation stories from further west: the culture hero (or heroes) is at the same time a trickster and a fool. He may breathe life into humans and be responsible for giving them important features of their daily life. But he may also have the lustful or thieving urges that give *him* his life. "All living things," one Sioux elder says, "are tied together with a common navel cord"—the tall mountains and streams, the corn and the grazing buffalo, the bravest hero and the deceitful Coyote.

RABBIT BOY

[WHITE RIVER SIOUX]

*This is a story of Rabbit Boy; in some tribes it is called the story of
Blood Clot Man. "As you know," Jenny Leading Cloud said, "we
Indians think of the earth and the whole universe as a never-ending
circle, and in this circle man is just another animal. The buffalo and
the coyote are our brothers; the birds, our cousins. Even the tiniest
ant, even a louse, even the smallest flower you can find—they are
all relatives. We end our prayers with the words* mitakuye oyasin—
*'all my relations'—and that includes everything that grows, crawls,
runs, creeps, hops, and flies on this continent. White people see
man as nature's master and conqueror, but Indians, who are close
to nature, know better."*

In the old, old days, before Columbus "discovered" us, as they say, we
were even closer to the animals than we are now. Many people could
understand the animal languages; they could talk to a bird, gossip with
a butterfly. Animals could change themselves into people, and people
into animals. It was a time when the earth was not quite finished, when
many kinds of mountains and streams, animals and plants came into
being according to nature's plan.

In these far-gone days, hidden from us as in a mist, there lived a
rabbit—a very lively, playful, good-hearted rabbit. One day this rabbit
was walking, enjoying himself, when he came across a clot of blood.
How it got there, nobody knows. It looked like a blister, a little bladder
full of red liquid. Well, the playful rabbit began toying with that clot of
blood, kicking it around as if it were a tiny ball.

Now, we Indians believe in Takuskanskan, the mysterious power of
motion. Its spirit is in anything that moves. It animates things and makes
them come alive. Well, the rabbit got into this strange moving power
without even knowing it, and the motion of being kicked around, or
rather the spirit of the motion—and I hope you can grasp what I mean
by that—began to work on the little blob of blood so that it took shape,
forming a little gut. The rabbit kicked it some more, and the blob began

to grow tiny hands and arms. The rabbit kept nudging it, and suddenly it had eyes and a beating heart. In this way the rabbit, with the help of the mysterious moving power, formed a human being, a little boy. The rabbit called him We-Ota-Wichasha, Much-Blood Boy, but he is better known as Rabbit Boy.

The rabbit took him to his wife, and both of them loved this strange little boy as if he were their only son. They dressed him up in a beautiful buckskin shirt, which they painted with the sacred red color and decorated with designs made of porcupine quills. The boy grew up happily among the rabbits. When he was almost a man, the old rabbit took him aside and said: "Son, I must tell you that you are not what you think you are—a rabbit like me. You are a human. We love you and we hate to let you go, but you must leave and find your own people."

Rabbit Boy started walking until he came to a village of human beings, where he saw boys who looked like himself. He went into the village. The people could not help staring at this strange boy in his beautiful buckskin clothes. "Where are you from?" they asked him. "I am from another village," said Rabbit Boy, though this was not true. There was no other village in the whole world, for as I told you, the earth was still in its beginning.

In the village was a beautiful girl who fell in love with Rabbit Boy, not only for his fine clothes, but also for his good looks and kind heart. Her people, too, wanted him to marry into the village, wanted a man with his great mystery power to live among them. And Rabbit Boy had a vision. In it he was wrestling with the sun, racing the sun, playing hand games with the sun—and always winning.

But, Iktome, the wicked Spider Man, the mean trickster, prankster, and witch doctor, wanted that beautiful girl for himself. He began to say bad things about Rabbit Boy. "Look at him," Iktome said, "showing off his buckskin outfit to us who are too poor to have such fine things." And to the men he also said: "How come you're letting him marry a girl from your village?" He also told them: "In case you want me to, I have a magic hoop to throw over that Rabbit Boy. It will make him helpless."

Several boys said, "Iktome is right." They were jealous of Rabbit Boy on account of his strange power, his wisdom and generosity. They began to fight him, and Spider Man threw his magic hoop over him. Though it had no effect on Rabbit Boy, he pretended to be helpless to amuse himself.

The village boys and young men tied Rabbit Boy to a tree with rawhide thongs. All the time, the evil Spider Man was encouraging them: "Let's take our butchering knives and cut him up!"

"Friends, *kola-pila*," said Rabbit Boy, "if you are going to kill me, let me sing my death song first." And he sang:

> *Friends, friends,*
> *I have fought the sun.*
> *He tried to burn me up,*
> *But he could not do it.*
> *Even battling the sun,*
> *I held my own.*

After the death song, the villagers killed Rabbit Boy and cut him up into chunks of meat, which they put in a soup pot. But Rabbit Boy was not hurt easily. A storm arose, and a great cloud hid the face of the sun, turning everything into black night.

When the cloud was gone, the chunks of meat had disappeared without a trace. But those who had watched closely had seen the chunks forming up again into a body, had seen him going up to heaven on a beam of sunlight. A wise old medicine man said, "This Rabbit Boy really has powerful medicine: he has gone up to see the sun. Soon he will come back stronger than before, because up there he will be given the sun's power. Let's marry him to that girl of ours."

But the jealous spider, Iktome, said, "Why bother about him? Look at me: I am much more powerful than Rabbit Boy! Here, tie me up too; cut me up! Be quick!" Iktome thought he remembered Rabbit Boy's song. He thought there was power in it—magic strength. But Iktome did not remember the words right. He sang:

> Friends, friends,
> I have fought the moon,
> She tried to fight,
> But I won.
> Even battling the moon,
> I came out on top.

They cut Iktome up, as he had told them, but he never came to life again. The spider had finally outsmarted himself. Evil tricksters always do.

—*Told by Jenny Leading Cloud in White River Rosebud*
Indian Reservation, South Dakota, 1967,
and recorded by Richard Erdoes.

BLOOD CLOT

[SOUTHERN UTE]

Unlike the previous tale, here the baby is born from a clot of buffalo blood and derives his power from the mighty buffalo tribe.

Long ago a very old man and his wife lived alone and hunted for game, but it was scarce and they were hungry. One day the man discovered some buffalo tracks and followed them to the place where the animal had stopped. There he found only a big clot of blood, which he wrapped in his shirt and carried home.

The old man told his wife to boil the blood, and she put it into the kettle with water from the creek. But before it came to a boil over the fire, they heard cries inside the kettle. The man ran up to it and pulled out a baby, a little boy, who had somehow formed out of the blood clot.

The old couple washed the baby and wrapped him up. By the next morning he had grown much larger, and that day he continued to grow until he could crawl about by himself. The second day he was able to walk a little; by the third day he was walking with ease. The couple called him Blood Clot and came to treat him as their son.

The old man made little arrows so that the child could learn to shoot. Soon Blood Clot needed larger arrows, and with them he began to hunt birds and other small game. He never brought the game home himself, but sent the old man for it. One day Blood Clot returned from hunting and said, "I have killed something with a striped back." The man went out and fetched an animal a little bigger than a mouse, which he cooked for the three of them. The next day the boy announced, "I have killed a white short-tailed animal." It was a cottontail, which the man also cooked.

The day after that, Blood Clot went farther and killed a badger. "I have killed an animal in a hole in the ground," he said, and the man brought the creature home and cooked it. The following day when the boy returned, he said, "I have killed an animal with black ears and a black tail." To the old man's joy, it was a female deer. The three of them ate and were happy.

Next Blood Clot said, "I have killed a big fellow with big antlers." It was an elk, so again the family feasted on meat. The old man gave the boy a full-sized bow and arrows, and Blood Clot went into the mountains and shot a mountain goat. "I have killed an animal with big horns in the mountains," he said when he came down. "Every day," the old man said proudly, "he kills a different kind of animal."

Now their troubles were over, and they had an easy time. Blood Clot killed a mountain lion. Then he tracked and shot an otter: "I have killed an animal with nice fur, living in the water." The old man tanned the skin to make strings for tying the boy's braids. The following day Blood Clot found a beaver: "I have killed a water animal with a tail of this size."

At last there came a day when Blood Clot said, "I want to visit the village where many people live. Before that, I will go on my last hunt for you, all day and all night. First I want you to tie up the tent, put rocks on the edge, and fasten the door lest the night wind carry it away. Though the wind will be strong, don't go outdoors and don't be afraid. I will call when you can come out."

The old couple obeyed, and he hunted all night while they were sleeping. About daybreak they heard a big noise, forerunner of a wind that threatened to tip over the tent. The man was frightened and wanted to go out, but the wife held him back, reminding him of what their son had said.

When daylight came, they heard their son's voice: "Come on out; I'll show you something." They unfastened the door and saw dead buffalo lying all around.

"I have done this for you," Blood Clot said. "Dry the meat and hides; save the meat and it will last you for a long time." The young man asked his mother to fix him a lunch, and she gave him pemmican. "Now my parents have plenty of food," he said. As he left, they cried and asked him to return.

Wearing buckskin leggings, carrying a quiver of mountain lion skin, Blood Clot began to travel. After a few days he reached the village. At the outskirts he asked for the chief's house, and a man told him, "It is in the center." There he found the chief with his wife and daughter. They invited him to sit down, and the chief asked him where he came from and what his tribe was.

"I don't know what tribe I belong to. I have come to visit you," Blood Clot replied. The chief stepped outdoors and shouted to the people to come and meet their visitor. The villagers were starving for lack of game, but all gathered at the chief's house and sat down.

The chief said, "Do any of you know the tribe of this young man?" People named the tribes—Deer, Elk, Otters, Beavers, and others. They asked him whether he belonged to any of these, but he thought not. At last one old man said, "I think I know from the power in him, although I may be mistaken. I think he is one of the Buffalo." Blood Clot thought about it, and finally agreed.

The people of the village asked Blood Clot to stay and marry the chief's daughter. He agreed to this as well, and the wedding was held.

That evening he asked his father-in-law to bring one arrow from the tipi. When the chief returned, Blood Clot told him to have all the tipis

fastened and to warn the people that they should stay indoors, for there would be a great storm. The chief told the villagers, and at daybreak when they heard a big noise, they cried out in fear but did not leave their tipis.

Then Blood Clot called to the chief, who came out to find dead buffalo before every lodge. At his son-in-law's bidding he summoned the whole village for a feast, and all were happy.

Blood Clot stayed there until one day when a group of villagers went out to hunt buffalo. Long before this, he had told his wife, "You know the Buffalo Calf? I am part of that, it is part of me, so you must never say the word 'calf.'" When the party killed some buffalo and were butchering, another herd came running past. His wife pointed and called, "Kill that calf!" Immediately Blood Clot jumped on his horse and galloped away, changing as he did so into a buffalo. His wife cried and attempted to catch him, but in vain. From that time on, Blood Clot ran with the buffalo.

—Based on a story reported by Robert Lowie in the 1920s.

■

CORN MOTHER

■

[PENOBSCOT]

What the buffalo represented to the nomadic tribes of the Plains, corn was to the planting people of the East and the Southwest— the all-nourishing sacred food, the subject of innumerable legends and the central theme of many rituals. Derived from a wild grass called teosintl, *corn was planted in Mexico's Tehuacan Valley as early as 8,000 years ago. The oldest corn found north of the border was discovered in New Mexico's Bat Cave. It is about 5,500 years old. The Hopis say: "Moing'iima makes corn. Everything grows on his body. He is short, about the height of a boy. He has a female partner. Every summer he becomes heavy, his body is full of vege- tables: watermelon, corn, squash. They grow in his body. When the Hopi plant, they invariably ask him to make the crop flourish; then their things come up, whether vegetables or fruit. When he shaves his body, the seeds come out, and afterward his body is thin. He used to live on this earth and go with the Hopi. When things grow*

When Kloskurbeh, the All-maker, lived on earth, there were no people yet. But one day when the sun was high, a youth appeared and called him "Uncle, brother of my mother." This young man was born from the foam of the waves, foam quickened by the wind and warmed by the sun. It was the motion of the wind, the moistness of water, and the sun's warmth which gave him life—warmth above all, because warmth is life. And the young man lived with Kloskurbeh and became his chief helper.

Now, after these two powerful beings had created all manner of things, there came to them, as the sun was shining at high noon, a beautiful girl. She was born of the wonderful earth plant, and of the dew, and of warmth. Because a drop of dew fell on a leaf and was warmed by the sun, and the warming sun is life, this girl came into being—from the green living plant, from moisture, and from warmth.

"I am love," said the maiden. "I am a strength giver, I am the nourisher, I am the provider of men and animals. They all love me."

Then Kloskurbeh thanked the Great Mystery Above for having sent them the maiden. The youth, the Great Nephew, married her, and the girl conceived and thus became First Mother. And Kloskurbeh, the Great Uncle, who teaches humans all they need to know, taught their children how to live. Then he went away to dwell in the north, from which he will return sometime when he is needed.

Now the people increased and became numerous. They lived by hunting, and the more people there were, the less game they found. They were hunting it out, and as the animals decreased, starvation came upon the people. And First Mother pitied them.

The little children came to First Mother and said: "We are hungry. Feed us." But she had nothing to give them, and she wept. She told them: "Be patient. I will make some food. Then your little bellies will be full." But she kept weeping.

Her husband asked: "How can I make you smile? How can I make you happy?"

"There is only one thing that will stop my tears."

"What is it?" asked her husband.

"It is this: you must kill me."

"I could never do that."

"You must, or I will go on weeping and grieving forever."

Then the husband traveled far, to the end of the earth, to the north he went, to ask the Great Instructor, his uncle Kloskurbeh, what he should do.

"You must do what she wants. You must kill her," said Kloskurbeh. Then the young man went back to his home, and it was his turn to weep. But First Mother said: "Tomorrow at high noon you must do it. After you have killed me, let two of our sons take hold of my hair and drag my body over that empty patch of earth. Let them drag me back and forth, back and forth, over every part of the patch, until all my flesh has been torn from my body. Afterwards, take my bones, gather them up, and bury them in the middle of this clearing. Then leave that place."

She smiled and said, "Wait seven moons and then come back, and you will find my flesh there, flesh given out of love, and it will nourish and strengthen you forever and ever."

So it was done. The husband slew his wife and her sons, praying, dragged her body to and fro as she had commanded, until her flesh covered all the earth. Then they took up her bones and buried them in the middle of it. Weeping loudly, they went away.

When the husband and his children and his children's children came back to that place after seven moons had passed, they found the earth covered with tall, green, tasseled plants. The plants' fruit—corn—was First Mother's flesh, given so that the people might live and flourish. And they partook of First Mother's flesh and found it sweet beyond words. Following her instructions, they did not eat all, but put many kernels back into the earth. In this way her flesh and spirit renewed themselves every seven months, generation after generation.

And at the spot where they had burned First Mother's bones, there grew another plant, broad-leafed and fragrant. It was First Mother's breath, and they heard her spirit talking: "Burn this up and smoke it. It is sacred. It will clear your minds, help your prayers, and gladden your hearts."

And First Mother's husband called the first plant *Skarmunal*, corn, and the second plant *utarmur-wayeh*, tobacco.

"Remember," he told the people, "and take good care of First Mother's flesh, because it is her goodness become substance. Take good care of her breath, because it is her love turned into smoke. Remember her and think of her whenever you eat, whenever you smoke this sacred plant, bcause she has given her life so that you might live. Yet she is not dead, she lives: in undying love she renews herself again and again."

—Retold from three nineteenth-century sources,
including Joseph Nicolar.

CREATION OF THE ANIMAL PEOPLE

[OKANOGAN]

The earth was once a human being: Old One made her out of a woman. "You will be the mother of all people," he said.

Earth is alive yet, but she has been changed. The soil is her flesh, the rocks are her bones, the wind is her breath, trees and grass are her hair. She lives spread out, and we live on her. When she moves, we have an earthquake.

After taking the woman and changing her to earth, Old One gathered some of her flesh and rolled it into balls, as people do with mud or clay. He made the first group of these balls into the ancients, the beings of the early world.

The ancients were people, yet also animals. In form some looked human while some walked on all fours like animals. Some could fly like birds; others could swim like fishes. All had the gift of speech, as well as greater powers and cunning than either animals or people. But deer were never among the ancients; they were always animals, even as they are today.

Besides the ancients, real people and real animals lived on the earth at that time. Old One made the people out of the last balls of mud he took from the earth. He rolled them over and over, shaped them like Indians, and blew on them to bring them alive. They were so ignorant that they were the most helpless of all the creatures Old One had made.

Old One made people and animals into males and females so that they might breed and multiply. Thus all living things came from the earth. When we look around, we see part of our mother everywhere.

The difficulty with the early world was that most of the ancients were selfish and some were monsters, and there was much trouble among them. They were also very stupid in some ways. Though they knew they had to hunt in order to live, they did not know which creatures were deer and which were people, and sometimes they ate people by mistake.

At last Old One said, "There will soon be no people if I let things go on like this." So he sent Coyote to kill all the monsters and other evil beings among the ancients and teach the Indians how to do things.

And Coyote began to travel on the earth, teaching the Indians, making life easier and better for them, and performing many wonderful deeds.

—*Reported by Ella Clark in the 1950s.*

■

STONE BOY

■

[BRULE SIOUX]

Depending on the individual storyteller, the Sioux legend of Stone Boy takes many different forms. The following version from the Cheyenne River Reservation was heard by Henry Crow Dog around 1910, when he was a child listening to the storytellers at the campfire.

■ |||||||||||||||||||||||||||||||||||||||||||||||||||||||||||||||||||||||||||||||||||| ■

Back in the great days of the Indians, a maiden and her five brothers lived together. People in those times had to look for food; it was their main occupation. So while the sister cooked and made clothes, the brothers spent their days hunting.

It happened once that this family moved their tipi to the bottom of a canyon. It was a strange, silent place, but there was water in a creek and the hunting was good. The canyon was cool in the summer and shielded from wind in the winter. Still, when the brothers went out hunting, the girl was always waiting for them. Waiting and listening, she heard noises. Often she thought they were footsteps, but when she looked outside, no one was there.

Then one evening, only four of the five brothers came back from hunting. They and the sister stayed awake all night, wondering what could have happened to the other. The next day when the men went hunting, only three returned. Again they and the sister stayed awake wondering. The next evening only two came home, and they and the girl were afraid.

In those early days the Indians had no sacred ceremonies or prayers to guide them, so it was hard for the maiden and her two brothers to watch through the night in that ghostly place. Again the brothers went out in the morning, and only a single one returned at night. Now the girl cried and begged him to stay home. But they had to eat, and so in the morning her last and youngest brother, whom she loved best of all, went out to hunt. Like the others, he did not come back. Now no one would bring the maiden food or water, or protect her.

Weeping, the girl left the canyon and climbed to the top of a hill. She wanted to die, but did not know how to. Then she saw a round pebble lying on the ground. Thinking that it would kill her, she picked it up and swallowed it.

With peace in her heart the maiden went back to the tipi. She drank some water and felt a stirring inside her, as if the rock were telling her not to worry. She was comforted, though she could not sleep for missing her brothers.

The next day she had nothing left to eat except some pemmican and berries. She meant to eat them and drink water from the creek, but she found she wasn't hungry. She felt as if she had been to a feast, and walked around singing to herself. The following day she was happy in a way she had never been before.

On the fourth day that the girl had been alone, she felt pain. "Now the end comes," she thought. "Now I die." She didn't mind; but instead of dying, she gave birth to a little boy.

"What will I do with this child?" she wondered. "How did it come? It must be that stone I swallowed."

The child was strong, with shining eyes. Though the girl felt weak for a while, she had to keep going to care for the new life, her son. She named him Iyan Hokshi, Stone Boy, and wrapped him in her brothers' clothes. Day after day he grew, ten times faster than ordinary infants, and with a more perfect body.

The mother knew that her baby had great powers. One day when he was playing outside the tipi, he made a bow and arrows, all on his own. Looking at his flint arrowhead, the mother wondered how he had done it. "Maybe he knows that he was a stone and I swallowed him," she thought. "He must have a rock nature."

The baby grew so fast that he was soon walking. His hair became long, and as he matured his mother became afraid that she would lose him as she had lost her brothers. She cried often, and though he did not ask why, he seemed to know.

Very soon he was big enough to go hunting, and when she saw this, his mother wept more than ever. Stone Boy come into the tipi. "Mother, don't cry," he said.

"You used to have five uncles," she said. "But they went out hunting. One after another, they did not come back." And she told him about his birth, how she had gone to the top of the hill and swallowed a stone, and how she had felt something moving inside her.

"I know," he said. "And I am going to look for your brothers, my uncles."

"But if you don't return," she sobbed, "what will I do?"

"I will come back," he told her. "I will come back with my uncles. Stay in the tipi until I do."

So the next morning Iyan Hokshi started walking and watching. He kept on till dusk, when he found a good place to sleep. He wandered for four days, and on the evening of the fourth day he smelled smoke. Iyan Hokshi, this Stone Boy, he followed the smell. It led him to a tipi with smoke coming from its smoke hole.

This tipi was ugly and ramshackle. Inside Iyan Hokshi could see an old woman who was ugly too. She watched him pass and, calling him over, invited him to eat and stay the night.

Stone Boy went into the tipi, though he was uneasy in his mind, and a little timid. He looked around and saw five big bundles, propped up on end, leaning against the tipi wall. And he wondered.

The old woman was cooking some meat. When it was done he ate it, though it didn't taste good. Later she fixed a dirty old buffalo robe for him to sleep on, but he sensed danger and felt wide awake.

"I have a backache," the woman said. "Before you go to sleep, I wish you would rub it for me by walking up and down my back. I am old and alone, and I have nobody to help with my pain."

She lay down, and Stone Boy began walking on her back. As he did, he felt something sticking up under her buckskin robe, something sharp like a knife or a needle or the point of a spear. "Maybe she used this sharp tool to kill my uncles," he thought. "Maybe she put poison from a snake on its point. Yes, that must be so."

Iyan Hokshi, having pondered, jumped high in the air, as high as he could, and came down on that old woman's back with a crash. He jumped and jumped until he was exhausted and the hag was lying dead with a broken back.

Then Iyan Hokshi walked over to the big bundles, which were wrapped in animal hides and lashed together with rawhide thongs. He unwrapped them and found five men, dead and dried like jerked meat, hardly human-looking. "These must be my uncles," he thought, but he didn't know how to bring them back to life.

Outside the ugly tipi was a heap of rocks, round gray stones. He found that they were talking and that he could understand them. "Iyan Hokshi, Stone Boy, you are one of us, you come from us, you come from Tunka, you come from Iyan. Listen; pay attention."

Following their instructions, he built a little dome-like hut out of bent willow sticks. He covered it with the old woman's buffalo robes and put the five dead, dried-up humans inside. Out in the open he built a big fire. He set the rocks right in the flames, picked up the old woman, and threw her in to burn up.

After the rocks glowed red-hot, Stone Boy found a deer antler and used it to carry them one by one into the little hut he had made. He picked up the old woman's water bag, a buffalo bladder decorated with quillwork, and filled it with water. He drew its rawhide tie tight and took it inside too. Then he placed the dried humans around him in a circle.

Iyan Hokshi closed the entrance of his little lodge with a flap of buffalo robe, so that no air could escape or enter. Pouring water from the bag over them, he thanked the rocks, saying, "You brought me here." Four times he poured the water; four times he opened the flap and closed it. Always he spoke to the rocks and they to him. As he poured, the little lodge filled with steam so that he could see nothing but the white mist in the darkness. When he poured water a second time, he sensed a stirring. When he poured the third time, he began to sing. And when he poured the fourth time, those dead, dried-up things also began to sing and talk.

"I believe they have come to life," thought Iyan Hokshi, the Stone Boy. "Now I want to see my uncles."

He opened the flap for the last time, watching the steam flow out and rise into the sky as a feathery cloud. The bonfire and the moonlight both shone into the little sweat lodge, and by their light he saw five good-looking young men sitting inside. He said, "*Hou, lekshi*, you must be my uncles." They smiled and laughed, happy to be alive again.

Iyan Hokshi said, "This is what my mother—your sister—wanted. This is what she wished for."

He also told them: "The rock saved me, and now it has saved you. Iyan, Tunka—rock—Tunka, Iyan. Tunkashila, the Grandfather Spirit, we will learn to worship. This little lodge, these rocks, the water, the fire—these are sacred, these we will use from now on as we have done here for the first time: for purification, for life, for *wichosani*, for health. All this has been given to us so that we may live. We shall be a tribe."

—*Told by Henry Crow Dog, February 26, 1968, at Rosebud,*
South Dakota, and recorded by Richard Erdoes.

Henry Crow Dog is a full-blooded Sioux elder with a majestic face, craggy as the Black Hills themselves. He is the grandson of the famous Crow Dog, a chief, warrior, and leader of the Ghost Dancers. The first Crow Dog once voluntarily drove 150 miles to his own hanging for killing his rival, Chief Spotted Tail, only to be freed on orders of the Supreme Court, which ruled that federal law had no jurisdiction on an Indian reservation.

THE POWERFUL BOY

■

[SENECA]

The Seneca, one of the Iroquois nations of the Northeast, have their own version of the all-conquering little one.

■ ||||||||||||||||||||||||||||||||||||||||||||||||||||||||||||||||| ■

A man and his wife lived with their five-year-old son in an ugly-looking lodge in the woods. One day the woman died giving birth to another boy, who was bright and lively but no longer than a person's hand. Thinking that the infant would not live, the father wrapped it carefully and placed it in a hollow tree outside the lodge. After that he burned the body of the mother.

Then as he had done before, the man went hunting every day. The five-year-old played around the lodge by himself, feeling lonely. After a time he heard crying from the hollow tree, for the baby too was lonely, and hungry as well. When he discovered his little brother, the boy made him some soup from deer intestines, which the baby drank with relish. Much stronger, the newborn crawled out of the tree, and the two played together. The older brother made a little coat out of fawn skin; when he put it on, the baby looked like a chipmunk scampering around.

When he came home, the father noticed that the deer intestines were gone and asked the boy what he had done with them. "Oh," said the child, "I was hungry."

Seeing a small track of very short steps around the fire, the father said, "Here are a boy's tracks. Who is it?" So his son confessed that he had found his little brother in a hollow tree, and that he had given him soup and made him a fawn-skin coat.

"Go and bring him," said the father.

"He's shy; he won't come for anything," the boy said.

"Well, we'll catch him. Ask him to hunt mice with you in the old stump behind the hollow tree, and I'll get him."

Gathering a great many mice, the man hid them in his clothes. Then he walked beyond the tree and crouched down so that he looked like an old stump.

The boy went to the tree and called, "Come on, let's catch some mice." The baby climbed out, and they rushed around the stump catching mice.

Wild with excitement, the tiny thing laughed and shouted; he had never had so much fun.

Suddenly the stump turned into a man, who caught the little one in his arms and ran to the lodge. The infant screamed and struggled, but it was no use; he couldn't get away, and he would not be pacified until his father put a small club into his hand and said. "Now hit that tree." The baby struck a great hickory. The tree fell. Then he laid about him with the club, and everything he hit at was either crushed or killed. He was delighted and stopped crying.

Now the baby stayed with his older brother while their father went hunting. "You must not go to the north while I'm away," the father told them. "Bad, dangerous people live there."

But when the father had left, the tiny one said to his brother, "Oh, let's go north; I want to see what's there."

The boys started off and walked until they came to wooded, marshy ground. Then they heard what sounded like many people calling, "My father! My father!" Actually they were frogs singing the frog song, "*Nohqwa! Nohqwa!*"

"Oh, these people want to hurt my father!" the little boy cried. He fixed himself a pile of red-hot stones and, hurling them at the frogs, killed every one.

When the boys came home, their father was very angry. "You must not go again," he said. "And you must not go west; it's dangerous there too."

But the next day when their father had left, the little boy said, "I want to see what's in the west; let's go there." So they traveled westward until they came to a tall pine tree, with a bed made of skins at the very top. "That's a strange place for a bed," the little boy said to his brother. "I'll climb up and look at it."

Up he went. In the bed at the top he found two naked, frightened children, a boy and a girl. He pinched the naked boy, who called out, "Father, Father! Some strange child has come and scared me nearly to death!"

Suddenly the voice of Thunder was heard in the far west. It rumbled toward them faster and faster until it reached the bed in the treetop. Raising his club, the little boy, the powerful one, struck Thunder and crushed his head, so that he fell dead to the ground.

Then the boy pinched the naked girl, which made her call, "Mother! Mother! Some strange boy is tormenting me!" Instantly the voice of Mother Thunder sounded in the west and grew louder until she stood by the tree. The powerful boy struck her on the head as he had done with her husband, and she fell dead.

The powerful one thought, "This Thunder boy would make a fine tobacco pouch for my father. I'll take him home." He struck the boy with his club and then threw both children to the ground.

The two brothers went home, and the tiny one said, "Oh, Father! I have brought you a splended pouch!"

"What have you done?" the father said when he saw the dead Thunder baby. "These Thunders have never harmed us. They bring rain and do us good, but now they will destroy us to revenge their children."

"Oh, they won't hurt us—I've killed the whole family," the powerful boy replied. So the father took the skin for a tobacco pouch, but he said, "You must never go north to the country where Stone Coat lives."

The next day the older brother would not disobey his father, so the powerful boy headed north by himself. About noon he heard the loud barking of Stone Coat's dog, which was as tall as a deer. Thinking that the master must be close by, the little boy jumped into the heart of a chestnut tree to hide. The dog kept barking, and Stone Coat came up to look around. "There's nothing here," he said, but the dog barked and stared at the tree. Finally Stone Coat struck the tree with his club and split it open.

"What a strange little fellow you are," Stone Coat said, looking at the boy as he came out. "You're not big enough to fill a hole in my tooth."

"Oh, I didn't come to fill holes in your teeth. I came to go home with you and see how you live," said the boy.

"All right, come on," Stone Coat said, and began walking with enormous steps. In his belt he carried two great bears, which seemed as small

as squirrels. Once in a while he would look far down and say to the boy running by his side, "You're a funny little creature!"

His lodge was huge and very long; the boy had never seen anything like it. Stone Coat skinned the two bears, put one before his visitor, and otok the other for himself. "You eat this bear," he said, "or I'll eat you and him together."

"If you don't eat yours before I eat mine, may I kill you?" asked the boy.

"Oh, yes," said Stone Coat.

The little boy cut off pieces of meat, cleaned them as fast as he could, and put them into his mouth. Then he ran out of the lodge to hide the meat. He kept running in and out, in and out, until all the flesh of his bear had disappeared. "You haven't finished yours yet," he said to Stone Coat. "I'm going to kill you!"

"Wait until I show you how to slide downhill," Stone Coat said, and took him to a long, slippery hillside which ended in a cave. Putting the boy in a wooden bowl. Stone Coat sent him down at great speed. But presently the powerful boy ran up the slope again.

"Where did you leave the bowl?" asked the surprised Stone Coat.

"Oh, I don't know—down there, I suppose," the boy replied.

"Well, let's see who can kick this log highest," said Stone Coat.

"You try first," said the little one.

The log was two feet thick and six feet long. Putting his foot under it, Stone Coat kicked the log up twice his own height. Then the boy, slipping his foot under the log, sent it whistling through the air. It was gone a long time. Then it came down on Stone Coat's head and crushed him to death.

"Come here," said the boy to Stone Coat's dog. The dog came, and the little one climbed on his back and rode home. "Now my father will have a fine hunting dog," he said.

When the father saw the dog, he cried, "What have you done? Stone Coat will kill us all!"

"I have killed Stone Coat. He won't trouble us any more," replied the boy, the powerful one.

"Now, boys," said the father, "you must never go to the southwest, the gambling place." But the next day about noon, the younger brother started walking southwest. He came to a beautiful opening in the woods, with a lean-to at the farther end. Sitting under the lean-to a man with a large head, much larger than a buffalo's, played dice for the heads of all who came along. He used wild-plumpits with designs on them for dice.

Crowds of people were betting in groups of three. When they lost, as all did, the big-headed man put the three persons to one side. Then he played with three more, and when they lost he put them with the first three, and so on—until he decided that the number was large enough. Then he got up and cut all their heads off.

As the boy approached, a number of people who had lost their bets were waiting to be killed. Hope came to them all, for they sensed that this child had great *orenda*—power, or medicine.

The boy took his place, and the game began immediately. When the big-headed man threw the dice, the bay caused some to remain in the dish and others to go high, so that the dice came to rest with different designs showing. But when the boy threw, the dice turned into wood-cocks, flew high, and came down as dice of the same design.

The two played until the boy won back all the people and the gambler lost his own big head, for the boy instantly cut it off. The whole crowd shouted, "Now you must be our chief!"

The boy said, "How could a little thing like me be a chief? Maybe my father would be willing to do it; I'll ask him." The boy went home with the story, but his father would not move to the land of gambling.

"Now," said the father, "you must never go to the east, where they play ball."

But the next day the boy traveled east until he came to a great, level country of beautiful plains. There the Wolf and the Bear clans were playing against the Eagle, the Turtle, and the Beaver clans.

The boy took the side of the Wolf and the Bear. "If you win," they told him, "you will own all this country." They played, and the boy won. "Now," they said, "you are the owner."

The powerful boy went home and told his father, "I have won all the beautiful country of the east; come and be chief of it."

His father consented and moved with his two boys to the country of the east, and there they lived. That is the story.

—*Based on a legend reported by Jeremiah Curtin and*
J. N. B. Hewitt around 1910.

While archeological evidence confirms that the Iroquois have inhabited upstate New York and northeastern Pennsylvania continuously for literally thousands of years, their cultural myths still include tales of a great migration into the beautiful country of the East from a previous homeland. This may refer to the arrival of other related tribes from the south and west who joined the core population during different periods.

GLOOSCAP AND THE BABY

[ALGONQUIAN]

For many Algonquian tribes, such as the Passamaquoddy of Maine,
the great Glooscap was First Man, culture hero, demiurge, trickster,
and god.

Glooscap, having conquered the Kewawkqu', a race of giants and magicians, and the Medecolin, who were cunning sorcerers, and Pamola, a wicked spirit of the night, besides hosts of fiends, goblins, cannibals, and witches, felt himself great indeed, and boasted to a woman that there was nothing left for him to subdue.

But the woman laughed and said: "Are you quite sure, Master? There is still one who remains unconquered, and nothing can overcome him."

In some surprise Glooscap inquired the name of this mighty one.

"He is called Wasis," replied the woman, "but I strongly advise you to have no dealings with him."

Wasis was only a baby, who sat on the floor sucking a piece of maple sugar and crooning a little song to himself. Now Glooscap had never married and was ignorant of how children are managed, but with perfect confidence he smiled at the baby and asked it to come to him. The baby

smiled back but never moved, whereupon Glooscap imitated a beautiful birdsong. Wasis, however, paid no attention and went on sucking his maple sugar. Unaccustomed to such treatment, Glooscap lashed himself into a rage and in terrible and threatening accents ordered Wasis to come to him at once. But Wasis burst into dire howls, which quite drowned the god's thundering, and would not budge for any threats.

Glooscap, thoroughly aroused, summoned all his magical resources. He recited the most terrible spells, the most dreadful incantations. He sang the songs which raise the dead, and those which send the devil scurrying to the nethermost depths. But Wasis merely smiled and looked a trifle bored.

At last Glooscap rushed from the hut in despair, while Wasis, sitting on the floor, cried, "Goo, goo!" And to this day the Indians say that when a baby says "Goo," he remembers the time when he conquered mighty Glooscap.

—From a tale reported by Lewis Spence around the turn
of the century.

THE OLD WOMAN OF THE SPRING

[CHEYENNE]

This tale about the gifts of corn and buffalo to the Cheyenne is related to the legend which follows it about Arrow Boy. In the Cheyenne manner, a storyteller will say, "Let's tie another story to the end of this one," and go on from there. North, as it is spoken of at the beginning of both tales, is a nostalgic reference to the Cheyenne hunting grounds in north-central America, from which they were driven by invading tribes, probably the Ojibway.

When the Cheyenne were still in the north, they camped in a large circle at whose entrance a deep, rapid spring flowed from a hillside. The spring provided the camp with water, but food was harder to find. The buffalo had disappeared, and many people went hungry.

One bright day some men were playing the game of ring and javelin in the center of the camp circle. They used a red and black hoop and four long sticks, two red and two black, which they threw at the hoop as it rolled along. In order to win, a player had to throw his stick through the hoop while it was still moving.

A large audience had already gathered when a young man came from the south side of the camp circle to join them. He wore a buffalo robe with the hair turned outward. His body was painted yellow, and a yellow-painted eagle breach-feather was fastened to his head. Soon another young man dressed exactly like the first came from the north side of the circle to watch the game. They were unacquainted, but when the two caught sight of each other they moved through the crowd to talk. "My friend," said the man from the south side, "you're imitating my dress. Why are you doing it?" The other man said, "It's you who are imitating me. Why?"

In their explanations, both men told the same story. They had entered the spring that flowed out from the hillside, and there they had been instructed how to dress. By now the crowd had stopped watching the game and gathered around to listen, and the young men told the people that they would go into the spring again and come out soon. As the crowd watched, the two approached the spring. The man from the south covered his head with his buffalo robe and entered. The other did the same.

The young men splashed through the water and soon found themselves in a large cave. Near the entrance sat an old woman cooking some buffalo meat and corn in two separate earthen pots. She welcomed them: "Grandchildren, you have come. Here, sit beside me." They sat down, one on each side of her, and told her that the people were hungry and that they had come to her for food. She gave them corn from one pot and meat from the other. They ate until they had had enough, and when they were through the pots were still full. Then she told them to look toward the south, and they saw that the land in that direction was covered with buffalo. She told them to look to the west, and they saw all kinds of animals, large and small, including ponies, though they knew nothing of ponies in those days. She told them to look toward the north, and they saw corn growing everywhere.

The old woman said to them, "All this that you have seen shall be yours in the future. Tonight I cause the buffalo to be restored to you. When you leave this place, the buffalo will follow, and your people will see them coming before sunset. Take this uncooked corn in your robes, and plant it every spring in low, moist ground. After it matures, you can feed upon it.

"Take also this meat and corn that I have cooked," she said, and when you have returned to your people, ask them to sit down to eat in the following order: First, all males, from the youngest to the oldest, with the exception of one orphan boy; second, all females, from the oldest to the youngest, with the exception of one orphan girl. When all are through eating, the rest of the food in the pots is to be eaten by the orphan boy and the orphan girl."

The two men obeyed the old woman. When they passed out of the spring, they saw that their entire bodies were painted red, and the yellow breath-feathers on their heads had turned red. They went to their people, who ate as directed of the corn and meat. There was enough for all, and the contents of the pots remained full until they were passed to the two orphan children, who ate all the rest of the food.

Toward sunset the people went to their lodges and began watching the spring closely, and in a short time they saw a buffalo leap out. The creature jumped and played and rolled, then returned to the spring. In a little while another buffalo jumped out, then another and another, and finally they came so fast that the Cheyenne were no longer able to count them. The buffalo continued to emerge all night, and the following day the whole country out in the distance was covered with buffalo. The buffalo scented the great camp. The next day the Cheyenne surrounded them, for though the men hunted on foot, they ran very fast.

For a time the people had an abundance of buffalo meat. In the spring they moved their camp to low, swampy land, where they planted the corn they had received from the medicine stream. It grew rapidly, and every grain they planted brought forth strong stalks bearing two to four ears of corn. The people planted corn every year after this.

One spring after planting corn, the Cheyenne went on a buffalo hunt. When they had enough meat to last for a long time, they returned to their fields. To their surprise, they found that the corn had been stolen by some neighboring tribe. Nothing but stalks remained—not even a kernel for seed. Though the theft had occurred about a moon before, the Cheyenne trailed the enemy's footprints for several days. They even fought with two or three tribes, but never succeeded in tracing the robbers or recovering the stolen crop. It was a long time before the Cheyenne planted any more corn.

—Based on a story reported by George A. Dorsey at the turn of the century.

The loss of corn described here may symbolize how the Cheyenne abandoned planting for buffalo hunting in the last half of the eighteenth century. The "wings" given the Plains tribes by the arrival of guns and horses at this time not only al-lowed them to move from being gatherers to being hunters (the reverse of the more common cultural evolution) but opened up the possibility of a more elaborate—and transportable—material culture—hence the term, golden age of the Plains Indians.

■

ARROW BOY

■

[CHEYENNE]

Arrow Boy, the wonderful boy, gives a magic performance still en-acted during Sioux Yuwipi ceremonies. in which the medicine man is tied up with a rawhide thong and covered with a star blanket (formerly a buffalo robe) while eerie lights flicker and invisible rattles and strange voices are heard. The pottery-making Pueblos have another version of this tale that they call the legend of the Water-Olla Boy.

■ ▏▏ ■

After the Cheyenne had received their corn, and while they were still in the north, a young man and woman of the tribe were married. The woman became pregnant and carried her child in the womb for four years. The people watched with great interest to see what would happen, and when the woman gave birth to a beautiful boy in the fourth year, they regarded him as supernatural.

Before long the woman and her husband died, and the boy was taken in by his grandmother, who lived alone. He learned to walk and talk very quickly. He was given a buffalo calf robe and immediately turned it inside out so that the hair side was outward, the way medicine men wore it.

Among the Cheyenne there were certain medicine men of extraor-dinary wisdom and superhuman powers. Sometimes they would come together and put up a lodge. Sitting in a large circle, they chanted and went through curious rituals, after which each man rose and performed wonders before the crowd.

One of these magic dances were held when the boy was about ten. He made his grandmother ask if he could take part, and the medicine men let him enter the lodge. "Where do you want to live?" the chief of the medicine men asked, meaning "Where do you want to sit?" Without ceremony the boy took his seat beside the chief. To the man who had ushered him in, the child gave directions to paint his body red and draw black rings around his face, wrists, and ankles.

The performance began at one end of the circle. When the boy's turn came, he told the people what he was going to do. He used sweet grass to burn incense. Then he passed his buffalo sinew bowstring east, south, west, and north through the smoke. He asked two men to assist him and told them to tie his bowstring around his neck, cover his body with his robe, and pull at the ends of the string. They pulled with all their might, but they could not move him. He told them to pull harder, and as they tugged at the string, his head was severed. It rolled out from under the robe, and the men put it back.

Next the men lifted the robe up. Instead of the boy, a very old man was sitting in his place. They covered the old man with the robe and pulled it away again, this time revealing a pile of human bones with a skull. A third time they placed the robe over the bones and lifted it. Nothing at all was there. But when for a fourth time they spread the robe over the empty space and removed it, the wonderful boy sat in his place is if nothing had happened.

After the magic dance, the Cheyenne moved their camp to hunt buffalo. When a kill had been made, the wonderful boy led a crowd of boys who went hunting for calves that might return to the place where they last saw their mothers. The boys found five or six calves, surrounded them, and killed a two-year-old with their arrows. They began to skin it very carefully with bone knives, keeping the hide of the head intact and leaving the hooves on, because the wonderful boy wanted the skin for a robe.

While they worked, a man driving a dog team approached them. It was Young Wolf, head chief of the tribe, who had come to the killing ground to gather what bones had been left. He said, "My children have favored me at last! I'll take charge of this buffalo; you boys go on off."

The children obeyed, except for the wonderful boy, who kept skinning as he explained that he wanted only the hide for a robe. The chief pushed the wonderful boy aside, but the boy returned and resumed skinning. Then the chief jerked the boy away and threw him down. The boy got up and continued his work. Pretending that he was skinning one of the hind legs, he cut the leg off at the knee and left the hoof on.

When the chief shouldered the boy out of the way and took over the work, the wonderful boy struck him on the back of the head with the buffalo leg. The chief fell dead.

The boys ran to the camp and told the story, which caused great excitement. The warriors assembled and decided to kill the wonderful boy. They went out to look for him near the body of their chief, but the boy had returned to camp. He was sitting in his grandmother's lodge while she cooked food for him in an earthen pot, when suddenly the whole tipi was raised by the warriors. Quickly the wonderful boy kicked the pot over, sending the contents into the fire. As the smoke billowed up, the boy rose with it. The old woman was left sitting alone.

The warriors looked around and saw the boy about a quarter of a mile away, walking off toward the east. They ran after him but could not seem to draw closer. Four times they chased him with no success, and then gave up.

People became afraid of the wonderful boy. Still, they looked for him every day and at last saw him on the top of a nearby hill. The whole camp gathered to watch as he appeared on the summit five times, each time in a different dress. First he came as a Red Shield warrior in a headdress made out of buffalo skin. He had horns, a spear, a red shield, and two buffalo tails tied to each arm. The second time he was a Coyote warrior, with his body painted black and yellow and with two eagle feathers sticking up on his head. The third time he appeared as a Dog Men warrior wearing a feathered headdress and carrying an eagle-bone whistle, a rattle of buffalo hoof, and a bow and arrows. The fourth time he was a Hoof Rattle warrior. His body was painted, and he had a rattle to sing by and a spear about eight feet long, with a crook at one end and the shaft at the other end bent in a semicircle. The fifth time his body was painted white, and on his forehead he wore a white owl skin.

After this the wonderful boy disappeared entirely. No one knew where he went, people thought him dead, and he was soon forgotten, for the buffalo disappeared and famine came to the Cheyenne.

During this time the wonderful boy traveled alone into the highest ranges of the mountains. As he drew near a certain peak, a door opened in the mountain slope. He passed through into the earth, and the opening closed after him.

There inside the mountain he found a large circle of men. Each represented a tribe and was seated beneath that tribe's bundle. They welcomed the wonderful boy and pointed out the one empty place under a bundle wrapped in fox skin. "If you take this seat, the bundle will be yours to carry back to the Cheyenne," the head man said. "But first you will remain here for four years, receiving instruction in order to become your tribe's prophet and counselor."

The wonderful boy accepted the bundle, and all the men gave thanks. When his turn came to perform the bundle ceremony, they took it down and showed him its sacred ceremonies, songs, and four medicine arrows, each representing certain powers. Then for four years under the mountain peak, they taught him prophecies, magic, and ceremonies for warfare and hunting.

Meanwhile the Cheyenne were weak with hunger, threatened by starvation. All the animals had died, and the people ate herbs. One day as the tribe was traveling in search of food, five children lagged behind to look for herbs and mushrooms.

Suddenly the wonderful boy, now a young man bearing the name of Arrow Boy, appeared before them. "My poor children, throw away those mushrooms," he said. "It is I who brought famine among you, for I was angry with your people when they drove me from their camp. I have returned to provide for you; you shall not hunger in the future. Go and gather some dried buffalo bones, and I will feed you."

The children ran away and picked up buffalo bones, and the wonderful boy, Arrow Boy, made a few passes that turned them into fresh meat. He fed the children with fat, marrow, liver, and other strengthening parts of the buffalo. When they had eaten all they wanted, he gave them fat and meat. "Take this to your people," he said. "Tell them that I, Motzeyouf, Arrow Boy, have returned."

Though the boys ran to the camp, Motzeyouf used his magic to reach it first. He entered the lodge of his uncle and lay down to rest, for he was tired. The uncle and his wife were sitting just outside, but they did not see Arrow Boy pass by.

The boys arrived in camp with their tale, which created great excitement. The uncle's wife went into the lodge to get a pipe, and it was then that she saw Arrow Boy lying covered with a buffalo robe. The robe, and his shirt, leggings, and moccasins, all were painted red. Guessing that he was Motzeyouf, the men went into the lodge, asked the stranger to sit up, and cried over him. They saw his bundle, and knowing that he had power, they asked him what they should do.

Motzeyouf told the Cheyenne to camp in a circle and set up a large tipi in the center. When this had been done, he called all the medicine men to bring their rattles and pipes. Then he went into the tipi and sang the sacred songs that he had learned. It was night before he came to the song about the fourth arrow. In the darkness the buffalo returned with a roar like thunder. The frightened Cheyenne went in to Arrow

Boy and asked him what to do. "Go and sleep," he said, "for the buffalo, your food, has returned to you." The roar of the buffalo continued through the night as long as he sang.

The next morning the land was covered with buffalo, and the people went out and killed all they wanted. From that time forth, owing to the medicine arrows, the Cheyenne had plenty to eat and great powers.

—Retold from a tale reported by George A. Dorsey in 1905.

The medicine arrows brought down from the mountains by Motzeyouf still exist and are cared for by the Arrow Keeper of the Southern Cheyenne in Oklahoma.

 # THE GREAT MEDICINE DANCE

[CHEYENNE]

The sun dance was the most important, solemn, and awe-inspiring ritual of the prairie tribes west of the Missouri. Sun dance is its Sioux name; the Cheyenne called it the new-life lodge, while for the Ponca it was the mystery dance. Closely related to the sun dance was the Okapi ceremony of the Mandans.

The dance took place once a year, at the height of summer. It lasted four days—longer, if the elaborate preparations are taken into account. In some tribes, such as the Sioux, the ritual involved the "piercing" of the dancers: the passing of sharpened skewers through the flesh of their chests and the performance of other kinds of self-torture. This is still the custom during Sioux sun dances today. In other tribes the ritual involved fasting and "looking at the sun" throughout the four long days. The most extreme form of self-torture occurred during the Okapi ceremony of the mandans, painted in great detail by Catlin in the 1830s. Dancers suffered—"they gave of their flesh so that the people might live." They underwent piercing in obedience to a vow, or to help a sick relative recover, or to bring a beloved son back unhurt from the warpath.

The dance was a celebration of the renewal of all life, "to make the grass grow and the buffalo and the people increase and thrive."

It was the one occasion when all the small hunting bands of a tribe came together, a time for old friends to talk and for young men to find wives.

◼ ▌▌▌ ◼

The Tsis-tsistas people have danced the great medicine dance for a long, long time, longer than anyone can remember or even imagine. The dance represents the making of this universe and was conceived and taught to the people by the Creator, Maheo, and his helper, Great Roaring Thunder. It portrays the making of the sun, moon, and stars; of rain, wind, and snow; of Grandmother Earth and the blue sky above her; of the mountains and rivers; of all living things, big and small. The dance is performed especially in times of starvation, distress, and widespread death. This, our most sacred ceremony, was brought to us by the Sutai medicine man Horns Standing Up, under the guidance of the Creator himself.

Long ago, when the earth and the people dwelling upon it were young, our tribe was starving. The earth itself was starving, for no rain was falling. Plants and trees wilted. Many rivers dried up. The animals were dying of hunger and thirst.

The Cheyenne had nothing to eat except some old, dried corn and their dogs, which used to carry their packs in those days before we had horses. There were not many dogs remaining, and very little corn. So the people left their old hunting grounds, left the land which had nourished them for generations, and started off in search of food. They went north, where the drought was less severe, but found little game and no buffalo at all.

One evening they came to a stream in which water still flowed. The leaders and old chiefs sat down beside this stream and sadly watched the thin, weary people pitching their tipis. Then it came to the chiefs, as in a vision, what ought to be done. They ordered all the men to go to the women, each man to the woman he felt most attracted to, and beg her to give him something to eat. The men did as they had been directed, and each chose the woman who was to feed him.

Among the warriors was a young medicine man. He went up to a beautiful woman who happened to be the wife of the head chief. She set a bowl of dog soup before him and waited for him to finish eating. Then he said: "I have chosen you from among all women to help me save our people. I want you to go north with me, as the medicine spirits have commanded. Take your dog teams and bring supplies for a long journey—now, right away!"

Though she was the chief's wife, the woman did what the medicine man had asked. She was ready to travel in no time, and the two left unobserved in the dark of night. Two days and one night they traveled without stopping, urging on the dogs who carried the travois with the tipi poles and hides and other things needed for survival.

At last they rested. The man told the woman to put up the lodge and to prepare two beds of soft, fragrant sage for them to sleep on. He said: "Make the tipi face the rising sun." He also told her that Maheo, the Creator, had sent him a vision revealing that the two of them must go north and bring back the great medicine lodge, Maheo's symbol of the universe, and with it a sacred ceremony which they would teach to the Cheyenne. "In my vision," he said, "Maheo promised that if the people accept and perform this holy ritual, the rains will fall again and the earth rejoice, the plants will bring forth green leaves and fruit, and the buffalo will return."

And so they traveled, the woman every evening pitching the tipi facing east and preparing the beds of sage on opposite sides of the tipi, the man sleeping on his bed, the woman on hers. One night she said: "How is this? You made me run away with you, but you never approach me as man approaches woman. Why did you make me go with you, then?"

He answered: "We must abstain from embracing until we enter the great mountain of the north and receive the sacred medicine dance. After we emerge from the mountain, I shall embrace you in a renewal-of-all-life ceremony by which people will continue to be born, generation after generation, through the woman-power of perpetuation."

At last they came to a vast, dark forest from whose center rose a cloud-wreathed mountain reaching far into the sky. Beyond the mountain they saw a lake of unending waters. They came to a large rock at the foot of the mountain, rolled the rock aside, and discovered an entrance. They went inside the mountain and, closing the opening behind them, found themselves in the mountain's great medicine lodge, which was wonderful to behold. Today the medicine tipi which the Cheyenne put up for their sun dances at Bear Butte is an imitation of that sacred mountain lodge.

The young man and the woman heard voices coming out of the mountaintop—the voices of Maheo the Creator and his helper Great Roaring Thunder. Instructing them in the holy ways to perform the sacred ceremony, Maheo spoke for four days. When they had learned all there was to know about the dance, the Creator, said:

Now you will leave and teach the people what I have taught you.

And if they perform the ceremonies in the right way, they will be favored for generations to come. The sun, the moon, the stars will move again in harmony. Roaring Thunder will bring soothing rain and winds. Corn and chokecherries will ripen again. Wild turnips and healing herbs will grow once more. All the animals will emerge from behind this mountain, herds of buffalo and antelope among them, and follow you back to your village and your people.

Take this sacred hat, *issiwun*, and wear it whenever you perform the sun dance. With *issiwun* you will control the animals—the buffalo, the antelope, the elk, the deer—who give themselves to the people for food. The Tsis-tsistas shall never be hungry again, but live in plenty. Put on this sacred buffalo hat as you leave, and Grandmother Earth will smile upon you forever.

And so the young medicine man of the Sutai and the good-looking woman left the mountain through the secret passage. As they rolled the rock aside and emerged, buffalo without numbers streamed out of the mountain behind them, and the earth brought forth green shoots. Herbs and plants sprouted under a gentle rain, and the earth was like new, glistening in freshness. Thus the man and woman walked sacredly, clad in buffalo robes painted red, and the medicine man wore his horned cap. Their dogs walked before them, dragging their travois poles, while behind them followed a thundering herd of buffalo, and after these came all manner of animals, male and female, big and small.

At the day's end the man and the woman put up their tipi and lay down on their beds of sage to rest, and all the animals settled down to rest also. And at some time during this journey back to their village, the man and the woman did lovingly what was necessary to ensure renewal and continuation of life through woman-power. Each morning during their travels, the man sang the sacred songs which the voice of Maheo had taught him.

At last one evening they arrived near the stream where the people were still camped, awaiting their return. The medicine man and the woman did not go into the village at once, but spent the night outside. In the morning the medicine man put on *issiwun* and entered the camp, accompanied by the woman. He told the people of all that had passed, told them that he had brought them the knowledge of the great medicine lodge and the great sacred dance, the songs and ceremonies that went with it, and above all, *issiwun*, the sacred buffalo hat which had the power to control the wandering of the animals. He told the people that if they performed the sacred sun dance, they would have plenty of buffalo to eat and would never suffer hunger again.

The people put up the medicine lodge according to the young man's instructions, painted their bodies in a sacred manner, and sang the right songs. The children made clay figures of buffalo, antelopes, and elk and brought them into the lodge as a symbol of life's renewal. Since then, whenever the little figures are placed inside the Medicine lodge during the dance, some of those animals will come near to gaze upon the sacred tipi, and some of their animal power will linger on. In the same way, our old friends, the Sioux people, fasten the figures of a man and a bison, both cut from buffalo hide, to their sacred sun dance pole. Then an eagle will come in and circle above the dancers to bless them.

Thus the Tsis-tsistas people performed the great medicine ceremony for the first time, and all was well again. And the people named the young medicine man Horns Standing Up, because the sacred hat has two horns at each side.

—*Told by Josie Limpy and Mrs. Medicine Bull,*
with the help of an interpreter, at Birney, Montana, in 1972.
Recorded by Richard Erdoes.

Some say that Horns Standing Up did not touch the beautiful woman until well after the sun dance was finished. And from this belief comes the custom that men refrain from having relations with women from the time of making the vow to dance until after the ceremony is over.

Josie Limpy was an old, chain-smoking lady belonging to the Sutai division of the Cheyenne tribe. She was, at the time, keeper of issiwun, the sacred buffalo hat, at the Northern Cheyenne Reservation. This story was actually related inside the tipi in which issiwun was kept.

■

THE ORIGIN OF
CURING CEREMONIES

■

[WHITE MOUNTAIN APACHE]

■ |||||||||||||||||||||||||||||||||||||||||||||||||||||||||||||||||||||||||||||||||||||| ■

This is how ceremonies started among us for the curing of sick people. Long, long ago, the earth was made. Then the One Who Made the Earth also planned for each person to have a piece of land that he could live on and call his own. Our people were living in one such place, but they didn't like that particular spot. So the One Who Made the Earth told them to move to a new location, and when they did, they slept well, and liked it, and lived in a good way.

Then two men among them became sick and grew weaker day by day. The people didn't do anything for them because no one knew then about illnesses and how to cure them. The One Who Made the Earth said, "Why don't you do something for those two men? Why don't you say some words over them?" But the people had no knowledge of curing ceremonies.

Four men among the people happened to be standing, one to the east, one to the south, one to the west, and one to the north. The One Who Made the Earth spoke to one of these men, telling him, "Everything on earth has power to cause its own kind of sickness, make its own trouble. There is a way to cure all these things." Now this man understood that knowledge was available. Then those four stood there. On the first night, the one standing on the east side began to chant a set prayer all by himself. On the second night, the one on the south started to drum and sing lightning songs. On the third night, the one on the west chanted a set prayer. On the fourth night, the one on the north began to drum and sing lightning songs. They did not conceive this pattern in their own minds; it was bestowed upon them by the One Who Made the Earth. It was as if the knowledge of what they should chant or sing had suddenly been transmitted to them from outside.

Then the One Who Made the Earth said to these four, "Why don't you go to the two sick men and say some words over them and make them well?" So those four went to where the two sick men were and worked over them, and they were cured. From that time on, we had curing ceremonies and knowledge of the different kinds of sickness that may be caused by various things. That's the way all curing ceremonies started.

—Based on a tale reported by Grenville Goodwin in 1939.

CREATION OF FIRST MAN AND FIRST WOMAN

[NAVAJO]

The first people came up through three worlds and settled in the fourth world. They had been driven from each successive world because they had quarreled with one another and committed adultery. In previous worlds they found no other people like themselves, but in the fourth world they found the Kisani or Pueblo people.

The surface of the fourth world was mixed black and white, and the sky was mostly blue and black. There were no sun, no moon, no stars, but there were four great snow-covered peaks on the horizon in each of the cardinal directions.

Late in the autumn they heard in the east the distant sound of a great voice calling. They listened and waited, and soon heard the voice nearer and louder than before. Once more they listened and heard it louder still, very near. A moment later four mysterious beings appeared. These were White Body, god of this world; Blue Body, the sprinkler; Yellow Body; and Black Body, the god of fire.

Using signs but without speaking, the gods tried to instruct the people, but they were not understood. When the gods had gone, the people discussed their mysterious visit and tried without success to figure out the signs. The gods appeared on four days in succession and attempted to communicate through signs, but their efforts came to nothing.

On the fourth day when the other gods departed, Black Body remained behind and spoke to the people in their own language: "You do not seem to understand our signs, so I must tell you what they mean. We want to make people who look more like us. You have bodies like ours, but you have the teeth, the feet, and the claws of beasts and insects. The new humans will have hands and feet like ours. Also, you are unclean; you smell bad. We will come back in twelve days. Be clean when we return."

On the morning of the twelfth day the people washed themselves well. Then the woman dried their skin with yellow cornmeal, the men with white cornmeal. Soon they heard the distant call, shouted four times, of the approaching gods. When the gods appeared, Blue Body and Black

Body each carried a sacred buckskin. White Body carried two ears of corn, one yellow, one white, each covered completely with grains.

The gods laid one buckskin on the ground with the head to the west, and on this they placed the two ears of corn with their tips to the east. Over the corn they spread the other buckskin with its head to the east. Under the white ear they put the feather of a white eagle; under the yellow ear the feather of a yellow eagle. Then they told the people to stand back and allow the wind to enter. Between the skins the white wind blew from the east and the yellow wind from the west. While the wind was blowing, eight of the gods, the Mirage People, came and walked around the objects on the ground four times. As they walked, the eagle feathers, whose tips protruded from the buckskins, were seen to move. When the Mirage People had finished their walk, the upper buckskin was lifted. The ears of corn had disappeared; a man and a woman lay in their place.

The white ear of corn had become the man, the yellow ear the woman, First Man and First Woman. It was the wind that gave them life, and it is the wind that comes out of our mouths now that gives us life. When this ceases to blow, we die.

The gods had the people build an enclosure of brushwood, and when it was finished, First Man and First Woman went in. The gods told them, "Live together now as husband and wife."

At the end of four days, First Woman bore hermaphrodite twins. In four more days she gave birth to a boy and a girl, who grew to maturity in four days and lived with one another as husband and wife. In all, First Man and First Woman had five pairs of twins, and all except the first became couples who had children.

In four days after the last twins were born, the gods came again and took First Man and First Woman away to the eastern mountain, dwelling place of the gods. The couple stayed there for four days, and when they returned, all their children were taken to the eastern mountain for four days. The gods may have taught them the awful secrets of witchcraft. Witches always use masks, and after they returned, they would occasionally put on masks and pray for the good things they needed— abundant rain and abundant crops.

Witches also marry people who are too closely related to them, which is what First Man and First Woman's children had done. After they had been to the eastern mountain, however, the brothers and sisters separated. Keeping their first marriages secret, the brothers now married women of the Mirage People and the sisters married men of the Mirage People. But they never told anyone, even their new families, the mysteries they had learned from the gods. Every four days the women bore children, who grew to maturity in four days, then married, and in their turn had children every four days. In this way many children of First Man and First Woman filled the land with people.

—Based on a legend reported by Washington Matthews
in 1897.

It is very common in origin stories around the world for the first people to be hermaphrodites or bisexuals. Religious scholars have been trying for years to find an explanation, but have not yet succeeded.

■

HOW MEN AND WOMEN GOT TOGETHER

■

[BLOOD-PIEGAN]

Old Man had made the world and everything on it. He had done everything well, except that he had put the men in one place and the women in another, quite a distance away. So they lived separately for a while.

Men and women did everything in exactly the same way. Both had buffalo jumps—steep cliffs over which they chased buffalo herds so that the animals fell to their death at the foot of the cliff. Then both the men and the women butchered the dead animals. This meat was their only food; they had not yet discovered other things that were good to eat.

After a while the men learned how to make bows and arrows. The women learned how to tan buffalo hides and make tipis and beautiful robes decorated with porcupine quills.

One day Old Man said to himself: "I think I did everything well, but I made one bad mistake, putting women and men in different places. There's no joy or pleasure in that. Men and women are different from each other, and these different things must be made to unite so that there will be more people. I must make men mate with women. I will put some pleasure, some good feeling into it; otherwise the men won't be keen to do what is necessary. I myself must set an example."

Old Man went over to where the women were living. He traveled for four days and four nights before he saw the women in their camp. He was hiding behind some trees, watching. He said to himself: "Ho, what a good life they're having! They have these fine tipis made of tanned buffalo hide, while we men have only brush shelters or raw, stinking, green hides to cover us. And look what fine clothes they wear, while we have to go around with a few pelts around our loins! Really, I made a mistake putting the women so far away from us. They must live with us and make fine tents and beautiful clothes for us also. I'll go back and ask the other men how they feel about this."

So Old Man went back to his camp and told the men what he had seen. When they heard about all the useful and beautiful things the women had, the men said: "Let's go over there and get together with these different human beings."

"It's not only those things that are worth having," said Old Man. "There's something else—a very pleasurable thing I plan on creating."

Now, while this was going on in the men's camp, the chief of the women's village had discovered the tracks Old Man had made while prowling around. She sent a young woman to follow them and report back. The young woman arrived near the men's camp, hid herself, and watched for a short while. Then she hurried back to the women as fast as she could and told everybody: "There's a camp over there with human beings living in it. They seem different from us, taller and stronger. Oh, sisters, these beings live very well, better than us. They have a thing shooting sharp sticks, and with these they kill many kinds of game— food that we don't have. They are never hungry."

When they heard this, all the women said: "How we wish that these strange human beings would come here and kill all kinds of food for us!" When the women were finishing their meeting, the men were already over the hill toward them. The women looked at the men and saw how shabbily dressed they were, with just a little bit of rawhide around their loins. They looked at the men's matted hair, smelled the strong smell coming from their unwashed bodies. They looked at their dirty skin. They said to each other: "These beings called men don't know how to live. They have no proper clothes. They're dirty; they smell. We don't want people like these." The woman chief hurled a rock at Old Man, shouting: "Go away!" Then all the women threw rocks and shouted "Go away!"

Old Man said: "It was no mistake putting these creatures far away from us. Women are dangerous. I shouldn't have created them." Then Old Man and all the men went back to their own place.

After the men left, the woman chief had second thoughts. "These poor men," she said, "they don't know any better, but we could teach them. We could make clothes for them. Instead of shaming them, maybe we could get them to come back if we dress as poorly as they do, just with a piece of hide or fur around our waist.

And in the men's camp, Old Man said: "Maybe we should try to meet these women creatures once more. Yes, we should give it another chance. See what I did on the sly." He opened his traveling bundle in which he kept his jerk meat and other supplies, and out of it took a resplendent white buckskin outfit. "I managed to steal this when those women weren't looking. It's too small for me, but I'll add on a little buffalo hide here and a little bear fur there, and put a shield over here, where it doesn't come together over my belly. And I'll make myself a feather headdress and paint my face. Then maybe this woman chief will look at me with new eyes. Let me go alone to speak with the women creatures first. You stay back a little and hide until I have straightened things out."

So Old Man dressed up as best he could. He even purified himself in a sweat bath which he thought up for this purpose. He looked at his reflection in the lake waters and exclaimed: "Oh, how beautiful I am! I never knew I was that good-looking! Now that woman chief will surely like me."

Then Old Man led the way back to the women's camp. There was one woman on the lookout, and even though the men were staying back in hiding, she saw them coming. Then she spotted Old Man standing alone on a hilltop overlooking the camp. She hurried to tell the woman chief, who was butchering with most of the other women at the buffalo jump. For this job they wore their poorest outfits: just pieces of rawhide with a hole for the head, or maybe only a strap of rawhide around the waist. What little they had on was stiff with blood and reeked of freshly slaughtered carcasses. Even their faces and hands were streaked with blood.

"We'll meet these men just as we are," said the woman chief. "They will appreciate our being dressed like them."

So the woman chief went up to the hill on which Old Man was standing, and the other women followed her. When he saw the woman chief standing there in her butchering clothes, her skinning flint knife still in her hand, her hair matted and unkempt, he exclaimed: "Hah! Hrumph! This woman chief is ugly. She's dressed in rags covered with blood. She stinks. I want nothing to do with a creature like this. And those other women are just like her. No, I made no mistake putting these beings far away from us men!" And having said this, he turned around and went back the way he had come, with all his men following him.

"It seems we can't do anything right," said the woman chief. "Whatever it is, those male beings misunderstand it. But I still think we should unite with them. I think they have something we haven't got, and we have something they haven't got, and these things must come together. We'll try one last time to get them to understand us. Let's make ourselves beautiful."

The women went into the river and bathed. They washed and combed their hair, braided it, and attached hair strings of bone pipes and shell beads. They put on their finest robes of well-tanned, dazzling white doeskin covered with wonderful designs of porcupine quills more colorful than the rainbow. They placed bone and shell chokers around their necks and shell bracelets around their wrists. On their feet they put fully quilled moccasins. Finally the women painted their cheeks with sacred red face paint. Thus wonderfully decked out, they started on their journey to the men's camp.

In the village of the male creatures, Old Man was cross and ill-humored. Nothing pleased him. Nothing he ate tasted good. He slept fitfully. He got angry over nothing. And so it was with all the men. "I don't know what's the matter," said Old Man. "I wish women were beautiful instead of ugly, sweet-smelling instead of malodorous, good-tempered instead of coming at us with stones or bloody knives in their hands."

"We wish it too," said all the other men.

Then a lookout came running, telling Old Man: "The women beings are marching over here to our camp. Probably they're coming to kill us. Quick everybody, get your bows and arrows!"

"No, wait!" said Old Man. "Quick! Go to the river. Clean yourselves. Anoint and rub your bodies with fat. Arrange your hair pleasingly. Smoke yourselves up with cedar. Put on your best fur garments. Paint your faces with sacred red color. Put bright feathers on your heads." Old Man himself dressed in quilled robe stolen from the women's camp which he had made into a war shirt. He wore his great chief's headdress. He put on his necklace of bear claws. Thus arrayed, the men assembled at the entrance of their camp, awaiting the women's coming.

The women came. They were singing. Their white quilled robes dazzled the men's eyes. Their bodies were fragrant with the good smell of sweet grass. Their cheeks shone with sacred red face paint.

Old Man exclaimed: "Why, these women beings are beautiful! They delight my eyes! Their singing is wonderfully pleasing to my ears. Their bodies are sweet-smelling and alluring!"

"They make our hearts leap," said the other men.

"I'll go talk to their woman chief," said Old Man. "I'll fix things up with her."

The woman chief in the meantime remarked to the other women: "Why, these men beings are really not as uncouth as we thought. Their rawness is a sort of strength. The sight of their arm muscles pleases my eyes. The sound of their deep voices thrills my ears. They are not altogether bad, these men."

Old Man went up to the woman chief and said, "Let's you and I go someplace and talk."

"Yes, let's do that," answered the woman chief. They went someplace. The woman chief looked at Old Man and liked what she saw. Old Man looked at the woman chief and his heart pounded with joy. "Let's try one thing that has never been tried before," he said to the woman chief.

"I always like to try out new, useful things," she answered.

"Maybe one should lie down, trying this," said Old Man.

"Maybe one should," agreed the woman chief. They lay down.

After a while Old Man said: "This is surely the most wonderful thing that ever happened to me. I couldn't ever imagine such a wonderful thing."

"And I," said the woman chief, "I never dreamed I could feel so good. This is much better, even, than eating buffalo tongues. It's too good to be properly described."

"Let's go and tell the others about it," said Old Man.

When Old Man and the woman chief got back to the camp, they found nobody there. All the male creatures and the women beings had already paired off and gone someplace, each pair to their own spot. They didn't need to be told about this new thing; they had already found out.

When the men and women came back from wherever they had gone, they were smiling. Their eyes were smiling. Their mouths were smiling, their whole bodies were smiling, so it seemed.

Then the women moved in with the men. They brought all their things, all their skills to the men's village. Then the women quilled and tanned for the men. Then the men hunted for the women. Then there was love. Then there was happiness. Then there was marriage. Then there were children.

—*Based on four fragments dating from 1883 to 1910.*

THE WELL-BAKED MAN

■

[PIMA]

The creation of the white man is depicted here, as in many other tales, as one of the Creator's slight mistakes.

■ ▏▏▏ ■

The Magician had made the world but felt that something was missing. "What could it be?" he thought. "What could be missing?" Then it came to him that what he wanted on this earth was some beings like himself, not just animals. "How will I make them?" he thought. First he built himself a *horno*, an oven. Then he took some clay and formed in into a shape like himself.

Now, Coyote was hanging around the way he usually does, and when Magician, who was Man Maker, was off gathering firewood, Coyote quickly changed the shape of that clay image. Man Maker built a fire inside the *horno*, then put the image in without looking at it closely.

After a while the Magician said: "He must be ready now." He took the image and breathed on it, whereupon it came to life. "Why don't you stand up?" said Man Maker. "What's wrong with you?" The creature barked and wagged its tail. "Ah, oh my, Coyote has tricked me," he said. "Coyote changed my being into an animal like himself."

"Coyote said, "Well, what's wrong with it? Why can't I have a pretty creature that pleases me?"

"Oh my, well, all right, but don't interfere again." That's why we have the dog; it was Coyote's doing.

So Man Maker tried again. "They should be companions to each other," he thought. "I shouldn't make just one." He shaped some humans who were rather like himself and identical with each other in every part.

"What's wrong here?" Man Maker was thinking. Then he saw. "Oh my, that won't do. How can they increase?" So he pulled a little between the legs of one image, saying: "Ah, that's much better." With his fingernail he made a crack in the other image. He put some pleasant feeling in them somewhere. "Ah, now it's good. Now they'll be able to do all the necessary things." He put them in the *horno* to bake.

"They're done now," Coyote told him. So Man Maker took them out and made them come to life.

"Oh my, what's wrong?" he said. "They're underdone; they're not brown enough. They don't belong here—they belong across the water someplace." He scowled at Coyote. "Why did you tell me they were done? I can't use them here."

So the Magician tried again, making a pair like the last one and placing them in the oven. After a while he said: "I think they're ready now."

"No, they aren't done yet," said Coyote. "You don't want them to come out too light again; leave them in a little longer."

"Well, all right," replied Man Maker. They waited, and then he took them out. "Oh my. What's wrong? These are overdone. They're burned too dark." He put them aside. "Maybe I can use them some other place across the water. They don't belong here."

For the fourth time Man Maker placed his images inside the oven. "Now, don't interfere," he said to Coyote, "you give me bad advice. Leave me alone."

This time the Magician did not listen to Coyote but took them out when he himself thought they were done. He made them come to life, and the two beings walked around, talked, laughed, and behaved in a seemly fashion. They were neither underdone nor overdone.

"These are exactly right," said Man Maker. "These really belong here; these I will use. They are beautiful." So that's why we have the Pueblo Indians.

—*Based on fragments recorded in the 1880s.*

■

THE WHITE BUFFALO WOMAN

■

[BRULE SIOUX]

The Sioux are a warrior tribe, and one of their proverbs says, "Woman shall not walk before man." Yet White Buffalo Woman is the dominant figure of their most important legend. The medicine man Crow Dog explains, "This holy woman brought the sacred buffalo calf pipe to the Sioux. There could be no Indians without it. Before she came, people didn't know how to live. They knew nothing. The Buffalo Woman put her sacred mind into their minds." At the ritual of the sun dance one woman, usually a mature and universally respected member of the tribe, is given the honor of representing Buffalo Woman.

Though she first appeared to the Sioux in human form, White Buffalo Woman was also a buffalo—the Indians' brother, who gave its flesh so that the people might live. Albino buffalo were sacred to all Plains tribes; a white buffalo hide was a sacred talisman, a possession beyond price.

■ ▮▮▮▮▮▮▮▮▮▮▮▮▮▮▮▮▮▮▮▮▮▮▮▮▮▮▮▮▮▮▮ ■

One summer so long ago that nobody knows how long, the Oceti-Shakowin, the seven sacred council fires of the Lakota Oyate, the nation, came together and camped. The sun shone all the time, but there was no game and the people were starving. Every day they sent scouts to look for game, but the scouts found nothing.

Among the bands assembled were the Itazipcho, the Without-Bows, who had their own camp circle under their chief, Standing Hollow Horn. Early one morning the chief sent two of his young men to hunt for game. They went on foot, because at that time the Sioux didn't yet have horses. They searched everywhere but could find nothing. Seeing a high hill, they decided to climb it in order to look over the whole country. Halfway up, they saw something coming toward them from far off, but the figure was floating instead of walking. From this they knew that the person was *wakan*, holy.

At first they could make out only a small moving speck and had to squint to see that it was a human form. But as it came nearer, they realized that it was a beautiful young woman, more beautiful than any they had ever seen, with two round, red dots of face paint on her cheeks. She wore a wonderful white buckskin outfit, tanned until it shone a long way in the sun. It was embroidered with sacred and marvellous designs of porcupine quill, in radiant colors no ordinary woman could have made. This *wakan* stranger was Ptesan-Wi, White Buffalo Woman. In her hands she carried a large bundle and a fan of sage leaves. She wore her blue-black hair loose except for a strand at the left side, which was tied up with buffalo fur. Her eyes shone dark and sparkling, with great power in them.

The two young men looked at her open-mouthed. One was overawed, but the other desired her body and stretched his hand out to touch her. This woman was *lila wakan*, very sacred, and could not be treated with disrespect. Lightning instantly struck the brash young man and burned him up, so that only a small heap of blackened bones was left. Or some say that he was suddenly covered by a cloud, and within it he was eaten up by snakes that left only his skeleton, just as a man can be eaten up by lust.

To the other scout who had behaved rightly, the White Buffalo

Woman said: "Good things I am bringing, something holy to your nation. A message I carry for your people from the buffalo nation. Go back to the camp and tell the people to prepare for my arrival. Tell your chief to put up a medicine lodge with twenty-four poles. Let it be made holy for my coming."

This young hunter returned to the camp. He told the chief, he told the people, what the sacred woman had commanded. The chief told the *eyapaha*, the crier, and the crier went through the camp circle calling: "Someone sacred is coming. A holy woman approaches. Make all things ready for her." So the people put up the big medicine tipi and waited. After four days they saw the White Buffalo Woman approaching, carrying her bundle before her. Her wonderful white buckskin dress shone from afar. The chief, Standing Hollow Horn, invited her to enter the medicine lodge. She went in and circled the interior sunwise. The chief addressed her respectfully, saying: "Sister, we are glad you have come to instruct us."

She told him what she wanted done. In the center of the tipi they were to put up an *owanka wakan*, a sacred altar, made of red earth, with a buffalo skull and a three-stick rack for a holy thing she was bringing. They did what she directed, and she traced a design with her finger on the smoothed earth of the altar. She showed them how to do all this, then circled the lodge again sunwise. Halting before the chief, she now opened the bundle. The holy thing it contained was the *chanunpa*, the sacred pipe. She held it out to the people and let them look at it. She was grasping the stem with her right hand and the bowl with her left, and thus the pipe has been held ever since.

Again the chief spoke, saying: "Sister, we are glad. We have had no meat for some time. All we can give you is water." They dipped some *wacanga*, sweet grass, into a skin bag of water and gave it to her, and to this day the people dip sweet grass or an eagle wing in water and sprinkle it on a person to be purified.

The White Buffalo Woman showed the people how to use the pipe. She filled it with *chan-shasha*, red willow-bark tobacco. She walked around the lodge four times after the manner of Anpetu-Wi, the great sun. This represented the circle without end, the sacred hoop, the road of life. The woman placed a dry buffalo chip on the fire and lit the pipe with it. This was *peta-owihankeshni*, the fire without end, the flame to be passed on from generation to generation. She told them that the smoke rising from the bowl was Tunkashila's breath, the living breath of the great Grandfather Mystery.

The White Buffalo Woman showed the people the right way to pray, the right words and the right gestures. She taught them how to sing the pipe-filling song and how to lift the pipe up to the sky, toward Grandfather, and down toward Grandmother Earth, to Unci, and then to the four directions of the universe.

"With this holy pipe," she said, "you will walk like a living prayer. With your feet resting upon the earth and the pipestem reaching into the sky, your body forms a living bridge between the Sacred Beneath and the Sacred Above. Wakan Tanka smiles upon us, because now we are as one: earth, sky, all living things, the two-legged, the four-legged, the winged ones, the trees, the grasses. Together with the people, they are all related, one family. The pipe holds them all together.

"Look at this bowl," said the White Buffalo Woman. "Its stone represents the buffalo, but also the flesh and blood of the red man. The buffalo represents the universe and the four directions, because he stands on four legs, for the four ages of creation. The buffalo was put in the west by Wakan Tanka at the making of the world, to hold back the waters. Every year he loses one hair, and in every one of the four ages he loses a leg. The sacred hoop will end when all the hair and legs of the great buffalo are gone, and the water comes back to cover the Earth.

The wooden stem of this *chanunpa* stands for all that grows on the earth. Twelve feathers hanging from where the stem—the backbone— joins the bowl—the skull—are from Wanblee Galeshka, the spotted eagle, the very sacred bird who is the Great Spirit's messenger and the wisest of all flying ones. You are joined to all things of the universe, for they all cry out to Tunkashila. Look at the bowl: engraved in it are seven circles of various sizes. They stand for the seven sacred ceremonies you will practice with this pipe, and for the Ocheti Shakowin, the seven sacred campfires of our Lakota nation."

The White Buffalo Woman then spoke to the women, telling them that it was the work of their hands and the fruit of their bodies which kept the people alive. "You are from the mother earth," she told them. "What you are doing is as great as what the warriors do."

And therefore the sacred pipe is also something that binds men and women together in a circle of love. It is the one holy object in the making of which both men and women have a hand. The men carve the bowl and make the stem; the women decorate it with bands of colored porcupine quills. When a man takes a wife, they both hold the pipe at the same time and red trade cloth is wound around their hands, thus tying them together for life.

The White Buffalo Woman had many things for her Lakota sisters in her sacred womb bag—corn, *wasna* (pemmican), wild turnip. She taught them how to make the hearth fire. She filled a buffalo paunch

with cold water and dropped a red-hot stone into it. "This way you shall cook the corn and the meat," she told them.

The White Buffalo Woman also talked to the children, because they have an understanding beyond their years. She told them that what their fathers and mothers did was for them, that their parents could remember being little once, and that they, the children, would grow up to have little ones of their own. She told them: "You are the coming generation, that's why you are the most important and precious ones. Some day you will hold this pipe and smoke it. Some day you will pray with it."

She spoke once more to all the people: "The pipe is alive; it is a red being showing you a red life and a red road. And this is the first ceremony for which you will use the pipe. You will use it to keep the soul of a dead person, because through it you can talk to Wakan Tanka, the Great Mystery Spirit. The day a human dies is always a sacred day. The day when the soul is released to the Great Spirit is another. Four women will become sacred on such a day. They will be the ones to cut the sacred tree—the *can-wakan*—for the sun dance."

She told the Lakota that they were the purest among the tribes, and for that reason Tunkashila had bestowed upon them the holy *chanunpa*. They had been chosen to take care of it for all the Indian people on this turtle continent.

She spoke one last time to Standing Hollow Horn, the chief, saying, "Remember: this pipe is very sacred. Respect it and it will take you to the end of the road. The four ages of creation are in me; I am the four ages. I will come to see you in every generation cycle. I shall come back to you."

The sacred woman then took leave of the people, saying: *"Toksha ake wacinyanktin ktelo—I shall see you again."*

The people saw her walking off in the same direction from which she had come, outlined against the red ball of the setting sun. As she went, she stopped and rolled over four times. The first time, she turned into a black buffalo; the second into a brown one; the third into a red one; and finally, the fourth time she rolled over, she turned into a white female buffalo calf. A white buffalo is the most sacred living thing you could ever encounter.

The White Buffalo Woman disappeared over the horizon. Sometime she might come back. As soon as she had vanished, buffalo in great herds appeared, allowing themselves to be killed so that the people might survive. And from that day on, our relations, the buffalo, furnished the people with everything they needed—meat for their food, skins for their clothes and tipis, bones for their many tools.

*—Told by Lame Deer at Winner, Rosebud Indian
Reservation, South Dakota, 1967.*

Two very old tribal pipes are kept by the Looking Horse family at Eagle Butte in South Dakota. One of them, made from a buffalo calf's leg bone, too fragile and brittle with age to be used for smoking, is said to be the sacred pipe which the Buffalo Maiden brought to the people. "I know," said Lame Deer. "I prayed with it once, long ago."

The turtle continent is North America, which many Indian tribes regard as an island sitting on the back of a turtle.

John Fire Lame Deer was a famous Sioux "holy man," grandson of the first Chief Lame Deer, a great warrior who fought Custer and died during a skirmish with General Miles. Lame Deer's son, Archie, is carrying on his work as a medicine man and director of the sun dance.

THE ORPHAN BOY AND THE ELK DOG

[BLACKFOOT]

The horse was introduced to this continent by the Spaniards when they arrived in the middle of the sixteenth century. Within two centuries the horses had been acquired by almost every tribe and had transformed the Indians' life. As there was no Indian word for horse, and it carried burdens like a dog, it was usually named Elk Dog, Spirit Dog, Sacred Dog, or Moose Dog.

In the days when people had only dogs to carry their bundles, two orphan children, a boy and his sister, were having a hard time. The boy was deaf, and because he could not understand what people said, they thought him foolish and dull-witted. Even his relatives wanted nothing to do with him. The name he had been given at birth, while his parents still lived, was Long Arrow. Now he was like a beaten, mangy dog, the kind who hungrily roams outside a camp, circling it from afar, smelling the good meat boiling in the kettles but never coming close for fear of being kicked. Only his sister, who was bright and beautiful, loved him.

Then the sister was adopted by a family from another camp, people who were attracted by her good looks and pleasing ways. Though they wanted her for a daughter, they certainly did not want the awkward, stupid boy. And so they took away the only person who cared about him, and the orphan boy was left to fend for himself. He lived on scraps thrown to the dogs and things he found on the refuse heaps. He dressed in remnants of skins and frayed robes discarded by the poorest people. At night he bedded down in a grass-lined dugout, like an animal in its den.

Eventually the game was hunted out near the camp that the boy regarded as his, and the people decided to move. The lodges were taken down, belongings were packed into rawhide bags and put on dog travois, and the village departed. "Stay here," they told the boy. "We don't want your kind coming with us."

For two or three days the boy fed on scraps the people had left behind, but he knew he would starve if he stayed. He had to join his people, whether they liked it or not. He followed their tracks, frantic that he would lose them, and crying at the same time. Soon the sweat was running down his skinny body. As he was stumbling, running, panting, something suddenly snapped in his left ear with a sound like a small crack, and a worm-like substance came out of that ear. All at once on his left side he could hear birdsongs for the first time. He took this worm-like thing in his left hand and hurried on. Then there was a snap in his right ear and a worm-like thing came out of it, and on his right side he could hear the rushing waters of a stream. His hearing was restored! And it was razor sharp—he could make out the rustling of a tiny mouse in dry leaves a good distance away. The orphan boy laughed and was happy for the first time in his life. With renewed courage he followed the trail his people had made.

In the meantime the village had settled into its new place. Men were already out hunting. Thus the boy came upon Good Running, a kindly old chief, butchering a fat buffalo cow he had just killed. When the chief saw the boy, he said to himself, "Here comes that poor good-for-nothing boy. It was wrong to abandon him." To the boy Good Running said: "Rest here, grandson, you're sweaty and covered with dust. Here, have some tripe."

The boy wolfed down the meat. He was not used to hearing and talking yet, but his eyes were alert and Good Running also noticed a change in his manner. "This boy," the chief said to himself, "is neither stupid nor crazy." He gave the orphan a piece of the hump meat, then a piece of liver, then a piece of raw kidney, and at last the very best kind of meat—a slice of tongue. The more the old man looked at the boy, the more he liked him. On the spur of the moment he said, "Grandson, I'm going to adopt you; there's a place for you in my tipi. And I'm going to make you into a good hunter and warrior." The boy wept, this time for joy. Good Running said, "They called you a stupid, crazy boy, but now that I think of it, the name you were given at birth is Long Arrow. I'll see that people call you by your right name. Now come along."

The chief's wife was not pleased. "Why do you put this burden on me," she said, "bringing into our lodge this good-for-nothing, this, slow-witted crazy boy? Maybe you're a little slow-witted and crazy yourself!"

"Woman, keep talking like that and I'll beat you! This boy isn't slow or crazy; he's a good boy, and I have taken him for my grandson. Look—he's barefooted. Hurry up, and make a pair of moccasins for him, and if you don't do it well I'll take a stick to you."

Good Running's wife grumbled but did as she was told. Her husband was a kind man, but when aroused, his anger was great.

So a new life began for Long Arrow. He had to learn to speak and to understand well, and to catch up on all the things a boy should know. He was a fast learner and soon surpassed other boys his age in knowledge and skills. At last even Good Running's wife accepted him.

He grew up into a fine young hunter, tall and good-looking in the quilled buckskin outfit the chief's wife made for him. He helped his grandfather in everything and became a staff for Good Running to lean on. But he was lonely, for most people in the camp could not forget that Long Arrow had once been an outcast. "Grandfather," he said one day, "I want to do something to make you proud and show people that you were wise to adopt me. What can I do?"

Good Running answered, "Someday you will be a chief and do great things."

"But what's a great thing I could do now, Grandfather?"

The chief thought for a long time. "Maybe I shouldn't tell you this," he said. "I love you and don't want to lose you. But on winter nights, men talk of powerful spirit people living at the bottom of a faraway lake. Down in that lake the spirit people keep mystery animals who do their work for them. These animals are larger than a great elk, but they carry the burdens of the spirit people like dogs. So they're called Pono-Kamita—Elk Dogs. They are said to be swift, strong, gentle, and beautiful beyond imagination. Every fourth generation, one of our young warriors has gone to find these spirit folk and bring back an Elk Dog for us. But none of our brave young men has ever returned."

"Grandfather, I'm not afraid. I'll go and find the Elk Dog."

"Grandson, first learn to be a man. Learn the right prayers and ceremonies. Be brave. Be generous and open-handed. Pity the old and the fatherless, and let the holy men of the tribe find a medicine for you which will protect you on your dangerous journey. We will begin by purifying you in the sweat bath."

So Long Arrow was purified with the white steam of the sweat lodge. He was taught how to use the pipe, and how to pray to the Great Mystery Power. The tribe's holy men gave him a medicine and made for him a shield with designs on it to ward off danger.

Then one morning, without telling anybody, Good Running loaded his best travois dog with all the things Long Arrow would need for traveling. The chief gave him his medicine, his shield, and his own fine bow and, just as the sun came up, went with his grandson to the edge of the camp to purify him with sweet-smelling cedar smoke. Long Arrow left un-

heard and unseen by anyone else. After a while some people noticed
that he was gone, but no one except his grandfather knew where and
for what purpose.

Following Good Running's advice, Long Arrow wandered southward.
On the fourth day of his journey he came to a small pond, where a
strange man was standing as if waiting for him. "Why have you come
here?" the stranger asked.

"I have come to find the mysterious Elk Dog."

"Ah, there I cannot help you," said the man, who was the spirit of
the pond. "But if you travel further south, four-times-four days, you
might chance upon a bigger lake and there meet one of my uncles.
Possibly he might talk to you; then again, he might not. That's all I
can tell you."

Long Arrow thanked the man, who went down to the bottom of the
pond, where he lived.

Long Arrow wandered on, walking for long hours and taking little
time for rest. Through deep canyons and over high mountains he went,
wearing out his moccasins and enduring cold and heat, hunger and
thirst.

Finally Long Arrow approached a big lake surrounded by steep pine-
covered hills. There he came face to face with a tall man, fierce and
scowling and twice the height of most humans. This stranger carried a
long lance with a heavy spearpoint made of shining flint. "Young one,"
he growled, "why did you come here?"

"I came to find the mysterious Elk Dog."

The stranger, who was the spirit of the lake, stuck his face right into
Long Arrow's and shook his mightly lance. "Little one, aren't you
afraid of me?" he snarled.

"No, I am not," answered Long Arrow, smiling.

The tall spirit man gave a hideous grin, which was his way of being
friendly. "I like small humans who aren't afraid," he said, "but I can't

help you. Perhaps our grandfather will take the trouble to listen to you. More likely he won't. Walk south for four-times-four days, and maybe you'll find him. But probably you won't." With that the tall spirit turned his back on Long Arrow and went to the bottom of the lake, where he lived.

Long Arrow walked on for another four-times-four days, sleeping and resting little. By now he staggered and stumbled in his weakness, and his dog was not much better off. At last he came to the biggest lake he had ever seen, surrounded by towering snow-capped peaks and waterfalls of ice. This time there was nobody to receive him. As a matter of fact, there seemed to be no living thing around. "This must be the Great Mystery Lake," thought Long Arrow. Exhausted, he fell down upon the shortgrass meadow by the lake, fell down among the wild flowers and went to sleep with his tired dog curled up at his feet.

When Long Arrow awoke, the sun was already high. He opened his eyes and saw a beautiful child standing before him, a boy in a dazzling white buckskin robe decorated with porcupine quills of many colors. The boy said: "We have been expecting you for a long time. My grandfather invites you to his lodge. Follow me."

Telling his dog to wait, Long Arrow took his medicine shield and his grandfather's bow and went with the wonderful child. They came to the edge of the lake. The spirit boy pointed to the water and said: "My grandfather's lodge is down there. Come!" The child turned himself into a kingfisher and dove straight to the bottom.

Afraid, Long Arrow thought, "How can I follow him and not be drowned?" But then he said to himself, "I knew all the time that this would not be easy. In setting out to find the Elk Dog, I already threw my life away." And he boldly jumped into the water. To his surprise, he found it did not make him wet, that it parted before him, that he could breathe and see. He touched the lake's sandy bottom. It sloped down, down toward a center point.

Long Arrow descended this slope until he came to a small, flat valley. In the middle of it stood a large tipi of tanned buffalo hide. The images of two strange animals were drawn on it in sacred vermillion paint. A kingfisher perched high on the top of the tipi flew down and turned again into the beautiful boy, who said, "Welcome. Enter my grandfather's lodge."

Long Arrow followed the spirit boy inside. In the back at the seat of honor sat a black-robed old man with flowing white hair and such power emanating from him that Long Arrow felt himself in the presence of a truly Great One. The holy man welcomed Long Arrow and offered him food. The man's wife came in bringing dishes of buffalo hump, liver, tongues, delicious chunks of deer meat, the roasted flesh of strange, tasty water birds, and meat pounded together with berries, chokecherries, and kidney fat. Famished after his long journey, Long Arrow ate with relish. Yet he still looked around to admire the furnishings of the tipi, the painted inner curtain, the many medicine shields, wonderfully wrought weapons, shirts and robes decorated with porcupine quills in rainbow colors, beautifully painted rawhide containers filled with wonderful things, and much else that dazzled him.

After Long Arrow had stilled his hunger, the old spirit chief filled the pipe and passed it to his guest. They smoked, praying silently. After a while the old man said: "Some came before you from time to time, but they were always afraid of the deep water, and so they went away with empty hands. But you, grandson, were brave enough to plunge in, and therefore you are chosen to receive a wonderful gift to carry back to your people. Now, go outside with my grandson."

The beautiful boy took Long Arrow to a meadow on which some strange animals, unlike any the young man had ever seen, were galloping and gamboling, neighing and nickering. They were truly wonderful to look at, with their glossy coats fine as a maiden's hair, their long manes and tails streaming in the wind. Now rearing, now nuzzling, they looked at Long Arrow with gentle eyes which belied their fiery appearance.

"At last," thought Long Arrow, "here they are before my own eyes, the Pono-Kamita, the Elk Dogs!"

"Watch me," said the mystery boy, "so that you learn to do what I am doing." Gracefully and without effort, the boy swung himself onto the back of a jet-black Elk Dog with a high, arched neck. Larger than any elk Long Arrow had ever come across, the animal carried the boy all over the meadow swiftly as the wind. Then the boy returned, jumped off his mount, and said, "Now you try it." A little timidly Long Arrow climbed up on the beautiful Elk Dog's back. Seemingly regarding him as feather-light, it took off like a flying arrow. The young man felt himself soaring through the air as a bird does, and experienced a happiness greater even than the joy he had felt when Good Running had adopted him as a grandson.

When they had finished riding the Elk Dogs, the spirit boy said to Long Arrow: "Young hunter from the land above the waters, I want you to have what you have come for. Listen to me. You may have noticed that my grandfather wears a black medicine robe as long as a woman's dress, and that he is always trying to hide his feet. Try to get a glimpse of them, for if you do, he can refuse you nothing. He will then tell you to ask him for a gift, and you must ask for these three things: his rainbow-colored quilled belt, his black medicine robe, and a herd of these animals which you seem to like."

Long Arrow thanked him and vowed to follow his advice. For four days the young man stayed in the spirit chief's lodge, where he ate well and often went out riding on the Elk Dogs. But try as he would, he could never get a look at the old man's feet. The spirit chief always kept them carefully covered. Then on the morning of the fourth day, the old one was walking out of the tipi when his medicine robe caught in the entrance flap. As the robe opened, Long Arrow caught a glimpse of a leg and one foot. He was awed to see that it was not a human limb at all, but the glossy leg and firm hoof of an Elk Dog! He could not stifle a cry of surprise, and the old man looked over his shoulder and saw that his leg and hoof were exposed. The chief seemed a little embarrassed, but shrugged and said: "I tried to hide this, but you must have been fated to see it. Look, both of my feet are those of an Elk Dog. You may as well ask me for a gift. Don't be timid; tell me what you want."

Long Arrow spoke boldly: "I want three things: your belt of rainbow colors, your black medicine robe, and your herd of Elk Dogs."

"Well, so you're really not timid at all!" said the old man. "You ask for a lot, and I'll give it to you, except that you cannot have all my Elk Dogs; I'll give you half of them. Now I must tell you that my black hair medicine robe and my many-colored belt have Elk Dog magic in them. Always wear the robe when you try to catch Elk Dogs; then they can't get away from you. On quiet nights, if you listen closely to the belt, you will hear the Elk Dog dance song and Elk Dog prayers. You must learn them. And I will give you one more magic gift: this long rope woven from the hair of a white buffalo bull. With it you will never fail to catch whichever Elk Dog you want."

The spirit chief presented him with the gifts and said: "Now you must leave. At first the Elk Dogs will not follow you. Keep the medicine robe and the magic belt on at all times, and walk for four days toward the north. Never look back—always look to the north. On the fourth day the Elk Dogs will come up beside you on the left. Still don't look back. But after they have overtaken you, catch one with the rope of white buffalo hair and ride him home. Don't lose the black robe, or you will lose the Elk Dogs and never catch them again."

Long Arrow listened carefully so that he would remember. Then the old spirit chief had his wife make up a big pack of food, almost too heavy for Long Arrow to carry, and the young man took leave of his generous spirit host. The mysterious boy once again turned himself into a kingfisher and led Long Arrow to the surface of the lake, where his faithful dog greeted him joyfully. Long Arrow fed the dog, put his pack of food on the travois, and started walking north.

On the fourth day the Elk Dogs came up on his left side, as the spirit chief had foretold. Long Arrow snared the black one with the arched neck to ride, and he caught another to carry the pack of food. They galloped swiftly on, the dog barking at the big Elk Dogs' heels.

When Long Arrow arrived at last in his village, the people were afraid and hid. They did not recognize him astride his beautiful Elk Dog but took him for a monster, half man and half animal. Long Arrow kept calling, "Grandfather Good Running, it's your grandson. I've come back bringing Elk Dogs!"

Recognizing the voice, Good Running came out of hiding and wept for joy, because he had given Long Arrow up for lost. Then all the others emerged from their hiding places to admire the wonderful new animals.

Long Arrow said, "My grandfather and grandmother who adopted me, I can never repay you for your kindness. Accept these wonderful Elk Dogs as my gift. Now we no longer need to be humble footsloggers, because these animals will carry us swiftly everywhere we want to go. Now buffalo hunting will be easy. Now our tipis will be larger, our possessions will be greater, because an Elk Dog travois can carry a load ten times bigger than that of a dog. Take them, my grandparents. I shall keep for myself only this black male and this black female, which will grow into a fine herd."

"You have indeed done something great, Grandson," said Good Running, and he spoke true. The people became the bold riders of the Plains and soon could hardly imagine how they had existed without these wonderful animals.

After some time Good Running, rich and honored by all, said to Long Arrow: "Grandson, lead us to the Great Mystery Lake so we can camp by its shores. Let's visit the spirit chief and the wondrous boy; maybe they will give us more of their power and magic gifts."

Long Arrow led the people southward and again found the Great Mystery Lake. But the waters would no longer part for him, nor would any of the kingfishers they saw turn into a boy. Nor, gazing down into the crystal-clear water, could they discover people, Elk Dogs, or a tipi. There was nothing in the lake but a few fish.

—Retold from George Bird Grinnell and other sources
around 1910.

SALT WOMAN IS REFUSED FOOD

[COCHITI]

Old Salt Woman had a grandson, and they were very poor. They came to Cochiti and went from house to house, but people turned them away. They were all busy cooking for a feast. At that time they used no salt.

When Salt Woman and her grandson had been to all the houses, they came to a place outside the pueblo where lots of children were playing. All the children came to see the magic crystal Salt Woman had in her hand. She led them to a piñon tree and told them each to take hold of a branch of the tree and swing themselves. Using her magic crystal, she turned them into the chaparral jays who live in piñon trees. "When we were in the pueblo, nobody would invite us to stay," Salt Woman said. "From now on you will be chaparral jays."

Salt Woman and her grandson went south and came to Santa Domingo, where they were well treated and fed. After they had eaten and were leaving, Salt Woman said, "I am very thankful for being given food to eat," and she left them some of her flesh. The people of the house ate it with their bread and meat. It tasted good—salty.

"At Cochiti," Salt Woman told them, "they treated me badly, and when I left, I took all the children outside the pueblo and changed them into chaparral jays roosting in a piñon tree. But to you I am grateful. Therefore remember that if I am in your food, it will always taste better. I will go southeast and stay there, and if any of you want more of my flesh you will find it at that place. And when you come to gather, let there be no laughing, no singing, nothing of that kind. Be quiet and clean." So she left Santo Domingo and went to Salt Lake, where we get salt today.

—From a legend recorded by Ruth Benedict in 1924.

The procuring of salt was and still is associated with a set of solemn ceremonies in the Southwest. The journey to the source is considered a great odyssey or pilgrimage, and those making this trip must undergo elaborate rituals and carefully observe strict taboos. When they return, the entire experience is described in detail, analyzed, and preserved by the rest of the tribe. The mythic figure associated with salt is almost always an old woman, as we see here, and she often provides it through her mucus, which is shared among the people.

THE SACRED WEED

[BLACKFOOT]

For longer than anyone knows, Indians throughout the Americas have smoked tobacco and other plants for pleasure and for praying. The smoke was the Great Spirit's breath taking the prayers up to the Ones Above. With a pipe in his hands, a man could speak nothing but the truth. Sir Walter Raleigh learned the use of tobacco from the Indians. When he first had a smoke in a London inn, the bartender, thinking that he was on fire, emptied a tankard of ale over him. To the white man, smoking became an addiction; but to the native American, pipe and tobacco were sacred and smoking was a holy ritual. A man who had killed a member of his own tribe could not smoke ritually with the others. He had to smoke a mean little pipe all by himself—hard punishment.

There once were four brothers, all spiritual men who had power. In a vision the oldest of them heard a voice saying: "Out there is a sacred weed; pick it and burn it." The man looked around, saw the strange weed, and put it in the fire. It gave off a very pleasing aroma.

Then the second brother had a dream in which a voice said: "Take this herb. Chop it fine. Put it into a hide bag." The man did what he was told, and the dry herb in his hide bag was wonderfully fragrant. The third brother had a vision in which he saw a man hollowing out a bone and putting the strange weed into it. A voice said, "Make four pipes like this," and the third brother carved four pipes out of an animal's leg bones.

Then the youngest of the four brothers had a vision. A voice told him: "You four men light your pipes and smoke. Inhale the smoke; exhale it. Let the smoke ascend to the clouds." The voice also taught him the songs and prayers that went with smoking.

So the four medicine men, born of the same mother, smoked together. This was the first time that men had ever smoked, and they sang and prayed together as they did so.

The brothers, who called the sacred weed *nawak'osis*, were meant to teach its use to the people. But *nawak'osis* made them powerful and wise and clear-minded, and they did not want to share it with others. They planted the sacred weed in a secret place that only they knew. They guarded the songs and prayers and rituals that went with smoking. They formed a Tobacco Society, just the four of them.

So there was anger, there was war, there was restlessness of spirit, there was impiety. *Nawak'osis* was meant to calm anger, to make men worship, to make peace, to ease the mind. But without the sacred herb, unity and peace were lacking.

A young man called Bull-by-Himself said to his wife: "These four powerful ones have been given something good to share with the people, but they are keeping it for themselves. So things are bad. I must find a way to plant and reap the sacred weed they call *nawak'osis*."

Bull-by-Himself and his wife went to a sacred lake and set up their tipi close by its shore. The man left every day to hunt and look for the plant *nawak'osis*. The woman stayed in the lodge to quill, tan, and prepare food. One day while she was alone, she heard somebody singing beautifully. She searched everywhere to find the source of the music and discovered that it was coming from a beaver house close by the shore. "It must be the beavers singing," she thought. "Their songs are lovely. I hope they don't stop."

Though her husband came home with plenty of meat, he had not found *nawak'osis*. The woman called his attention to the music, but he said, "I hear nothing. It's your imagination."

"No," she said, "I can hear it clearly. Put your ear to the beaver house." He did, but still heard nothing.

Then the wife took her knife and made a hole in the beaver lodge. Through it they could not only hear the beavers sing, but also watch them performing a strange, beautiful dance.

"My young brothers," the wife called to them, "be of a sharing spirit. Teach me your wonderful song and your medicine!"

The Beavers answered: "Close the hole you have made, because it lets the cold in. Then we'll come out and visit you." So she sealed their wall up, and that night four beavers came to Bull-by-Himself's lodge. As soon as they were inside they turned themselves into humans—four nice-looking young men. One asked: "What have you come here for?"

"I have come," said Bull-by-Himself, "to find the sacred weed called *nawak'osis*."

"Then this is the right place," said the man-beavers. "We are water people, and *nawak'osis* is water medicine. We will give you this sacred herb, but first you must learn the songs, the prayers, the dances, the ceremonies that go with it."

"There are four powerful men in our tribe," said Bull-by-Himself, "who have the medicine and the knowledge, but keep them from us."

"Ah," said the man-beavers, "that is wrong. This sacred weed is meant to be shared. Here is what you must do. By day, go out and get the skin of every four-legged and two-legged creature that lives in and around the water—except, of course, beaver. You must get the skins of the muskrat and otter, of the duck and kingfisher, of all creatures like that, because they represent water. Sun and water mean life. Sun begets life, and water makes it grow."

So every day Bull-by-Himself went out for the skins, while his wife scraped, tanned, and smoked them. And every night the four man-beavers came to teach them the prayers, songs, and dances that go with *nawak'osis*. After a while the beavers said: "Now all is ready. Now you have all the skins, and now you have the knowledge. Make the skins, which represent water power, into a bag, into a medicine bundle. Tomorrow night we'll come again for the last time to tell you what to do."

The following night the beavers came as they had promised. They brought with them the sacred weed *nawak'osis*. The top of the stalks was covered with little round seeds, and the man-beavers put the seeds into the medicine bundle the woman had prepared.

"It's planting time now," said the Beavers. "Don't touch *nawak'osis* before you're ready to plant. Choose a place where there is not too much shade and not too much sunlight. Mix plenty of brown earth with plenty of black earth, and keep the soil loose. Say the prayers we have taught you. Then you, Bull-by-Himself, must take a deer horn and with its point make holes in the earth—one hole for each seed. And you, his wife, must use a buffalo-horn spoon to drop one seed into each hole. Keep singing the songs we taught you all the while. Then both of you dance lightly over this earth, tamping down the seeds. After that you just wait for *nawak'osis* to grow. Now we have taught you everything. Now we go." The nice-looking young men left, turning back into beavers as they went.

Bull-by-Himself and his wife planted the sacred weed as they had been told. The four medicine-men brothers said to one another: "What can this man, Bull-by-Himself, and his wife be planting? Their songs sound familiar." They sent somebody to find out, and this person came back saying: "They are planting *nawak'osis*, doing it in a sacred manner."

The four powerful men began to laugh. "No, it can't be. It's some useless weed they're planting. No one but us can plant *nawak'osis*. No one but us can use it. No one but us has its power."

But when it was time to harvest *nawak'osis*, a great hailstorm destroyed the secret tobacco patch of the four medicine brothers. Nothing was left, and they had not saved a single seed. They said to each other: "Perhaps this man and his wife did plant *nawak'osis* after all. Perhaps the hail hasn't destroyed their tobacco patch."

Again the four brothers sent someone to find out, and that person came back saying: "This man and his wife had no hail on their field. Here is what they have been growing." He showed the brothers some leaves. "It is indeed *nawak'osis*," they said, shaking their heads in wonder.

Thus with the help of the beaver people, Bull-by-Himself and his wife brought the sacred tobacco to the tribes, who have been smoking it in a sacred manner ever since.

—Retold from several nineteenth-century sources.

HOW GRANDFATHER PEYOTE CAME TO THE INDIAN PEOPLE

[BRULE SIOUX]

Vision quests in which an individual seeks spiritual power are common to many Indian tribes. The peyote plant is often used by the Sioux and Cheyenne in the rituals associated with such quests— the sweat lodge, a solitary vigil, a flesh offering. The plant is often considered to be a human spirit and is a sacrament in the Native American Church, founded by a Comanche chief in the last century. Henry Crow Dog, the father of the man who told this story, was among those who introduced the peyote religion to the Sioux in the 1920s.

This is how Grandfather Peyote came to the Indian people. Long ago, before the white man, there was a tribe living far south of the Sioux in a land of deserts and mesas. These people were suffering from a sickness, and many died of it. One old woman had a dream that she would find a herb, a root, which would save her people.

The woman was old and frail but, taking her little granddaughter, she went on a vision quest to learn how to find this sacred herb. They walked away from the camp until they were lost. Arriving at the top of a lonely hill, the grandmother made a brush shelter for herself and the young one. Without water or food they were weak, and as night fell they huddled together, not knowing what to do.

Suddenly they felt the wingbeats of a huge bird, an eagle flying from the east toward the west. The old woman raised her arms and prayed to the eagle for wisdom and power. Toward morning they saw the figure of a man floating in the air about four steps above their heads. The old woman heard a voice: "You want water and food and do not know where to find it. I have a medicine for you. It will help you."

This man's arm was pointing to a spot on the ground about four steps from where the old woman was sitting. She looked and saw a peyote plant—a large Grandfather Peyote Plant with sixteen segments. She did not know what it was, but she took her bone knife and cut the green part off. And there was moisture, the peyote juice, the water of life. The old woman and her granddaughter drank it and were refreshed.

The sun went down again and the second night came. The old woman prayed to the spirit: "I am sacrificing myself for the people. Have pity on me. Help me!"

And the figure of the man appeared again, hovering above her as before, and she heard a voice saying: "You are lost now, but you will find your people again and you will save them. When the sun rises two more times, you will find them."

The grandmother ate some more of the sacred medicine and gave some to the girl. And a power entered them through the herb, bringing them knowledge and understanding and a sacred vison. Experiencing this new power, the old woman and her granddaughter stayed awake all night. Yet in the morning when the sun rose and shone upon the hide bag with the peyote, the old one felt strong. She said, Grand-daughter, pray with this new herb. It has no mouth, but it is telling me many things."

During the third night the spirit came again and taught the old woman how to show her people the proper way to use the medicine. In the morning she got up, thinking: "This one plant won't be enough to save my people. Could it have been the only herb in this world? How can I find more?"

Then she heard many small voices calling, "Over here, come over

here. I'm the one to pick." These were peyote plants guiding her to their hiding places among the thorn bushes and chaparral. So the old woman and the girl picked the herbs and filled the hide bag with them.

At nightfall once more they saw the spirit man, silhouetted against the setting sun. He pointed out the way to their camp so that they could return quickly. Though they had taken no food or water for four days and nights, the sacred medicine had kept them strong-hearted and strong-minded.

When they arrived home, their relatives were happy to have them back, but everybody was still sick and many were dying. The old woman told the people: "I have brought you a new sacred medicine which will help you."

She showed the men how to use this *pejuta*, this holy herb. The spirit had taught her the ceremony, and the medicine had given her the knowledge through the mind power which dwells within it. Under her direction the men put up a tipi and made a fire. At that time there was no leader, no roadman, to guide them, and the people had to learn how to perform the ceremony step by step, from the ground up.

Everybody, men and women, old and young, ate four buttons of the new medicine. A boy baby was breast nursing, and the peyote power got into him through his mother's milk. He was sucking his hand, and he began to shake it like a gourd rattle. A man sitting next to the tipi entrance got into the power and caught a song just by looking at the baby's arm.

A medicine man took a rattle of rawhide and began to shake it. The small stones inside the rattle were the voice of Grandfather Peyote, and everybody understood what it was saying. Another man grabbed a drum and beat it, keeping time with the song and the voice inside the rattle. The drumming was good, but it did not yet have the right sound, because in that first ceremony there was no water in the drum.

One woman felt the spirit telling her to look for a cottonwood tree. After the sun rose, all the people followed her as Grandfather Peyote guided her toward the west. They saw a rabbit jumping out of a hole inside a dried-up tree and knew that that this was the sacred cottonwood.

They cut down the tree and hollowed out the trunk like a drum where the rabbit hole had been. At the woman's bidding they filled it with fresh spring water—the water of life.

On the way back to camp, a man felt the power telling him to pick up five smooth, round pebbles and to cover the drum with a piece of tanned moose hide. He used the pebbles to make knobs around the rim of the drum so that he could tie the hide to it with a rawhide thong. And when he beat the drum it sounded good, as if a spirit had gotten hold of it.

When night came, the people made a fire inside the tipi and took the medicine again. Guided by peyote power, the old woman looked into the flames and saw a heart, like the heart-shaped leaf of the cottonwood tree. Thus she knew that the Great Spirit, who is also in Grandfather Peyote, wanted to give his heart to the red men of this continent. She told the man tending the fire to form the glowing embers into the shape of a heart, and the people all saw it beat in rhythm with the drum. A little later, one helper who was under the spirit power saw that the hide rope formed a star at the bottom of the drum. He shaped the glowing coals of the fire into a star and then into a moon, because the power of the star and the spirit of the moon had come into the tipi.

One man sitting opposite the door had a vision in which he was told to ask for water. The old woman brought fresh, cool water in a skin bag, and they all drank and in this way came under the power. Feeling the spirit of the water, the man who was in charge of the fire shaped the embers into the outline of a water bird, and from then on the water bird became the chief symbol of the holy medicine.

Around the fire this man made a half-moon out of earth, and all along the top of it he drew a groove with his finger. Thus he formed a road, the road of life. He said that anybody with the gift of *wacankiyapi*, which means having love and heart for the people, should sit right there.

And from that day on, the man who is running a meeting was called the "roadman."

In this way the people made the first peyote altar, and after they had drunk the water, they thanked the peyote. Looking at the fire in the shape of the sacred water bird, they prayed to the four directions, and someone sprinkled green cedar on the fire. The fragrant, sweet-smelling smoke was the breath of Grandfather Peyote, the spirit of all green and growing things.

Now the people had everything they needed: the sacred herb, the drum, the gourd, the fire, the water, the cedar. From that moment on, they learned to know themselves. Their sick were cured, and they thanked the old woman and her grandchild for having brought this blessing to them. They were the Comanche nation, and from them the worship of the sacred herb spread to all the tribes throughout the land.

—*Told by Leonard Crow Dog at Winner, Rosebud Indian*
Reservation, South Dakota, 1970.

■

THE VISION QUEST

■

[BRULE SIOUX]

The vision quest is a tradition among the Plains people. A man or woman seeking the way on the road of life, or trying to find the answer to a personal problem, may go on a vision quest for knowledge and enlightenment. This may mean staying on top of a hill or inside a vision pit, alone, without food or water, for as long as four days and nights. It is hard, but if the spirit voices reveal or confer a vision that shapes a person's life, then the quest is worth all the suffering.

The following tale, however, treats the vision quest with less than complete solemnity, with Sioux medicine man Lame Deer's characteristic quirks.

A young man wanted to go on a *hanbleceya*, or vision seeking, to try for a dream that would give him the power to be a great medicine man.

Having a high opinion of himself, he felt sure that he had been created to become great among his people and that the only thing lacking was a vision.

The young man was daring and brave, eager to go up to the mountaintop. He had been brought up by good, honest people who were wise in the ancient ways and who prayed for him. All through the winter they were busy getting him ready, feeding him *wasna*, corn, and plenty of good meat to make him strong. At every meal they set aside something for the spirits so that they would help him to get a great vision. His relatives thought he had the power even before he went up, but that was putting the cart before the horse, or rather the travois before the horse, as this is an Indian legend.

When at last he started on his quest, it was a beautiful morning in late spring. The grass was up, the leaves were out, nature was at its best. Two medicine men accompanied him. They put up a sweat lodge to purify him in the hot, white breath of the sacred steam. They santified him with the incense of sweet grass, rubbing his body with sage, fanning it with an eagle's wing. They went to the hilltop with him to prepare the vision pit and make an offering of tobacco bundles. Then they told the young man to cry, to humble himself, to ask for holiness, to cry for power, for a sign from the Great Spirit, for a gift which would make him into a medicine man. After they had done all they could, they left him there.

He spent the first night in the hole the medicine men had dug for him, trembling and crying out loudly. Fear kept him awake, yet he was cocky, ready to wrestle with the spirits for the vision, the power he wanted. But no dreams came to ease his mind. Toward morning before the sun came up, he heard a voice in the swirling white mists of dawn. Speaking from no particular direction, as if it came from different places, it said: "See here, young man, there are other spots you could have picked; there are other hills around here. Why don't you go there to cry for a dream? You disturbed us all night, all us creatures, animals and birds; you even kept the trees awake. We couldn't sleep. Why should you cry here? You're a brash young man, not yet ready or worthy to receive a vision."

But the young man clenched his teeth, determined to stick it out, resolved to force that vision to come. He spent another day in the pit, begging for enlightenment which would not come, and then another night of fear and cold and hunger.

The young man cried out in terror. He was paralyzed with fear, unable to move. The boulder dwarfed everything in view; it towered over the vision pit. But just as it was an arm's length away and about to crush him, it stopped. Then, as the young man stared openmouthed, his hair standing up, his eyes starting out of his head, the boulder ROLLED UP THE MOUNTAIN, all the way to the top. He could hardly believe what he saw. He was still cowering motionless when he heard the roar and ramble again and saw that immense boulder coming down at him once more. This time he managed to jump out of his vision pit at the last moment. The boulder crushed it, obliterated it, grinding the young man's peace pipe and gourd rattle into dust.

Again the boulder rolled up the mountain, and again it came down. "I'm leaving, I'm leaving!" hollered the young man. Regaining his power of motion, he scrambled down the hill as fast as he could. This time the boulder actually leapfrogged over him, bouncing down the slope, crushing and pulverizing everything in its way. He ran unseeingly, stumbling, falling, getting up again. He did not even notice the boulder rolling up once more and coming down for the fourth time. On this last and most fearful descent, it flew through the air in a giant leap, landing right in front of him and embedding itself so deeply in the earth that only its top was visible. The ground shook itself like a wet dog coming out of a stream and flung the young man this way and that.

Gaunt, bruised, and shaken, he stumbled back to his village. To the medicine men he said: "I have received no vision and gained no knowledge." He returned to the pit, and when dawn arrived once more, he heard the voice again: "Stop disturbing us; go away!" The same thing happened on the third morning. By this time he was faint with hunger,

thirst, and anxiety. Even the air seemed to oppress him, to fight him. He was panting. His stomach felt shriveled up, shrunk tight against his backbone. But he was determined to endure one more night, the fourth and last. Surely the vision would come. But again he cried for it out of the dark and loneliness until he was hoarse, and still he had no dream.

Just before daybreak he heard the same voice again, very angry: "Why are you still here?" He knew then that he had suffered in vain; now he would have to go back to his people and confess that he had gained no knowledge and no power. The only thing he could tell them was that he got bawled out every morning. Sad and cross, he replied "I can't help myself; this is my last day, and I'm crying my eyes out. I know you told me to go home, but who are you to give me orders? I don't know you. I'm going to stay until my uncles come to fetch me, whether you like it or not."

All at once there was a rumble from a larger mountain that stood behind the hill. It became a mighty roar, and the whole hill trembled. The wind started to blow. The young man looked up and saw a boulder poised on the mountain's summit. He saw lightning hit it, saw it sway. Slowly the boulder moved. Slowly at first, then faster and faster, it came tumbling down the mountainside, churning up the earth, snapping huge trees as if they were little twigs. And the boulder WAS COMING RIGHT DOWN ON HIM! I have made the spirits angry. It was all for nothing."

"Well, you did find out one thing," said the older of the two, who was his uncle. "You went after your vision like a hunter after buffalo, or a warrior after scalps. You were fighting the spirits. You thought they owed you a vision. Suffering alone brings no vision nor does courage, nor does sheer will power. A vision comes as a gift born of humility, of wisdom, and of patience. If from your vision quest you have learned nothing but this, then you have already learned much. Think about it."

—*Told by Lame Deer at Winner, Rosebud Indian*
Reservation, South Dakota, 1967, and recorded by
Richard Erdoes.

PART TWO

THE PLACE OF EMERGENCE

TALES OF WORLD CREATION

The world did not always exist as we know it today, and the myths which describe its creation are associated with (and as varied as) those about the rise of culture. The primordial environment is for almost all tribes a watery one, from which different beings bring up mud to make the earth. In Southwestern tales, four or five worlds of different colors or elements are stacked one on top of the other, and people climb up a reed or stalk through a hole in the ceiling of one dying world into the next, newborn one. People in the Northwest tell of descending through a hole in the sky (associated with the smoke hole of a tipi) to emerge into the present world. Countless characters enter into the action—true gods and spirits; monsters and dragons; elks, bears, eagles, and other birds. Even the trickster Coyote tries his hand at creation.

The creation myth of the Iroquois, reflected in those of many other cultures, combines several of these elements. The daughter of the Sky Chief is pushed down through a hole in the sky into a world that is covered with water, but she is saved from drowning by water fowls, who convince the great turtle below to harbor her. Toad dives for mud and makes the earth on the back of the great turtle. It is this daughter who, impregnated by the west wind, gives birth to the gentle, creative Tsentsa and his cruel brother, Taweskare, who kills his mother in childbirth as he kicks his way through her side.

The twins who combine both good and evil recur across the continent. Among the Yuma, it is Kokomaht, the all-father, who is good, while his blind brother, the subterranean Bakothal, personifies evil. The twins can also be two girls, or brother and sister. Manabozho, White Rabbit, is the creation hero of the Great Lakes region; he is also one of a set of twins who are both animal and human, his brother being Wolf.

In the California region, the culture hero may find himself floating in a boat in the chaos of primeval water. He sends animals to dive down to the bottom for a dab of mud and creates the present world from that. He also creates another character, frequently Coyote, who in turn makes man from wood or clay and gives him life. Animals are created next, and the world is ordered. The theft of light or fire is a prominent theme, as is the establishment of the earth's topography.

In the North Pacific and the plateau east of the Rockies to the Cascades, various heroes act through a similar cycle of events. From southern Vancouver Island north, Raven is the hero; in the Gulf of Georgia area it is Mink; and in Washington and Oregon it is Blue Jay. The cycle opens with the birth of a child after a spiritual conception; he is then adopted by a chief. The myths follow his adventures as he steals fire, light, water, and animals for his people, and gives animals and objects the forms they have today.

In the Southwest, creation myths are closely related to a complex ceremonialism that distinguishes these tribes from those of the rest of North America. We have already seen tales that describe the origin of ceremonies such as the corn dance. In creation stories of the Southwest, life emerges from lower worlds, with people fashioned from the creator's skin. There are twin heroes here as well, and struggles with primeval monsters.

Common themes and images of creation are widespread across North America, for myths migrate as freely as people. The theme of primeval water covering a not-yet-created earth is perhaps the most prevalent, found in every area except that of the Eskimo, while only the Southwest lacks the episode of a diving creature fashioning the earth from mud. The California regions and the Southwest share tales of the original world parents, Earth and Sky, and the creation of men from rubbings of skin. Among tribes of the Trans-Mississippi West, the determination of the seasons is a prominent theme, and there are many stories across the continent which describe how the four winds came to be. While stories of a creator and of the formation of the universe (which follow in Part Three) tend to be more fragmentary, there is clear and universal concern for the beginning of mankind and the foundation of the world in which humans live.

THE GOOD TWIN AND
THE EVIL TWIN

[YUMA]

This is how it all began. There was only water—there was no sky, there was no land, only nothingness. Then out of the waters rose a mist, and it became the sky. Still there were no sun, no moon, no stars—just darkness. But deep down in the waters lived Kokomaht, the Creator. He was bodiless, nameless, breathless, motionless, and he was two beings —twins.

Then the waters stirred and rushed and thundered, and out of the spray and foam rose the first twin, the good twin. With closed eyes he cleaved the waves and came to the surface. He stood upon the waters, opened his eyes, and saw. There he named himself Kokomaht—All-Father.

And from beneath the waters a second voice called out to Kokomaht: "Brother, how did you rise? With eyes open or with eyes closed?"

Bakotahl was the evil twin, and Kokomaht wanted to make it more difficult for him to do harm. So Kokomaht lied to him, saying: "I opened my eyes while I was under water." The second twin opened his eyes as he rose, and when he reached the surface he was blind. Kokomaht said: "I name you Bakotahl—the Blind One."

Then Kokomaht said: "Now I shall make the four directions." He pointed with his finger and took four steps, walking on the water. Then he stood still for a while and said, "Ho, this is north." Then he went back to his starting place, and in the same manner made the west, the south, and the east—always taking four steps in each direction and always returning to the center.

"Now," Kokomaht said, "I shall make the earth."

Blind Bakotahl answered: "I don't think you have the power to do this."

"Certainly I have," said Kokomaht.

"Let me try to make the earth first," asked Bakotahl.

"Certainly not," said Kokomaht.

Kokomaht stirred the waters into a foaming whirlpool with his hand.

They frothed and swelled and bubbled, and when they subsided there was land. And Kokomaht sat down upon it.

Bakotahl was angry because he would have liked to create the earth, but he said nothing and settled down by Kokomaht's side. The Blind Evil One said to himself: "I shall make something with a head, with arms and legs. I can make it out of the earth." Bakotahl formed something resembling a human being, but it was imperfect. Instead of hands and feet there were lumps; it had neither fingers nor toes. Bakotahl hid it from Kokomaht.

Then Kokomaht said: "I feel like making something." Out of mud he shaped a being that was perfect. It had hands and feet, fingers and toes, even fingernails and toenails. Kokomaht waved this being four times toward the north and then stood it on its feet. It moved, it walked, it was alive: it was a man. Kokomaht made another being in the same way, and it was alive: it was a woman.

Bakotahl went on trying to make humans, piecing together seven beings out of earth. All were imperfect. "What are you making?" Kokomaht asked.

"People," answered Bakotahl.

"Here," said Kokomaht, "feel these people I've made. Yours have no hands or feet. Here; feel; mine have fingers, thumbs, to work, to fashion things, to draw bows, to pick fruit." Kokomaht examined the beings Bakotahl had formed. "These are no good," he said, and stamped them to pieces. Bakotahl was so enraged that he dove down deep beneath the waters amid rumblings and thunderings. From the depths he sent up the whirlwind, bringer of all evil. Kokomaht stepped on the whirlwind and killed it—except for a little whiff that slipped out from under his foot. In it were contained all the sicknesses which plague people to this day.

So Kokomaht was by himself except for the two beings he had made. These were the Yumas, and in the same way that he had created them, Kokomaht now made the Cocopahs, the Dieguieños, and the Mojaves. In pairs he created them. Then he rested. Four tribes he had created. After having rested, he made four more tribes: the Apaches, the Maricopas, the Pimas, and the Coahuilas. In all, he made twenty-four kinds of people. The white people he left for last.

The one he had made first, the Yuma man, said to Kokomaht: "Teach us how to live."

"You must learn how to increase," said Kokomaht. In order to teach them, he begat a son. Out of nothing, without help from a woman, he sired him and named him Komashtam'ho. He told men and women not to live apart, but to join together and rear children.

Still something was missing. "It is too dark," said Kokomaht. "There should be some light." So he made the moon, the morning star, and all the other stars. Then he said, "My work is done. Whatever I have not finished, my son Komashtam'ho will finish."

Now, among the beings Kokomaht had made was Hanyi, the Frog. She was powerful; fire could not destroy her. She envied Kokomaht his power and thought to destroy him. Kokomaht knew this because he knew the thoughts of all the beings he had made, but he said to himself: "I taught the people how to live. Now I must teach them how to die, for without death there will soon be too many people on the earth. So I will permit Frog to kill me."

Hanyi burrowed down underneath the spot where Kokomaht was standing and sucked the breath out of his body through a hole in the earth. Then Kokomaht sickened and lay down to die. He called all the people to come to him, and all came except the white man, who stayed by himself in the west.

The white man was crying because his hair was faded and curly and his skin pale and washed out. The white man was always pouting and selfish. Whatever he saw, he had to have at once. He had been created childish and greedy. Komashtam'ho, tired of hearing the white man crying, went over to him and tied two sticks together in the form of a cross. "Here, stop crying," he said. "Here's something for you to ride on." The white man straddled these sticks and they turned into a horse, so the greedy one was satisfied—for a while.

For the last time now Kokomaht taught the people. "Learn how to die," he told them, and expired.

"I have to make what my father could not finish," said Komashtam'ho. He spat into his hand and from his spittle made a disk. He took it and threw it up into the sky toward the east. It began to shine. "This is the sun," Komashtam'ho told the people. "Watch it move; watch it lighting up the world."

Then Komashtam'ho prepared to burn the body of his father, but since there were no trees yet, he had no wood. Komashtam'ho called out: "Wood, come into being! Wood, come alive! Wood, come here to where I stand." Wood came from everywhere and formed itself into a great funeral pyre.

Before he died, Kokomaht had told Coyote: "Friend, take my heart. Be faithful. Do what I tell you." Coyote misunderstood Kokomaht and thought that he was supposed to eat the heart. Komashtam'ho knew this because he could see into Coyote's mind. So he told Coyote: "Go get a spark from the sun to light a fire."

As soon as Coyote was gone, Komashtam'ho took a sharpened stick and twirled it in some soft wood until he sparked a flame. "Look, my people," he said, "this is the way to make fire. Quick now, before Coyote comes back." With these words he lit the funeral pyre. The people did not lament for Kokomaht because they did not yet understand what death was. But before the flames had consumed the body, Coyote returned and leapt up quick as a flash to seize Kokomaht's heart. He ran off with it, and though all the other animals and the people too chased after him, he was too fast for them.

Komashtam'ho called after Coyote: "You have done something bad. You will never amount to anything. You will be a wild man without a house to live in. You will live by stealing, and for your thefts the people will kill you."

After Kokomaht's body had been burned, the people asked Komashtam'ho: "When will Kokomaht come back."

"He will never come back," he told them. "He is dead. He let himself be killed because if he had gone on living, then all you people would also live forever, and soon there would be no room left on the earth. So from now on, everybody will die sometime."

Then all the people began to lament. They wept for Kokomaht and for themselves. They did not want to believe that he would never come back. As they sat grieving, they saw a little whirlwind like a dust devil rising from the spot where Kokomaht had been burned. "What is it? What can it be?" they cried.

Komashtam'ho told them: "It is the spirit of Kokomaht. His body died, but his soul is alive. He will go someplace—north or south, east or west—somewhere his spirit will dwell. He will never tire, he will never be hungry or thirsty, and though we weep because he has died, Kokomaht's spirit will be happy always."

And Komashtam'ho instructed the people in the nature of death. "When you die, you will be again with those you love who have gone before you. Again you will be young and strong, though you might have been old and feeble on the day you died. In the spirit land the corn will

grow and all will be happy, whether they were good or bad when they were alive. So death is not something to be afraid of." And when they heard this, the people stopped weeping and smiled again.

Then Komashtam'ho chose one man, Marhokuvek, to help him put the world in order. The first thing that Marhokuvek did was to say, "Ho, you people, as a sign that you mourn the death of your father Kokomaht, you should cut your hair short." Then all the people, animals, and birds did as they had been told. The animals at this time were people also: they looked like humans. But when he saw them Komashtam'ho said: "These animals and birds don't look well with their hair cut," and changed them into coyotes and deer, into wild turkeys and roadrunners—into the animals and birds we have now.

After some time, Komashtam'ho let fall a great rain, the kind that never stops. There was a flood in which many of the animals were drowned. Marhokuvek was alarmed. "Komashtam'ho, what are you doing?" he cried.

"Some of these animals are too wild. Some have big teeth and claws and are dangerous. Also, there are simply too many of them. So I am killing them off with this flood."

"No, Komashtam'ho, stop the flood," pleaded Marhokuvek. "The people need many of these animals for food. They like to hear the songs of the birds. Rain and flood make the world too cold, and the people can't stand it."

So Komashtam'ho made a big fire to cause the waters to evaporate. The fire was so hot and fierce that even Komashtam'ho himself was slightly burned. Ever since that time, the deserts around here have been hot, and the people are used to the warmth.

After that, he called the people together and told them: "Over there is your father Kokomaht's house. We must pull it down, because when a man dies, the spirits of his house and of all his belongings follow him to the spirit land. So people must destroy all the things he owned in this life so that their spirits can serve him in the other world. Also, after a man has died, it is not good to look upon the things that he used to own. One sees his house, but he who dwelt in it is gone. One sees his water olla, but he who owned it is no longer here to lift it to his lips. It makes people sad, and they sicken with grief and longing. Therefore you Yuma people must always burn the house and possessions of those who die, and you must move to another dwelling where nothing reminds you of the dead. Also, never again mention the name of him who is gone. He belongs to another life, while you must start on a new one." And from that time on, the Yuma have followed these rules.

Komashtam'ho took a huge pole, smashed the house of Kokomaht, and rooted up the ground on which it had stood. Water welling up from the rut made by the pole became the Colorado River. And in it swam the beings that Bakotahl—the Blind Evil One—had formed, the creatures without hands or feet, toes or fingers. These were the fish and other water animals.

Now Kahk, the Crow, was a good planter and reaper. He brought corn and all kinds of useful seeds from the four corners of the world. He flew south to the great water, stopping four times on the way and crying: "Kahk, kahk!" Each time he did this, a big mountain arose. After the overflow of the river which Komashtam'ho had made, Crow brought many seeds from the south for the people to plant.

The tribes had been scattered over all the world, but Komashtam'ho kept the Yuma near him because they were the special people he loved. "Listen closely," he said to them. "I cannot stay with you forever. I am now only one, but soon I will become four. My name will no longer be Komashtam'ho. I will turn myself into four eagles—the black eagle of the west, the brown eagle of the south, the white eagle of the east, and the fourth eagle, whose name is 'unseen,' because no man has ever caught a glimpse of him."

When Komashtam'ho had turned himself into the four eagles, he dwelt no longer among the Yuma in the shape of a man. He kept watch over them, however, and in their dreams he gave them power from Kokomaht. Thus Kokomaht advises the people through Komashtam'ho and tells them while they sleep: "Think about me, think of what I taught you. Sick people especially should follow my teachings."

Now Bakotahl, the Evil Blind One, is under the earth and does bad things. Usually he lies down there quietly, but sometimes he turns over. Then there is a great noise of thunder, the earth trembles and splits open, and mountainsides crack, while flames and smoke shoot out of their summits. Then the people are afraid and say: "The Blind Evil One is stirring down below."

Everything that is good comes from Kokomaht, and everything evil comes from Bakotahl. This is the tale—how it was, and how it is, and how it will be.

—Retold from several sources, among them Natalie Curtis's report in 1909.

THE JICARILLA GENESIS

[JICARILLA APACHE]

In the beginning the earth was covered with water, and all living things were below in the underworld. Then people could talk, the animals could talk, the trees could talk, and the rocks could talk.

It was dark in the underworld, and eagle plumes were used for torches. The people and the animals that go about by day wanted more light, but the night animals—the bear, the panther, and the owl—wanted darkness. After a long argument they agreed to play the thimble-and-button game, and if the day animals won there would be light, but if the night animals won it would always be dark.

The game began. The magpie and the quail, who love the light and have sharp eyes, watched until they could see the button through the thin wood of the hollow stick that served as a thimble. This told the people where the button was, and in the first round, the people won. The morning star came out and the black bear ran and hid in the darkness. They played again, and the people won. It grew bright in the east and the brown bear ran and hid in a dark place. They played a third time, and the people won. It grew brighter in the east and the mountain lion slunk away into the darkness. They played a fourth time, and again the people won. The sun came up in the east, and it was day, and the owl flew away and hid.

Even though it was light now, the people still didn't see much because they were underground. But the sun was high enough to look through a hole and discover that there was another world—this earth. He told the people, and they all wanted to go up there. They built four mounds to help them reach the upper world. In the east they mounded the soil and planted it with all kinds of fruits and berries that were colored black. In the south they heaped up another mound and planted all kinds of fruits that were blue. In the west they built a mound that they planted with yellow fruits. In the north they planted the mound with fruits of variegated colors.

The mounds grew into mountains and the bushes blossomed, fruited, and produced ripened berries. One day two girls climbed up to pick berries and gather flowers to tie in their hair. Suddenly the mountains stopped growing. The people wondered, and they sent Tornado to learn the cause. Tornado went everywhere and searched into every corner, and at last he found the two girls and brought them back to their people. But the mountains did not grow any more, and this is why a boy stops growing when he goes with a woman for the first time. If he never did, he would continue to grow taller.

The mountains had stopped growing while their tops were still a long way from the upper world. So the people tried laying feathers crosswise to make a ladder, but the feathers broke under weight. The people made a second ladder of larger feathers, but again they were too weak. They made a third ladder of eagle feathers, but even these would not bear much weight. Then a buffalo came and offered his right horn, and three others also contributed their right horns. The horns were strong and straight, and with them the people were able to climb up through the hole to the surface of the earth. But the weight of all those humans bent the buffalo horns, which have been curved ever since.

Now the people fastened the sun and moon with spider threads so that they could not get away, and sent them up into the sky to give light. And since water covered the whole earth, four storms went to roll the waters away. The black storm blew to the east and rolled up the waters into the eastern ocean. The blue storm blew to the south and rolled up the waters in that direction. The yellow storm rolled up the waters in the west, and the varicolored storm went to the north and rolled up the waters there. So the tempests formed the four oceans in the east, the south, the west, and the north. Having rolled up the waters, the storms returned to where the people were waiting, grouped around the mouth of the hole.

The Polecat first went out, when the ground was still soft, and his legs sank in the black mud and have been black ever since. They sent the Tornado to bring him back, because it wasn't time. The badger went out, but he too sank in the mud and got black legs, and Tornado called him back. Then the beaver went out, walking through the mud and swimming through the water, and at once began to build a dam to save the water still remaining in pools. When he did not return, Tornado found him and asked why he had not come back.

"Because I wanted to save the water for the people to drink," said the beaver.

"Good," said Tornado, and they went back together. Again the people waited, until at last they sent out the gray crow to see if the time had come. The crow found the earth dry, and many dead frogs, fish, and reptiles lying on the ground. He began picking out their eyes and did not return until Tornado was sent after him. The people were angry when they found he had been eating carrion, and they changed his color to black.

But now the earth was all dry, except for the four oceans and the lake in the center, where the beaver had dammed up the waters. All the people came up. They traveled east until they arrived at the ocean; then they turned south until they came again to the ocean; then they went west to the ocean, and then they turned north. And as they went, each tribe stopped where it wanted to. But the Jicarillas continued to circle around the hole where they had come up from the underworld. Three times they went around it, when the Ruler became displeased and asked them where they wished to stop. They said, "In the middle of the earth." So he led them to a place very near Taos and left them, and there near the Taos Indians, the Jicarillas made their home.

—Based on a tale reported by James Mooney in the 1890s.

WHEN GRIZZLIES WALKED UPRIGHT

[MODOC]

Before there were people on the earth, the Chief of the Sky Spirits grew tired of his home in the Above World, because the air was always brittle with an icy cold. So he carved a hole in the sky with a stone and pushed all the snow and ice down below until he made a great mound that reached from the earth almost to the sky. Today it is known as Mount Shasta.

Then the Sky Spirit took his walking stick, stepped from a cloud to the peak, and walked down to the mountain. When he was about half-way to the valley below, he began to put his finger to the ground here and there, here and there. Wherever his finger touched, a tree grew. The snow melted in his footsteps, and the water ran down in rivers.

The Sky Spirit broke off the small end of his giant stick and threw the pieces into the rivers. The longer pieces turned into beaver and otter; the smaller pieces became fish. When the leaves dropped from the trees, he picked them up, blew upon them, and so made the birds. Then he took the big end of his giant stick and made all the animals that walked on the earth, the biggest of which were the grizzly bears.

Now when they were first made, the bears were covered with hair and had sharp claws, just as they do today, but they walked on two feet and could talk like people. They looked so fierce that the Sky Spirit sent them away from him to live in the forest at the base of the mountain.

Pleased with what he'd done, the Chief of the Sky Spirits decided to bring his family down and live on the earth himself. The mountains of snow and ice became their lodge. He made a big fire in the center of the mountain and a hole in the top so that the smoke and sparks could fly out. When he put a big log on the fire, sparks would fly up and the earth would tremble.

Late one spring while the Sky Spirit and his family were sitting round the fire, the Wind Spirit sent a great storm that shook the top of the mountain. It blew and blew and roared and roared. Smoke blown back into the lodge hurt their eyes, and finally the Sky Spirit said to his youngest daughter, "Climb up to the smoke hole and ask the Wind Spirit to blow more gently. Tell him I'm afraid he will blow the mountain over."

As his daughter started up, her father said, "But be careful not to stick your head out at the top. If you do, the wind may catch you by the hair and blow you away."

The girl hurried to the top of the mountain and stayed well inside the smoke hole as she spoke to the Wind Spirit As she was about to climb back down, she remembered that her father had once said you could see the ocean from the top of their lodge. His daughter wondered what the ocean looked like, and her curiosity got the better of her. She poked her head out of the hole and turned toward the west, but before she could see anything, the Wind Spirit caught her long hair, pulled her out of the mountain, and blew her down over the snow and ice. She landed among the scrubby fir trees at the edge of the timber and snow line, her long red hair trailing over the snow.

There a grizzly bear found the little girl when he was out hunting food for his family. He carried her home with him, and his wife brought her up with their family of cubs. The little red-haired girl and the cubs ate together, played together, and grew up together.

When she became a young woman, she and the eldest son of the grizzly bears were married. In the years that followed they had many children, who were not as hairy as the grizzlies, yet did not look exactly like their spirit mother, either.

All the grizzly bears throughout the forests were so proud of these new creatures that they made a lodge for the red-haired mother and her children. They placed the lodge near Mount Shasta—it is called Little Mount Shasta today.

After many years had passed, the mother grizzly bear knew that she would soon die. Fearing that she should ask the Chief of the Sky Spirits to forgive her for keeping his daughter, she gathered all the grizzlies at the lodge they had built. Then she sent her oldest grandson in a cloud to the top of Mount Shasta, to tell the Spirit Chief where he could find his long-lost daughter.

When the father got this news he was so glad that he came down the mountainside in giant strides, melting the snow and tearing up the land under his feet. Even today his tracks can be seen in the rocky path on the south side of Mount Shasta.

As he neared the lodge, he called out, "Is this where my little daughter lives?"

He expected his child to look exactly as she had when he saw her last. When he found a grown woman instead, and learned that the strange creatures she was taking care of were his grandchildren, he became very angry. A new race had been created that was not of his making! He frowned on the old grandmother so sternly that she promptly fell dead. Then he cursed all the grizzlies:

"Get down on your hands and knees. You have wronged me, and from this moment all of you will walk on four feet and never talk again."

He drove his grandchildren out of the lodge, put his daughter over his shoulder, and climbed back up the mountain. Never again did he come to the forest. Some say that he put out the fire in the center of his lodge and took his daughter back up to the sky to live.

Those strange creatures, his grandchildren, scattered and wandered over the earth. They were the first Indians, the ancestors of all the Indian tribes.

That's why the Indians living around Mount Shasta would never kill a grizzly bear. Whenever a grizzly killed an Indian, his body was burned on the spot. And for many years all who passed that way cast a stone there until a great pile of stones marked the place of his death.

—*Reported by Ella Clark in 1953.*

OLD MAN COYOTE MAKES
THE WORLD

[CROW]

Here the trickster takes on the mysterious powers of a Creator, leaving aside his clowning ways for a moment.

How water came to be, nobody knows. Where Old Man Coyote came from, nobody knows. But he was, he lived. Old Man Coyote spoke: "It is bad that I am alone. I should have someone to talk to. It is bad that there is only water and nothing else." Old Man Coyote walked around. Then he saw some who were living—two ducks with red eyes.

"Younger brothers," he said, "is there anything in this world but water and still more water? What do you think?"

"Why," said the ducks, "we think there might be something deep down below the water. In our hearts we believe this."

"Well, younger brothers, go and dive. Find out if there is something. Go!"

One of the ducks dove down. He stayed under water for a long, long time.

"How sad!" Old Man Coyote said. "Our younger brother must have drowned."

"No way has he drowned," said the other duck. "We can live under water for a long time. Just wait."

At last the first duck came to the surface. "What our hearts told us was right," he said. "There is something down there, because my head bumped into it."

"Well, my younger brother, whatever it may be, bring it up."

The duck dived again. A long time he stayed down there. When he came up, he had something in his beak. "Why, what can this be?" Old Man Coyote took it. "Why, this is a root," he said. "Where there are roots, there must be earth. My younger brother, dive again. If you find something soft, bring it up."

The duck went down a third time. This time he came up with a small lump of soft earth in his bill. Old Man Coyote examined it. "Ah, my younger brother, this is what I wanted. This I will make big. This I will spread around. This little handful of mud shall be our home."

Old Man Coyote blew on the little lump, which began to grow and spread all over. "What a surprise, elder brother!" said the ducks. "This is wonderful! We are pleased."

Old Man Coyote took the little root. In the soft mud he planted it. Then things started to grow. Grasses, plants, trees, all manner of food Old Man Coyote made in this way. "Isn't this pretty?" he asked. "What do you think?"

"Elder brother," answered the ducks, "this is indeed very pretty. But it's too flat. Why don't you hollow some places out, and here and there make some hills and mountains. Wouldn't that be a fine thing?"

"Yes, my younger brothers. I'll do as you say. While I'm about it, I will also make some rivers, ponds, and springs so that wherever we go, we can have cool, fresh water to drink."

"Ah, that's fine, elder brother," said the ducks after Old Man Coyote had made all these things. "How very clever you are."

"Well, is something still missing, younger brothers? What do your hearts believe?"

"Everything is so beautiful, elder brother. What could be missing?"

"Companions are missing," Old Man Coyote said. "We are alone. It's boring."

He took up a handful of mud, and out of it made people. How he did this, no one can imagine. The people walked about. Watching them, Old Man Coyote was pleased, but the ducks were not so happy. "Elder brother," they said, "you have made companions for yourself, but none for us."

"Why, that's true. I forgot it." Right away he made all kinds of ducks. "There, my younger brothers, now you can be happy."

After a while Old Man Coyote remarked: "Something's wrong here."

"But everything is good. We're no longer bored. What could be wrong?"

"Why, don't you see, I've made all these people men, and all the ducks I made are male. How can they be happy? How can they increase?"

Forthwith he made women. Forthwith he made female ducks. Then there was joy. Then there was contentment. Then there was increase. That's the way it happened.

Old Man Coyote walked about on the earth he had made. Suddenly he encountered Cirape, the coyote. "Why, younger brother, what a wonderful surprise! Where did you come from?"

"Well, my elder brother, I don't know. I exist. That's all. Here I am. Cirape, I call myself. What's your name?"

"Old Man Coyote, they call me." He waved his hand: "All that you see around you, I made."

"You did well. But there should be some animals besides ducks."

"Yes, you're right, come to think of it. Now, I'll pronounce some animal names. As soon as I say one, that animal will be made." Old Man Coyote named buffalo, deer, elk, antelopes, and bear. And all these came into being.

After some time the bear said to Old Man Coyote: "Why did you make me? There's nothing to do. We're all bored."

"I have made females for you. This should keep everybody busy."

"Well, elder brother, one can't do that all the time."

"Yes, you're right; it's true. Well, I'll think of something. I'll make a special bird."

From one of the bear's claws he made wings. From a caterpillar's hair he made feet. From a bit of buffalo sinew he made a beak. From leaves he made a tail. He put all these things together and formed a prairie chicken. Old Man Coyote instructed it: "There are many pretty birds. You I haven't made pretty, but I gave you a special power. Every dawn as the sun rises, you shall dance. You will hop and strut with your head down. You will raise your tail and shake it. Spreading your wings, you shall dance—thus!"

At once the prairie chicken danced. All the animals watched, and soon they began to dance too. Now there was something to keep them amused. But the bear still wasn't satisfied. "I gave you a claw to make part of this prairie chicken," he told Old Man Coyote. "Why didn't you give me my own dance? I don't want to dance like a chicken."

"Well, all right, cousin. I'll give you a dance of your own. Thus and thus, this way and that, you shall dance."

"Old Man Coyote," the bear kept complaining, "how can I dance? Something is missing."

"How can something be missing? I've made everything."

"There should be some kind of sound to dance to."

"Why, you're right. There should be." Forthwith Old Man Coyote made a little grouse and gave him a song. Then he made a drum—how, no man can imagine. The little grouse sang and drummed, and everybody danced.

"Why should this no-account prairie chicken dance?" asked the bear. "Why should all those little, no-account animals dance? I alone should have this dance power."

"Why, they're happy. The chokecherries are ripe, the sun is shining. All of them feel like dancing. Why should you be the only one?"

"I am big and important. So I alone should dance."

"Why, listen to him, how he talks! Be polite to me who made you."

"Ho! You didn't make me. I made myself."

"How impolite!" said Old Man Coyote. "He is threatening the little animals with his big claws." He told the bear: "You're not fit to live among us. You will stay in a den by yourself and eat decayed, rotten things. In winter you will sleep, because the less we see of you, the better." So it was.

One day Old Man Coyote and Cirape were walking and talking. "Something you forgot," Cirape said to Old Man Coyote.

"How could I have forgotten something?"

"Why, those people you made. They live poorly. They should have tools, tipis to live in, a fire to cook by and warm themselves."

"You're right. Why didn't I think of that?" Forthwith he made a fire with lightning and the people rejoiced.

"Now everything is finished. What do you think?"

"Oh, elder brother, the people should have bows and arrows and spears for better hunting. Often they starve."

"That's so. I'll give out weapons."

"Elder brother, give weapons, but only to the people, not to the animals."

"Why shouldn't the animals have bows and arrows too?"

"Don't you see? The animals are swift; they already have big claws, teeth, and powerful horns. The people are slow. Their teeth and nails are not very strong. If animals had weapons, how could the people survive?"

"Why, my younger brother, you think of everything." Forthwith he gave the people bows and spears. "Younger brother, are you satisfied now?"

"No, not at all. There's only one language, and you can't fight somebody who speaks your language. There should be enmity; there should be war."

"What are wars good for?"

"Oh, my respected elder brother, sometimes you're just not thinking. War is a good thing. Say you're a young warrior. You paint yourself with vermilion. You wear a fine war shirt. You start. You sing war songs. You have war honors. You look at the good-looking young girls. You look at the young women whose husbands have no war honors. They look back at you. You go on the warpath. You steal the enemy's horses. You steal his women and maidens. You count coup, do brave deeds. You are rich. You have gifts to give away. They sing songs honoring you. You have many loves. And by and by you become a chief."

"Ah, Cirape, my younger brother, you've hit upon something." Old Man Coyote divided the people into tribes, giving them different languages. Then there was war, then there was horse stealing, then there was counting coup, then there was singing of honoring songs.

After a long time, Old Man Coyote was walking with Cirape again. "You are very clever, my younger brother, but there are some things you don't know. Let me tell you: When we marry a young woman, when we take her to wife secretly, how satisfying it is! What pleasure it gives us!"

"Yes, my elder brother, just so. That's how it is with me."

"Ah, but after some years, after you have lived with one woman for a while, you lose interest. You are yearning for someone new. So you steal someone else's wife. In this back-and-forth wife stealing that goes on in our tribe, has some fellow ever made off with your wife? A proud young warrior, maybe?"

"Why yes, my elder brother. It was such a man who took a plump, pleasing young wife away from me. It would have been better if an enemy from another tribe had done it. It would have been easier to bear if she were far away where I couldn't see them together."

"Well, younger brother, if she would come back, would you take her?"

"What, take her back? Never! I have honor, I respect myself. How could I do such a thing?"

"Ah, Cirape, how foolish you are. You know nothing. Three times my wife has been abducted, and three times I have taken her back. Now when I say 'come,' she comes. When I say 'go,' she goes. Whenever I tell her to do something, she remembers that she has been stolen. I never have to remind her. She is eager to please. She fulfills my every desire. Under the blanket she's a hot one—she has learned things. This is the best wife, the best kind of loving."

"That's how you feel. But people mock you. They look at you sideways and laugh behind your back. They say: 'He has taken what another one threw away.'"

"Ah, younger brother of mine, what do I care if they laugh behind my back when, under our buffalo robe, I am laughing for my own reasons? Let me tell you, there's nothing more satisfying than having a wife who has been stolen once or twice. Tell me: Do they steal ugly old wives, or young and pretty ones?"

So because of Old Man Coyote's sensible advice, there was mutual wife stealing among the Crows in the old days. And that's why Crow men ever since have taken back wives they had already divorced. In one way or another, everything that exists or that is happening goes back to Old Man Coyote.

—*Based on a number of anthropological accounts, including*
Robert Lowie's The Crow Indians.

■

HOW THE SIOUX CAME TO BE

■

[BRULE SIOUX]

■ |||||||||||||||||||||||||||||||||||||||||||||||||||||||||||||||||||||||||||| ■

This story was told to me by a Santee grandmother. A long time ago, a really long time when the world was still freshly made, Unktehi the water monster fought the people and caused a great flood. Perhaps the

Great Spirit, Wakan Tanka, was angry with us for some reason. Maybe he let Unktehi win out because he wanted to make a better kind of human being.

Well, the waters got higher and higher. Finally everything was flooded except the hill next to the place where the sacred red pipestone quarry lies today. The people climbed up there to save themselves, but it was no use. The water swept over that hill. Waves tumbled the rocks and pinnacles, smashing them down on the people. Everyone was killed, and all the blood jelled, making one big pool. The blood turned to pipestone and created the pipestone quarry, the grave of those ancient ones. That's why the pipe, made of that red rock, is so sacred to us. Its red bowl is the flesh and blood of our ancestors, its stem is the backbone of those people long dead, the smoke rising from it is their breath. I tell you, that pipe, that *chanunpa*, comes alive when used in a ceremony; you can feel power flowing from it.

Unktehi, the big water monster, was also turned to stone. Maybe Tunkashila, the Grandfather Spirit, punished her for making the flood. Her bones are in the Badlands now. Her back forms a long, high ridge, and you can see her vertebrae sticking out in a great row of red and yellow rocks. I have seen them. It scared me when I was on that ridge, for I felt Unktehi. She was moving beneath me, wanting to topple me.

Well, when all the people were killed so many generations ago, one girl survived, a beautiful girl. It happened this way: When the water swept over the hill where they tried to seek refuge, a big spotted eagle, Wanblee Galeshka, swept down and let her grab hold of his feet. With her hanging on, he flew to the top of a tall tree which stood on the highest stone pinnacle in the Black Hills. That was the eagle's home. It became the only spot not covered with water. If the people had gotten up there, they would have survived, but it was a needle-like rock as smooth and steep as the skyscrapers you got now in the big cities. My grandfather told me that maybe the rock was not in the Black Hills; maybe it was Devil's Tower, as white men call it—that place in Wyoming. Both places are sacred.

Wanblee kept that beautiful girl with him and made her his wife. There was a closer connection then between people and animals, so he could do it. The eagle's wife became pregnant and bore him twins, a boy and a girl. She was happy, and said: "Now we will have people again. *Washtay*, it is good." The children were born right there, on top of that cliff.

When the waters finally subsided, Wanblee helped the children and their mother down from his rock and put them on the earth, telling them: "Be a nation, become a great Nation—the Lakota Oyate." The boy and girl grew up. He was the only man on earth, she the only woman of child-bearing age. They married; they had children. A nation was born.

So we are descended from the eagle. We are an eagle nation. That is good, something to be proud of, because the eagle is the wisest of birds. He is the Great Spirit's messenger; he is a great warrior. That is why we always wore the eagle plume, and still wear it. We are a great nation. It is I, Lame Deer, who said this.

—Told by Lame Deer in Winner, South Dakota, in 1969,
and recorded by Richard Erdoes.

■

PUSHING UP THE SKY

■

[SNOHOMISH]

Chief William Shelton, who relates this story, says he was told it as a child by his family elders to teach him what could be accomplished if people work together.

■ ▮▮▮▮▮▮▮▮▮▮▮▮▮▮▮▮▮▮▮▮▮▮▮▮▮▮▮▮▮▮▮▮▮▮▮▮▮ ■

The Creator and Changer first made the world in the East. Then he slowly came westward, creating as he came. With him he brought many languages, and he gave a different one to each group of people he made.

When he reached Puget Sound, he liked it so well that he decided to go no further. But he had many languages left, so he scattered them all around Puget Sound and to the north. That's why there are so many different Indian languages spoken there.

These people could not talk together, but it happened that none of them were pleased with the way the Creator had made the world. The sky was so low that the tall people bumped their heads against it. Sometimes people would do what was forbidden by climbing up high in the trees and, learning their own words, enter the Sky World.

Finally the wise men of all the different tribes had a meeting to see what they could do about lifting the sky. They agreed that the people should get together and try to push it up higher.

"We can do it," a wise man of the council said, "if we all push at the same time. We will need all the people and all the animals and all the birds when we push."

"How will we know when to push?" asked another of the wise men. "Some of us live in this part of the world, some in another. We don't all talk the same language. How can we get everyone to push at the same time?"

That puzzled the men of the council, but at last one of them suggested that they use a signal." When the time comes for us to push, when we have everything ready, let someone shout 'Ya-hoh.' That means 'Lift together!' in all our languages."

So the wise men of the council sent that message to all the people and animals and birds and told them on what day they were to lift the sky. Everyone made poles from the giant fir trees to use in pushing against the sky.

The day for the sky lifting came. All the people raised their poles and touched the sky with them. Then the wise men shouted, "Ya-hoh!" Everybody pushed, and the sky moved up a little.

"Ya-hoh," the wise men shouted a second time, and everybody pushed with all his strength. The sky moved a few inches more. "Ya-hoh," all shouted, and pushed as hard as they could push.

They kept on shouting "Ya-hoh" and pushing until the sky was in the place where it is now. Since then, no one has bumped his head against it, and no one has been able to climb into the Sky World.

Now, three hunters had been chasing four elks during all the meetings and did not know about the plan. Just as the people and animals and birds were ready to push the sky up, the three hunters and the four elks came to the place where the earth nearly meets the sky. The elks jumped into the Sky World, and the hunters ran after them. When the sky was lifted, elks and hunters were lifted too.

In the Sky World they were changed into stars, and at night even now you see them. The three hunters form the handle of the Big Dipper. The middle hunter has his dog with him—now a tiny star. The four elks make the bowl of the Big Dipper.

Some other people were caught up in the sky in two canoes, three men in each of them. And a little fish also was on its way up into the Sky World when the people pushed. So all of them have had to stay there ever since. The hunters and the little dog, the elk, the little fish, and the men in the two canoes are stars, even though they once lived on earth.

We still shout "Ya-hoh!" when doing hard work together or lifting something heavy like a canoe. When we say "Hoh!" all of us use all the strength we have. Our voices have a higher pitch on that part of the word, and we make the o very long—"Ya-hooooh!"

—Reported by Ella Clark in 1953.

■

EMERGING INTO THE UPPER WORLD

■

[ACOMA]

This legend reflects the matrilineal society of the Western Pueblos; Ia'tik, the All-Mother, herself makes the gods she wishes to believe in.

■ |||||||||||||||||||||||||||||||||||||||||||||||||||||||||||||||||||||||||||||||||||||| ■

In the beginning two female human beings were born. There was land already, but no one knows how long it had existed. The two girls were born underground at a place called Cipapu. There was no light, but as they grew up they became aware of each other through touch. Being in the dark, they grew slowly.

When they had reached adulthood, a spirit, Tsitctinako, spoke to them and gave them nourishment. Slowly they began to think for themselves. One day they asked the spirit to appear to them and say whether it was male or female. But Tsitctinako replied only that it was not allowed to meet them.

The women asked the spirit why they had to live in the dark without knowing each other by name. It told them that they were under the earth (*nuk'timi*), and that they must be patient until everything was ready for them to go up into the light. During the long time that they waited, Tsitctinako taught them their language.

One day the sisters found two baskets full of presents: seeds of all kinds, and little images of many animals. Tsitctinako told them that the baskets had been sent by their father, whose name was Utc'tsiti, and that he wanted them to take his gifts up into the light.

Tsitctinako said, "You have the seeds of four types of trees. Plant them; you will use the trees to climb up." Because the sisters could not see, they felt each object in their baskets and asked, "Is this it?" and Tsitctinako answered yes or no. In that way they identified the four seeds and then buried them in their underground world. All sprouted, but the trees grew very slowly in the dark. The women themselves slept for a long time, and whenever they woke, they felt the trees to find out how tall they were. A certain pine grew faster than the others, and after a very long while it pushed a hole through the earth and let in a little light.

However, the hole was not large enough for the women to pass through. With Tsitctinako's help they found the image of an animal called *dyu·p* (badger) in their baskets. Commanding the badger to come alive, the sisters asked him to climb the tree and dig around the edges of the hole. They warned him not to go out in the light, so he climbed up, enlarged the hole, and returned directly. Thanking him, they said, "As a reward, you will come up with us into the light and live in happiness."

Next Tsitctinako helped them sort through the baskets until they found *tawai'nu* (the locust). They gave him life, asked him to smooth the hole by plastering it, and warned him not to go into the light. But the locust, having smoothed the hole, was curious and slipped out to look around before he returned. Three times the women asked him if he had gone out, and three times the locust said no. When they asked a fourth time, he admitted that he had.

"What is it like?" they asked him. "It's just *tsi'iti*, laid out flat," he replied. "From now on," they said, "you will be known as Tsi·k'a. You may come up with us, but for your disobedience you will be allowed to see the light for only a short time. Your home will be in the ground. You will soon die, but you will be reborn each season."

A shaft of light now reached into the place where the two sisters lived.

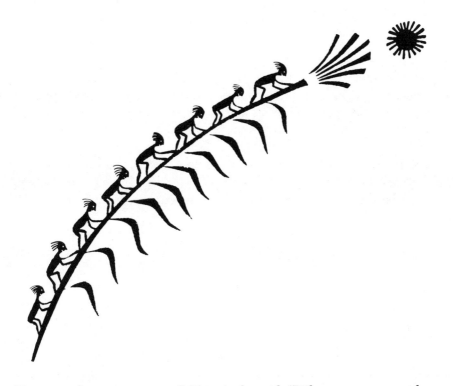

"It is time for you to go out," Tsitctinako said. "When you come to the top, wait for the sun to rise. That direction is called *ha'nami*, east. Pray to the sun with pollen and sacred cornmeal, which you will find in your baskets. Thank it for bringing you to the light. Ask for long life and happiness, and for success in the purpose for which you were created."

Tsitctinako taught them the prayers to say and the creation song to sing. Then the humans, followed by the badger and the locust, climbed the pine tree. Stepping out into the light, the sisters put down their baskets and for the first time saw what they contained. Gradually the sky grew lighter, and finally the sun came up. As they faced it their eyes hurt, for they were not accustomed to strong light.

Before they began to pray, Tsitctinako told them that their right side, the side their best arm was on, would be known as south, and the left north. At their backs was west, the direction in which the sun would go down. Underground they had already learned the direction *nuk'um'*, down. (Later they asked where their father was, and Tsitctinako said, "*Tyunami*—four skies above.")

As they waited to pray to the sun, the girl on the right moved her best hand and was named Ia'tik, which means "Bringing to life." Now name your sister," Tsitctinako told her. Ia'tik was perplexed at first, but then she noticed that her sister's basket was fuller than her own. So she called her sister Nao'tsiti—"More of everything in the basket."

They prayed and sang the creation song, and for the first time they asked Tsitctinako why they had been created. The spirit replied, "It was not I but your father, Utc'tsiti, who made you. He made the world, the sun, the sky, and many other things, but he is not yet satisfied. For this reason he has made you in his image. You will rule over the world and create the things he has given you in the baskets."

"And who are you?" they asked Tsitctinako. "And why don't you become visible to us so that we can see you and live together?"

"I am female like you," the spirit replied. "But I don't know how to live like a human being. Your father has sent me to teach you, and I will always look after you."

When it became dark at the end of the first day, the sisters were frightened. They thought that Tsitctinako had betrayed them, but she explained, "This is the way it will always be. The sun will go down and a new sun will come up in the east tomorrow. Rest and sleep while it is dark." So the sisters slept, and the next day the sun rose. Happy to feel its warmth, they prayed to it as they had been taught.

Tsitctinako asked Nao'tsiti which clan she wished to belong to. Nao'tsiti said, "I see the sun; my clan will be the Sun clan." The spirit asked Ia'tik what clan she wanted. It'tik had noticed that her basket contained the seed from which the sacred meal was made, and she said, "My clan will be Ya'ka-Hano, the Red Corn clan."

The sun was too bright for Ia'tik; it hurt her eyes. She tilted her head sideways so that her hair hung as a sunscreen, producing a reddish shade on her face. "The sun has not appeared for you," Tsitctinako observed. "See how it shines on Nao'tsiti, and how white she looks." Hastily Ia'tik also bared her face to the sun. But it did not make her as white as Nao'tsiti, and Ia'tik's mind was slowed down, while Nao'tsiti's was made quick. Even so, both always remembered to do everything Tsitctinako taught them.

"From now on," Tsitctinako told the sisters, "you will rule in every direction, north, west, south, and east. Bring everything in your baskets to life for Utc'tsiti has created you to help him complete the world. Now is the time to plant the seeds."

So far the sisters had not eaten food, and they did not understand what the seeds in their baskets were for. "First plant the corn, and when it grows, it will produce a part that you can eat," Tsitctinako said. Highly interested, the two women watched the growing corn every day. The spirit showed them where the pollen formed so that they could continue to offer pollen and cornmeal every morning to the sun. And they always did, though sometimes Nao'tsiti was a little lazy.

After a while the corn turned hard and ripe. Ia'tik carefully picked two ears without hurting the plant; Nao'tsiti yanked two off, and Ia'tik told her to handle it more gently. Tsitctinako had said that the corn must be cooked, but the sisters did not understand what "cooked" meant until a red light dropped from the sky that evening. Explaining that it was fire, the spirit taught them to scoop some of the flames up on a flat rock and feed them with branches from the pine tree.

Following Tsitctinako's directions, they roasted the corn and seasoned it with salt from their baskets. Nao'tsiti grabbed some and ate it, exclaiming how good it was. Then she gave a piece to Ia'tik, and so it was that the two women had their first meal. "You have been fasting for a long time, and your father has nourished you," the spirit told them. "Now you will eat in order to live."

The sisters learned to give life to their salt by praying to the earth, whereupon salt appeared in each of the four directions. Then Tsitctinako taught them their first song for creating an animal—a mouse. When they had sung it, they said, "Come to life, mouse," and their mouse image breathed. "Go and increase," they told it, and it ran away and soon bred many offspring. Tsitctinako showed them how to take one back, kill it, and roast it with the corn and salt. They prayed to their father and offered him little pieces of the meal before they ate. There was not much food on the mouse, but they thought it was good.

Looking into their baskets for larger animals to eat, the women found images of a rat, a mole, and a prairie dog. "Before you give life to them," Tsitctinako said, "you must plant grass for their food." The sisters took grass seed and scattered it north, west, south, and east—and grass immediately covered the ground. Then they gave life to the animals, telling each its name as it began to breathe. Before commanding them to run away and increase, they told the three creatures to live in the ground, because there was no shade on earth.

"Now we are going to make the mountains," Tsitctinako said, and showed them how to throw a certain stone from the basket toward the north while speaking certain words. There a large mountain arose. They did the same in the other directions, and mountains appeared all around them. "Now that you have the mountains," the spirit said, "you must clothe them with growing things." From the trees they had planted underground the sisters took seeds which they scattered in all the directions. "These will be tall trees," Tsitctinako said, "and large enough to form the logs you will use to build houses."

There were many seeds left in their baskets. The women planted the food-yielding trees—piñon, cedar, oak, and walnut—with the prayer, "Grow on this mountain and yield fruit for food. Your places are in the mountains. You will grow and be useful." They planted other seeds, such as pumpkin, squash, and beans, that Tsitctinako said would be important to them. As these crops ripened, she showed them which parts to eat.

The sisters too were growing, and they needed more food. They began to bring the larger animals to life: first rabbits, jackrabbits, antelope, and water deer; then deer, elk, mountain sheep, and buffalo. They told the buffalo to live in the plains, the elk and deer in the mountains, and the sheep on the very high mountain slopes. They ate their meat and enjoyed the new tastes, and always they prayed to their father before they began a meal.

The sisters made mountain lions, wolves, wildcats, and bears—strong beasts that hunted the same game the humans used. They made birds— eagles and hawks, which hunted small game, and little birds whose bright colors beautified the country. They made the wild turkey, and told it not to fly. They told the smaller birds to eat various seeds on the mountains and plains.

Tsitctinako pointed out that there were still fish, snakes, and turtles to be created, and the sisters gave life to all these and tried them for food. They found that some were good to eat and others were not, but whenever they ate they prayed first to their father. So it happened that many animals came alive in the world.

Ia'tik was always ready to use her seeds and images, but Nao'tsiti was selfish about the things in her basket. Now Nao'tsiti had many left, and she said she wanted a chance to give life to more of her images. "I am the elder," Ia'tik replied. "You are younger than I." "Is that true?" Nao'tsiti said. "I thought we were created at the same time. Let's put it to the test: tomorrow let's see for which of us the sun rises first."

Ia'tik agreed to the test, but she was afraid that her sister would get the better of her in some way. She went to a white bird she knew called co'eka (the magpie) and asked it to fly quickly into the east and use its wings to shade the sun from Nao'tsiti. The magpie flew fast and far, for Ia'tik had told it not to stop. But it began to feel hungry, and when it passed over a lion's kill, it could not resist landing. The carcass, a deer, had a hole in its side. The bird put its head into the gash to eat the intestines, and then flew on without noticing that its white feathers were soiled and bloody.

The magpie did reach the east before the sun had risen. It spread its wings on the sun's left side, creating shade over Nao'tsiti. In this way it happened that the sun struck Ia'tik first, and Nao'tsiti was very angry.

Ia'tik whispered to the magpie that it must never tell. Then she saw its filthy plumage and said, "Because you stopped and ate, from this day on you will eat carrion, and your feathers will be spotted instead of white."

Both sisters were now having selfish thoughts. Nao'tsiti was full of plans to outwit Ia'tik, but Ia'tik watched her and anticipated everything. Nao'tsiti saw that Ia'tik was not happy; Ia'tik noticed that Nao'tsiti wandered off alone.

Tsitctinako had told them that their father forbade them to think about having children. She promised that other humans would be born to them at the appropriate time. But now Nao'tsiti met a snake who said, "Why are you sad? If you bore a child in your likeness, you wouldn't have to be lonely just because you and your sister don't get along."

"What can I do?" Nao'tsiti asked.

"Go to the rainbow; he will show you."

Soon afterward Nao'tsiti was sitting alone on a rock when it rained. It was so hot that the rain cracked on the ground, and she lay on her back to receive the drops. As the water dripped into her, the rainbow did his work and she conceived without knowing it. Ia'tik noticed that her sister was growing very fat, and after a time Nao'tsiti bore two children, both boys.

Very angry, Tsitctinako came to them. "Why have you disobeyed your father?" she said. "For your sin, he is taking me away. You are alone now."

Tsitctinako left them, but instead of feeling sorry, the two sisters found that they were happier. It turned out that Nao'tsiti disliked one of her children, so Ia'tik took him and brought him up. The two women still did not get along, but they were so busy with the children that it hardly mattered.

When the children were almost grown, Nao'tsiti said to her sister, "We aren't really happy together. Let's divide what remains in our baskets and separate. I still have many things, though they require a lot of work." Nao'tsiti pulled out sheep and cows, seeds for wheat and vegetables, and many metals. But Ia'tik refused them, saying they would be too difficult to take care of. Nao'tsiti looked again in her basket and found something written. She offered it, but Ia'tik did not want the gift of writing either. "You should have taken some of the things I offered," Nao'tsiti said. "In a long time we will meet again, and then you will desire my possessions. We'll still be sisters, but I'll have the better of you again."

Taking the boy she had brought up, Nao'tsiti disappeared into the east. Ia'tik said to the other boy, "We will continue to live here with everything our father has given us." The years passed, and Tia'muni, as she called him, grew up to become her husband. Ia'tik bore him a girl who was entered into the clan of her sister, the Sun clan. After the fourth day of the baby's birth, Ia'tik put some pollen and sacred corn-meal into its hands and took it to pray to the sun. And with the many children that Ia'tik bore afterwards, she followed this same ritual that she herself had been taught when she came up into the light.

Ia'tik's children lived together and began to increase. Their mother ruled over them, for she had her own power now that Tsitctinako was gone. But Ia'tik wished to create some other rulers, so she made the spirits of the seasons by taking earth from her baskets and giving it life. First she made the spirit of winter, which she told, "You will live in the north mountain and give life to everything in the wintertime." Next she created the spirit of spring and sent him to the west mountain. The spirit of summer she sent to the south mountain and the spirit of autumn to the east mountain. These four spirits were ugly, not at all like the chil-dren she had borne. She taught each one what to do: winter was to bring snow, spring would warm up the world, summer would heat the world, and autumn would dislike the smell of plants and fruits and work to destroy them. And Ia'tik taught her children how to pray to these spirits for moisture, warmth, ripening, and frost.

Taking dirt from her basket, Ia'tik next gave life to the gods. The first one she created she named Tsitsenuts. "You are very handsome," she said, "but I will give you a mask that makes you different from us humans." She fashioned it from buffalo skin, colored it with different kinds of earth, and decorated it with feathers. Around Tsitsenuts' neck she hung a wildcat skin, and she painted his body. She gave him a skirt, a belt, and moccasins, put cords on each wrist, and painted buffalo skins on his arms. On his calves she bound spruce branches.

"You see that I have created many other gods," she told him. "I ap-point you their ruler; you will initiate the others." She gave him weeds

of the soapwood plant for the initiation and then spoke to them all: "From now on, wear the costumes I have made for you. You are rain gods, created to call the rain when you dance before my people. They will worship you for all time." And after she had instructed each of the gods and given each his costume and a prayer, she told them that they would have a sacred chamber in each of the four mountains. And so everything was as it should be.

—*Based on a legend reported by C. Daryll Forde in 1930,*
and on various oral accounts.

The Hopis tell this as the tale of Bahana, the lost White Brother, replacing the sisters with brothers throughout. This version from Acoma shows Spanish influence in the mention of "sin," a concept unknown on this continent until after Columbus; the role of the snake in tempting Nao-tsiti may also be colored by knowledge of the Bible.

■

EARTH MAKING

■

[CHEROKEE]

The Cherokee are one of the very few Indian tribes who conceive of the sun as female. This version is unusual for the Cherokee because it refers to Sun as "he."

■ |||||||||||||||||||||||||||||||||||||||||||||||||||||||||||||||||||||||||||||||| ■

Earth is floating on the waters like a big island, hanging from four raw-hide ropes fastened at the top of the sacred four directions. The ropes are tied to the ceiling of the sky, which is made of hard rock crystal. When the ropes break, this world will come tumbling down, and all living things will fall with it and die. Then everything will be as if the earth had never existed, for water will cover it. Maybe the white man will bring this about.

Well, in the beginning also, water covered everything. Though living creatures existed, their home was up there, above the rainbow, and it was crowded. "We are all jammed together," the animals said. "We need more room." Wondering what was under the water, they sent Water Beetle to look around.

Water Beetle skimmed over the surface but couldn't find any solid footing, so he dived down to the bottom and brought up a little dab of soft mud. Magically the mud spread out in the four directions and became this island we are living on—this earth. Someone Powerful then fastened it to the sky ceiling with cords.

In the beginning the earth was flat, soft, and moist. All the animals were eager to live on it, and they kept sending down birds to see if the mud had dried and hardened enough to take their weight. But the birds all flew back and said that there was still no spot they could perch on.

Then the animals sent Grandfather Buzzard down. He flew very close and saw that the earth was still soft, but when he glided low over what would become Cherokee country, he found that the mud was getting harder. By that time Buzzard was tired and dragging. When he flapped his wings down, they made a valley where they touched the earth; when he swept them up, they made a mountain. The animals watching from above the rainbow said, "If he keeps on, there will be only mountains," and they made him come back. That's why we have so many mountains in Cherokee land.

At last the earth was hard and dry enough, and the animals descended. They couldn't see very well because they had no sun or moon, and someone said, "Let's grab Sun from up there behind the rainbow! Let's get him down too!" Pulling Sun down, they told him, "Here's a road for you," and showed him the way to go—from east to west.

Now they had light, but it was much too hot, because Sun was too close to the earth. The crawfish had his back sticking out of a stream, and Sun burned it red. His meat was spoiled forever, and the people still won't eat crawfish.

Everyone asked the sorcerers, the shamans, to put Sun higher. They pushed him up as high as a man, but it was still too hot. So they pushed him farther, but it wasn't far enough. They tried four times, and when they had Sun up to the height of four men, he was just hot enough. Everyone was satisfied, so they left him there.

Before making humans, Someone Powerful had created plants and animals and had told them to stay awake and watch for seven days and seven nights. (This is just what young men do today when they fast and prepare for a ceremony.) But most of the plants and animals couldn't manage it; some fell asleep after one day, some after two days, some after three. Among the animals, only the owl and the mountain lion were still awake after seven days and nights. That's why they were given the gift of seeing in the dark so that they can hunt at night.

Among the trees and other plants, only the cedar, pine, holly, and laurel wer still awake on the eighth morning. Someone Powerful said to them: "Because you watched and kept awake as you had been told, you will not lose your hair in the winter." So these plants stay green all the time.

After creating plants and animals, Someone Powerful made a man and his sister. The man poked her with a fish and told her to give birth. After seven days she had a baby, and after seven more days she had another, and every seven days another came. The humans increased so quickly that Someone Powerful, thinking there would soon be no more room on this earth, arranged things so that a woman could have only one child every year. And that's how it was.

Now, there is still another world under the one we live on. You can reach it by going down a spring, a water hole; but you need underworld people to be your scouts and guide you. The world under our earth is exactly like ours, except that it's winter down there when it's summer up here. We can see that easily, because spring water is warmer than the air in winter and cooler than the air in summer.

—*Told at a Cherokee treaty council meeting in New York City, 1975.*

THE EARTH DRAGON

[NORTHERN CALIFORNIA COAST]

Before this world was formed, there was another world with a sky made of sandstone rock. Two gods, Thunder and Nagaicho, saw that old sky being shaken by thunder.

"The rock is old," they said. "We'll fix it by stretching it above, far to the east."

They stretched the sandstone, walking on the sky to do it, and under each of the sky's four corners they set a great rock to hold it up. Then they added the different things that would make the world pleasant for people to live in. In the south they created flowers. In the east they put clouds so that people wouldn't get headaches from the sun's glare. To form the clouds they built a fire, then opened a large hole in the sky so that the clouds could come through. In the west they made another opening for the fog to drift in from the ocean.

Now the two gods were ready to create people. They made a man out of earth and put grass inside him to form his stomach. They used another bundle of grass for his heart, round pieces of clay for the liver and kidneys, and a reed for the windpipe. They pulverized red stone and mixed it with water to form his blood. After putting together man's parts, they took one of his legs, split it, and turned it into a woman. Then they made a sun to travel by day and a moon to travel by night.

But the creations of the gods did not endure, for every day and every night it rained. All the people slept. Floodwaters came, and great stretches of land disappeared. The waters of the oceans flowed together; animals of all kinds drowned. Then the waters completely joined, and there were no more fields or mountains or rocks, only water. There were no trees or grass, no fish or land animals or birds. Human beings and animals all had been washed away.

The wind no longer blew through the portals of the world, nor was there snow, or frost, or rain. It did not thunder or lightning, since there were no trees to be struck. There were neither clouds nor fog, nor did the sun shine. It was very dark.

Then the earth dragon, with its great, long horns, got up and walked down from the north. It traveled underground, and the god Nagaicho rode on its head. As it walked along through the ocean depths, the water outside rose to the level of its shoulders. When it came to shallower places it turned its head upward, and because of this there is a ridge near the coast in the north upon which the waves break. When it came to the middle of the world, in the east under the rising sun, it looked up again, which created a large island near the coast. Far away to the south it continued looking up and made a great mountain range.

In the south the dragon lay down, and Nagaicho placed its head as it should be and spread gray-colored clay between its eyes and on each horn. He covered the clay with a layer of reeds, then spread another layer of clay. On it he put some small stones, and then set blue grass, brush, and trees in the clay.

"I have finished," he said. "Let there be mountain peaks on the earth's head. Let the waves of the sea break against them."

The mountains appeared, and brush sprang up on them. The small stones he had placed on earth's head became large, and the head itself was buried from sight.

Now people appeared, people who had animal names. (Later when Indians came to live on the earth, these "first people" were changed into their animal namesakes.) Seal, Sea Lion, and Grizzly Bear built a dance house. One woman by the name of Whale was fat, and that is why there are so many stout Indian women today.

The god Nagaicho caused different sea foods to grow in the water so that the people would have things to eat. He created seaweed, abalones, mussels, and many other things. Then he made salt from ocean foam. He caused the water of the ocean to rise up in waves and said that the ocean would always behave that way. He arranged for old whales to float ashore so that people would have them to eat.

He made redwoods and other trees grow on the tail of the great dragon, which lay to the north. He carved out creeks by dragging his foot through the earth so that people would have good fresh water to drink. He created many oak trees to provide acorns to eat. He traveled all over the earth making it a comfortable place for men.

After he had finished, he and his dog went walking to see how the new things looked. When they arrived back at their starting point in the north, he said to his dog: "We're close to home. Now we'll stay here."

So he left this world where people live, and now he inhabits the north.

—Based on E. W. Gifford's 1930 account.

Because so many California tribes were shattered so early on by contact with Europeans, decimated by disease and displaced from their traditional lands, many of their stories have been recorded only as fragments, and it is often difficult to attribute some to specific tribes. We can only note the general region of origin.

■

PEOPLE BROUGHT IN A BASKET

■

[MODOC]

■ |||||||||||||||||||||||||||||||||||||||||||||||||||||||||||||||||||||||||||||||||||||||| ■

Kumush, Old Man of the Ancients, went down with his daughter to the underground world of the spirits. It was a beautiful world, reached by one long, steep road. In it were many spirits—as many as all the stars in the sky and all the hairs on all the animals in the world.

When night came, the spirits gathered in a great plain to sing and dance. When daylight came, they returned to their places in the house, lay down, and became dry bones.

After six days and six nights in the land of the spirits, Kumush longed for the sun. He decided to return to the upper world and to take some of the spirits with him to people his world.

With a big basket in hand, he went through the house of the spirits and chose the bones he wished to take. Some bones he thought would be good for one tribe of people, others for another.

When he had filled his basket, Kumush strapped it to his back and together with his daughter started up the steep road to the upper world. Near the top he slipped and stumbled, and the basket fell to the ground. At once the bones became spirits again. Shouting and singing, they ran back to their house in the spirit world, lay down, and became dry bones.

A second time Kumush filled his basket with bones and started toward the upper world. A second time he slipped, and the spirits, shouting and singing, returned to the underground world. A third time he filled his basket with bones. This time he spoke to them angrily. "You just think you want to stay here. When you see my land, a land where the sun shines, you'll never want to come back to this place. There are no people up there, and I know I'll get lonesome again."

A third time Kumush and his daughter started up the steep and slippery road with the basket. When he came near the edge of the upper world, he threw the basket ahead of him, onto level ground. "Indian bones!" he called out.

Then he uncovered the basket and selected the bones for the kinds of Indians he wanted in certain places. As he threw them, he named them. "You shall be the Shastas," he said to the bones he threw westward. "You shall be brave warriors."

"You also shall be brave warriors," he said to the Pit River Indians and the Warm Springs Indians.

To the bones he threw a short distance northward, he said, "You shall be the Klamath Indians. You'll be as easy to frighten as women are. You won't be good warriors."

Last of all he threw the bones which became the Modoc Indians. To them he said, "You will be the bravest of all. You will be my chosen people. Though you'll be a small tribe and though your enemies are many, you will kill all who come against you. You kill keep my place when I have gone. I, Kumush, have spoken."

To all the people created from the bones of the spirits, Kumush said,

"You must send certain men to the mountains. There they must ask to be made brave or to be made wise. There, if they ask for it, they will be given the power to help themselves and to help all of you."

Then Kumush named the different kinds of fish and beasts that the people should eat. As he spoke their names, they appeared in the rivers and lakes, on the plains and in the forests. He named the roots and the berries and the plants that the people should eat. He thought, and they appeared.

He divided the work of the people by making this law: "Men shall fish and hunt and fight. Women shall get wood and water, gather berries and dig roots, and cook for their families. This is my law."

So Kumush finished the upper world and his work in it. Then with his daughter, he went to the place where the sun rises, at the eastern edge of the world. He traveled along the sun's road until he reached the middle of the sky. There he built a house for himself and his daughter. There they live even today.

—Reported by Ella Clark in 1953.

 ## GREAT MEDICINE MAKES A BEAUTIFUL COUNTRY

[CHEYENNE]

In this epic tale, a number of different incidents in Cheyenne history from the last four hundred years are all merged into a single account of a tribe's evolution told in terms of great migrations, tragic losses, and natural disasters.

In the beginning the Great Medicine created the earth, and the waters upon the earth, and the sun, moon, and stars. Then he made a beautiful country to spring up in the far north. There were no winters, with ice and snow and bitter cold. It was always spring; wild fruits and berries grew everywhere, and great trees shaded the streams of clear water that flowed through the land.

In this beautiful country the Great Medicine put animals, birds, insects, and fish of all kinds. Then he created human beings to live with the other creatures. Every animal, big and small, every bird, big and small, every fish, and every insect could talk to the people and understand them. The people could understand each other, for they had a common language and lived in friendship. They went naked and fed on honey and wild fruits; they were never hungry. They wandered everywhere among the wild animals, and when night came and they were weary, they lay down on the cool grass and slept. During the days they talked with the other animals, for they were all friends.

The Great Spirit created three kinds of human beings: first, those who had hair all over their bodies; second, white men who had hair all over their heads and faces and on their legs; third, red men who had very long hair on their heads only. The hairy people were strong and active. The white people with the long beards were in a class with the wolf, for both were the trickiest and most cunning creatures in that beautiful world. The red people were good runners, agile and swift, whom the Great Medicine taught to catch and eat fish at a time when none of the other people knew about eating meat.

After a while the hairy people left the north country and went south, where all the land was barren. Then the red people prepared to follow the hairy people into the south. Before they left the beautiful land, however, the Great Medicine called them together. On this occasion, the first time the red people had all assembled in one place, the Great Medicine blessed them and gave them some medicine spirit to awaken their dormant minds. From that time on they seemed to possess intelligence and know what to do. The Great Medicine singled out one of the men and told him to teach his people to band together, so that they all could work and clothe their naked bodies with skins of panther and bear and deer. The Great Medicine gave them the power to hew and shape flint and other stones into any shape they wanted—into arrow- and spearheads and into cups, pots, and axes.

The red people stayed together ever afterwards. They left the beautiful country and went southward in the same direction the hairy people had taken. The hairy people remained naked, but the red people clothed themselves because the Great Medicine had told them to. When the red men arrived in the south, they found that the hairy people had scattered and made homes inside of hills and in caves high up in the mountains. They seldom saw the hairy men, for the hairy ones were afraid and went inside their caves when the red men came. The hairy people had pottery and flint tools like those of the red men, and in their caves they slept on beds made out of leaves and skins. For some reason they decreased in numbers until they finally disappeared entirely, and today the red men cannot tell what became of them.

After the red men had lived in the south for some time, the Great Medicine told them to return north, for the barren southland was going to be flooded. When they went back to that beautiful northern land, they found that the white-skinned, long-bearded men and some of the wild animals were gone. They were no longer able to talk to the animals, but this time they controlled all other creatures, and they taught the panther, the bear, and similar beasts to catch game for them. They increased in numbers and became tall and strong and active.

Then for a second time the red people left the beautiful land to go south. The waters had gone, grass and trees had grown, and the country had become as beautiful as the north. While they were living there, however, another flood swept over the land and scattered the red men. When the great waters at last sank and the ground was dry, the red people did not come together again. They traveled in small bands, just as they had done in the beginning before the Great Medicine told them to unite. The flood destroyed almost everything, and they were on the point of starvation. So they started back to their original home in the north as they had done before. But when they reached the north country this time, they found the land all barren. There were no trees, no living animals, not a fish in the water. When the red people looked upon their once-beautiful home, the men cried aloud and all the women and children wept. This happened in the beginning, when the Great Medicine created us.

The people returned to the south and lived as well as they could, in some years better, in others worse. After many hundreds of years, just before the winter season came, the earth shook, and the high hills sent forth fire and smoke. During that winter there were great floods. The people had to dress in furs and live in caves, for the winter was long and cold. It destroyed all the trees, though when spring came there was a new growth. The red men suffered much and were almost famished when the Great Medicine took pity on them. He gave them corn to plant and buffalo for meat, and from that time there were no more floods and no more famines. The people continued to live in the south, and they grew and increased. There were many different bands with different languages, for the red men were never united after the second flood.

The descendants of the original Cheyenne had men among them who were magicians with supernatural wisdom. They charmed not only their own people, but also the animals that they lived on. No matter how fierce or wild the beast, it became so tame that people could go up to it and handle it. This magic knowledge was handed down from the

original Cheyenne, who came from the far north. Today Bushy Head is the only one who understands that ancient ceremony, and the Cheyenne consider him equal in rank to the medicine-arrow keeper and his assistants.

—Based on George A. Dorsey's account in 1905.

In this remarkable tale is stored the memory of much that has happened to the Cheyenne over many hundreds of years. It symbolically relates how they were once driven from their old hunting grounds in north-central America in the late 1600s, probably by the Ojibway, who had firearms from their French allies. It also describes the eighteenth or nineteenth century division of the Cheyenne into two separate bands (one of which, the Sutai, still retain certain ceremonial roles). The gaining and losing of corn may symbolize their giving up planting for buffalo hunting in the last half of the eighteenth century. The tale reflects as well the Cheyenne's ever-present yearning for the cool, beautiful north country after white authorities removed the whole tribe to a hot and unhealthy reservation in the south, following Little Big Horn. It was from this sorry existence that in the 1880s Dull Knife led a group of sick and starving people on their back to North Montana, where those who survived were permitted at last to remain.

THE WHITE DAWN OF THE HOPI

[HOPI]

A very long time ago, there was nothing but water on the earth. In the east a Huruing Wuhti, one of the goddesses of rocks, clay, minerals, and other hard substances, lived in the ocean. Her house was a kiva, like the kivas of the Hopi today. Two fox skins, one gray, one yellow, were usually tied to the ladder leading into the house. In the west lived another Huruing Wuhti in a similar kiva, with a turtle-shell rattle attached to her ladder.

The sun rose and set on this world of water. Shortly before he appeared in the east, he dressed himself in the skin of the gray fox, creating the white dawn of the Hopi. After a little while he took off the gray skin and put on the yellow skin, which brightened the sky into the yellow dawn of the Hopi. Then he rose, emerging from the opening in the north end of the kiva in which the Huruing Wuhti lived. When he had crossed the sky and arrived in the west, he announced his arrival at the western Huruing Wuhti's kiva by fastening the rattle on the top of the ladder beam. Then he entered the kiva, passed through an opening in its north end, and continued his course eastward under the water.

By and by, the two goddesses caused the waters to recede eastward and westward so that some dry land appeared. The sun passing over the land noticed that no living being could be seen. When he mentioned this to the goddesses, the one in the west invited the one in the east to come and talk about it. The Huruing Wuhti of the east traveled west over a rainbow, and the two deities deliberated and decided to create a little bird. The Huruing Wuhti of the east made a wren of clay and covered it up with a piece of *möchápu*, native cloth. Both goddesses sang a song over it, and after a while a live bird came forth. Since the sun always passed over the middle of the earth, the deities thought that he might not have seen living creatures in the north or the south. They sent the little wren to fly all over the earth, but it returned and said that no living being existed anywhere. (Actually Spider Woman, Kóhkang Wuhti, lived in a kiva somewhere in the southwest at the edge of the water, but the little bird failed to notice her.)

The deity of the west proceeded to make many birds of different kinds, covering them with the same cloth under which the wren had been brought to life. Both Huruing Wuhtis again sang a song over them, and presently the birds began to move under the cover. The goddesses took them out, taught every bird the sound that it should make, and let them scatter in all directions.

Next the Huruing Wuhti of the west made different kinds of animals in the same way, teaching them their own sounds or languages and sending them forth to inhabit the earth. Now the goddesses decided that they would create human beings. The Huruing Wuhti of the east fashioned first a white woman and then a white man out of clay and brought them to life. She made two tablets of a hard substance (tradition does not tell whether it was stone or clay), drew characters on them with a wooden stick, and handed them to the man and woman. The humans did not know what the tablets said, so the deity rubbed the palms of her hands first against the palms of the woman and then against the palms of the man. Suddenly the couple understood the meaning of the tablets. Then the deities taught them their language, after which the goddess of the east took them out of the kiva and led them over a rainbow to her home in the east. They stayed four days, and Huruing Wuhti told them to go and select a place to live. They traveled around a while and, finding a good field, built a small, simple house, similar to those of the Hopi.

Soon the Huruing Wuhti of the west told the eastern goddess, "All this is not finished yet." By then Spider Woman had heard what they were doing, and she also created a man and woman of clay. But she taught them Spanish and fashioned two burros for them, and the couple settled down near her.

Spider Woman continued to create people in the same manner, giving a different language to each pair. But she forgot to make a woman for a certain man, and this is the reason why today there are always some single men. Then as she continued turning out people, she found that she had failed to create a man for a certain woman. "Oh my!" she said, and told the woman, "Somewhere there is a single man who went away. Find him and if he accepts you, live with him. If he doesn't, both of you will have to stay single. Do the best you can."

The two finally found each other, and the woman said, "Where shall we live?"

The man answered, "Why, anywhere." He went to work and built a house for them, but before long they began to quarrel.

"I want to live alone," the woman said. "I can cook for myself."

"Yes, but who will get the wood for you and work the fields?" the man said. "We had better stay together." They made up, but it didn't last. They quarreled, separated, came together again, separated again. If they had managed to get along, all the Hopi would live in peace today. But other couples learned quarreling from them; this is why there are so many arguments between husbands and wives.

These were the kind of people that Spider Woman created—rough-mannered. The Huruing Wuhti of the west heard about it and soon called the goddess of the east to come over. "I don't want to live here alone," the deity of the west said. "I want some good people around me." So she created a number of people, always in pairs. But wherever Spider Woman's people came into contact with them, there was trouble. Human beings at that time led a nomadic life, feeding mostly on game. Whenever they found rabbits or antelope or deer, they would kill and eat. This led to many quarrels.

Finally the goddess of the west said to the people: "You stay here; I'm going to live in the middle of the ocean in the west. When you want anything, pray to me there." Her people were sorrowful, but she left them. The Huruing Wuhti of the east did the same, and that's the reason why their kivas are never seen today. Hopi who want something from them must deposit their prayer offerings in the village. And when they say their prayers, they think of the two goddesses who live far away, but who, the Hopi believe, still remember them.

—*Based on a story reported in 1905 by H. R. Voth.*

CREATION OF THE
YAKIMA WORLD

[YAKIMA]

In the beginning of the world, all was water. Whee-me-me-ow-ah, the Great Chief Above, lived up in the sky all alone. When he decided to make the world, he went down to the shallow places in the water and began to throw up great handfuls of mud that became land.

He piled some of the mud so high that it froze hard and made the mountains. When the rain came, it turned into ice and snow on top of the high mountains. Some of the mud was hardened into rocks. Since that time the rocks have not changed—they have only become harder.

The Great Chief Above made trees grow on the earth, and also roots and berries. He made a man out of a ball of mud and told him to take fish from the waters, and deer and other game from the forests. When the man became lonely, the Great Chief Above made a woman to be his companion and taught her how to dress skins, how to find bark and roots, and how to make baskets out of them. He taught her which berries to gather for food and how to pick them and dry them. He showed her how to cook the salmon and the game that the man brought.

Once when the woman was asleep, she had a dream, and in it she wondered what more she could do to please the man. She prayed to the Great Chief Above for help. He answered her prayer by blowing his breath on her and giving her something which she could not see or hear, smell or touch. This invisible something was preserved in a basket. Through it, the first woman taught her daughters and granddaughters the designs and skills which had been taught her.

But in spite of all the things the Great Chief Above did for them, the new people quarreled. They bickered so much that Mother Earth was angry, and in her anger she shook the mountains so hard that those hanging over the narrow part of Big River fell down. The rocks, falling into the water, dammed the stream and also made rapids and waterfalls. Many people and animals were killed and buried under the rocks and mountains.

Someday the Great Chief Above will overturn those mountains and rocks. Then the spirits that once lived in the bones buried there will go back into them. At present those spirits live in the tops of the mountains, watching their children on the earth and waiting for the great change which is to come. The voices of these spirits can be heard in the mountains at all times. Mourners who wail for their dead hear spirit voices reply, and thus they know that their lost ones are always near.

We did not know all this by ourselves; we were told it by our fathers and grandfathers, who learned it from their fathers and grandfathers. No one knows when the Great Chief Above will overturn the mountains. But we do know this: the spirits will return only to the remains of people who in life kept the beliefs of their grandfathers. Only their bones will be preserved under the mountains.

—*Reported by Ella Clark in 1953.*

CHILDREN OF THE SUN

[OSAGE]

Way beyond the earth, a part of the Osage lived in the sky. They wanted to know where they came from, so they went to the sun. He told them that they were his children. Then they wandered still farther and came to the moon. She told them that she gave birth to them, and that the sun was their father. She said that they must leave the sky and go down to live on earth. They obeyed, but found the earth covered with water. They could not return to their home in the sky, so they wept and called out, but no answer came from anywhere. They floated about in the air, seeking in every direction for help from some god; but they found none.

The animals were with them, and of these the elk inspired all creatures with confidence because he was the finest and most stately. The Osage appealed to the elk for help, and he dropped into the water and began to sink. Then he called to the winds, and they came from all quarters and blew until the waters went upward in mist.

At first only rocks were exposed, and the people traveled on the rocky places that produced no plants to eat. Then the waters began to go down until the soft earth was exposed. When this happened, the elk in his joy rolled over and over, and all his loose hairs clung to the soil. The hairs grew, and from them sprang beans, corn, potatoes, and wild turnips, and then all the grasses and trees.

—From Alice Fletcher and Francis LaFléche, who recorded
this myth in 1911.

THE VOICE, THE FLOOD, AND THE TURTLE

[CADDO]

Once there was a chief whose wife, to the fear and wonder of the people, gave birth to four little monsters. The elders said: "These strange children will bring great misfortune. It would be better to kill them right now, for the sake of the tribe."

"No way will we kill them," said their mother. "These children will turn out all right, by and by."

But they didn't turn out all right. The small monsters grew fast, much faster than ordinary children, and became very big. They had four legs and arms each. They hurt other children; they upset tipis; they tore up buffalo robes; they befouled people's food.

A wise man, who could see things in his mind which had not yet happened, said: "Kill these strange bad things before they kill you."

But their mother said: "Never. They'll be fine young men some day."

They never became fine young men; instead they started killing and eating people. At that point all the men in the village rushed at them to do away with them, but by then it was too late. The monsters had become too big and too powerful to be killed.

They grew taller and taller. One day they went into the middle of the camp and stood back to back, one facing east, one facing south, one facing west, and one facing north. Their backs grew together, and they became one.

As they grew higher and higher, most people took refuge near the monsters' feet, where the huge creatures could not bend down to catch them. But people who stayed farther off were seized by mile-long arms, killed, and eaten. The four monsters, now grown together, rose up to the clouds, and their heads touched the sky.

Then the man who could see into the future heard a voice telling him to set up a hollow reed and plant it in the ground. The man did, and the reed grew bigger and bigger very fast. In no time it rose to touch the sky. The man heard the voice again, saying: "I will make a great flood. When the signs of bad things coming appear, you and your wife climb up inside this hollow cane. Be naked as you were born, and take with you a pair of all the good animals in order to save them."

The man asked: "What sign will you be sending?"

"When all the birds in the world—birds of the woods, the sea, the deserts, and the high mountains—form up into a cloud flying from north to south, that will be the sign. Watch for the cloud of birds."

One day the man looked up and saw a big cloud made up of birds traveling from north to south. At once he and his wife moved up into the hollow reed, taking with them all the animals they wished to save.

Then it began to rain and did not stop. Waters covered the earth and kept rising until only the top of the hollow cane and the heads of the monsters were left above the surface.

Inside the hollow reed, the man and his wife heard the voice again: "Now I shall send Turtle to destroy the monsters."

The monsters' heads were saying to each other: "Brothers, I'm getting tired. My legs are weakening. I can't keep standing much longer."

The floods swirled around them with strong currents that almost swept them away. Then the Great Turtle began digging down underneath the monsters' feet. It uprooted them, and they could not keep their footing but broke apart and toppled over. They fell down into the waters, one sinking toward the north, one toward the east, one toward the south, and one toward the west. Thus the four directions came into being.

After the monsters had drowned, the waters subsided. First the mountaintops reappeared, then the rest of the land. Next came hard-blowing winds that dried the earth. The man climbed down to the bottom of the hollow reed and opened the hole at its foot. He looked out. He stuck out his hand and felt around. He said to his wife: "Come out. Everything is dry."

So they emerged, followed by all the animals. They left the reed, which collapsed and disappeared. But when they stepped out on the earth, it was bare; nothing was growing.

The wife said: "Husband, there's nothing here and we are naked. How shall we live?"

The man said: "Go to sleep." They lay down and slept, and when they woke the next morning, all kinds of herbs had sprung up around them.

The second night while they slept, trees and bushes grew. Now there was firewood to keep them warm, and all kinds of woods for making bows and arrows.

During the third night green grass covered the earth, and animals appeared to graze on it.

The man and his wife went to sleep a fourth time and woke up inside a grass hut. They stepped out and found a stalk of corn. Then they heard the voice say: "This will be your holy food." It told the woman how to plant and harvest the corn and ended with: "Now you have everything you need. Now you can live. Now you will have children and form a new generation. If you, woman, should plant corn, and something other than corn comes up, then know that the world will come to its end."

After that, they never heard the voice again.

—*Retold from various sources.*

■

A TALE OF ELDER BROTHER

■

[PIMA]

■ |||||||||||||||||||||||||||||||||||||||||||||||||||||||||||||||||||||||||||| ■

You people desired to capture Elder Brother so that you might destroy him, so you went to Vulture. He made a miniature earth, shaping the mountains, routing the water courses, and placing the trees, and in four days he completed his task. Mounting the zigzag ladders of his house he flew forth and circled about until he saw Elder Brother. Vulture saw the blue flames issuing from Brother's heart and knew that he was invulnerable. In his turn Elder Brother knew what had made the earth, and wished to kill him.

Elder Brother, as he regained consciousness, rose on hands and feet and swayed unsteadily from side to side. He looked at the land about him, and at first it seemed a barren waste, but as he recovered from his bewilderment he saw the wonderful world Vulture had built.

Looking about him he saw a river toward the west along which grew arrow bushes. From these he cut four magic sticks; placing his hand on these he blew smoke over them, whereupon magic power shone forth from between his fingers. He was much pleased with this and laughed softly to himself. He rubbed his magic bag of buckskin four times with each of the four sticks and then put them in and tied it. Then, with his strength fully recovered, Elder Brother began to move. He arose and crushed all mortal magicians; the orator, the warrior, the industrious, and the provident woman, and even ground his own house into the earth. Then he sank beneath the surface of the earth. He reappeared in the east and made a transparent trail back to the place where he had gone down. About the base of his mountains the water began to seep forth; entering, he came out with spirit refreshed. Taking all waters, even those covered with water plants, he dipped his hands in and made downward passes. Touching the large trees he made downward sweeps with his hands.

Going to the place where he had killed Eagle he sat down looking like a ghost. A voice from the darkness asked, "Why are you here?" He answered sadly that despite all that he had done for them the people hated him. He went on to the east, renewing his power four times at the place where the sun rises. He blew his hot breath upon the people, which like a weight held them where they were. He went along with the sun on his journey, traveling along the south border of the trail where there was a fringe of beads, feathers, strings of down, and flowers. He jerked the string holding these so that they fell and made the magicians jump. Later he did the same thing in the north.

On his journey along the sun's orbit Elder Brother came to Talking Tree. "Why do you come like a ghost?" asked Tree. He replied, "Despite all I have done for the people they hate me." Tree broke one of its middle branches and cut a notch around it to form a war club and gave it to him. Then Tree broke a branch on the south side and made a bundle of ceremonial sticks from it for him. He saw a trail toward the south and another toward the north bordered with shells, feathers, down, and flowers, and he turned them all over.

Arriving at the drinking place of the sun, he knelt down and saw a dark-blue stone. He left there the sticks cut from the arrow bush which he knew contained all his enemies' power, but he kept in his grasp the sticks cut from Talking Tree. Toward the south were strewn necklaces, earrings, feathers, strings of down, and flowers, all of which he jerked and threw face down. Toward the north he threw down the same objects, and as they struck the earth the magicians jumped again. Reaching the place where the sun sets he slid down four times before he reached the place where Earth Doctor lived.

"Why do you come looking like a ghost?" asked the god. "Despite all that I have done for them the people hate me," he answered. By Earth Doctor's order the wind from the west caught him up and carried him far to the east, then brought him back and violently tossed him back down to earth. The south wind carried him to the north; the east wind carried him to the west; the wind from the zenith carried him to the sky; all carelessly dropped him back down again. From his cigarette containing two kinds of roots Earth Doctor blew smoke upon the breast of Elder Brother, whereupon green leaves sprang forth and he gained consciousness. Earth Doctor cleared the ground for a council and then picked up Elder Brother as he would have taken up a child and put him in his house.

Earth Doctor sent Gray Gopher up through the earth to emerge in the east by the white water where lay the eagle tail. He came out by the black water where lay the raven feathers. He came out by the blue water where lay the bluebird's feathers. He came out by the yellow water where lay the hawk feathers. He found so many people that he feared they could not be conquered. But he gnawed the magic power of their leader until he weakened it. Then he returned to the council in the nether world, where his power as a magician was recognized, and he was placed on a mat with Elder Brother.

The people were now ready to do whatever Elder Brother desired of them and, like fierce predatory animals or birds of prey, they poured out of the underworld and fell upon the people of the upper world, whom they conquered without difficulty. The victors swept the property and everything relating to the conquered from the face of the earth.

Consider the magic power which abode with me and which is at your service.

—*Based on Frank Russell's 1908 report on the Pimas.*

This fantastic tale of creation and violence features several related episodes in the life of the great Pima culture hero, Elder Brother, whose task it is to assert order in the primordial chaos. Elder Brother fixes the features of the landscape, he brings elements of Pima culture, and he struggles with representatives of predation and evil, vanquishing them or, in turn, being killed himself and rising to live on another day. The Pima tell such stories not as self-contained tales but in a narrative chain, one incident suggesting the next, achieving an episodic progression with neither beginnings nor ends.

PART THREE

THE EYE OF THE GREAT SPIRIT

TALES OF THE SUN, MOON, AND STARS

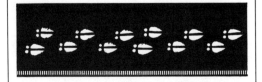

Just as trees, ponds, clouds, and rocks are thought of as living beings, so the sun, moon, and stars in their firmament are depicted in Indian mythology as alive and endowed with human passions and yearnings. The sun, the father of light who begets all living things upon mother earth, the illuminator of the primordial darkness, is life giver as well as destroyer. The sun is usually male, though it is female among the Juchi, Cherokees, and Eskimos (all of whom regard the moon as male). In the tales of many tribes, the sun makes love to mortal women, sometimes marries, and has offspring by them.

The great shining orb is the ultimate fertilizing agent in the universe, usually the embodiment of the male principle, though not necessarily the god at the center of religion. There may be other chief deities or super-natural phenomena and spirits which represent different powers. Tales depict mortal men and women turning themselves into the morning and evening stars, or even into the moon, and taking on lovers and spouses in those guises. In historical times, the only instance of human sacrifice among the Plains tribes occurred among the Skidi-Pawnee who, once a year, sacrificed a girl captive to the morning star. Representing the evening star, protectress of all growing things, the maiden was painted half red and half black (symbolizing day and night) and ritually shot to death with arrows to send her to her celestial husband. Very old people among the Sioux still tell of ancestors who, participating in a ghost dance in 1890, fell down in a trance and in that state of unconsciousness traveled to the morning or evening star, waking up with star flesh or moon flesh in their clenched fists.

The creation myth of the Bella Coola relates how the fierce Bear of Heaven guarded the place of sunrise. At the place of sunset an immense pillar upheld the sky. The sun's path was a bridge as wide as the distance between the winter, the "place where the sun sits down," and summer, the "place where the sun stands up." Three dancing slaves accompany him on his path, and whenever he drops his torch, an eclipse plunges the earth into darkness.

Indian myths, like those in every other culture, grapple with the basic paradoxes at the center of the human world, and certain primal themes emerge which we in the West have often come to associate with Greek prototypes, even though their evolution has been wholly separate on this continent. Thus one Northwest Coast myth closely resembles the Helios-Phaeton story of ancient Greece. A woman conceives by sitting in the sun's beams, and her son matures in one year. He shoots arrows into the sky and climbs up the ladder they form to visit his father. After pestering his father, he is finally permitted to carry the flaming disk along the appointed path, but tottering under his heavy burden, he gets too close to earth. The oceans boil, the forests catch fire, and everything bursts into flames. The father quickly steps in to assume the load, and the presumptuous boy is turned into a mink.

Other themes include Promethean thefts and an Orpheus-like journey to the underworld in an attempt to defy the finality of death, seen in the story of a Cherokee tribe trying to help a grieving female sun retrieve her dead daughter.

The sun can also be reduced to a small object stolen from the other side of the world by a trickster or friendly animal to bring light to a tribe living in darkness.

Whether they are hunters or planters, people who live close to nature are keen observers of the stars and planets. They study the sky to determine the right time for planting and harvesting, or to discover where to find game at certain times of the year. The prehistoric mound builders of Kahokia, in what is now eastern Missouri, had their own Stonehenge, an astronomical observatory consisting of a circle of upright poles. Among the prehistoric ruins of Chaco Canyon in New Mexico, one kiva—a large, partially underground, circular ceremonial chamber—is so constructed that on the day of the summer solstice, and on this day only, a shaft of light shines through a slit in its stone wall.

From the spiral image of the sun chipped into a rock wall in the Southwestern United States to the Plains Tunkashila, Grandfather, whose sunbeams impregnated the Mother Goddess so that she gave birth to gods, humans, and animals alike, the sun plays a radiant role in Indian mythology. He is Shakuru of the Pawnees, who gives health and strength to warriors. He is Paiyatemu of the Keres, regulating the seasons and determining the time for planting and harvesting. He is Ataksak of the North, the personification of joy, clothed in raiments of brilliant cords, whose body shines even in death. He is T'ahn of the Tewa, with his face surrounded by rays of feathers. He is the shining, piercing embodiment of the Sioux Wakan Tanka, the Great Spirit, who is in and of everything.

SUN CREATION

[BRULE SIOUX]

*Far from being relics, Indian myths are still told on winter nights,
and as some of the old tales die, new legends are being born according to a medicine man's dreams or visions. It is a rare privilege to
be present as a legend's birth, as with this one, told for the first
time by Leonard Crow Dog in 1981.*

This story has never been told. It is in no book or computer. It came to
me in a dream during a vision quest. It is a story as old as the beginning
of life, but it has new understandings according to what I saw in my
vision, added to what the grandfathers told me—things remembered,
things forgotten, and things re-remembered. It comes out of the World
of the Minds.

Some people say we are descended from Adam and Eve, but there was
no Adam or Eve in our creation. Some people try to tell us that we were
born with the burden of original sin, but that is an alien white man's
concept. Sin was not in the mind of the universe of our creators or the
created.

When this world came into being seven million eons ago, it was composed of numberless hoops, skeletons with no substance. Land, the whole
earth, had yet to be made. All was orbits within orbits within orbits. The
world on which we are sitting now, our earth, was made up of sixteen
sacred hoops. There was no earth, no land, but there were planets and
stars. Above all there was the great sun. He controlled all the orbit
powers. He had the sole power to communicate, to talk planet-talk between the universes, stars, and orbits.

The sun had seven shadows, and in them he recreated himself. The
seventh shadow was the important one. The sun looked at it and saw
that its design was different. This shadow was the creator of the red
man's land.

Then the great sun called to all the orbits, planets, and stars: "Come
to the sixteen hoops! Come to the sixteen hoops!" and they all went to
the place the sun had appointed and made earth-plan talk. The sun would
not allow them to leave until they were done. And that great ball called

earth, the earth planet himself, said to the sun: "Instruct us in the way of the universe." For this purpose and for this reason the orbs and the orbits talked to each other. They related to each other and that was the first relation-making feast, the first *alonwanpi* of the universe.

And one of the orbits, the east, asked the sun: "Why have you called us to come here? What have you called me for?"

"I have called you because you shall take part in this creation. You will breathe into these sixteen hoops. You will breathe into them with your Takuskanskan, the moving power, the quickening power which is part of the Wakan Wichohan, the big sacred work we must do."

And the orbit which is called the south asked the sun: "Why did you call me? I have come with my planets and my orbits and you must tell me what to do." In this manner the orbits talked.

Then the west asked: "Sun, why have you called all the orbits and planets here? What is the purpose?"

"I have called you here in a sacred manner, for a sacred purpose: To help me make this earth, this land. To breathe into these sixteen hoops."

The north said: "What is that thing you call land, what is this thing you call earth? What have I to do with it?"

The great sun replied: You are the living moisture; you are the atmosphere; you are the north. You will be the caretaker of this earth. You will make the seasons in all eternity."

And the power from the north answered: "Hou, hou!" This was the echo of the echos of all the universe, and it reverberated throughout the hoops and orbits.

So the sacred four-direction powers breathed their life-giving breath into this earth we are sitting on. The sixteen hoops were still skeleton hoops; you could see through them, walk through, float through; they had no substance yet.

The sun again called all the powers and planets to crowd around the earth and breathe into it, and this was the beginning of the red man's life. All the powers of the universe participated in its creation, but there arrived among them in a whirlwind an unknown power right out of the center of the universes. Its name was Unknowingly, and it also breathed into the sixteen hoops. All the powers breathed fire and the other elements into this land, and when they had finished, one and a half million eons of creation had passed.

The sun looked at the earth. Everywhere he saw beauty and light. He saw the art designs of the universe, the creation art of the planets, and land painting. The sun gathered parts of all the riches of all the universes and put them into this newly created world; nothing was wasted.

But the earth was bare. It was a bald-headed world. No life was on it yet; it was rock, a far-shining crystal.

The Great Unknown Power, the Grandfather Power, Unknowingly, was part of the sun and the sun was part of him. Unknowingly was seen-unseen and had many forms. He spoke: "Ho! Aho! Now it is done. This is the Great Way of the Great Spirit talking." And of the earth he said: "This will be my seat. This will be my backrest." In the earth he planted the seed of life, a planting that took half a million eons of creation time.

First Unknowingly planted trees, the kind that never change, that are always green: the pine and the cedar. They are the green relations of the universe, and we still use the cedar as incense in our ceremonies. In his mind this tree planting was done in the blink of an eye, but it lasted a million and a half eons of creation time. At that point the sun did not move yet, did not rise and did not go down, just stood in one place. The sun looked at the earth covered with green and said: "It is beautiful. I am satisfied." Then the great sun made the four seasons for north to take care of, and when he had finished, another half-million eons of creation time had passed. And no birds had yet been created; just our green relations.

The trees spoke to each other. Every day and every moment they were talking, and they are still talking now in an unknown language which humans do not understand. When a little child emerges from the womb, the first thing it does is to cry and cry. It too is speaking in an unknown language—tree language, universe language, survival language. Though the newborn later forgets, he knows at birth that we have to survive to take care of this world, to live in a sacred manner after the original instruction.

When three million eons of creation time had passed, the great sun looked down from his orbit and thought: "This is unique. Everything moves in the Great Way. Caretakers, the sacred four directions, have been appointed, and they are doing well what they are supposed to do." And he looked at a tree and saw that a big branch was broken off. He said: "Ton, Ton, Tonpi. Birth giving. It's time for creating people, for forming them up in pairs."

Don't call us Indians; call us Birth People, because that is what we are.

The sun thought: "Everything looks nice, and birthing is about to take place, but somebody should be the caretaker of this Birth people land. The four-direction powers already take care of the planet, but I want a special caretaker for the hemisphere upon which I shall put the red man." At that time he did not think of it as Mother Earth but as the Planet of the Universes, the Orb of Planification. Because there was no mother yet, no man or woman; just the colors of the four directions and

the plants, and the intelligence of powers, the intelligence of Tunkashila.

The great sun called loudly: "Unknowing, you always arrive unknowingly. Come unknowlingly from your seat." And Unknowingly arrived with lightning and with powers that no human could scientifically analyze, that could not be computed, powers sacred and secret, the oldest, the most innate. Unknown was a shadow who spoke with lightning, with thundering. The great sun, *anpetu-wi*, still stood idle, fixed in his place from the moment of creation. Then suddenly, at billions of miles an hour, the sun began to move. Moving, he released glowing gases, the energy of the fire without end, life-giving warmth. Unknowingly was right beside him at that moment of creation time. (Were he and the sun one? Were they two? Was he the sun's seventh shadow?)

Unknowingly said: "Now we are going to make a human out of all these elements. We will take the vein of the cedar tree to create a man who will be the caretaker of this land. His name shall be Ikche Wichasha —the Wild Natural Two-Legged, the wild, free human. Unknowingly was the seventh shadow of the sun, and he spoke the lightning language to communicate his wishes. If the shadow walked through this room here, you couldn't see him, but you would somehow feel his presence and you would have a new vision.

Unknowingly called the whirlwind. "Yumni-Omni, Tate Yumni, arrive!"

Whirlwind arrived with a thundering moan—the earth-birthing sound. The sun, from his eye of eyes, his eye of the universe, made tears flow. When one tear hit the earth, it turned into a blood clot, a *we-ota*. It was as yet only a shadow, but for four generations this shadow developed itself. The whirlwind enfolded him, hit him, helping him to become a body. He was We-Ota-Wichasha, Blood Clot Boy, and he was almost seven feet tall. When the whirlwind hit him, supernatural knowledge went into him, as well as the power of speech and the knowledge of language. And when Blood Clot received these powers, he became a man. The sun was content, saying: "Now a caretaker has been created for this land."

We-Ota-Wichasha developed not only into one man, but into seven nations of the seven ore colors. Today we have only four colors—the red man, the white man, the black man, and the yellow man. What happened to the other three kinds of men? Where did they go?

One was Kosankiya—a great planet, with plants, with animals, with humans. Kosankiya is the darkness of every blue. He said: "I shall be the nest maker. I shall be the upholder of the dome. I shall be the blue sky." He is still here, whether it is day or night. That vault above us makes himself dark at night, blue during the day.

And where is the second one? His name is Edam, Hota Edam, Hotanka —the Great Voice blazing forth. Where does he come from? He is floating in the voids. He is red, an art design. You can see him among the thunder clouds sometimes. And he is the Wakinyan, the great thunderbird, the winged part of the sixteen sacreds. He is still here.

And still one is missing; where is he? Look carefully, for he is the spirit of the land, the yellow spearhead of the earth powers. He is Wo-Wakan, the supernatural.

Together with the four races of mankind, the Above, the Below, and the Winged Spirit form the seven generations. None are missing. And we are part of them. They include us, they include everything; even a pebble or a tiny insect is gathered up in the sacred hoop.

Now, the sun had given Blood Clot Man the intelligence of the divine human being. He was a medicine, for the sun had shed tears and sweated as during a sweat-lodge purification. Out of the winds, out of the whirl-wind, out of the sacred breath of the universe Blood Clot had been made. He was not created in nine months, like the child you and your woman begot, but over millions of years. Yet even in your baby, a little of that lightning power and star breath is being passed on.

At this time the earth was a crystal inhabited by a great intelligence and overblanketed by the sun and the shadows he had created. Its shining center was crystal, glass, and mica, but it was solid now. You could not pierce it or walk through it, for the skeleton had been covered with flesh, green flesh. Next Wakan Tanka, Tunkashila, formed animals in pairs, to give their flesh so that man could live. And then it was time to create woman. There was no moon then; it was still the period of sacred newness. The sun again called all the planets and supernaturals, and when they had assembled, the sun, in a bright flash, took out one of his eyes. He threw it on the wind of his vision into a certain place, and it became the moon. And on this new orb, that eye-planet, he created woman. "You are a planet virgin, a moon maiden," he told her. "I have touched you and made you out of my shadow. I want you to walk on the earth." This happened in darkness at the time of a new moon.

"How will I walk over to that land?" asked the woman. So the sun created woman power and woman understanding. He used the lightning to make a bridge from the moon to the earth, and the woman walked on the lightning. Her crossing took a long time.

Now the maker of the universe had created man and woman and given them a power and a way that has never been changed. Doing that, the sun had used up another million eons of creation time. He instructed the woman in her tasks, which she accomplished through her dreams, through her visions, through her special powers.

The Great Spirit had created the woman to be with the man, with We-Ota-Wichasha—but not right away. They had to make contact slowly, get used to each other, understand each other for the survival of their caretaking. Tunkashila let blood roll into her. She walked on the lightning, but she also walked on a blood vein reaching from the moon to the earth. This vein was a cord, a birth cord that went into her body, and through it she is forever connected with the moon. And nine months of creation were given to her. At first she was without feeling, for love was created in her and inside the man long after their bodies had been formed. They did not live as we do today but were a part of the land, taking care of it even while it took care of them.

The man and the woman began to communicate with each other and talked for many years. Then inside them a feeling emerged. Even before they touched each other they felt a vibration, womb understanding. So by the powers of the great sun, by the powers of Tunkashila, it was given to them to understand that they were man and woman, creators themselves. That understanding came to the man through lightning, through the sun blood that was in him, and it came to the woman through that birth cord which connects her to the moon and whose power she still feels at her moon time.

"You are the caretaker of the generations, you are the birth giver," the sun told the woman. "You will be the carrier of this universe."

The man and the woman did what they were meant to do after sacred nature's way, and twins were born to them, two little boys. They were not born in a hospital or a tipi but in the natural way, the woman crouching, gripping her birthing stick, with a soft deerskin waiting to receive her womb offerings. The sun dome was their dwelling, not a tipi or a house. Their roof was the sky vault. And that is why we, the red people, the Ikche Wichasa, are the oldest people on this hemisphere, living here since the beginning of time with the understanding and power given to us.

At the moment they were born, the twins already had that understanding and power. When they were old enough (and they grew faster than humans do now), they climbed to the top of a high hill for their vision quest, which lasted sixteen days and sixteen nights. They did not purify themselves in a sweat lodge before and after they cried for a dream, because everything was still pure. On the mountain one of the twins heard the voice of Tunkashila and answered, "Hou!" And Tunkashila showed him the path to making and keeping a flame—*peta owihankeshni*, the fire without end. And ultimately from the vision came the first sweat lodge. The one twin received this great vision, the other twin a lesser one. And each of them followed his own dream.

We-Ota-Wichasha and First Woman begat other children, boys and girls from whom sprang many nations. The twin who had received the great vision also had a son, begotten with the help of a sunbeam. When that son was old enough he too went up on a high hill for his vision quest, and the hill turned itself into a nest. "Ikcheha, Ikchewi, Ikche Wichasha, that will be your name," he heard a voice saying. "Ikche Wichasha, that is who you are,"—and that is what we Sioux have called ourselves ever since. Mark what is in this name: *che*, the male organ; *wi*, the sun; and *sha*, red. Together they mean "wild, common man," a natural free human, an earth man. But all those syllables and meanings are put in to show that we are the original red sun people. Ho He!

And the son of the twin made the first fire and built the first sweat lodge. Then he went to his parents and said. "I must leave you. I am appointed to take care of the winds of this universe." He began walking up the hill on which he had performed his vision quest and, before the eyes of his father and mother and of We-Ota-Wichasha and First Woman, he turned himself into an eagle. The eagle-son flew off with a gift from the Great Spirit—the four seasons. They accompanied him in the shapes of the bald eagle, the spotted eagle, the golden eagle, and the northern eagle.

We-Ota-Wichasha and First Woman saw their grandson fly away, circling higher and higher. And they went up to the mountaintop which had become a nest and found that he had left them gifts. A bow and arrow were lying there, and a rock, a spider web, and a gourd rattle. They found a fire stick and a small fire burning brightly. The eagle had scratched it out of the rock with his claw, striking a spark from the flint.

These things had been shadows out of a vision, and eagle-son's understanding had brought them into being, making them real. All the sacred survival things fitted themselves into the hands of We-Ota-Wichasha and First Woman, and through them were given to the red man, together with the knowledge of how to use them. And when these First Parents brought the things back to their small camp, they found it swarming with people in many camp circles of many tribes. And to them all, We-Ota-Wichasha and First Woman imparted the vision and the dream and the sacred things and the understanding. And at that moment the seven million eons of creation were ended.

—*Told by Leonard Crow Dog on Grass Mountain at*
Rosebud Indian Reservation, South Dakota, March 18, 1981,
and recorded by Richard Erdoes.

Leonard Crow Dog, Henry Crow Dog's son, is a well-known Sioux medicine man and a "road man" of the Native American Church.

WALKS-ALL-OVER-THE-SKY

[TSIMSHIAN]

This is an older and more traditional tale about the sun and moon,
in contrast with the contemporary vision of the previous story.

In the beginning, before anything that lives in our world was created, there was only the chief in the sky. The chief had two sons and a daughter, and his people were numerous. But there was no light in the sky—only emptiness and darkness.

The chief's eldest son was named Walking-About-Early, the second son was called The-One-Who-Walks-All-Over-the-Sky, and the daughter was Support-of-Sun. They were all very strong, but the younger boy was wiser and abler than the elder.

It made the younger son sad to see the sky always so dark, and one day he took his brother and went to cut some good pitch wood. They bent a slender cedar twig into a ring the size of a person's face, then tied the pitch wood all around it so that it looked like a mask. They lit the wood, and The-One-Who-Walks-All-Over-the-Sky put on the mask and went to the east.

Suddenly everyone saw a great light rising. As the people watched and marveled, the chief's younger son ran from east to west, moving swiftly so that the flaming mask would not burn him.

Every day the second son repeated his race and lit up the sky. Then the whole tribe assembled and sat down to a council. "We're glad your child has given us light," they told the chief. "But he's too quick; he ought to slow down a little so we can enjoy the light longer."

The chief told his son what the people had said, but Walks-All-Over-the-sky replied that the mask would burn up before he reached the west. He continued to run very fast, and the people continued to wish he would go slower, until the sister said, "I'll try and hold him back a little."

The next time Walks-All-Over-the-Sky rose in the east and started on his journey, Support-of-Sun also started from the south. "Wait for me!" she cried, running as hard as she could. She intercepted her brother in the middle of his race and held him briefly until he could break free. That's why the sun today always stops for a little while in the middle of the sky. The people shouted for joy, and Support-of-Sun's father blessed her.

But the chief was displeased with Walking-About-Early because he was not as smart and capable as his younger brother. The father expressed his disappointment, and Walking-About-Early was so mortified that he flung himself down and cried. Meanwhile his brother, the sun, came back tired from his daily trip and lay down to rest. Later when everybody was asleep, Walking-About-Early rubbed fat and charcoal over his face. He woke his little slave and said, "When you see me rising in the east, jump up and shout, 'Hurrah! He has arisen!'"

Then Walking-About-Early left, while Walks-All-Over-the-Sky slept deeply, his face shedding light out of the smoke hole. Suddenly Walking-about-Early rose in the east, and his charcoaled face reflected the smoke hole's luster. The little slave jumped up and shouted, "Hurrah! He has arisen!"

Several people asked him, "Why are you so noisy, bad slave?" The slave jumped up and down, pointing to the east. The people looked up and saw the rising moon, and they too shouted, "Hurrah!"

Time passed, and animals were created to live in our world below. At last all the animals assembled to hold a council. They agreed that the sun should run from east to west, that he should be the light of day, and that he should make everything grow. The moon, they decided, should walk at night. Then they had to set the number of days that would be in a month. The dogs were wiser than the other animals and spoke first. "The moon shall rise for forty days," they said.

All the animals were silent. The dogs sat together talking secretly among themselves and thinking about what they had said. The wisest dog, their spokesman, was still standing. He was counting up to forty on his fingers, when the porcupine suddenly struck him on the thumb. "Who can live if there are forty days to each month?" the porcupine said. "The year would be far too long. There should be only thirty days in a month."

The rest of the animals agreed with the porcupine. And as a result of this council, each month has thirty days and there are twelve months in a year. By now the animals were disgusted with the dogs and banded together to drive them away. For this reason dogs hate all the creatures of the woods, and most of all the porcupine, who struck the wise dog's thumb with its spiny tail and humiliated him in the council. And because of the porcupine's blow, a dog's thumb now stands opposite to his other fingers.

Before that long-ago council ended, the animals also named the following months:

> *Between October and November, Falling-Leaf Month*
> *Between November and December, Taboo Month*
> *Between December and January, The Intervening Month*
> *Between January and February, Spring Salmon Month*
> *Between February and March, Month When Olachen Is Eaten*
> *Between March and April, When Olachen Is Cooked*
> *Between May and June, Egg Month*
> *Between June and July, Salmon Month*
> *Between July and August, Humpback-Salmon Month*
> *Between September and October, Spinning Top Month*

In addition, the animals divided the year into four seasons—spring, summer, autumn, and winter.

New things were also happening in the sky. When Walks-All-Over-the-Sky was asleep, the sparks that flew out of his mouth became the stars. And sometimes when he was glad, he painted his face with his sister's red ochre, and then people knew what kind of weather was coming. If his red paint colored the sky in the evening, there would be good weather the next day, but a red sky in the morning meant that storms were coming. And that's still true, people say.

After the sky had been furnished with the sun, moon, and stars, the chief's daughter, Support-of-Sun, was cast down because she had played such a small part in the creation. Sadly she wandered westward into the water, and her clothes became wet. When she returned, she stood near her father's great fire to warm herself. She wrung the water out of her garments and let it drip onto the flames, making a great cloud of steam that floated out of the house. It settled over the land and moderated the hot weather with damp fog. Her father blessed her, for the whole tribe enjoyed it. And to this day, all fog comes from the west.

The chief was glad when he saw that all three of his children were wise. Now it was the duty of the moon, Walking-About-Early, to rise and set every thirty days so that people may know the year. The sun, Walks-All-Over-the-Sky, was charged with creating all good things, such as fruit, and making everything plentiful. And the chief's daughter, Support-of-Sun, served by refreshing the hot earth with cool fog.

—Based on a version recorded by Franz Boas in 1916.

Some Northwest tribes did indeed have slaves, as this story suggests; the status could be inherited from one generation to the next, and they were looked upon as their owners' possessions, to be killed if the owner wished. Since the Tsimshians lived in the Northwest, the fog that came from the West refers, naturally, to the weather rolling in from the Pacific Ocean.

■

THREE-LEGGED RABBIT
FIGHTS THE SUN

■

The origin of this tale is not precise. Ella Clark only notes that it comes from a Western Rocky Mountain tribe.

Once there was a rabbit with only three legs, but he made a wooden leg for himself so that he could move fast.

At the time the sun was very hot, and Rabbit said to himself, "I'll go and see what the problem is." As he hopped along toward Sun, he found it getting hotter every day.

"The only thing on earth that doesn't burn," said Rabbit, "is cactus." So he made a house of cactus to stay in during the day, and he traveled only at night.

When he came to the east, he rose early in the morning and ran toward the place where Sun should appear. He saw the ground boiling and knew that Sun was ready to come up. Rabbit stopped, sat down, and took out his bow and arrows.

When Sun was about halfway out of the earth, Rabbit shot. His first arrow hit the heart and killed Sun. Rabbit stood over the corpse and cried: "The white part of your eye will be clouds." And it was.

"The black part of your eye will be the sky."

And it was.

"Your kidney will be a star, your liver the moon, and your heart the dark."

And they were.

Then Rabbit said to Sun, "You will never be too hot again, for now you are only a big star."

Sun has never been too hot since, and after that day, rabbits have had brown spots behind their ears and on their legs. Their rabbits' fur was scorched during their journey, long, long ago, to see why Sun was so hot.

—Told by Ella Clark in 1966.

■

COYOTE STEALS THE SUN AND MOON

■

[ZUNI]

■ |||||||||||||||||||||||||||||||||||||||||||||||||||||||||||||||||||||||||||||||||||| ■

Coyote is a bad hunter who never kills anything. Once he watched Eagle hunting rabbits, catching one after another—more rabbits than he could

eat. Coyote thought, "I'll team up with Eagle so I can have enough meat."
Coyote is always up to something.

"Friend," Coyote said to Eagle, "we should hunt together. Two can
catch more than one."

"Why not?" Eagle said, and so they began to hunt in partnership.
Eagle caught many rabbits, but all Coyote caught was some little bugs.

At this time the world was still dark; the sun and moon had not yet
been put in the sky. "Friend," Coyote said to Eagle, "no wonder I can't
catch anything; I can't see. Do you know where we can get some light?"

"You're right, friend, there should be some light," Eagle said. "I think
there's a little toward the west. Let's try and find it."

And so they went looking for the sun and moon. They came to a big
river, which Eagle flew over. Coyote swam, and swallowed so much
water that he almost drowned. He crawled out with his fur full of mud,
and Eagle asked, "Why don't you fly like me?"

"You have wings, I just have hair," Coyote said. "I can't fly without
feathers."

At last they came to a pueblo, where the Kachinas happened to be
dancing. The people invited Eagle and Coyote to sit down and have
something to eat while they watched the sacred dances. Seeing the power
of the Kachinas, Eagle said, "I believe these are the people who have
light."

Coyote, who had been looking all around, pointed out two boxes, one
large and one small, that the people opened whenever they wanted light.
To produce a lot of light, they opened the lid of the big box, which
contained the sun. For less light they opened the small box, which held
the moon.

Coyote nudged Eagle. "Friend, did you see that? They have all the
light we need in the big box. Let's steal it."

"You always want to steal and rob. I say we should just borrow it."

"They won't lend it to us."

"You may be right," said Eagle. "Let's wait till they finish dancing
and then steal it."

After a while the Kachinas went home to sleep, and Eagle scooped
up the large box and flew off. Coyote ran along trying to keep up, panting, his tongue hanging out. Soon he yelled up to Eagle, "Ho, friend,
let me carry the box a little way."

"No, no," said Eagle, "you never do anything right."

He flew on, and Coyote ran after him. After a while Coyote shouted
again: "Friend, you're my chief, and it's not right for you to carry the
box; people will call me lazy. Let me have it."

"No, no, you always mess everything up." And Eagle flew on and Coyote ran along.

So it went for a stretch, and then Coyote started again. "Ho, friend, it isn't right for you to do this. What will people think of you and me?"

"I don't care what people think. I'm going to carry this box."

Again Eagle flew on and again Coyote ran after him. Finally Coyote begged for the fourth time: "Let me carry it. You're the chief, and I'm just Coyote. Let me carry it."

Eagle couldn't stand any more pestering. Also, Coyote had asked him four times, and if someone asks four times, you better give him what he wants. Eagle said, "Since you won't let up on me, go ahead and carry the box for a while. But promise not to open it."

"Oh, sure, oh yes, I promise." They went on as before, but now Coyote had the box. Soon Eagle was far ahead, and Coyote lagged behind a hill where Eagle couldn't see him. "I wonder what the light looks like, inside there," he said to himself. "Why shouldn't I take a peek? Probably there's something extra in the box, something good that Eagle wants to keep to himself."

And Coyote opened the lid. Now, not only was the sun inside, but the moon also. Eagle had put them both together, thinking that it would be easier to carry one box than two.

As soon as Coyote opened the lid, the moon escaped, flying high into the sky. At once all the plants shriveled up and turned brown. Just as quickly, all the leaves fell off the trees, and it was winter. Trying to catch the moon and put it back in the box, Coyote ran in pursuit as it skipped away from him. Meanwhile the sun flew out and rose into the sky. It drifted far away, and the peaches, squashes, and melons shriveled up with cold.

Eagle turned and flew back to see what had delayed Coyote. "You fool! Look what you've done!" he said. "You let the sun and moon escape, and now it's cold." Indeed, it began to snow, and Coyote shivered. "Now you teeth are chattering," Eagle said, "and it's your fault that cold has come into the world."

It's true. If it weren't for Coyote's curiosity and mischief making, we wouldn't have winter; we could enjoy summer all the time.

—*Based on a story reported by Ruth Benedict in 1935.*

Day and night (as represented by the sun and moon) are metaphorically associated with summer and winter; hence the release of the moon brings death and desolation to the world. Coyote of course completely disrupts the seasonal cycle by interfering with the heavenly progression. The Kachinas mentioned were at the time of this story demi-gods, supernatural intermediaries, mostly benign, who regularly visited the pueblos and established elaborate rituals that included festive dances for the people.

KEEPING WARMTH IN A BAG

[SLAVEY]

In the beginning before there were people, there was a long winter. The sun remained hidden by low, black clouds. It never stopped snowing. The sky was black and the earth was white with snow and ice. After this had been going on for three years, all the animals got together for a big council about what they should do. They were freezing and starving to death. All the four-legged animals, the winged ones, and the scaly creatures of the sea attended.

The animals agreed that it was the lack of heat, the absence of warmth, which made the winter go on and on. They saw that no bears had come to the council and realized that, in fact, no bears had been seen for three years. One wise animal said: "Maybe the bears have something to do with our suffering. Maybe they're keeping the warmth to themselves. Let's go and find out." So they formed a search party consisting of the wolf, the fox, the wolverine, the bobcat, the mouse, the pike, and the dogfish.

At this time the bears were living in an upper world high above the earth. The search party was lucky enough to find a hole in the sky through which the animals could enter. Wandering about in the upper world, they came to a lake. On its shore stood a hut with a fire burning in front of it, and inside they found two bear cubs huddling together.

"Where is your mother?" the animals asked.

"She went out hunting," answered the little bears.

The visitors looked around and saw a number of bags hanging from poles. The bobcat pointed to the first one and asked: "What's in this bag?"

"Our mother keeps rain in that one," answered the cubs.

"And in this one?" inquired the mouse.

"It's full of winds."

"Ah, and that one over there?" said the fox.

"Oh, she keeps fog in that one."

"And this one here," said the wolverine. "What does she keep in this bag?"

"Oh, we can't tell," said the cubs. "It's a secret. Mother told us not to let anybody know what's in that bag."

"Oh, come on, we're friends," said the wolf. "You can tell us."

"No, no! Mother would beat us if we tell."

"But she doesn't have to find out," said the bobcat. "We won't tell on you."

"Well, in that case," said the cubs, "this is the bag where she keeps the heat."

"Thank you, kind little bears," said the mouse. "You've told us all we wanted to know."

The party of animals went outside and held a council. They resolved to hide so that the old bear would not see them when she came home. But first the mouse jumped into the bear's canoe and gnawed almost entirely through the handle of the paddle. At last they saw the mother on the far side of the lake. The bobcat quickly ran around the lake and, changing himself into a plump caribou calf, appeared in front of the mother.

"Quick, quick, children!" the bear mother shouted. "Help me catch this caribou for our dinner!" The cubs came scrambling out and scurried to their mother as fast as they could run. The bobcat lured them deep into the forest. Meanwhile the other animals went into the hut, jerked the bag down from its pole, and made off with it, pulling and tugging.

The caribou-bobcat ran back to the lake and jumped into the water, where it swam toward the hut on the opposite shore. The bear mother leapt into her canoe and paddled furiously after it, but halfway across the lake her paddle snapped in two at the spot where the mouse had gnawed it. The bear pitched into the water and upset the canoe. In the meantime the bobcat reached the shore and assumed his usual shape. "Hurry!" he told the others. "That bear will be after us."

The animals took turns pulling the heavy bag full of heat toward the opening that led to their world below. When one of them got tired, he passed the burden to another. By then the old bear was hot after them, and all the bigger animals were exhausted. But the pike and the dogfish were still fresh, and at the very last moment, with the bear's teeth snapping at their heels, they managed to pull the bag through the hole in the sky. The whole party slipped safely through the opening.

As soon as they were down in their own world, they tore the bag open. At once the heat rushed out, spreading in every direction, melting the snow and ice, dispersing the black clouds, and making the sun shine again. However, the melting water caused a great flood which covered the world and threatened to drown all living creatures. At this time the earth had a giant tree which reached high into the sky, almost to the world above. To save themselves the animals climbed up to its highest branches and cried, "Somebody help us!"

Out of nowhere appeared a giant fish who drank up all the flood water, in the process himself becoming a great mountain. After that the sun dried up the land, the trees covered themselves with leaves, the flowers bloomed, and it was summer again, to the joy of all creatures.

—Based on a tale reported by Robert Bell at the
turn of the century.

■

THE HOPI BOY AND THE SUN

■

[HOPI]

Where cultures overlap—as in areas of the Southwest, with its mixture of Hispanic, Pueblo, and nomadic traditions—legends are often modified and reshaped in the retelling. This story, related in 1920 by a Zuni elder who may have been part Hispanic, gives a curious twist to Hopi tales of the sun. Besides the traditional Hopi elements such as the trail of sacred cornmeal and the sun's fox skin, it embodies the fear and antagonism felt by the Pueblo farmers toward the marauding nomadic tribes. At the same time, it is full of things unknown to the Pueblos before the coming of the Spaniards, such as peaches, silver bracelets, and the ocean itself.

■ |||||||||||||||||||||||||||||||||||||||||||||||||||||||||||||||||||||||||||| ■

A poor Hopi boy lived with his mother's mother. The people treated him with contempt and threw ashes and sweepings into his grandmother's house, and the two were very unhappy. One day he asked his grandmother who his father was.

"My poor boy, I don't know," she replied.

"I must find him," the boy said. "We can't stay in this place; the people treat me too badly."

"Grandchild, you must go and see the sun. He knows who your father is."

On the following morning the boy made a prayer stick and went out. Many young men were sitting on the roof of the kiva, the underground ceremonial chamber. They sneered when they saw him going by, though one of them remarked, "Better not make fun of him! I believe the poor little boy has supernatural power."

The boy took some sacred meal made of pounded turquoise, coral, shell, and cornmeal, and threw it upward. It formed a trail leading into the sky, and he climbed until the trail gave out. He threw more of the sacred meal upward, and a new trail formed. After he had done this twelve times, he came to the sun. But the sun was too hot to approach, so the boy put new prayer sticks into the hair at the back of his head, and the shadow of their plumes protected him from the heat.

"Who is my father?" he asked the sun.

"All children conceived in the daytime belong to me," the sun replied. "But as for you, who knows? You are young and have much to learn."

The boy gave the sun a prayer stick and, falling down from the sky, landed back in his village.

One the following day he left home and went westward, hoping to begin learning. When he came to the place where Holbrook, Arizona, now stands, he saw a cottonwood tree and chopped it down. He cut a length of the trunk to his own height, hollowed it out, and made a cover for each end. Then he put in some sweet cornmeal and prayer sticks and decided he was ready to go traveling. Climbing into the box, he closed the door and rolled himself into the river.

The box drifted for four days and four nights, until finally he felt it strike the shore at a place where two rivers join. He took the plug out of a peephole he had made and saw morning light. But when he tried to get out, he couldn't open the door, no matter how hard he pushed. He thought he would have to die inside.

In the middle of the afternoon a rattlesnake-girl came down to the river. When she discovered the box, she took off her mask and looked into the peephole. "What are you doing here?" she asked the boy.

"Open the door! I can't get out," he said.

The girl asked, "How can I open it?"

"Take a stone and break it."

So the girl broke the door, and when the Hopi boy came out, she took him to her house. Inside he saw many people—young and old, men and women—and they were all rattlesnakes.

"Where are you going?" they asked him.

"I want to find my father," the boy replied.

The girl said, "You can't go alone; I'll go with you."

She made a small tent of rattlesnake skins and carried it to the river. They crawled into the tent and floated for four days and four nights. Finally they reached the ocean, and there they say a meteor fall into the sea on its way to the house of the sun. They asked the meteor to take them along.

In this manner they reached the sun's house, where they found an old woman working on turquoise, coral, and white shell. She was the moon, the mother of the sun.

"Where is my father?" the boy asked.

"He has gone out," the moon replied, "but he will be home soon."

The sun arrived in the evening, and the old woman gave him venison and wafer bread. After he had eaten, he asked the boy, "What do you want here?"

The boy replied, "I want to know my father."

"I think you are my son. And when I go into the other world, you shall accompany me," the sun said this time. And early the next morning, he said, "Let's go!" He opened a door in the ground, and they went out.

Seating himself on a stool of crystal, the son took a fox skin and held it up. Daylight appeared. After a while he put the fox skin down and held up the tail feathers of a macaw, and the yellow rays of sunrise streamed out. When at last he let them down, he said to the boy. "Now let's go!"

The sun made the boy sit behind him on the stool, and they went out into another world. After traveling for some time, they saw people with long ears, Lacokti ianenakwe. They used their ears as blankets to cover themselves when they slept. The sun remarked, "If bluebird droppings fall on those people, they die."

"How is that possible?" the boy said. "How can people be killed that way? Let me kill the birds!"

The sun said, "Go ahead! I'll wait."

The boy jumped down, took a small cedar stick, and killed the bluebirds. Then he roasted them over a fire and ate them. The people shouted, "Look at this boy! He's eating Navahos!"

"No," said the boy, "these aren't Navahos, they're birds." Then he went back to the sun, and they traveled on.

About noon they came to another town. The sun said, "Look! The Apache are coming to make war on the people."

The boy saw a whirlwind moving along. When wheat straw was blown against the legs of the people, they fell dead. "How can people be killed by wheat straw?" he said. "Let me go down and tear it up."

The sun said, "I'll wait."

The boy jumped down, gathered the wheat straw, and tore it up. The people said, "Look at this boy, how he kills the Apache!"

"These aren't Apache," the boy replied, "they're wheat straws." Then he went back to the sun.

They came to another town, where the Hopi boy saw people with very long hair reaching down to their ankles. They had a large pot with onions tied to its handles. Inside it thin mush was cooking and boiling over, and when it hit a person, he died. The sun said, "Look at the Jicarilla Apache, how they kill people!"

"No," said the boy, "that's not Jicarilla Apache; it's mush. I'll go down and eat it."

The sun said, "I'll wait."

Then the boy jumped down, dipped the mush out of the pot, took the onions from the handles, and ate the mush with the onions. The people said, "Look how this boy eats the brains, hands, and feet of the Jicarilla Apache!"

The boy said, "This isn't Jicarilla Apache! It's corn mush. Come and eat with me!"

"No! they said. "We're not cannibals; we don't eat Apache warriors!" Then the boy went back to the sun, and they traveled on.

Finally they came to the house of the sun in the east. There the sun's sister gave them venison stew for supper. After they had eaten, the sun said to his sister, "Wash my son's head!"

The sun's sister took a large dish, put water and yucca suds into it, and washed the boy's head and body. Then she gave him new clothing, the same kind that the sun was wearing—buckskin trousers, blue moccasins, blue bands of yarn to tie under the knees, a white sash and belt of fox skin, turquoise and shell earrings, a white shirt, silver arm rings, bead bracelets, and a bead necklace. She put macaw feathers in his hair and a *miha*, sacred blanket, over his shoulder, and gave him a quiver of mountain lion skin.

Then the sun told him, "Go ahead! I'm going to follow you." The boy opened the door in the ground and went out. He sat down on the crystal stool, took the fox skin, and held it up to create the dawn. Then he put it down and raised the macaw feathers, holding them up with the palms of his hands stretched forward until the yellow rays of sunrise appeared. After that he dropped his hands and went on into the upper world. As he did, the people of Laguna, Isleta, and the other eastern pueblos looked eastward and sprinkled sacred meal. The sun behind him said, "Look at the trails, the life of the people! Some are short, others are long. Look at this one! He is near the end of his trail; he's going to die soon." The boy saw an Apache coming, and in a short time the Apache had killed that man whose trail had been so short. The Hopi boy said to the sun, "Let me go and help the people!"

"I'll wait," the sun replied.

The boy jumped down into the territory where the Laguna people were fighting the Apache. He told the people to wet their arrow points with saliva and hold them up to the sun, for this would help them in battle. The boy himself killed ten Apaches, then went back to his father.

They traveled on, and when they saw a group of Navahos setting out to make war on the Zuni, the boy killed them. He and his father crossed the land of his own people, the Hopi, and then came to Mexican territory.

A Mexican was playing with his wife. When the sun saw them, he threw the Mexican aside and cohabited with the woman. "I don't need a wife," he told his son, "because all the women on earth belong to me. If a couple cohabits during the daytime, I interfere as I just did. So I'm the father of all children conceived in the daytime."

In the evening the sun entered his house in the west. By then the boy wanted to go back to his own people, so the sun's mother made a trail of sacred flour, and the boy and the rattlesnake-woman went back eastward over it. At noon they came to the rattlesnakes' home. The rattlesnake-woman said, "I want to see my father and mother. After that, let's go on." They entered the house, and she told her relatives that the Hopi boy was her husband. Then they resumed their journey.

That evening they arrived in the Hopi village. The boy made straight for his grandmother's house, but an old chief said, "Look at the handsome man going into that poor home!" He invited the boy into his own house, but the boy replied, "No, I'm going here." The war chief said, "We don't want you in that dirty house."

"The house is mine," the boy replied, "so tell your people to clean it up. When all of you treated me badly, I went up to the sun and he helped me."

On the following evening the boy appeared before a village council and told all that had happened to him. "You must teach the people how to act rightly. The sun says that you should forbid all bad actions." The people accepted his words, and everyone worked hard at cleaning his house. In return the boy gave peaches, melons, and wafer bread to the poor. Every evening after sunset the women would come with their dishes, and he would offer them venison stew and peaches. He said to the chief, "I teach the people the right way to live. Even if you are my enemy, I must show you how to behave well."

Twin children, a boy and a girl, were born to his wife. They had the shape of rattlesnakes, but they were also humans.

—Based on a legend reported by Franz Boas in 1922.

■

A GUST OF WIND

■

[OJIBWAY]

This story has many variations. The following version is notable because Stone Boy, sometimes conceived when his mother swallows a pebble, appears in creation legends from several Plains tribes.

■ |||||||||||||||||||||||||||||||||||||||||||||||||||||||||||||||||||||||||||||| ■

Before there was a man, two women, an old one and her daughter, were the only humans on earth. The old woman had not needed a man in order to conceive. Ahki, the earth, also was like a woman—female—but not as she is now, because trees and many animals had not yet been made.

Well, the young woman, the daughter, took her basket out one day to go berrying. She had gathered enough and was returning home when a sudden gust of wind lifted her buckskin dress up high, baring her body. Geesis, the sun, shone on that spot for a short moment and entered the body of the young woman, though she hardly noticed it. She was aware of the gust of wind but paid no attention.

Time passed. The young woman said to the old one: "I don't know what's wrong with me, but something is." More time passed. The young woman's belly grew bigger, and she said: "Something is moving inside me. What can it be?"

"When you were going berrying did you meet anyone?" The old woman asked.

"I met nobody. The only thing that happened was a big gust of wind which lifted my buckskin dress. The sun was shining."

The old woman said: "I think you're going to have a child. Geesis, the sun, is the only one who could have done it, so you will be the mother of a sun child."

The young woman gave birth to two boys, both *manitos*, supernaturals. They were the first human males on this earth—Geesis's sons, sons of the sun.

The young mother made cradleboards and put the twins in these, hanging them up or carrying them on her back, but never letting the babies touch the earth. Why didn't she? Did the Old Woman tell her not to? Nobody knows. If she had put the cradleboards on the ground, the babies would have walked upright from the moment of their birth, like deer babies. But because their mother would not let them touch earth for some months, it now takes human babies a year or so to walk. It was that young woman's fault.

One of the twins was Stone Boy, a rock. He said: "Put me in the fire and heat me up until I glow red hot." They did, and he said: "Now pour cold water over me." They did this also. That was the first sweat bath. The other boy, named Wene-boozhoo, looked like all human boys. He became mighty and could do anything; he even talked to the animals and gave them their names.

—*Told by David Red Bird in New York City, 1974, and*
recorded by Richard Erdoes.

David Baker Red Bird is a young Green Bay Indian with a great sense of humor. He is a well-known singer and musician.

DAUGHTER OF THE SUN

[CHEROKEE]

Many Indian legends, such as the two previous selections, depict the sun as a male being who impregnates mortal women. The Cherokees are one of three tribes who view the sun as female. In this classic tale with an Orpheus theme, the sun is an old woman with a grown daughter and human emotions.

The sun lived on the other side of the sky vault, but her daughter lived in the middle of the sky, directly above the earth. Every day as the sun was climbing along the sky arch to the west, she used to stop at her daughter's house for dinner.

Now, the sun hated the people of this earth, because they never looked straight at her without squinting. She said to her brother, the moon, "My grandchildren are ugly; they screw up their faces whenever they see me.

But the moon said, "I like my younger brothers; I think they're handsome." This was because they always smiled pleasantly at his mild glow in the night sky.

The sun was jealous of the moon's popularity and decided to kill the people. Every day when she got near her daughter's house, she sent down such sultry heat that fever broke out and people died by the hundreds. When everyone had lost some friend and it seemed as if no one would be spared, the humans went for help to the Little Men. These men, who were friendly spirits, said that the only way the people could save themselves was to kill the sun.

The Little Men made medicine to change two humans into snakes—the spreading adder and the copperhead—who could hide near the daughter's door and bite the old sun. The snakes went up to the sky and lay in wait until the sun arrived for dinner. But when the spreading adder was about to spring, her bright light blinded him and he could only spit out yellow slime, as he does to this day when he tries to bite. The sun called him a nasty thing and went into the house, and the copperhead was so discouraged that he crawled off without trying to do anything.

The people, still dying from the terrible heat, went a second time to the Little Men for help. Again the Little Men made medicine and changed one man into the great Uktena, the water monster, and another into a rattlesnake. As before, the serpents had instructions to kill the old sun when she stopped at her daughter's house. Uktena was large and fierce, with horns on his head, and everyone thought he would be sure to succeed. But the rattlesnake was so eager that he raced ahead and coiled up just outside the house. When the sun's daughter opened the door to look for her mother, he struck and she fell dead in the doorway. Forgetting to wait for the old sun, he went back to the people, and Uktena was so angry at the rattlesnake's stupidity that he went back too.

Since then we pray to the rattlesnake and don't kill him, because he wishes people well and never tries to bite if we don't disturb him. But Uktena grew angrier and more dangerous all the time. He became so venomous that if he even looked at a man, the man's whole family would die. Eventually the people held a council and decided that he was just too dangerous, so they sent him to Galun'lati, the end of the world, where he still is.

When the sun found her daughter dead, she shut herself up in the house and grieved. Now the people were no longer dying from the heat, but they lived in darkness. Once more they sought help from the Little Men, who said that in order to coax the sun out, they must bring her daughter back from Tsusgina'i. This is the ghost country, which lies in Usunhi'yi, the Darkening Land in the west.

The people chose seven men to make the journey. The Little Men told the seven to take a box, and told each man to carry a sourwood rod a handbreadth long. When they got to Tsusgina'i, the Little Men explained, they would find all the ghosts at a dance. They should stand outside the circle, and when the sun's daughter danced past them, they must strike her with the rods and she would fall to the ground. Then they could put her in the box and bring her back to her mother. But they must not open the box, even a crack, until they arrived home.

The seven men took the rods and the box and traveled west for seven days until they came to the Darkening Land. There they found a great crowd of ghosts having a dance, just as if they were alive. The sun's daughter was in the outside circle. As she danced past them, one of the seven men struck her with his rod. As she swung around a second time, another touched her with his rod, and then another and another, until at the seventh round she fell out of the ring. The men put her into the box and closed the lid, and the other ghosts never seemed to notice what had happened.

The seven took up the box and started home toward the east. In a while the girl came to life again and begged to be let out, but the party went on without answering. Soon she called again and said she was hungry, but they did not reply. When at last the group was very near home, the daughter of the sun cried that she was smothering and begged them to raise the lid just a little. Now they were afraid that she was really dying, so they barely cracked the lid to give her air. There was a fluttering sound, and something flew past them into the bushes. Then they heard a redbird cry, "Kwish! Kwish! Kwish!" Shutting the lid, they went on again. But when they arrived at the settlements and opened the box, it was empty.

So we know that the redbird is the daughter of the sun. And if the party had kept the box closed, as the Little Men told them to, they could have brought her home safely, and today we would be able to recover our friends from the Ghost Country. Because the seven opened the box, however, we can never bring back people who die.

The sun had been hopeful when the party had started off for the Darkening Land, but when they came back without her daughter, she wept until her tears caused a great flood. Fearing that the world would be drowned, the people held another council and decided to send their handsomest young men and women to amuse the sun and stop her crying. This group danced before her and sang their best songs, but for a long time she kept her face bowed and paid no attention. At last when the drummer suddenly changed the song, she looked up and was so pleased at the sight of the beautiful young people that she forgot her grief and smiled.

—Based on James Mooney's account in the 1890s.

■

GRANDMOTHER SPIDER STEALS THE SUN

■

[CHEROKEE]

■ ‖‖‖ ■

In the beginning there was only blackness, and nobody could see anything. People kept bumping into each other and groping blindly. They said: "What this world needs is light."

Fox said he knew some people on the other side of the world who had plenty of light, but they were too greedy to share it with others. Possum said he would be glad to steal a little of it. "I have a bushy tail," he said. "I can hide the light inside all that fur." Then he set out for the other side of the world. There he found the sun hanging in a tree and lighting everything up. He sneaked over to the sun, picked out a tiny piece of light, and stuffed it into his tail. But the light was hot and burned all the fur off. The people discovered his theft and took back the light, and ever since, Possum's tail has been bald.

"Let me try," said Buzzard. "I know better than to hide a piece of stolen light in my tail. I'll put it on my head." He flew to the other side of the world and, diving straight into the sun, seized it in his claws. He put it on his head, but it burned his head feathers off. The people grabbed the sun away from him, and ever since that time Buzzard's head has remained bald.

Then Grandmother Spider said, "Let me try!" First she made a thick-walled pot out of clay. Next she spun a web reaching all the way to the other side of the world. She was so small that none of the people there noticed her coming. Quickly Grandmother Spider snatched up the sun, put it in the bowl of clay, and scrambled back home along one of the strands of her web. Now her side of the world had light, and everyone rejoiced.

Spider Woman brought not only the sun to the Cherokee, but fire with it. And besides that, she taught the Cherokee people the art of pottery making.

—From a tale reported by James Mooney in the 1890s.

THE STORY OF THE CREATION

[DIEGUEÑOS]

When Tu-chai-pai made the world, the earth was the woman, the sky was the man. The sky came down upon the earth. The world in the beginning was pure lake covered with bulrushes. Tu-chai-pai and Yo-Ko-mat-is, his brother, sat together, stooping far over, bowed down under the weight of the sky. The Maker said to the brother, "What am I going to do?"

"I do not know," said Yo-ko-mat-is.

"Let us go a little farther," said the Maker.

Then they went a little farther and sat down again. "Now, what am I going to do?" said Tu-chai-pai.

"I don't know."

All this time Tu-chai-pai knew what he would do, but he was asking the brother.

Then he said, "We-hicht, we-hicht, we-hicht," three times; and he took tobacco in his hand, and rubbed it fine, and blew upon it three times, and every time he blew, the heavens rose higher above their heads. Then the Maker told his brother to do the same thing, and he did. The heavens went high, and there was the sky. Then they did it both together, "We-hicht, we-hicht, we-hicht"; and both took the tobacco, and rubbed it, and puffed upon it, and sent the sky up.

Then they placed the north, south, east, and west. Tu-chai-pai made a line upon the ground.

"Why do you make that line?"

"I am making the line from east to west, and I name them thus, Y-nak, east; A-uk, west. Now you may make it from north to south."

Then Yo-ko-mat-is was thinking.

"Why are you thinking?"

"Oh, I must think; but now I have arranged it. I draw a line thus (a crossline), and I name it Ya-wak, south; Ka-tulk, north."

"Why have we done this?"

"I don't know."

"Then I will tell you. Three or four men are coming from the east, and from the west three or four Indians are coming."

The boy asked, "And do four men come from the north, and two or three men come also from the south?"

Then Tu-chai-pai said, "Now I am going to make hills and valleys, and little hollows of water."

"Why are you making all these things?"

The Maker said, "After a while, when men come and are walking back and forth in the world, they will need to drink water, or they will die." He had already put the ocean down in its bed, but he made these little waters for the people.

Then he made the forests, and said, "After a while men will die of cold unless I make wood for them to use. What are we going to do now?"

"I don't know."

"We're going to dig up some mud and make the Indians first." And he formed the men and did it well, but he didn't do such a good job on the women because they were hard to make, and it took a long time. He gave beards to the men and boys, but not to the women. After the Indians he made the Mexicans, and he finished all his creating. Then he called out very loud, "You can never die, and you can never be tired, but you shall walk all the time." After that he made them so that they could sleep at night, and need not walk around all the time in the darkness. At last he told them that they must travel toward the east, toward the light.

The people walked in darkness till he made the light. Then they came out and searched for the light, and when they found it they were glad. Then he called out to Yo-ko-mat-is, "You may make the moon, as I have made the sun. Sometime it is going to die. When it grows very small, men may know that it is going to die, and at that time all men, young and old, must run races."

All the people talked about the matter, and they understood that they must run these races, and that Tu-chai-pai was looking at them to see that they did this. After the Maker did all this, he did nothing more, but he was thinking many days.

—*Based on a tale reported by Constance Goddard du Bois*
in 1901.

THE FOOLISH GIRLS

[OJIBWAY]

In the world long ago, some people were camping in birchbark lodges. There were two very foolish girls who always slept outside the lodge, in the open. Self-respecting girls didn't do this, only foolish, man-hungry ones. So there they were, lying outside, looking at the sky, giggling.

One of the girls said to the other, "Look at those stars, the white one and the red one."

"I'd like to sleep with a star. They must be good lovers, real hot ones," said the other.

"Me too—I want a star under the blanket with me," said her friend. "I'll take the red star to bed, and you can have the white one."

"All right," said her companion, and they drifted off to sleep. When they awoke, they found themselves in an upper world—in star country. The stars were men, and they spoke to the girls: "You wanted to sleep with us. Well, here we are; let's do it!"

So they did. The girl who had chosen the red star found that he was a vigorous young man, and he kept her busy all night. She was content. Not so the other, because her star, the white star, was very old. His hair was white, and he couldn't perform very well. She said to her friend, "Let's swap husbands for a while," but the friend didn't want to.

So they lived for a time with their chosen stars. Then the one who had married the young redheaded star began to complain: "This man wears me out. It's too much; I can't stand doing it all the time."

The other said, "This star lover of mine is so old that he can't do anything."

And after having stayed there for a long while, they both concluded that it wasn't as much fun being with star men as they had imagined. All the stars did was eat star food, sleep with the girls, and shine. They didn't play games; they didn't hunt. The girls became bored and homesick. It was winter, and one said to the other, "Down in our country they're playing snow-snake now. I wish I could be there."

Old Woman sat on a hole in the sky all the time. Once when those foolish girls passed by, she moved a little bit and let them look down through the hole. They saw their village and watched the people playing snow-snake. They heard singing and dancing coming up through the hole, and they felt very sad.

"How can we get down there?" they asked. Old Woman gave them plants of various kinds and said, "Twist them into fibers. Make a long rope. That's the only way to get down where you came from."

For days the girls twisted fibers into ropes. They needed a very, very long rope, and they got tired. They were lazy as well as foolish, and they said, "Surely this rope is long enough. No use working any more." They went to their two star men and told them: "We want to visit our folks down there, just for a little while. Then you can haul us up again."

Of course they didn't mean it. They had discovered that sleeping with stars was no different from sleeping with humans. Now they wanted young Ojibway men, they were so foolish and fickle.

"Hold these ropes; help us down," they told the stars. But the ropes were too short, which is what comes of being lazy. The cords reached almost all the way down, but not quite—just to the top of a very, very high tree, the highest tree in the world. At its tip was an abandoned eagle nest, and there the two foolish ones were stuck. "Oh! What are we going to do? How are we going to get down?"

They saw a bear passing by below. "Hey, Bear, you sure must be looking for some women to sleep with. If you get us down safely, you can do it with us!" The bear saw that these girls were good-looking, but he was wise and noticed that they were also very foolish and forward. He wanted nothing to do with them. He pretended he couldn't climb, though he could easily have made it up the tree. The bear went off, not even looking back.

Next a buffalo passed under the tree. "Hey, Powerful One," the girls shouted, "get us down from here. If you do, you can sleep with us." Seeing that the girls were pretty, the buffalo didn't care whether they were stupid or not. He tried to climb up, tried a long time, but couldn't do it. He gave up and shouted to the girls, "Hooves are no good for this kind of thing. Get somebody with claws!" Then he went off.

The third one to pass by was Old Man Coyote. "Hey, friend!" the girls called down to him, "Do you want some good-looking young women to sleep with? You can, if you get us down."

"I sure would like to," shouted Old Man Coyote, "but I have a young, jealous wife. She gets mean if I fool around with the girls." And he went off too.

The fourth one to pass under that tree was Wolverine, who is so ugly no girl will sleep with him. "Hey, Handsome," the two girls called, "you sure are a good-looking man. Get us down from here, and you can enjoy us."

They didn't have to say it twice; with his powerful claws Wolverine shinnied up that largest of all trees in no time. He threw the first girl down and immediately made love to her. There was no use resisting, he was so strong and greedy. Then he did the same with the second girl. He had never had such a good time, but they enjoyed it a lot less, since Wolverine was the ugliest man they had ever seen. "Friend," one girl said to the other, "I think we've done a dumb thing. When I get home I'll never sleep outside the lodge again."

"How right you are," said the other girl. "This man is truly ugly, and so rough that it really hurts. I'm never sleeping outside again, either."

But they had a problem, because after making love to them, Wolverine always fed them and then carried them back up, willy-nilly, to that eagle's nest. He didn't want them to get away—ever. He knew when he had a good thing.

One day when Wolverine was out hunting, what did those suffering girls see from their nest but Wolverine Woman. Wolverine Woman hadn't met up with Wolverine Man yet, and she was so ugly, truly surpassingly ugly, that no man wanted her.

"Hey, beautiful woman down there," the two girls called, "up here, Doll Baby! If you get us down and take our place in this nest, we promise you a handsome young man to sleep with. He comes up here to make love to us, but we're humans and we have to get home to our people. But he's such a nice man, we don't want to disappoint him. He should have a good woman to sleep with."

"You're absolutely right," answered Wolverine Woman, "and so generous! I sure would like to meet that handsome man."

Wolverine Woman got those two girls down safely, and they hurried off as fast as they could. They had never run so hard in their lives.

At night Wolverine Man arrived, climbed the tree, and got Wolverine Woman down. He was in such a hurry he didn't even notice that there was only one woman in the eagle nest. He made love to her all night, and when dawn finally came, Wolverine Woman said, "You're not as handsome as I was told."

Wolverine Man saw that he had been tricked. "You're not a raving beauty either," he told her.

"Let's stop this," she said. "Face it: we're incredibly ugly. Nobody else would have us, so let's stay together."

"I guess you're right," said Wolverine Man, so they stayed together. There's nobody so ugly that he can't find a mate.

When the two girls played that trick on Wolverine Man, it was the first time they stopped being foolish and got smart.

—*Told by David Red Bird in New York City, 1974, and recorded by Richard Erdoes.*

MOON RAPES HIS SISTER SUN

[INUIT]

This violent story tells of a stormy encounter between a female sun and a male moon.

In the old days, when everything began, a brother lived with his sister in a large village which had a dance house. At night it was lit with stone lamps burning seal oil, and once the sister was dancing and singing there when a big wind blew all the lamps out. While everything was black, a man copulated with her. She struggled against him, but he was too strong, and it was too dark to see who he was.

Thinking he might come again, before she went back there next she blackened the palms of her hands with soot. Again a great gust of wind blew out all the lamps. Again that man threw her upon her back, got on top of her, and entered her. But this time she smeared his back with soot. When the lamps were rekindled, she looked for the one with a sooty back and was enraged to see that it was her brother.

She cried, "Such things are not done! Such things are unheard of!"

She was so angry that she took her sharp knife and cut off both her breasts. Flinging them at her brother, she cried, "As you seem to enjoy me, as you seem to have a taste for my body, eat these!"

She grabbed a brightly burning torch and, maddened and wild-eyed, ran out of the dance house into the dark night. Her brother snatched up another torch and ran after her, but stumbled and fell down in the snow. The snow put out the flames of his torch so that only its embers flickered feebly.

Then a big windstorm lifted both the sister and her brother high up into the sky. The girl was turned into the sun, and her brother into the Moon. She stays as far away from him as she can. As long as the moon shines, she hides herself, coming out only after he is gone. If the brother had not let his torch fall into the snow, the moon would be as bright as the sun.

—Retold from four nineteenth-century sources.

■

SUN TEACHES VEEHO A LESSON

■

[CHEYENNE]

■ ▥▥▥▥▥▥▥▥▥▥▥▥▥▥▥▥▥▥▥▥▥▥▥▥▥▥▥▥▥▥ ■

Sun had beautiful, wonder-working leggings which could set the prairie on fire and drive the game toward the hunter's bow. Veeho, the clever trickster, greatly admired them, and one day when he came to visit, he sneaked off with them when Sun was not looking.

Chuckling, Veeho said to himself, "Now I can work many miracles and be the world's greatest hunter."

Toward evening he was tired from running so fast and far. "Sun can't catch up with me now," he decided. Rolling up the magic leggings and placing them under his head for a pillow, he lay down to sleep. He slept well, but in the morning he found himself back inside Sun's tipi. Veeho is so stupid he didn't know that all the world is contained within Sun's lodge. But though he was surprised to wake up there after having run so far and fast, he is hard to embarrass.

Sun smiled and said: "What are you doing with my leggings?"

Veeho may be stupid, but he is never at a loss for an answer. He said, "I just put my head on them to sleep softly. I knew you wouldn't mind."

"I don't mind," said Sun. "You can use them as a pillow if you want to." Sun knew very well that Veeho was lying, as usual, and meant to steal the wonder-working leggings again. But he only said, "Well, I must go walk my daily path."

"Don't hurry back," said Veeho. "I'll keep an eye on your lodge."

Once he could no longer see Sun, Veeho ran off with the leggings again, this time twice as fast and twice as far. Again he went to sleep, and again woke to find himself back inside Sun's tipi.

Sun laughed and told Veeho, "If you're that fond of my leggings, you can keep them. Let's pretend that I'm holding a giveaway feast and that you got these as a present."

Veeho was overjoyed. "I never meant to steal these beautiful leggings, friend Sun. You know me—I'm always up to some trick; I was only fooling. But now that you've given them to me of your own free will, I gladly accept."

Veeho could hardly wait to get away from Sun's lodge and put on the leggings. Wearing them, he ran over the prairie and ignited the grass to drive the buffalo toward him. But Veeho did not have Sun's power; he couldn't handle such a big fire, and it scorched his soles and blistered his feet. "Friend Sun, come and help me!" he cried. "Help your poor friend! Where are you, Sun? Come put the fire out!"

But Sun pretended not to hear, and soon Veeho's leggings were on fire. Crying from pain, he plunged into the nearest stream. By then it was too late; the leggings were ruined and Veeho's legs blistered.

When Veeho begged Sun to make him a new pair of leggings, Sun said, "Even I can't make magic leggings but once. I'm sorry, friend. Be more careful in the future."

Sun could easily have made another pair, of course, but then Veeho wouldn't have learned a lesson.

—*Told by Strange Owl in Birney, Montana, and recorded by Richard Erdoes.*

Veeho is a prototype trickster, and the word is used today to mean white man. In a Blackfoot variation of this tale, Sun visits the same retribution on Old Man, who has stolen his porcupine-quill leggings.

The Strange Owl family are traditional Cheyennes who live in Birney, Montana, on the Lame Deer Cheyenne Reservation, and in other Western states. Many members of this family are known for their fine beadwork and knowledge of Indian crafts.

LITTLE BROTHER
SNARES THE SUN

[WINNEBAGO]

At the beginning when the earth was new, the animals were the chiefs. They were more powerful than humans, whom they hunted, killed, and ate. Finally they killed all the people except one girl and her little brother, who lived in hiding. The brother was very small, no bigger than a newborn child, but the girl was normal in size. Because she was so much bigger, she took care of him and did all the work.

One winter day the girl had to go out and gather food in the woods. To keep Little Brother occupied, she gave him her bow and arrows. "Hide until a snowbird comes," she told him. "Wait until he looks for grubs in that huge dead tree. Then kill him with one of your arrows."

She went off, and the snowbird came, but Little Brother's arrows missed him. "It doesn't matter," the sister said when she came home. "Try again tomorrow." The next day she went into the forest again. Once more the bird came, and this time the boy's arrow hit and killed him. Proudly he showed the bird to his sister when she returned at night.

"Sister, I want you to skin the snowbird and stretch the hide," he said. "I'll be killing more birds, and when we have enough skins, you can make a feather robe for me."

"But what shall we do with the meat?" asked the girl. At that time people ate only berries and other green things, because they didn't hunt; it was the animals who hunted them.

"Make soup out of it," said Little Brother, who was clever in spite of his size. Every day for ten days he shot a snowbird, and his sister made him a fine feather robe from the skins.

"Sister, are there no other people in this world?" he asked one day. "Are we the only ones?"

"There may be others," she said, "but we don't dare go looking for them. Terrible animals would stalk and kill us."

But Little Brother was consumed with curiosity. So when his sister went off to gather food again, he set out to look for other humans. He walked a long time but met neither people nor animals. He got so tired that he lay down in a spot where the sun had melted the snow away. While he was sleeping, the sun rose and shot fiery rays upon Little

Brother. Waking up, the boy found that his feather robe had scorched and tightened around him so that he couldn't move. To free himself he had to tear it apart, ruining it. He shook his fists and shouted, "Sun, I'll get even! Don't think you're so high that I can't get at you! Do you hear me up there?"

Angry and sad, Little Brother returned home. He wept when he told his sister how the sun had spoiled his feather robe. He lay down on his right side for ten days and refused to eat or drink. Still fasting, he lay on his left side for another ten. After twenty days he got up and told his sister to make a snare for him to catch the sun. She had only a short length of dried deer sinew, and out of that she made a noose. "I can't catch the sun with this little thing," he said.

So the girl made a string for him out of her hair, but he said, "This isn't long or strong enough."

"Then I'll have to make a snare out of something secret," she said. She went out and gathered many secret things and twisted them into a strong cord. The moment he saw it, Little Brother said, "This is the one!" To wet the cord he drew it through his lips again and again, so that it grew longer and stronger.

Then Little Brother waited until the middle of the night, when it is darkest. He went out and found the hole through which the sun would rise, and at its entrance he set his snare. When the sun came up at the usual time, he was caught and held fast, and there was no day that day. There was no light, no warmth.

Even though the animals were the chiefs who had killed and eaten the people, they were afraid. They called a council of all their elders and talked for a long time. At last they decided that the biggest and most fearsome of all the animals should go and gnaw through the cord holding the sun. This animal was Dormouse, who was not small, as it is now, but big as a mountain. Even so, Dormouse was afraid of the sun. "What you want me to do is dangerous," she said, "but I'll try."

Dormouse went to the place where the sun rises and found him in the snare. Struggling to free himself, the sun had grown hotter. As Dormouse approached, the hair on her back smoked and was singed off, but she crouched down and began to gnaw at the cord. She chewed and chewed and after a long time managed to bite it in two.

Freed at last, the sun rose at once and made everything bright again. But the heat had shriveled Dormouse down to her present size, and the sun's rays had half blinded her. So she was given the name of Kug-e-been-gwa-kwa, Blind Woman.

Though brave Dormouse had freed the sun, everybody realized that Little Brother, who had snared the sun, was the wisest being in this world, and the one with the greatest power. Since that time the humans have been the chiefs over the animals, the hunters instead of the hunted.

—Told by David Red Bird in New York City.

In a Canadian Métis variation of this tale, the sun's rays are too close and burn the earth, so First Real Boy snares him in a pit and plunges the world into darkness. When First Boy goes to imprison the moon too, he himself is tricked into the trap and now hangs forever from a tree, taking the sun's proper place.

■

THE SCABBY ONE
LIGHTS THE SKY

■

[TOLTEC]

This thousand-year-old myth comes from Central rather than North America, but it is included here as a touching counterpoint to tales of sun worship from north of the Rio Grande. Nanautzin, a Toltec Prometheus, offers his own life to bring light into the world, underscoring the tradition of sacrifice, especially self-sacrifice and self-torture, which figures in the worship of the sun in some Indian cultures even in North America.

■ ▬▬▬▬▬▬▬▬▬▬▬▬▬▬▬▬▬▬▬▬ ■

Five worlds and five suns were created one after the other. There were the suns of earth, fire, air, water, and rock. The first world was destroyed because its people acted wrongfully: they were devoured by ocelots, and their sun also died. The second sun, the pure orb, saw his human beings changed into monkeys for their lack of wisdom. Next came the sun of fire, whose world was destroyed by flames, earthquakes, and volcanic eruptions because the people living in it were impious and did not sacrifice to the gods. The fourth world perished in a great flood which also drowned its sun. Before the dawn of the fifth, our present world, all the gods assembled in darkness to decide who should have the honor—and a dangerous honor it turned out to be—to light up the fifth world, and with it the fifth sun. One god named Tecciztecatl volunteered, thinking to get much praise from the other gods. After days of purification, the gods built a huge fire on the top of a pyramid and told Tecciztecatl: "Light up the world!"

"How?" asked Tecciztecatl, dressed in irridescent hummingbird feathers and jewels of gold and turquoise.

"By jumping into the fire, O Tecciztecatl," said the gods.

But Teccitztecatl was afraid; he didn't want to be burned up. Four times he tried to immolate himself, and four times the heat, the flames, and his fear drove him back.

Then the lowliest of all the gods, Nanautzin, dressed in humble garments of woven reeds, misshapen, ugly, and covered with scabs, offered to renew the world and light up the sun by jumping into the fire. None of the gods had paid him the slightest attention before, but now they all cried with one voice:

"O, Scabby One, be thou he who brings back the Sun!"

Without a moment's hesitation Nanautzin hurled himself into the

flames, burning up with a great crackling sound, his blazing garments of reeds lighting up the sky. And ashamed of his cowardice, Tecciztecatl followed his example and was cremated also. At once the sun rose to light up the new fifth world, and it was the despised Scabby One, brave Nanautzin, who by his death had given life to the sun.

—*Based on Nahua versions of a lost Toltec legend.*

PLAYING A TRICK ON THE MOON

[SNOQUALMIE]

Long ago, Snoqualm, or Moon, was chief of the heavens. One day he said to Spider, "Make a rope of cedar bark and stretch it from the earth to the sky."

Soon Fox and Blue Jay found the rope and climbed up it. Late at night they came to the place where it was fastened to the underside of the sky. Blue Jay picked a hole in the sky, and the two of them crawled through.

Blue Jay flew to a tree, and Fox found himself in a lake. There he changed himself into Beaver. Moon had set a trap in the lake, and Beaver got caught in the trap. Next morning Moon took Beaver out of the trap, skinned him, stretched his skin out to dry, and threw the body into a corner of the smokehouse.

The next night Beaver waited until Moon was asleep and snoring loudly. Then he got up, took his skin from the place where it was stretching, and put it back on. While Moon was still snoring, he examined the house and the sky world.

Outside he found a great forest of fir and pine and cedar trees. He pulled some of them up by their roots and then, with his spirit powers, made them small enough to carry under one arm. Under his other arm he put Moon's tools for making daylight. He took some fire from below the smoke hole, put ashes and leaves and bark around it, and carried it in one hand. He found the sun hidden in Moon's house and carried it away in his other hand.

Then Beaver found the hole Blue Jay had made, changed himself back to Fox again, and went down the rope to the earth. There he gave the fire to the people. He set out the trees. He made the daylight. He set the sun in its place so it would give light and heat to all. The people were happy because of the things Fox brought from the sky.

By this time Moon had awakened. When he found the beaver skin gone and the sun stolen, he was very angry. He knew that one of the earth people had tricked him. Noticing footprints around the house, he followed them to the top of the rope Spider had made.

"I'll follow him to the earth world," Moon thought.

But as he started down, the rope broke. Both Moon and rope fell down in a heap and were transformed into a mountain.

Today the peak is called Mount Si. The face of Snoqualm, Moon, can still be seen on one of its rocky walls. The trees which Fox brought down from the sky and planted have become the great forests of the Cascade Mountains.

—Recorded by Ella Clark in 1953.

Mount Si is a solitary, sharp peak in what is today the Snoqualmie National Forest, east of Seattle, Washington.

■

THE THEFT OF LIGHT

■

[TSIMSHIAN]

This sun-stealing legend features Raven the Giant, a favorite hero of many Northwest Coast tribes.

■ ▏▎▍▌▋▊▉ ■

At one time there was always darkness, never daylight. Giant put on his raven skin and left the heavens, flying across the water for a long time. When he was very tired, he dropped a little round stone that his father the chief had given him. It fell into the sea and turned into a large rock, where he lighted to rest. Then he flew east again until he reached the mainland at the mouth of the Skeena River, and there he scattered salmon roe and trout roe, saying, "Let every river and creek have all kinds of fish!" Opening a dried sea-lion bladder that he had packed with fruits, he strewed them over the land and said, "Let every mountain, hill, valley, and plain be filled with these!"

When the sky in this world of darkness was clear, a little light came from the stars, but when it was cloudy there was only black night. The people were distressed by this, and Giant was too when he realized how hard it would be to get food in the dark. There was light where he had come from, and he made up his mind to bring it down. Putting on his raven skin, he flew upward until he found the hole in the sky and went through. He took off the raven skin and placed it near the hole, then traveled until he came to a spring near the house of the chief of heaven. There he sat down and waited.

Soon the chief's daughter appeared with a small bucket to fetch water. When Giant saw her coming to the spring, he transformed himself into the leaf of a cedar and floated on the water. Without noticing the leaf, she dipped it up with some water and swallowed it.

After a short time she was with child, and soon she gave birth to a boy. The chief and his wife were delighted and took care of the baby as he grew strong and began to creep about. Then, however, he began to cry, "Hama, hama!" all the time. Nothing they could do would soothe him, until finally the chief called his wise men together and asked them why the baby was crying.

One of the men listened to the cries and understood them. He told the chief, "He is crying for the *mā*." This was the box in which the daylight was kept and which hung in one corner of the chief's house. It was what Giant had remembered when he descended to our world. The chief immediately ordered it taken down and placed near the fire. Suddenly the boy stopped crying and began to roll the *mā* about inside the house. He played with it for four days, until the chief became so used to the child's games that he did not notice them. Then the boy (who was, of course, Giant) grabbed the *mā*, put it on his shoulders, and ran out of the house. Seeing him, someone said, "Giant is running away with the *mā*!" and all the hosts of heaven pursued him. But he reached the hole in the sky, put on the raven skin, and flew down carrying the *mā*, and his pursuers went back home.

This time Giant started at the mouth of the Nass River and traveled up it in the dark. After a while he heard the noise of some people, who were catching *olachen* in bag nets from their canoes. Holding the *mā*, Giant sat on the shore and asked them to throw him one of their fish. They refused, calling him a liar, for though he was wearing his raven skin, they knew it was Giant.

"Throw me one, or I'll break the *mā*!" Giant said. Still they scolded and taunted him. Giant repeated his request four times and then broke the *mā*. Suddenly there was daylight. The north wind began to blow hard, and all the fishermen, who were actually frogs, were driven downriver until they arrived at a large, mountainous island. Here the frogs tried to climb up, but they were frozen by the icy wind and turned into stones that stuck to the rock. They are there to this day, and to this day all the world has daylight.

—Based on a legend reported by Franz Boas in 1916.

■

COYOTE PLACES THE STARS

■

[WASCO]

■ ||||||||||||||||||||||||||||||||||||||||||||||||||||||||||||||||||||||||||||||||||||| ■

One time there were five wolves, all brothers, who traveled together. Whatever meat they got when they were hunting they would share with Coyote. One evening Coyote saw the wolves looking up at the sky.

"What are you looking at up there, my brothers?" asked Coyote.

"Oh, nothing," said the oldest wolf.

Next evening Coyote saw they were all looking up in the sky at something. He asked the next oldest wolf what they were looking at, but he wouldn't say. It went on like this for three or four nights. No one wanted to tell Coyote what they were looking at because they thought he would want to interfere. One night Coyote asked the youngest wolf brother to tell him, and the youngest wolf said to the other wolves, "Let's tell Coyote what we see up there. He won't do anything."

So they told him. "We see two animals up there. Way up there, where we cannot get to them."

"Let's go up and see them," said Coyote.

"Well, how can we do that?"

"Oh, I can do that easy," said Coyote. "I can show you how to get up there without any trouble at all."

Coyote gathered a great number of arrows and then began shooting them into the sky. The first arrow stuck in the sky and the second arrow stuck in the first. Each arrow stuck in the end of the one before it like that until there was a ladder reaching down to the earth.

"We can climb up now," said Coyote. The oldest wolf took his dog with him, and then the other four wolf brothers came, and then Coyote. They climbed all day and into the night. All the next day they climbed. For many days and nights they climbed, until finally they reached the sky. They stood in the sky and looked over at the two animals the wolves had seen from down below. They were two grizzly bears.

"Don't go near them," said Coyote. "They will tear you apart." But the two youngest wolves were already headed over. And the next two youngest wolves followed them. Only the oldest wolf held back. When the wolves got near the grizzlies, nothing happened. The wolves sat down and looked at the bears, and the bears sat there looking at the wolves. The oldest wolf, when he saw it was safe, came over with his dog and sat down with them.

Coyote wouldn't come over. He didn't trust the bears. "That makes a nice picture, though," thought Coyote. "They all look pretty good sitting there like that. I think I'll leave it that way for everyone to see. Then when people look at them in the sky they will say, 'There's a story about that picture,' and they will tell a story about me."

So Coyote left it that way. He took out the arrows as he descended so there was no way for anyone to get back. From down on the earth Coyote admired the arrangement he had left up there. Today they still look the same. They call those stars Big Dipper now. If you look up there you'll see that three wolves make up the handle and the oldest wolf, the one in the middle, still has his dog with him. The two youngest wolves make up the part of the bowl under the handle, and the two grizzlies make up the other side, the one that points toward the North Star.

When Coyote saw how they looked, he wanted to put up a lot of stars. He arranged stars all over the sky in pictures and then made the Big Road across the sky with the stars he had left over.

When Coyote was finished he called Meadowlark over. "My brother," he said, "When I am gone, tell everyone that when they look up into the sky and see the stars arranged this way, I was the one who did that. That is my work."

Now Meadowlark tells that story about Coyote.

—*Told by Barry Lopez in 1977.*

DEER HUNTER AND
WHITE CORN MAIDEN

■

[TEWA]

Long ago in the ancient home of the San Juan people, in a village whose ruins can be seen across the river from present-day San Juan, lived two magically gifted young people. The youth was called Deer Hunter because even as a boy, he was the only one who never returned empty-handed from the hunt. The girl, whose name was White Corn Maiden, made the finest pottery, and embroidered clothing with the most beautiful designs, of any woman in the village. These two were the handsomest couple in the village, and it was no surprise to their parents that they always sought one another's company. Seeing that they were favored by the gods, the villagers assumed that they were destined to marry.

And in time they did, and contrary to their elders' expectations, they began to spend even more time with one another. White Corn Maiden began to ignore her pottery making and embroidery, while Deer Hunter gave up hunting, at a time when he could have saved many of his people from hunger. They even began to forget their religious obligations. At the request of the pair's worried parents, the tribal elders called a council. This young couple was ignoring all the traditions by which the tribe had lived and prospered, and the people feared that angry gods might bring famine, flood, sickness, or some other disaster upon the village.

But Deer Hunter and White Corn Maiden ignored the council's pleas and drew closer together, swearing that nothing would ever part them. A sense of doom pervaded the village, even though it was late spring and all nature had unfolded in new life.

Then suddenly White Corn Maiden became ill, and within three days she died. Deer Hunter's grief had no bounds. He refused to speak or eat, preferring to keep watch beside his wife's body until she was buried early the next day.

For four days after death, every soul wanders in and around its village and seeks forgiveness from those whom it may have wronged in life. It is a time of unease for the living, since the soul may appear in the form of a wind, a disembodied voice, a dream, or even in human shape. To prevent such a visitation, the villagers go to the dead person before burial and utter a soft prayer of forgiveness. And on the fourth day after death, the relatives gather to perform a ceremony releasing the soul into the spirit world, from which it will never return.

But Deer Hunter was unable to accept his wife's death. Knowing that he might see her during the four-day interlude, he began to wander around the edge of the village. Soon he drifted farther out into the fields, and it was here at sundown of the fourth day, even while his relatives were gathering for the ceremony of release, that he spotted a small fire near a clump of bushes.

Deer Hunter drew closer and found his wife, as beautiful as she was in life and dressed in all her finery, combing her long hair with a cactus brush in preparation for the last journey. He fell weeping at her feet, imploring her not to leave but to return with him to the village before the releasing rite was consummated. White Corn Maiden begged her husband to let her go, because she no longer belonged to the world of the living. Her return would anger the spirits, she said, and anyhow, soon she would no longer be beautiful, and Deer Hunter would shun her.

He brushed her pleas aside by pledging his undying love and promising that he would let nothing part them. Eventually she relented, saying that she would hold him to his promise. They entered the village just as their relatives were marching to the shrine with the food offering that would release the soul of White Corn Maiden. They were horrified when they saw her, and again they and the village elders begged Deer Hunter to let her go. He ignored them, and an air of grim expectancy settled over the village.

The couple returned to their home, but before many days had passed, Deer Hunter noticed that his wife was beginning to have an unpleasant odor. Then he saw that her beautiful face had grown ashen and her skin dry. At first he only turned his back on her as they slept. Later he began to sit up on the roof all night, but White Corn Maiden always joined him. In time the villagers became used to the sight of Deer Hunter racing among the houses and through the fields with White Corn Maiden, now not much more than skin and bones, in hot pursuit.

Things continued in this way, until one misty morning a tall and imposing figure appeared in the small dance court at the center of the village. He was dressed in spotless white buckskin robes and carried the biggest bow anyone had ever seen. On his back was slung a great quiver with the two largest arrows anyone had ever seen. He remained standing at the center of the village and called, in a voice that carried into every home, for Deer Hunter and White Corn Maiden. Such was its authority that the couple stepped forward meekly and stood facing him.

The awe-inspiring figure told the couple that he had been sent from the spirit world because they, Deer Hunter and White Corn Maiden, had violated their people's traditions and angered the spirits; that because they had been so selfish, they had brought grief and near-disaster to the village. "Since you insist on being together," he said, "you shall have your wish. You will chase one another forever across the sky, as visible reminders that your people must live according to tradition if they are to survive." With this he set Deer Hunter on one arrow and shot him low into the western sky. Putting White Corn Maiden on the other arrow, he placed her just behind her husband.

That evening the villagers saw two new stars in the west. The first, large and very bright, began to move east across the heavens. The second, a smaller, flickering star, followed close behind. So it is to this day, according to the Tewa; the brighter one is Deer Hunter, placed there in the prime of his life. The dimmer star is White Corn Maiden, set there after she had died; yet she will forever chase her husband across the heavens.

—Translated from the Tewa by Alfonso Ortiz.

P A R T   F O U R

ORDEALS
OF THE HERO

M O N S T E R S   A N D
M O N S T E R   S L A Y E R S

We have already met a variety of culture heroes and heard how they created races or brought corn or fire to their people. Here they take center stage as dragon slayers and giant killers, calling on a wealth of fabulous powers to meet the tests which are strewn in their path in the guise of monsters, ogres, witches, and demons. The particular trials to which the hero is subjected vary widely across the continent, though most cultures tell of an ogre on a cliff; of a ferocious guardian animal who must be evaded; of a gluttonous monster (often in the shape of a bull or bear) that swallows people into its unfillable stomach; and of some kind of trial by fire or heat. Regional variations reflect specific cultures, so that one finds the harpooning test in North Pacific tales, while in the central woodlands or Great Lakes region, toboggans figure prominently. The stories themselves often merge with creation myths, using the incidents of the heros' adventures to explain the features of the natural landscape, relics of a battle long ago.

The Indian hero displays awesome talents; he can change into any shape he wants or make himself invisible at will. His supernatural powers often come to him from earth and sky spirits in dreams, or are given to him by magicians. He may have to seize power by conquering another supernatural, perhaps the first in a series of tests he faces; sometimes he simply steals it, showing his cunning as well as his strength. The tokens or medicine he receives are associated with contemporary ceremonies as well, particularly in the Southwest.

The birth of a hero is shrouded in mystery. His mother may be visited in a dream or impregnated in some other unusual fashion; the hero is often the son of the sun or the morning star, and will display human desires and frailties as well as traits of his divine heritage. The child-hero grows up rapidly, and even at age six or seven he may be a match for any monster or giant. Daring and inquisitive, he quickly demonstrates that he will not be controlled by his parents. In one case, a brother and sister must fight off an attack *by* a parent.

The Indian hero relates comfortably to the natural world; he speaks to animals and they speak to him, often revealing knowledge or aiding him in other ways. He assumes their shape, and they carry or hide him. Often the hero himself is an animal, or rather a human who is at the same time an animal, like Old Man Coyote, Bear-Man, Spider Woman, or the ferocious Man-Eagle.

Europeans enter some of these tales obliquely, as beings (some evil, some benign) from another place who may have special powers or such gifts as metal tools and weapons. A few epic tales of the Northeast coast reflect as well the slow but steadily intrusive influence of European sagas on Indian storytellers.

Though the hero may win the day, it is his terrifying opponent who gives vitality to these tales. Monsters and dragons come in all shapes— and can, of course, shift shapes at will. Common to many tribes is the great water monster, Unktehi or Uncegila to the Sioux, whose huge fossil bones are strewn across the Badlands of Nebraska and the Dakotas. Many tribes east and west tell about No Body, the Great Rolling Head, a creature who rolls over prairies and mountains, crushing all in his path, seizing and devouring men with his enormous teeth. Other heros have had to contend with the likes of Yeitso, the terrible giant of the East; Delgeth, a monstrous flesh-eating antelope; or with huge, man-eating birds. The Tlingit hero Stone Ribs, protected by his magic halibut skin, fights the Lord of Killer Whales, and there are always wicked witches and ghosts ready to prey on an unsuspecting human. Evil may enter the world in the guise of a single creature, but its family multiplies quickly, and there is never an end to the trials of a true hero.

GLOOSCAP FIGHTS THE
WATER MONSTER

[PASSAMAQUODDY, MICMAC, AND MALISEET]

Glooscap yet lives, somewhere at the southern edge of the world. He never grows old, and he will last as long as this world lasts. Sometimes Glooscap gets tired of running the world, ruling the animals, regulating nature, instructing people how to live. Then he tells us: "I'm tired of it. Good-bye; I'm going to make myself die now." He paddles off in his magic white canoe and disappears in misty clouds. But he always comes back. He cannot abandon the people forever, and they cannot live without him.

Glooscap is a spirit, a medicine man, a sorcerer. He can make men and women smile. He can do anything.

Glooscap made all the animals, creating them to be peaceful and useful to humans. When he formed the first squirrel, it was as big as a whale. "What would you do if I let you loose on the world?" Glooscap asked, and the squirrel attacked a big tree, chewing it to pieces in no time. "You're too destructive for your size," said Glooscap, and remade him small. The first beaver also was as big as a whale, and it built a dam that flooded the country from horizon to horizon. Glooscap said, "You'll drown all the people if I let you loose like this." He tapped the beaver on the back, and it shrank to its present size. The first moose was so tall that it reached to the sky and looked altogether different from the way it looks now. It trampled everything in its path—forests, mountains, everything. "You'll ruin everything," Glooscap said. "You'll step on people and kill them." Glooscap tapped the moose on the back to make it small, but the moose refused to become smaller. So Glooscap killed it and recreated it in a different size and with a different look. In this way Glooscap made everything as it should be.

Glooscap had also created a village and taught the people there everything they needed to know. They were happy hunting and fishing. Men and women were happy making love. Children were happy playing. Parents cherished their children, and children respected their parents. All was well as Glooscap had made it.

The village had one spring, the only source of water far and wide,

that always flowed with pure, clear, cold water. But one day the spring ran dry; only a little bit of slimy ooze issued from it. It stayed dry even in the fall when the rains came, and in the spring when the snows melted. The people wondered, "What shall we do? We can't live without water." The wise men and elders held a council and decided to send a man north to the source of the spring to see why it had run dry.

This man walked a long time until at last he came to a village. The people there were not like humans; they had webbed hands and feet. Here the brook widened out. There was some water in it, not much, but a little, though it was slimy, yellowish, and stinking. The man was thirsty from his walk and asked to be given a little water, even if it was bad.

"We can't give you any water," said the people with the webbed hands and feet, "unless our great chief permits it. He wants all the water for himself."

"Where is your chief?" asked the man.

"You must follow the brook further up," they told him.

The man walked on and at last met the big chief. When he saw him he trembled with fright, because the chief was a monster so huge that if one stood at his feet, one could not see his head. The monster filled the whole valley from end to end. He had dug himself a huge hole and dammed it up, so that all the water was in it and none could flow into the stream bed. And he had fouled the water and made it poisonous, so that stinking mists covered its slimy surface.

The monster had a mile-wide, grinning mouth going from ear to ear. His dull yellow eyes started out of his head like huge pine knots. His body was bloated and covered with warts as big as mountains. The monster stared dully at the man with his protruding eyes and finally said in a fearsome croak: "Little man, what do you want?"

The man was terrified, but he said: "I come from a village far down-stream. Our only spring ran dry, because you're keeping all the water for yourself. We would like you to let us have some of this water. Also, please don't muddy it so much."

The monster blinked at him a few times. Finally he croaked:

> *Do as you please,*
> *Do as you please,*
>
> *I don't care,*
> *I don't care,*
>
> *If you want water,*
> *If you want water,*
>
> *Go elsewhere!*

The man said, "We need the water. The people are dying of thirst." The monster replied:

> *I don't care,*
> *I don't care,*
>
> *Don't bother me,*
> *Don't bother me,*
>
> *Go away,*
> *Go away,*
>
> *Or I'll swallow you up!*

The monster opened his mouth wide from ear to ear, and inside it the man could see the many things that the creature had killed. The monster gulped a few times and smacked his lips with a noise like thunder. At this the man's courage broke, and he turned and ran away as fast as he could.

Back at his village the man told the people: "Nothing can be done. If we complain, this monster will swallow us up. He'll kill us all."

The people were in despair. "What shall we do?" they cried. Now, Glooscap knows everything that goes on in the world, even before it happens. He sees everything with his inward eye. He said: "I must set things right. I'll have to get water for the people!"

Then Glooscap girded himself for war. He painted his body with paint as red as blood. He made himself twelve feet tall. He used two huge clamshells for his earrings. He put a hundred black eagle feathers and a hundred white eagle feathers in his scalp lock. He painted yellow rings around his eyes. He twisted his mouth into a snarl and made himself look ferocious. He stamped, and the earth trembled. He uttered his fearful war cry, and it echoed and re-echoed from all the mountains. He grasped a huge mountain in his hand, a mountain composed of flint, and from it made himself a single knife sharp as a weasel's teeth. "Now I am going," he said, striding forth among thunder and lightning, with mighty eagles circling above him. Thus Glooscap came to the village of the people with webbed hands and feet.

"I want water," he told them. Looking at him, they were afraid. They brought him a little muddy water. "I think I'll get more and cleaner water," he said. Glooscap went upstream and confronted the monster. "I want clean water," he said, "a lot of it, for the people downstream."

Ho! Ho!
Ho! Ho!

All the waters are mine!
All the waters are mine!

Go away!
Go away!

Or I'll kill you!

"Slimy lump of mud!" cried Glooscap. "We'll see who will be killed!" They fought. The mountains shook. The earth split open. The swamp smoked and burst into flames. Mightly trees were shivered into splinters.

The monster opened its huge mouth wide to swallow Glooscap. Glooscap made himself taller than the tallest tree, and even the monster's mile-wide mouth was too small for him. Glooscap seized his great flint knife and slit the monster's bloated belly. From the wound gushed a mighty stream, a roaring river, tumbling, rolling, foaming down, down, down, gouging out for itself a vast, deep bed, flowing by the village and on to the great sea of the east.

"That should be enough water for the people," said Glooscap. He grasped the monster and squeezed him in his mighty palm, squeezed and sqqueezed and threw him away, flinging him into the swamp. Glooscap had squeezed this great creature into a small bullfrog, and ever since, the bullfrog's skin has been wrinkled because Glooscap squeezed so hard.

—*Retold from several nineteenth-century sources.*

LITTLE-MAN-WITH-
HAIR-ALL-OVER

[MÉTIS]

Little-Man was hairier than a skunk. Hair grew out of his nose and nostrils. He had thick, matted hair between his buttocks. He was not particularly good-looking and he smelled as if he didn't wash often, but he was a merry fellow who laughted a lot, and he never had any trouble finding pretty girls to share his blanket. He was always on the move, eager to discover new things.

Little-Man-with-Hair-All-Over was small, but he succeeded in everything he did. He was tough in a fight, so they called for him whenever there was something dangerous to do. When a bear monster went on a rampage, ripping up lodges with his huge claws and eating the people inside, Little-Man-with-Hair-All-Over had no trouble killing it. For this his grateful people gave him a magic knife.

One time when Little-Man was traveling, he met two brothers and asked what they were up to. "We're looking for adventure," they answered.

"That's exactly what I'm doing. Let's join up and travel together," said Little-Man. "What do they call you?"

"My name is Smoking Mountain," said one. "I'm the oldest. This one here is Broken War Club."

The three wandered on together and after a while came to a fine, large lodge with plenty of buffalo robes lying around. Outside there were racks with jerk meat, and someone had left a large cooking kettle. But the lodge was deserted; there was no trace of any human beings.

"I like this place," said Little-Man. "Let's stay a while."

"Somebody must own it," said Smoking Mountain.

"Well," said Little-Man, "if someone comes and claims it, I won't mind; and if nobody shows up I won't mind either." So they stayed.

Little-Man said to Smoking Mountain: "Let's go hunting. Broken War Club can stay and cook some of that jerk meat for supper." So the two of them took their bows and arrows and went.

But when the hunters came back to camp, there was no supper. Broken War Club was lying under a buffalo robe moaning and groaning.

"What's the matter with you?" asked Little-Man. "You look as if you've been in a fight."

"I'm too embarrassed to tell," answered Broken War Club.

"Suit yourself," said Little-Man, and they ate some cold jerk meat.

The next day Little-Man-with-Hair-All-Over said to Broken War Club: "Let's go out and hunt. Smoking Mountain can stay here and cook." But when the two came back, they found Smoking Mountain also lying under a buffalo robe moaning and groaning. "What happened to you, friend?" asked Little-Man. "You look as if you've been in a fight."

"I'm too ashamed to tell," answered Smoking Mountain.

"You two are some fine cooks!" remarked Little-Man. Again they ate their jerk meat cold.

The next morning Little-Man told the brothers: "You go out and hunt; I'll stay and cook." And when the brothers came home with their meat, they found a fine supper waiting.

"Has anybody been here?" Smoking Mountain asked.

"Under that robe over there." said Little-Man, pointing to a buffalo robe on the floor, "there's a large flat stone, and under the stone there's a hole. Someone lifted the stone, came out of the hole, and crept out from under the robe."

"And what happened then?" asked the brothers.

"The same thing that happened to you. An ugly dwarf, only as big as my hand but monstrously strong, tried to beat me up with his whip. So that's why you were moaning and groaning. And you were ashamed to tell because he was so small."

"Ah," said the brothers, "he whipped you too."

"No," said Little-Man, "I didn't give him the chance. I killed him and threw him down that hole."

Smoking Mountain pushed aside the robe, lifted up the stone, and peeked down. "This is a very deep hole," he said. "It must lead to that dwarf's home. I wish I could go down and find out."

Little-Man-with-Hair-All-Over said: "That's easy." He took hold of the big cooking kettle and fastened a long rawhide rope to its handle. "Climb into this kettle," he told Smoking Mountain, "and we'll let you down. Then we'll draw you up and you can tell us about it." They lowered Smoking Mountain down the hole and after a while pulled him up.

Smoking Mountain reported: "I landed right on top of that dwarf; you really fixed him good. It was dark and damp down there, and I could hear a strange noise like an animal snorting. I didn't feel comfortable in that place."

"Let me down," said Broken War Club. "I'm not afraid."

So they let him down and after a while pulled him up. He said: "I went a little farther. There's a door down there, a kind of hole in a cave wall, covered with a rock. I heard the noise too—it sounds like a deep growl rather than a snort. I didn't want to go in there."

"Let me down," said Little-Man-with-Hair-All-Over.

After they had lowered him, Little-Man found the entrance door and listened to the growling snort, or snorting growl. He rolled the rock out of the way and found himself in a cave-like room face to face with a two-headed monster. The monster growled: "Where is my son? Have you seen him? He is only so big . . ."

"That must be the dwarf I killed," said Little-Man-with-Hair-All-Over. "I left his body outside."

At this the monster roared and attacked. Little-Man managed to cut off one of its heads with his magic knife, but the monster continued fighting just as savagely. They struggled until Little-Man succeeded in cutting off the other head.

Looking past the monster's corpse, Little-Man saw another door opposite the first one. It too was stopped up with a big rock. From behind came a truly terrifying growling, snorting, and snuffling, as from a horde of strange beasts.

"I wonder who that can be," he thought, rolling the rock out of the way. In the next room he found a scaly man-monster with three heads, all three of which were snorting and growling and snuffling at the same time.

"Where is my son, the one with two heads?" the monster asked.

"Grandfather—or is it grandfathers?—he is dead. I had to kill him, because otherwise, I think he would have killed me. He was mad because I killed his son—your grandson, probably—the evil little dwarf with the whip."

At this the three-headed monster hurled himself at Little-Man. The three heads foamed at the lips, snarled and bit. "One at a time, one at a time," said Little-Man as he cut the three heads off one after the other.

"They really made me sweat," said Little-Man, looking around. He discovered yet another door, behind which he heard howling, shuffling, snarling, and growling. "This is getting boring," he said as he rolled the rock aside and met a horny-skinned, four-headed man-monster. This one asked no questions but immediately jumped at Little-Man with four sets of teeth biting, snapping, and tearing. The monster's skin was so tough, especially at the necks, that it resisted the magic knife. Even when Little-Man had finally cut off three of the four heads, the man-monster fought as fiercely as ever. The fourth head was the toughest; it bit a good-sized piece out of Little-Man's shoulder before he managed to cut it off. Panting, exhausted, Little-Man-with-Hair-All-Over kicked the giant body of the monster and said, "There, you wicked little thing!"

Again he looked around and saw a door. "Not again!" he said. But he listened and behind it he heard the sweet song of young girls. "This is much better," said Little-Man-with-Hair-All-Over as he rolled the last rock aside. He stepped into the last chamber and found three very pretty young women.

"Are the monsters out there relatives of yours?" asked Little-Man.

"No, no, in no way!" answered the maidens. "These horrible monsters have been keeping us prisoner for their own pleasure. We've been having a hard life."

"I believe it," he said.

"Handsome young warrior," said one of the girls, "surely you've come to free us."

"I don't know about handsome," said Little-Man, "but free you I will."

"And you are handsome," said the bold girl. "I like a little, hairy, lusty fellow."

"Then you've met the right man," he said. He looked around and saw wonderful things that the monsters had taken from their victims: buckskin robes decorated with multicolored porcupine quills, well-made weapons, war bonnets of eagle feathers, and much wore.

"Enough here for three friends to divide," said Little-Man, "and isn't it a lucky coincidence that there are three of you and three of us? For I have two friends waiting in the lodge above."

"Better and better," said the three good-looking girls.

Little-Man-with-Hair-All-Over gathered up the many fine things in a bundle and walked to the hole underneath the lodge. "Ho, friends," he hollered, "here are some good things for us to divide!" He placed the bundle in the kettle, and the two brothers in the lodge pulled it up. They called down, "Are you coming up now?"

"Not yet," he answered. "First pull up three young pretty ones well worth meeting." The brothers lowered the kettle and, one by one, drew up the women. Then Little-Man called out: "I'm coming up now." He climbed into the kettle. When they had pulled him halfway up, Broken War Club said to Smoking Mountain: "Let's drop him back down. Then we can keep these pretty girls and all the fine things for ourselves."

"No," said Smoking Mountain, "Little-Man has been a good friend to us." But Broken War Club had already cut the rawhide rope, and Little-Man fell all the way down with a big clatter. He was stunned, but recovered quickly, saying: "Some fine friends I chose!"

Without the rope and the kettle, Little-Man-with-Hair-All-Over had a hard time climbing up into the lodge. He tried four times before he finally did it. "Now I'll find these no-good brothers," he said.

Traveling along what he believed to be the trail of Smoking Mountain and Broken War Club, Little-Man heard some people quarreling. He followed the sound and came upon the body of a big elk, over which a wasp, a worm, and a woodpecker were squabbling. "My friends," Little-Man-with-Hair-All-Over told them, "there's enough here for all. Let me settle this for you and stop all the fuss." He gave the bones to the woodpecker, the fat to the wasp, and the meat to the worm, and everyone was satisfied.

"Thank you, uncle, for settling this matter and making peace between us," they said. "In return, if you ever find yourself in trouble, you can assume any of our shapes: you can turn yourself into a worm, a wasp, or a woodpecker."

"Thank you, I appreciate it," said Little-Man.

Always following the trail, he came at last to a lodge standing in a clearing of the forest. At once he turned himself into a woodpecker, flew up to a pole above the smoke hole, and looked down. "Ah," he said to himself, "Here are the two no-good brothers talking to the three girls." Then he turned himself into a wasp and flew down into the lodge, where he settled on the shoulder of the bold girl. Nobody noticed him. The bold girl said: "I'm still angry with you men. It was mean to drop that nice little fellow. He was brave, and I was fond of him. I hope he's well, wherever he is."

Smoking Mountain added, "Yes, it wasn't right. I tried to stop it, but this one here had already cut the rope."

Broken War Club just laughed. "Brother, don't talk like a fool. It was so funny, dropping that hairy, useless man down there and listening to him squeal. Look at all the riches I got for us, and look at these pretty girls who, thanks to me, make our nights pleasant. Yes, I still have to laugh when I think of the hairy one clattering down, squealing."

"I don't remember having squealed," said Little-Man-with-Hair-All-Over, quickly turning himself back into a man. "Let's see who'll be squealing now."

Broken War Club tried to run away, but Little-Man seized him by the hair and cut his throat with the magic knife. Then he kicked Smoking Mountain in the backside. "Coward! You could have defied your younger brother and gotten me out of that hole. If you ever cross my path again, I'll kill you the way I killed this one." Smoking Mountain slunk away.

Then Little-Man turned to the women. "Good-looking girls, will you take me for a husband? I'm man enough for three. I'm small, but not everywhere."

"Handsome one," said the bold girl, "since we three are sisters, it's only fitting for us to have one husband." So Little-Man-with-Hair-All-Over married the girls, and they were all very happy together.

After Little-Man had lived with them for a while, he said: "My dears, I'm not made to stay always in one place. Now and then I just have to roam and discover things. I've left enough meat, pemmican, tongues, and back fat to last you a good many days. I won't be away for long, so don't be afraid."

Thus Little-Man-with-Hair-All-Over went traveling again. He came to a lodge, inside which a pretty young woman was crying. He went in and asked: "Good-looking one, what's the matter?"

"A slimy water monster is keeping me prisoner, and I hate his embraces. I've tried and tried to run away, but he always catches me and drags me back."

"Dry your tears," said Little-Man, "I'll kill this monster and marry you. I already have three wives, but I can easily take care of one more."

"I'd like that," said the woman, "but no one can kill him."

"I can kill any monster with my magic knife. I am forever rescuing pretty maidens imprisoned by evil monsters; I'm quite used to it."

"You can't kill this one, even with a magic knife, because he's many monsters in one. There's a secret way to kill him, and if you don't happen to know it, he'll kill you."

'And what is this secret way?"

"I don't know; I've never had a chance to ask. But tonight the monster comes back, and I'll try to get it out of him. Hide yourself in the meantime."

"That's easy," said Little-Man, turning into a woodpecker and flying to the top pole above the smoke hole.

At nightfall the water monster returned. Looking down from his perch, Little-Man thought: "This is indeed an ugly, slimy monster!"

The creature threw some meat to the girl, saying: "I just drowned and ate some humans, so I'm full, but here's some antelope meat for you."

"Just what I like," said the girl. "You know, that horn coming out of your forehead is dirty; let me clean it for you. It's really quite handsome."

"You're pleasant today for a change," said the monster," instead of scowling and sour-faced. Perhaps you're beginning to appreciate me."

"How could anyone not appreciate you?" said the girl. "Tell me, so that in case of trouble I can help you: what's the only way to kill you?"

The monster grinned horribly and said: "Well, here I am, the great water monster. If you kill me, a huge grizzly bear will come out of me, and out of him a smaller brown bear, and out of him a panther, and out of the panther a wolf, and out of the wolf a wolverine, and out of that a fox, and out of that a rabbit. Out of the rabbit will come a quail, and out of the quail an egg. Only by dashing this egg against the horn in my forehead can I be killed."

Little-Man heard it all. At once he flew down into the lodge, resumed his own shape, and attacked the great water monster with his magic knife. One after the other, he killed all the animals coming out of the monster, and at last dashed the egg against the monster's horn.

"You're brave and powerful," said the girl. "I'm yours."

So Little-Man-with-Hair-All-Over took her as his fourth wife and carried her home to his lodge, together with all the treasures which the monster had amassed through robbing and murder. And Little-Man had been right: he was man enough for four wives, with a little left over.

—Told by Jean Desjarlais in New York City, 1971, and recorded by Richard Erdoes.

Jean Desjarlais also calls himself "Oohosis"—the owl—because the owl is a messenger. He was one of many Native Americans who occupied Alcatraz Island in 1970–1971, and he now lives in the Arctic regions of northern Canada.

HOW MOSQUITOES CAME TO BE

■

[TLINGIT]

■ |||||||||||||||||||||||||||||||||||||||||||||||||||||||||||||||||||||||||||| ■

Long ago there was a giant who loved to kill humans, eat their flesh, and drink their blood. He was especially fond of human hearts. "Unless we can get rid of this giant," people said, "none of us will be left," and they called a council to discuss ways and means.

One man said, "I think I know how to kill the monster," and he went to the place where the giant had last been seen. There he lay down and pretended to be dead.

Soon the giant came along. Seeing the man lying there, he said: "These humans are making it easy for me. Now I don't even have to catch and kill them; they die right on my trail, probably from fear of me!"

The giant touched the body. "Ah, good," he said, "this one is still warm and fresh. What a tasty meal he'll make; I can't wait to roast his heart."

The giant flung the man over his shoulder, and the man let his head hang down as if he were dead. Carrying the man home, the giant dropped him in the middle of the floor right near the fireplace. Then he saw that there was no firewood and went to get some.

As soon as the monster had left, the man got up and grabbed the giant's huge skinning knife. Just then the giant's son came in, bending low to enter. He was still small as giants go, and the man held the big knife to his throat. "Quick, tell me, where's your father's heart?" "Tell me or I'll slit your throat!"

The giant's son was scared. He said: "My father's heart is in his left heel."

Just then the giant's left foot appeared in the entrance, and the man swiftly plunged the knife into the heel. The monster screamed and fell down dead.

Yet the giant still spoke. "Though I'm dead, though you killed me, I'm going to keep on eating you and all the other humans in the world forever!"

"That's what you think!" said the man. "I'm about to make sure that

you never eat anyone again." He cut the giant's body into pieces and burned each one in the fire. Then he took the ashes and threw them into the air for the winds to scatter.

Instantly each of the particles turned into a mosquito. The cloud of ashes became a cloud of mosquitoes, and from their midst the man heard the giant's voice laughing, saying: "Yes, I'll eat you people until the end of time."

And as the monster spoke, the man felt a sting, and a mosquito started sucking his blood, and then many mosquitoes stung him, and he began to scratch himself.

—*Retold from English source, 1883.*

■

HIAWATHA THE UNIFIER

■

[IROQUOIS]

Hiawatha (Haion-Hwa-Tha—He-Who-Makes-Rivers) is thought to have been a statesman, lawgiver, shaman, and unifier who lived around 1570. According to some sources, he was born a Mohawk and sought refuge among the Onondaga when his own tribe at first rejected his teachings. His efforts to unite the Iroquois tribes were opposed by a formidable chieftain, Wathatotarho, whom he eventually defeated and who killed Hiawatha's daughter in revenge.

■ ▏▏▏ ■

The slumber of Ta-ren-ya-wa-gon, Upholder of Heavens, was disturbed by a great cry of anguish and woe. He looked down from his abode to earth and saw human beings moaning with terror, pursued by horrifying monsters and cruel, man-devouring giants. Turning himself into a mortal, Ta-ren-ya-wa-gon swiftly descended to earth and, taking a small girl by the hand, told the frightened humans to follow him. By trails known only to him, he led the group of shivering refugees to a cave at the mouth of a great river, where he fed them and told them to sleep.

After the people had somewhat recovered under his protection, Ta-ren-ya-wa-gon again took the little girl by the hand and led them toward the rising sun. The band traveled for many days until they came to the confluence of two mighty rivers whose waters, white with spray, cascaded over tremendous rocks. There Ta-ren-ya-wa-gon halted and built a longhouse for himself and his people.

For years they lived there, content and growing fat, their children turning into strong men and handsome women. Then Ta-ren-ya-wa-gon, the Sky Upholder became mortal, gathered the people around him and spoke: "You, my children, must now spread out and become great nations. I will make your numbers like the leaves of a forest in summertime, like pebbles on the shore of the great waters." And again he took one little girl by the hand and walked toward the setting sun, all the people following him.

After a long journey they came to the banks of a beautiful river. Ta-ren-ya-wa-gon separated a few families from the rest and told them to build a longhouse at that spot and found a village. "You shall be known by the name of Te-ha-wro-gah, Those-of-Divided-Speech," he told them, and they grew into the Mohawk tribe. And from the moment he had named them, their language changed and they could no longer understand the rest of the people.

To the Mohawks Ta-ren-ya-gon gave corn, beans, squash, and tobacco, together with dogs to help them hunt game. He taught them how to plant and reap and pound corn into meal. He taught them the ways of the forest and the game, for in that long-ago time, people did not yet know all these things. When he had fully instructed them and given them the necessities of life, Ta-ren-ya-wa-gon again took one little girl by the hand and traveled with the remaining people toward the sunset.

After a long journey they halted in a beautiful well-watered valley surrounded by forests, and he commanded another group to build their village at that spot. He gave them what was necessary for life, taught them what they needed to know, and named them Ne-ha-wre-ta-go, the Big-Tree people, for the great forests surrounding them. And these people, who grew into the Oneida nation, also spoke a tongue of their own as soon as he had named them.

Then once more Ta-ren-ya-wa-gon took a little girl's hand and wandered on, always toward the setting sun, and the rest of the people followed him. They came to a big mountain which he named O-nun-da-ga-o-no-ga. At its foot he commanded some more families to build a longhouse, and he gave them the same gifts and taught them the same things that he had the others. He named them after the mountain towering above them and also gave them a speech of their own. And these people became the Onondaga nation.

Again with a small girl at his side, Ta-ren-ya-wa-gon wandered on, leading the people to the shores of a lake sparkling in the sun. The lake was called Go-yo-gah, and here still another group built their village, and they became the Cayugas.

Now only a handful of people were left, and these Ta-ren-ya-wa-gon led to a lake by a mountain called Ga-nun-da-gwa. There he settled them, giving them the name of Te-ho-ne-noy-hent—Keepers of the Door. They too received a language of their own and grew into the mighty Seneca nation.

There were some among the people who were not satisfied with the places appointed to them by the Upholder of Heavens. These wandered on toward the setting sun until they came to a river greater than all others, a river known as the Mississippi. They crossed it on a wild grapevine that formed a bridge from bank to bank, and after the last of them had crossed over, the vine tore asunder. None could ever return, so that this river divided the western from the eastern human beings.

To each nation the Upholder of Heavens gave a special gift. To the Senecas he gave such swift feet that their hunters could outrun the deer. To the Cayugas he gave the canoe and the skill to guide it through the most turbulent waters. To the Onondagas he gave the knowledge of eternal laws and the gift to fathom the wishes of the Great Creator. To the Oneidas he gave skills in making weapons and weaving baskets, while to the Mohawks he gave bows and arrows and the ability to guide the shafts into the hearts of their game and their enemies.

Ta-ren-ya-wa-gon resolved to live among the people as a human being. Having the power to assume any shape, he chose to be a man and took the name of Hiawatha. He chose to live among the Onondagas and took a beautiful young woman of that tribe for his wife. From their union came a daughter, Mni-haha, who surpassed even her mother in beauty and womanly skills. Hiawatha never ceased to teach and advise, and above all he preached peace and harmony.

Under Hiawatha the Onondagas became the greatest of all tribes, but the other nations founded by the Great Upholder also increased and prospered. Traveling in a magic birchbark canoe of dazzling whiteness, which floated above waters and meadows as if on an invisible bird's wings, Hiawatha went from nation to nation, counseling them and keeping man, animal, and nature in balance according to the eternal laws of the manitous. So all was well and the people lived happily.

But the law of the universe is also that happiness alternates with sorrow, life with death, prosperity with hardship, harmony with disharmony. From out of the north beyond the Great Lakes came wild tribes, fierce, untutored nations who knew nothing of the eternal law; peoples who did not plant or weave baskets or fire clay into cooking vessels. All they knew was how to prey on those who planted and reaped the fruits of their labor. Fierce and pitiless, these strangers ate their meat raw, tearing it apart with their teeth. Warfare and killing were their occupation. They burst upon Hiawatha's people like a flood, spreading devastation wherever they went. Again the people turned to Hiawatha for help. He advised all the nations to assemble and wait his coming.

And so the five tribes came together at the place of the great council fire, by the shores of a large and tranquil lake where the wild men from the north had not yet penetrated. The people waited for Hiawatha one day, two days, three days. On the fourth day his gleaming-white magic canoe appeared, floating, gliding above the mists. Hiawatha sat in the stern guiding the mystery canoe, while in the bow was his only child, his daughter.

The sachems, elders, and wise men of the tribes stood at the water's edge to greet the Great Upholder. Hiawatha and his daughter stepped ashore. He greeted all he met as brothers and spoke to each in his own language.

Suddenly there came an awesome noise, a noise like the rushing of a hundred rivers, like the beating of a thousand giant wings. Fearfully the people looked upward. Out of the clouds, circling lower and lower, flew the great mystery bird of the heavens, a hundred times as big as the largest eagles, and whenever he beat his wings he made the sound of a thousand thunderclaps. While the people cowered, Hiawatha and his daughter stood unmoved. Then the Great Upholder laid his hands upon his daughter's head in blessing, after which she said calmly, "Farewell, my father." She seated herself between the wings of the mystery bird, who spiraled upwards and upwards into the clouds and at last disappeared into the great vault of the sky.

The people watched in awe, but Hiawatha, stunned with grief, sank to the ground and covered himself with the robe of a panther. Three days he sat thus in silence, and none dared approach him. The people wondered whether he had given his only child to the manitous above as a sacrifice for the deliverance of his people. But the Great Upholder would never tell them, would never speak of his daughter or of the mystery bird who had carried her away.

After having mourned for three days, Hiawatha rose on the morning of the fourth and purified himself in the cold, clear waters of the lake. Then he asked the great council to assemble. When the sachems, elders, and wise men had seated themselves in a circle around the sacred fire, Hiawatha came before them and said:

What is past is past; it is the present and the future which concern us. My children, listen well, for these are my last words to you. My time among you is drawing to the end.

My children, war, fear, and disunity have brought you from your villages to this sacred council fire. Facing a common danger, and fearing for the lives of your families, you have yet drifted apart, each tribe thinking and acting only for itself. Remember how I took you from one small band and nursed you up into many nations. You must reunite now and act as one. No tribe alone can withstand our savage enemies, who care nothing about the eternal law, who sweep upon us like the storms of winter, spreading death and destruction everywhere.

My children, listen well. Remember that you are brothers, that the downfall of one means the downfall of all. You must have one fire, one pipe, one war club.

Hiawatha motioned to the five tribal firekeepers to unite their fires with the big sacred council fire, and they did so. Then the Great Upholder sprinkled sacred tobacco upon the glowing embers so that its sweet fragrance enveloped the wise men sitting in the circle. He said:

Onondagas, you are a tribe of mighty warriors. Your strength is like that of a giant pine tree whose roots spread far and deep so that it can withstand any storm. Be you the protectors. You shall be the first nation.

Oneida, your men are famous for their wisdom. Be you the counselors of the tribes. You shall be the second nation.

Seneca, you are swift of foot and persuasive in speech. Your men are the greatest orators among the tribes. Be you the spokesmen. You shall be the third people.

Cayuga, you are the most cunning. You are the most skilled in the building and managing of canoes. Be you the guardians of our rivers. You shall be the fourth nation.

Mohawk, you are foremost in planting corn and beans and in building longhouses. Be you the nourishers.

You tribes must be like the five fingers of a warrior's hand joined in gripping the war club. Unite as one, and then your enemies will recoil before you back into the northern wastes from whence they came. Let my words sink deep into your hearts and minds. Retire now to take counsel among yourselves, and come to me tomorrow to tell me whether you will follow my advice.

On the next morning the sachems and wise men of the five nations came to Hiawatha with the promise that they would from that day on be as one nation. Hiawatha rejoiced. He gathered up the dazzling white feathers which the great mystery bird of the sky had dropped and gave the plumes to the leaders of the assembled tribes. "By these feathers," he said, "you shall be known as the Ako-no-shu-ne, the Iroquois." Thus with the help of Hiawatha, the Great Unifier, the mighty League of the Five Nations was born, and its tribes held sway undisturbed over all the land between the great river of the west and the great sea of the east.

The elders begged Hiawatha to become the chief sachem of the united tribes, but he told them: "This can never be, because I must leave you. Friends and brothers, choose the wisest women in your tribes to be the future clan mothers and peacemakers, let them turn any strife arising among you into friendship. Let your sachems be wise enough to go to such women for advice when there are disputes. Now I have finished speaking. Farewell."

At that moment there came to those assembled a sweet sound like the rush of rustling leaves and the song of innumerable birds. Hiawatha stepped into his white mystery canoe, and instead of gliding away on the waters of the lake, it rose slowly into the sky and disappeared into the clouds. Hiawatha was gone, but his teachings survive in the hearts of the people.

—Retold from Victorian sources.

In 1714, the Tuscarora tribe joined the Iroquois League, which had been in existence since the fifteenth century and which now became known as well as the Six Nations. The League was a powerful force in what is now northeast Pennsylvania and upstate New York until the Revolutionary War, when they sided with the British. After the Treaty of Fort Stanwix in 1784, the League's strength was effectively broken, though it has never formally disbanded.

THE LIFE AND DEATH
OF SWEET MEDICINE

[NORTHERN CHEYENNE]

In this version of the medicine arrow story, Sweet Medicine rather than Arrow Boy brings the Cheyenne their religion, their social codes, and their political unity.

A long time ago the people had no laws, no rules of behavior—they hardly knew enough to survive. And they did shameful things out of ignorance, because they didn't understand how to live.

There was one man among them who had a natural sense of what was right. He and his wife were good, hard-working people, a family to be proud of. They knew how to feel ashamed, and this feeling kept them from doing wrong.

Their only child was a daughter, beautiful and modest, who had reached the age when girls begin to think about husbands and making a family. One night a man's voice spoke to her in a dream: "You are handsome and strong, modest and young. Therefore Sweet Root will visit you."

Dismissing it as just a dream, the girl went cheerfully about her chores the next day. On the following night, however, she heard the voice again: "Sweet Root is coming—woman's medicine which makes a mother's milk flow. Sweet Root is coming as a man comes courting."

The girl puzzled over the words when she awoke, but in the end shrugged her shoulders. People can't control their dreams, she thought, and the idea of a visit from a medicine root didn't make sense.

On the third night the dream recurred, and this time it was so real that a figure seemed to be standing beside the buffalo robe she slept on. He was talking to her, telling her: "Sweet Root is coming; he is very near. Soon he will be with you."

On the fourth night she heard the same voice and saw the same figure. Disturbed, she told her mother about it the next morning. "There must be something in it," she said. It's so real, and the voice is so much like a man's voice."

"No, it's just a dream," said her mother. "It doesn't mean anything."

But from that time on, the girl felt different. Something was stirring, growing within her, and after a few months her condition became obvious: she was going to have a baby. She told her parents that no man had touched her, and they believed her. But others would not be likely to, and the girl hid her condition. When she felt the birth pangs coming on, she went out into the prairie far from the camp and built herself a brush shelter. Doing everything herself, she gave birth to a baby boy. She dried the baby, wrapped him in soft moss, and left him there in the wickiup, for in her village a baby without a father would be scorned and treated badly. Praying that someone would find him, she went sadly home to her parents.

At about the same time, an old woman was out searching the prairie for wild turnips, which she dug up with an animal's shoulder blade. She heard crying, and following the sound, came to the wickiup. She was overjoyed to find the baby, as she had never had one of her own. All around the brush shelter grew the sweet root which makes a mother's milk flow, so she named the boy Sweet Medicine. She took him home to her shabby tipi even though she had nothing to offer him but love.

In the tipi next to the old woman's lived a young mother who was nursing a small child, and she agreed to nurse Sweet Medicine also. He grew faster and learned faster than ordinary children and was weaned in no time. When he was only ten years old, he already had grown-up wisdom and hunting skill far in advance of his age. But because he had no family and lived at the edge of the camp in a poor tipi, nobody paid any attention to Sweet Medicine's exceptional powers.

That year there was a drought, very little game, and much hunger in the village. "Grandmother," Sweet Medicine said to the old woman, "find me an old buffalo hide—any dried-out, chewed-up scrap with holes in it will do."

The woman searched among the refuse piles and found a wrinkled, brittle piece that the starving dogs had been chewing on. When she brought it to Sweet Medicine, he told her, "Take this to the stream outside the camp, wash it in the flowing water, make it pliable, scrape it clean." After she had done this Sweet Medicine took a willow wand and bent it into a hoop, which he colored with sacred red earth paint. He cut the buffalo hide into one long strip and wove it back and forth over the hoop, making a kind of net with an opening in the center. Then he cut four wild cherry sticks, sharpened them to a point, and hardened them in the hearth fire.

The next morning he said: "Grandmother, come with me. We're going to play the hoop-and-stick game." He took the hoop and the cherry-wood sticks and walked into the middle of the camp circle. "Grandmother, roll this hoop for me," he said. She rolled the hoop along the ground and Sweet Medicine hurled his pointed sticks through the center of it, hitting the right spot every time. Soon a lot of people, men and women, boys and girls, came to watch the strange new game.

Then Sweet Medicine cried: "Grandmother, let me hit it once more and make the hoop into a fat buffalo calf!"

Again he threw his stick like a dart, again the stick went through the center of the hoop, and as it did so the hoop turned into a fat, yellow buffalo calf. The stick had pierced its heart, and the calf fell down dead. "Now you people will have plenty to eat," said Sweet Medicine. "Come and butcher this calf."

The people gathered and roasted chunks of tender calf meat over their fires. And no matter how many pieces of flesh they cut from the calf's body, it was never picked clean. However much they ate, there was always more. So the people had their fill, and that was the end of the famine. It was also the first hoop-and-stick game played among the Cheyenne. This sacred game has much power attached to it, and it is still being played.

A boy's first kill is an important happening in his life, something he will always remember. After killing his first buffalo a boy will be honored by his father, who may hold a feast for him and give him a man's name. There would be no feast for Sweet Medicine; all the same, he was very happy when he killed a fat, yellow buffalo calf on his first hunt. He was skinning and butchering it when he was approached by an elderly man, a chief too old to do much hunting, but still harsh and commanding. "This is just the kind of hide I have been looking for," said the chief. "I will take it."

"You can't have a boy's first hide," said Sweet Medicine. "Surely you must know this. But you are welcome to half of the meat, because I honor old age."

The chief took the meat but grabbed the hide too and began to walk off with it. Sweet Medicine took hold of one end, and they started a tug-of-war. The chief used his riding whip on Sweet Medicine, shouting: "How dare a poor nothing boy defy a chief?" As he whipped Sweet Medicine again and again across the face, the boy's fighting spirit was aroused. He grabbed a big buffalo leg bone and hit the old man over the head.

Some say Sweet Medicine killed that chief, others say the old man just fell down stunned. But in the village the people were angry that a mere boy had dared to fight the old chief. Some said, "Let's whip him," others said, "Let's kill him."

After he had returned to the old woman's lodge, Sweet Medicine sensed what was going on. He said: "Grandmother, some young men of the warrior societies will come here to kill me for having stood up for myself." He thanked her for her kindness to him and then fled from the village. Later when the young warriors came, they were so angry to find the boy gone that they pulled the lodge down and set fire to it.

The following morning someone saw Sweet Medicine, dressed like a Fox warrior, standing on a hill overlooking the village. His enemies set out in pursuit, but he was always just out of their reach and they finally retired exhausted. The next morning he appeared as an Elk warrior, carrying a crooked coupstick wrapped in otter skin. Again they tried to catch and kill him, and again he evaded them. They resumed their futile chase on the third morning, when he wore the red face paint and feathers of a Red Shield warrior, and on the fourth, when he dressed like a Dog soldier and shook a small red rattle tied with buffalo hair at his pursuers. On the fifth day he appeared in the full regalia of a Cheyenne chief. That made the village warriors angrier than ever, but they still couldn't catch him, and after that they saw him no more.

Wandering alone over the prairie, the boy heard a voice calling, leading him to a beautiful dark-forested land of many hills. Standing apart from the others was a single mountain shaped like a huge tipi: the sacred medicine mountain called Bear Butte. Sweet Medicine found a secret opening which has since closed (or perhaps was visible to him alone) and entered the mountain. It was hollow inside like a tipi, forming a sacred lodge filled with people who looked like ordinary men and women, but were really powerful spirits.

"Grandson, come in, we have been expecting you," the holy people said, and when Sweet Medicine took his seat, they began teaching him the Cheyenne way to live so that he could return to the people and give them this knowledge.

First of all, the spirits gave him the sacred four arrows, saying: "This is the great gift we are handing you. With these wonderful arrows, the tribe will prosper. Two arrows are for war and two for hunting. But there is much, much more to the four arrows. They have great powers. They contain rules by which men ought to live."

The spirit people taught Sweet Medicine how to pray to the arrows, how to keep them, how to renew them. They taught him the wise laws of the forty-four chiefs. They taught him how to set up rules for the warrior societies. They taught him how women should be honored. They taught him the many useful things by which people could live, survive, and prosper, things people had not yet learned at that time. Finally they taught him how to make a special tipi in which the sacred arows were to be kept. Sweet Medicine listened respectfully and learned well, and finally an old spirit man burned incense of sweet grass to purify both Sweet Medicine and the sacred arrow bundle. Then the Cheyenne boy put the holy bundle on his back and began the long journey home to his people.

During his absence there had been a famine in the land. The buffalo had gone into hiding, for they were angry that the people did not know how to live and were behaving badly. When Sweet Medicine arrived at the village, he found a group of tired and listless children, their ribs sticking out, who were playing with little buffalo figures they had made out of mud. Sweet Medicine immediately changed the figures into large chunks of juicy buffalo meat and fat. "Now there's enough for you to eat," he told the young ones, "with plenty left over for your parents and grandparents. Take the meat, fat, and tongues into the village, and tell two good young hunters to come out in the morning to meet me."

Though the children carried the message and two young hunters went out and looked everywhere for Sweet Medicine the next day, all they saw was a big eagle circling above them. They tried again on the second and third days with no success, but on the fourth morning they found Sweet Medicine standing on top of a hill overlooking the village. He told the two: "I have come bringing a wonderful gift from the Creator which the spirits inside the great medicine mountain have sent you. Tell the people to set up a big lodge in the center of the camp circle. Cover its floor with sage, and purify it with burning sweet grass. Tell everyone to go inside the tipi and stay there; no one must see me approaching."

When at last all was ready, Sweet Medicine walked slowly toward the village and four times called out: "People of the Cheyenne, with a great power I am approaching. Be joyful. The sacred arrows I am bringing." He entered the tipi with the sacred arrow bundle and said: "You have not yet learned how to live in the right way. That is why the Ones Above were angry and the buffalo went into hiding." The two young hunters lit the fire, and Sweet Medicine filled a deer-bone pipe with sacred tobacco. All night through, he taught the people what the spirits inside the holy mountain had taught him. These teachings established the way of the Tsistsistas, the true Cheyenne nation. Toward morning Sweet Medicine sang four sacred songs. After each song he smoked the pipe, and its holy breath ascended through the smoke hole up into the sky, up to the great mystery.

At daybreak, as the sun rose and the people emerged from the sacred arrow lodge, they found the prairie around them covered with buffalo. The spirits were no longer angry. The famine was over.

For many nights to come, Sweet Medicine instructed the people in the sacred laws. He lived among the Cheyenne for a long time and made them into a proud tribe respected throughout the Plains.

Four lives the Creator had given him, but even Sweet Medicine was not immortal. Only the rocks and mountains are forever. When he grew old and feeble and felt that the end of his appointed time was near, he directed the people to carry him to a place near the Sacred Bear Butte. There they made a small hut for him out of cottonwood branches and cedar lodge poles covered with bark and leaves. They spread its floor with sage, flat cedar leaves, and fragrant grass. It was a good lodge to die in, and when they placed him before it, he addressed the people for the last time:

> I have seen in my mind that some time after I am dead—and may the time be long—light-skinned, bearded men will arrive with sticks spitting fire. They will conquer the land and drive you before them. They will kill the animals who give their flesh that you may live, and they will bring strange animals for you to ride and eat. They will introduce war and evil, strange sicknesses and death. They will try to make you forget Maheo, the Creator, and the things I taught you, and will impose their own alien, evil ways. They will take your land little by little, until there is nothing left for you. I do not

like to tell you this, but you must know. You must be strong when that bad time comes, you men, and particularly you women, because much depends on you, because you are the perpetuators of life and if you weaken, the Cheyenne will cease to be. Now I have said all there is to say.

Then Sweet Medicine went into his hut to die.

—Told by members of the Strange Owl family on the Lame Deer Indian Reservation, Montana, 1967, and recorded by Richard Erdoes.

THE QUILLWORK GIRL AND HER SEVEN STAR BROTHERS

[CHEYENNE]

In another Cheyenne tale, the buffalo are villains instead of benevolent animals who give their flesh so that people may live.

Hundreds of years ago there was a girl who was very good at quillwork, so good that she was the best among all tribes everywhere. Her designs were radiant with color, and she could decorate anything—clothing, pouches, quivers, even tipis.

One day this girl sat down in her parents' lodge and began to make a man's outfit of white buckskin—war shirt, leggings, moccasins, gauntlets, everything. It took her weeks to embroider them with exquisite quillwork and fringes of buffalo hair marvellous to look at. Though her mother said nothing, she wondered. The girl had no brothers, nor was a young man courting her, so why was she making a man's outfit?

As if that wasn't strange enough, no sooner had she finished the first outfit than she began working on a second, then on a third. She worked all year until she had made and decorated seven complete sets of men's clothes, the last a very small one. The mother just watched and kept wondering. At last after the girl had finished the seventh outfit, she spoke to her mother. "Someplace, many days' walk from here, live seven brothers," she said. "Someday all the world will admire them. Since I am an only child, I want to take them for my brothers, and these clothes are for them."

"It is well, my daughter," her mother said. "I will go with you."

"This is too far for you to walk," said the girl.

"Then I will go part of the way," said her mother.

They loaded their strongest dogs with the seven bundles and set off toward the north. "You seem to know the way," said the mother.

"Yes. I don't know why, but I do," answered the daughter.

"And you seem to know all about those seven young men and what makes them stand out from ordinary humans."

"I know about them," said the girl, "though I don't know how."

Thus they walked, the girl seeming sure of herself. At last the mother said, "This is as far as I can go." They divided the dogs, the girl keeping two for her journey, and took leave of each other. Then the mother headed south back to her village and her husband, while the daughter continued walking into the north.

At last the daughter came to a lone, painted, and very large tipi which stood near a wide stream. The stream was shallow and she waded across it, calling: "It is I, the young-girl-looking-for-brothers, bringing gifts."

At that a small boy about ten years old came out of the tipi. "I am the youngest of seven brothers," he told the girl. "The others are out hunting buffalo, but they'll come back after a while. I have been expecting you. But you'll be a surprise to my brothers, because they don't have my special gifts of knowing and of 'No Touch.'"

"What is the gift of no touch?" asked the girl.

"Sometime you'll find out. Well, come into the tipi."

The girl gave the boy the smallest outfit, which fitted him perfectly and delighted him with its beautiful quillwork.

"I shall take you all for my brothers," the girl told him.

"And I am glad to have you for a sister," answered the boy.

The girl took all the other bundles off her two dogs' backs and told them to go back to her parents, and at once the dogs began trotting south.

Inside the tipi were seven beds of willow sticks and sage. The girl unpacked her bundles and put a war shirt, a pair of leggings, a pair of moccasins, and a pair of gauntlets upon each of the older brothers' beds. Then she gathered wood and built a fire. From her packs she took dried meat, dried chokecherries, and kidney fat, and cooked a meal for eight.

Toward evening just as the meal was ready, the six older brothers appeared laden with buffalo meat. The little boy ran outside the lodge and capered, kicking his heels and jumping up and down, showing off his quilled buckskin outfit.

"Where did you get these fine clothes?" the brothers asked.

"We have a new sister," said the child. "She's waiting inside, and she has clothes for you too. She does the most wonderful quillwork in the world. And she's beautiful herself!"

The brothers greeted the girl joyfully. They were struck with wonder at the white buckskin outfits she had brought as gifts for them. They were as glad to have a sister to care for as she was to have brothers to cook and make clothes for. Thus they lived happily.

One day after the older brothers had gone out to hunt, a light-colored buffalo calf appeared at the tipi and scratched and knocked with his hoof against the entrance flap. The boy came out and asked it what it wanted.

"I am sent by the buffalo nation," said the calf. "We have heard of your beautiful sister, and we want her for our own."

"You can't have her," answered the boy. "Go away."

"Oh well, then somebody bigger than I will come," said the calf and ran off jumping and kicking its heels.

The next day when the boy and the sister were alone again, a young heifer arrived, lowing and snorting, rattling the entrance flap of the tipi.

Once more the child came out to ask what she wanted.

"I am sent by the buffalo nation," said the heifer. "We want your beautiful sister for ourselves."

"You can't have her," said the boy. "Go away!"

"Then somebody bigger than I will come," said the heifer, galloping off like the calf before her.

On the third day a large buffalo cow, grunting loudly, appeared at the lodge. The boy came out and asked, "Big buffalo cow, what do you want?"

"I am sent by the buffalo nation," said the cow. "I have come to take your beautiful sister. We want her."

"You can't have her," said the boy. "Go away!"

"Somebody very big will come after me," said the buffalo cow, "and he won't come alone. He'll kill you if you don't give him your sister." With these words the cow trotted off.

On the fourth day the older brothers stayed home to protect the girl. The earth began to tremble a little, then to rock and heave. At last appeared the most gigantic buffalo bull in the world, much larger than any you see now. Behind him came the whole buffalo nation, making the earth shudder. Pawing the ground, the huge bull snorted and bellowed like thunder. The six older brothers, peering out through the entrance hole, were very much afraid, but the little boy stepped boldly outside. "Big, oversized buffalo bull, what do you want from us?" he asked.

"I want your sister," said the giant buffalo bull. "If you won't give her to me, I'll kill you all."

The boy called for his sister and older brothers to come out. Terrified, they did so.

"I'll take her now," growled the huge bull.

"No," said the boy, "she doesn't want to be taken. You can't have her. Go away!"

"In that case I'll kill you now," roared the giant bull. "I'm coming!"

"Quick, brother, use your special medicine!" the six older brothers cried to the youngest.

"I am using it," said he. "Now all of you, catch hold of the branches of this tree. Hurry!" He pointed to a tree growing by the tipi. The girl and the six brothers jumped up into its branches. The boy took his bow and swiftly shot an arrow into the tree's trunk, then clasped the trunk tightly himself. At once the tree started to grow, shooting up into the sky in no time at all. It all happened much, much quicker than it can be told.

The brothers and the girl were lifted up in the tree branches, out of reach of the buffalo. They watched the herd of angry animals grunting and snorting, milling around the tree far below.

"I'll chop the tree down with my horns!" roared the giant buffalo. He charged the tree, which shook like a willow and swayed back and forth. Trying not to fall off, the girl and the brothers clutched the branches. The big bull had gouged a large piece of wood from the trunk.

The little boy said, "I'd better use one more arrow." He shot an arrow high into the treetop, and again the tree grew, shooting up another thousand feet or so, while the seven brothers and the girl rose with it.

The giant buffalo bull made his second charge. Again his horns stabbed into the tree and splintered wood far and wide. The gash in the trunk had become larger.

The boy said, "I must shoot another arrow." He did, hitting the treetop again, and quick as a flash the tree rose another thousand feet.

A third time the bull charged, rocking the tree, making it sway from side to side so that the brothers and the girl almost tumbled out of their branches. They cried to the boy to save them. The child shot a fourth arrow into the tree, which rose again so that the seven young men and the girl disappeared into the clouds. The gash in the tree trunk had become dangerously large.

"When that bull charges again, he will shatter this tree," said the girl. "Little brother, help us!"

Just as the bull charged for the fourth time, the child loosed the single arrow he had left, and the tree rose above the clouds.

"Quick, step out right on the clouds. Hurry!" cried the little boy. "Don't be afraid!"

The bull's head hit the tree trunk with a fearful impact. His horns cut the trunk in two, but just as the tree slowly began to topple, the seven brothers and the girl stepped off its branches and into the sky.

There the eight of them stood. "Little brother, what will become of us now? We can never return to earth; we're up too high. What shall we do?"

"Don't grieve," said the little boy, "I'll turn all of us into stars."

At once the seven brothers and the girl were bathed in radiant light. They formed themselves into what the white men call the big dipper. You can see them there now. The brightest star is the beautiful girl, who is filling the sky with glimmering quillwork, and the star twinkling at the very end of the dipper's handle is the little boy. Can you see him?

—*Told by one of the Strange Owl family in Birney,*
Montana, 1972, and recorded by Richard Erdoes.

■

ROLLING HEAD

■

[WINTU]

Among the Wintu a menstruating woman was considered unclean,
but at the same time she was recognized as having extraordinary
magical powers which she could use to harm others, purposely or
not. Proper rituals were needed to prevent disaster and to restore her.

■ |||||||||||||||||||||||||||||||||||||||||||||||||||||||||||||||||||||||||||||||||||||| ■

Long ago there was a village filled with people. They lived in the flat-lands on both the west and the east sides of the river. The younger of the chief's two daughters had just reached puberty, and her parents were planning to call a puberty dance.

In the evening the father spoke to the other women. "Early in the morning go strip bark for a maple-bark apron," he said. "But don't take my younger daughter with you. Go secretly."

So the women got up very early and stole away. Quite far north they went, and some even climbed uphill and crossed the ridge to the north.

Later the girl who had reached puberty woke up and, though it was forbidden, followed the others. When she reached them, they were stripping bark. She went up to them and began cutting maple bark too.

All at once she struck her little finger with a splinter. Her older sister came up to her and wiped the blood with dead leaves. The other women said, "When will it leave off? The blood cannot stop flowing." Afraid of what had happened, they ran back to the village. They reached the house and told the father, "She got stuck with a splinter while stripping bark." And the old man said, "She doesn't listen to me."

The girl and her older sister were left behind alone. The younger one, who stood downhill to the north, now sucked blood and spat it out. Then more blood came, and though she sucked and sucked, she could not stop the flow. Meanwhile the sun began to set. She kept on sucking until early evening, unable to help herself. Suddenly she happened to swallow blood and smelled the fat. It tasted sweet. So she ate her little finger, and then ate her whole hand. Then devoured both her hands. Then she ate her leg, ate both her legs. Then she ate up her whole body. Then her head alone was left. It went rolling over the ground, with her sister still beside her.

In the village the chief said, "From the north she'll come. Put on your clothes, people. Get your weapons. We must go." And the people dressed themselves and got their weapons. And from the north they saw her come, rolling toward her father's house. She arrived in the early evening and lay there. After she had rested a while, she bounced up to the west across the river to the flat on the west, where she threw the people into her mouth. Without stopping, she turned the village upside down as she devoured them all. Then she fell to the east across the river and lay there, and the next morning she threw the people who lived on the eastern flat into her mouth and ate them, devoured them all. Only her eldest sister she left for a while. And she went about the world, and when she saw people, she threw them into her mouth and ate them. Each evening she came home, each morning she went about the world looking for people. Always she went searching.

One day she climbed up to the northern edge of the sky and looked all over the world, but she saw no one. So in the evening she came home, and the next morning she got up and threw her sister into her mouth. Then she went on her way until she reached the edge of a big creek which she did not know how to cross. A man was sitting on the other side. She called to him, and he threw a bridge over. She was crossing, and when she had gone halfway he jerked it, and it went down at Talat. And she fell into the river, and a riffle pike jumped and swallowed her. And it is finished. That is all.

—Based on a myth reported by Cora DuBois and
Dorothy Demetracopoulou in 1931.

■

SON OF LIGHT
KILLS THE MONSTER

■

[HOPI]

■ |||||||||||||||||||||||||||||||||||||||||||||||||||||||||||||||||||| ■

Man-Eagle, a frightful monster, had laid waste to the whole country. With his sharp talons he seized women and girls, wives and maidens. He flew off with them to his home above the clouds, where he abused them for four nights before eating them up.

Among those abducted by Man-Eagle was the young wife of Son of

Light. Within hours this hero was on their trail, and along the way he met the Piñon Maidens, dressed in grass and piñon bark. With them were Spider Woman and Mole.

"Where are you going?" these spirit people asked Son of Light. "Man-Eagle has stolen my wife," he answered. "I am going to rescue her, but I have to get there in a hurry before he kills her."

"This is bad," said Spider Woman, "but never fear, I'll help you." And to the Piñon Maidens she said: "You girls gather piñon resin and shape it into a copy of Man-Eagle's flint-arrowhead shirt that no weapon can penetrate. Be quick."

The Piñon Maidens gathered the resin and made a shirt exactly like Man-Eagle's, and when they had finished it, Spider Woman sprinkled sacred corn pollen over it and chanted an invocation. Then she turned herself into a tiny spider no bigger than a grain of salt and crawled up on Son of Light's right ear. "Here I am," she said, "Where I can tell you what to do if you get into trouble. The next step is up to Mole."

Mole burrowed a passage through the mountain up to the top so that Son of Light could get to the summit without being seen. When they came out onto the mountaintop, they saw that they were still far below Man-Eagle's home in the clouds. Spider Woman said, "I'll call some good birds to help us."

The first to answer her call was the spotted eagle. Son of Light, Mole, and Spider Woman climbed onto his back, and he spread his wings and began circling upwards. Higher and higher he flew, until at last he was exhausted. "I can go no farther," he said.

Spider Woman then called on the hawk, who came at once, flying wing tip to wing tip with the spotted eagle. Mole and Son of Light, with Spider Woman still perched on his right ear, walked over the wings onto the hawk's back. The hawk carried them higher, but after a while his strength gave out too. "This is as high as I can go," he said.

Spider Woman called for the gray hawk to take over. Again Son of Light, Mole, and Spider Woman changed birds, and the gray hawk flew up higher than the others. Still it was not high enough, and the three friends transferred to the back of the red hawk, best of all fliers.

The red hawk flew through a hole in the clouds right to the white house that was the home of Man-Eagle. Thanking the red hawk for carrying them so far, Son of Light, Spider Woman, and Mole got down and walked boldly up to the house.

"Look at the ladder to the entrance," said Spider Woman to Son of Light. "Its rungs are sharp obsidian knives. They'll cut your fingers off if you try to get up there."

"What shall we do?" asked Son of Light.

"Go pick some sumac berries," Spider Woman said. Son of Light gathered the berries and returned to her. "Now feed them to Horned Toad over there," she said.

Son of Light popped the berries into the wide mouth of Horned Toad, who chewed them into a gooey paste which he spit into the palm of Son of Light's hand.

"Now smear what Horned Toad has given you on the sharp edges of the rungs," Spider Woman told him. As Son of Light smeared the edges, they immediately became blunt so that he could climb up without having his fingers cut off. Spider Woman was still behind his right ear, while little Mole had buried himself in Son of Light's hair. With his two hidden companions, Son of Light stepped inside Man-Eagle's home.

The first thing he saw was Man-Eagle's magic flint-arrowhead shirt hanging from a viga. Quick as a flash Son of Light hung the counterfeit shirt on that rafter and put the real shirt on. They were so alike that not even Son of Light could tell them apart. He went into the second room and found his wife, her hands tied behind her back.

"I've come to free you," he told her.

"Flee!" she cried. "Run quickly! No one who enters here ever leaves alive."

"Don't be afraid," he answered, untying her hands. "We'll come out of here alive and happy."

Man-Eagle was asleep in the next room, but Spider Woman was carrying a "hear nothing" charm which prevented their noise from reaching his ears. Unaware that strangers were in his house, he awoke and put on his flint-arrow shirt, then went into the next room. "Now I will enjoy the beautiful girl," he thought, but instead found himself face to face with Son of Light. "Who are you?" asked Man-Eagle. "How dare you come here!"

"You have stolen my wife, and I am taking her back now."

"Maybe you will, and maybe you won't," said Man-Eagle. "You're speaking big words, but first you'll have a contest with me."

"What kind of contest?" inquired Son of Light.

"A smoking contest," said Man-Eagle. The monster brought out a huge pipe, as long as a good-sized man, and filled it with tobacco. "We will both smoke this," he told Son of Light, "and whoever weakens and faints is the loser. If you lose, I have the right to kill you and possess your wife. If you win, you can take her back."

Now, Man-Eagle's magic tobacco was poisonous enough to stun anyone who was not used to it, though it no longer had an effect on him. But while Man-Eagle explained the rules of the contest, Mole quickly burrowed a hole in the floor underneath the spot on which Son of Light was sitting. Mole made a passage all the way down through the earth to the outside, and as the man and the monster puffed away, the smoke passed right through Son of Light and through the hole into the outside air. The two smoked and smoked, until Man-Eagle got dizzy from his own magic tobacco and had to stop. Son of Light, on the other hand, was unaffected.

Filled to the bursting point with smoke, Man-Eagle stepped outside the house to clear his head. Son of Light followed, and they both saw dense clouds of smoke covering the whole sky. "I wonder how he did it," thought Man-Eagle. Aloud he said: "Well, you win this contest, but this is only the first. Now comes the second."

Man-Eagle brought forth two huge elk antlers. "Take this one," he told Son of Light, "and I'll take the other. Each of us will try and break his own in two. If you fail to break yours with your hands, I shall kill you and possess your wife."

The antler that Man-Eagle had given his rival was actually a magical piece of stone—the hardest stone in the world. The antler that Man-Eagle had kept for himself was a false antler made of brittle wood.

Quick as a flash just before the contest began, Spider Woman exchanged the two elk antlers. She did it with such lightning speed that not even the eye of Man-Eagle could follow her. The rivals took up their antlers, and Son of Light broke his easily, but Man-Eagle could not break his however hard he tried. "I wonder how he did that," thought the monster. He was not so sure of himself now.

"Well, this was just child's play, something to warm us up," said Man-Eagle. "Now for our third contest."

"What is it this time?" asked Son of Light.

"Step outside with me," said Man-Eagle. They went out, and the monster pointed to two huge pine trees near his house. "You choose one of these trees and I will choose the other, and he who fails to pull his tree up by the roots loses the contest. If I win, I'll kill you and possess your wife."

"So be it," answered Son of Light.

Man-Eagle chose the tree which he thought had the shallower roots. "Remember," he told Son of Light, "if you fail to pull up your tree—trunk, branches, roots, and all—you lose, no matter what I do."

During these preparations, Mole had burrowed underneath Son of Light's tree and gnawed through all the roots. Son of Light pulled it up easily, while Man-Eagle could not uproot his. "It pleased me to let you win once more," he told Son of Light, "but you must win the fourth and last contest." To himself he said: "I wonder how he did it. This young man is really strong."

"What do you propose?" asked Son of Light.

"Watch me," answered Man-Eagle. He began carrying into his biggest room heaps of food—meat of all kinds, *piki* bread and cornbread of all kinds, mush and gruel of all kinds, squash and bean dishes of all kinds—baskets, pots, cups, and dippers full of food. Making two mountains of it all, he told Son of Light: "This is your heap and that over there is mine. You must eat your heap all at once, without leaving a single scrap. If you can't do it, I'll kill you and possess your wife." "I'm sure to win this one," Man-eagle said to himself. "The young man is puny compared with me; he can't absorb all this food."

Again Mole had dug a tunnel underneath Son of Light. As quickly as Son of Light emptied a dish, the food passed through him and through the tunnel to some place outside the house. In no time Son of Light had eaten the whole mountain of meat, corn, squash, beans, *piki*, and mush. Man-Eagle tried to match him dish for dish, but could not.

"Well," said Son of Light, "Now I'll take my wife and go home."

"Not quite yet," said Man-Eagle. "In the end it comes down to this: Which of us is invulnerable? Which of us can withstand the flames of a mighty fire? I can. Can you? We shall see."

Man-Eagle made two huge piles of dry wood. "You sit on this one, and I'll sit on that," he said. "Your wife can set fire to them once we're in position. If you can withstand the fire, then I'll do whatever you say."

"Now," thought Man-Eagle, "I can get rid of this upstart. My magic flint-arrowhead shirt is fireproof, but the young fellow will burn up."

Son of Light's wife set fire to the two woodpiles. Of course, son of Light was wearing the real magic flint-arrowhead shirt. Coated with ice, clear and cold like crystal, it protected him from the flames. In the process part of the ice melted and extinguished the fire. But the shirt of Man-Eagle made out of resin, ignited in a flash which so thoroughly consumed Man-Eagle that only his ashes remained.

Then Spider Woman whispered into Son of Light's ear: "Take this wonderful medicine of mine in your mouth and spurt it all over Man-Eagle's ashes."

Son of Light did what Spider Woman said, and as he spat the medicine over the ashes, Man-Eagle arose, transformed into a good-looking man.

Spider Woman addressed this eagle turned into a man: "Have you learned your lesson? Will you stop killing and eating people? Will you stop stealing and abusing wives and maidens? Will you promise?"

Eagle-turned-into-Man said: "I promise. I will never do evil again, never."

Son of Light joyfully claimed his wife, while Spider Woman brought all the Hopi people whom Man-Eagle had killed back to life again. Then they all got on the backs of the eagle, hawk, gray hawk, and red hawk, and these friendly birds carried them safely back to their homes.

—Retold from various nineteenth-century versions.

THE COMING OF THUNDER

[MIWOK]

Bear's sister-in-law, Deer, had two beautiful fawn daughters. Bear was a horrible, wicked woman, and she wanted the fawns for herself. So this is what she did.

One day she invited Deer to accompany her when she went to pick clover. The two fawns remained at home. While resting during the day after having gathered much clover, Bear offered to pick lice from Deer's head. While doing so she watched her chance, took Deer unaware, and bit her neck so hard that she killed her. Then she devoured her, all except the liver. This she placed in the bottom of a basket filled with clover, and took it home. She gave the basket of clover to the fawns to eat.

When they asked where their mother was, she replied, "She will come soon. You know she's always slow and takes her time in coming home."

So the fawns ate the clover, but when they reached the bottom of the basket, they discovered the liver. Then they knew their aunt had killed their mother.

"We had better watch out, or she will kill us too," they said to one another.

They decided to run away and go to their grandfather. So the next day when Bear was out, they got together all the baskets and awls which belonged to Deer and departed. They left one basket, however, in the house.

When Bear returned and found the Fawns missing, she hunted for their tracks and set out after them. After she had trailed them a short distance, the basket they had left at home whistled. Bear ran back to the house, thinking the fawns had returned. But she could not find them and so set out again, following their tracks.

The fawns meanwhile had proceeded on their journey, throwing awls and baskets in different directions. These awls and baskets whistled. Each time she heard them, Bear thought that the fawns were whistling, and she left the trail in search of them. And each time that Bear was fooled in this manner, she became angrier and angrier.

She shouted in her anger: "Those girls are making a fool of me. When I capture them, I'll eat them."

The awls only whistled in response, and Bear ran toward the sound. No one was there.

Finally, the fawns, far ahead of Bear, came to the river. On the opposite side they saw Daddy Longlegs. They asked him to stretch his leg across the river so that they could cross safely, because Bear had killed their mother and they were fleeing from her. He did, and when Bear at last came to the river, Daddy Longlegs stretched his leg over again.

But just as the wicked aunt of the two fawns, walking on his leg, reached the middle of the river, Daddy Longlegs gave his leg a sudden twitch and threw her into the water.

However, Bear did not drown. She managed to swim to shore, where she again started in pursuit of the fawns. But the fawns were far ahead of their aunt and soon reached their grandfather's house. Their grandfather was Lizard. They told him of the terrible fate which had overtaken their mother.

"Where is Bear?" he asked them.

"She is following us and will soon be here," they replied.

Upon hearing this, Lizard threw two large white stones into the fire and heated them. When Bear arrived outside Lizard's house, she could not find an entrance. She asked Lizard how she should come in, and he told her that the only entrance was through the smoke hole. She must climb on the roof and enter that way, he said, and when she did, she must close her eyes tightly and open her mouth wide.

Bear followed these instructions, for Lizard had told her that the two fawns were in his house. As Bear entered, eyes closed and mouth open, Lizard took the red-hot stones from the fire and thrust them down her throat. Bear rolled from the top of Lizard's house and landed on the ground dead.

Lizard skinned her and dressed her hide, after which he cut it in two pieces, one large and one small. The larger piece he gave to the older fawn, the smaller piece to the younger. Then Lizard instructed the girls to run about and see what kind of noise was made by Bear's skin. The girls proceeded to run, and the pieces of skin crackled loudly. Lizard, watching them, laughed and said to himself, "The girls are all right. They are Thunders. I think I had better send them up to the sky."

When the fawns came to Lizard to tell him that they were going to return home, he said, "Don't go home. I have a good place for you in the sky."

So the girls went to the sky, and Lizard could hear them running about up there. Their aunt's skin, which they had kept, makes the loud noises that we call thunder. Whenever the fawn girls (Thunders, as Lizard called them) run around in the sky, rain and hail fall.

—*Reported by Edward W. Gifford in 1930.*

The Miwok were master basket makers and had elaborate containers used in gathering and leaching acorns, transporting other food and goods, and in many other facets of their daily life. When the fawns fled from their aunt, therefore, they would naturally be sure to take with them not just their valuable baskets but the awls with which they fashioned the coils from which they wove and decorated them.

■

WAKINYAN TANKA, THE GREAT THUNDERBIRD

■

[BRULE SIOUX]

John (Fire) Lame Deer, a Sioux medicine man, was about seventy when he told this tale and like "A Legend of Devil's Tower" it bears the hallmarks of his own crusty, evocative vision.

■ |||||||||||||||||||||||||||||||||||||||||||||||||||||||||||||||||||||||||||||||| ■

Wakinyan Tanka, the great thunderbird, lives in his tipi on top of a high mountain in the sacred Paha Sapa, the Black Hills. The whites call it Harney Peak, but I don't think he lives there anymore since the *wasichu*, the whites, have made these hills into a vast Disneyland. No,

I think the thunder beings have retreated to the farthest end of the earth, where the sun goes down, where there are no tourists and hot-dog stands.

The Wakinyan hates all that is dirty. He loves what is clean and pure. His voice is the great thunderclap, and the smaller rolling thunders that follow his booming shouts are the cries of his children, the little thunderbirds. Four paths lead to the mountain on which the Wakinyan dwell. A butterfly guards the entrance at the East side. A Bear guards the West, a Deer the North, and a beaver the South.

There are four large, old Thunderbirds. The Great Wakinyan of the West is the first and foremost among them. He is clothed in clouds. His body has no form, but he has giant, four-jointed wings. He has no feet, but enormous claws. He has no head, but a huge, sharp beak with rows of big, pointed teeth. His color is black.

The second Wakinyan of the North is red. The third Thunderbird of the East is yellow. The fourth hunderbird of the South is white, though there are some who say that its colors are blue. That one has no eyes or ears, yet he can see and hear. How that can be is a mystery. From time to time a holy man catches a glimpse of a Wakinyan in his dreams, but always only a part of it. No one sees the Thunderbird whole, not even in a vision, so the way we think a Thunderbird looks is pieced together from many dreams and visions.

The Great Wakinyan's tipi stands beside the tallest of all cedar trees. That's why we use its foliage for the "cedaring," the "smoking up," in our ceremonies which call for sweet-smelling incense to purify our houses and ourselves. Inside the Wakinyan's tipi is a nest made of dry bones. In it lies the giant egg from which the little thunderbirds are hatched. The egg is bigger than the whole state of South Dakota.

You cannot see the Wakinyan because they are wrapped in robes of dark clouds, but you can feel their presence. I have often felt it. During a vision quest they may come and try to frighten you, to see whether you have enough courage to go through your "crying for a dream"— your four days and nights of fasting and listening and staying awake on top of a lonely hill. They test you this way, but the Wakinyan are good spirits. They like to help the people, even if they scare you sometimes.

Everything in nature moves in a certain way that whites call clockwise. Only the thunder beings move in a contrary manner—counterclockwise. That's their way; they do everything differently. That's why, if you dream of the Wakinyan, you become a *heyoka*: an upside-down, hot-cold, forward-backward man. This gives you power, but you don't want to stay a *heyoka* for long, so we have a ceremony through which you can become your old self again.

The Wakinyan's symbol is the zig-zag lightning, forked at the ends, which I use in some of my rituals. It's a design I like and to which I feel in some way related, because a *heyoka* is also a sacred clown, and there is some of that clown nature within me.

The thunder beings are guardians of the truth. When you're holding thesacred pipe and you swear on it, you can say nothing but the truth. If you lie, the Wakinyan will kill you with their lightning bolts.

So thunderbirds stand for rain, and fire, and the truth, and as I said before, they like to help the people. In contrast, Unktehi, the great water monster, did not like human beings from the time they were put on this earth. Unktehi was shaped like a giant scaly snake with feet. She had a huge horn coming out of the top of her head, and she filled the whole of the Missouri River from end to end. The little water monsters, who lived in smaller streams and lakes, likewise had no use for humans.

"What are these tiny, lice-like creatures crawling all over the place?" they asked. "What are these blood-clot people creeping out of the red pipestone? We don't want them around!"

The Great Unktehi could place her body and puff it up in such a way that it made the great Missouri overflow, and her children, the little water monsters, did the same with their streams and lakes. So they caused a great flood that spread over the whole country, killing most of the people. Only a few escaped to the top of the highest mountain, and even there the waves threatened to sweep them off.

Then the great thunderbird spoke: "What's to be done? I like these humans. They respect us; they pray to us. If they dream of us, they get a little of our power, and that makes them relatives of ours, in a way. Even though they are small, helpless, and pitiful, Grandfather put them on this earth for some purpose. We must save them from Unktehi!"

Then began the great battle between the thunderbirds and the evil water monsters. It lasted many years, during which the earth trembled and the waters burst forth in mighty torrents, while the night was like day because of the flashes of lightning. The Wakinyan have no bodies as we imagine them—no limbs or hands or feet—but they have enormous claws. They have no mouths, but they have big, sharp teeth. They have no eyes, but lightning bolts somehow shoot out of the eyes which are not there. This is hard to explain to a *wasichu*.

The Wakinyan used their claws, their teeth, their lightning to fight the water monsters. The Wakinyan Tanka grappled with the Great Unktehi and the little thunder children were pitted against the smaller water monsters. The battle was not only long but desperate, for the Unktehi had spikes at the tip of their powerful tails that could gouge out fearful wounds as they roared and thrashed.

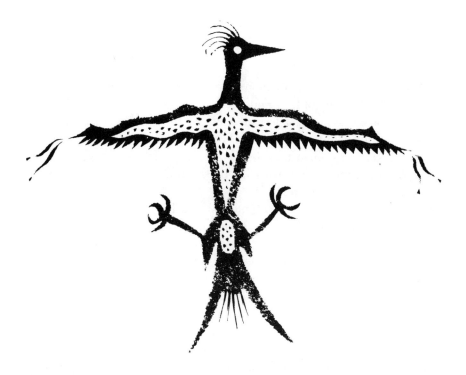

At last the Wakinyan Tanka called to the little thunderbirds: "My children, the Unktehi are winning. This close body-to-body fighting favors them!"

All the thunder beings retreated to the top of their sacred mountain and took council together. The Great Wakinyan said: "Our country is the air. Our power comes from the sky. It was wrong to fight the Unktehi on their own ground, on the earth and in the water where they are all-powerful. Come, my children, follow me!"

Then all the thunderbirds flew up into the sky. "When I give the signal," said the Wakinyan Tanka, "let's use our lightning and thunderbolts together!"

So the thunder beings shot off all their bolts at the same instant. The forests were set on fire, and flames consumed everything except the top of the rock on which the humans had taken refuge. The waters boiled and then dried up. The earth glowed red-hot, and the Unktehi, big and small, burned up and died, leaving only their dried bones in the Mako Sicha, the Badlands, where their bones turned to rock.

Until then the Unktehi had represented the water power, and now this power was taken by the Thunderbirds. And the few humans who survived climbed down from their high rock, praising the Wakinyan for saving them. These few again peopled the earth, and all was well. The battle and the victory of the Wakinyan took place in the first of the great four ages—the age of Tunka, the Rock.

When I was young, hardly more than a boy, I went after some horses which had somehow got lost. Following their tracks into the Badlands, I searched for many hours. I lost all sense of time and was surprised by nightfall, sudden and pitch-black. The clouds that were covering the moon and stars split open in a thunderstorm. Hailstones as big as moth-balls blanketed the ground with icy mush, and I thought that I might freeze to death in the summer.

I happened to be in a narrow gulch, where I was in danger of drowning from the rush of water. As best I could, I began scrambling up toward a high ridge. I couldn't see except when there was a flash of lightning, and the earth was crumbling under me. Somehow I made it.

The thunder never stopped, and the lightning became almost continuous. I could smell the *wakangeli*, the electricity, all around; it made my hair stand up. The thunder was deafening. I straddled the ridge as if I were riding a horse. I could see enough in the lightning to know that I was very high up and the canyon was a long way down, and I was afraid of being blown off the ridge and hurled into that black nothingness. My teeth chattering, my legs and hands clamped to the razorback ridge, I moved inch by inch as I tried to get out of there.

But I felt the presence of the Wakinyan, heard them talking to me through the thunder: "Don't be afraid! Hold on! You'll be all right."

At last the storm ended, and finally dawn came. Then I saw that I was straddling a long row of petrified bones, the biggest I had ever seen. I had been moving along the spine of the Great Unktehi. Stiff with cold, I waited until the sun warmed me. Then I scrambled down and ran toward home. I forgot all about the horses; I never found them. And I searched many times for the ridge deep inside the Badlands that formed Unktehi's spine. I wanted to show it to my friends, but I never found the ridge either.

—*Told by Lame Deer in 1969 in Winner, Rosebud*
Indian Reservation, South Dakota, and recorded by
Richard Erdoes.

COYOTE KILLS THE GIANT

[FLATHEAD]

Coyote was walking one day when he met Old Woman. She greeted him and asked where he was headed.

"Just roaming around," said Coyote.

"You better stop going that way, or you'll meet a giant who kills everybody."

"Oh, giants don't frighten me," said Coyote (who had never met one). "I always kill them. I'll fight this one too, and make an end of him."

"He's bigger and closer than you think," said Old Woman.

"I don't care," said Coyote, deciding that a giant would be about as big as a bull moose and calculating that he could kill one easily.

So Coyote said good-bye to Old Woman and went ahead, whistling a tune. On his way he saw a large fallen branch that looked like a club. Picking it up, he said to himself, "I'll hit the giant over the head with this. It's big enough and heavy enough to kill him." He walked on and came to a huge cave right in the middle of the path. Whistling merrily, he went in.

Suddenly Coyote met a woman who was crawling along on the ground. "What's the matter?" he asked.

"I'm starving," she said, "and too weak to walk. What are you doing with that stick?"

"I'm going to kill the giant with it," said Coyote, and he asked if she knew where he was hiding.

Feeble as she was, the woman laughed. "You're already in the giant's belly."

"How can I be in his belly?" asked Coyote. "I haven't even met him."

"You probably thought it was a cave when you walked into his mouth," the woman said, and sighed. "It's easy to walk in, but nobody ever walks out. This giant is so big you can't take him in with your eyes. His belly fills a whole valley."

Coyote threw his stick away and kept on walking. What else could he do? Soon he came across some more people lying around half dead. "Are you sick?" he asked.

"No," they said, "just starving to death. We're trapped inside the giant."

"You're foolish," said Coyote. "If we're really inside this giant, then the cave walls must be the inside of his stomach. We can just cut some meat and fat from him."

"We never thought of that," they said.

"You're not as smart as I am," said Coyote.

Coyote took his hunting knife and started cutting chunks out of the cave walls. As he had guessed, they were indeed the giant's fat and meat, and he used it to feed the starving people. He even went back and gave some meat to the woman he had met first. Then all the people imprisoned in the giant's belly started to feel stronger and happier, but not completely happy. "You've fed us," they said, "and thanks. But how are we going to get out of here?"

"Don't worry," said Coyote. "I'll kill the giant by stabbing him in the heart. Where is his heart? It must be around here someplace."

"Look at the volcano puffing and beating over there," someone said. "Maybe it's the heart."

"So it is, friend," said Coyote, and began to cut at this mountain.

Then the giant spoke up. "Is that you, Coyote? I've heard of you. Stop this stabbing and cutting and let me alone. You can leave through my mouth; I'll open it for you."

"I'll leave, but not quite yet," said Coyote, hacking at the heart. He told the others to get ready. "As soon as I have him in his death throes, there will be an earthquake. He'll open his jaw to take a last breath, and then his mouth will close forever. So be ready to run out fast!"

Coyote cut a deep hole in the giant's heart, and lava started to flow out. It was the giant's blood. The giant groaned, and the ground under the people's feet trembled.

"Quick, now!" shouted Coyote. The giant's mouth opened and they all ran out. The last one was the wood tick. The giant's teeth were closing on him, but Coyote managed to pull him through at the last moment.

"Look at me," cried the wood tick, "I'm all flat!"

"It happened when I pulled you through," said Coyote. "You'll always be flat from now on. Be glad you're alive."

"I guess I'll get used to it," said the wood tick, and he did.

—Based on a tale reported by Louisa McDermott in 1901.

A LEGEND OF DEVIL'S TOWER

[SIOUX]

This is another characteristically tongue-in-cheek tale from Lame Deer.

Out of the plains of Wyoming rises Devil's Tower. It is really a rock, visible for a hundred miles around, an immense cone of basalt which seems to touch the clouds. It sticks out of the flat prairie as if someone had pushed it up from underground.

Of course, Devil's Tower is a white man's name. We have no devil in our beliefs and got along well all these many centuries without him. You people invented the devil and, as far as I am concerned, you can keep him. But everybody these days knows that towering rock by this name, so Devil's Tower it is. No use telling you its Indian name. Most tribes call it Bear Rock. There is a reason for that—if you see it, you will notice on its sheer sides many, many streaks and gashes running straight up and down, like scratches made by giant claws.

Well, long, long ago, two young Indian boys found themselves lost in the prairie. You know how it is. They had played shinny ball and whacked it a few hundred yards out of the village. And then they had shot their toy bows still farther out into the sagebrush. And then they had heard a small animal make a noise and had gone to investigate. They had come to a stream with many colorful pebbles and followed that for a while. They had come to a hill and wanted to see what was on the other side. On the other side they saw a herd of antelope and, of course, had to track them for a while. When they got hungry and thought it was time to go home, the two boys found that they didn't know where they were. They started off in the direction where they thought their village was, but only got farther and farther away from it. At last they curled up beneath a tree and went to sleep.

They got up the next morning and walked some more, still headed the wrong way. They ate some wild berries and dug up wild turnips, found some chokecherries, and drank water from streams. For three days they walked toward the west. They were footsore, but they survived. Oh, how they wished that their parents, or aunts and uncles, or elder brothers and sisters would find them. But nobody did.

On the fourth day the boys suddenly had a feeling that they were being followed. The looked around and in the distance saw Mato, the bear. This was no ordinary bear, but a giant grizzly so huge that the two boys would make only a small mouthful for him, but he had smelled the boys and wanted that mouthful. He kept coming close, and the earth trembled as he gathered speed.

The boys started running, looking for a place to hide, but there was no such place and the grizzly was much, much faster than they. They stumbled, and the bear was almost upon them. They could see his red, wide-open jaws full of enormous, wicked teeth. They could smell his hot, evil breath.

The boys were old enough to have learned to pray, and they called upon Wakan Tanka, the Creator: "Tunkashila, Grandfather, have pity, save us."

All at once the earth shook and began to rise. The boys rose with it. Out of the earth came a cone of rock going up, up, up until it was more than a thousand feet high. And the boys were on top of it.

Mato the bear was disappointed to see his meal disappearing into the clouds. Have I said he was a giant bear? This grizzly was so huge that he could almost reach to the top of the rock when he stood on his hind legs. Almost, but not quite. His claws were as large as a tipi's lodge poles. Frantically Mato dug his claws into the side of the rock, trying to get up, trying to get those boys. As he did so, he made big scratches in the sides of the towering rock. But the stone was too slippery; Mato could not get up. He tried every spot, every side. He scratched up the rock all around, but it was no use. The boys watched him wearing himself out, getting tired, giving up. They finally saw him going away, a huge, growling, grunting mountain of fur disappearing over the horizon.

The boys were saved. Or were they? How were they to get down? They were humans, not birds who could fly. Some ten years ago, mountain climbers tried to conquer Devil's Tower. They had ropes, and iron hooks called pitons to nail themselves to the rock face, and they managed to get up. But they couldn't get down. They were marooned on that giant basalt cone, and they had to be taken off in a helicopter.

In the long-ago days the Indians had no helicopters. So how did the two boys get down? The legend does not tell us, but we can be sure that the Great Spirit didn't save those boys only to let them perish of hunger and thirst on the top of the rock.

Well, Wanblee, the eagle, has always been a friend to our people. So it must have been the eagle that let the boys grab hold of him and carried them safely back to their village. Or do you know another way?

—Told by Lame Deer in Winner, Rosebud Sioux Indian
Reservation, South Dakota, 1969, and recorded by
Richard Erdoes.

■

THE FLYING HEAD

■

[IROQUOIS]

■ ▦▦▦▦▦▦▦▦▦▦▦▦▦▦▦▦▦▦▦▦▦▦▦▦ ■

In days long past, evil monsters and spirits preyed upon humans. As long as the sun was shining, the monsters hid unseen in deep caves, but on stormy nights they came out of their dens and prowled the earth. The most terrible of all was the great Flying Head. Though only a scowling, snarling head without a body, it was four times as tall as the tallest man. Its skin was so thick and matted with hair that no weapon could penetrate it. Two huge bird wings grew from either side of its cheeks, and with them it could soar into the sky or dive down, floating, like a buzzard. Instead of teeth, the Flying Head had a mouth full of huge, piercing fangs with which it seized and devoured its prey. And everything was prey to this monster, every living being, including people.

One dark night a young woman alone with her baby was sitting in a longhouse. Everybody had fled and hidden, because someone had seen the great Flying Head darting among the treetops of the forest. The young mother had not run away because, as she said to herself, "Someone must make a stand against this monster. It might as well be me." So she sat by the hearth, building a big fire, heating in the flames a number of large, red-hot, glowing stones.

She sat waiting and watching, until suddenly the Flying Head appeared in the door. Grinning horribly, it looked into the longhouse, but she pretended not to see it and acted as if she were cooking a meal. She made believe that she was eating some of the red-hot rocks, picking them up with a forked stick and seeming to put them into her mouth. (In reality she passed them behind her face and dropped them on the ground.) All the while she was smacking her lips, exclaiming: "Ah, how good this is! What wonderful food! Never has anyone feasted on meat like this!"

Hearing her, the monster could not restrain itself. It thrust its head deep inside the lodge, opened its jaws wide, and seized and swallowed in one mighty gulp the whole heap of glowing, hissing rocks. As soon as it had swallowed, the monster uttered a terrible cry which echoed throughout the land. With wings flapping the great Flying Head fled screaming, screaming, screaming over mountains, streams and forest, screaming so that the biggest trees were shaking, screaming until the earth trembled, screaming until the leaves fell from the branches. At last the screams were fading away in the distance, fading, fading, until at last they could no longer be heard. Then the people everywhere could take their hands from their ears and breathe safely. After that the Flying Head was never seen again, and nobody knows what became of it.

—Retold from a 1902 tale.

THE FIRST SHIP

[CHINOOK]

In this curious tale, obviously based on an actual incident, the Indians consider the Wasichu, the white men, as monstrous as any ogres or demons.

An old woman in a Clatsop village near the mouth of Big River mourned the death of her son. For a year she grieved. One day she stopped her crying and took a walk along the beach where she had often gone in happier days.

As she was returning to the village, she saw a strange something out in the water not far from shore. At first she thought it was a whale. When she came nearer, she saw two spruce trees standing upright on it.

"It's not a whale," she said to herself, "it's a monster."

When she came near the strange thing that lay at the edge of the water, she saw that its outside was covered with copper and that ropes were tied to the spruce trees. Then a bear came out of the strange thing and stood on it. It looked like a bear, but the face was the face of a human being.

"Oh, my son is dead," she wailed, "and now the thing we have heard about is on our shore."

Weeping, the old woman returned to her village. People who heard her called to others, "An old woman is crying. Someone must have struck her."

The men picked up their bows and arrows and rushed out to see what was the matter.

"Listen!" an old man said.

They heard the woman wailing, "Oh, my son is dead, and the thing we have heard about is on our shore."

All the people ran to meet her. "What is it? Where is it?" they asked.

"Ah, the thing we have heard about in tales is lying over there." She pointed toward the south shore of the village. "There are two bears on it, or maybe they are people."

Then the Indians ran toward the thing that lay near the edge of the water. The two creatures on it held copper kettles in their hands. When the Clatsop arrived at the beach, the creatures put their hands to their mouths and asked for water.

Two of the Indians ran inland, hid behind a log awhile, and then ran back to the beach. One of them climbed up on the strange thing, entered it, and looked around inside. It was full of boxes, and he found long strings of brass buttons.

When he went outside to call his relatives to see the inside of the thing, he found that they had already set fire to it. He jumped down and joined the two creatures and the Indians on shore.

The strange thing burned just like fat. Everything burned except the iron, the copper, and the brass. Then the Clatsop took the two strange-looking men to their chief.

"I want to keep one of the men with me," said the chief.

Soon the people north of the river heard about the strange men and the strange thing, and they came to the Clatsop village. The Willapa came from across the river, the Chehalis and the Cowlitz from farther north, and even the Quinault from up the coast. And people from up the river came also—the Klickitat and others farther up.

The Clatsop sold the iron, brass, and copper. They traded one nail for a good deerskin. For a long necklace of shells they gave several nails. One man traded a piece of brass two fingers wide for a slave.

None of the Indians had ever seen iron or brass before. The Clatsop became rich selling the metal to other tribes.

The two Clatsop chiefs kept the two men who came on the ship. One stayed at the village called Clatsop, and the other stayed at the village on the cape.

—Reported by Franz Boas in 1894.

CHASE OF THE SEVERED HEAD

[CHEYENNE]

Once in a lonely lodge there lived a man, his wife, and two children—a girl and a boy. In front of the lodge, not far off, was a great lake, and a plain trail leading from the lodge down to the shore where the family used to go for water.

Every day the man went hunting, but before starting he would paint the woman red all over, coating her face, her arms, and her whole body with this sacred medicine to protect her from harm. After he departed, she would leave the children alone in the lodge and go for water; when she returned with it, the red paint was always gone and her hair was unbraided. She would manage to get back with her water just before her husband arrived. Not being a good hunter, he never brought any meat.

Though he asked her no questions, her husband thought it strange that every night the paint that he had put on his wife in the morning had disappeared. One day he said to his daughter, "What does your mother do every day? When I go out, I paint her, and when I get back, she has no paint on."

The girl replied, "Whenever you start out hunting, she goes for water, and she is usually away for a long time."

The next day, the man painted his wife as usual and then took his bow and arrows and left the lodge. But instead of going off hunting, he went down to the lake shore, dug a hole in the sand, and buried himself, leaving a little place where he could look out.

The man had not been hidden long when he saw his wife coming with a bucket. When she was near the water's edge, she slipped off her dress, unbraided her hair, sat down on the shore, and said, "*Na shu eh'*, I am here." Soon the man saw the water begin to move, and a *mih'ni*, a water spirit, rose from it, crawled out on the land, crept up to the woman, wrapped itself about her, and licked off all the red paint that was on her body.

The man emerged from his hiding place and rushed down to the pair. With his knife he cut the monster to pieces and cut off his wife's head. The pieces of the monster crept and rolled back into the water and were never seen again. The man cut off the woman's arms at the elbow and her legs at the knees. Saying, "Take your wife!" he threw these pieces and her head into the water. Then he opened the body, extracted a side of her ribs, and skinned it.

Returning to the lodge, he said, "Ah, my little children, I have had good luck; I have killed an antelope and brought back some of the meat. Where is your mother?"

The children answered, "Our mother has gone to bring water."

"Well," he said, "since I killed my meat sooner than I thought, I carried it back to camp. Your mother will be here pretty soon. In the meantime I'll cook something for you to eat before I go out again." He cooked a kettle of meat and took it to the children, who both ate. The little boy, who was the younger and the last one to suckle, said to his sister, "This tastes like mother!"

"Oh," said his sister, "keep still; this is antelope meat." After the children had finished, the little girl saved some of the meat for the mother to eat when she returned.

The father got his moccasins and other things together and started off, intending never to come back. He was going to look for his tribe's camp.

After he had gone, the children were sitting in the lodge, the girl making moccasins and putting porcupine quills on them. Suddenly they heard a voice outside say, "I love my children, but they don't love me; they have eaten me!"

The girl said to her brother, "Look out the door and see who is coming." The boy looked out and then cried, very much frightened, "Sister, here comes our mother's head!"

"Shut the door," cried the girl. The little boy did so. The girl picked up her moccasins and her quills—red, white, and yellow—rolled them up, and seized her root digger. Meanwhile the head had rolled against the door. "Daughter, open the door," it called. The head would strike the door, roll partway up the lodge, and then fall back again.

The girl and her brother ran to the door, pushed it open, and stood to the side. The head rolled into the lodge and clear across it to the back. The girl and boy jumped out, the girl closed the door, and both children ran away as fast as they could. As they ran, they heard the mother calling to them from the lodge.

They ran, and they ran, and at last the boy called, "Sister, I'm tired; I can't run any longer." The girl took his robe and carried it for him, and they ran on.

At last as they reached the top of the divide, they looked back, and there they could see the head coming, rolling along over the prairie. Somehow it had gotten out of the lodge. The children kept running, but at last the head had almost overtaken them. The little boy was frightened nearly to death, as well as exhausted.

The sister said, "This running is almost killing my brother. When I was a little girl playing, sometimes the prickly pears were so thick on the ground that I couldn't get through them." As she said this, she scattered behind her a handful of the yellow porcupine quills. At once there appeared a great bed of tall prickly pears with great yellow thorns. This cactus patch was strung out for a long way in both directions across the trail they had made.

When the head reached that place, it rolled up on the prickly pears and tried to roll over them, but kept getting caught in the thorns. For a long time it kept trying and trying to work its way through, and at last it did get loose from the thorns and passed over. But by this time the girl and the boy had gone a long distance.

After a while, however, they looked back and again saw the head coming. The little boy almost fainted. He kept calling out, "Sister, I'm tired; I can't run any longer."

When the sister heard him, she said while she was running, "When I was a little girl, I often used to find the bullberry bushes very thick." As she said this, she threw behind her a handful of the white quills, and where they touched the ground a huge grove of thick, thorny bullberry bushes grew up. They blocked the way, and the head stopped there for a long time, unable to pass through the bushes.

The children ran on and on, toward the place where the tribe had last been camped. But at length they looked back and saw the head coming again.

The little boy called out, "Sister, I'm tired; I can't run any longer." Again the girl threw quills behind—this time the red ones—and a great thicket of thorny rosebushes sprang up and stopped the head.

Again the children went a long way, but at last they saw the head coming, and the boy called out: "Sister, I'm tired." Then the sister said, "When I was a little girl playing, I often came to small ravines that I couldn't cross." She stopped and drew the point of her root digger over the ground in front of her. This made a little groove in the dirt, and she placed the root digger across the groove. Then she and her brother walked over on the root digger, and when they had crossed, the furrow became wider and wider and deeper and deeper. Soon it was a great chasm with cut walls, and at the bottom they could see a little water trickling.

"Now," said the girl, "we will run no longer; we will stay here."

"No, no," said the boy, "let's run."

"No," said the girl, "I will kill our mother here."

Presently the head came rolling up to the edge of the ravine and stopped. "Daughter," it said, "where did you cross? Place your root digger on the ground so that I can cross too." The girl attempted to do so, but the boy pulled her back every time. At last she managed to lay the root digger down, and the head began rolling over. But when it was halfway across, the girl tipped the stick, the head fell into the ravine, and the ravine closed on it.

After this the children started on again to look for the people. At last they found the camp and drew near it. Before they arrived, however, they heard a man's loud voice. As they came closer, they saw that it was their father speaking. He was walking about the camp and telling everyone that while he was out hunting, his two children had killed and eaten their mother. He warned the people that if the children came to the camp, they should not be allowed to enter.

When they heard this, the children were frightened. Still, they didn't know what else to do but go on into the camp. The people immediately caught them and tied their hands and feet. And the next day the whole tribe moved away and left the children there, still tied.

In the camp there was an old, old dog who knew what had happened and took pity on the children. The night of their arrival, she went into a lodge, stole some sinew, a knife, and an awl, and took them into a hole where she had her pups.

The next day after all the people had gone, the children heard a dog howling. Presently the old, old dog approached them. "Grandchildren," she said, "I pity you and have come to help you."

The girl said, "Untie me first, and I can untie my brother." So the old dog began to gnaw at the rawhide strings around the girl's hands. The animal had no teeth and could not cut the cords, but they became wet and began to slip. The girl kept working her hands and at last got them free. She untied her legs and then freed her brother. That evening they walked about through the camp and picked up old moccasins to wear. Both children were crying, and so was the dog. They all sat on the hill near the camp and cried bitterly, for they had nothing to eat, no place to sleep, and nothing to cover themselves with, and winter was coming. The girl and the dog sat weeping with their heads hanging down, but the boy was looking about. Presently he said, "Sister, see that wolf; it's coming straight toward us!"

"It's useless for me to look," said the girl. "I couldn't kill him by looking at him, so we can't eat him."

"But look, Sister," said the boy, "he's coming right up to us'"

At last the girl raised her head, and when she looked at the wolf, it fell dead. Then the dog brought the tools that she had stolen before the tribe left. With the knife they cut the wolf up, and from its skin they made a bed for the dog.

The children stayed in the abandoned camp, living well now, while the people in the new camp were starving. The children kept a large fire burning day and night and used big logs so that it never went out.

But after they had eaten the wolf, they began to feel hungry again. The girl became very unhappy, and one day as she sat crying, with the dog sitting beside her and the boy standing and looking about, he said, "Sister, look at that antelope coming!"

"No," said the girl, "it's useless for me to look; looking will do no good."

"But look even so," said the boy. "Perhaps it will do as the wolf did." The girl looked, and as with the wolf, the antelope fell dead. They cut it up and used its skin to make a bed for themselves. They ate the flesh and fed the old dog on the liver. The girl would chew pieces up fine for the toothless animal.

At last the antelope was all eaten, and again they grew hungry. Again the boy saw a strange-looking animal—this time an elk, which fell dead before the girl's look. She stretched the elk hide, which they used for a shelter. With the sinews the dog had stolen, they sewed their moccasins and mended their clothing.

When the elk meat ran out, the boy saw a buffalo coming straight to their shelter, and the girl killed it by a look. They cut up the meat and used the hide to make a larger and better shelter, where they stayed until winter came and snow began to fall.

One night when the girl went to bed, she said, "I wish that I might see a lodge over there in that sheltered place in the morning. I could sleep there with my brother and the dog, on a bed in the back of the lodge. I could make a bow and some arrows, so that my brother could kill the buffalo close to the camp when they gather in the underbrush during bad weather." She also wished that her brother might become a young man, and that they might have meat racks in the camp and meat on them.

In the morning when the boy got up and looked out, he said, "Sister, our lodge is over there now." It was in the very place the girl had wished. They moved their possessions and their fire over to it, and when the boy entered the lodge, he was a young man. That winter he killed many buffalo and they had plenty of meat.

One night as she was going to bed, the girl made another wish. "Brother," she said, "our father has treated us very badly. He caused us to eat our mother, and he had us tied up and deserted by the people. I wish we knew how to get word to the camp, and I wish we had two bears that we could tell to eat our father."

Next morning when the girl got up, two bears were sitting in the lodge on either side of the door. "Hello, my animals," she said. "Arise and eat." After giving them food, she went out to one of the meat racks and pulled off a piece of bloody fat. She called to a raven that was sitting in a tree near by: "Come here; I want to send you on an errand." When the raven had flown to her, she said, "Go and look for the camp of my people. Fly about among the lodges and call them. And when the people come out and ask each other, 'What's that raven doing? And what is he carrying?' drop this piece of fat into the thick of the crowd. Then tell them that the people you came from have great scaffolds of meat."

The raven took the piece of fat in his bill and flew away. He found the camp and flew about, calling and calling, and a number of men sitting her and there began to say to each other, "What's that raven carrying?" The raven dropped the meat, and someone who picked it up said, "Why, it's fresh fat."

Then the raven said, "Those people whom you threw away are still in the old camp, and they have scaffolds of meat like this." Then the raven flew back to the girl.

An old man began crying out to the people as he walked through the camp: "Those children whom we threw away have plenty of meat! They are in the old camp, and now we must move back to it as quickly as we can." The people tore down their lodges, packed up, and started back. Some of the young men went ahead in little groups of threes and fours, and when they reached the children's camp, the girl fed them and gave them meat to carry back to the others. All the trees about the lodge were covered with meat, and buffalo hides were stacked in great piles.

After a while the whole village arrived and camped not far from the children's lodge, and everyone began to come to the lodge for food. The girl sent word to her father to hold off until all the rest had been fed, so that he could come and take his time instead of eating in a hurry.

She said to the bears, "I'm going to send for your food last. After that person gets here and has eaten, I'll say, "There's your food," as he goes out of the lodge. Then you may eat him up."

In the evening when the last of the people was leaving the lodge, she said to her brother, "Tell everyone not to come anymore tonight; it is my father's turn now."

When the father came and they fed him, he said happily, "Oh, my children, you're living well here; you have plenty of meat and tongues and back fat." He did not eat everything his daughter had set before him. "I'll take all this home for my breakfast," he said.

After he had left the lodge, the girl said to the bears, "There's your food; eat him up!" The bears sprang after the father and pulled him down. He called to his daughter to take her animals away, but they killed him and began to drag him back to the lodge. The girl said, "Take him off somewhere else and eat him, and what you don't eat, throw into the stream."

What the bears did not eat they threw in the creek, and then they washed their hands, and no one ever knew what had become of the father. Since that time, bears have eaten human flesh when they could.

The boy and the girl returned to the camp, and always afterward lived well there.

—*Based on an account by George Bird Grinnell in 1903.*

■

UNCEGILA'S SEVENTH SPOT

■

[BRULE SIOUX]

Legends in many tribes tell of the awful wickedness and eventual death of Uncegila, the great water monster, also known as Unktehi. Now only her bones are left, strewn across the Badlands of Nebraska and the Dakotas, but they still have power to make strong medicine.

■ ▯▯ ■

When the earth was young, an evil witch was transformed into the huge snakelike monster Uncegila. She was as long as a hundred horses placed head to tail. Her body was thicker than the biggest tree trunk in the world, and her scales were of glittering mica. She had one curved horn coming out of her head. Along her back ran a crest that sparkled like dancing flames, while her vast side was adorned with a row of round spots in many colors. The only way to kill Uncegila was to shoot a magic medicine arrow through the seventh spot from her head. Behind that one small circle lay her ice-cold heart, made of a flashing red crystal.

Many brave warriors wanted to kill Uncegila, not only to free the people from her evil doings but also to acquire her sparkling heart. Whoever possessed it would have more power than anyone in the world. He could charm any woman he desired into his lodge and under his blanket. He could see deeply into the future. He would always find buffalo and never be hungry.

Although so many wanted to kill Uncegila, there were obstacles. The first sight of her would blind a man, a day later he would go mad, two days later he would foam at the mouth, and on the fourth day he would be dead. And it was not only he who would die, but all the members of his family. So there were not many who dared go to that great fathomless black pool which was Uncegila's home.

Two brave twin boys discussed their chances of killing this monster. The younger had been blinded by an accident, so that he had only empty sockets instead of eyes. And he said, "Elder brother, who saw the light of the world a second before me, I think I can kill Uncegila. Looking at her can do me no harm, and you can lead me to her home."

"But brother," said his twin, "how could you aim at the seventh spot behind Uncegila's head?"

"Someplace in the Paha Sapa, the Black Hills, lives Old Ugly Woman, who owns arrows which never fail to hit their targets. Maybe she will give them to us."

So the two boys went off to find Old Ugly Woman. They searched for a long time, the older brother leading his blind twin. High in the mountains they came at last to a *wakan*, a mysterious place. It was a cave under an overhanging cliff into which strange designs of mystery animals had been scratched. This was the home of Old Ugly Woman. She welcomed the two young men: "Come in, twin brothers who wish to fight Uncegila. Come in first of all to rest, eat, drink, and smoke." She was friendly enough, giving them sweet pemmican and dried meat, berry soup, and all those good things. She had a pipe and sacred tobacco, so they smoked. Then Old Ugly Woman asked what they wanted, even though she already knew.

"Old Ugly Woman," said the older twin, "we have come to ask for your magic medicine arrows. Without them we can't kill Uncegila, and that's what we most want to do."

"What will you give me, brave young men, for my arrows that never fail to hit?"

"Old Ugly Woman," they said, "Take pity on us. We are poor and own nothing valuable. We know you have power enough without the arrows, and we hoped that you would have a generous heart."

"Well, young men, there is something you can give. I am old. It has been a very long time since I was with a young, strong, good-looking boy. Sleep with me, give me a little pleasure once more in my old age, and you may have my magic medicine arrows.

The older twin, the one who could see, whispered to the younger: "This woman is old and wrinkled and bald, without a tooth left in her mouth. She is indeed very, very ugly. I don't think I could do it, but you, you're blind; what does it matter to you how she looks?"

"You're right; "I'll sacrifice myself," the blind one whispered back.

So the one who could see went out, while the blind one prepared to make love to Old Ugly Woman. And as he embraced her, Old Ugly Woman turned into a beautiful young, hot girl. She told the young man: "*Hokshila*, my boy, it's a great thing you've done for me—freed me from this wrinkled outer shell that a bad witch forced me to wear. *Pilamaya*, thank you, very much."

When the other twin came back and saw the beautiful young woman, he wanted to sleep with her too. But she told him: "*Koshkalaka*, young man, you wouldn't touch me when I was old and ugly; you shan't touch me now when I am young and pretty."

For four days and nights Old Ugly Woman, newly turned Young Pretty Woman, purified these boys and also purified the arrows, burning sweet grass and powdered cedar leaves and fanning them. Then she said: "Young men, take these arrows and free the people from the evil monster. But be careful when you cut out Uncegila's heart; it's so cold that it will burn your hands right off. Make yourselves gauntlets of thick hide in order to carry it. Also, the heart will speak, asking you for four things. You must refuse four times; but after that, you must do as the heart wishes. In addition, you must share the power it will give you." And to the younger twin she said: "*Hokshila*, one day you will see again. Then come back to me."

The twins, with the elder leading the way, set out to look for Uncegila. They walked for many days, almost to the end of the world. Then the one who could see found a slimy trail winding in big curves toward a huge, dark lake.

"That must be the home of Ungelica," he said to the blind one. "The trail leads right into the water. Now we'll sit and wait. Keep your bow and medicine arrows ready, and as soon as I see the very tip of Uncegila's horn coming out of the water, I'll tell you and turn away as fast as I can. Then count slowly to four times four, to allow time for the horn, the head, and the neck up to to seventh spot to rise above the surface. Then shoot."

They waited. At last from the bottomless lake came a swirling, bubbling, and foaming, and the tiniest tip of Uncegila's horn broke the water.

"She's coming up; count and shoot well!" said the elder, quickly averting his head. The blind twin counted to four times four, then let fly a magic medicine arrow, and another, and another. He shot all four of the mystery arrows, and one after the other they pierced the monster's side at the seventh spot.

Now Uncegila writhed in her death throes. The water of the lake turned to blood and boiled, overflowing and drenching the twins as they cowered on a little hill above. There was a long thrashing and rumbling and fearful noises and mighty groans, until at last all was still.

"Uncegila must be dead!" said the older twin. "I'll go and see. Old Ugly Woman turned into Young Pretty Woman said that looking at the monster can't hurt people once she is dead." He looked, he marveled, he could hardly believe his eyes when he stood before Uncegila's huge, glittering, flaming body. Then with his knife he exposed the still-beating heart of red crystal. Feeling the icy blast emanating from it, he put on his thick hide gauntlets and seized it. He had the sensation of strange powers streaming from the crystal into his body. Even through the thick gloves he could feel its coldness, so he wrapped it in his robe before taking it to his blind brother.

Then they heard a muffled sound as the heart spoke through the blanket. It said sternly: "Don't cut the horn off my head." Remembering the warning that Old Ugly Woman had given them, the elder brother at once began cutting, and with great labor managed to sever the horn at its base. If he had not, Uncegila would have come to life again.

"So you cut off my horn after all," said the monster's heart. "At least be so kind as to stick the tip of it into my wound, the one your arrows made in my side, at the seventh spot." The twins would not do this, and if they had, Uncegila would have come back to life.

"Go and cut a piece from my body. Roast and eat it," the heart said. If they had obeyed, of course, the poison would have killed them instantly.

"Take sacred tobacco and make a thin trail around the lake. You can at least do that for me," the heart said next. Had they been foolish enough to do this, all of Uncegila's many children, the smaller water monsters, would have come out of their streams and pools to kill the twins.

"We have refused four times to do what the monster's heart asked. From now on, we must fulfill its requests," said the younger brother.

And the heart spoke again, saying: "Blind one, put some of my blood on your eyelids."

The older twin went down to the monster's body and scooped up a little of Uncegila's blood with his horn spoon. He smeared some of the blood on his brother's eyelids, and at once new eyes formed, and the brother could see.

The twins took the crystal heart back to their camp. Following the heart's instructions, they dug a deep shaft to keep it in, and over the shaft they built a special twenty-skin lodge painted with a likeness of Uncegila. Daily the heart was fed with the blood of deer and other animals, and daily it was turned to face in another direction. The heart kept inventing more ceremonies for the brothers to perform. "If you ever refuse to do what I tell you," the heart said, "not only will I deprive you of my power, but I will become a blazing ball of fire and burn you up."

"It's good to have power," the younger twin said to his brother, "but too much power can become burdensome."

Yet the heart made the twins powerful indeed. They could foretell the future. Their lodges were always full of meat. No woman could resist them. They were generous, feeding their people with the game that was easy for them to catch. They were made chiefs. The older married; in fact he took four wives, who gave him strong sons. "Younger brother," he asked his twin, "why haven't you taken a woman, or two or three, into your lodge, as a great chief should? It's not good to be alone, not to have a woman sharing one's blanket."

The younger twin answered: "I haven't taken wives because, I think, I've always been in love with Old Ugly Woman turned Young Pretty Woman. I don't really want anyone but her. I think I'll go back to the cave where she lives and ask her to be my wife. I was blind when she gave us the magic arrows, but you know the way. Lead me."

The twins went alone to find the medicine woman. When they came to the *wakan p*lace where she had lived, they could feel her power, but Old Ugly Woman turned Young Pretty Woman was no longer there. She had disappeared without a trace. Where the cave had been, there was now only the smooth face of the cliff. Sadly the brothers returned home. "There are plenty of other women you can have," said the elder, but this did not cheer his brother up.

Sometime after they had returned home, the younger twin said to the elder: "I'm tired of these great powers the monster's heart is giving us. I'm bored always finding buffalo. I'm bored always hitting the target with my arrows, unfailingly killing all the game that this power puts in my way. The thrill of the hunt is missing. I'm tired of all the good-looking girls, and women, and even other men's wives who try to creep into my lodge. The pleasure of wooing is gone. Besides, my mind is still on that medicine women, the ugly one who turned beautiful. I'm tired of having the power to see into the future. I might learn the time and manner of my death, of our deaths, and I don't want to brood over these thnigs. I'm just tired of power; I want to be like other men."

"I'm tired of it, too," said the older. "I'm tired of feeding the monster's heart and carrying out its endless wishes. But there's a simple way to rid ourselves of this unwanted power. Remember, the woman also told us never to let anybody else set eyes on the heart, or the power would be taken away from us."

At once the brothers called out to all the people around them: "Ho, haven't you always wondered what we keep in this special tipi—the tipi we never allowed you to go in? Come on, we'll show you the big secret." They invited the whole crowd inside and let them look into the deep shaft at Uncegila's cold, red crystal heart. And when all eyes were on it, this heart screamed loudly and burst into a blinding ball of fire, consuming itself so that only ashes remained, while from the bottom of the hole came the noise of some big animal thrashing in water. And that was the end of it.

"I feel much better now," said the younger to the older twin.

"And I feel as if a heavy load had been taken off me," his brother said.

So these two lived happily, taking good and bad as it came, as most men do.

—*Told by George Eagle Elk in 1968 at Parmelee,*
South Dakota, and recorded by Richard Erdoes.

George Eagle Elk was an old, respected "yuwipi" medicine man. He lived in a tiny trailer shell on the Rosebud Sioux Reservation.

PART FIVE

COUNTING COUP

WAR AND THE WARRIOR CODE

War for many Indians was an exciting but dangerous sport. In a way it resembled a medieval tournament, governed by strict rules of conduct. The battlefield became an arena for an intensely personal competition of honor in which a young man might make a name for himself and earn the eagle feathers which signified adulthood. One could be killed in this game, but killing enemies was not the reason why men went to war. Total war resulting in the extinction of a tribe was almost unknown and generally abhorred.

War parties were formed as much for personal as for political reasons; a few young men would be attracted to an experienced leader whose medicine they considered good. There was no stigma attached if a man refused to come because he had had a discouraging dream or another token of bad medicine. Leaders had no inherent power to command or enforce obedience, only the sway of their prestige or charisma. In battle, every man behaved more or less as his own warrior code dictated. Lives were not squandered for small gains, If possible, for every life was precious to people living in small hunting bands, and a single man killed would be sorely missed. A leader lost standing if he lost a man, even if his foray was otherwise successful.

The conduct of war was a ceremonial affair, full of magic and ritual. Men rode to war with protective medicine bundles, miracle-working pebbles, or medicine shields, their horses covered with sacred gopher dust or painted with lightning designs—all intended to make the wearer arrow- or bullet-proof, and to give his horse supernatural speed.

The main object in any battle—and the only way to gain honors— was to "count coup," to reckon one's brave deeds. Killing a man from an ambush with a gun was no coup because it was easy—even a coward could do it. But riding up on an unwounded and fully armed enemy, and touching him with the hand or with one's coupstick, was a great

feat. Stealing horses right under the enemy's nose was also a fine coup. Coups had to be witnessed in order to be recognized, though in a few tribes a man could swear upon the pipe or some other sacred object that what he said was true. A warrior's eagle feathers were notched, split, or dotted with paint to indicate what kind of coups he had counted, how many enemies he had slain, or how often and in what way he had been wounded. Coups were proudly boasted of around campfires, their stories and details told and retold. In some tribes a young man could not aspire to marry unless he had counted coup.

Three of these tales describe the bravery of women, including the great Buffalo-Calf-Road-Woman, heroine of the Battle of the Rosebud, which was fought just before Little Bighorn in 1876, in Montana.

Most young men belonged to one of their tribe's several warrior societies, each with its own legend of origin, its own way of dressing, its special paraphernalia, songs, and ceremonies. One became a member on invitation or by being sponsored by an older warrior, often a relative. In some tribes one could "buy into" a society by a gift of horses or other valuables, but generally leaders were interested only in brave young men who would do credit to the group as a whole.

In some societies such as the Sioux Kit Foxes (Tokala) or the Cheyenne Dog soldiers, there were death-defying men who, during a battle, pinned their sashes to the ground as a sign that they would fight it out on the spot until victory or death. A wounded prisoner, if he had shown himself particularly brave, might be spared and adopted into the tribe of his captors.

All but one of these ten tales come from the Plains Indians, who still have the most highly ritualized war-story tradition in North America. The Lakota/Dakota people held out from the 1850s through the 1890s in the longest heroic resistance to the incursion of white armies, and no other tribes have so carefully recorded the heroic deeds of warriors—on tipis, war shields, embroidery, and of course, in the body of legends which are told today. When populations are reduced to living on reservations, ancient deeds of valor become even more crucial to the preservation of a positive identity. In the East, the process of tale collecting was so corrupted by the prejudices of the collectors that many important war and other stories have been lost, with the exception of some Iroquois legends. The Southwestern desert people have traditionally been too peaceful to generate a large body of war myths, though some tales of Apache and Navajo raids do still exist.

LITTLE MOUSE COUNTING COUP

[BRULE SIOUX]

This is a children's song which Lame Deer made up and from time to time improved upon. It was composed in the old style of warrior songs, with archaic words, and translated as well as Lame Deer and Richard Erdoes could manage.

Ho! Kola pila, *friends! it has come to pass.*
Black face paint I crave; horses I crave.
Friends, I, Itunkala the Mouse, on the warpath I go.
Behold my steed, Washin the Bullfrog,
Behold me, Itunkala, on the far-jumping frog!
Me, Mouse, myself riding; me, Itunkala, first in war!
Friends, a grass-blade; as coupstick I carry it,
A stiff grass-blade to count coup; on Igmu the Cat.
Igmu, I am coming; in a warlike manner I ride.
Igmu, your horses, your scalp, I am craving.

Friends, Igmu, the great Cat; I fought him.
Friends, kola pila; Igmu I feared not.
My long tail, friends, I pinned to the ground,
Sash wearer I, Fox warrior I; I Itunkala, Mouse.
First coup I counted; first strike on Igmu.
For a scalp, friends, one of his whiskers I took;
Behold! Igmu's whiskers I bring; long whiskers I am bringing.
Nice-looking girls: prepare a feast!
Friends, Hoka-hey! Igmu I vanquished,
But friends, where is my tail?

(In Igmu's stomach. Friends, pity me!)

TWO BULLETS AND TWO ARROWS

[BRULE SIOUX]

This is Henry Crow Dog speaking. Here is how my grandfather, the first Crow Dog, got his name. He was a chief about to lead a raiding party into Hante Paha Wakan—now called Cedar Valley in South Dakota. Before riding out, he had a vision; he saw a white horse in the clouds that gave him the sacred horse power. As a result, his pony became *shunkaka-luzahan*, the swiftest horse in the band.

But that wasn't all of the vision. The chief heard the voice of *shunk-manitu*, the coyote, saying: "I am the One!" Then his horse suddenly pricked up his ears, and the wind whistled through the two eagle feathers the chief was wearing. The feathers spoke, telling him: "There's a man standing on that hill over there, between the two trees." The chief and his companions clearly saw the man, who raised his hands and then was gone. The chief dispatched two scouts, one to the north and one to the south, but they returned saying that they had seen no one.

"This man on the hill must have been a *wanagi*, a ghost," the chief said. "He tried to warn us, but what did he warn us of? I don't know. I'm a warrior about to lead a raid, and I can't bother over much about ghosts." So they rode out and came to a river. The chief decided to camp there so that if enemies came, the riverbank would prevent them from surrounding his party.

During the night the chief heard the coyote howl four times. *Shunk-manitou* was telling him: "Something bad is going to happen to you!" The chief understood and gathered the men of his party together. There were some Tokala, some Kit Fox warriors, there. They sang a strong-heart song:

> *I am a Fox.*
> *I am supposed to die.*
> *I already threw my life away.*
>
> *Something daring,*
> *Something dangerous,*
> *I wish to do.*

They painted their faces black. They made themselves sacred. They prepared to fight and to die. They said that it would be a good day for a man to give his life.

At dawn the enemy attacked. There were some wasichu, some white settlers, led by a blue-coated soldier, and many Crow scouts and Absaroka warriors helping them. Indians helping whites to fight Indians! This was indeed a bad thing.

In the chief's party, however, were many famous warriors. There was Two Strikes—Numpa Kachpa—who got his name when he shot with one bullet two white soldiers riding on the same horse. Kills-in-Water was there, and Hollow Horn Bear's son, and Kills-in-Sight. Two Crow scouts wounded Kills-in-Sight and shot his horse from under him. The chief went to him at a dead run, killed the traitors, counted first coup on them, and put Kills-in-Sight on his own fast horse. Kills-in-Sight whipped the horse, which took off with him hanging onto it. The horse was so fast that no enemy could come near, and it carried Kills-in-Sight safely home.

On foot now, the chief was looking around, hoping to catch himself one of the riderless Crow horses, when he took two enemy arrows, one high on his chest right under the collar bone, the other in his side. The second arrow went deep, right into his bladder. He broke off the arrows with his hand, and Hollow Horn Bear's son and two others of the band came to help, though they too had been wounded. Their horses all had at least one arrow in them.

The chief told them: "No use bothering with me; I'm hurt bad. I can't live, so save yourselves!" Still, they caught a fallen man's horse and put the chief on it, saying: "Be strong. Hold on!" Then the Absaroka and some wasichu swooped down upon them and they had a hard time forcing their way through. Fighting for their lives against many, they lost sight of their chief. They thought he must have been killed and rode home talking of the bad things that had happened.

The chief had been riding, but he soon became so weak from loss of blood that he fell off the pony. Lying in the snow in great pain, he hardly had the strength to sing his death song. He was all alone, with neither friend nor enemy in sight.

Suddenly two coyotes came, growling but gently. They said: "We know you!" and kept him warm during the night by lying on either side of him. They licked the blood off his face. They brought him deer meat to make him strong and a sacred wound medicine which they told him to apply where the arrows had hit him. The medicine made his flesh tender and caused it to open up so that he could pull out the arrowheads and what was left of the shafts. The medicine brought by the coyotes

cured the chief, and the meat they gave him made him strong. When he was able to walk, a crow came flying and guided him home. All the people marveled on seeing him and hearing his story.

Sometimes after the chief had recovered, he went out alone to hunt and was ambushed by a war party of Pahanis. These enemies had guns, and the chief took two bullets, one in the arm and one in the ribs. The second touched his lungs so that in later life he was always somewhat weak in the chest.

He managed to get far enough away on his fast horse to be safe from the Pahanis, but then he could ride no further. He got down from his horse and stretched himself on the ground. "This time I die for sure," he said to himself.

But again the two coyotes came, bringing meat and bullet medicine, nursing and warming him for four days until his strength returned and his wounds were a little better. And again the crow came flying, watching over the man, warning him when enemies were close, guiding him to the place where his horse had strayed. So once more the chief came back alive from the dead.

Then he made himself a shield from the neck skin of a buffalo and, using sacred procedures, painted two arrowheads and two circles representing bullets on it. This was his *wotawe*, his crest and protection, because after he had survived these four wounds, and after he had made the shield, nothing further could ever hurt him.

And then also he took his last name—Kangi Shunka, Crow Coyote—which the white census takers misunderstood and made into Crow Dog. You can stand on a name like this.

—*Told by Henry Crow Dog on Rosebud Indian Reservation,*
South Dakota, in 1969, and recorded by Richard Erdoes.

A CHEYENNE BLANKET

[PAWNEE]

The Cheyennes, like other Indians, do not speak to each other when they are away from the camp. If a man leaves the village and sits or stands by himself on the top of a hill, it is a sign that he wants to be alone, perhaps to meditate, perhaps to pray. No one speaks to him or goes near him.

There was once a Pawnee boy who went off on the warpath to the Cheyenne camp. Somehow he had obtained a Cheyenne blanket. He came close to the camp, hid himself, and waited. About the middle of the afternoon he left his hiding place and walked to the top of the hill overlooking the village. He had his Cheyenne blanket wrapped about him and over his head, with only a little hole for his eyes. He stood quietly watching the camp for an hour or two.

Men began coming in from buffalo hunting, some of them leading packhorses loaded with meat. One hunter was riding a horse packed with meat while he led another packhorse and a black spotted horse that was his running horse. Running horses are ridden only on the chase or on war parties, and after being used they are taken down to the river to be carefully washed and groomed. When the Pawnee boy saw the spotted horse, he knew that this was the one he wanted. The hunter led the animal to his lodge, dismounted and handed the ropes to his women, and went inside.

Then the Pawnee made up his mind what he would do. He started down the hill into the village and went straight to the lodge where the women were unloading the meat. Walking up to them, he reached out and took the ropes of the spotted horse and one of the packhorses. The women fell back, doubtless thinking that he was one of the owner's relatives come to take the running horse down to the river. The Pawnee could not speak Cheyenne, but as he turned away he mumbled something, "M-m-m-m-," in a low voice, and then walked toward the river. As soon as he had gone down over the bank and out of sight, he jumped on the spotted horse, rode into the brush, and soon was away with the two animals, stolen out of the Cheyenne camp in broad daylight.

*—Based on a story collected by George Bird Grinnell
in the 1880s.*

THE WARRIOR MAIDEN

■

[ONEIDA]

■ ▏▏ ■

Long ago, in the days before the white man came to this continent, the Oneida people were beset by their old enemies, the Mingoes. The invaders attacked the Oneida villages, stormed their palisades, set fire to their longhouses, laid waste to the land, destroyed the cornfields, killed men and boys, and abducted the women and girls. There was no resisting the Mingoes, because their numbers were like grains of sand, like pebbles on a lake shore.

The villages of the Oneida lay deserted, their fields untended, the ruins of their homes blackened. The men had taken the women, the old people, the young boys and girls into the deep forests, hiding them in secret places among rocks, in caves, and on desolate mountains. The Mingoes searched for victims, but could not find them. The Great Spirit himself helped the people to hide and shielded their places of refuge from the eyes of their enemies.

Thus the Oneida people were safe in their inaccessible retreats, but they were also starving. Whatever food they had been able to save was soon eaten up. They could either stay in their hideouts and starve, or leave them in search of food and be discovered by their enemies. The warrior chiefs and sachems met in council but could find no other way out.

Then a young girl stepped forward in the council and said that the good spirits had sent her a dream showing her how to save the Oneida. Her name was Aliquipiso and she was not afraid to give her life for her people.

Aliquipiso told the council: "We are hiding on top of a high, sheer cliff. Above us the mountain is covered with boulders and heavy sharp rocks. You warriors wait and watch here. I will go to the Mingoes and lead them to the spot at the foot of the cliff where they all can be crushed and destroyed."

The chiefs, sachems, and warriors listened to the girl with wonder. The oldest of the sachems honored her, putting around her neck strands of white and purple wampum. "The Great Spirit has blessed you, Aliquipiso, with courage and wisdom," he said. "We, your people, will always remember you."

During the night the girl went down from the heights into the forest below by way of a secret path. In the morning, Mingoe scouts found her wandering through the woods as if lost. They took her to the burned and abandoned village where she had once lived, for this was now their camp. They brought her before their warrior chief. "Show us the way to the place where your people are hiding," he commanded. "If you do this, we shall adopt you into our tribe. Then you will belong to the victors. If you refuse, you will be tortured at the stake."

"I will not show you the way," answered Aliquipiso. The Mingoes tied her to a blackened tree stump and tortured her with fire, as was their custom. Even the wild Mingoes were astonished at the courage with which the girl endured it. At last Aliquipiso pretended to weaken under the pain. "Don't hurt me any more," she cried, "I'll show you the way!"

As night came again, the Mingoes bound Aliquipiso's hands behind her back and pushed her ahead of them. Don't try to betray us," they warned. "At any sign of it, we'll kill you." Flanked by two warriors with weapons poised, Aliquipiso led the way. Soundlessly the mass of Mingoe warriors crept behind her through thickets and rough places, over winding paths and deer trails, until at last they arrived beneath the towering cliff of sheer granite. "Come closer, Mingoe warriors," she said in a low voice, "gather around me. The Oneidas above are sleeping, thinking themselves safe. I'll show you the secret passage that leads upwards." The Mingoes crowded together in a dense mass with the girl in the center. Then Aliquipiso uttered a piercing cry: "Oneidas! The enemies are here! Destroy them!"

The Mingoes scarcely had time to strike her down before huge boulders and rocks rained upon them. There was no escape; it seemed as if the angry mountain itself were falling on them, crushing them, burying them. So many Mingoe warriors died there that the other bands of Mingoe invaders stopped pillaging the Oneida country and retired to their own hunting grounds. They never again made war on Aliquipiso's people.

The story of the girl's courage and self-sacrifice was told and retold wherever Oneidas sat around their campfires, and will be handed down from grandparent to grandchild as long as there are Oneidas on this earth.

The Great Mystery changed Aliquipiso's hair into woodbine, which the Oneidas call "running hairs" and which is a good medicine. From her body sprang honeysuckle, which to this day is known among her people as the "blood of brave women."

—*Based on the version told by W. W. Canfield in 1902.*

THE SIEGE OF COURTHOUSE ROCK

■

[WHITE RIVER SIOUX]

■ ▏▏ ■

Nebraska is green and flat, a part of the vast corn belt. There are farms everywhere, and silos, and the land does not look like the West at all. But as you travel on toward the setting sun, you find three great, wild rocks which rise out of the plains. First you come to Chimney Rock, towering like a giant needle on the prairie. It was a famous landmark for the settlers in their covered wagons as they traveled west on the Oregon trail or took the more southerly route to the Colorado goldfields.

Then you come to the twins—Courthouse Rock and Jailhouse Rock. Formed of yellowish stone, they are covered with yucca plants and sagebrush. Mud swallows nest in the rock faces. If you climb one of the twins, there is a wonderful view of the plains all around. And westward beyond the plains rise the chalk cliffs and the sandhills of Nebraska, home of many western Sioux.

A long time ago a Sioux war party surprised a war party of Pahani near Courthouse Rock. We Sioux had been fighting many battles with the Pahani. The whites had pushed nations like ours, whose homeland was further east near the Great Lakes, westward into the prairie and the hunting grounds of other tribes. Maybe the Pahani were there before us; who knows? At any rate, now we were hunting the same herds in the same place, and naturally we fought.

I guess there must have been more of us than of the Pahani, and they retreated to the top of Courthouse Rock to save themselves. Three sides of Courthouse Rock go straight up and down like the sides of a skyscraper. No one can climb them. Only the fourth side had a path to the top, and it could be easily defended by a few brave men.

Thus the Pahani were on the top and the Sioux at the foot of Courthouse Rock. The Sioux chief told his warriors: "It's no use trying to storm it. Only three or four men can go up that path abreast, so even women and children could defend it. But the Pahani have no water, and soon they'll run out of food. They can stay up there and starve or die of thirst, or they can come and fight us on the plain. When they climb down, we can kill them and count many coups on them." The Sioux settled down to wait at the foot of the rock.

On the summit, as the Sioux chief expected, the Pahani suffered from hunger and thirst. They grew weak. Though there was little hope for them, they had a brave leader who could use his head. He knew that three sides of the rock were unguarded but that one would have to be a bird to climb down them. On one of the three steep sides, however, there was a round bulge jutting out from the rock face. "If we could fasten a rope to it, we could let ourselves down," he thought. But the outcropping was too smooth, round, and wide to hold a lasso.

Then the Pahani leader tried his knife on the rock bulge. He found that the stone was soft enough for the knife to bite easily into, and he began patiently whittling a groove around the bulge. He and his men worked only at night so that the Sioux wouldn't see what they were up to. After two nights they had carved the groove deep enough. When they tied all their rawhide ropes together, they found that the line would reach to the ground.

On the third night the Pahani leader tied one end of the rope around the bulge in the rock. He himself tested it by climbing all the way down and then up again, which took most of the night.

On the next and fourth night, he told his men: "Now we do it. Let the youngest go first." The Pahani climbed down one by one, the youngest and least accomplished first, so that a large group could belay them, and the older and more experienced warriors later. The leader came down last. The Sioux did not notice them at all, and the whole party stole away.

The Sioux stayed at the foot of the rock for many days. They themselves grew hungry, because they had hunted out all the game. At last a young, brave warrior said: "They must be all dead up there. I'm fed up with waiting; I'll go up and see." He climbed the path to the top and shouted down that nobody was up there.

That time the joke was on us Sioux. It's always good to tell a story honoring a brave enemy, especially when the story is true. Are there any Pahani listening?

—*Told by Jenny Leading Cloud at White River, Rosebud*
Indian Reservation, South Dakota, 1967.
Recorded by Richard Erdoes.

CHIEF ROMAN NOSE
LOSES HIS MEDICINE

■

[WHITE RIVER SIOUX]

The Lakota and the Shahiyela—the Sioux and the Cheyenne—have been good friends for a long time. Often they have fought shoulder to shoulder. They fought the white soldiers on the Bozeman Road, which we Indians called the Thieves' Road because it was built to steal our land. They fought together on the Rosebud River, and the two tribes united to defeat Custer in the big battle of the Little Bighorn. Even now in a barroom brawl, a Sioux will always come to the aid of a Cheyenne and vice versa. We Sioux will never forget what brave fighters the Cheyenne used to be.

Over a hundred years ago the Cheyenne had a famous war chief whom the whites called Roman Nose. He had the fierce, proud face of a hawk, and his deeds were legendary. He always rode into battle with a long warbonnet trailing behind him. It was thick with eagle feathers, and each stood for a brave deed, a coup counted on the enemy.

Roman Nose had a powerful war medicine, a magic stone he carried tied to his hair on the back of his head. Before a fight he sprinkled his war shirt with sacred gopher dust and painted his horse with hailstone patterns. All these things, especially the magic stone, made him bullet-proof. Of course he could be slain by a lance, a knife, or a tomahawk, but not with a gun. And nobody ever got the better of Roman Nose in hand-to-hand combat.

There was one thing about Roman Nose's medicine: he was not allowed to touch anything made of metal when eating. He had to use horn or wooden spoons and eat from wooden or earthenware bowls. His meat had to be cooked in a buffalo's pouch or in a clay pot, not in a white man's iron kettle.

One day Roman Nose received word of a battle going on between white soldiers and Cheyenne warriors. The fight had been swaying back and forth for over a day. "Come and help us; we need you" was the message. Roman Nose called his warriors together. They had a hasty meal, and Roman Nose forgot about the laws of his medicine. Using a metal spoon and a white man's steel knife, he ate buffalo meat cooked in an iron kettle.

The white soldiers had made a fort on a sandspit island in the middle of a river. They were shooting from behind and they had a new type of rifle which was better and could shoot faster and farther than the Indians' arrows and old muzzle-loaders.

The Cheyenne were hurling themselves against the soldiers in attack after attack, but the water in some spots came up to the saddles of their horses and the river bottom was slippery. They could not ride up quickly on the enemy, and they faced murderous fire. Their attacks were repulsed, their losses heavy.

Roman Nose prepared for the fight by putting on his finest clothes, war shirt, and leggings. He painted his best horse, with hailstone designs, and he tied the pebble which made him bulletproof into his hair at the back of his head. But an old warrior stepped up to him and said: "You have eaten from an iron kettle with a metal spoon and a steel knife. Your medicine is powerless; you must not fight today. Purify yourself for four days so that your medicine will be good again."

"But the fight is today, not in four days," said Roman Nose. "I must lead my warriors. I will die, but only the mountains and the rocks are forever." He put on his great warbonnet, sang his death song, and then charged. As he rode up to the whites' cottonwood breastwork, a bullet hit him in the chest. He fell from his horse; his body was immediately lifted by his warriors, and the Cheyenne retreated with their dead chief. To honor him in death, to give him a fitting burial, was more important than to continue the battle.

All night the soldiers in their fort could hear the Cheyennes' mourning songs, the keening of the women. They too knew that the great chief Roman Nose was dead. He had died as he had lived. He had shown that sometimes it is more important to act like a chief than to live to a great old age.

—Told by Jenny Leading Cloud at White River, Rosebud
Indian Reservation, South Dakota, 1967.
Recorded by Richard Erdoes.

BRAVE WOMAN COUNTS COUP

[WHITE RIVER SIOUX]

Over a hundred years ago, when many Sioux were still living in what now is Minnesota, there was a band of Hunkpapa Sioux at Spirit Lake under a chief called Tawa Makoce, meaning His Country. It was his country, too—Indian country, until the white soldiers with their cannon finally drove the Lakota tribes across the Mni Shoshay: The Big Muddy, the Missouri.

In his youth the chief had been one of the greatest warriors. Later, when his fighting days were over, he was known as a wise leader, invaluable in council, and as a great giver of feasts, a provider for the poor. The chief had three sons and one daughter. The sons tried to be warriors as mighty as their father, but that was a hard thing to do. Again and again they battled the Crow Indians with reckless bravery, exposing themselves in the front rank, fighting hand to hand, until one by one they all were killed. Now only his daughter was left to the sad old chief. Some say her name was Makhta. Others call her Winyan Ohitika, Brave Woman.

The girl was beautiful and proud. Many young men sent their fathers to the old chief with gifts of fine horses that were preliminary to marriage proposals. Among those who desired her for a wife was a young warrior named Red Horn, himself the son of a chief, who sent his father again and again to ask for her hand. But Brave Woman would not marry. "I will not take a husband," she said, "until I have counted coup on the Crows to avenge my dead brothers." Another young man who loved Brave Woman was Wanblee Cikala, or Little Eagle. He was too shy to declare his love, because he was a poor boy who had never been able to distinguish himself.

At this time the Kangi Oyate, the Crow nation, made a great effort to establish themselves along the banks of the upper Missouri in country which the Sioux considered their own. The Sioux decided to send out a strong war party to chase them back, and among the young men riding out were Red Horn and Little Eagle. "I shall ride with you," Brave Woman said. She put on her best dress of white buckskin richly decorated with beads and porcupine quills, and around her neck she wore a choker of dentalium shells. She went to the old chief. "Father," she said, "I must go to the place where my brothers died. I must count coup for them. Tell me that I can go."

The old chief wept with pride and sorrow. "You are my last child," he said, "and I fear for you and for a lonely old age without children to comfort me. But your mind has long been made up. I see that you must go; do it quickly. Wear my warbonnet into battle. Go and do not look back."

And so his daughter, taking her brothers' weapons and her father's warbonnet and best war pony, rode out with the warriors. They found an enemy village so huge that it seemed to contain the whole Crow nation—hundreds of men and thousands of horses. There were many more Crows than Sioux, but the Sioux attacked nevertheless. Brave Woman was a sight to stir the warriors to great deeds. To Red Horn she gave her oldest brother's lance and shield. "Count coup for my dead brother," she said. To Little Eagle she gave her second brother's bow and arrows. "Count coup for him who owned these," she told him. To another young warrior she gave her youngest brother's war club. She herself carried only her father's old, curved coupstick wrapped in otter fur.

At first Brave Woman held back from the fight. She supported the Sioux by singing brave-heart songs and by making the shrill, trembling war cry with which Indian women encourage their men. But when the Sioux, including her own warriors from the Hunkpapa band, were driven back by overwhelming numbers, she rode into the midst of the battle. She did not try to kill her enemies, but counted coup left and right, touching them with her coupstick. With a woman fighting so bravely among them, what Sioux warrior could think of retreat?

Still, the press of the Crows and their horses drove the Sioux back a second time. Brave Woman's horse was hit by a musket bullet and went down. She was on foot, defenseless, when Red Horn passed her on his speckled pony. She was too proud to call out for help, and he pretended not to see her. Then Little Eagle came riding toward her out of the dust of battle. He dismounted and told her to get on his horse. She did, expecting him to climb up behind her, but he would not. "This horse is wounded and too weak to carry us both," he said.

"I won't leave you to be killed," she told him. He took her brother's bow and struck the horse sharply with it across the rump. The horse bolted, as he intended, and Little Eagle went back into battle on foot. Brave Woman herself rallied the warriors for a final charge, which they made with such fury that the Crows had to give way at last.

This was the battle in which the Crow nation was driven away from the Missouri for good. It was a great victory, but many brave young men died. Among them was Little Eagle, struck down with his face to the enemy. The Sioux warriors broke Red Horn's bow, took his eagle feathers from him, and sent him home. But they placed the body of Little Eagle on a high scaffold on the spot where the enemy camp had been. They killed his horse to serve him in the land of many lodges. "Go willingly," they told the horse. "Your master has need of you in the spirit world."

Brave Woman gashed her arms and legs with a sharp knife. She cut her hair short and tore her white buckskin dress. Thus she mourned for Little Eagle. They had not been man and wife; in fact he had hardly dared speak to her or look at her, but now she asked everybody to treat her as if she were the young warrior's widow. Brave Woman never took a husband, and she never ceased to mourn for Little Eagle. "I am his widow," she told everyone. She died of old age. She had done a great thing, and her fame endures.

—Told by Jenny Leading Cloud at White River, Rosebud
Indian Reservation, South Dakota, 1967.
Recorded by Richard Erdoes.

SPOTTED EAGLE AND BLACK CROW

[WHITE RIVER SIOUX]

This story of two warriors, of jealousy, and of eagles was first told by the great Mapiya Luta—Chief Red Cloud of the Oglalas.

Many lifetimes ago there lived two brave warriors. One was named Wanblee Gleshka, Spotted Eagle. The other was Kangi Sapa, Black Crow. They were friends but, as it happened, were also in love with the same girl, Zintkala Luta Win—Red Bird. She was beautiful as well as accomplished in tanning and quillwork, and she liked Spotted Eagle best, which made Black Crow unhappy and jealous.

Black Crow went to his friend and said: "Let's go on a war party against the Pahani. We'll get ourselves some fine horses and earn eagle feathers."

"Good idea," said Spotted Eagle, and the two young men purified themselves in a sweat bath. They got out their war medicine and their shields, painted their faces, and did all that warriors should do before a raid. Then they rode out against the Pahani.

The raid did not go well. The Pahani were watchful, and the young warriors could not get near the herd. Not only did they fail to capture any ponies, they even lost their own mounts while they were trying to creep up to the enemy's herd. Spotted Eagle and Black Crow had a hard time escaping on foot because the Pahani were searching for them everywhere. At one time the two had to hide underwater in a lake and breathe through long, hollow reeds which were sticking up above the surface. But at least they were clever at hiding, and the Pahani finally gave up the hunt.

Traveling on foot made the trip home a long one. Their moccasins were tattered, their feet bleeding. At last they came to a high cliff. "Let's go up there," said Black Crow, "and find out whether the enemy is following us." Clambering up, they looked over the countryside and saw that no one was on their trail. But on a ledge far below them they spied a nest with two young eagles in it. "Let's get those eagles, at least," Black Crow said. There was no way to climb down the sheer rock wall, but Black Crow took his rawhide lariat, made a loop in it, put the rope around Spotted Eagle's chest, and lowered him.

When his friend was on the ledge with the nest, Black Crow said to himself: "I can leave him there to die. When I come home alone, Red Bird will marry me." He threw his end of the rope down and went away without looking back or listening to Spotted Eagle's cries.

At last it dawned on Spotted Eagle that his friend had betrayed him, that he had been left to die. The lariat was much too short to lower himself to the ground; an abyss of three hundred feet lay beneath him. He was alone with the two young eagles, who screeched angrily at the strange, two-legged creature that had invaded their home.

Black Crow returned to his village. "Spotted Eagle died a warrior's death," he told the people. "The Pahanis killed him." There was loud wailing throughout the village, because everybody had liked Spotted Eagle. Red Bird slashed her arms with a sharp knife and cut her hair to make her sorrow plain to all. But in the end because life must go on, she became Black Crow's wife.

Spotted Eagle, however, did not die on his lonely ledge. The eagles got used to him, and the old eagles brought plenty of food—rabbits,

prairie dogs, and sage hens—which he shared with the two chicks. Maybe it was the eagle medicine in his bundle which he carried on his chest that made the eagles accept him. Still, he had a very hard time on that ledge. It was so narrow that he had to tie himself to a little rock sticking out of the cliff to keep from falling off in his sleep. In this way he spent some uncomfortable weeks; after all, he was a human being and not a bird to whom a crack in the rock face is home.

At last the young eagles were big enough to practice flying. "What will become of me now?" thought the young man. "Once the fledglings have flown the nest, the old birds won't bring any more food." Then he had an inspiration, and told himself, "Perhaps I'll die. Very likely I will. But I won't just sit here and give up."

Spotted Eagle took his little pipe out of his medicine bundle, lifted it up to the sky, and prayed: "Wakan Tanka, *onshimala ye*: Great Spirit, pity me. You have created man and his brother, the eagle. You have given me the eagle's name. Now I will try to let the eagles carry me to the ground. Let the eagles help me; let me succeed."

He smoked and felt a surge of confidence. Then he grabbed hold of the legs of the two young eagles. "Brothers," he told them, "you have accepted me as one of your own. Now we will live together, or die together. Hoka-hey!" and he jumped off the ledge.

He expected to be shattered on the ground below, but with a mighty flapping of wings, the two young eagles broke his fall and the three landed safely. Spotted Eagle said a prayer of thanks to the ones above.

Then he thanked the eagles and told them that one day he would be back with gifts and have a giveaway in their honor.

Spotted Eagle returned to his village. The excitement was great. He had been dead and had come back to life. Everybody asked him how it happened that he was not dead, but he wouldn't tell them. "I escaped," he said, "that's all." He saw his love married to his treacherous friend and bore it in silence. He was not one to bring strife and enmity to his people, to set one family against the other. Besides, what had happened could not be changed. Thus he accepted his fate.

A year or so later, a great war party of the Pahani attacked his village. The enemy outnumbered the Sioux tenfold, and Spotted Eagle's band had no chance for victory. All the warriors could do was fight a slow rear-guard action to give the aged, the women, and the children time to escape across the river. Guarding their people this way, the handful of Sioux fought bravely, charging the enemy again and again, forcing the Pahani to halt and regroup. Each time, the Sioux retreated a little, taking up a new position on a hill or across a gully. In this way they could save their families.

Showing the greatest courage, exposing their bodies freely, were Spotted Eagle and Black Crow. In the end they alone faced the enemy. Then, suddenly, Black Crow's horse was hit by several arrows and collapsed under him. "Brother, forgive me for what I have done," he cried to Spotted Eagle, "let me jump on your horse behind you."

Spotted Eagle answered: "You are a Kit Fox member, a sash wearer. Pin your sash as a sign that you will fight to the finish. Then, if you survive, I will forgive you; and if you die, I will forgive you also."

Black Crow answered: "I am a Fox. I shall pin my sash. I will win here or die here." He sang his death song. He fought stoutly. There was no one to release him by unpinning him and taking him up on a horse. He was hit by lances and arrows and died a warrior's death. Many Pahani died with him.

Spotted Eagle had been the only one to watch Black Crow's last fight. At last he joined his people, safe across the river, where the Pahani did not follow them. "Your husband died well," Spotted Eagle told Red Bird.

After some time had passed, Spotted Eagle married Red Bird. And much, much later he told his parents, and no one else, how Black Crow had betrayed him. "I forgive him now," he said, "because once, long ago, he was my friend, and because he died as a warrior should, fighting for his people, and also because Red Bird and I are happy now."

After a long winter, Spotted Eagle told his wife when spring came again: "I must go away for a few days to fulfill a promise. And I have to go alone." He rode off by himself to that cliff and stood again at its foot, below the ledge where the eagles' nest had been. He pointed his sacred pipe to the four directions, then down to Grandmother Earth and up to the Grandfather, letting the smoke ascend to the sky, calling out: "Wanblee, Mishunkala, little Eagle Brothers, hear me."

High above in the clouds appeared two black dots, circling. These were the eagles who had saved his life. They came at his call, their huge wings spread royally. Swooping down, uttering a shrill cry of joy and recognition, they alighted at his feet. He stroked them with his feather fan, thanked them many times, and fed them choice morsels of buffalo meat. He fastened small medicine bundles around their legs as a sign of friendship, and spread sacred tobacco offerings around the foot of the cliff. Thus he made a pact of friendship and brotherhood between Wan-blee Oyate—the eagle nation—and his own people. Afterwards the stately birds soared up again into the sky, circling motionless, carried by the wind, disappearing into the clouds. Spotted Eagle turned his horse's head homeward, going back to Red Bird with deep content.

> —*Told by Jenny Leading Cloud in White River, Rosebud*
> *Indian Reservation, South Dakota, 1967.*
> *Recorded by Richard Erdoes.*

WHERE THE GIRL SAVED HER BROTHER

[CHEYENNE]

In the summer of 1876, the two greatest battles between soldiers and Indians were fought on the plains of Montana. The first fight was called the Battle of the Rosebud. The second, which was fought a week later, was called the Battle of the Little Bighorn, where General Custer was defeated and killed. The Cheyennes call the Battle of the Rosebud the Fight Where the Girl Saved Her Brother. Let me tell you why.

Well, a hundred years ago, the white men wanted the Indians to go into prisons called "reservations," to give up their freedom to roam and hunt buffalo, to give up being Indians. Some tamely submitted and settled down behind the barbed wire of the agencies, but others did not.

Those who went to the reservations to live like white men were called "friendlies." Those who would not go were called "hostiles." They weren't hostile, really. They didn't want to fight; all they wanted was to be left alone to live the Indian way, which was a good way. But the soldiers would not leave them alone. They decided to have a great roundup and catch all "hostiles," kill those who resisted, and bring the others back to the agencies as prisoners.

Three columns of soldiers entered the last stretch of land left to the red man. They were led by Generals Crook, Terry, and Custer. Crook had the most men with him, about two thousand. He also had cannon and Indian scouts to guide him. At the Rosebud he met the united Sioux and Cheyenne warriors.

The Indians had danced the sacred sun dance. The great Sioux chief and holy man, Sitting Bull, had been granted a vision telling him that the soldiers would be defeated. The warriors were in high spirits. Some men belonging to famous warrior societies had vowed to fight until they were killed, singing their death songs, throwing their lives away, as it was called. They painted their faces for war. They put on their finest outfits so that if they were killed, their enemies would say: "This must have been a great chief. See how nobly he lies there."

The old chiefs instructed the young men how to act. The medicine men prepared protective charms for the fighters, putting gopher dust on their hair or painting their horses with hailstone designs. This was to render them invisible to their foes, or to make them bulletproof. Brave Wolf had the most admired medicine—a mounted hawk that he fastened to the back of his head. He always rode into battle blowing his eagle-bone whistle—and once the fight started, the hawk came alive and whistled too.

Many proud tribes were there besides the Cheyenne—the Hunkpapa, the Minniconjou, the Oglala, the Burned Thighs, the Two Kettles. Many brave chiefs and warriors came, including Two Moons, White Bull, Dirty Moccasins, Little Hawk, Yellow Eagle, and Lame White Man. Among the Sioux was the great Crazy Horse, and Sitting Bull—their holy man, still weak from his flesh offerings made at the sun dance— and the fierce Rain-in-the-Face. Who can count them all! What a fine sight they were!

Those who had earned the right to wear warbonnets were singing, lifting them up. Three times they stopped in their singing, and the fourth time they put the bonnets on their heads, letting the streamers fly and trail behind them. How good it must have been to see this!

Crazy Horse of the Oglala shouted his famous war cry: "A good day to die, and a good day to fight! Cowards to the rear, brave hearts—follow me!"

The fight started. Many brave deeds were done, many coups counted. The battle swayed to and fro. More than anybody else's, this was the Cheyenne's fight. This was their day. Among them was a brave young girl, Buffalo-Calf-Road-Woman, who rode proudly beside her husband, Black Coyote. Her brother, Chief Comes-in-Sight, was in the battle too. She looked for him and at last saw him surrounded, his horse killed from under him. Soldiers were aiming their rifles at him, while their Crow scouts circled around him and waited for an opportunity to count coups. But he fought them off with courage and skill.

Buffalo-Calf-Road-Woman uttered a shrill, high-pitched war cry. She raced her pony into the midst of the battle, into the midst of the enemy. She made the spine-chilling, trilling, trembling sound of the Indian woman encouraging her man during a fight. Chief Comes-in-Sight jumped up on her horse behind her. Buffalo-Calf-Road-Woman laughed with joy and the excitement of battle, and all the while she sang. The soldiers were firing at her, and their Crow scouts were shooting arrows at her horse, but it moved too fast for her and her brother to be hit. Then she turned her horse and raced up the hill from which the old chiefs and the medicine men were watching the battle.

The Sioux and Cheyenne saw what she was doing, and then the white soldiers saw it too. They all stopped fighting and watched the brave girl saving her brother's life. The warriors raised their arms and set up a mighty shout—a long undulating war cry that made one's hair stand up on end. And even some of the soldiers threw their caps in the air and shouted "Hurrah!" in honor of Buffalo-Calf-Road-Woman.

The battle was still young. Not many men had been killed on either side, but the white general was thinking: "If their women fight like this, what will their warriors be like? Even if I win, I will lose half my men." And so General Crook retreated a hundred miles or so. He was to have joined up with Custer, Old Yellow Hair; but when Custer had to fight the same Cheyenne and Sioux a week later, Crook was far away and Custer's regiment was wiped out. So in a way, Buffalo-Calf-Road-Woman contributed to that battle too.

Many who saw what she had done thought that she had counted the biggest coup of all—not taking life, but giving it. That's why the Indians call the Battle of the Rosebud the Fight Where the Girl Saved Her Brother.

The spot where Buffalo-Calf-Road-Woman counted her coup has long since been plowed under. A ranch now covers it. But the memory of her deed will last as long as there are Indians. This is not a fairy tale, but it sure is a legend.

—Told by Rachel Strange Owl, Birney, Montana,
with the assistance of two or three others. Recorded by
Richard Erdoes.

■

TATANKA IYOTAKE'S
DANCING HORSE

■

[BRULE SIOUX]

As the teller of this tale puts it, "By dancing and singing the right songs, the Lakota people thought that they could bring back the good old buffalo-hunting days, the days before the whites came, the days before smallpox, reservations, and too little to eat. So they danced."

■ ▯▯▯▯▯▯▯▯▯▯▯▯▯▯▯▯▯▯▯▯▯▯▯▯▯▯▯▯▯▯▯ ■

The ghost dance was peaceful, but the whites thought of it as the signal for a great Indian uprising. They asked the army for help, and in the end many unarmed ghost dancers, mostly women and children, were killed at Wounded Knee. We Indians think that the white people were afraid of the ghost dance because they had a bad conscience, having taken away half of the remaining Indian land just a few years before. People with bad consciences live in fear, and they hate most those whom they have wronged. Thus it was with the ghost dance.

At the time, Sitting Bull lived on the Standing Rock Reservation in North Dakota with his Hunkpapa people. He was not, as some people think, the war leader who had defeated Custer on the Little Big Horn. He was a holy man, the spiritual leader of the Sioux nation. He got along well with some whites, even had a few white friends, but he always said: "I want the white man beside me, not above me." Sitting Bull, or Tatanka Iyotake, as he is called in Sioux, was a proud and dignified man, and nobody's slave.

Now, at some time before 1890, Sitting Bull had joined Buffalo Bill's Wild West Show. He had traveled all over the country. In New York he could often be seen sitting on a doorstep on Broadway, giving nickels to poor street urchins and saying that white folks did not know how to take care of their children. He also said that all children—red, white, black, yellow—were alike in their innocence, and that if grown-ups could remain children in their hearts, all would be well. Sitting Bull and Buffalo Bill became friends. When the circus show was over, Buffalo Bill presented his friend Tatanka Iyotake with a fine sombrero, which the Indian holy man wore from then on. Buffalo Bill Cody also gave Sitting Bull his favorite circus horse. It was white and could do many tricks.

At that time the Great White Father in Washington, and the white agents who ruled the reservations, thought that the solution to what they called the "Indian problem" was for Indians to behave like whites: to speak and dress like whites, to become Christians and worship like whites, to own property and work like whites, to marry whites, and to be swallowed up by white society. The "problem" would be solved by simply having no more Indians, by letting them disappear into the great American melting pot.

Sitting Bull opposed this. He did not want the Indians to die out. He wanted them to remain true to their old ways, to go on worshiping the Great Spirit, to continue speaking their own language and singing their old Sioux songs. And because Sitting Bull was a Wichasha Wakan, a medicine man, the most respected one among the Lakota people, many Indians rallied around him. Thus he became the center of the resistance to being swallowed up by the culture of the whites. And thus he became the enemy of those who wanted to make the Indians into white men.

They said that he stood in the path of progress, and the ghost dance trouble seemed a good opportunity to get rid of the old chief. He was accused of siding with the dancers and protecting them. The white reservation chief sent out the Indian police, forty-three of them, to arrest

Sitting Bull. If he resisted and was killed, so much the better. The police force was made up of what we now call "apples," men who are red outside and white inside. They were led by Lieutenants Shave Head and Bull Head.

The police came to arrest the great leader before dawn on an icy winter morning. The ground was covered with snow. They burst into his one-room log cabin with their six-shooters drawn. They dragged him naked from beneath his buffalo robe and pushed him outside; they would not even let him dress properly. They kept pushing at him as they put handcuffs on. The commotion awoke Sitting Bull's friends and relatives in the cabins nearby. Led by the old chief's friend and adopted brother Chase-the-Bear, they came boiling out of their huts and tipis. A woman's voice rose in a song:

> *Sitting Bull,*
> *You were a warrior once,*
> *What are you going to do now?*

The old chief stopped abruptly. He pushed the policemen away, saying: "I won't go!"

Immediately one of the police chiefs shot him through the body, and an all-out fight to the death began. It is always said that a fight between Indians and whites is one thing, but when Sioux fights Sioux, watch out! The police tried to act like whites, but once the fight started, they became Indian warriors again. And among Sitting Bull's friends were some of the bravest warriors, who had fought in many famous battles. When it was over, fifteen people lay dead or dying in the snow, among them Sitting Bull, Chase-the-Bear, and the two police chiefs.

When the white horse heard the shooting, it thought it was back in the circus during the Wild West Show. It began dancing and prancing, sitting on its haunches and raising up its front legs, jumping around, bowing, curtsying, doing all the tricks it had been taught. In this way it honored its dead master in the only way it knew. All who saw it said that the horse was possessed, *wakan*, in the spirit way, because it was unhurt even though it had danced through a hail of bullets. The white horse kept dancing for a while after the fight was over and the bloody scene was silent. Thus Tatanka Iyotake, the great Sitting Bull, and his favorite white horse became part of the legend of our people.

—*Told by George Eagle Elk at Parmelee, Rosebud*
Indian Reservation, South Dakota, 1969.
Recorded by Richard Erdoes.

In 1890 the messianic ghost dance religion swept the Plains tribes. Originating with a vision of the Paiute prophet Wovoka, and heralded by such signs as a frightening eclipse of the sun, the ghost dance was a religion of despair. It gave hope to a people who had been deprived of their ancient hunting grounds and were starving on the reservations. Ghost dancers performed a special round dance, holding hands and singing ghost dance songs. Their shirts, painted with the images of stars, the moon and sun, and magpies, were supposed to make them bulletproof. Dancers swooned and fell down in a trance. Afterwards they declared that they had been in a beautiful land teeming with buffalo, and that they had met their long-dead relatives. The ghost dance, so Wovoka said, would change the world back into what it was before the white man came.

PART SIX

THE SOUND OF FLUTES

TALES OF LOVE AND LUST

Like the rituals of war, the rituals of love demand serious attention. Courtship in different Indian tribes may involve ordeals or tests for the beloved, unpleasant or burdensome responsibilities, sacrifices for one's commitment, or even death itself in the name of love. The tales are by turns tragic, ribald, earthy, and poetic. They tell of contests both exciting and hilarious—great water battles in the Northwest, antics of Coyote and Iktome in the desert. Hair-raising trials of endurance test a vowed commitment, and the rewards are not always as the lovers might have anticipated.

As in tales with other themes, the usual divisions in the natural world are blurred. Human lovers become mountains, stars, and trees. A maiden marries a merman, while a man weds the moon. Alliances between animals and humans are common in many tribes' myths. They appear to be most popular in the North Pacific Coast tribes, where a whale takes a human wife, and among the Plains Indians, whose legends often feature a buffalo or bear. Many more tales of such encounters will come in Part Seven. Often the animal spouses behave better toward their mates than their human counterparts, and in a graceful version of the European "Beauty and the Beast" tale, a dreadful sea serpent teaches a temperamental woman about love and tolerance.

Speaking of love and sex, the Sioux medicine man Lame Deer once said, "Love is sacred, and sex is sacred too. The two things are not apart; they belong together." The missionaries' prudish attitudes toward sex always puzzled the Indians, who even as children generally took sexual expression in its many forms for granted. There are no "dirty words" in Indian languages, and therefore no separate category of "obscene" concepts. Plains tribesmen often had names like Testicles or Penis, bestowed like any other title of honor after a vision or special event.

On the Plains, seducing a pretty girl was almost like counting coup. A man might draw figures on his courting robe to indicate his conquests, much as he would draw scenes of his feats in war on his tipi. Note that the Plains people were no more promiscuous than whites—they simply lacked hypocrisy in sexual matters. If a Sioux girl did not wish to make love (and many did not), she simply tied a hair rope in a certain way between her legs, and no man would dare touch her.

In many tribes, the flute was an instrument used only for courting. Its sound was said to resemble the call of the elk, whose powerful medicine made a man irresistible. If a man drew elk tracks on a small mirror and then flashed the sun's rays from it onto a girl's face or heart, she was immediately his. There are also tales of men whose flutes and melodies had such power that any woman who heard them would follow the sound and surrender herself to the player. The Sioux even tell of women who were so excited by their lovers' music that their noses started to bleed.

Faithlessness is not a theme dealt with lightly; great value is placed on the loyalty of a spouse, even under duress. One Apache women falsely accused of infidelity and banished still remains so steadfast in her commitment to her husband that she returns in the guise of a warrior to rescue him and his entire tribe.

Not all courtship or lovemaking is solemn, of course. The sacred clowns of the Southwest, the Koyemshi and Koshare, often enlivened feasts and dances with antics that mimicked sexual acts or made erotic jokes. These pantomimes had religious undertones, touching on rituals associated with the renewal of life. And of course, among almost all tribes, the antics of the trickster lend themselves perfectly to ribald or erotic themes.

THE LEGEND OF THE FLUTE

[BRULE SIOUX]

Well, you know our flutes; you've heard their sound and seen how beautifully they are made. That flute of ours, the *siyotanka*, is for only one kind of music—love music. In the old days the men would sit by themselves, maybe lean hidden, unseen, against a tree in the dark of night. They would make up their own special tunes, their courting songs.

We Indians are shy. Even if he was a warrior who had already counted coup on an enemy, a young man might hardly screw up courage enough to talk to a nice-looking *winchinchala*—a girl he was in love with. Also, there was no place where a young man and a girl could be alone inside the village. The family tipi was always crowded with people. And naturally, you couldn't just walk out of the village hand in hand with your girl, even if hand holding had been one of our customs, which it wasn't. Out there in the tall grass and sagebrush you could be gored by a buffalo, clawed by a grizzly, or tomahawked by a Pawnee, or you could run into the Mila Hanska, the Long Knives, namely the U.S. Cavalry.

The only chance you had to met your *winchinchala* was to wait for her at daybreak when the women went to the river or brook with their skin bags to get water. When that girl you had your eye on finally came down the water trail, you popped up from behind some bush and stood so she could see you. And that was about all you could do to show her that you were interested—standing there grinning, looking at your moccasins, scratching your ear, maybe.

The *winchinchala* didn't do much either, except get red in the face, giggle, maybe throw a wild turnip at you. If she liked you, the only way she would let you know was to take her time filling her water bag and peek at you a few times over her shoulder.

So the flutes did all the talking. At night, lying on her buffalo robe in her parents' tipi, the girl would hear that moaning, crying sound of the *siyotanka*. By the way it was played, she would know that it was her lover who was out there someplace. And if the elk medicine was very strong in him and her, maybe she would sneak out to follow that sound and meet him without anybody noticing it.

The flute is always made of cedarwood. In shape it describes the long neck and head of a bird with an open beak. The sound comes out of the beak, and that's where the legend comes in, the legend of how the Lakota people acquired the flute.

Once many generations ago, the people had drums, gourd rattles, and bull-roarers, but no flutes. At that long-ago time a young man went out to hunt. Meat was scarce, and the people in his camp were hungry. He found the tracks of an elk and followed them for a long time. The elk, wise and swift, is the one who owns the love charm. If a man possesses elk medicine, the girl he likes can't help sleeping with him. He will also be a lucky hunter. This young man I'm talking about had no elk medicine.

After many hours he finally sighted his game. He was skilled with bow and arrows, and had a fine new bow and a quiver full of straight, well-feathered, flint-tipped arrows. Yet the elk always managed to stay just out of range, leading him on and on. The young man was so intent on following his prey that he hardly noticed where he went.

When night came, he found himself deep inside a thick forest. The tracks had disappeared and so had the elk, and there was no moon. He realized that he was lost and that it was too dark to find his way out. Luckily he came upon a stream with cool, clear water. And he had been careful enough to bring a hide bag of *wasna*—dried meat pounded with berries and kidney fat—strong food that will keep a man going for a few days. After he had drunk and eaten, he rolled himself into his fur robe, propped his back against a tree, and tried to rest. But he couldn't sleep; the forest was full of strange noises, the cries of night animals, the hooting of owls, the groaning of trees in the wind. It was as if he heard these sounds for the first time.

Suddenly there was an entirely new sound, of a kind neither he nor anyone else had ever heard before. It was mournful and ghost-like. It made him afraid, so that he drew his robe tightly about himself and reached for his bow to make sure that it was properly strung. On the other hand, the sound was like a song, sad but beautiful, full of love, hope, and yearning. Then before he knew it, he was asleep. He dreamed that the bird called *wagnuka*, the redheaded woodpecker, appeared singing the strangely beautiful song and telling him: "Follow me and I will teach you."

When the hunter awoke, the sun was already high. On a branch of the tree against which he was leaning, he saw a redheaded woodpecker. The bird flew away to another tree, and another, but never very far, looking back all the time at the young man as if to say: "Come on!" Then once more he heard that wonderful song, and his heart yearned to find the singer. Flying toward the sound, leading the hunter, the bird flitted through the leaves, while its bright red top made it easy to follow. At last it lighted on a cedar tree and began hammering on a branch, making a noise like the fast beating of a small drum. Suddenly there was a gust of wind, and again the hunter heard that beautiful sound right above him.

Then he discovered that the song came from the dead branch that the woodpecker was tapping with his beak. He realized also that it was the wind which made the sound as it whistled through the holes the bird had drilled.

"*Kola*, friend," said the hunter, "let me take this branch home. You can make yourself another."

He took the branch, a hollow piece of wood full of woodpecker holes that was about the length of his forearm. He walked back to his village bringing no meat, but happy all the same.

In his tipi the young man tried to make the branch sing for him. He blew on it, he waved it around; no sound came. It made him sad, he wanted so much to hear that wonderful new sound. He purified himself in the sweat lodge and climbed to the top of a lonely hill. There, resting with his back against a large rock, he fasted, going without food or water for four days and nights, crying for a vision which would tell him how to make the branch sing. In the middle of the fourth night, *wagnuka*, the bird with the bright-red top, appeared, saying, "Watch me," turning himself into a man, showing the hunter how to make the branch sing, saying again and again: "Watch this, now." And in his dream the young man watched and observed very carefully.

When he awoke, he found a cedar tree. He broke off a branch and, working many hours, hollowed it out with a bowstring drill, just as he had seen the woodpecker do it in his dream. He whittled the branch into the shape of a bird with a long neck and an open beak. He painted the top of the bird's head with *washasha*, the sacred red color. He prayed. He smoked the branch up with incense of burning sage, cedar, and sweet grass. He fingered the holes as he had seen the man-bird do in his vision, meanwhile blowing softly into the mouthpiece. All at once there was the song, ghost-like and beautiful beyond words drifting all the way to the

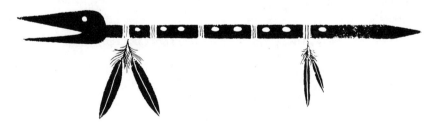

village, where the people were astounded and joyful to hear it. With the help of the wind and the woodpecker, the young man had brought them the first flute.

In the village lived an *itanchan*—a big chief. This *itanchan* had a daughter who was beautiful but also very proud, and convinced that there was no young man good enough for her. Many had come courting, but she had sent them all away. Now, the hunter who had made the flute decided that she was just the woman for him. Thinking of her he composed a special song, and one night, standing behind a tall tree, he played it on his *siyotanka* in hopes that it might have a charm to make her love him.

All at once the *winchinchala* heard it. She was sitting in her father's tipi, eating buffalo-hump meat and tongue, feeling good. She wanted to stay there, in the tipi by the fire, but her feet wanted to go outside. She pulled back, but the feet pulled forward, and the feet won. Her head said, "Go slow, go slow!" but the feet said, "Faster, faster!" She saw the young man standing in the moonlight; she heard the flute. Her head said, "Don't go to him; he's poor." Her feet said, "Go; run!" and again the feet prevailed.

So they stood face to face. The girl's head told her to be silent, but the feet told her to speak, and speak she did, saying: "*Koshkalaka*, young man, I am yours altogether." So they lay down together, the young man and the *winchinchala*, under one blanket.

Later she told him: "*Koshkalaka*, warrior, I like you. Let your parents send a gift to my father, the chief. No matter how small, it will be accepted. Let your father speak for you to my father. Do it soon! Do it now!"

And so the two fathers quickly agreed to the wishes of their children. The proud *winchinchala* became the hunter's wife, and he himself became a great chief. All the other young men had heard and seen. Soon they too began to whittle cedar branches into the shape of birds' heads with long necks and open beaks. The beautiful love music traveled from tribe to tribe, and made young girls' feet go where they shouldn't. And that's how the flute was brought to the people, thanks to the cedar, the woodpecker, and this young man, who shot no elk, but knew how to listen.

—*Told by Henry Crow Dog in New York City, 1967, and
recorded by Richard Erdoes.*

TEACHING THE MUDHEADS
HOW TO COPULATE

■

[ZUNI]

Practically all Indian pueblos of the Southwest have their sacred clowns—the Koshare, Koyemshi, or Chiffonetti, depending on the tribe. Among the Zuni they are known as the Koyemshi, or more colloquially, the Mudheads. In intervals between solemn, exalted masked dances, the clowns appear to do ridiculous things and make ribald jokes, often at the expense of the local missionary or the white tourist. They provide relief from rituals that are highly emotional, sometimes even a little frightening. But their occasionally gross antics are really only the comic counterpart of solemnity, the underscoring of the duality of life. Clowning is serious business, because the Mudheads too are holy people. Their performance is not an antithesis to solemn rites, but an integral part of them.

The Mudheads are not very bright. Long ago they didn't know many things, even very simple, everyday actions. So a man tried to instruct them.

He tried to teach them how to go up a ladder. He showed them how to do it, and they tried to copy him, but they couldn't. One tried to go up the ladder with his feet upmost, standing on his head. Another tried to climb the back of the ladder. A third kept falling through the rungs, while a fourth got all tangled in the rungs. They just couldn't do it.

Then the man tried to teach them how to build a house. He showed them the right way to do it, and they tried to imitate his actions. But one started with the roof and made the others hold up the ceiling while he tried to build downward from it. Another put together a house with no doors and windows. He built it from the inside, and when he wanted to go out, he found he had walled himself in. The others had to break down the walls to let him out. Still another made the mud bricks out of sand. When it rained, his house collapsed into a sandpile. Try as they would, the Mudheads just couldn't do it right.

Then the man tried to show them a really simple thing—how to sit on a chair. They watched and tried to do as he did. One sat on top of the chair back and tumbled over. Another sat underneath the chair.

Another sat on the chair with his back to the front. A fourth tried to sit upside down with his head where his rump ought to have been. They just couldn't get the point.

"Well," said their instructor, "I'll try one thing more. I'm going to show you how to copulate." There was a fat old woman who hadn't had a man in her for a long time. "They can all practice on me," she said, "I don't mind." So she lifted up her manta and bent over, and the instructor copulated with her in the simplest way—from the back as dogs do. The Mudheads watched closely, and then they all wanted to try. But none of them could find the right opening. One did it in the anus, another in the knee bend, another in the arm bend, another in the armpit, another in the navel, another in the ear. They tried and tried. They really wanted to do it right, but they couldn't. "I give up on you," said the instructor. The fat old woman just laughed.

—Told in several versions during a sacred clown dance and pantomime at Zuni Pueblo, 1964, and recorded by Richard Erdoes.

THE FIGHT FOR A WIFE

[ALEUT]

Once upon a time there was a boy who lived all alone, far from other people. He had a habit of lifting stones, at first small ones, then larger and larger ones as he grew and became stronger. When he was old enough to marry, he decided to go out in the world to get a wife, peaceably if he could, but if not, then by fighting for her.

After several days' paddling, he came by night to a village. In one hut he saw a light, so he went there and found a young girl who gave him something to eat and a place to sleep.

The whole village heard that a stranger had arrived. Soon an old man presented himself and shouted through the window of the hut: "Our champion would like to try his strength with the new arrival." The girl explained the meaning of the challenge to the young man and advised him to accept.

The first test consisted of a hunt for beluga. Watched by all the people, the village champion and the stranger went off, each in his own boat. In the evening when they returned, it was the newcomer who had killed the largest number of the animals and was declared the winner.

On the following day another challenge was delivered in the same manner. This time the contest was a boat race around a large island facing the village. When the rivals met on the beach, their *bidarkas*—boats—were side by side. Between them was placed a bow and arrow, to be used by the victor on the vanquished.

The two men got away together, and for a time the contest was in doubt as first one and then the other took the lead. But as the race progressed, the local champion gradually drew ahead of his rival until they lost sight of one another. So certain of the outcome were the old men on the shore that they did not even stay to see the finish. But the newcomer spoke to his boat, which was made of beluga skin, and commanded it to change into the beluga, swim under the water, and overtake the other boat. When the young man was close to shore, he and his boat came up, assumed their usual shapes, and landed.

When the local champion had lost sight of his rival, he had slowed up because he felt certain of victory. Great was his astonishment and fright when he saw the young stranger on the beach with the bow in his hand. He had little time to think, for the twice-victorious hero shot him. While the hero was eating supper at the young girl's home, an old man came to ask him to go to the beach and withdraw the arrow from the defeated champion, since no one else could do it. The newcomer went to the beach and pulled the arrow out, and the villager became well again.

On the evening of the third day, the young man was challenged once more, this time to a wrestling match in the village Large House. In its center was a fenced-in pit containing many bones and shaman worms. The victor was to throw his opponent into the pit, where the worms would eat him. Life, love, glory hung on the outcome, and both men fought hard and long. In this contest the young man's strength, derived from lifting stones, proved decisive. With a skillful movement he picked the local champion off his feet and heaved him into the pit.

The crowd declared the young man to be the new village champion. He went to the home of his defeated rival to claim the spoils of war, which included two wives, furs—all the luxurious possessions of a rich man.

—*Based on F. A. Golder's account of 1909.*

TEETH IN THE
WRONG PLACES

[PONCA-OTOE]

When Coyote was roaming around for adventures, looking for great deeds to do, someone told him of an evil sorceress, an old woman who lived with her two wicked daughters. Many young men went there to sleep with the daughters, who were very handsome, but none was ever seen alive again.

Coyote said, "That's just the place I want to go."

"Be careful," said the person who had told him about it. "Whatever you do, don't sleep with these girls. It would kill you, or so I've been told."

"How could sleeping with two pretty women kill a man?" thought Coyote, and off he went.

The old woman was very nice to him when he arrived, her two daughters were very beautiful. "Come in, come in, the mother said. "You're a good-looking young man, just the kind of person I'd like to have for a son-in-law."

Coyote went into the tipi with his bow and quiver. "Sit down, sit down," the old woman said. "You'll get something good to eat. My daughters will serve you."

The girls brought Coyote many good dishes—buffalo hump, tongues, all kinds of meat. One of the daughters, the older one, said: "You sure are handsome." Coyote thought to himself: "My informant was wrong; these are good people."

By nightfall, Coyote was full of good food and getting drowsy. "You must be tired after your journey," the old woman said. "And it's cold outside. Lie down to sleep between my two daughters—they'll keep you warm."

Coyote snuggled between the two girls. He felt amorous, but he wondered. In the dark the face of the younger girl brushed his; she was whispering in his ear: "Pretty soon my sister will ask you to sleep with her. I'm supposed to ask you too, but you mustn't do it."

"Why not?" asked Coyote.

"The old woman is a witch," said the girl. "She's not really my mother; I'm her prisoner, though the other girl is her daughter. This witch has put teeth into both our vaginas, and when a man comes to visit she gets him to copulate with us. Then these teeth take hold of his penis and chew it to bits. Once he puts it in, he can't pull it out no matter how hard he tries. You should hear those poor young men cry; they cry until they die."

"Why do you tell me this?"

"I like you and I hate doing the old woman's dirty work. After the poor young men are dead, she takes all their things. She likes robbing them, but she likes hearing them die even better."

"I don't believe you."

"Then listen. Do you hear the noise?"

"Yes, I do hear it, a strange noise."

"It's the grinding of the sharp teeth inside our vaginas."

Coyote heard the grinding. He believed what the girl said.

Coyote and the girl pretended to sleep. After a while the older girl, the old woman's daughter, pulled at his sleeve. "Strong young man," she whispered, "you must be hot for us. Let me make you happy. Get on top of me. Quick, get into me;" Coyote could hear the teeth gnashing furiously inside her vagina.

"I've been thinking of nothing else since I first saw you, pretty one," said Coyote, "but let me get my clothes off."

"Hurry up," said the impatient girl. "Don't dawdle. Put it in!"

Coyote took hold of a thick, long stick still warm from the fire, and stuck it deep into that wicked girl's vagina.

"Oh, a real man at last," said the girl, "how good it feels. A real big one for a change!" The teeth inside her were chewing, and wood splinters were flying out of her all over Coyote. "Whew!" he thought. "This is really something!" Quickly he grabbed an arrow from his quiver and thrust it deep into the girl before the teeth could snap shut. The teeth closed upon the shaft near the feathers, but it was too late: the arrow-head had already reached the evil girl's heart, and she died.

Then Coyote went over to the old woman and killed her with his knife. He told the younger girl: "You've saved my life, so come with me and I'll marry you."

"How can you?" said the girl. "I'd like to be your wife, but I have these teeth in the wrong place."

"I'll take care of that," Coyote told her, "so come on."

They started off for Coyote's house and walked all one day. When evening came, Coyote build a brush shelter for the two of them. He put sage into it for a bed. "Now I'm going to make love to you," he said.

"No, never!" said the girl. "It would kill you."

"Well, of course, first I have to knock your teeth out," said Coyote. "And not the ones in your head!"

So he knocked out the teeth in the girl's vagina—except for one blunt tooth that was very thrilling when making love. They were happy, Coyote and this girl.

—Told in New York City by a pixyish old lady who would like to remain anonymous. Recorded by Richard Erdoes.

THE STOLEN WIFE

[TEWA]

Once upon a time in the village of Cu-oh-chi-tae lived an untidy old man and an untidy old lady. Also living with them were their grandson Tiny Flower, his wife White Corn, and the young couple's baby girl.

The cold weather was coming on. To prepare for the winter Tiny Flower went to the mountains every day and hunted deer. One morning soon after he had left the house, White Corn picked up her water jar and took it to Green Willow Lake. There she filled the jar. And as she leaned over the water, she spotted a magic stick under the surface and pulled it out.

This stick belonged to the governor of the Yellow Kachina people. He was a personage with great powers, whose duty it was to make rain, thunder, and clouds every day in the four directions. Although the governor lived far from the lake, his power was such that he had been able to watch White Corn from his home. Seeing how beautiful she was, he had used his magic stick to fly to her.

Now he jumped out from behind a bush and cried, "You can't take that stick! It belongs to me."

Laughing, White Corn darted away, and the governor chased her around and around the lake. She enjoyed being run after by the handsome stranger, while the governor was wishing that he could have the beautiful woman for his wife. Out of breath, White Corn finally came to a stop and handed him his stick.

"Lady White Corn, may I have some of your water?"

White Corn offered him her filled jar, and he drank some and gave it back. "If a person drinks from the jar and doesn't finish it all," said White Corn, "the custom is to pour water on him."

Now it was the governor who darted away and White Corn who chased him. But he didn't run very fast, and he enjoyed having her splash him with water.

"Lady White Corn, wouldn't you like to go to my place?"

"Where do you live?"

"Not far. I live at the top of Flint-Covered Mountain."

"Yes! I'll go with you." White Corn emptied her water jar and placed it upside down at the edge of the lake.

Both the governor and White Corn sat on the magic stick, and in moments they reached the top of Flint-Covered Mountain. On the rooftop of the governor's house was a ladder made of cedarwood. The two climbed down the ladder into the house.

At once the governor said, "Lady White Corn, this is my home, and now it's yours too!" White Corn had been tricked. Like it or not, she had to stay with the governor.

When Tiny Flower returned home and found that his wife had gone, he dropped everything he was carrying and hurried to his grandparents. "My son," said his grandfather, "we found her jar turned upside down at the lake. We have looked and asked all over, but no one has seen her."

Tiny Flower searched again for his wife and visited almost every home in the village, but he learned nothing. The baby cried and cried. The grandparents had been taking her to be fed by nursing mothers in the village, but still she cried day and night. The best that the old couple and Tiny Flower could do was carry her back and forth, back and forth, trying to soothe her.

Days passed, and Tiny Flower grew sadder and sadder. He lay on the rooftop and grieved. Even his arrow bag made of mountain-lion skin lay empty on the floor where he had dropped it the first night he returned.

"You must go to Grandmother Spider," his grandfather said at last. "She will know where White Corn is, because she can spin her web into all parts of the earth."

Carrying gifts, including a little bag of blue cornmeal, Tiny Flower set out to visit Grandmother Spider. He reached her house after many days of walking. "Grandmother, this is a home of reverence, a home of respect, and I have entered it humbly," he said after she had invited him in. "My heart is heavy, sad thoughts disturb my mind, and with your permission I would like to tell you of my troubles." And he spoke of his missing wife and crying baby.

"My son," said Grandmother Spider, "your wife is at the top of Flint-Covered Mountain, where the governor of the Yellow Kachina people took her."

"I must get her," he said.

"First go home, cleanse yourself with holy water, and fill your bag with arrows," she said. "Then return to me and I will give you instructions and some of my medicine."

Tiny Flower traveled quickly and reached home in four days. He cleansed himself carefully and rose the next morning before the sun was up. After offering blue cornmeal to the Great Spirit, he started out again. In three days he arrived at Grandmother Spider's.

"My son, take this pipe, this bag of tobacco, and this medicine stick," she said. "Just before you reach the governor's house, bite a piece off the medicine stick, mix it with your saliva, and rub it on your body. Use the pipe and tobacco when the governor challenges you to match his powers. If you win, you can take your wife away, but if you lose, he will keep White Corn."

Tiny Flower thanked Grandmother Spider, who blessed him and told him not to be afraid. Then, putting the pipe, the bag of tobacco and the medicine stick in his quiver, he went on his way.

His journey took several days, for he had to pass Shoo-fan-ne and Dee-Oaa Cwe-ye Mountains. Then he followed the Trail of the Bears, which led to the top of Flint-Covered Mountain.

Tiny Flower quickly found the governor's house and saw that smoke was coming out of it. So he climbed to the roof and stamped on it violently.

Out came White Corn. "Oh, my husband!" she said. "Why are you here? The governor of the Yellow Kachina people is so cruel and so powerful that something awful will happen to you!"

"Don't be afraid," Tiny Flower said. "I've come to take you home."

"First you must wait for the governor," replied White Corn. "I belong to him now, and he would be so angry if he found me missing that he would hunt us down and kill us for sure. He has gone to the south to make thunder and rain, but he comes home for dinner at noon."

White Corn gave Tiny Flower some cornbread while they waited, and at noon the governor arrived.

"I smell ashes, I smell ashes!" he said in a loud voice. "White Corn, you've fed someone here!"

"No, no, there's no one here! Who would dare come?"

"I know you have someone. Where is he?"

"Well, someone is here," White Corn confessed. "It's my husband; he came to take me home."

Angrily the governor asked, "Where is he?"

"In the next room," she said in a husky voice.

"Why doesn't he come out? Call him."

Out came Tiny Flower at that moment.

"Aha! Look who's here—Tiny Flower the deer hunter. We shall see which of us is the better man, and the one of us who has more power will keep White Corn."

"Poor me; I don't have any magical powers or know any tricks," Tiny Flower replied, "but I must do what you say."

The governor pointed to the center of the room. "Sit on top of this flagstone," he said, and Tiny Flower did as he was told.

"White Corn, stand beside me." And White Corn moved to the governor's side.

The governor prepared a pipe, lit it, and gave it to Tiny Flower. "Here; smoke this."

Puff, puff, puff, puff, went the smoke as Tiny Flower pulled on the pipe. Soon he began to feel dizzy. He swayed back and forth and to the sides; swayed to the right, then to the left. But he did not fall over.

"You must know something! You must know something!" cried the governor.

"I know nothing. I don't live by the night; poor me, the things I do are done in the daytime. So how could I know the things of the spirits?"

Seeing that the tobacco had not worked, the governor began to sing. White Corn joined in, and together they sang:

> Aaa, aaa, ya ma; a-ya-ma, a-ya-ma,
> Aaa, aaa, ya ma; a-ya-ma.
>
> *Tiny Flower man, if you are a man,*
> *Your beloved wife you can take*
> *With you, with you.*
>
> *If you are not a man, here, this*
> *Lightning you can take with you.*

And the governor of the Yellow Kachina struck at Tiny Flower with a bolt of lightning. However, it just missed him. Four times the governor and White Corn sang, and four times the bolt of lightning missed Tiny Flower. The governor had failed. Now it was up to Tiny Flower to test the powers that Grandmother Spider had given him.

Tiny Flower said, "It's your turn to sit on the stone." As the governor seated himself, Tiny Flower told White Corn to tighten her belt and the laces of her moccasins. Then he prepared the tiny pipe that he had from Grandmother Spider and told the governor to smoke it.

"Ho, ho, ho! What can this little thing do to me? It's so small I might swallow the whole thing." He took one puff and became dizzy. He took three more: puff, puff, puff, and over on the floor rolled the governor.

Tiny Flower and White Corn sang:

> Aaa, aaa, ya ma; a-ya-ma, a-ya-ma,
> Aaa, aaa, ya ma; a-ya-ma,
>
> *Yellow Kachina governor man,*
> *If you are a man, my beloved wife*
> *You can have, you can have.*
>
> *If you are not a man, here, this*
> *Lightning you can take with you.*

And Tiny Flower struck at the governor with a bolt of lightning, which did not miss but split him in two. Four times Tiny Flower and White Corn sang, and four times the governor was hit by lightning.

Tiny Flower tore the governor's body into four pieces, then took White Corn by the hand and left the house.

"Be brave and strong, my wife. I am taking you home."

Hand in hand, White Corn and Tiny Flower ran along the top of Flint-Covered Mountain. Soon they came to the Trail of the Bears, which led them down into the valley and back to Grandmother Spider's house. There they stopped just long enough to thank her and return her medicine. And she told them to hurry, because she knew that the governor was coming back to life.

Sure enough, in the distance Tiny Flower and White Corn saw a small white cloud. The governor was just beginning to breathe again. It was not long before the sky darkened and thunder and lightning began to play all around White Corn and Tiny Flower as they ran.

When they passed the river with red water, rain had caught up with them. By the time they reached Yunque, it was falling faster and faster. Tiny Flower urged White Corn to keep running, for they were just a mile away from home.

The Rio Grande was the next river they crossed, and hail began to fall. All kinds of birds were circling above them, but they kept running. They had only a few hundred yards to go when the hail became so heavy that they could not move.

Tiny Flower and White Corn lay on the ground, and all the birds that had been following—crows, eagles, hawks, owls, sparrows, and more—swooped down and protected the man and woman with their spread wings. The birds that were on top of this great canopy were struck by hail and became spotted, while the ones underneath, like the crows, kept their solid colors. When the rain and hail stopped, Tiny Flower promised the birds that in the next four days he would bring them four deer to eat.

Then the couple reached home at last. The grandparents and the baby girl rejoiced, and White Corn was so happy that she cried. As the legend goes, it is because of her return that white corn still grows in the village of San Juan.

—Told at San Juan Pueblo, New Mexico, in the early
1960s and translated from the Tewa by Alfonso Ortiz.

■

TOLOWIM WOMAN AND
BUTTERFLY MAN

■

[MAIDU]

■ |||||||||||||||||||||||||||||||||||||||||||||||||||||||||||||||||||||||||||||||||||| ■

A Tolowim woman went out to gather food. She took her child with her, and while she worked, she stuck the point of the cradleboard in the ground and left the child alone. A large butterfly flew past, and she started after it and chased it for a long time. She would almost catch it, and then just miss. She thought, "Perhaps I can't run fast enough because of this heavy thing," and she threw away her deerskin robe. But still she never could quite overtake the creature. Finally she threw away her apron too and hurried on, chasing the butterfly till night came. Then, her child forgotten, she lay down under a tree and went to sleep.

When she awoke in the morning, she found a man lying beside her. He said, "You have followed me this far; perhaps you would like to follow me always. If so, you must pass through a lot of my people." Without thinking of her child at all, the woman rose and followed the butterfly man. By and by they came to a large valley, whose southern side was full of butterflies. When the two reached the edge of the valley, the man said, "No one has ever before come through this valley alive. But you'll be safe if you don't lose sight of me. Follow closely."

They traveled for a long time. "Keep tight hold of me; don't let go," the butterfly man said again and again. When they come halfway through the valley, other butterflies swarmed about them in great numbers. They flew every way, all around the couple's heads and in their faces, for they wanted to get the Tolowim woman for themselves. She watched them for a long time, holding tightly to her new husband. But at last, unable to resist, she let go of him and reached out to seize one of the others. She missed that one and she tried to grab now one, now the other, but always failed, and so she wandered in the valley forever, dazed and lost.

She died there, and the butterfly man she had lost went on through the valley to his home. And now when people speak of the olden times, they say that this woman lost her lover, and tried to get others but lost them, and went crazy and died.

—Based on a tale reported by Roland Dixon in 1904.

APACHE CHIEF PUNISHES HIS WIFE

[TIWA]

The Yellow House people were traveling. They stopped by a lake, and to reach the deep water they put down a buffalo head to step on. The chief's wife, who was a good-looking woman, picked up her basket and went to fetch some water. When she came to the lake she looked at the head and said, "My father, what a handsome man you were! I would like to have seen you alive. What a pity you're being trampled in this mud!"

As she finished speaking, up sprang a big white buffalo. He said, "I'm the man you speak of. I am White Buffalo Chief. I want to take you with me. Sit on my head between my horns!" She left her water basket right there, and climbed up.

The sun was going down, and the chief's wife did not come home. "Something has happened" he said. "I should go and see." When he got to the lake, he found the basket, and looking around, saw his wife's track and the track of a big buffalo leading to the east. He said, "The buffalo head has taken my wife!" He went back to his camp and for many days made arrows. When he had enough, he set out to find his wife.

As he walked, he nearly stepped on the house of Spider Old Woman. She said, "Sho! sho! sho! My grandchild, don't step on me! Grandchild, you are Apache-Chief-Living-Happily; what are you doing around here?"

"Grandmother, I am looking for my wife. Buffalo Chief took her away. Can you help me?"

"He is a powerful person, but I will give you medicine. Go now to Gopher Old Woman."

He went along, and on the plain he came to Gopher's house. Said Gopher Old Woman, "What are you doing around here? You are Apache-Chief-Living-Happily. Why are you here?"

"Yes, grandmother, I was living happily when my wife went to get water. Buffalo stole her. I am going after her, and I would like to ask you for help."

Gopher Old Woman said, "My grandson, your wife now has as husband a powerful man. He is White Buffalo Chief. She is the tribe's female in-law, and when they go to sleep, she is in the middle and they lie close around her. Her dress is trimmed with elk teeth, and it makes such a noise that it will be difficult to get her out. You go to the edge of where they lie, and I will do the rest."

Apache Chief came to the buffalo territory and hid to watch them. White Buffalo Chief had the stolen wife dancing, and the buffalo sang:

Ya he a he
Ya he iya he
Ya he e ya
He ya hina he
Hina ye ne
He mah ne!

The Apache crept near the dance and spat out the medicine Spider Old Woman had given, and all the buffalo went to sleep. Gopher Old

Woman burrowed underground to the girl's ear and said, "I have come for you. Apache-Chief-Living-Happily is waiting outside the herd."

The girl said, "My present husband is a powerful man. My dress is made of elk teeth, and it makes such a noise that it will wake my husband." Gopher told her to gather the dress up under her arms. Then Gopher led the way, and they slipped through the group of sleeping buffalo.

Her husband was waiting. "I have come for you," he said, "You are my wife and I want to take you back." And she told him they must hurry to a safe place.

The plain was large. As they came to three cottonwood trees, they could feel the earth trembling. White Buffalo had waked up and was shouting to his clan, "Someone took my wife!" The herd followed the track toward the trees.

Apache Chief said to the first cottonwood, "Brother, the buffalo are coming. I want you to hide us." The tree said, "Go to your next brother! I am old and soft." He went to the next tree. "Brother, the buffalo are coming. I want you to hide us!" The tree said, "Go to your next brother." He went to the third tree, a young tree with one branch. "Apache Chief," it said, "come up into my branches and I will help you."

After they were safely up, the wife said she had to urinate. Apache Chief folded up his buffalo hide and told her to urinate on it, but her water leaked through. The buffalo were passing, the dust was rising, and the earth was trembling. In the rear of the pack were a shabby old buffalo and a small one. As they came under the tree, the little buffalo said, "Grandfather, I can smell the water of our daughter-in-law." They looked up and saw the man and woman in the tree.

The old buffalo said, "Grandchild, you are fast. Run on and tell the first one you reach, and each will tell the next one." Soon the whole herd had turned back. Each one in succession butted the tree, and Apache Chief tried to shoot them.

Then White Buffalo Chief took a running start and crashed against the tree. The young cottonwood was nearly down, and Apache Chief could not kill White Buffalo Chief.

Crow was calling above them, "Kaw, kaw kaw!"

Apache Chief said angrily to Crow, "Why are you calling out when I am in such a bad way?"

"I came to tell you to shoot him in the anus. That's where his life is." So the Apache shot White Buffalo Chief in the anus and killed him.

He and his wife came from the tree, and he started to butcher the buffalo beside a little fire. The tears ran down her cheek.

"Are you crying because I'm butchering White Buffalo?"

"No, I'm crying from the smoke."

Apache Chief kept on butchering. He looked at her again and said, "You are crying!"

"No, it's just the smoke."

He stared at her. "You are crying! After all our trouble, you still want this man! Now you die with him! And he took his bow and arrow and shot her.

"I am Apache Chief, chief of a roaming tribe," he said. "I will wander over these plains watching the earth, and if any woman leaves her husband, what I have done to my wife may be done to her."

—*Based on a tale recorded by Elsie Clews Parsons in 1940.*

Like other tales told in pueblos near Taos, New Mexico, this Tiwa story features Apache characters. Taos, because of its proximity to the Plains area, had a close relation to the tribes of that region, and they have shared many elements in their culture, this story being one of them. The Yellow House people refer to people who settled toward the East, nearer the sun.

THE HUSBAND'S PROMISE

[TEWA]

This tale from San Juan Pueblo in New Mexico is a graceful varia-
tion on the same theme as "Deer Hunter and Corn Maiden."

There lived in the village of San Juan a young man, Ca-peen, and a
maiden, Willow Flower. These two were deeply in love, and on the
day of their wedding they promised each other that as long as they were
alive, they would never part.

The couple built a home on the edge of the village and lived happily
together for three moons, until one day the lovely maiden became ill.
The young husband did everything to help her get well, but instead she
became worse, and in a short time she was dead.

The young husband was despondent. He could not understand why
she had to go so soon, after she had promised that she would never
leave him. When many moons had passed, however, he was learning
to live with his grief. At night he did not have much to do and would
usually visit his parents. One night as he was walking back across town
to his own home, he noticed a light burning in the distance beyond the
village. For several days he saw the light shining at the same spot around
midnight, and it began to bother him. Even during the day as he worked,
he would think about it.

One night he said to himself, "I must go to see this light and find
out what it is." It took him about an hour to reach the place, and much
to his surprise he found a house there. Frightened, but curious to know
who lived in it, he decided to peep through the window. He was
astounded to see his lovely wife. She was standing by the fireplace combing her beautiful black hair, which came down to her knees.

Ca-peen said, "Aha, at last I have found her! The light was kept
burning for me to see. Why didn't I come before? And I wonder where
she is going, all dressed up!"

Now his wife finished combing her hair and was putting on her
snow-white moccasins. "I must speak to her before she leaves," said
Ca-peen. Up the stairs he went. Standing in the only entrance to the
house, he saw her poised to ascend the ladder that led to the rooftop.

"What are you doing here?" she said immediately. Before he could reply, she added, "You might as well come in."

Ca-peen slowly descended the stairs. He told her how he had seen the light for a number of nights and decided to investigate. "If I had known you lived here," he said, "I would have come sooner."

"Well," said Willow Flower, "you can't stay any longer. You must go."

"I don't understand. What are you thinking? Remember the promise we made when we got married—that we would never part? And now that I've found you, I will stay."

Angrily Willow Flower replied, "You can't stay here. You do not belong with me, and until your time comes, you cannot be with me. Go, before it's too late."

Ca-peen insisted on staying, and this led to a long quarrel. At last Willow Flower said, "All right; you can stay for the night—provided that you are a man."

"I am a man," retorted Ca-peen.

"In that case, you will stay with me until the morning. And if you are still here then, I will go home with you to the village. Do you agree?"

"Yes, I agree," said Ca-peen.

Willow Flower prepared a bed on the floor, and they both went to sleep.

About three o'clock in the morning, Ca-peen was awakened by a pungent odor that stung his nostrils. It was coming from the body of his wife. Soon Ca-peen could no longer tolerate the odor of rotten flesh. Slowly he got out of bed and put on his clothes.

He said to himself, "If I leave before she wakes, I will be free."

Very quietly he went up the stairs. Just as he reached the last step, Willow Flower woke up and cried, "Come back, you coward! You have failed to keep your end of the bargain, and now you must pay the penalty."

Ca-peen was not yet ready to join the people of death, so he jumped off the rooftop and ran toward home with all his might.

But Willow Flower was swift as the wind, and in no time she was out of the house and running after him.

As Ca-peen came to the Rio Grande he met the old medicine man from the village, who was on his way to the mountains in search of game. The old man said, "What's wrong, my son? Are you running away from someone? You look as if something awful has happened to you."

Ca-peen could hardly talk, but he finally managed to gasp, "I'm running away from Willow Flower."

"So you are," said the old medicine man. "You've never learned to mind your own business, and now this has happened to you."

"Old Medicine Man, you must help me. You are a powerful one; send me where Willow Flower can't catch me."

The old man said, "There's no place on earth that will hide you from Willow Flower. I'll shoot you into the sky, which has plenty of room for you to run. Come, jump into the shaft of this special arrow."

Ca-peen did as he was told. "Ca-peen, are you comfortable in there?"

"Yes, Old Man."

"Get ready. Now I'm going to shoot you into the sky, where Willow Flower will never catch you."

"Twang!" went the old medicine man's bowstring, and off into the sky flew Ca-peen.

With Ca-peen on his way, the old medicine man returned to his own trail. A few minutes later he met Willow Flower.

"Good morning, my child," said the medicine man. "Where are you going?"

"I am running after Ca-peen. Have you seen him?"

"Yes, I talked to him near the river a few minutes ago."

"You are a powerful one; tell me where he is heading."

"Ca-peen is now in the sky. If you want to catch him, that's where you'll have to go."

"Please shoot me into the sky with your strong bow," said Willow Flower. So the old medicine man put her into one of his special arrows and shot her to the sky.

To this day, Willow Flower is chasing Ca-peen. Tonight if the stars are out, just look to the west and you will see two bright ones about a foot apart. The first is Ca-peen, and the one behind is Willow Flower, chasing her husband.

—*Told at San Juan Pueblo, New Mexico, in the early 1960s and translated from the Tewa by Alfonso Ortiz.*

THE MAN WHO
MARRIED THE MOON

■

[ISLETA PUEBLO]

*This story, prepared for a popular magazine at the turn of the cen-
tury, blends Pueblo folklore with late-Victorian language and sen-
sibilities. Corn maidens are both malevolent (as in this tale) and
beneficent spirits who give themselves as food so that the people
may live.*

■ ▍▍▍ ■

Long before the first Spaniards came to New Mexico, Isleta stood
where it stands today—on a lava ridge that defies the gnawing current
of the Rio Grande. In those far days, Nah-chu-rú-chu, "The Bluish
Light of Dawn," dwelt in Isleta, and was a leader of his people. A
weaver by trade, his rude loom hung from the dark rafters of his room;
and in it he wove the strong black mantas or robes like those which are
the dress of Pueblo women to this day.

Besides being very wise in medicine, Nah-chu-rú-chu was young, and
tall, and strong, and handsome. All the girls of the village thought it a
shame that he did not care to take a wife. For him the shyest dimples
played, for him the whitest teeth flashed out, as the owners passed him
in the plaza; but he had no eyes for them. Then, in the custom of the
Tiwa, bashful fingers worked wondrous fringed shirts of buckskin, or
gay awl sheaths, which found their way to his house by unknown
messengers.

But Nah-chu-rú-chu paid no more attention to the gifts than to the
smiles, and just kept weaving and weaving—such mantas as were never
seen in the land of the Tee-wahn before or since.

Two of his admirers were sisters who were called, in Tiwa language,
Ee-eh-ch-chóo-ri-ch'áhm-nin—the Yellow Corn Maidens. They were
both young and pretty, but they "had the evil road," or were witches,
possessed of a magic power which they always used for ill. When all
the other girls gave up, discouraged at Nah-chu-rú-shu's indifference,
the Yellow Corn Maidens kept coming day after day, trying to win his
notice. At last the matter became so annoying to Nah-chu-rú-chu that
he hired the deep-voiced town crier to go through all the streets and
announce that in four days Nah-chu-rú-chu would choose a wife.

For dippers to take water from the big earthen jars, the Tiwa used then, as they use to-day, queer little *omates* made of a gourd. But Nah-chu-rú-chu, being a great medicine man and very rich, had a dipper of pure pearl, shaped like the gourds, but wonderfully precious.

"On the fourth day," proclaimed the crier, "Nah-chu-rú-chu will hang his pearl *omate* at his door, when every girl who will may throw a handful of cornmeal at it. And she whose meal is so well ground that it sticks to the *omate*, she shall be the wife of Nah-chu-rú-chu!"

When this strange news came rolling down the still evening air, there was a great scampering of little moccasined feet. The girls ran out from hundreds of gray adobe houses to catch every word; and when the crier had passed on, they ran back into the storerooms and began to ransack the corn bins for the biggest, evenest, and most perfect ears. Shelling the choicest, each took her few handfuls of kernels to the sloping *metate*, and with the *mano*, or hand stone, scrubbed the blue grist up and down and up and down till the hard corn was a soft blue meal. All the next day, and the next, and the next, they ground it over and over again, until it grew finer than ever flour was before; and every girl felt sure that her meal would stick to the *omate* of the handsome young weaver. The Yellow Corn Maidens worked hardest of all; day and night for four days they ground and ground, with all the magic spells they knew.

Now, in those far-off days the moon had not gone into the sky to live, but was a maiden of Isleta. And a very beautiful girl she was, but blind of one eye. She had long admired Nah-chu-rú-chu, but was always too maidenly to try to attract his attention as the other girls had done; and at the time when the crier made his proclamation, she happened to be away at her father's ranch. It was only upon the fourth day that she returned to town, and in a few moments the girls were to go with their meal to test it upon the magic dipper. The two Yellow Corn Maidens were just coming from their house as she passed, and they told her what was to be done. They were very confident of success, and hoped to pain her. They laughed derisively as she went running to her home.

By this time a long file of girls was coming to Nah-chu-rú-chu's house, outside whose door hung the pearl *omate*. Each girl carried in her hand a little jar of meal. As they passed the door, one by one, each took from the jar a handful and threw it against the magic dipper. But each time the meal dropped to the ground, and left the pure pearl undimmed and radiant as ever.

At last came the Yellow Corn Maidens, who had waited to watch the failure of the others. As they came where they could see Nah-chu-rú-chu sitting at his loom, they called: "Ah! here we have the meal that will stick!" and each threw a handful at the *omate*. But it did not stick at all;

and still from his seat Nah-chu-rú-chu could see, in the shell's mirror-like surface, all that went on outside.

The Yellow Corn Maidens were very angry, and instead of passing on as the others had done, they stood there and kept throwing and throwing at the *omate*, which smiled back at them with undiminished luster.

Just then, last of all, came the moon, with a single handful of meal which she had hastily ground. The two sisters were in a fine rage by this time, and mocked her, saying:

"Hoh! Páh-hlee-oh, Moon, you poor thing, we are very sorry for you! Here we have been grinding our meal for four days and still it will not stick, and we did not tell you till today. How then can you ever hope to win Nah-chu-rú-chu? Puh, you silly little thing!"

But the moon paid no attention whatsoever to their taunts. Drawing back her little dimpled hand, she threw the meal gently against the pearl *omate*, and so fine was it ground that every tiniest bit of it clung to the polished shell, and not a particle fell to the ground!

When Nah-chu-rú-chu saw that, he rose up quickly from his loom and came and took the moon by the hand, saying: "You are she who shall be my wife. You shall never want for anything, since I have very much." And he gave her many beautiful mantas, and cotton wraps, and fat boots of buckskin that wrap round and round, that she might dress as the wife of a rich chief. But the Yellow Corn Maidens, who had seen it all, went away vowing vengeance on the moon.

Nah-chu-rú-chu and his sweet moon-wife were very happy together. There was no other such housekeeper in all the pueblo as she, and no other hunter brought home so much buffalo meat from the vast plains to the east, nor so many antelopes, and black-tailed deer, and jack rabbits from the Manzanos, as did Nah-chu-rú-chu. But constantly he was saying to her:

"Moon-wife, beware of the Yellow Corn Maidens, for they have the evil road and will try to do you harm; but you must always refuse to do whatever they propose."

And always the young wife promised.

One day the Yellow Corn Maidens came to the house and said: "Friend Nah-chu-rú-chu, we are going to the llano, the plain, to gather amole." (Amole is a soapy root the Pueblos use for washing.) "Will you not let your wife go with us?"

"Oh, yes, she may go," said Nah-chu-rú-chu. But taking her aside, he said: "Now be sure that while you are with them, you refuse whatever they may propose."

The moon promised, and started away with the Yellow Corn Maidens.

In those days there was only a thick forest of cottonwoods where now the smiling vineyards, gardens, and orchards of Isleta are spread, and to reach the llano the three women had to go through the forest. In the very center of it they came to a deep *pozo*—a square well, with steps at one side leading down to the water's edge.

"Ay!" said the Yellow Corn Maidens, "How hot and thirsty is our walk! Come, let us get a drink of water."

But the moon, remembering her husband's words, said politely that she did not wish to drink. They urged in vain, but at last, looking down into the *pozo*, they called:

Oh, moon-friend, moon-friend! Come and look in this still water, and see how pretty you are!"

The moon, you must know, has always been just as fond of looking at herself in the water as she is to this very day; and forgetting Nah-chu-rú-chu's warning, she came to the brink and looked down upon her fair reflection. But at that very moment the two witch sisters pushed her head foremost into the *pozo*, and drowned her; and then they filled the well with earth, and went away as happy as wicked hearts can be.

As the sun crept along the adobe floor, closer and closer to his seat, Nah-chu-rú-chu began to look oftener from his loom to the door. When the shadows were very long, he sprang suddenly to his feet, and walked to the house of the Yellow Corn Maidens with long, long strides.

"Yellow Corn Maidens," he asked them very sternly, "where is my little wife?"

"Why, isn't she at home?" asked the wicked sisters, as if greatly surprised. "She got enough amole long before we did."

"Ah," groaned Nah-chu-rú-chu within himself, "it is as I thought—they have done her ill."

But without a word to them he turned on his heel and went away.

From that hour all went wrong at Isleta; for Nah-chu-rú-chu held the well-being of all his people, even unto life and death. Paying no attention to what was going on about him, he sat motionless upon the topmost crosspiece of the *estufa* (the kiva, or sacred council chamber ladder—the highest point in all the town) with his head bowed upon his hands. There he sat for days, never speaking, never moving. The children who played along the streets looked up with awe to the motionless figure, and ceased their boisterous play. The old men shook their heads gravely, and muttered: "We are in evil times, for Nah-chu-rú-chu is mourning, and will not be comforted; and there is no more rain, so that our crops are dying in the fields. What shall we do?"

At last all the councilors met together, and decided that there must be another effort made to find the lost wife. It was true that the great

Nah-chu-rú-chu had searched for her in vain, and the people had helped him; but perhaps someone else might be more fortunate. So they took some of the sacred smoking weed wrapped in a corn husk and went to the eagle, who has the sharpest eyes in all the world. Giving him the sacred gift, they said:

"Eagle-friend, we see Nah-chu-rú-chu in great trouble, for he has lost his moon-wife. Come, search for her, we pray you, to discover if she be alive or dead."

So the eagle took the offering, and smoked the smoke prayer; and then he went winging upward into the sky. Higher and higher he rose, in great upward circles, while his keen eyes noted every stick, and stone, and animal on the face of all the world. But with all his eyes, he could see nothing of the lost wife; and at last he came back sadly, and said:

"People-friends, I went up to where I could see the whole world, but I could not find her."

Then the people went with an offering to the coyote, whose nose is sharpest in all the world, and besought him to try and find the moon. The coyote smoked the smoke prayer, and started off with his nose to the ground, trying to find her tracks. He trotted all over the earth; but at last he too came back without finding what he sought.

Then the troubled people got the badger to search, for he is the best of all the beasts at digging (it was he whom the Trues employed to dig the caves in which the people first dwelt when they came to this world). The badger trotted and pawed, and dug everywhere, but he could not find the moon; and he came home very sad.

Then they asked the osprey, who can see furthest under water, and he sailed high above the lakes and rivers in the world, till he could count the pebbles and the fish in them, but he too failed to discover the lost moon.

By this time the crops were dead and sere in the fields, and thirsty animals walked crying along the river. Scarcely could the people themselves dig deep enough to find water to keep them alive. They were at a loss, but at last they thought: We will go now to the P'ah-ku-ee-teh-ay-deh (the water-goose grandfather, which means turkey buzzard), who can find the dead—for surely she is dead, or the others would have found her.

So they went to him, and besought him. The turkey buzzard wept when he saw Nah-chu-rú-chu still sitting there upon the ladder, and said: "Truly it is sad for our great friend; but for me, I am afraid to go, since they who are more mighty than I have already failed. Yet I will try." And spreading his broad wings, he went climbing up the spiral ladder of the sky. Higher he wheeled, and higher, till at last not even the eagle could see him. Up and up, till the sun began to singe his head, and not even the eagle had ever been so high. He cried with pain, but still he kept mounting—until he was so close to the sun that all the feathers were burned from his head and neck. But he could see nothing, and at last, frantic with the burning, he came wheeling downward. When he got back to the *estufa* where all the people were waiting, they saw that his head and neck had been burned bare of feathers—and from that day to this the feathers would never grow out again.

"And did you see nothing?" they all asked, when they had bathed his burns.

"Nothing," he answered, "except that when I was halfway down, I saw in the middle of yon cottonwood forest a little mound covered with all the beautiful flowers in the world."

"Oh!" cried Nah-chu-rú-chu, speaking for the first time, "Go, friend, and bring me one flower from the very middle of the mound."

Off flew the buzzard, and in a few minutes returned with a little white flower. Nah-chu-rú-chu took it and, descending from the ladder in silence, walked solemnly to his house, while all the wondering people followed.

When Nah-chu-rú-chu came inside his home once more, he took a new manta and spread it in the middle of the room. Laying the wee white flower tenderly in its center, he put another manta above it. Then, dressing himself in the splendid buckskin suit that the lost wife had made him, and taking in his right hand the sacred *guaje*, rattle, he seated himself at the head of the mantas and sang:

"*Shú-nah, shú-nah! Ai-ay, ai-ay, ai-ay-ay.* Seeking her, seeking her! There-away, there-away."

When he had finished the song, all could see that the flower had begun to grow, so that it lifted the upper manta a little. Again he sang, shaking his gourd; and still the flower kept growing. Again and again he sang; and when he had finished for the fourth time, it was plain to all that a human form lay between the two mantas. And when he sang his song the fifth time, the form sat up and moved. Tenderly he lifted away the upper cloth; and there sat his sweet moon-wife, fairer than ever, and alive as before!

For four days the people danced and sang in the public square. Nah-chu-rú-chu was happy again; and now the rain began to fall. The choked earth drank and was glad and green, and the dead crops came to life.

When his wife told him what the witch sisters had done, he was very angry; and that day he made a beautiful hoop to play the hoop game. He painted it, and put many strings across it, and decorated it with beaded buckskin.

"Now," said he, "the wicked Yellow Corn Maidens will come to congratulate you, and will pretend not to know where you were. You must not speak of that, but invite them to go out and play a game with you."

In a day or two the witch sisters did come, with deceitful words; and the moon invited them to go out and play a game. They went up to the edge of the llano, and there she let them get a glimpse of the pretty hoop.

"Oh, give us that, moon-friend," they teased. But she refused. At last, however, she said: "Well, we will play the hoop game. I will stand here, and you there; and if, when I roll it to you, you catch it before it falls upon its side, you may have it."

So the witch sisters stood a little way down the hill, and she rolled the bright hoop. As it came trundling to them, both grasped it at the same instant; and lo! instead of the Yellow Corn Maidens, there were two great snakes, with tears rolling down ugly faces. The moon came and put upon their heads a little of the pollen of the corn blossom (still used by Pueblo snake charmers) to tame them, and a pinch of sacred meal for their food.

"Now," she said, "you have the reward of treacherous friends. Here shall be your home among these rocks and cliffs forever, but you must never be found upon the prairie; and you must never bite a person. Remember you are women, and must be gentle."

And then the moon went home to her husband, and they were very happy together. As for the sister snakes, they still dwell where she bade them, and never venture away; though sometimes the people bring them to their houses to catch mice, for these snakes never hurt a person.

—*Published by Charles F. Lummis in* St. Nicholas Magazine
in 1897.

In view of Pueblo esteem for snakes, the sisters' punishment was a mild one. Some Pueblo tribes view snakes as rain bringers, and the heroes of Pueblo myths sometimes marry snake maidens, as in "The Hopi Boy and the Sun." According to a government report of 1900: "The superstitious regard of these Indians for snakes, inasmuch as they hold a prominent part in religious rites, protects them and renders them abundant among the villages. A snake on being found in the pueblo is merely carried off on sticks and laid outside of man's immediate range." Notice that when the wicked corn maidens were turned into snakes, they became gentler and kinder beings.

WHY MOLE LIVES UNDERGROUND

[CHEROKEE]

A man was in love with a woman who disliked him and wanted nothing to do with him. He tried in every way to win her favor, but with no success. At last he grew discouraged and made himself sick thinking about it.

Mole came along, and finding the man so low in his mind, asked what the trouble was. The man told him the whole story, and when he had finished, Mole said: "I can help you. Not only will she like you, but she'll come to you of her own free will."

That night, burrowing underground to the place where the girl was in bed asleep, Mole took out her heart. He came back by the same way and gave the heart to the discouraged lover, who couldn't see it even when it was in his hand. "There," said Mole. "Swallow it, and she will be so drawn to you that she has to come."

The man swallowed the heart, and when the girl woke up she somehow thought of him at once. She felt a strange desire to be with him, to go to him that minute. She couldn't understand it, because she had always disliked him, but the feeling grew so strong that she was compelled to find the man and tell him that she loved him and wanted to be his wife. And so they were married.

All the magicians who knew them both were surprised and wondered how it had come about. When they found that it was the work of Mole, whom they had always thought too insignificant to notice, they were jealous and threatened to kill him. That's why Mole hid under the ground and still doesn't dare to come up.

—*Based on a tale reported by James Mooney in the 1890s.*

A LEGEND OF MULTNOMAH FALLS

Many years ago the head chief of the Multnomah people had a beautiful young daughter. She was especially dear to her father because he had lost all his sons in fighting, and he was now an old man. He chose her husband with great care—a young chief from his neighbors, the Clatsop people. To the wedding feast came many people from tribes along the lower Columbia and south of it.

The wedding feast was to last for several days. There were swimming races and canoe races on the river. There would be bow-and-arrow contests, horse racing, dancing, and feasting. The whole crowd was merry, for both the maiden and the young warrior were loved by their people.

But without warning the happiness changed to sorrow. A sickness came over the village. Children and young people were the first victims; then strong men became ill and died in one day. The wailing of women was heard throughout the Multnomah village and the camps of the guests.

"The Great Spirit is angry with us," the people said to each other. The head chief called together his old men and his warriors for counsel and asked gravely, "What can we do to soften the Great Spirit's wrath?"

Only silence followed his question. At last one old medicine man arose. "There is nothing we can do. If it is the will of the Great Spirit that we die, then we must meet our death like brave men. The Multnomah have ever been a brave people."

The other members of the council nodded in agreement—all except one, the oldest medicine man. He had not attended the wedding feast and games, but he had come in from the mountains when he was called by the chief. He rose and, leaning on his stick, spoke to the council. His voice was low and feeble.

"I am a very old man, my friends; I have lived a long, long time. Now you will know why. I will tell you a secret my father told me. He was a great medicine man of the Multnomah, many summers and many snows in the past.

"When he was an old man, he told me that when I became old, the

Great Spirit would send a sickness upon our people. All would die, he said, unless a sacrifice was made to the Great Spirit. Some pure and innocent maiden of the tribe, the daughter of a chief, must willingly give her life for her people. Alone, she must go to a high cliff above Big River and throw herself upon the rocks below. If she does this, the sickness will leave us at once."

Then the old man said, "I have finished; my father's secret is told. Now I can die in peace."

Not a word was spoken as the medicine man sat down. At last the chief lifted his head. "Let us call in all the maidens whose fathers or grandfathers have been headmen."

Soon a dozen girls stood before him, among them his own loved daughter. The chief told them what the old medicine man had said. "I think his words are the words of truth," he added.

Then he turned to his medicine men and his warriors, "Tell our people to meet death bravely. No maiden shall be asked to sacrifice herself. The meeting has ended."

The sickness stayed in the village, and many more people died. The daughter of the head chief sometimes wondered if she should be the one to give her life to the Great Spirit. But she loved the young warrior— she wanted to live.

A few days later she saw the sickness on the face of her lover. Now she knew what she must do. She cooled his hot face, cared for him tenderly, and left a bowl of water by his bedside. Then she slipped away alone, without a word to anyone.

All night and all the next day she followed the trail to the great river. At sunset she reached the edge of a cliff overlooking the water. She stood there in silence for a few moments, looking at the jagged rocks far below. Then she turned her face toward the sky and lifted up her arms. She spoke aloud to the Great Spirit.

"You are angry with my people. Will you make the sickness pass away if I give you my life? Only love and peace and purity are in my heart. If you will accept me as a sacrifice for my people, let some token hang in the sky. Let me know that my death will not be in vain and that the sickness will quickly pass."

Just then she saw the moon coming up over the trees across the river. It was the token. She closed her eyes and jumped from the cliff.

Next morning, all the people who had expected to die that day arose from their beds well and strong. They were full of joy. Once more there was laughter in the village and in the camps of the guests.

Suddenly someone asked, "What caused the sickness to pass away? Did one of the maidens—?"

Once more the chief called the daughters and granddaughters of the headmen to come before him. This time one was missing.

The young Clatsop warrior hurried along the trail which leads to Big River. Other people followed. On the rocks below the high cliff they found the girl they all loved. There they buried her.

Then her father prayed to the Great Spirit, "Show us some token that my daughter's spirit has been welcomed into the land of the spirits."

Almost at once they heard the sound of water above. All the people looked up to the cliff. A stream of water, silvery white, was coming over the edge of the rock. It broke into floating mist and then fell at their feet. The stream continued to float down in a high and beautiful waterfall.

For many summers the white water has dropped from the cliff into the pool below. Sometimes in winter the spirit of the brave and beautiful maiden comes back to see the waterfall. Dressed in white, she stands among the trees at one side of Multnomah Falls. There she looks upon the place where she made her great sacrifice and thus saved her lover and her people from death.

—Reported by Ella Clark in 1953.

THE INDUSTRIOUS DAUGHTER WHO WOULD NOT MARRY

[COCHITI]

An old woman and an old man were living in the village, and they had an only daughter. They were very poor. When the girl grew up and began to wonder how she could take care of her father and mother, she said to herself, "I will pick up cotton that has been thrown away." She gathered cotton scraps, combed them, spun them, and rolled the yarn into a ball. When she had enough, she knit a pair of footless stockings. She showed them to her father and mother and said, "I worked hard to make them, and I think it will help us."

Next she tried knitting a pair of openwork stockings—the sort of leggings, now made of twine, that women wear for the deer dance. She hung them on the clothes pole and called her parents to see what she had learned.

"Now I will try to make a big white manta," she said. Picking up more scraps, she combed them and spun them and wound the yarn into balls. Then threaded her loom and began to weave. When she had finished, she decided to embroider it with different colors. She dyed her yarn and sat sewing on the white manta by the window. By this time the daughter had grown to be a large, handsome girl. While she was embroidering, the young men came around to talk to her about marriage, but she was not interested. She said, "I take care of my father and mother and myself." When the manta was finished, she presented it to her parents, and her mother hung it over the clothes pole.

"Now I will make a white ball-fringed sash," she said. She laid the threads horizontally and began weaving. While she was working, the boys would come to the window and watch, but she paid no attention. When she finished, she took it to her parents, and her mother hung it on the pole.

"Now I will make a small white manta for a dancer's sash," she said. She threaded her loom, wove it, and embroidered it at both ends. Her parents were very happy that their daughter had such initiative.

"I am going to make a belt," the girl said. She collected more cotton scraps and went out to pick the plants that are used in dyeing the yarn yellow. She saved urine in a very large jar, and when it was full, dipped some out into a bowl. She pounded up bluestone, wet it with the urine, and poured it into the big jar. Then she threw the yarn into the big jar, and when she took it out on the third day, it was blue as blue could be.

Next, after boiling the yellow dye plants, the girl dipped the yarn into the dye water. She said to her father, "Shall I take them all out? For I might make the belt only of blue and yellow." Her father said, "Yes; when you take the yarn out, hang it over a rafter end, and in the lower loops put the rubbing stone so the yarn will dry straight. Then when you die, they won't stretch you out like that." Then she dyed some yarn red, wove her belt, and finished it. "When you finish the belt, stretch it well, so they won't stretch you when you die," her father told her. This is the advice they give all Indian girls when they weave.

Now the girl sent her father and mother out to sell what she had made, and when they got home, she was spinning again. "Did you have good luck?" she asked, and they said they had sold them all.

Soon the people in the village were coming to the girl's house to buy whatever they wanted. The young men bought so many ball-fringed sashes and small embroidered mantas that at last everybody had a complete dancing costume. Then they said, "Let's have a great dance before her house and see which of us she will choose to dance with." So they dressed for the dance and gathered in front of her house. She was sitting in the doorway embroidering a white manta when they began to dance. But she said, "Why do you think I am the only girl in the village? You are all calling me." She didn't even lift her head as the dance ended and they left. She finished embroidering the manta and gave it to her mother, who hung it over the pole.

The family sat by the fireplace, and her father said, "Rest yourself, my daughter." "I can't help working," she replied. "I like it." Even as she was sitting there, she was pulling cotton apart. She heard the noise of the rattles approaching and said, "They're coming again! They make a great noise!" It was the rainbow dance, but she didn't watch. Some of the dancers came to the house and said, "We're surprised that you don't even care to look up when we dance." They went home, but she kept working.

Next day the young men began to come to ask her to marry them. Each brought a large manta and a small manta and a belt, but she refused them all. "Thank you, but I can make those myself," she said. "I know how to make whatever I want."

"What can we do to persuade her to marry us?" they said. "Let's all draw pretty things on our houses." Soon all the young men were busy painting rainbows all over their houses, some on the walls and some on the ladders. Some made little stone birds, set them on both sides of the ladder rungs, and painted them in all colors. The next day she went all through the village, but she didn't care for the rainbows or birds or sunflowers. "I take care of myself and my parents," she said. "I don't need anything more, and I want to stay where I am."

Next the young men thought they would tempt her with corn. On top of their roofs they made piles of all the different-colored ears: blue, white, red, dark red, yellow, and many others. As she walked through the village, she looked at the piles, and the young men all trembled with hope. But she didn't care for any of it. "I tell you boys, I never want to marry. I make my own clothing, and I live very well."

So at last the boys said, "We won't court her any more; she doesn't care for young men."

Coyote heard about this and said, "She'll have to go with me. I shall offer her nothing at all, but she will belong to me. I'll go to the mountains to fetch a black currant branch."

He went to his house and took his white buckskin moccasins, the skunk skin to tie around his ankles, the openwork stockings, the small white manta for his kilt, white and red yarn to tie around his arms, his white shell beads, his abalone shell, his paint pot, his long parrot-tail feathers, his short parrot-tail feathers, his downy feathers, and his gourd rattle. He did all these up in a bundle and started off. As he went, he came to the place where the black currants grow. He took some and said, "Come along, Payatamu."

Arriving at the girl's village, he went not to her house but to another one. "Hello," he said, but no one answered, for nobody was there. He went into the inner room and laid down his bundle. "Now come, Payatamu!" He stamped four times rapidly with his foot, and drew on his white buckskin moccasins. He looked down at his feet. "Do I look pretty? Yes, I look pretty," he said. He stamped four times and put on his lace stockings, and he said, "Do I look pretty? Yes, I look pretty." He stamped four times, put the skunk skin around his ankles, and said, "Do I look pretty? Yes, I look pretty." And so he proceeded as he put on each of the things in his bundle. When he was all dressed, he said, "Come, Payatamu, see if I can get that girl. I shall not dance before her house, but in the center of Little Plaza." And before he went out, picked up the bunch of black currants in his left hand.

He went into the center of Little Plaza and began to dance. When they heard the sound of the rattle, everybody looked out and saw a boy dancing. Hearing somebody singing, the girl threw down the white manta she was embroidering and went out. "What a fine-looking boy!" she said. "I've never seen him before; I wonder who he is." She walked into the center of Little Plaza, and she spied his bunch of black currants, of which she was very fond. Then she said to Coyote, "Give me the black currant branch, and I'll take you to my house."

The boys of the village said to her, "What a dirty, miserable girl you are! Why will you take such a little bit of black currants and let him sleep with you? We've offered you so much more, but you wouldn't even look at it."

But the girl kept right on and led the dancer to her house. She called to her father and mother, "Here comes Payatamu."

Her mother exclaimed, "Oh, my dear daughter! What a mischief you have done!"

"My dear mother, he has a branch of great black currants. You know how I love black currants, and it's a long time since I've eaten any."

Payatamu stayed the night and had intercourse with her, and she gave birth to little coyotes. She was a fine-looking girl, but no one in the village cared about her looks by then.

Coyote said to the girl's father and mother, "I shall take my wife and child to my home." The couple set out and on their journey came near

High Bank. There was a big hole in the ground, and Coyote said, "Let me go in first." The girl asked, "How can you go in? It's so small." But he managed, and next the two little coyotes entered, and then the mother peeped through. Inside was a house just as good as her parents' home. Coyote had as many mantas, and embroidered mantas, and openwork stockings and belts as she had. So she went in, and they lived there ever after.

—Collected by Ruth Benedict in 1924.

■

THE WOMAN WHO
MARRIED A MERMAN

■

[COOS]

■ |||||||||||||||||||||||||||||||||||||||||||||||||||||||||||||||||||||||||||||||||||| ■

In a village named Takimiya there lived five brothers and a sister. Many men from different places wished to marry the girl, but she did not want to get married. It was her custom to go swimming every day in a little creek. One day while returning from her swim, she noticed that she was pregnant. Her brothers demanded to know how it had happened, but she could not give them an answer because she did not understand it herself.

She gave birth to a boy, a fretful baby who cried all the time. They did everything to try and soothe him, but nothing worked. At their wits' end, her brothers finally told her to put the child outdoors. He immediately stopped crying. After a while the mother went out to check on him and noticed, to her surprise, that he was eating a piece of seal meat which someone had strung on a small stick for him. She looked around to see who could have done it, but nobody was there. When she took the child into the house, he started to cry again and would not let anybody sleep. So her brothers told her to take him out again and suggested that she hide and watch what happened.

The mother lay hidden outside for a whole day without seeing anyone. Suddenly toward evening a man appeared and told her to follow him, because he was her husband. At first she refused, fearing that her relatives would not know where she had gone. But after he promised that she would be safe, she took the baby in her arms and went with him. They approached the creek, and her husband told her to hang onto his belt and keep her eyes closed. Together they plunged into the water. Soon they came to the bottom of the sea—to a village inhabited by many Indians. Her husband was one of the five sons of the village chief, and the couple lived there happy and satisfied.

The boy grew up, and like many boys on dry land, he loved to play with arrows. His mother would make them for him, meanwhile telling him that his uncles, who lived above the water, had lots of arrows. One day the boy asked her to take him to his land uncles to get some arrows. The father objected to this, but he finally allowed his wife to go up alone. Wearing five sea-otter hides, she started out early one morning. As soon as her brothers saw her, they thought she was a real otter, and they began to shoot arrows at her from the shore. Having been hit repeatedly, the otter would sink, then surface again with the arrows gone. The otter swam up and down the river, and many people in canoes kept shooting at it, but nobody could kill it.

Eventually everybody gave up the chase except the oldest brother, who followed the otter until it reached the beach. Coming nearer, he caught the shape of a woman beneath the skins and recognized her at once as his lost sister. She told him that she had been the sea otter, and showed him the arrows that the people had shot at her. "I came to get them for my boy," she said. "My husband is the son of a chief. Whenever the tide is low, you can see our house right in the middle of the ocean." She gave him the five sea-otter skins, and he gave her as many arrows as she could carry.

Before going down into the water, she told him, "Tomorrow morning you will find a whale on the beach, right in front of your landing." And it happened just as she said. The whale landed on the beach, and the men divided its meat among all the people.

A few months later the woman came again to her relatives, and her brothers noticed that her shoulders were turning scaly and dark like those of a sea serpent. She stayed a while, and then returned to her water home, but she never came ashore again and was seen no more. Long afterwards, many sea serpents came into the harbor. Thinking that they too may have come after arrows, the people kept on shooting at them. They never returned again, but every summer and winter they would put ashore two whales as a gift to their kinsmen above the sea.

—*Based on a myth reported by Harry St. Clair in 1909.*

COYOTE'S STRAWBERRY

[CROW]

Out walking, Old Man Coyote spied a group of good-looking girls picking wild strawberries. "Ah, these pretty young things!" he said. Quickly he buried himself in the earth among some strawberry bushes and let only the tip of his penis protrude.

Soon the girls came to those bushes. "There's a big berry here," said one girl, "different from the others." She tried to pluck it, but it wouldn't come loose. "This berry has deep roots," she said.

All the other girls came and tried to pick the strawberry. Some pulled at it, some nibbled at it. "Oh, my," said one, "this berry weeps." "No," said another girl, "it has milk in it." A third said: "Since we can't pick it, let's look for a sharp piece of flint and cut it off."

The girls searched and found a flint, but when they came back to the berry patch, the strange strawberry had disappeared. "It must have been some trick by that nasty Old Man Coyote," the girls said to each other. One said: "Yes, I'm sure it was Coyote. We'll have to get even."

One day the girls went to a place along the trail where Old Man Coyote always went hunting. They took their dresses off and smeared themselves with blood from some meat they had been given to cook. Looking as if they had been raped and slain by enemies, they lay there, face down, naked, and bloody.

Pretty soon Old Man Coyote came along. When he saw the girls with blood all over them, he was scared. "Oh my, oh my!" he said. "What enemy has done this? What shall I do? Maybe the enemy is still around and will come and kill me. Oh my! I must find out how long these girls have been dead. If their corpses are old, then surely the enemy is far away."

He bent down and started feeling and smelling the girls' bodies. Whenever he came near one of the girls' backsides, she farted right into Old Man Coyote's face. He said: "Oh, my, I think I am safe. These girls must have been dead a long time, they smell so bad!"

Then all the girls jumped up laughing, shouting: "Old Man, this time the joke was on you."

—Based on two stories told in 1899 and 1903.

THE FAITHFUL WIFE AND
THE WOMAN WARRIOR

■

[TIWA]

Here is another Pueblo tale featuring Apache characters.

A long time ago a band of Apache lived in a place called Namtsuleta, or Yellow Earth. In the band were two young men: Blue Hawk, son-in-law to the tribe, who was married to the daughter of the head chief, and Red Hawk, his friend.

Their tribe was fighting with a fearful and dangerous tribe that lived far away, and the two young men meant to go there and get some scalps. One day they packed their horses and started out. When they camped that night, they talked of what was ahead and what they had left behind.

Red Hawk, the unmarried boy, said to his friend, "As women do, your wife is probably sleeping with another man tonight."

"You may think that, but I never would," said Blue Hawk. "My wife is true to me."

"I'll bet I could go back tonight and sleep with your wife!"

"My friend, you can go back, but she won't accept you."

"I bet she will."

"Well, go and try!" And they bet their pack horses, their food, everything they had with them, and everything they had at home.

So Red Hawk returned to the village and hung around Blue Hawk's tipi. He saw his friend's wife sitting outside, but she never looked at him. Though he kept smiling at her, she ignored him so completely that he was afraid to speak to her.

"She must be as true as my friend said," the boy thought. When he realized that he was going to lose the bet, he went to an old woman in the village. He told her everything—about the two friends' journey and their wager, then about the wife's coldness and his shame.

"Is there any way I can see the girl unclothed?" he asked. "Or if not, can you find out what her body looks like? I'll pay well."

"Yes my grandson, I will find out for you."

Limping along with a cane, her toes sticking out of her shoes, the old woman shuffled past the wife's tipi. "Poor old grandmother!" said Blue Hawk's wife, looking out. She had someone bring the woman inside and fix her a bed of skins in the corner. It was from there late at night that the old one, watching through a hole in her blanket, managed to see the girl undressing.

Blue Hawk's wife had a long golden braid in the center of her abdomen which she unplaited, brushed out, braided up again, and wound around her body five times. As the girl bent and turned, the old one saw that she had a kind of black mark on her backbone.

At daybreak the old woman got up. "Granddaughter, I am going home to feed my turkeys," she said. And she returned to her own house, where Red Hawk had spent the night, and reported all she had seen.

Red Hawk rode back to his friend's camp. "I slept with your wife!" he said, but Blue Hawk would not believe it. "Well, she has long golden hair on the center of her abdomen and a black mark on her backbone."

Silently Blue Hawk dropped his head.

"My friend, you gave your word, and the words of a man are worth a great deal," Red Hawk said.

Then Blue Hawk spoke. "There are my pack horses and my money and everything I was carrying. Take all. We will go back and I will give you everything, money, horses, cattle, and house."

So they returned to the village, and Blue Hawk presented his friend with all his possessions, as one would when making funeral offerings. His wife kept asking, "What are you doing? Why are you giving everything to that boy?" He did not reply but went quietly to work making a huge rawhide trunk. In it he put money, food, and cooking gear.

At last Blue Hawk spoke to his wife. He was going to take a trip on the plains, he said—a long pleasure trip to the water. He asked her to dress in her finest clothes, and then he put her into the trunk too. "I made this case to keep you from the heat of the sun, so you won't get burned," he said.

Blue Hawk hitched a cart to the horses, set out on the trip, heaved the trunk into the first large river they came to, and went back to the tribe. Everyone asked where he had taken his wife and why he had given all his property to Red Hawk, but he would not say.

His silence was not pleasing to the girl's father, the head chief. He worked to make a hole down to the underworld, and then he arranged for his son-in-law to fall into that hole.

On the large river into which Blue Hawk had thrown the trunk, there was a fisherman who hooked something heavy. "A big fish," he said as he slowly pulled. He drew it to the edge of the river, dragged it out, and found that it was a rawhide trunk. To his amazement, a very pretty girl lay inside. He wanted to take her to his camp, but before she would go, the girl insisted on switching clothes with him.

The fisherman's band of Apaches were preparing to go to war, and

the girl, dressed in the man's clothes, joined the warriors when they started off early the next morning. On the journey the young men talked among themselves about the handsome, well-dressed stranger. "His eyes look like a girl's," one said. "He moves like a girl," another said. That night when they made camp, a boy finally said, "I'll make friends and see if he is a boy or girl."

Now, the woman had told them that she was a medicine man, and she put her tent apart from the others. She said her medicine was the sun, which is why she carried a white eagle feather. The boy who wanted to make friends went over to her tent and asked if he could sleep there. After they went to bed, the boy stayed awake all night waiting for the stranger to fall asleep, but she never did. Whenever he moved slowly toward her and put his arm over her, she would say, "Don't do that!" After a while he would try again, and she would say, "Why don't you go to sleep?" That way they passed the night. In the morning the boy confessed his failure to the other warriors, and the next night another young man made the same unsuccessful attempt. Every night of the journey, a different boy tried fruitlessly to discover the stranger's true sex.

Finally the band of warriors reached enemy country. The medicine man ordered his tent pitched apart from theirs and warned them to stay inside their tents and be silent. Once she was alone, the girl spat medicine in the direction of the hostile tribe and in this way, with no assistance, killed off all their enemies.

She gave a war whoop, at which all the young men emerged from their tents. "I fought a big battle and killed them all," she announced.

"Now I will go to the dead and cut off their ears, every one, and take their shields, bows and arrows, and war clubs." She did, and took their scalps too. When the war party returned home with the scalps, the grateful chief picked out a young warrior to escort her back to her home, but she refused a guard and asked only for a good horse.

At last she took off her man's clothes, and there she was, the faithful wife whose husband had thrown her into the river. "Though I am a girl," she said, "I did all the fighting for your young warriors. I killed your enemies—here you have their scalps and ears and weapons. My husband was once Blue Hawk, but you shut him up in the dark because of the trick that Red Hawk played on him. Now bring him to me!"

When they brought Blue Hawk, his wife embraced him and cried, because he looked so thin and sad. "You were beaten," she said, "by letting Red Hawk convince you that he knew my body. He deceived you. You know I love you honestly, truly. Now go and get Red Hawk and the old woman!"

The wrongdoers were brought before the couple and the head chief. The girl said to her father, "Tell your boys to get the wildest ponies in the camp!" They fetched the two wildest horses, and she ordered them to tie Red Hawk to the tail of one and the old woman to the tail of the other. Then they turned the horses loose. Off they went, kicking and jumping, and tore Red Hawk and the old woman to pieces, away from the camp.

—*Based on a tale reported by Elsie Clews Parsons in 1940.*

■

COYOTE AND THE
MALLARD DUCKS

■

[NEZ PERCÉ]

■ |||||||||||||||||||||||||||||||||||||||||||||||||||||||||||||||||||||| ■

Coyote was traveling up the river when he saw five mallard duck girls swimming on the other side. He hid himself in the bushes and became aroused right away. Then he thought out a plan to satisfy himself.

Coyote lengthened his penis and let it fall into the river. It floated on top of the water. Coyote didn't like this, so he pulled it back in and tied a rock to it to keep it below the surface of the water. He threw his penis back in and tied a smaller rock to it. This was just right. It floated just below the surface of the water, where no one could see it. He sent it across to where the girls were swimming. He began copulating with the oldest girl.

Now, these girls did not know what was wrong with their older sister, the way she was moving around in the water and making strange sounds. Then they saw what was happening and they grabbed the penis and tried to pull it out. When they couldn't, they got out on the bank and held down their older sister and tried to pull it out that way, but they couldn't and they began laughing about it.

When Coyote had satisfied himself, he called over to the girls and said, "My sisters, what is the problem over there?" They told him. He said, "Cut the thing off with some wire grass." They did, and Coyote cut the other end off where he was and the middle section of the penis fell in the river and became a ledge.

The eldest girl became ill then. Coyote went down the river a short distance, swam across and then came upstream to the girls' camp where the oldest girl was almost dead.

The girls recognized Coyote and said, "Coyote, the medicine man, has come." They asked him to cure the sick girl. He told them that he would do it, but they had to close up all the chinks in the lodge so no one could see in and steal his medicine by watching. He told them to leave him alone with the girl for a while.

He got the sisters together around the lodge and told them to sing a song and keep time on a log with sticks. "Keep time on the log very carefully, for now I am going to take it out."

Coyote began singing, "I will stick it back on, I will stick it back on." He went into the lodge and copulated again with the mallard duck girl and recovered the end of his penis. The girl was cured.

After that everyone said the medicine of Coyote was very powerful.

—Told by Barry Lopez in 1977.

THE GREEDY FATHER

[KAROK]

Famine descended, and the people were hungry. A man decided he would go fishing to get food for his family. He left the house at dawn. As the sun rose, it shone on the water. Suddenly the string attached to the fishnet quivered. The man hauled out the net and discovered a huge salmon, which he put down in back of the fishery.

Then he thought, "I'm so hungry, I think I'll just cook it up right now." So he cleaned it and cut off the tail, putting it to one side. Then he cooked the salmon, and when he devoured it all, only realizing afterwards what he had done.

Then he went home, carrying just the tail. When he was some distance from home, he began shouting, "Here children, this is the tail! There were a lot of beggars on the way who got the rest."

Then the children ran out, shouting, "Hurray, we're going to eat! Hurray, we're going to eat!"

The next day he went fishing again. Again he caught a big salmon, and he ate it on the spot. Again he went home and shouted, "Here, children, this is the tail! There were a lot of beggars."

Now his wife began to suspect that he was holding out on them. When he went fishing again the next day, she told her children, "You stay here. I'm following him." When she arrived at the fishery, he had just pulled out a big salmon. He cut off the tail and put it down a little way off. Then he made a fire and cooked it. He was about to eat it.

The woman ran back upriver, and she gathered her children together and told them they were leaving. They climbed uphill, and when the father returned, they heard him shouting below them, "Here, children, this is the tail! There were a lot of beggars." But he heard only silence. He shouted again. He ran indoors, and found only mice squeaking. Then he jumped out of the house, still shouting about the tail and the beggars. He looked uphill and finally saw where they had climbed.

His wife shouted down to him, "Eat alone there, just like you have been all along! He followed them, getting closer and closer, and still shouting. When he caught up with them, his wife told him, "You'll be eating only mud in the creeks. But we will be sitting around in front of rich people."

And he reached out to grab the littlest one, but the child turned into a bear lily. He grabbed another and it turned into a hazel bush. He grabbed the wife; she turned into a pine tree. Finally he fell down back to the banks of the water, and you'll see him like that now, eating mud on the edge of creeks. He became a water ouzel, a small gray bird which we call "moss eater." But his wife and his children line up in front of rich people, baskets in the deerskin dance.

—Based on a tale reported by William Bright in 1957.

KULSHAN AND HIS TWO WIVES

[LUMNI]

Komo Kulshan, a very tall and handsome young man, had two wives, as was the custom of his tribe. One was named Clear Sky; the other, Fair Maiden.

For several years Clear Sky was Kulshan's favorite wife. She was the more beautiful of the two, and she had borne him three children. Fair Maiden was less beautiful, but she was always gentle and kind. At last she won Kulshan's love through kindness, though as a result she gained Clear Sky's dislike. Clear Sky had a jealous and bitter nature. Soon there was quarreling in the lodge.

One day Clear Sky scolded Komo Kulshan at great length and concluded, "You should love me more than Fair Maiden. I am the mother of your children."

Kulshan smiled and said nothing.

Clear Sky became angrier. "I'm going away," she said. "I'll leave you and the children and go away."

She expected him to answer, "Don't go away. You're the mother of my children, and I love you most. Don't go."

But Kulshan did not beg her to stay. Though he loved her and didn't want her to leave, he was too proud to say so.

Instead he told her, "If you want to, you may go as soon and as far as you wish."

Slowly, taking her time, Clear Sky packed her things. She packed all her seeds and bulbs, packed her roots and berries, packed all her flowering plants. At last she was finished, and her children cried loudly when they saw her leaving. This pleased Clear Sky, who felt sure that Kulshan would call her back when she had gone a little distance.

She started down the mountain valley slowly, alone. When she had gone a short distance, she stopped and looked back. But Kulshan did not say, "Come home."

She went a little farther and paused on a hill to look back at Kulshan and the children. When she stood on tiptoe, she could see them. But still Kulshan did not say, "Come back, Clear Sky."

She went on farther south. She was still among the hills and mountains, mountains not so high as Komo Kulshan. He still did not call her, though she stood on the very tips of her toes. Farther south she climbed to the top of a high hill, rose on tiptoe, and made herself as tall as she could. That way she could just see Kulshan and the children, and they could see her.

By this time she had stretched herself so often that she had become much taller. Sure now that her husband did not want her to return, she decided to make camp where she was. At least on a clear day she would be able to see her family. So she put down her packs and took out all the seeds and bulbs and roots. She planted them around her, and there she stayed, cultivating them.

Fair Maiden lived with Kulshan for a long time. One day she said to him: "I want to visit my mother. I'm going to have a baby, and I want to see my mother."

"How can you go to your mother?" asked Kulshan. "There's no trail, nothing but rocks and trees and mountains between us and Whulge."

"I don't know how I can get there, but you'll have to make a passage-way for me. I want to see my mother."

So Komo Kulshan called together all the animals that have claws—the beavers, the marmots, the cougars, the bears, even the rats and mice and moles—and told them to dig a big ditch. The animals dug a deep one that was wide enough for two canoes to pass. Then Kulshan turned all the water from the mountains near him into the ditch until there was enough to float a fair-sized canoe. Today the stream is called the Nooksack River.

Before starting, Fair Maiden gathered many kinds of food to take with her. Then she went down the river and out into the salt water of Whulge.

She ate mussels at one of the islands and left some there. That's why mussels are found on the same island today. She ate clams at another island and left some there. She ate camas at another, and that's why a lot of camas grow on Matia Island today. She ate devilfish and berries at another island and left some. At every island on her journey she left some kind of fish or root or berry, and that's why the Indian names for these islands are the names of food.

When she got to Flat Top Island, she decided to stay somewhere near it. She stood looking over the water for a long time, trying to choose the best place. The winds blew round her tall figure and made a number of whirlpools. The whirlpools sucked many people in, even some who lived far away, and devoured them.

Fair Maiden kept on standing there, and the winds kept blowing round her. At last the Changer came to her and said, "Why don't you lie down? If you stand, the winds will create whirlpools, and the whirlpools will suck all the people in."

So Fair Maiden lay down, and the Changer transformed her into Spieden Island. When her child was born, it was a small island of the same shape as Spieden and lying beside it. Today it is called Sentinel Island.

Kulshan, left with his children in the mountains of the Northwest coastal range, kept stretching upward, trying to see his wives. So did his children. The three of them grew taller and taller and became high mountains. One is Shuksan, a little east of Kulshan and almost as tall. Some people say the others are Twin Sisters, a little west and south of Kulshan.

A long journey south of them stands their mother, Clear Sky. You know her as Mount Rainier. The seeds and roots she planted there grew and spread, and that's why the lower slopes bloom with flowers of every color. Often on a clear day or night, the mountain dresses in sparkling white and looks with longing at Komo Kulshan and the mountain children near him.

—*Reported by Ella Clark in 1953.*

MEN AND WOMEN
TRY LIVING APART

[SIA]

Before Ut'sĕt, Mother of the People, left this world, she selected six Sia women and sent one to the north, one to the west, one to the south, one to the east, one to the zenith, and one to the nadir, and told them to make their homes at these points for all time. That way they would be near the cloud rulers of the cardinal points, and they could intercede for all the people of Ha'arts. Ut'sĕt told her people to remember these women in times of need, and they would appeal to the cloud people for them.

The Sia alone followed the command of Ut'sĕt and took the straight road, while all other pueblos advanced by various routes to the center of the earth. After Ut'sĕt's departure the Sia traveled some distance and built a village of beautiful white stone, where they lived,   declared, for a long duration. At one time all the parents suffered tragically at the hand of the *ti'ämoni*, who, objecting to the increase of his people, caused all children to be put to death. The Sia had scarcely recovered from this calamity when another serious difficulty arose.

The Sia women worked hard all day, grinding meal and singing; and at sundown, when the men returned to the houses, the women would often abuse them, saying: "You are no good; you do not care to work. All you want to do is be with women all the time. If you would allow four days to pass between, the women would care more for you."

The men replied: "You women really want to be with us all day and all night. If you could have the men only every four days, you would be very unhappy."

The women retorted: "It is you men who would be unhappy if you could be with the women only every four days."

And the fight grew angrier and angrier. The men cried: "Were it ten days, twenty days, thirty days that we remained apart from you, we'd never be unhappy." The women replied: "We think not, but we women would be very contented to remain away from you men for sixty days." And the men said: "We men would be happy to remain apart from you women for five moons." The women, growing more excited, cried: "You do not speak the truth; we women would be contented to be separated from you ten moons." The men retorted: "We men could remain away from you women twenty moons and be very happy." You do not speak the truth," said the women, "for you wish to be with us all the time, day and night."

Three days they quarreled and on the fourth day the women finally took themselves to one side of the pueblo, while the men and boys gathered on the other side, each forming their own kiva, or ceremonial chamber. The women had a great talk and the men held a council. They were both furious with one another.

The *ti'amoni*, who presided over the council, said: "Perhaps you will each be contented if you and the women try living apart." And on the following morning he had all the men and male children who were not being nourished by their mothers cross the great river which ran by the village, the women remaining in the village. The men departed at sunrise, and the women were delighted. They said: "We can do all the work; we understand the men's work and we can work like them." The men said to each other: "We can do the things the women did for us." As they left the village the men called to the women: "We leave you to yourselves, perhaps for one year, perhaps for two, and perhaps longer. Who knows how it will work out? After all, men are not so amorous as you."

It took a long time for the men to cross the river, as it was very wide. The *ti'amoni* led the men and remained with them. The women were compelled by the *ti'amoni* to send their male infants over the river as soon as they ceased nourishing them. For two moons the men and women were very happy. The men were busy hunting and had all the game they could eat, but the women had no animal food. The men grew stout and the women very thin. At the expiration of the first ten moons some of the women were sad away from the men. As the second year passed, more of the women wanted the men, but the men seemed perfectly satisfied with the way things were. After three years the women more and more wished for the men, but the men were only slightly desirous of the women.

When the fourth year was half gone, the women called to the *ti'amoni*, saying: "We want the men to come to us." The female children had grown up like reeds; they had no flesh on them. The morning after the women begged the *ti'amoni* for the return of the men, they recrossed the river to live again with the women, and in four days after their return the women had recovered their flesh.

—*Based on Matilda Cox Stevenson's report of 1889.*

A CONTEST FOR WIVES

■

[COCHITI]

At Amatsushe they were living; Old Coyote and Old Coyote Woman lived on one side of the hill and Old Beaver and Old Beaver Woman lived on the other. They visited each other every night. One night it was snowing, deep, and Old Coyote said to his wife, "I shall go to Old Brother Beaver to invite him to go hunting, and to make plans for exchanging our wives."

When Coyote got there, he called, "Hello." Beaver answered, "Hello, come in and sit down." They sat together by the fireplace to smoke.

Coyote said, "I came to tell you we are to go hunting. If we kill any rabbits we'll bring them to our wives. I'll bring mine to your wife, and you can bring yours to mine."

"All right," Old Beaver agreed.

"You go first," said Coyote.

"No, you go first. This is your invitation; you invited me," Beaver insisted.

"All right, I shall go early in the morning."

Coyote said to Old Beaver Woman, "In the morning I am going hunting for you."

"All right. I shall sing the song so that you will kill many rabbits." Old Beaver Woman started to fix the supper. She wanted it ready for his return. Old Coyote was gone for the whole day. It was evening, and he did not come home at all. Sitting near the fireplace, Old Beaver Woman waited and waited. She started to sing her song:

> Old Coyote, Old Coyote, come sleep with me,
> Come have intercourse with me,
> Ai-oo-ai-oo.

Old Beaver said, "What are you singing about? He won't kill anything, for he isn't any hunter." Coyote killed nothing, and Beaver Woman waited and waited but Coyote never came.

Next day it was Old Beaver's turn to go hunting. He went to tell Old Coyote Woman that she must wait for him, for he was going to hunt rabbits for her. "All right," she said. And he killed so many that he could hardly carry them.

In the morning Beaver came into Coyote's house and said, "Old Coyote Woman, here are the rabbits." She took them and said, "Thank you, thank you, Old Man Beaver."

They went straight into the inner room, and Old Man Coyote was left by himself in the front room. He was very angry. They gave him his supper, and when he had finished, they went in to bed.

Old Beaver Man started to have intercourse with Old Coyote Woman. Old Coyote Woman cried out, and Old Coyote called out, "Old Beaver, don't hurt my wife." Old Coyote Woman answered, "Shut up, Old Man Coyote! It's because I like it that I'm crying out."

When he had finished, Old Beaver Man came out. He said to Old Coyote, "We won't keep bad feelings against each other; this was your plan. I shall always wait for you at my house whenever you want to visit me." And they were as good neighbors as ever.

—*Recorded by Ruth Benedict in 1931.*

THE SERPENT OF THE SEA

■

[ZUNI]

■

■ ▮▮▮▮▮▮▮▮▮▮▮▮▮▮▮▮▮▮▮▮▮▮▮▮▮▮▮▮▮▮▮▮▮ ■

"Let us abide with the ancients tonight!" exclaims the elder.
"Be it well," reply the listeners.

In the times of our forefathers there was a village under Thunder Mountain called Home of the Eagles. It is now in ruins: the roofs gone, the ladders decayed, the hearths cold. But when it was alive, it was the home of a beautiful maiden, the daughter of the priest-chief. Though beautiful, she had one strange trait: she could not endure the slightest speck of dust or dirt upon her clothes or person.

A sacred spring of water lay at the foot of the terrace on which the town stood. Now we call it the Pool of the Apaches, but then it was sacred to Kolowissi, the Serpent of the Sea. Washing her clothes and bathing herself over and over, the maiden spent almost all her time at this spring. The defilement of his waters, their contamination by the dirt of her apparel and the dun of her person, angered Kolowissi. He devised a plan to punish her.

When the maiden next came to the spring, she was startled to find a smiling baby boy gurgling and splashing in the water. Of course it was the Sea Serpent who, like the other gods, can assume any form at his pleasure. The girl looked all around—north, south, east, and west—but saw no trace of a person who might have left the beautiful child. "Whose can it be?" she wondered. "Only a cruel mother would leave her baby here to die!"

The maiden talked softly to the child, took him in her arms, and carried him up the hill to her house. There she brought him into her room, where she lived apart from her family because of her loathing of dust and dirt. As she played with him, laughing at his pranks and smiling into his face, he answered her in baby fashion with coos and smiles of his own.

Meanwhile her younger sisters had prepared the evening meal and were waiting for her. "Where can she be?" they asked.

"Probably at the spring, as usual!" said their father. "Run down and call her."

But the youngest sister could not find her at the spring, so she came home and climbed to the maiden's private room at the top of the house. And there the maiden was, sitting on the floor and playing with the beautiful baby.

On hearing this the father was silent and thoughtful, for he knew that the waters of the spring were sacred. When the rest of the family started to climb the ladder to see the child, he called them back.

"Do you suppose any real mother would leave her baby in a spring?" he said. "This is not as simple as it seems." And since the maiden would not leave the child, they ate without her.

Upstairs the baby began to yawn. Growing drowsy herself, the girl put him on the bed and fell asleep beside him.

The maiden's sleep was real, the baby's a pretense. He lay quietly and began to lengthen, drawing himself out, extending longer and longer. Slowly the Serpent of the Sea appeared, like a nightmare come true. He was so huge that he had to coil himself round and round the room, filling it with scaly, gleaming circles. Placing his enormous head near the maiden's, Kolowissi surrounded her with his coils and finally took his own tail into his mouth.

So the night passed. In the morning when breakfast was ready and the oldest sister had not come down, the others grew impatient.

"Now that she has the child, nothing else matters to her," the old man said. "A baby is enough to absorb any woman's attention."

But the smallest sister climbed up to the room and called her. Receiving no answer, she pushed the door, first gently and then with all her might. She could not move it and began to be frightened. Running to the skyhole over the room where the others were sitting, she cried for help.

Everyone except the father rushed up, and pushing together, cracked the door just enough to catch a glimpse of the serpent's great scales. Then they screamed and ran back down.

The father, priest and sage that he was, told them quietly, "I expected as much. I thought it was impossible for a woman to be so foolish as to leave her child in a spring. But it's not impossible, it seems, for another woman to be so foolish as to take such a child to her bosom."

Climbing up to her room, he pushed against the door and called, "Oh Kolowissi, it is I who speak to you—I, your priest. I pray you, let my child come to me again, and I will make atonement for her errors. She is yours; but let her return to us once more."

Hearing this, the Serpent of the Sea began to loosen his coils. The whole building, the whole village, shook violently, and everyone trembled with fear.

At last the maiden awoke and cried piteously for help. As the coils unwound, she was able to rise. The great serpent bent the folds of his body nearest the doorway so that they formed an arch for her to pass under. She was half stunned by the din of the monster's scales, which rasped against one another like the scraping of flints under the feet of a rapid runner.

Once clear of the writhing mass, the maiden was away like a deer. Tumbling down the ladder and into the room below, she threw herself on her mother's breast.

But the priest remained, praying to the serpent. He ended with: "It shall be as I have said; she is yours!"

He and the two warrior-priests of the town called together all the other priests in sacred council. Performing the solemn rites, they prepared plumes, prayer wands, and offerings of treasure. After four days of ceremonies, the old priest called his daughter and told her that she must give these offerings, together with the most precious of them all, herself, to the Serpent of the Sea. She must renounce her people and her home and dwell in the house of Kolowissi in the Waters of the World.

"Your deeds tell me," said her father, "that this has been your desire. For you brought this fate on yourself by using the sacred water for profane purposes."

The maiden wept and clung to her mother's neck. Then, shivering with terror, she left her childhood home. In the plaza they dressed her in sacred cotton robes, elaborately embroidered, and adorned her with earrings, bracelets, beads, and other precious things. Amidst the lamentations of the people, they painted her cheeks with red spots as if for a dance. They made a road of sacred meal toward the distant spring known as the Doorway of the Serpent of the Sea. Four steps toward this spring they marked out sacred terraces on the ground at the west of the plaza. And when they had finished the sacred road, the old priest, without one tear, told his daughter to walk out on it and call the serpent to come.

At once the door opened and the Serpent of the Sea descended from the maiden's room, where he had been waiting. Without using ladders, he lowered his head and breast down to the ground in great undulations. He placed his heavy head on the maiden's shoulder, and the priests said, "It is time."

Slowly, cowering beneath her burden, the maiden started toward the west. Whenever she staggered with fear and weariness and was about to wander from the path, the serpent gently pushed her onward and straightened her course.

They went toward the river trail and followed it, then crossed over the Mountain of the Red Paint, and still the serpent was not completely uncoiled from the maiden's room. Not until they were past the mountain did his tail emerge.

Suddenly Kolowissi drew himself together and began to assume a new shape. Before long his serpent form contracted and shortened until he lifted his head from the maiden's shoulder and stood up, a beautiful young man in sacred ceremonial dress! He slipped his serpent scales, now grown small, under his flowing mantle. In the snake's hoarse hiss he said: "Are you tired, girl?" She never replied, but plodded on with her eyes cast down.

In a gentler voice he said, "Are you weary, poor maiden?" Rising taller, walking a little behind her, he wrapped his scales more closely in his blanket. He repeated in a still softer voice, "Are you weary, poor maiden?"

At first she dared not look around, though the voice sounded so changed, so kind. Yet she still felt the weight of the serpent's head on her shoulder, for she had become used to the heavy burden and could not tell that it had gone. At last, however, she turned and saw a splendid, brave young man, magnificently dressed.

"May I walk by your side?" he asked. "Why don't you speak?"

"I am filled with fear and shame," said she.

"Why? What do you fear?"

"I came away from my home with a terrifying creature, and he rested his head upon my shoulder, and even now I feel it there." She lifted her hand to the place where it had been, still fearing that she would find it.

"But I came all the way with you," said he, "and I saw no such creature."

She stopped and looked at him. "You came all the way? Then where has the serpent gone?"

He smiled and replied, "I know where he has gone."

"Ah, my friend, will he leave me alone now? Will he let me return to my people?"

"No, because he thinks too much of you."

"Where is he?"

"He is here," said the youth, smiling and placing his hand on his heart. "I am he."

"I don't believe it!" cried the maiden.

He drew the shriveled serpent scales out from under his mantle. "I am he, and I love you, beautiful maiden! Won't you come and stay with me? We will live and love one another not just now, but forever, in all the Waters of the World."

And as they journeyed on, the maiden quite forgot her sadness, and soon she forgot her home too. She followed her husband into the Doorway of the Serpent of the Sea and lived with him ever after.

—*Based on Frank Hamilton Cushing's version of 1931.*

PART SEVEN

COYOTE LAUGHS AND CRIES

TRICKSTER TALES

Stories about tricks and pranks, especially when played by the lowly, small, and poor on the proud, big, and rich, have delighted audiences from the dawn of storytelling. In Europe, Reynard the Fox (or the German Reinecke Fuchs) is the trickster par excellence, whose exploits were related by illiterate storytellers on market days or written down in elaborate form by some of the world's great authors.

The trickster is a rebel against authority and the breaker of all taboos. He is what the best-behaved and most circumspect person may secretly wish to be. He is, especially in the western areas of North America, at the same time imp and hero—the great culture bringer who can also make mischief beyond belief, turning quickly from clown to creator and back again.

In Indian America it is not the fox but Coyote who is the great trickster. His exploits are recounted from Alaska down to the southern deserts, from the Atlantic all the way to the Pacific Coast. Raven, Mink, Rabbit, Blue Jay, and other animals also take their turn playing the prankster and troublemaker. Besides animals, there are human or semihuman tricksters—Old Man of the Blackfeet and Crow, Iktome the Sioux Spider Man, Veeho or Vihio of the Cheyenne, Manabozho of the central woodlands and Great Lakes regions, and Whisky Jack of the Cree and Saultaux. Even when a tribe has another such trickster of its own, Coyote often appears as his comrade and fellow mischief-maker.

In the Plains and plateau areas, where Coyote takes center stage, most tales bear witness to his cleverness alternating with buffoonery, his lechery, his craft in cheating and destroying his enemy, and his voracious appetite and unending need to keep poaching game. In the North Pacific Coast area, the emphasis is more on Coyote's cleverness than his stupidity. Coyote often poses as a woman and marries a man (presumably to be fed and taken care of); he also transforms himself into a fish so he can steal a valuable harpoon or fishhook. His gluttony and lust are well represented, too. In all regions, Coyote periodically gets his comeuppance —even if, as in one story here, it takes several lifetimes.

Shorn of the various surface features from different cultures, Coyote and his kin represent the sheerly spontaneous in life, the pure creative spark that is our birthright as human beings and that defies fixed roles or behavior. He not only represents some primordial creativity from our earlier days, but he reminds us that such celebration of life goes on today, and he calls us to join him in the frenzy. In an ordered world of objects and labels, he represents the potency of nothingness, of chaos, of freedom —a nothingness that makes something of itself. There is great power in such a being, and it has always been duly recognized and honored by Indian people.

Coyote also reminds us of another salient element in Indian philosophy: there is laughter amid tears, and sadness tucked away in a raucous tale. The Sioux medicine man Lame Deer said, "Coyote, Iktome, and all clowns are sacred. They are a necessary part of us. A people who have so much to cry about as Indians do also need their laughter to survive."

COYOTE, IKTOME, AND THE ROCK

[WHITE RIVER SIOUX]

Coyote was walking with his friend Iktome. Along their path stood Iya, the rock. This was not just any rock; it was special. It had those spidery lines of green moss all over it, the kind that tell a story. Iya had power.

Coyote said: "Why, this is a nice-looking rock. I think it has power." Coyote took off the thick blanket he was wearing and put it on the rock. "Here, Iya, take this as a present. Take this blanket, friend rock, to keep you from freezing. You must feel cold."

"Wow, a giveaway!" said Iktome. "You sure are in a giving mood today, friend."

"Ah, it's nothing. I'm always giving things away. Iya looks real nice in my blanket."

"His blanket, now," said Iktome.

The two friends went on. Pretty soon a cold rain started. The rain turned to hail. The hail turned to slush. Coyote and Iktome took refuge in a cave, which was cold and wet. Iktome was all right; he had his thick buffalo robe. Coyote had only his shirt, and he was shivering. He was freezing. His teeth were chattering.

"*Kola*, friend of mine," Coyote said to Iktome, "go back and get me my fine blanket. I need it, and that rock has no use for it. He's been getting along without a blanket for ages. Hurry; I'm freezing!"

Iktome went back to Iya, saying: "Can I have that blanket back, please?"

The rock said: "No, I like it. What is given is given."

Iktome returned and told Coyote: "He won't give it back."

"That no-good, ungrateful rock!" said Coyote. "Has he paid for the blanket? Has he worked for it? I'll go get it myself."

"Friend," said Iktome, "Tunka, Iya, the rock—there's a lot of power there! Maybe you should let him keep it."

"Are you crazy? This is an expensive blanket of many colors and great thickness. I'll go talk to him."

Coyote went back and told Iya: "Hey, rock! What's the meaning of this? What do you need a blanket for? Let me have it back right now!"

"No," said the rock, "what is given is given."

"You're a bad rock! Don't you care that I'm freezing to death? That I'll catch a cold?" Coyote jerked the blanket away from Iya and put it on. "So there; that's the end of it."

"By no means the end," said the rock.

Coyote went back to the cave. The rain and hail stopped and the sun came out again, so Coyote and Iktome sat before the cave, sunning them-selives, eating pemmican and fry-bread and *wojapi*, berry soup. After eating, they took out their pipes and had a smoke.

All of a sudden Iktome said: "What's that noise?"

"What noise? I don't hear anything."

"A crashing, a rumble far off."

"Yes, friend, I hear it now."

"Friend Coyote, it's getting stronger and nearer, like thunder or an earthquake."

"It is rather strong and loud. I wonder what it can be."

"I have a pretty good idea, friend," said Iktome.

Then they saw the great rock. It was Iya, rolling, thundering, crashing upon them.

"Friend, let's run for it!" cried Iktome; "Iya means to kill us!"

The two ran as fast as they could while the rock rolled after them, coming closer and closer.

"Friend, let's swim the river. The rock is so heavy, he sure can't swim!" cried Iktome. So they swam the river, but Iya, the great rock, also swam over the river as if he had been made of wood.

"Friend, into the timber, among the big trees," cried Coyote. "That big rock surely can't get through this thick forest." They ran among the trees, but the huge Iya came rolling along after them, shivering and splintering the big pines to pieces, left and right.

The two came out onto the flats. "Oh! Oh!" cried Iktome, Spider Man. "Friend Coyote, this is really not my quarrel. I just remembered, I have pressing business to attend to. So long!" Iktome rolled himself into a tiny ball and became a spider. He disappeared into a mousehole.

Coyote ran on and on, the big rock thundering close at his heels. Then Iya, the big rock, rolled right over Coyote, flattening him out al-together.

Iya took the blanket and rolled back to his own place, saying: "So there!"

A *wasichu* rancher riding along saw Coyote lying there all flattened out. "What a nice rug!" said the rancher, picking Coyote up, and he took the rug home.

The rancher put Coyote right in front of his fireplace. Whenever Coyote is killed, he can make himself come to life again, but it took him the whole night to puff himself up into his usual shape. In the morning the rancher's wife told her husband: "I just saw your rug running away."

Friends, hear this: always be generous in heart. If you have something to give, give it forever.

—Told by Jenny Leading Cloud in White River, Rosebud
Indian Reservation, South Dakota, 1967.
Recorded by Richard Erdoes.

■

WHAT'S THIS? MY BALLS FOR YOUR DINNER?

■

[WHITE RIVER SIOUX]

■ |||||||||||||||||||||||||||||||||||||||||||||||||||||||||||||||||||||||||||||||||| ■

Iktome, the wicked Spider Man, and Shunk-Manitou, Coyote, are two no-good loafers. They lie, they steal, they are greedy, they are always after women. Maybe because they are so very much alike, they are friends, except when they try to trick each other.

One day Iktome invited Coyote for dinner at his lodge. Ikto told his wife: "Old Woman, here are two fine, big buffalo livers for my friend Coyote and myself. Fry them up nicely, the way I like them. And get some *timpsila*, some wild turnips, on the side, and afterwards serve us up some *wojapi*, some berry soup. Use chokecherries for that. Coyote always likes something sweet after his meal."

"Is that all?" asked Iktome's wife.

"I guess so; I can't think of anything else."

"There's no third liver for me?" the wife inquired.

"You can have what's left after my friend Coyote and I have eaten," said Iktome. "Well, I'll go out for a while; maybe I can shoot a fine, plump duck too. Coyote always stuffs himself, so one liver may not be enough for him. But watch this good friend of mine; don't let him stick his hands under your robe. He likes to do that. Well, I go now. Have everything ready for us; Coyote never likes to wait."

Iktome left and his old woman got busy cooking. "I know who's always stuffing himself," she thought. "I know whose hands are always busy feeling under some girl's robe. I know who can't wait—it's that no-good husband of mine."

The fried livers smelled so wonderful that the wife said to herself: "Those greedy, stingy, overbearing men! I know them; they'll feast on these fine livers, and a few turnips will be all they leave for me. They have no consideration for a poor woman. Oh, that liver here looks so good, smells so good; I know it tastes good. Maybe I'll try a little piece, just a tiny one. They won't notice."

So the wife tasted a bit of the liver, and then another bit, and then another, and in no time at all that liver was gone. "I might as well eat the other one too," the wife said to herself, and she did.

"What will I do now?" she thought. "When Iktome finds out, he'll surely beat me. But it was worth it!"

Just then Coyote arrived. He had dressed himself up in a fine beaded outfit with fringed sleeves. "Where is my good friend Iktome?" he asked. "What's he up to? Probably nothing good."

"How are you, friend?" said the woman, "My husband, Iktome, is out taking care of some business. He'll be back soon. Sit down; be comfortable."

"Out on business—you don't say!" remarked Coyote, quickly sticking his hand under the woman's robe and between her legs.

"Iktome told me you'd try to do that. He told me not to let you."

"Oh, Iktome and I are such good friends," said Coyote, "we share everything." He joked, he chucked the woman under the chin, he tickled her under the arms, and pretty soon he was all the way in her; way, way up inside her.

"It feels good," said the woman, "but be quick about it. Iktome could be back any time now."

"You think he'd mind, seeing we are such good friends?"

"I'm sure he would. You'd better stop now."

"Well, all right. It smells very good here, but I see no meat cooking, just some *timpsila*. Meat is what I like."

"And meat is what you'll get. One sees this is the first time that you've come here for dinner; otherwise you'd know what you'll get. We always serve a guest the same thing. Everybody likes it."

"Is it really good?"

"It's more than good. It's *lila washtay*, very good."

Coyote smacked his lips, his mouth watering. "I can't wait. What is it? Tell me!"

"Why, your *itka*, your *susu*, your eggs, your balls, your big hairy balls! We always have the balls of our guests for dinner."

"Oh my! This must be a joke, a very bad joke."

"It's no joke at all. And I'd better cut them off right now with my big skinning knife, because it's getting late. Ikto gets mad when I don't have his food ready—he'll beat me. And there I was, fooling around with you instead of doing my cooking. I'll do it right now; drop your breechcloth. You won't feel a thing, I do this so fast. I have practice."

The woman came after Coyote with the knife in her hand.

"Wait a bit," said Coyote. "Before you do this, let me go out and make some water. I'll be right back," and saying this, he ran out of the lodge. But he didn't come back. He ran and ran as fast as his feet would carry him.

Just then Iktome came back without any ducks; he had caught nothing. He saw Coyote running away and asked, "Old Woman, what's the matter with that crazy friend of mine? Why is he running off like that?"

"Your good friend is very greedy. He doesn't have the sharing spirit," his wife told Iktome. "Never invite him again. He has no manners. He doesn't know how to behave. He saw those two fine buffalo livers, which I cooked just as you like them, and didn't want to share them with you. He grabbed both and made off with them. Some friend!"

Iktome rushed out of the lodge in a frenzy, running after Coyote as fast as he could, shouting: "Coyote! *Kola!* Friend! Leave me at least one! Leave one for me! For your old friend Iktome!"

Coyote didn't stop. He ran even faster than Ikto. Running, running, he looked back over his shoulder and shouted: "Cousin, if you catch me, you can have both of them!"

—Told by one of the Left Handed Bull family in
White River, Rosebud Indian Reservation, and recorded by
Richard Erdoes.

COYOTE AND WASICHU

[BRULE SIOUX]

There was a white man who was such a sharp trader that nobody ever got the better of him. Or so people said, until one day a man told this *wasichu*: "There's somebody who can outcheat you anytime, anywhere."

"That's not possible," said the *wasichu*. "I've had a trading post for many years, and I've cheated all the Indians around here."

"Even so, Coyote can beat you in any deal."

"Let's see whether he can. Where is Coyote?"

"Over there, that tricky-looking guy."

"Okay, all right, I'll try him."

The *wasichu* trader went over to Coyote. "Hey, let's see you outsmart me."

"I'm sorry," said Coyote, "I'd like to help you out, but I can't do it without my cheating medicine."

"Cheating medicine, hah! Go get it."

"I live miles from here and I'm on foot. But if you'd lend me your fast horse?"

"Well, all right, you can borrow it. Go on home and get your cheating medicine!"

"Well, friend, I'm a poor rider. Your horse is afraid of me, and I'm afraid of him. Lend me your clothes; then your horse will think that I am you."

Well, all right. Here are my clothes; now you can ride him. Go get that medicine. I'm sure I can beat it!"

So Coyote rode off with the *wasichu*'s fast horse and his fine clothes, while the *wasichu* stood there bare-assed.

—*Told at Grass Mountain, Rosebud Indian Reservation,*
South Dakota, 1974.

HOW BEAVER STOLE FIRE
FROM THE PINES

[NEZ PERCÉ]

Once, before there were any people in the world, the different animals and trees lived and moved about and talked together just like human beings. The pine trees had the secret of fire and guarded it jealously, so that no matter how cold it was, they alone could warm themselves. At length an unusually cold winter came, and all the animals were in danger of freezing to death. But all their attempts to discover the pines' secret were in vain, until Beaver at last hit upon a plan.

At a certain place on Grande Ronde River in Idaho, the pines were about to hold a great council. They had built a large fire to warm themselves after bathing in the icy water, and sentinels were posted to prevent intruders from stealing their fire secret. But Beaver had hidden under the bank near the fire before the sentries had taken their places, and when a live coal rolled down the bank, he seized it, hid it in his breast, and ran away as fast as he could.

The pines immediately raised a hue and cry and started after him. Whenever he was hard pressed, Beaver darted from side to side to dodge his pursuers, and when he had a good start, he kept a straight course. The Grande Ronde River preserves the direction Beaver took in his flight, and this is why it is tortuous in some parts of its course and straight in others.

After running for a long time, the pines grew tired. So most of them halted in a body on the river banks, where they remain in great numbers to this day, forming a growth so dense that hunters can hardly get through. A few pines kept chasing Beaver, but they finally gave out one after another, and they remain scattered at intervals along the banks of the river in the places where they stopped.

There was one cedar running in the forefront of the pines, and although he despaired of capturing Beaver, he said to the few trees who were still in the chase, "We can't catch him, but I'll go to the top of the hill yonder and see how far ahead he is." So he ran to the top of the hill and saw Beaver just diving into Big Snake River where the Grande Ronde enters it. Further pursuit was out of the question. The cedar stood and watched Beaver dart across Big Snake River and give fire to some willows on the opposite bank, and recross farther on and give fire to the birches, and so on to several other kinds of trees. Since then, all who have wanted fire have got it from these particular trees, because they have fire in them and give it up readily when their wood is rubbed together in the ancient way.

Cedar still stands alone on the top of the hill where he stopped, near the junction of Grande Ronde and Big Snake rivers. He is very old, so old that his top is dead, but he still stands as a testament to the story's truth. That the chase was a very long one is shown by the fact that there are no cedars within a hundred miles upstream from him. The old people point him out to the children as they pass by. "See," they say, "here is old Cedar standing in the very spot where he stopped chasing Beaver."

—*Based on an account in the*
Journal of American Folk-Lore, *1890.*

In a Jicarilla Apache version of this story, it is Fox who tricks the fireflies out of their fire secret. Arriving from the sky, flying on the back of a wild goose, Fox makes the first drum ever. Beating it, he teaches the fireflies how to dance. Their watchfulness relaxes as they sway to the rhythm of the drum, and they dance themselves into a trance. Fox steals their fire by putting glowing embers in his bushy tail, and with his tail burning like a torch, he brings fire to the human beings.

■

THE RAVEN

■

[ATHAPASCAN]

Among a number of Athapascan-speaking tribes of the Northwest Coast and Alaskan tribes, Raven is not only a powerful supernatural creator, but also a trickster.

There once lived an old couple who wished to see their only daughter married to a rich man. When anyone arrived at their camp, the old man sent his son down to the landing to count the bone beads on the stranger's clothing, so that he could be received according to his rank.

One day the boy came running in saying that a man had come who would make a good brother-in-law, for he had a number of fine beads. The mother went down to the riverbank and saw a richly dressed stranger whom she also thought would make a suitable husband. She noticed that the shore was wet and muddy, so she got some bark and tore it into strips for the stranger to walk upon. She invited him to enter their tipi and seated him next to the girl.

The visitor pointed to a dog that was tied in the corner of the lodge and said, "I can't eat while that animal is in here." Thinking that only a very great personage would be so particular, the woman took the dog out into the forest and killed it. The next morning as she went for wood, she noticed that the earth around the dog's body was marked with bird tracks and that its eyes had been picked out. She returned to camp and insisted that all the people take off their moccasins and show their feet, because she had heard that Raven could deceive people by appearing in human form. The stranger, who was indeed Raven, took his moccasins off and slipped them on again so quickly that his scaly bird feet were not noticed.

The girl had agreed to marry Raven, and he demanded that she leave with him at once, before he could be found out. Promising that they would return in a few days, he took his bride down to his canoe.

As soon as the couple set off down the river, it began to rain. Raven was seated in front of the woman, who noticed that the rain was washing something white off his back. This made her suspicious, and she resolved to escape. Reaching forward, she succeeded in tying the tail of Raven's coat to a crossbar of the canoe. Then she asked to be set ashore for a minute, saying that she would come right back. Her husband told her not to go far, but she started to run for home as soon as she was out of sight among the trees.

After a while Raven decided to follow her. He found that his tail was tied, and to get free he had to resume his true form. As he flew over the girl, he cried out, "Once more I cheat you," then caw-cawed and glided away. The girl got home safely and told her mother that her rich husband was Raven, who had come to them covered with lime, which the rain had melted.

Raven was always cheating the people, so they finally took his beak away from him. After a time he went up the river and made a raft, which he loaded with moss. Floating down to the camps on it, he told the people that his head was sore where his beak had been torn off, and that he was lying in the moss to cool it. Then he went back upriver and made several more rafts. When the people saw these floating down toward them, they thought that a large group of warriors was coming to help Raven regain his beak. They held a council and decided to send a young girl to take the beak to an old woman who lived alone at some distance from the camp.

Raven, who had concealed himself among them and heard the council's plans, waited until the girl came back. Then he went to the old woman and told her that the girl wanted her to return the beak to him. Suspecting nothing, the old woman gave him his beak. He put it on and flew away, cawing with pleasure at his success. The warriors who had been on the rafts proved to be nothing but the tufts or hummocks of bog moss which are commonly known as *têtes de femmes*.

—*Retold from an account in the*
Journal of American Folk-Lore, *1900.*

■

THE BLUEBIRD AND COYOTE

■

[PIMA]

■ ▏▏ ■

The bluebird was once a very ugly color. But there was a lake where no river flowed in or out, and the bird bathed in it four times every morning for four mornings. Every morning it sang:

There's a blue water, it lies there.
I went in.
I am all blue.

On the fourth morning it shed all its feathers and came out of the lake in its bare skin, but on the fifth morning it came out with blue feathers.

All this while Coyote had been watching the bird. He wanted to jump in and get it, but he was afraid of the water. On that fifth morning he said, "How is it that all your ugly color has come out and now you are blue and gay and beautiful? You're more beautiful than anything that flies in the air. I want to be blue too."

Coyote was at that time a bright green. "I went in four times," said the bird, and taught Coyote the song. So Coyote went in four times, and the fifth time he came out as blue as the little bird.

That made him feel very proud. As he walked along, he looked on every side to see if anyone was noticing how fine and blue he was. He looked to see if his shadow was blue too, and so he was not watching the road. Presently he ran into a stump so hard that it threw him down in the dirt, and he became dust-colored all over. And to this day all coyotes are the color of dirt.

—A story reported by Frank Russell in 1908.

■

ADVENTURES OF GREAT RABBIT

■

[ALGONQUIAN]

Among the Micmac and Passamaquoddy of the Northeast coast it is Mahtigwess the Rabbit who is a powerful trickster. Rabbit has m'téoulin, great magical powers.

■ |||||||||||||||||||||||||||||||||||||||||||||||||||||||||||||||||||| ■

Wildcat is mean and ferocious. He has a short tail and big, long, sharp fangs, and his favorite food is rabbit. One day when Wildcat was hungry, he said to himself: "I'm going to catch and eat Mahtigwess, Great Rabbit, himself. He's plump and smart, and nothing less will do for my dinner." So we went hunting for Great Rabbit.

Now, Great Rabbit can sense what others are thinking from a long way off, so he already knew that Wildcat was after him. He made up his mind that he would use his magic power against Wildcat's strength. He picked up a handful of wood chips, threw them ahead of himself, and jumped after them, and because Great Rabbit is *m'téoulin*, every jump was a mile. Jumping that far, of course, he left very few tracks to follow.

Wildcat swore a mighty oath that he would catch Great Rabbit, that he would find him even if Mahtigwess had fled to the end of the world. At that time Wildcat had a beautiful long tail, and he swore by it: "Let my tail fall off—may I have just a little stump for a tail—if I fail to catch Great Rabbit!"

After a mile he found Rabbit's tracks. After another mile he found some more tracks. Wildcat was not altogether without magic either, and he was persevering. So mile by mile, he kept on Rabbit's trail.

In fact, Wildcat was drawing closer and closer. It grew dark and Great Rabbit grew tired. He was on a wide, empty plain of snow, and there was nothing to hide behind except a little spruce tree. He stomped on the snow and made himself a seat and bed of spruce boughs.

When Wildcat came to that spot, he found a fine, big wigwam and stuck his head through the door. Sitting inside was an old, gray-haired chief, solemn and mighty. The only strange thing about him was that he had two long ears standing up at each side of his head.

"Great Chief," said Wildcat, "have you by any chance seen a biggish rabbit running like mad?"

"Rabbits? Why of course, there are hundreds, thousands of rabbits hereabouts, but what's the hurry? It's late and you must be tired. If you want to hunt rabbits, start in the morning after a good night's sleep. I'm a lonely man and enjoy the company of a respected personage like you. Stay overnight; I have a fine rabbit stew cooking here."

Wildcat was flattered. "Big Chief, I am honored," he said. He ate a whole kettle full of tasty rabbit stew and then fell asleep before the roaring fire.

Wildcat awoke early because he was freezing. He found himself alone in the midst of a huge snowfield. Nothing was there, no wigwam, no fire, no old chief; all he could see were a few little spruce boughs. It had been a dream, an illusion created by Great Rabbit's magic. Even the stew had been an illusion, and Wildcat was ravenous.

Shivering in the icy wind, Wildcat howled: "Rabbit has tricked me again, but I'll get even with him. By my tail, I swear I'll catch, kill, and eat him!"

Again Great Rabbit traveled with his mile-wide jumps, and again Wildcat followed closely. At nightfall Rabbit said to himself: "Time to rest and conjure something up." This time he trampled down a large area and spread many pine boughs around.

When Wildcat arrived, he found a large village full of busy people, though of what tribe he couldn't tell. He also saw a big wooden church painted white, the kind the French Jesuits were putting up among some tribes. Wildcat went up to a young man who was about to enter the church. "Friend, have you seen a biggish rabbit hereabouts, running away?"

"Quiet," said the young man, "we're having a prayer meeting. Wait until the sermon is over." The young man went into the church, and Wildcat followed him. There were lots of people sitting and listening to a gray-haired preacher. The only strange thing was the two long ears sticking up at each side of the priest's cap. He was preaching a very, very long sermon about the wickedness of ferocious wild beasts who tear up victims with their big, sharp fangs and then devour them. "Such savage fiends will be punished for their sins," said this preacher over and over.

Wildcat didn't like the long sermon, but he had to wait all the same. When the preaching was over at last, he went up to the priest with the long ears and asked: "Sir, have you seen a very sacred, biggish rabbit hereabouts?"

"Rabbits!" exclaimed the preacher. "We have a wet, foggy cedar swamp nearby with thousands of rabbits."

"I don't mean just any rabbit; I'm speaking of Great Rabbit."

"Of him I know nothing, friend. But over there in that big wigwam lives the wise old chief, the Sagamore. Go and ask him; he knows everything."

Wildcat went to the wigwam and found the Sagamore, an imposing figure, gray-haired like the preacher, with long white locks sticking up on each side of his head. "Young man," said the Sagamore gravely, "what can I do for you?"

"I'm looking for the biggish Great Rabbit."

"Ah! Him! He's hard to find and hard to catch. Tonight it's too late, but tomorrow I'll help you. Sit down, dear man. My daughters will give you a fine supper."

The Sagamore's daughters were beautiful. They brought Wildcat many large wooden bowls of the choicest food, and he ate it all up, because by now he was very hungry. The warmth of the fire and his full stomach made him drowsy, and the Sagamore's daughters brought him a thick white bearskin to sleep on. "You people really know how to treat a guest," said Wildcat as he fell asleep.

When he awoke, he found himself in a dismal, wet, foggy cedar swamp. Nothing was there except mud and icy slush and a lot of rabbit tracks. There was no village, no church, no wigwam, no Sagamore, no beautiful daughters. They had all been a mirage conjured up by Great Rabbit. The fine food had been a mirage too, and Wildcat's stomach was growling. He was ankle-deep in the freezing swamp. The fog was so thick he could hardly see anything. Enraged, he vowed to find and kill Great Rabbit even if he should die in the attempt. He swore by his tail, his teeth, his claws—by everything dear to him. Then he hastened on.

That night Wildcat came to a big longhouse. Inside, it was like a great hall, and it was full of people. On a high seat sat the chief, who wore two long white feathers at each side of his head. This venerable leader also had beautiful daughters who fed all comers, for Wildcat had stumbled into the midst of a great feast.

Exhausted and panting, he gasped, "Has any one seen the bi-big-biggish G-G-Great Ra-Rab-Rabbit?"

"Later, friend," said the chief with the two white feathers. "We are feasting, dancing, singing. You seem exhausted, poor man! Sit down; catch your breath. Rest. Eat."

Wildcat sat down. The people were having a singing contest, and the chief on his high seat pointed at Wildcat and said, "Our guest here looks like a fine singer. Perhaps he will honor us with a song."

Wildcat was flattered. He arose and sang:

> *Rabbits!*
> *How I hate them!*
> *How I despise them!*
> *How I laugh at them!*
> *How I kill them!*
> *How I scalp them!*
> *How I eat them!*

"A truly wonderful song," said the chief. "I must reward you for it. Here's what I give you." And with that the chief jumped up from his high seat, jumped over Wildcat's head, struck him a blow with his toma-hawk, kept on jumping with mile-long leaps—and all was gone. The longhouse, the hall, the people, the daughters: none remained. Once more Wildcat found himself alone in the middle of nowhere, worse off than ever, for he had a gash in his scalp where Great Rabbit had hit him with the tomahawk. His feet were sore, his stomach empty. He could hardly crawl. But he was more infuriated than ever. "I'll kill him!" he growled, "I'll give my life! And the tricks are over; he won't fool me again!"

That night Wildcat came to two beautiful wigwams. In the first was a young woman, obviously a chief's daughter. In the other was someone whom Wildcat took for her father, an elderly, gray-haired, gentle-looking man with two scalp locks sticking up at the sides of his head.

"Come in, come in, poor man," said the gray-haired host. "You're wounded! My daughter will wash and cure that cut. And we must build up your strength. I have a fine broth here and a pitcher full of wine, the drink Frenchmen make. It has great restorative powers."

But Wildcat was suspicious. "If this is Great Rabbit in disguise again, he won't fool me," he promised himself.

"Dear sir," said Wildcat, "I hesitate to mention it, but the two scalp locks sticking up at the sides of your head look very much like rabbit's ears."

"Rabbit's ears? How funny!" said the old man. "Know, friend, that in our tribe we all wear our scalp locks this way."

"Ah," said Wildcat, "but your nose is split exactly like a rabbit's nose."

"Don't remind me, friend. Some weeks ago I was hammering wampum beads, and the stone I was using to pound them on broke in half. A sharp piece flew up and split my nose—a great misfortune, because it does disfigure me."

"It does indeed. A pity. But why are your soles so yellow, like a rabbit's soles?"

"Oh, that's nothing. I prepared some tobacco yesterday, and the juice stained my palms yellow."

Then Wildcat said to himself: "This man is no rabbit."

The old man called his daughter, who washed Wildcat's wound, put a healing salve into it, and bathed his face. Then the old man gave him a wonderfully strengthening broth and a large pitcher of sweet wine.

"This wine is really good," said Wildcat, "the first I ever tasted."

"Yes, these white people, these Frenchmen, are very clever at making good things to drink."

When Wildcat awoke, he found, of course, that he had been tricked again. The food he had eaten was rabbit pellets, the wine was stale water in a half-wilted pitcher plant. Now it was only his great hatred that kept Wildcat going, but go he did, like a streak, on Rabbit's tail.

Mahtigwess, Great Rabbit, had only enough m'téoulin, enough magic power, left for one more trick. So he said to himself: "This time I'd better make it good!"

Great Rabbit came to a big lake and threw a chip of wood into the water. Immediately it turned into a towering ship, the kind white men build, with tall sides, three masts, white sails, and colored flags. That ship was pierced on each side with three rows of heavy cannon.

When Wildcat arrived at this lake, he saw the big ship with its crew. On deck was the captain, a gray-haired man with a large, gold-trimmed, cocked hat that had fluffy white plumes right and left.

"Rabbit!" cried Wildcat, "I know you! You're no French captain; you're Great Rabbit. I know you, Mahtigwess! I am the mighty Wildcat, and I'm coming to scalp and kill you now!"

And with that, Wildcat jumped into the lake and swam toward the ship. Then the captain, who indeed was Mahtigwess, the Great Rabbit, ordered his men to fire their muskets and the three rows of heavy cannon. Bullets went whistling by Wildcat; cannonballs flew toward him; the whole world was spitting thunder and fire.

Wildcat had never before faced white men's firearms; they were entirely new to him. It didn't matter that ship, cannon, muskets, cannonballs, bullets, fire, noise, and smoke were merely illusions conjured up by Rabbit. To Wildcat they were real, and he was scared to death. He swam back to shore and ran away. And if he hasn't died, he is running still.

And yes, as Wildcat had sworn by his tail to catch and kill Rabbit, his tail fell off, and ever since then this kind of big wildcat has a short, stumpy tail and is called a bobcat.

—*Based on an account by Charles G. Leland, 1884.*

TURKEY MAKES THE CORN AND COYOTE PLANTS IT

[WHITE MOUNTAIN APACHE]

Long ago when all the animals talked like people, Turkey overheard a boy begging his sister for food. "What does your little brother want?" he asked the girl. "He's hungry, but we have nothing to eat," she said.

When Turkey heard this, he shook himself all over. Many kinds of fruits and wild food dropped out of his body, and the brother and sister ate these up. Turkey shook himself again, and a variety of corn that is very large dropped out of his feathers. He shook himself a third time, and yellow corn dropped out. And when he shook himself for the fourth time, white corn dropped out.

Bear came over, and Turkey told him, "I'm helping to feed my sister and my brother, over there." Bear said, "You can shake only four times to make food come out of you, but I have every kind of food on me, from my feet to my head."

Bear shook himself, and out of his fur dropped juniper berries. He shook himself again, and out dropped a cactus that is good to eat. Then he shook out acorns, then another kind of cactus, then Gambel oak acorns, then blue oak acorns, then piñon nuts, then a species of sumac, then manzanita berries, then wild mulberries, then *saguaro* fruit.

Turkey said to the boy and girl, "I have four kinds of corn seeds here for you, and this is a good place to plant them." The sister and brother cut digging sticks and made holes with them. In the holes they planted all their corn seeds. The next day the corn had already come up and was about a foot and a half high. The girl said, "We still have some squash seeds here," so they planted them too.

The boy and girl asked Turkey for more corn seed. "The corn is coming up nicely," they said, "so we want to make another farm and plant more corn there." Turkey gave them the seed, and they left him to look after their first fields while they started off to make the other farm.

When they came back, they heard Turkey hollering at the corn field. They ran down there and saw him dragging one wing along the ground on the side toward them. There were snakes on the other side of him, and he pretended to have a broken wing to lure the snakes away and shield the boy and girl. The squash plants had young squash on them, and the corn had grown tall and formed ears and tassels. The tassels had pollen in them, and the snakes had come to gather the pollen out of the corn plants. Turkey told the boy and girl to stay away from the corn for four days, when the snakes would be finished. At the end of the four days, the corn was ripe. Turkey told them, "This will be the only time when the corn will come up in four days. From now on it will take quite a while." And it does.

By now the brother and sister had planted corn three times, and they gave seeds to other people. Then Slim Coyote came and asked for some. "The corn you planted is growing well, and the ears are coming out on it," he said. "I'd like to have some seeds to plant for myself."

Coyote would have to do lots of work if he wanted to raise his corn, but that wasn't his plan. "These other people here plant their corn, and after it's grown, they have to cook it. Me, I'm not going to do it that way. I'll cook my corn first and then plant it, so I won't have to bother to cook it when it's ripe." Here's where Coyote made a big mistake. He cooked his corn, ate some, and planted quite a patch of the rest. He felt pretty good about it. "Now I've done well for myself. You people have to cook your corn after you plant it, but mine will be already cooked," he said.

After planting, he went off with the rest of the people to gather acorns, but when they returned to their fields, Coyote's had nothing growing on it at all. He said angrily, "You people must have taken the hearts out of the corn seeds you gave to me." "No, we didn't do that," they told him, "but you cooked the heart out of them before you planted."

Coyote asked for more seeds and planted them the right way this time. So his corn grew: the day after he planted, it was up about a foot and a half. He felt good.

The people who had planted their corn at the beginning were harvesting now and tying it up into bundles. Coyote saw these and wanted some. People got mad at Coyote because he was always asking them for corn. "I just want some green ears to feed my children," he would say. "As soon as my corn is ripe, I'll pay you back."

The other people had all their corn in and stripped now, but their squashes were still growing in the field. Coyote stole their squash, and the people all came to his camp. They wanted to know if he was the one who was stealing their squash. Coyote pretended to get angry. "You're always blaming me for stealing everything. There are lots of camps over there. Why do you have to choose mine to come to with your accusations?" But the people knew about Coyote's thieving ways.

"From now on, don't make your farm near us. Move away and live someplace else!" they said.

"All right. There are several of you that I was going to repay with corn, but I won't do it now that you've treated me this way," he said. So Coyote's family lived poorly, and they never bothered to cook anything before they ate it.

—Based on Grenville Goodwin's version of 1939.

COYOTE TAKES WATER
FROM THE FROG PEOPLE

[KALAPUYA]

Coyote was out hunting and he found a dead deer. One of the deer's rib bones looked just like a big dentalia shell, and Coyote picked it up and took it with him. He went up to see the frog people. The frog people had all the water. When anyone wanted any water to drink or cook with or to wash, they had to go and get it from the frog people.

Coyote came up. "Hey, frog people, I have a big dentalia shell. I want a big drink of water—I want to drink for a long time."

"Give us that shell," said the frog people, "and you can drink all you want."

Coyote gave them the shell and began drinking. The water was behind a large dam where Coyote drank.

"I'm going to keep my head down for a long time," said Coyote, "because I'm really thirsty. Don't worry about me."

"Okay, we won't worry," said the frog people.

Coyote began drinking. He drank for a long time. Finally one of the frog people said, "Hey, Coyote, you sure are drinking a lot of water there. What are you doing that for?"

Coyote brought his head up out of the water. "I'm thirsty."

"Oh."

After a while one of the frog people said, "Coyote, you sure are drinking a lot. Maybe you better give us another shell."

"Just let me finish this drink," said Coyote, putting his head back under water.

The frog people wondered how a person could drink so much water. They didn't like this. They thought Coyote might be doing something.

Coyote was digging out under the dam all the time he had his head under water. When he was finished, he stood up and said, "That was a good drink. That was just what I needed."

Then the dam collapsed, and the water went out into the valley and made the creeks and rivers and waterfalls.

The frog people were very angry. "You have taken all the water, Coyote!"

"It's not right that one people have all the water. Now it is where everyone can have it."

Coyote did that. Now anyone can go down to the river and get a drink of water or some water to cook with, or just swim around.

—Told by Barry Lopez in 1977.

■

HOW THE PEOPLE GOT ARROWHEADS

■

[SHASTA]

■ |||||||||||||||||||||||||||||||||||||||||||||||||||||||||||||||||||||||||||| ■

In the days when the first people lived, they used to go hunting with arrows that had pine-bark points. They did not know where to get obsidian, or they would have used it, for obsidian made a sharp, deadly point which always killed the animals that were shot.

Ground Squirrel was the only one who knew that Obsidian Old Man lived on Medicine Lake, and one day he set out to steal some obsidian. Taking a basket filled with roots, he went into Obsidian Old Man's house and offered him some. Obsidian-Old-Man ate the roots and liked them so much that he sent Ground Squirrel out to get more. While Ground Squirrel was digging for them, Grizzly Bear came along.

"Sit down," Grizzly Bear said. "Let me sit in your lap. Feed me those roots by the handful."

Ground Squirrel was very much afraid of huge Grizzly Bear, so he did as he was told. Grizzly Bear gobbled the roots and got up. "Obsidian Old Man's mother cleaned roots for someone," he said as he went away.

Ground Squirrel returned to Obsidian Old Man, but there were only a few roots left to give him. Ground Squirrel told him what Grizzly Bear had done and what he had said as he departed. Obsidian Old Man was extremely angry at the insult to his dead mother.

"Tomorrow we will both go to find roots," he said.

So early next morning they set off. Obsidian Old Man hid near the place where Ground Squirrel started digging. Soon Ground Squirrel's basket was filled, and then along came Grizzly Bear.

"You dug all these for me!" he said. "Sit down!"

Ground Squirrel sat down, as he had the day before, and fed Grizzly Bear roots by the handful. But just then Grizzly Bear saw Obsidian Old Man draw near, and the bear got up to fight. At each blow, a great slice of the grizzly's flesh was cut off by the sharp obsidian. Grizzly Bear kept fighting till he was all cut to pieces, and then he fell dead. So Ground Squirrel and Obsidian Old Man went home and ate the roots and were happy. Early next morning, Obsidian Old Man was awakened by Ground Squirrel's groaning.

"I am sick. I am bruised because that great fellow sat upon me. Really, I am sick," he was groaning.

Obsidian Old Man was sorry for Ground Squirrel. "I'll go and get wood," he said to himself. "But I'll watch him, for he may be fooling me. These people are very clever."

So he went for wood, and on the way he thought, "I had better go back and look."

When he crept back softly and peeped in, he saw Ground Squirrel lying there, groaning.

"He is really sick," Obsidian Old Man said to himself, and went off in earnest—this time for wood.

But Ground Squirrel was very clever; he had been fooling all the time. As soon as Obsidian Old Man was far away, he got up. Taking all the obsidian points and tying them up in a bundle, he ran off.

As soon as Obsidian Old Man returned, he missed Ground Squirrel. He dropped the wood, ran after him, and almost caught him, but Ground Squirrel ran into a hole in the ground. As he went, he kicked the earth into the eyes of the old man, who was digging fast, trying to catch him.

After a while Obsidian Old Man gave up and left. Ground Squirrel came out the other end of the hole, crossed the lake, and went home.

He emptied the bundle of points on the ground and distributed them to everyone. All day long the people worked, tying them onto arrows. They threw away all the old bark points, and when they went hunting they used the new arrow points and killed a great many deer.

—*Based on a tale recorded by E. W. Gifford in 1930.*

IKTOME AND THE
IGNORANT GIRL

■

[BRULE SIOUX]

A pretty *winchinchala* had never been with a man yet, and Iktome was eager to sleep with her. He dressed himself up like a woman and went looking for the girl. He found her about to cross a stream. "*Hou mashke,* how are you, friend," he said. "Let's wade across together." They lifted their robes and stepped into the water.

"You have very hairy legs," said the girl to Iktome.

"That's because I am older. When women get older, some are like this."

The water got deeper and they lifted their robes higher. "You have a very hairy backside," said the *winchinchala* to Iktome. "Yes, some of us are like that," answered Iktome.

The water got still deeper and they lifted their robes up very high. "What's that strange thing dangling between your legs?" asked the girl, who had never seen a naked man.

"Ah," complained Iktome, "it's a kind of growth, like a large wart."

"It's very large for a wart."

"Yes. Oh my! An evil magician wished it on me. It's cumbersome; it's heavy; it hurts; it gets in the way. How I wish to be rid of it!"

"My elder sister," said the girl, "I pity you. We could cut this thing off."

"No, no, my younger sister. There's only one way to get rid of it, because the evil growth was put there by a sorcerer."

"What might this be, the way to get rid of it?"

"Ah, *mashke,* the only thing to do is to stick it in there, between your legs."

"Is that so? Well, I guess, women should help each other."

"Yes, *pilamaye,* thanks, you are very kind. Let's get out of this water and go over there where the grass is soft."

Spider Man made the girl lie down on the grass, got on top of her, and entered her. "Oh my," said the girl, "it sure is big. It hurts a little."

"Think how it must hurt me!" said Iktome, breathing hard.

"It hurts a little less now," said the girl. Iktome finished and got off the girl. The *winchinchala* looked and said: "Indeed, it already seems to be smaller."

"Yes, but not small enough yet," answered Spider Man. "This is hard work. Let me catch my breath, then we must try again." After a while he got on top of the girl once more.

"It really isn't so bad at all," said the ignorant *winchinchala*, "but it seems to have gotten bigger. It is indeed a powerful magic."

Iktome did not answer her. He was busy. He finished. He rolled off. "There's little improvement," said the girl.

"We must be patient and persevere," answered Iktome. So after a while they went at it again.

"Does it hurt very much, *mashke?*" the girl asked Iktome.

"Oh my, yes, but I am strong and brave," answered Iktome, "I can bear it."

"I can bear it too," said the girl.

"It really isn't altogether unpleasant," said the girl after they did it a fourth time, "but I must tell you, elder sister, I don't believe you will ever get rid of this strange thing."

"I have my doubts too," answered Spider Man.

"Well," said the ignorant *winchinchala*, "one could get used to it."

"Yes, *mashke*," answered Iktome, "one must make the best of it, but let's try once more to be sure."

—Told in Pine Ridge, South Dakota, and recorded by
Richard Erdoes.

COYOTE FIGHTS A LUMP OF PITCH

[WHITE MOUNTAIN APACHE]

Even long ago, when our tribe and animals and birds lived together near white people, Coyote was always in trouble. He would visit among the camps, staying in one for a while and then moving on, and when he stayed at Bear's camp, he used to go over at night to a white man's fields and steal the ears off the wheat.

When the white man who owned the farm found out what Coyote was up to, he trailed him long enough to locate his path into the field. Then he called all the white men to a council, and they made a figure of pitch just like a man and placed it in Coyote's path.

That night when Coyote went back to steal wheat again, he saw the pitch man standing there. Thinking it was a real person, he said, "Gray eyes—" he always talked like a Chiricahua Apache—"Get to one side and let me by. I just want a little wheat. Get over, I tell you." The pitch man stayed where he was. "If you don't move," Coyote said, "you'll get my fist in your face. Wherever I go on this earth, if I hit a man with my fist, it kills him." The pitch man never stirred. "All right, then I'm going to hit you." Coyote struck out, but his fist stuck fast in the pitch, clear to his elbow.

"What's the matter?" Coyote cried. "Why have you caught my hand? Turn loose or you'll get my other fist. If I hit a man with that one, it knocks all his wits out!" Then Coyote punched with his other fist, and this arm got stuck in the pitch also. Now he was standing on his two hind legs.

"I'm going to kick you if you keep holding me, and it'll knock you over." Coyote delivered a powerful kick, and his leg went into the pitch and stuck. "This other leg is worse still, and you're going to get it!" he said. He kicked, and his leg stuck into the pitch.

Now Coyote's legs were fast in the pitch; only his tail was free. "If I whip you with my tail, it will cut you in two. So turn me loose!" But the pitch man just stood there. Coyote lashed the pitch with his tail and got it stuck also. Only his head was free, and he was still talking with it. "Why do you hold me this way? I'll bite you in the neck and kill you, so you'd better turn me loose." When the pitch did nothing, Coyote bit it and got his mouth stuck, and there he was.

In the morning the farmer put a chain around Coyote's neck, took him out of the pitch, and led him to the house. "This is the one who has been stealing from me," he said to his family. The white people held a meeting to discuss what they should do with Coyote. They decided to put him into a pot of boiling water and scald him, so they set the water on to heat and tied Coyote up at the side of the house.

Pretty soon Coyote saw Gray Fox coming along, loafing around the farmer's yard, looking for something to steal from the white man. Coyote called him over. "My cousin," he said, "there are lots of things cooking for me in that pot," though of course the pot was only heating water to scald him in. "There are potatoes, coffee, bread, and all kinds of food for me. It'll soon be done, and the white people are going to bring them to me. You and I can eat them together, but you must help me first. Can you put this chain around your neck while I go and urinate behind that bush?" Fox agreed and, taking the chain off Coyote, put it on his own neck. As soon as Coyote was out of sight behind the bush, he ran off.

After a while the water was good and hot, and the white men came out to Gray Fox. "He seems so little! What happened? He must have shrunk, I guess," they said. They lifted him up and threw him into the pot. Now the hot water boiled his hair right off, leaving Gray Fox bright red and hairless. They took off the chain and threw him under a tree, where he lay motionless until evening. When it got dark and cold, he woke up and started off.

After a while Gray Fox came to Bear's camp and asked, "Where is Coyote?" Bear replied that Coyote always went for his water to some springs above Bear's camp at midnight. So Gray Fox ran off to the springs and hid himself.

Now at midnight Coyote came as usual to the spring, but when he put his head to the water to drink, Gray Fox jumped him. "Now I'm going to kill you and eat you," the fox said. The moon was shining from the sky down into the water, and Coyote, pointing to its reflection, replied, "Don't talk like that, when we can both eat this delicious 'ash bread' down there. All we have to do is drink all the water, and we can take the bread out and have a feast."

They both started to lap up the water, but soon Coyote was merely pretending to drink. Gray Fox drank lots, and when he was full, he got cold. Then Coyote said, "My cousin, some white people left a camp over here, and I'm going to look for some old rags or quilts to wrap you up in. Wait for me." So Coyote started off, and as soon as he was out of sight, he ran away.

—*Based on Grenville Goodwin's version of 1939.*

ALWAYS-LIVING-AT-THE-COAST

■

[KWAKIUTL]

Reported here is another dangerous amorous encounter similar to that in "Teeth in the Wrong Places."

■ ▨▨▨▨▨▨▨▨▨▨▨▨▨▨▨▨▨▨▨▨▨▨▨ ■

Coyote was paddling his canoe down the coast when some people called out to him from the beach.

"Coyote, where are you going?"

"I am going to marry the daughter of Always-Living-at-the-Coast."

"Only a crazy person would do something like that."

That made Coyote angry, and he paddled to the shore. He turned all the people into birds, and then he turned the flock of birds into deer.

"You will be the deer that men need," he said and departed.

Soon he passed some other people who were standing on the beach.

"Coyote, where are you headed?"

He told them.

"You should watch out, then. The bones of those who have tried to marry this woman are piled up high."

Coyote appreciated their concern. He came ashore and put mussels and salmon in the water, which is why you still go to this place for those things today.

A while later some other people called out to him, asking him where he was going. He told them.

The chief then said, "Be careful, Coyote. All my young men have gone there to marry this woman, and none of them have come back."

Coyote came ashore and filled the waters along this beach with mussels, and gave the people roasted salmon to eat.

At a place called Copper Bottom, Coyote put ashore again and walked through the woods to a village, where he saw an old woman steaming clover roots.

The woman was blind, but right away she smelled him.

"Coyote! What are you doing here?" she asked.

He reached over and took a handful of clover roots to eat.

"What's this? Who's taking my clover roots?"

"Can't you see?"

The woman explained that she was blind. Coyote then took some pine gum and chewed it and then spit it into the woman's eyes.

"Can you see now?"

"Yes. I can see well."

Coyote told her where he was going. She told him to be careful and gave him some food to take with him.

Coyote went on until he came to a woman working on a canoe. He went over and pinched the feet of her baby. The child began to cry, and the woman said, "Don't touch my child. He has never cried."

She went back to working on the canoe, chipping at the inside, but she cut a hole through the bottom.

"Look what you've done. Are you blind?" asked Coyote.

"Yes I am," answered the woman.

Coyote chewed some pine gum and spat into her eyes. And then she could see.

"Where are you going?" asked the woman.

"I am going to marry the daughter of Always-Living-at-the-Coast."

"You should be careful with her: she has teeth in her vagina. This is how she kills all the young men who come to see her. Take my stone chisel, and when you go to bed with her, stick this up in there and break the teeth off."

The woman rubbed Coyote's back with a stone and gave him the masks of the wren, the deer, the mountain goat, and the grizzly bear.

Coyote put on a mask that made him look older and went into the country of Always-Living-at-the-Coast, where he sat down by a river. He had not been there long when the man's daughter, Death-Bringing Woman, came by with her friends and saw him.

"Oh, he would make a good slave," she said. "Let's take him with us." So they took Coyote back to camp with them. That night Death-Bringing Woman asked Coyote to sleep with her.

Coyote could hear the sound of grinding teeth coming from under her clothes. When he got into bed with her, he heard the sound of rattle-snakes. He pushed the stone chisel in and twisted it sharply, and broke off all the teeth in Death-Bringing Woman's vagina. Then Coyote took off his mask. He said he was Coyote and he had come to marry her. They slept together.

The next night they arrived at the house of Always-Living-at-the-Coast. That night Always-Living-at-the-Coast heard laughing coming from his daughter's bedroom. He got up from his bed and came into her room.

"Who is that you're laughing with, my daughter?"

"This is my husband. Welcome him."

Always-Living-at-the-Coast welcomed Coyote and returned to his room. The next morning Always-Living-at-the-Coast split some cedar and stripped the bark, and made a snare trap. Then he went into his daughter's bedroom and said, "Son-in-law, I want you to jump through that door into the center of the house." Coyote put on his deer mask and jumped through the door of the room right into the trap, where the deer died.

"It serves him right, coming into my house and embarrassing me like this," said the old man.

But Coyote took off the mask of the deer and went back into his wife's room.

That night the old man heard his daughter laughing again.

The next morning he made another cedar bark trap and told his son-in-law to jump through the door into the center of the house. Coyote put on the mask of the mountain goat and jumped into the trap, where he died at once. When the old man went out, Coyote took off the mask of the mountain goat and returned to his wife.

That night Always-Living-at-the-Coast heard the sounds of two people making love again and he called out, "Who's in there with you, daughter?"

"My husband," she answered.

The next morning the old man did as he had done before, making the trap and telling his son-in-law to jump into the dimness where it was concealed. This time Coyote put on the mask of the grizzly bear and went out into the other room and crushed the trap. Then he sat down to eat.

The old man was still thinking how he might kill his son-in-law. He asked Coyote to go with him by canoe across an inlet to the other shore where they would begin work on another canoe.

Coyote and the old man paddled across the water and went into the woods, where they felled a tree and began splitting the log. Coyote took up some alderwood and chewed on it while he worked. They were working along like this when Always-Living-at-the-Coast dropped his hammer into the split. He asked Coyote, who was smaller, to go down into the crack and get the hammer. When Coyote went in, the old man quickly knocked out the wedges holding the split open. Coyote spit out the alderwood, which looked like blood, and the old man thought his son-in-law was dead.

"This serves you right for thinking you could come and marry my daughter," he said, and left.

Coyote put on the mask of the wren and flew up out of the crack. He caught up with Always-Living-at-the-Coast.

"Why did you leave me behind there, Father-in-law? The log closed up and I was almost trapped."

"Oh, I'm glad to see you! I almost cried myself to death when it happened. I was going home now to tell my daughter. I thought you were dead. I'm glad you got out; I didn't think it was possible."

They both got into the old man's canoe and started paddling toward home. Coyote was chewing a piece of wood. When it was soft, he took it out, carved it into the shape of a killer whale, and threw it into the water. "You will be the killer whales of future generations," he said.

Just then the killer whales came up out of the water and snatched Always-Living-at-the-Coast out of the canoe.

When he got home, Death-Bringing Woman asked him where her father was, and Coyote said he didn't know. Later the woman had a son. One morning Coyote took his son and went away.

—Reported by Barry Lopez, 1977.

■

GLOOSCAP GRANTS
THREE WISHES

■

[ALGONQUIAN]

Even the great Glooscap can behave like a trickster, especially when people ask him for the frivolous.

■ ▐▐▐ ■

When men had heard that Glooscap, the lord of men and beasts, would grant a wish to anyone who could come to him, three Indians resolved to attempt the journey. One was a Maliseet from St. John, and the other two were Penobscots from Old Town. The path was long and the way hard, and they suffered much during the seven years that it took them. But while they were still three months' journey from his home, they heard the barking of his dogs, and as they drew nearer day by day, the noise was louder. And so after great trials, they found him, and he made them welcome and entertained them.

Before they went, he asked them what they wanted. And the eldest, an honest, simple man with no standing at home because he was a bad hunter, said he wanted to be a master at catching and killing game. Then Glooscap gave him a flute, or magic pipe, which pleases every ear and has the power of persuading every animal to follow him who plays it. The man thanked the lord and left.

The second Indian, on being asked what he would have, replied, "the love of many women." And when Glooscap asked how many, he said, "I don't care how many, just so there are enough and more than enough." The god seemed displeased to hear this but, smiling, gave the man a bag which was tightly tied and told him not to open it until he reached home. So the second Indian thanked the lord and left.

The third Indian was a gay and handsome but foolish young fellow whose whole heart was set on making people laugh. When asked what he chiefly wanted, he said he would like to be able to make a certain quaint and marvelous sound, like breaking wind or belching, which was frequently heard in those primitive times among all the Wabanaki. The effect of this noise is such that they who hear it always burst out laughing. And to him Glooscap was also affable, securing from the woods a certain magic root which, when eaten, would create the miracle the young man sought. But Glooscap warned him not to touch the root until he got home. Elated, the man thanked the lord and left.

It had taken the three Indians seven years to get there, but seven days were all they needed to return home. Yet only one of the men ever saw his lodge again. This was the hunter, who trudged through the woods with his pipe in his pocket and peace in his heart, happy to know that as long as he lived he would always have venison in his larder.

But the man who loved women, yet had never even won a wife, was anxious to know whether Glooscap's magic would work. He hadn't gone very far into the woods before he opened the bag. And there flew out by the hundreds, like white doves swarming about him, beautiful girls with black, burning eyes and flowing hair. Wild with passion, they threw their arms around him and kissed him as he responded to their embraces. But they crowded thicker and thicker, wilder and more passionate. He asked them to give him air, but they would not, and he tried to escape, but he could not; and so, panting, crying for breath, he smothered. And those who came that way found him dead, but what became of the girls no man knows.

Now, the third Indian went merrily along the path when all at once it flashed on his mind that Glooscap had given him a present. And without the least thought of Glooscap's warning, he drew out the root and ate it. Scarcely had he done this before he realized that he had the power of uttering the weird and mystic sound to perfection. It rang over the hills and woke the distant echoes until it was answered by a solemn owl, and the young man felt that it was indeed wonderful. So he walked on gayly, trumpeting as he went, happy as a bird.

But by and by he began to feel weary of his performance. Seeing a deer, he drew an arrow, stole closer, and was just about to shoot when in spite of himself the wild, unearthly sound broke forth like a demon's warble. The deer bounded away, and the young man cursed. By the time he reached Old Town half dead with hunger, he was not much to laugh over, though at first the Indians did chuckle, which cheered him up a little. But as the days went on they wearied of his joke and began to avoid him. His unpopularity made him feel that his life was a burden, and he went into the woods and killed himself.

—From a legend reported in 1884 by Charles G. Leland.

COYOTE'S RABBIT CHASE

■

[TEWA]

Here is another version of the Cochiti "Contest for Wives."

■ ||||||||||||||||||||||||||||||||||||||||||||||||||||||||||||||||||||||||||||||||||| ■

Coyote got up early one morning feeling unusually full of pep. He trotted along the ridge of a wash just as the sun was beginning to appear on the distant horizon. As he ran, he spotted a small, lumbering figure moving slowly below him. He loped down to see who it was and recognized Badger. "Greetings, brother!" he called. Quietly Badger wished him a good morning.

Coyote had already hatched a plot to get the best of Badger, so as the two paused to visit, Coyote said: "Brother, it's such a fine day that we shouldn't waste it just wandering around. Why don't we have a contest and a wager? Let's each spend the day hunting rabbits, and at sunset we'll return to this spot with our catch. Whoever kills the most rabbits gets to spend the night with the other's wife. What do you say, brother Badger?" At first Badger did not think this was such a good idea, but fearing that Coyote would call him a coward, he accepted.

As the two set out in opposite directions, Coyote felt there was no way he could lose. While he ran, he imagined how it would be to spend the night with Badger Woman. After a while he spotted a jackrabbit nibbling grass in a shady spot. He took off after it, yelling "Yip! Yip! Yip!"

Now, this jackrabbit had also just emerged from his hole, and he too was full of pep on this morning. He led Coyote a merry daylong chase up and down washes, over hills, and through forests. Coyote was serenely confident, thinking, "This jackrabbit should be all I need to beat old Badger, so slow, so cumbersome, so nearsighted. I doubt whether he'd catch anything if he had a whole year." In this fashion the day slowly waned.

Just before sunset Coyote finally wore the jackrabbit down and caught it. He hurried back to the rendezvous with Badger feeling quite sure of himself.

Meanwhile, Badger had hatched a plan of his own. Soon after their parting, he hurried to a system of rabbit holes that he knew were nearby, and at the first one he began to dig with his powerful claws and muscles.

In short order he caught several half-asleep rabbits. By the time he made his way through the entire tunnel system, he had twelve of them. These he laid out in a row above the tunnels as fast as he caught them, so while Coyote was just getting into his jackrabbit chase, Badger already had twelve rabbits.

Badger leisurely took several trips to carry his catch to the rendezvous, and then he searched until he found a spot of shade to wait for Coyote. He was surprised when Coyote appeared, worn out and dripping with perspiration, carrying one jackrabbit. When Coyote spotted Badger's catch, he realized that his trick had backfired.

That night Coyote had to remain outside his own den while Badger made endless love to his wife. Throughout the night these lovemaking sessions were marked with howls of pain from Coyote Woman, because Badger has a drill-shaped penis which hurt her terribly. Coyote didn't sleep at all that night, and the next morning his wife, very sore from the exertions of the evening, said: "Old man! You think you're so smart! You lose contests and I have to pay for your stupidity!"

—Translated from the Tewa by Alfonso Ortiz

■

COYOTE GETS RICH OFF THE WHITE MEN

■

[WHITE MOUNTAIN APACHE]

■ |||||||||||||||||||||||||||||||||||||||||||||||||||||||||||||||||||||||||||||||||| ■

Once when Coyote was visiting various camps, he and Bobcat heard about a white man who was making some whisky. They went together to the man's house and managed to steal some, and after they had run a short distance with it, they stopped to drink. Then Coyote said, "My cousin, I feel so good, I'd like to holler!" "No, we're still close to those white men," Bobcat said. "I won't holler loud, cousin," Coyote said. They kept arguing and drinking. Finally Bobcat said, "All right then, holler quietly." Coyote intended to holler softly, but before he knew it he got carried away and was hollering as loud as he could.

Now, the white men heard the noise and headed right toward him.

Bobcat had enough whisky in him to feel good, but Coyote was really drunk. When the white men surrounded them, Bobcat got up and sailed over the nearest man with one jump. In a second jump he leaped over all the rest and got away. So they arrested Coyote and took him in chains to the town jail. Later on, Bobcat used to visit Coyote from time to time, and once they arrested Bobcat and had them both locked up for quite a while.

One day the two prisoners watched some white men breaking horses in front of the jail. There was one horse that no one could get close to, and Coyote boasted, "I could saddle that horse right away." The prison guard told the men what Coyote had said, and they decided to let him out and see what he could do.

Now Coyote knew horse power, and when he had used it with the horse, it wasn't wild any more. He got on and rode it around and then thought he would have some fun. The horse balked, and though he kicked it gently with his heel, it wouldn't move. Coyote told the white people to put on a fancy saddle. They brought out a brand new one with taps and saddle bags and everything on it, just as he wanted. He put it on the animal, remounted, and kicked it, but gently, so it wouldn't move. "This horse is thinking about a nice white bridle and bit and lines, all covered with silver," said Coyote. Actually the horse was ready to go, but Coyote kept holding him in. The men brought a fine bridle and put it on the horse. Then Coyote dismounted the horse and said, "I want you to fill the saddle bags with crackers and cheese; that's what the horse wants. Also, I have to wear a good white shirt and vest, and a big show hat, and a pair of white-handled pistols in a belt. That's what the horse likes. And good silver spurs: the horse wants these also." They brought all this finery for Coyote and filled the saddle bags.

Now Coyote got on the horse. Ahead by the gate were some American soldiers. He kicked the horse hard and started for the soldiers at a gallop, making it look as if the horse were running away with him. The soldiers moved back, and he and the horse tore through the gate and disappeared.

Later Coyote sat down by a spring under a walnut tree, thinking about the soldiers that he knew were after him. He swept the ground clean under the tree and strung his money up on its branches. Pretty soon the soldiers came along, and Coyote said, "I'm going to tell you about this tree. Money grows on it, and I want to sell it. Want to buy?"

The soldiers were interested, and Coyote told them, "It takes a day for the money to grow and ripen. Today's crop is mine, but tomorrow it's all yours. I'll sell you this fine tree for all your pack mules." Coyote was always thinking about eating, and he hoped the packs held food.

The soldiers agreed to the terms, and Coyote got a big rock and threw it against the trunk. Most of the money fell to the ground. "See, it only ripens at noon," he said. "You have to hit it just at noon." He whacked the tree again, and the rest of the money dropped out. Now it was all on the ground, and the white men helped him pick it up and put it in sacks. They turned all their pack mules over, and he started off.

Coyote traveled for the rest of the day and all night, until he was in another country. Meanwhile the soldiers camped under the walnut tree waiting for noon. Then the officer told the soldiers to hit the tree, and they pounded it hard. When no money fell out, the officer ordered it chopped down, cut into lengths, and split up, in case the money was inside. No matter what they did, they couldn't find even five cents.

That night one of Coyote's mules got hungry and started to bray. Irritated at the noise, he killed every mule that brayed, until at last he had killed them all. So when he came to a white man's house, he bought a burro from him.

Now Coyote was always thinking about how he could swindle someone, and the burro gave him another idea. Returning to his old home in the mountain, he put a lot of money up the burro's rear end, then kicked the animal in the belly so that it expelled all the money. He tried it again, and it worked as before. "This burro is going to make me lots of money," he thought.

Coyote put his money in the burro's rear end and started for town, where he went to the big man in charge. "Look at this wonderful burro! His excrement is money, and it comes out of him every day." Coyote always talked like a Chiricahua.

"Let's see him do it," the head man said.

"All right, see for yourself. The first money that comes out is mine, but after that it's all yours." Coyote started kicking the burro in the belly, and his money fell out. He gathered it up. "Now it's yours," he said. "Tomorrow at the same time, he'll do it again." They paid him lots of money, and he went on his way.

On the following day when the time came, the white men brought the burro out and kicked him. He merely broke wind. They kicked him all day till evening, then said, "We might just as well kill this burro and look inside him." So they cut him open, but there wasn't a sign of money inside.

—*Based on a tale reported in 1939 by Grenville Goodwin.*

IKTOME SLEEPS WITH HIS
WIFE BY MISTAKE

[BRULE SIOUX]

Iktome was dissatisfied. He was restless. Looking at his wife, he thought: "This woman has become old. She has become ugly. Her face is wrinkled. Her breasts are sagging. She's all dried up. It's no fun sleeping with a woman like that. I must have a young, pretty girl. I must have a young girl soon."

His wife was looking at him. She knew him well, and she knew that look on his face. She said to herself: "That no-good husband of mine! He's thinking of some young, nice-looking *winchinchala*, not of giving me a little pleasure. I'll fix him!"

"Well, I'll go out now," said Iktome. "I have things to do."

"I bet," said his wife.

Iktome was looking for a young girl to seduce. He saw one he liked: young and handsome, with laughing eyes, a laughing mouth, and clear, smooth skin. She wore a fine white doeskin outfit with little bells attached to it, so that she made a pleasing sound when she moved.

"This is the one," thought Ikto, "the one I shall sleep with tonight." He went up to the girl and said, "Pretty young *winchinchala*, is this your tipi you are standing in front of?"

The girl just laughed.

"I have many pretty things I could give you."

The girl just laughed.

"Tonight after everybody has gone to sleep, I'll creep into your tipi. You be on the left side of the door."

The girl just laughed.

"I am a great lover," boasted Iktome. "You have no idea of the pleasures that await you."

The girl just laughed. She did not take Ikto seriously, he was so comical. But Iktome took her laughter for assent.

"Well, I'll go now. Tonight I'll make love to you. Don't forget—at the left side of the door."

From her tipi Iktome's wife had watched it all. After Ikto was gone, the wife went up to the girl.

"*Winchinchala*," she said, "has that no-good man asked you to sleep with him tonight?"

"Yes," said the merry girl and laughed.

"I knew it. In this tipi here?"

"Yes, in this tipi."

"Where do you sleep?"

"He told me to sleep on the left side, close by the door."

"*Winchinchala*, let's you and me change places with each other. Let's exchange clothes."

"What will you give me?" asked the girl.

"Why, this nice choker of red and blue beads."

"And what else?"

"These fine, big hair strings made of rare dentalium shells."

"Oh my, these are pretty! All right, let's change places tonight."

So, the *winchinchala* put on Ikto's wife's clothes and went into his tipi to sleep, while Ikto's wife took her place. That night after everyone had gone to sleep, Iktome crept into the pretty girl's tipi. At the left side he heard a woman stir, heard a slight tinkling of bells. He crept over there.

"Oh pretty girl," he whispered, "it's me, your lover Ikto."

There was giggling in the dark.

"Oh pretty one, how fresh your mouth tastes, not like the mouth of my aged wife."

There was more giggling.

"Ah, how nice it is to fondle a firm young breast, not a sagging one like my wife's."

There was more giggling.

"Oh, pretty young one! How full of fire you are! How ardently you make love, not just lying there like dead, like my old woman does it."

There was more giggling.

"Oh, how pleasingly moist, how wet, how juicy this is! Not dry like my wife's."

There was more giggling and squirming.

"Ah! Aaaah! Oh! Oooooh!"

More giggling and squirming.

"Well, this was certainly enjoyable. Oh my! Yes, this was fun. Well, I must go now. Maybe pretty soon we'll do this again."

There was a last giggle.

"I wonder whether this *winchinchala* ever opens her mouth except to giggle," thought Ikto. He was panting. He went home very slowly because the woman he had slept with had tired him out. By the time he got to his tipi, his wife and the pretty girl had already exchanged places again. They were now where they belonged. Iktome lay down beside his wife and fell asleep. In the morning when he awoke, his wife was already up and about.

"Old Woman," he said, "I'm hungry. Give me something good to eat."

"I'll give you something," said his wife and hit him hard with her turnip digger.

"Stop! stop! you crazy woman! What are you doing?"

"So my mouth isn't fresh!" And she hit him again.

"Oh, Oh, Oh Have pity on me!"

"So my skin is wrinkled!" She was beating him all over.

"Oh! oh! oh! Don't do that. It hurts, stop!"

"So my breasts are sagging!" The blows were coming thick and fast.

"Oh! oh! you're killing me!"

"So I'm not a hot one, you say. I just lie there like dead!" and she hit him a real good one.

"Oh, you're killing me!"

"So I'm all dried up. I'm not pleasingly moist!" She was hitting Iktome harder than ever.

"Have pity! I'll never sleep with anyone but you!"

"Liar," she said and kept on whacking him.

Iktome managed at last to crawl out of the tipi and get away from her. He was running, afraid his wife would catch up with him. A long way off he stopped, hurting so much all over that he could hardly move. His mind was hurt, too.

"So I slept with my ugly old woman," he thought. "So she tricked me. Oh my! I'm losing my touch. If I don't watch out I'll make love to an old she-monster next. I must be more observant in the future."

After a while he got hungry. Nobody fed him. Then he limped humbly back to his tipi. He entered cooing, making sweet talk: "Old Woman, you're still the prettiest. Be peaceful. Didn't I give you a good time last night? What's for breakfast?"

—*Recorded by Richard Erdoes while listening to stories*
around a powwow campfire, July 7, 1971, in
Pine Ridge, South Dakota.

HOW TO SCARE A BEAR

■

[TEWA]

■ |||||||||||||||||||||||||||||||||||||||||||||||||||||||||||||||||||||||||||||||||| ■

Long ago and far away this did not happen. On top of Red Rock Hill, lived a little rabbit. Prickly pears were his favorite food, and every day he would hunt for them along the east bank of the Rio Grande. Eventually he ate all the prickly pears on that bank, so he cast his hungry eyes across the river. He said to himself, "I'll bet plenty of them grow over there. Now, how am I going to get across the river to look?"

The rabbit knew the river was too deep and too wide for him to swim on his own, and he sighed, "Oh, how I wish that Uncle Fast Water, who moves the current, were here to take me across."

Fast Water heard and replied, "Child, I'm lying right here. What can I do for you?"

The little rabbit leaped toward the sound. "Uncle, so this is where you live!"

"Yes, this is the place," said his uncle. "What kind of work do you want from me?"

"I want to cross the river to pick prickly pears, but the water is too deep and too wide for me. Will you help me get across?"

Fast Water agreed, so the little rabbit sat on top of his head. "Splash! Splash! Splash!" went the water, and quickly the two were on the other side. "Be sure and call me when you want to come back," Fast Water said when they landed.

The rabbit wanted to get home before night fell, so he wasted no time but went right to picking and eating prickly pears.

Then Brother Bear appeared. "Little Rabbit!"

"Yes, Brother Bear?"

"My! What a pretty necklace you have."

"Yes, isn't it?"

"I want to make a bet with you for that necklace," said Brother Bear. "I'm willing to bet my red necklace for yours. If I win, you'll give me yours, and if you win, I'll give you mine." Little rabbit agreed, and they arranged to meet at noon the next day in the same spot.

That afternoon the little rabbit returned to the river, and his uncle easily carried him back across the water.

"Tomorrow you must wait for me, Uncle. I have placed a bet with Brother Bear, and I'll need you to carry me across the river again!"

"I'll wait for you," replied his uncle. "I know you'll win."

The next day the little rabbit got up early and hurried to meet Brother Bear. Because of his early start, he arrived first and decided to stroll in the woods. As he was hopping around, he spotted an old horse bell that still had a dried-up piece of leather tied to it. He hung it around his neck, and with each jump the bell went "Clank! Clank!" The little rabbit said to himself, "I think this bell will come in very handy with Brother Bear." And he hid the bell carefully in the woods.

When noon came, Brother Bear appeared. "You're here early," he said.

"Yes," answered the little rabbit, but he said nothing more.

The two picked a place in the dense wooded area to have their contest. Then Brother Bear made a circle on the ground with a stick.

"Little Rabbit, you can go first," said Brother Bear.

"Oh, no," said the little rabbit. "You wanted to bet, and you should go first."

"Yes, I'll go first. I'll bet you I'm the braver of us two. See that circle? You sit in it, and if you move even a little from where you're sitting I win."

Little Rabbit sat down, and Brother Bear took off into the woods. A few minutes later the rabbit heard strange sounds:

Aaah . . . Aaaah . . . Aaah . . .
Tweet . . . Tweet . . . Tweet . . .

Aaah . . . Aaaah . . . Aaah . . .
Tweet . . . Tweet . . . Tweet . . .

"I know that's Brother Bear," thought the little rabbit. "He's trying to scare me, but I won't move."

Closer and closer came the strange sounds. Suddenly, with a crash, a great big tree came tumbling down and barely missed the little rabbit.

"You moved! You moved! I saw you move!" shouted Brother Bear.

"No, I didn't move. Come and see for yourself," answered the rabbit.

Brother bear couldn't find any foot marks and had to agree that the little rabbit had not moved at all.

Little Rabbit said to Brother Bear, "Now you must sit in this circle as I did in yours." The rabbit drew a circle, and Brother Bear sat in it.

Leaving Brother Bear sitting in the circle, the rabbit headed into the woods. He just put the old horse bell around his neck and headed toward the place where Brother Bear was waiting.

After he had hopped a few steps, the little rabbit stopped, rang the horse bell, and sang:

> *Ah nana-na——Ah nana-na——*
> *Is cha-nay——Cha nana-ne——*
> *Coo ha ya*
> *Where are you sitting, my bear friend?*

When Brother Bear heard this, he thought, "That's not my friend Little Rabbit. This is something else altogether."

Coming closer to the circle where Brother Bear was sitting, the little rabbit rang his horse bell louder and sang his song once more.

Brother Bear, growing really frightened, stood up and ran. The little rabbit jumped out and called, "You've lost! Let me have your necklace!"

As the story goes, the little rabbit defeated Brother Bear. And today if you see a rabbit around the Tewa country, and if he has a red ring around his neck, you can be sure that the rabbit is descended from the little rabbit who won Brother Bear's pretty red necklace.

—*Translated from the Tewa by Alfonso Ortiz*

■

COYOTE STEALS SUN'S TOBACCO

■

[WHITE MOUNTAIN APACHE]

■ |||||||||||||||||||||||||||||||||||||||||||||||||||||||||||||||||||||||||||||| ■

One day Slim Coyote started out to Sun's house. When he got there Sun was not home, but his wife was. "Where is my cousin Sun?" he asked. Sun's wife said that he had gone out and was not home yet. Coyote saw Sun's tobacco bag hanging up on the side of the house. "I came to smoke and talk with my cousin," said Slim Coyote, "so give me a smoke while I'm waiting. He won't mind, he's my cousin." Coyote was talking to Sun's wife as if she were his mother-in-law. She handed him the tobacco bag, and he used it to fill his own little buckskin bag. Then he quickly hid his bag and rolled a cigarette, so that he actually got off with a lot of Sun's tobacco without her noticing. "Since my cousin hasn't come back yet, I guess I won't wait after all," Coyote told her, and started home.

Pretty soon Sun arrived. "Who's been here and gone again?" he asked, looking at his depleted tobacco bag. "Somebody who said he was your cousin," answered his wife. She told him what had happened, and Sun was very angry. "I'll get that fellow," he said. He went out front where he had Black Wind Horse tied, and saddled him up and set off after Coyote. Black Wind Horse could fly, and when he traveled he made a noise like lightning. A light rain started to fall and covered up Coyote's tracks, but Sun could still follow the thief by the ashes from his cigarette. It kept raining, and pretty soon the tobacco Coyote had with him started to grow. Soon it was putting out leaves, then flowers. At last it ripened and dried, and the wind scattered the seeds everywhere. When Sun saw this, he gave up chasing Coyote and went home.

When Coyote got back to the Apache camp where he was living, he kept his tobacco for himself and wouldn't give any away. The people kept asking him for a little smoke, but he said no. The Apache held a council on how to get Coyote's tobacco away from him, and they decided to pretend to give him a wife.

"We're going to give you a wife," they told him, and Coyote said, "You're trying to fool me." "No we're not," they said, "we're really going to give you a wife." They set up a new wickiup for Coyote, dressed a young boy as a girl, and told the boy not to let Coyote touch him till just before dawn. They made a bed in the new wickiup, and Coyote felt so good that he gave them all his tobacco.

Just about dusk the boy dressed as a girl went over and sat down beside Coyote in his new wickiup. Slim Coyote was so excited he could not stand up but just crawled around on the ground. "Why don't you come to bed?" he said to his bride. "Let's hurry and go to bed." But the boy just sat there. After a while, when Coyote was more and more impatient, the boy lay down by him but not close to him. "I want you to lie close," Coyote said, and tried to touch the boy. But the boy said, "Don't!" and pushed Coyote's hand away.

This kept up all night, until just before dawn Coyote made a grab and caught hold of the boy's penis. He let go right away and jumped back. "Get away from me; get back from me; you're a boy, not a girl," he said. Then Coyote got up and called the people. "You lied to me," he said. "You didn't give me a wife at all. Give me my tobacco back!" But no matter how loudly he yelled, they wouldn't do it. This is the way the people first got tobacco.

—Based on a legend reported by Grenville Goodwin in 1939.

■

DOING A TRICK WITH EYEBALLS

■

[NORTHERN CHEYENNE]

■ |||||||||||||||||||||||||||||||||||||||||||||||||||||||||||||||||||||||||||||||||||||||| ■

Veeho is like some tourists who come into an Indian village not knowing how to behave or what to do, trying to impress everybody.

One day Veeho met a medicine man with great powers. This man thought to amuse Veeho—and himself—with a little trick. "Eyeballs," he shouted, "I command you to fly out of my head and hang on that tree over there." At once his eyeballs shot out of his head and in a flash were hanging from a tree branch. Veeho watched open-mouthed. "Ho! Eyeballs!" cried the medicine man, "now come back where you belong!" And quick as lightning, the eyeballs were back where they ought to be.

"Uncle," said Veeho, "please give me a little of your power so that I too can do this wonderful trick." To himself Veeho was thinking, "Then I can set up as a medicine man; then people will look up to me, especially good-looking girls; then people will give me many gifts!"

"Why not?" said the medicine man. "Why not give you a little power to please you? But, listen, Veeho, don't do this trick more than four times a day, or your eyeballs won't come back."

"I won't," said Veeho.

Veeho could hardly wait to get away and try out this stunning trick. As soon as he was alone, he ordered: "Eyeballs, hop on that ledge over there. Jump to it!" And the eyeballs did.

Veeho couldn't see a thing. "Quickly, eyeballs, back into your sockets!" The eyeballs obeyed. "Boy, oh boy," Veeho said to himself, "what a big man I am. Powerful, really powerful." Soon he saw another tree.

"Eyeballs, up into that tree, quick!" For a second time the eyeballs did as they were told. "Back into the skull!" Veeho shouted, snapping his fingers. And once more the eyeballs jumped back. Veeho was enjoying himself, getting used to this marvellous trick. He couldn't stop. Twice more he performed it. "Well, that's it for today," he said.

Later he came to a big village and wanted to impress the people with his powers. "Would you believe it, cousins," he told them, "I can make my eyeballs jump out of my head, fly over to that tree, hang themselves from a branch, and come back when I tell them." The people, of course, didn't believe him; they laughed. Veeho grew angry. "It's true, it's true!" he cried. "You stupid people, I can do it."

"Show us," said the people.

"How often have I done this trick?" Veeho tried to remember. "Four times? No, no. The first time was only for practice; it doesn't count. I can still show these dummies something." And he commanded: "Eyeballs, hang yourselves on a branch of that tree!" The eyeballs did, and a great cry of wonder and astonishment went up. "There, you louts, didn't I tell you?" said Veeho, strutting around, puffing himself up. After a while he said: "All right, eyeballs, come back!" But the eyeballs stayed up in the tree. "Come back, come back, you no-good eyeballs," Veeho cried again and again, but the eyeballs stayed put. Finally a big fat crow lighted on that tree and gobbled them up. "Mm, good," said the crow, "very tasty." The people laughed at Veeho, shook their heads, and went away.

Veeho was blind now. He didn't know what to do. He groped through the forest. He stumbled. He ran into trees. He sat down by a stone and cried. He heard a squeaking sound. It was a mouse calling other mice. "Mouse, little mouse," cried Veeho, "I am blind. Please lend me one of your eyes so that I can see again."

"My eyes are tiny," answered the mouse, "much too tiny. What good would one of them do you? It wouldn't fit." But Veeho begged so pitifully that the mouse finally gave him an eye, saying: "I guess I can get along with the other one."

So Veeho had one eye, but it was very small indeed. What he saw was just a tiny speck of light. Still, it was better than nothing.

Veeho staggered on and met a buffalo. "Buffalo brother," he begged, "I have to get along with just this one tiny mouse eye. How can a big man like me make do with that? Have pity on me, brother, and lend me one of your big, beautiful eyes."

"What good would one of my eyes do you?" asked the buffalo. "It's much too big for your eye hole." But Veeho begged and wept and wheedled until the buffalo said: "Well, all right, I'll let you have one.

I can't stand listening to you carrying on like that. I guess I can get by with one eye."

And so Veeho had his second eye. The buffalo bull's eye was much too big. It stuck out of its socket like a shinny ball boys like to play with. It made everything look twice as big as his own eyes had. And since the mouse eye saw everything ten times smaller, Veeho got a bad headache. But what could he do? It was better than being blind. "It's a bad mess, though," said Veeho.

Veeho went back to his wife and lodge. His wife looked at him. "I believe your eyes are a little mismatched," she told him. And he described all that had happened to him. "You know," she said, "I think you should stop fooling around, trying to impress people with your tricks."

"I guess so," said Veeho.

—Told by Rachel Strange Owl in Birney, Montana, 1971,
and recorded by Richard Erdoes.

IKTOME HAS A BAD DREAM

[BRULE SIOUX]

Once in the middle of the night, Iktome woke up in a cold sweat after a bad dream. His friend Coyote, who was visiting, noticed something wrong. "Friend, what's the matter," he asked.

"I had a very bad dream," said Iktome.

"What did you dream of?"

"I dreamed I saw a very pretty *winchinchala* about to take a bath in the stream."

"It doesn't sound like a very bad dream," said Coyote.

"This girl was taking her clothes off. I saw her naked. She had a very fine body."

"My friend, decidedly, this is not a bad dream."

"I dreamed I was hiding behind some bush at quite a distance from her. As I watched her, my penis began to grow. It grew exceedingly long. It was winding toward her like a long snake."

"There's nothing wrong with this dream."

"My penis was like a long, long rope. It went all the way over to that girl. It went into the water. It touched her."

"*Kanji*, cousin, let me tell you, I wish I had such a dream."

"Now, my friend, the tip of my penis entered that girl. She didn't even notice it at first."

"*Kola*, I'm telling you, this is a fine dream."

"Then my penis entered the girl all the way. She seemed to like it."

"This is as good a dream as I ever heard of, my friend."

"Just at that moment I heard a great noise. I had been so excited in my dream that I hadn't noticed a team of horses pulling a big wagon. It was right on top of me, a *wasichu's*—a white man's—wagon. It was coming at a dead run, and the white man was whipping his horses. This wagon was very heavy, my friend, it had heavy wheels of iron. It was going between me and that girl . . ."

"Friend, you were right. This is indeed a very bad dream," said Coyote.

—Told in a bar at Winner, South Dakota, 1969, and
recorded by Richard Erdoes.

■

HOW COYOTE GOT HIS CUNNING

■

[KAROK]

Kareya was the god who in the very beginning created the world. First he made the fishes in the ocean; then he made the animals on land; and last of all he made a man. He had, however, given all the animals the same amount of rank and power.

So he went to the man he had created and said, "Make as many bows and arrows as there are animals. I am going to call all the animals together, and you are to give the longest bow and arrow to the one that should have the most power, and the shortest to the one that should have the least."

So the man set to work making bows and arrows, and at the end of nine days he had turned out enough for all the animals created by Kareya. Then Kareya called them all together and told them that the man would come to them the next day with the bows, and the one to whom he gave the longest would have the most power.

Each animal wanted to be the one to get the longest bow. Coyote schemed to outwit the others by staying awake all night. He thought that if he was the first to meet the man in the morning, he could get the longest bow for himself. So when the animals went to sleep, Coyote lay down and only pretended to sleep. About midnight, however, he began to feel genuinely sleepy. He got up and walked around, scratching his eyes to keep them open. As time passed, he grew sleepier. He resorted to skipping and jumping to keep awake, but the noise waked some of the other animals, so he had to stop.

About the time the morning star came up, Coyote was so sleepy that he couldn't keep his eyes any longer. So he took two little sticks and sharpened them at the ends, and with these he propped his eyelids open. Then he felt it was safe to sleep, since his eyes could watch the morning star rising. He planned to get up before the star was completely up, for by then all the other animals would be stirring. In a few minutes, however, Coyote was fast asleep. The sharp sticks pierced right through his eyelids, and instead of keeping them open, they pinned them shut. When the rest of the animals got up, Coyote lay in a deep sleep.

The animals went to meet the man and receive their bows. Cougar was given the longest, Bear the next-longest, and so on until the next-to-last bow was given to Frog.

The shortest bow was still left, however.

"What animal have I missed?" the man cried.

The animals began to look about, and they soon spied Coyote lying fast asleep. They all laughed heartily and danced around him. Then they led him to the man, for Coyote's eyes were pinned together by the sticks and he could not see. The man pulled the sticks out of Coyote's eyes and gave him the shortest bow. The animals laughed so hard that the man began to pity Coyote, who would be the weakest of them all. So he prayed to Kareya about Coyote, and Kareya responded by giving Coyote more cunning than any other animal. And that's how Coyote got his cunning.

—*A tale reported by E. W. Gifford in 1930.*

COYOTE AND THE
TWO FROG WOMEN

[ALSEA]

Coyote had no wife, and nobody wanted him. So one day he decided that he would go to the coast to look for dried salmon to buy.

He wasn't gone long when he came upon two frog women who were digging in the ground for camas. They called, "Where are you going?" He acted as if he didn't hear. When they had yelled at him for a third time, he seemed to pay attention. "What do you want?" "Nothing. We've just been trying to ask you a question." "What is it?" "Where are you going?" "I'm going to the coast to look for salmon." "All right; are you going to leave us some on your way back?" "Certainly," said Coyote. So he went on.

Now he was thinking, "I wonder how I'm going to play a trick on those two?" He hadn't gone far when he saw some yellow-jacket wasps hanging on a branch. He went to their nest, took it off the tree, and closed it so that the yellow jackets could not fly out. Then, slipping it into his basket, he opened the nest again and tied the basket so that the wasps could fly around inside but not come out.

Coyote put the basket on like a pack and went back to the women digging for camas. He didn't seem to pay any attention to them, so they shouted, "Hey, are you on your way home?" "Yes, I am on my way home." "How much salmon are you bringing back?" "Not very much." "You promised to leave some behind for us two." "All right, come and get it."

They came up, and he began to untie his pack. "You two put your heads inside this basket!" They did, whereupon he kicked the pack. The yellow jackets came out so angry that they stung the two frog women to death.

After the women had died, Coyote took off their vulvas and went on. Now whenever he felt like intercourse, he dug a hole in the ground, put those vulvas there, and then did it.

Pretty soon the two women came to life again. One began to examine herself and cried, "My vulva is gone! How about you?" The other looked, and hers was gone too! They agreed that it was Coyote who played the trick on them.

For this reason frogs, they say, have no female organs.

—Based on a tale from 1901.

■

COYOTE DANCES WITH A STAR

■

[CHEYENNE]

■ |||||||||||||||||||||||||||||||||||||||||||||||||||||||||||||||||||||||| ■

Because the Great Mystery Power had given Coyote much of his medicine, Coyote himself grew very powerful and very conceited. There was nothing, he believed, that he couldn't do. He even thought he was more powerful than the Great Mystery, for Coyote was sometimes wise but also a fool. One day long ago, it came into his mind to dance with a star. "I really feel like doing this," he said. He saw a bright star coming up from behind a mountain, and called out: "Hoh, you star, wait and come down! I want to dance with you."

The star descended until Coyote could get hold of him, and then soared up into the sky, with Coyote hanging on for dear life. Round and round the sky went the star. Coyote became very tired, and the arm that was holding onto the star grew numb, as if it were coming out of its socket.

"Star," he said, "I believe I've done enough dancing for now. I'll let go and be getting back home."

"No, wait; we're too high up," said the star. "Wait until I come lower over the mountain where I picked you up."

Coyote looked down at the earth. He thought it seemed quite near. "I'm tired, star; I think I'll leave now; we're low enough," he said, and let go.

Coyote had made a bad mistake. He dropped down, down, down. He fell for a full ten winters. He plopped through the earth clouds at last, and when he finally hit ground, he was flattened out like a tanned, stretched deerskin. So he died right there.

Now, the Great Mystery Power had amused himself by giving Coyote several lives. It took Coyote quite a few winters, however, to puff himself up again into his old shape. He had grown quite a bit older in all that time, but he had not grown less foolish. He boasted: "Who besides me could dance with stars, and fall out of the sky for ten long winters, and be flattened out like a deer hide, and live to tell the tale? I am Coyote. I am powerful. I can do anything!"

Coyote was sitting in front of his lodge one night, when from behind the mountain there rose a strange kind of star, a very fast one, trailing a long, shining tail. Coyote said to himself: "Look at that fast star; what fun to dance with him!" He called out: "Ho, strange star with the long tail! Wait for me; come down; let's dance!"

The strange, fast star shot down, and Coyote grabbed hold. The star whirled off into the vastness of the universe. Again Coyote had made a bad mistake. Looking up from his lodge into the sky, he had had no idea of that star's real speed. It was the fastest thing in the universe. It whirled Coyote around so swiftly that first one and then the other of his legs dropped off. Bit by bit, small pieces of Coyote were torn off in this mad race through the skies, until at last only Coyote's right hand was holding onto that fast star.

Coyote fell back down to earth in little pieces, a bit here and a bit there. But soon the pieces started looking for each other, slowly coming together, forming up into Coyote again. It took a long time—several winters. At last Coyote was whole again except for his right hand, which was still whirling around in space with the star. Coyote called out: "Great Mystery! I was wrong. I'm not as powerful as you. I'm not as powerful as I thought. Have pity on me!"

Then the Great Mystery Power spoke: "Friend Coyote. I have given you four lives. Two you have already wasted foolishly. Better watch out!"

"Have pity on me," wailed Coyote. "Give me back my right hand."

"That's up to the star with the long tail, my friend. You must have patience. Wait until the star appears to you, rising from behind the mountain again. Then maybe he will shake your hand off."

"How often does this star come over the mountain?"

"Once in a hundred lifetimes," said the Great Mystery.

—Retold from several North Californian fragments.

PART EIGHT

‖‖‖

FOUR LEGS, TWO LEGS, AND NO LEGS

‖‖‖

STORIES OF ANIMALS AND OTHER PEOPLE

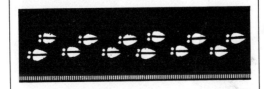

Animals are a swarming, talkative presence in the folklore of every Indian tribe. The number of tales in which they figure should not be surprising, given their major role in Indian mythology and religion. Their medicines are powerful, as are the emblems and tokens associated with them. We have seen a number of animals depicted as the creators of the universe and of the human race, and they freely move in and out of stories now as tricksters, now as culture bringers. In the Indian imagination there is no division between the animal and human spheres; each takes the other's clothing, shifting appearances at will. Animals of different species speak freely not only to one another, but to humans as well. Some of today's medicine men still claim to understand the language of certain animals. When a television interviewer laughed at Lame Deer's suggestion that he could understand birds, he replied: "In your Good Book a lady talks to a snake. I, at least, speak to eagles."

In the effort to merge the human and animal realms, marriages between the two are the natural result. All cultures across the continent depict bear spouses, and in addition to the buffalo (in the southwest and Plains) and the whale (in the northwest), the dog husband is also popular. In one story he is canine by day and human by night. When his wife has dog children, her tribe deserts her, but they return when it appears that these dog-boys are prospering far better than the starving humans. Such marriages are regarded with varying degrees of sympathy by the new human and animal in-laws, and don't necessarily fare better or worse than normal ones.

Even though animals were essentially sacred, they still provided an important food source. Folklore supplies vivid emblematic links between nourishment and the relations of humans and animals. In British Columbia there is a story of a young man who marries a deer, magically becomes one himself, and provides venison to feed his people. Hunting was a solemn, ritual-laden undertaking. Before starting out, men of many tribes observed careful rules requiring fasts and sexual abstinence, and they performed elaborate ceremonies to secure a successful hunt. Among the Pueblos, further rituals were performed after a deer was slain, to thank the deer for letting itself be caught and to ensure future luck in the hunt. Thus animals and humans find themselves bound together in a living web of mutual aid and respect.

THE GREAT RACE

[CHEYENNE]

When the Great Mystery created the earth and all living things upon it, the people and the animals lived in peace. None, neither people nor animals, ate flesh. Now it happened in the course of many seasons that the buffalo began to think they were the most powerful beings in the world. They came to believe that this gave them the right to kill and eat other animals, and people as well. Then the people said: "This isn't fair; we humans and the buffalo were created equal. But if it happens that one or the other must be the most powerful, then it should be us!"

The buffalo said. "Let's get this settled. We should have a contest to see whether we eat you or you eat us. How about a race?"

The people said: "But in a race you have an unfair advantage; two legs can't compete with four. Suppose we let the birds race for us. They have wings, you have four legs, that makes it more even."

The buffalo said: "Agreed. We'll choose our fastest runner, and you choose some birds to race for you."

Then some of the other animals said: "We should have a chance to race too."

"That's right, it's only fair," said the buffalo and the people. So all living things went to a place at the edge of the Black Hills called Buffalo Gap. There they lined up for the race.

As their contestant the buffalo had chosen Running Slim Buffalo Woman, a young cow who was the fastest of all animals and had never been beaten in a footrace.

To race for them the human beings had chosen four birds: a hummingbird, a meadowlark, a hawk, and a magpie.

In those early days of the world, the birds and animals had no color. Now for the race they all painted themselves carefully, each creature according to its own medicine, its own vision. For example, the skunk painted a white stripe on its back, the black-tailed deer painted its tail

black, the antelope took some red-brown earth and, mixing it with water, painted its whole hide. And as all the creatures painted themselves for this great race, so they have looked ever since.

Then the signal to race was given, and the crowd of runners started toward a hill which was the halfway point. Running Slim took off in a flash, with the buffalo cheering her on. For a while Hummingbird flew along with her, but soon he fell back exhausted and Meadowlark took over. Still, Running Slim kept far ahead, leading the great mass of racers with their thundering hooves. Though they had already covered a great distance, Running Slim was fresh.

By the time Running Slim reached the halfway point, she and the lark were far ahead of the field. At the hill the umpires were shouting: "Now turn and race back to the starting point, to Buffalo Gap!" The Lark heard this and thought: "I can't make it that far." He dropped out of the race, but already Hawk was coming on strongly.

Now Hawk, acknowledged to be the fastest of the birds, suddenly shot ahead of Running Slim. The people shouted for joy—but not for long. Hawk's endurance did not match his swiftness, and the sudden spurt exhausted him.

Again Running Slim came on, thundering ahead. With her deep chest, powerful legs, and great lungs, it seemed that she could keep up the pace forever. Then far in the rear a little black and white dot could be seen, coming up, flying hard. This was Magpie, a slow bird but strong-hearted and persevering. The buffalo herd paid no attention to Magpie; they were cheering their runner while the people watched silently.

Some of the racers were running so hard now that blood spurted from their mouths and nostrils. It colored the earth beneath, which has ever remained red along the trail where the race was run.

At last Buffalo Gap came into sight. Powerful and confident as she was, Running Slim herself was beginning to slow down, though it was hardly noticeable. Even she was not even aware of it, but ran along feeling sure that she would win. Then very slowly, imperceptibly, Magpie began to gain on her.

Buffalo Gap was closer now, though still a good way off, thought Slim Running. She could feel herself tiring. The buffalo were grunting and stomping, trying to encourage her. Magpie was still behind, but coming on steadily.

Now Buffalo Gap was near. Running Slim Buffalo Woman was really tired, but she gathered all her strength for the last spurt, thundering along, her heart close to bursting. By then, however, Magpie had come up even with her.

Both the buffalo and the people were cheering their racers on, calling out to them, yelling and stomping. So the two were speeding up, putting the very last of their strength into it—Running Slim Buffalo Woman and Magpie. Thus they neared the sticks, painted red, planted in the earth, which marked the finishing line. It was not until they were a hand breadth away from those sticks, at the last moment, that Magpie finally shot ahead. The people gave a great shout of happiness, and both racers fell exhausted.

So the humans had won and the buffalo had lost. And ever since the people have respected the magpie, never hunting it or eating it. So the people became more powerful than the buffalo and all the other animals, and from that time on, people have hunted the buffalo for their food.

—Recorded by Richard Erdoes on the Crow agency
during the intertribal Crow fair, summer 1968.

■

ORIGIN OF THE
GNAWING BEAVER

■

[HAIDA]

The Haida of the Queen Charlotte Islands off the coast of British
Columbia were great hunters of whales and sea otters.

■ ▏▎▍▌▋▊▉▊▋▌▍▎▏▏▎▍▌▋▊▉▊▋▌▍▎▏ ■

There was a great hunter among the people living at Larhwiyip on the Stikine River. Ever on the alert for new territories, he would go away by himself for long periods and return with quantities of furs and food. He had remained single, although he was very wealthy and his family begged him to take a wife. As a true hunter, he observed all the fasts of cleanliness and kept away from women.

One day when he returned from a hunting trip, he said, "I am going to take a wife now. After that I will move to a distant region where I hear that wild animals are plentiful." So he married a young woman from a neighboring village who, like himself, was clever and scrupulous in observing the rules. When the time came for them to go on their hunting trips, they both kept the fasts of purification, and the hunter got even more furs and food than he had before.

Some time later, he said to his wife, "Let's go to a new country, where we'll have to stay a long time." After many days of traveling, they came to a strange land. The hunter put up a hut, where they lived while he built a house. When he had finished it, he and his wife were happy. They would play with each other every night.

Soon he said to her, "I'm going to my new hunting grounds for two days and a night. I will return just before the second night." In his new territory he made snares in his trapline, and when these were set, he went home just before sunset on the second day. His wife was very happy, and again they played together all through the night. After several days, he visited his snares and found them full of game. He loaded his canoe and came back, again before dark on the second day. Very happy, he met his wife, and they both worked to prepare the furs and meat. When they had finished, he set out once more, saying, "This time I intend to go in a new direction, so I will be away for three sleeps." And he did, and rejoiced in being with his wife again when he returned.

To amuse herself when she was alone, the woman went down to the little stream flowing by the lodge. She spent most of her time bathing and swimming around in a small pool while her husband was away. As soon as he returned, she would play with him. Now he said, "Since you've become used to being alone, I'm going on a longer trip." By then he had enlarged his hunting house, and it was full of furs and food.

The woman again took to her swimming. Soon she found the little pool too small for her, so she built a dam by piling up branches and mud. The pool became a small lake, deep enough for her to swim in at ease. Now she spent nearly all her time in the new lake and felt quite happy. When her husband returned, she showed him the dam she had made,

and he was pleased. Before going away once more, he said, "I'll be gone a long time, now that I know you're not afraid of being alone."

The woman built a little house of mud and branches in the center of the lake. After a swim she would go into it and rest. At night she would return to the hunting house on land, but as soon as she waked in the morning, she would go down to the lake again.

Eventually she slept in her lake lodge all night, and when her husband came back, she felt uncomfortable staying with him at the house. Now she was pregnant and kept more to herself, and she preferred to stay in her lake lodge even when her husband was at home. To pass the time, she enlarged the lake by building the dam higher. She made another dam downstream, and then another, until she had a number of small lakes all connected to the large one in which she had her lodge.

The hunter went away on a last long journey. He had enough furs and food to make him very wealthy, and he planned that they would move back to his village after this trip. The woman, whose child was due any day, stayed in the water all the time and lived altogether in the lodge. By now it was partly submerged, and its entrance was under water.

When the hunter returned this time, he could not find his wife. He looked all over, searching the woods day after day without discovering a trace of her. He was at a loss, unwilling to go back to his people without knowing her fate, for fear that her family might want to kill him. He returned sadly to his hunting house every night and each morning resumed the search.

One evening at dusk, he remembered that his wife had spent much of her time in the water. "Perhaps she traveled on downstream," he thought. The next day he walked down to the lake that his wife had dammed and went around it, but he saw nothing of her.

After many days of searching, the hunter retraced his steps. When he came to the large lake, he sat down and began to sing a dirge. Now he knew that something had happened to his wife; she had been taken by a supernatural power. While he was singing and crying his dirge, a figure emerged from the lake. It was a strange animal, in its mouth a stick which it was gnawing. On each side of the animal were two smaller ones, also gnawing sticks.

Then the largest figure, which wore a hat shaped like a gnawed stick, spoke. "Don't be so sad! It is I, your wife, and your two children. We have returned to our home in the water. Now that you have seen me, you will use me as a crest. Call me the Woman-Beaver, and the crest Remnants-of-Chewing-Stick. The children are First Beaver, and you will refer to them in your dirge as the Offspring of Woman-Beaver."

After she had spoken, she disappeared into the waters, and the hunter saw her no more. At once he packed his goods, and when his canoe was filled, traveled down the river to his village.

For a long while he did not speak to his people. Then he told them what had happened and said, "I will take this as my personal crest. It shall be known as Remnants-of-Chewing-Stick, and forever remain the property of our clan, the Salmon-Eater household." This is the origin of the Beaver crest and the Remnants-of-Chewing-Stick.

—Based on two versions of the same myth, reported by
William Beynon in 1949 and by Marius Barbeau in 1953.

HOW THE CROW CAME
TO BE BLACK

[BRULE SIOUX]

In days long past, when the earth and the people on it were still young, all crows were white as snow. In those ancient times the people had neither horses nor firearms nor weapons of iron. Yet they depended upon the buffalo hunt to give them enough food to survive. Hunting the big buffalo on foot with stone-tipped weapons was hard, uncertain, and dangerous.

The crows made things even more difficult for the hunters, because they were friends of the buffalo. Soaring high above the prairie, they could see everything that was going on. Whenever they spied hunters approaching a buffalo herd, they flew to their friends and, perching between their horns, warned them: "Caw, caw, caw, cousins, hunters are coming. They are creeping up through that gully over there. They are coming up behind that hill. Watch out! Caw, caw, caw!" Hearing this, the buffalo would stampede, and the people starved.

The people held a council to decide what to do. Now, among the crows was a huge one, twice as big as all the others. This crow was their leader. One wise old chief got up and made this suggestion: "We must capture the big white crow," he said, "and teach him a lesson. It's either that or go hungry." He brought out a large buffalo skin, with the head and horns still attached. He put it on the back of a young brave, saying: "Nephew, sneak among the buffalo. They will think you are one of them, and you can capture the big white crow."

Disguised as a buffalo, the young man crept among the herd as if he were grazing. The big, shaggy beasts paid him no attention. Then the hunters marched out from their camp after him, their bows at the ready. As they approached the herd, the crows came flying, as usual, warning the buffalo: "Caw, caw, caw, cousins, the hunters are coming to kill you. Watch out for their arrows. Caw, caw, caw!" and as usual, all the buffalo stampeded off and away—all, that is, except the young hunter in disguise under his shaggy skin, who pretended to go on grazing as before.

Then the big white crow came gliding down, perched on the hunter's shoulders, and flapping his wings, said: "Caw, caw, caw, brother, are you deaf? The hunters are close by, just over the hill. Save yourself!" But the young brave reached out from under the buffalo skin and grabbed the crow by the legs. With a rawhide string he tied the big bird's feet and fastened the other end to a stone. No matter how the crow struggled, he could not escape.

Again the people sat in council. "What shall we do with this big, bad crow, who has made us go hungry again and again?"

"I'll burn him up!" answered one angry hunter, and before anybody could stop him, he yanked the crow from the hands of his captor and thrust it into the council fire, string, stone and all. "This will teach you," he said.

Of course, the string that held the stone burned through almost at once, and the big crow managed to fly out of the fire. But he was badly singed, and some of his feathers were charred. Though he was still big, he was no longer white. "Caw, caw, caw," he cried, flying away as quickly as he could, "I'll never do it again; I'll stop warning the buffalo, and so will all the Crow nation. I promise! Caw, caw, caw."

Thus the crow escaped. But ever since, all crows have been black.

—*Told by Good White Buffalo at Winner,*
Rosebud Indian Reservation, South Dakota, 1964.
Recorded by Richard Erdoes.

THE GIRL WHO
MARRIED RATTLESNAKE

[POMO]

At a place called Cobowin there was a large rock with a hole in it, and many rattlesnakes lived inside this hole. Nearby at Kalesima there was a village with four large houses, and in the one with a center pole lived a girl. In the spring when clover was just right to eat, this girl went out to gather some. While she was working, she was watched by a rattlesnake.

The snake followed her back to the village, and close to her house he transformed himself into a handsome young man with a net on his head and fine beads around his neck. Then he climbed up onto the top of the house and came down the center pole. The family was surprised to see him, but he told the girl that he wanted to marry her. He remained with the family overnight and the following morning went home again. He arrived and left like this for four days; then on the fifth evening he came back, but this time did not change his form. He simply slithered into the house and began conversing just as before. The girl's mother, waiting for her daughter's suitor, said she heard someone talking in the house. She took a light and looked in the place where she heard the sound, and there was Rattlesnake. He shook his snake's head, and she dropped the light and ran in terror.

On the following morning Rattlesnake took the girl home with him, and there she remained. In time she bore him four boys. Whenever these children saw any people from the village, they would coil to strike, but their mother would say, "No, you mustn't bite your relatives." And the children would obey her.

As the four rattlesnake boys grew older, they also grew more curious, and one day they came in from playing and asked their mother, "Why don't you talk the way we do? Why are you different?"

"I'm not a rattlesnake, like you and your father," she replied. "I'm a human being."

"Aren't you afraid of our father?" asked the boys, and she shook her head.

Then the oldest said that he had heard the other rattlesnakes discussing her differences and deciding to crawl over her body to find out what kind of creature she was. While this might have alarmed another human, the rattlesnake's wife was not at all afraid. When the other rattlesnakes came, she calmly let them crawl over her.

Then she said to her oldest boy, "It's impossible for you to become a human being, and though I'm not really human any longer, I must go back to my parents and tell them what has happened." And so she returned to the house with the center pole and said to her parents, "This is the last time that I will be able to talk to you and the last time that you can talk with me." Her father and mother were sad, but they said nothing until the daughter started to leave. Then her mother ran and caught her by the door, brought her back into the house, and wept over her because she was so changed. But the girl shook her body, and suddenly she was gone. No one knew how or where she went, but they think she returned to Rattlesnake's house and has lived there ever since.

—*Based on a legend recorded by Samuel Barrett in 1933.*

■

WHY THE OWL HAS BIG EYES

■

[IROQUOIS]

■ ▏▏▏ ■

Raweno, the Everything-Maker, was busy creating various animals. He was working on Rabbit, and Rabbit was saying: "I want nice long legs and long ears like a deer, and sharp fangs and claws like a panther."

"I do them up the way they want to be; I give them what they ask for," said Raweno. He was working on Rabbit's hind legs, making them long, the way Rabbit had ordered.

Owl, still unformed, was sitting on a tree nearby and waiting his turn. He was saying: "Whoo, whoo, I want a nice long neck like Swan's, and beautiful red feathers like Cardinal's, and a nice long beak like Egret's, and a nice crown of plumes like Heron's. I want you to make me into the most beautiful, the fastest, the most wonderful of all the birds."

Raweno said: "Be quiet. Turn around and look in another direction. Even better, close your eyes. Don't you know that no one is allowed to watch me work?" Raweno was just then making Rabbit's ears very long, the way Rabbit wanted them.

Owl refused to do what Raweno said. "Whoo, whoo," he replied, "nobody can forbid me to watch. Nobody can order me to close my eyes. I like watching you, and watch I will."

Then Raweno became angry. He grabbed Owl, pulling him down from his branch, stuffing his head deep into his body, shaking him until his eyes grew big with fright, pulling at his ears until they were sticking up at both sides of his head.

"There," said Raweno, "that'll teach you. Now you won't be able to crane your neck to watch things you shouldn't watch. Now you have big ears to listen when someone tells you what not to do. Now you have big eyes—but not so big that you can watch me, because you'll be awake only at night, and I work by day. And your feathers won't be red like cardinal's, but gray like this"—and Raweno rubbed Owl all over with mud—"as punishment for your disobedience." So Owl flew off, pouting: "Whoo, whoo, whoo."

Then Raweno turned back to finish Rabbit, but Rabbit had been so terrified by Raweno's anger, even though it was not directed at him, that he ran off half done. As a consequence, only Rabbit's hind legs are long, and he has to hop about instead of walking and running. Also, because he took fright then, Rabbit has remained afraid of most everything, and he never got the claws and fangs he asked for in order to defend himself. Had he not run away then, Rabbit would have been an altogether different animal.

As for Owl, he remained as Raweno had shaped him in anger—with big eyes, a short neck, and ears sticking up on the sides of his head. On top of everything, he has to sleep during the day and come out only at night.

—*Retold from various nineteenth-century sources.*

■

THE OWL HUSBAND

■

[PASSAMAQUODDY]

In many tribes the owl has a sinister meaning. In the Northwest the owl calls out the names of men and women who will die soon.

Among the Sioux, Hin-Han the owl guards the entrance to the Milky Way over which the souls of the dead must pass to reach the spirit land. Those who fail the owl's inspection because they do not have the proper tattoo on their wrists or elsewhere are thrown into the bottomless abyss. Among some nations, on the other hand, the owl is a wise and friendly spirit, an advisor and warning giver. A Passamaquoddy tale depicts the owl as having love medicine and a magic love flute—powers that the Plains people attribute to the elk.

■ ▏▎▍▌▋▊▉▊▋▌▍▎▏▎▍▌▋▊▉▊▋▌▍▎▏▎▍▌▋▊▉▊▋▌▍▎▏▎▍▌▋▊▉ ■

A man and his wife lived at the edge of their village near a stream. They had a beautiful daughter whom many young men wished to marry, but she was proud, and no suitor pleased her. Her father, caught between his daughter's haughtiness and the rejected suitors' anger, hoped to appease both by promising to give his daughter to the man who could make the embers of his hearth fire blaze up by spitting on it. Naturally, since spitting tends to put a fire out rather than kindle it, none of the young men succeeded.

There lived in the village an old woman whom many suspected of possessing evil powers, and their suspicions were well grounded. In reality she was an owl in disguise, and her nephew, the great horned owl, ruled the whole tribe of these bad and scheming birds. Because he wanted the haughty girl for his wife, he assumed the shape of a good-looking young hunter and went to his aunt for help. "Here," she said, and gave him a magic potion to drink. "This will enable you to fulfill that old man's condition."

The handsome young hunter went at once to the lodge where the girl lived. He found her father entertaining the tribal elders, among them the chief of the village.

"Old man," said the owl in disguise, "is it true that you will give me your daughter if I can make your fire blaze up by spitting on these hot ashes?"

"Certainly, young man," said her father, "if you can do that, I will indeed let you have her." The suitor spit on the glowing embers, which immediately blazed into a mighty flame reaching to the ceiling of the lodge, shooting up through the smoke hole, thrusting far into the sky. Since the girl could not refuse after her father made his promise in front of the elders and the chief, the hunter seized her by the hand and took her with him to his lodge.

There her owl husband spread out soft bear robes for her and did all a young bridegroom should do for a beloved wife. When the girl woke after her first night as a married woman, she gazed at her sleeping husband and discovered something awful. His ears stuck up from his long, thick black hair, and his yellowish eyes, which he kept half open even in sleep, had pupils that contracted at intervals into narrow slits. The girl sat for a long time petrified with fear, because now she knew that the handsome young hunter was the terrible great horned owl himself.

The spell was broken when the husband's aunt entered and nudged the girl. "What's the matter?" she asked. "Why are you sitting there staring at him like this?" Then the girl let out a piercing scream and fled.

The whole village tried to console the young woman for the shocking trick that had been played upon her. The great horned owl left the neighborhood, because now everybody knew who he really was. However, he still hoped to regain his beautiful wife by tricking her a second time.

The owl chief waited a while for the villagers to forget their fear and suspicion. Then he changed himself once more into a young man, also good-looking, but very different in appearance from his former disguise. He killed a moose and an elk, dragged the meat to the village, and announced to the people: "I have come as a friend from another camp nearby. I belong to your people and speak the same language, and I want to live among you. I am a great hunter and a generous man. I am putting up a lodge, and I have much meat, so I invite everybody to a feast."

At first the haughty young woman and her parents were suspicious and did not want to accept the invitation. But all the people said: "Why, he's just a good-natured stranger. It would be impolite not to go." So they went.

While the villagers were feasting, the newcomer said: "Let's tell stories. Has anybody had something strange, remarkable, or funny happen to him?" When it was the proud girl's turn, she looked straight at the host and said: "My story must be told in a whisper, so in order to hear it, you must all put your hair back and uncover your ears." The guests smiled and did as she said, but the host did not. "My hearing is keen," he told her. "I can understand a whisper from a great distance. I don't need to uncover my ears."

But everyone laughed and called: "Uncover them! uncover them!"

"I'm your host," he replied. "You're being rude and impolite. Stop making all that noise!"

But they cried even louder: "Uncover them! Uncover them!"

At this the host grew very angry and shouted: "All right! Here, look!" Throwing back his hair, he uncovered ears that were standing up like horns. With cries of terror, the guests rushed out of the lodge.

The great horned owl's aunt was as angry as he. "This young wife of yours is far too clever," she told him. "We must make something to outwit her." Having the power of a great sorceress, she created a magic flute that would lure any girl into the arms of the man who played it. "With this, nephew," she said, "she won't be able to stop herself from coming to you."

The great horned owl, again disguised as a man, tried to carry out his aunt's scheme. But the haughty young woman and her parents were now so wary that they had put their lodge right in the center of the village and never strayed far. The weeks went by as he waited for his opportunity, and still the horned owl could not manage to come near his wife.

At last one day this proud girl said to herself: "It's been so long that the great horned owl has surely forgotten about me. He has given up, while my fear of him is still imprisoning me. It's time for me to go out and walk in the woods, the way I used to do."

In a bad mood, the great horned owl was sitting high in a crotch of a huge tree. "I'm wasting my time," he thought. "My wife is so afraid of me that she stays in the middle of the village. It's hopeless; I must stop thinking about her." Brooding, he saw someone coming through the woods. With his sharp owl's eyes he recognized her, though he could hardly believe it. His heart began to beat very fast.

The proud girl came right to the foot of the big tree. Unaware of her husband's presence, she sat down and said to herself, "How good to be out in the forest again without feeling afraid. How I enjoy this!" Then she heard some sweet sounds that soon formed into a wonderful song— magical, alluring, bewitching. She abandoned herself to the sound of the flute. "I could never resist the player who makes this wonderful music," she thought.

Then the Great Horned Owl swooped softly down upon her, seizing her gently in his huge talons, carrying her off to the village of the owls. There they lived as man and wife, and the haughty girl eventually became used to being married to the great horned owl. Women have to get used to their husbands, no matter who they are.

—*Based on a legend reported in 1883 by Charles G. Leland.*

THE DOGS HOLD AN ELECTION

■

[BRULE SIOUX]

■ ||||||||||||||||||||||||||||||||||||||||||||||||||||||||||||||||| ■

We don't think much of the white man's elections. Whoever wins, we Indians always lose. Well, we have a little story about elections. Once a long time ago, the dogs were trying to elect a president. So one of them got up in the big dog convention and said: "I nominate the bulldog for president. He's strong. He can fight."

"But he can't run," said another dog. "What good is a fighter who can't run? He won't catch anybody."

Then another dog got up and said: "I nominate the greyhound, because he sure can run."

But the other dogs cried: "Naw, he can run all right, but he can't fight. When he catches up with somebody, what happens then? He gets the hell beaten out of him, that's what! So all he's good for is running away."

Then an ugly little mutt jumped up and said: "I nominate that dog for president who smells good underneath his tail."

And immediately an equally ugly mutt jumped up and yelled: "I second the motion."

At once all the dogs started sniffing underneath each other's tails. A big chorus went up:

"Phew, he doesn't smell good under his tail."

"No, neither does this one."

"He's no presidential timber!"

"No, he's no good, either."

"This one sure isn't the people's choice."

"Wow, this ain't my candidate!"

When you go out for a walk, just watch the dogs. They're still sniffing

underneath each other's tails. They're looking for a good leader, and they still haven't found him.

—*Told by Lame Deer at Winner,*
Rosebud Indian Reservation, South Dakota, 1969.
Recorded by Richard Erdoes.

■

THE SNAKE BROTHERS

■

[BRULE SIOUX]

■ |||||||||||||||||||||||||||||||||||||||||||||||||||||||||||||||||||||||||||||||||||||||| ■

For a long time people have been saying that somewhere near Soldier's Creek a giant rattlesnake has its den. It is supposed to be a full twelve feet long, and very old. Nobody has seen it for years, but some people have smelled it and heard its giant rattles. It smells something powerful, they say.

We Sioux think of rattlesnakes as our cousins. They always give warning before they strike, as if they wanted to say: "Uncle, don't step on me; then we'll get along."

A long time ago, so long that it is not on our oldest winter count, there were four brothers, all of them young and good hunters, who went out scouting for buffalo. They had not hunted long before they saw a lone buffalo and killed him with their arrows.

All at once they heard a voice, the voice of the buffalo making human talk: "Take the meat to nourish yourselves, but put the skin, head, hooves, and tail together, every part in its place. Do this for sure."

The youngest brother said: "Let's do as the voice told us."

But the other three didn't want to bother. "That was a foolish voice," they said, "maybe no voice at all—maybe we only imagined it. We'll take the skin home, and it will make a fine winter robe." The youngest brother had to argue long and hard—finally had to take the skin and offer to fight them for it—before they let him do what the voice had directed.

While the other three feasted on buffalo hump and lay down to get some rest, the youngest brother went to the top of a hill and spread out the skin, skull, hooves, and tail—just as the voice had told them. He said a prayer to the buffalo, who gave his flesh so that the people might live.

As he prayed, all the parts of the buffalo joined together before his eyes and came alive again, forming themselves into a whole animal once more. It was a fine, strong buffalo, who bellowed loudly and then walked slowly away to disappeare into the hills. The youngest brother watched the buffalo as long as his eyes could follow it. Only then did he join the others round the fire.

He ate some of what his brothers had left. But they had taken the best meat—the tongue and back fat—and made fun of him for having missed it. They said: "Now we're going up the hill to get the skin back, whether you like it or not." But the skin and the other parts were gone, and they would not believe the youngest brother when he told them what had happened. "You're trying to fool us," they said. "You buried it all somewhere."

After that, the four brother stretched out to sleep. In the middle of the night the oldest woke up, saying: "What's that noise I hear every time I move?" It was a rattling sound that came from his feet. He looked down, and in the dim light of the dying fire, saw that his feet had grown rattles. He called to the others: "Help! Something has happened to my feet!"

But only the youngest brother came to look; the others tried but could not. "Something's the matter with my legs too," cried the second-oldest, whose feet had stuck together so that he could not force them apart. "And look at mine!" cried the third brother. His legs were not only joined together but rounded, like a snake's tail. "I think we are being punished," said the oldest brother, "for not having obeyed that voice."

While they were talking, the change moved up to their hips. "Now I know we are being punished," said the second brother. "We are being turned into snakes." "My body is already covered with scales!" cried the third brother. By then the change had moved up to their necks.

"Don't worry, *misunkala*, younger brother," said the other three. "Though we are snakes, we remain your brothers. We will always look after our village and our people. You see that hill over there? It has a big hole—the entrance to the home of the snakes. We will go in there, but whenever you need help, stand outside and call us. Come to see us in a little while: alone at first, the second time with all the people. Now we must leave you." They could not say more, because their heads were changing into snakes' heads that could only hiss.

"Elder brothers," said the youngest, weeping, "It was your fate to become snakes. I believe this was destined to happen to you, that the

Great Spirit planned it so. I will come back as you have told me to, first alone, then with the rest of the people. Goodbye."

He saw that his snake brothers had trouble crawling like snakes; they still had to learn how. Though they were as big and heavy as people, he dragged them one by one to the hole in the hillside. When they were at the entrance to their snake home, they began to wiggle. The youngest brother watched them crawl in and disappear, one after the other. He heard them rattle, and then the sound of their rattles grew fainter and fainter and at last stopped. He dried his tears and gathered up the buffalo meat to take to the people. After all, that was what he had come to do.

When he reached the lodges of his people, he told them: "You see me come back alone. My three older brothers are gone, but do not mourn for them. They are still alive, though they have been turned into snakes, as the Great Spirit willed. They now live inside the hill which is the snakes' home, and there you will meet them someday."

Four-times-four days later, the youngest brother prepared to go with a war party against the Pahani on a horse-stealing raid. He painted his face black for war. Then he took his best pony and rode out to the hill where he had left his brothers. Standing before the hole at the foot of the hill, he called: "Elder brothers, I have come alone, as you have told me, and I need your help."

At once the big head of a giant rattlesnake thrust out of the hole. Its tongue flickered in and out as if in greeting. The young man knew that this was his eldest brother. Then two more big snakes' heads appeared, and he could sense that these were his second and third brothers. They crawled up to him, putting their heads on his arms and shoulders, hissing at him and looking at him with their yellow eyes.

"Brothers, I need your help," he said. "I am going to count coup upon the Pahani."

Many more snakes came out of the hole and set up a mighty rattling which made the earth tremble. One of the big snakes, the oldest brother, went back into the hole and reappeared pushing a medicine bundle before him.

"Eldest brother," said the youngest, "I know that you are bringing me snake medicine. It will give me speed and enable me to wiggle out of bad situations. It will make me feared by the enemy. It will cause me to strike swiftly with a deadly weapon. Thank you, my brothers."

It was as he had said. In war he struck quickly, with the speed of a rattlesnake. His enemies were afraid of him. He counted many coups on them and returned unharmed with a crowd of Pahani horses. The people were happy, and he told them: "Now we must give thanks to my elder brothers."

So all the people went with him to the hill which was the snakes' home. There he called for his elder brothers to show themselves, and they appeared with much hissing and rattling. The people made offerings to them of tobacco and good red meat, and the snake brothers were contented. From then on, they protected the people with powerful snake medicine every time they had to go to war.

And from then on, the people were successful in everything they undertook. If the rattlesnake brothers have not died in the meantime, they are still helping us today. That's why we never kill rattlesnakes.

—Told by Lame Deer at Winner,
Rosebud Indian Reservation, South Dakota, 1969.
Recorded by Richard Erdoes.

BUTTERFLIES

[PAPAGO]

One day the Creator was resting, sitting, watching some children at play in a village. The children laughed and sang, yet as he watched them, the Creator's heart was sad. He was thinking: "These children will grow old. Their skin will become wrinkled. Their hair will turn gray. Their teeth will fall out. The young hunter's arm will fail. These lovely young girls will grow ugly and fat. The playful puppies will become blind, mangy dogs. And those wonderful flowers—yellow and blue, red and purple—will fade. The leaves from the trees will fall and dry up. Already they are turning yellow." Thus the Creator grew sadder and sadder. It was in the fall, and the thought of the coming winter, with its cold and lack of game and green things, made his heart heavy.

Yet it was still warm, and the sun was shining. The Creator watched the play of sunlight and shadow on the ground, the yellow leaves being carried here and there by the wind. He saw the blueness of the sky, the whiteness of some cornmeal ground by the women. Suddenly he smiled. "All those colors, they ought to be preserved. I'll make something to gladden my heart, something for these children to look at and enjoy."

The Creator took out his bag and started gathering things: a spot of sunlight, a handful of blue from the sky, the whiteness of the cornmeal, the shadow of playing children, the blackness of a beautiful girl's hair, the yellow of the falling leaves, the green of the pine needles, the red, purple, and orange of the flowers around him. All these he put into his bag. As an afterthought, he put the songs of the birds in, too.

Then he walked over to the grassy spot where the children were playing. "Children, little children, this is for you," and he gave them his bag. "Open it; there's something nice inside," he told them.

The children opened the bag, and at once hundreds and hundreds of colored butterflies flew out, dancing around the children's heads, settling on their hair, fluttering up again to sip from this or that flower. And the children, enchanted, said that they had never seen anything so beautiful.

The butterflies began to sing, and the children listened smiling.

But then a songbird came flying, settling on the Creator's shoulder, scolding him, saying: "It's not right to give our songs to these new, pretty things. You told us when you made us that every bird would have his own song. And now you've passed them all around. Isn't it enough that you gave your new playthings the colors of the rainbow?"

"You're right," said the Creator. "I made one song for each bird, and I shouldn't have taken what belongs to you."

So the Creator took the songs away from the butterflies, and that's why they are silent. "They're beautiful even so!" he said.

—*Retold from various sources.*

THE REVENGE OF
BLUE CORN EAR MAIDEN

[HOPI]

A long time ago, two maidens lived in Oraibi. They were close friends and often ground corn at one another's houses. Their friendship ended abruptly, however, when they both fell in love with the same young man. One of them, Yellow Corn Ear Maiden, had supernatural powers, and she made up her mind to destroy her rival, Blue Corn Ear Maiden. Early one morning the two girls carried their jugs to get water from Spider Spring, northeast of the village. On the way back they came to a sand hill, and Yellow Corn Ear Maiden said, "Let's sit down and rest for a while."

After a time she said: "Let's play catch. You run down the hill, and I'll throw something at you, and you throw it back." She drew from her bosom a pretty little wheel that gleamed with all the colors of the rainbow. When her friend reached the foot of the hill, Yellow Corn Ear Maiden threw the wheel at her, but it was so heavy that Blue Corn Ear Maiden collapsed on the ground when she caught it. When she stood up again, she was a coyote. Yellow Corn Ear Maiden laughed and said, "That's what you get for quarreling with me!" She shooed the coyote away, took her own jug, and went back to the village.

Sadly the coyote climbed the hill and tried to pick up her jug, but without hands she couldn't. She sat down and cried until evening. After dark she tried to enter the village, but the dogs drove her away. She made a large circuit around the village and tried to go in from another side, but she was again driven away by the dogs. By this time she was getting very hungry, so she went off to the west hoping to find something to eat.

It was the fall of the year, and the people were busy in the fields working on their crops. Carefully she crept up to one of the homemade shelters in which the farmers lived, found two roasted ears of corn that had been left on top, and ate them right up. She tried a third time to enter the village, but when the dogs smelled her and drove her away, she knew she wouldn't be able to get home as long as she looked and smelled like a coyote.

She wandered through the entire night, until she arrived at a place which belonged to two Qooqoqlom Kachinas who were hunting in that region. In their hut she found plenty of baked rabbit meat and entrails, and lots of rabbit skins. Starving but also exhausted, she ate a little meat and a bit of entrail (which she did not like very much). Since the two hunters had already eaten and left for the hunt, she decided to stay in their hut and rest all day.

In the evening the two Qooqoqlom hunters returned. With their keen eyes and ears, they knew even as they approached that something was wrong. One of them peeked in and whispered, "There is a coyote in our hut and he's eaten some of our meat." He got his bow and arrows and was aiming at the intruder, when the other one said, "No, let's try to capture him alive and take him home to our grandmother, Spider Woman." So they went in but, much to their surprise, they heard the coyote sob and saw tears trickling from its eyes. Even they were touched by the sight, and one of them took a large piece of meat from his pouch, broke it in two, and gave a portion to the visitor, who ate it with relish. They then decided to go back home that evening. They tied up the meat and the skins, and also tied the feet of the coyote. Loading everything upon their backs, they returned to Kachina Gap, a short distance northwest of Oraibi.

As soon as they arrived, they called to Spider Woman, "Grandmother, we have brought you an animal. Come and help us lift it off our backs." She was delighted with her present, and placed the coyote with the rabbit meat near the fireplace. Then the woman looked closely at the wretched animal and exclaimed, "Alas! That poor one! This is no coyote. Thankfully you have not killed it. Where did you find it?" They told her how they had found and captured it in their hunting hut. She sent one of the men into the village after some *tomóala* a potent plant; the other one she sent to the woods to fetch a few juniper branches.

While they were gone she boiled some water, and when the man with the *tomóala* returned, she poured the water into a vessel and hooked one *tomóala* pod into the coyote's neck and another one into her back. She then plunged the animal into the water and covered her with a piece of native cloth. Placing her hand upon the cover, Spider Woman took hold of the two hooks and kept twisting and turning them until she had pulled off the skin of the coyote. When she threw aside the cloth, there was Blue Corn Ear Maiden, still in her original clothes, her hair tied in whorls just as it had been when she left the village. The woman asked how she had met this fate, and the maiden told her the whole story. Spider Woman comforted her, saying, "That Yellow Corn Ear Maiden is bad, but you will have your revenge."

At this point, the other hunter returned with the juniper branches. She took the maiden, together with the branches and the water, into another room and there bathed her, then gave her some corn, which the maiden ground into meal. The maiden stayed there for several days, until Spider Woman told her that her mother was very sick with worry and that she should go home. But first Spider Woman called together a number of Kachinas who lived nearby and told them all that had happened. "I want you to return her to her house," she said, and they were willing. She dressed the maiden in wonderful finery, put her hair into fresh whorls, and placed over her shoulders a new *atoo*. She instructed her to have her father make *bahos*, prayer sticks, and a number of *nakwakwosis* as prayer offerings to the leader of the Kachinas and the leader of the singing. Lastly, she gave her a plan to deal with Yellow Corn Ear Maiden. So off they set, the maiden walking in the rear of the line of Kachinas.

At early dawn, the so-called white dawn, they arrived near the house of the village chief, where the Pongowe kiva is at present situated; there they performed their first dance, singing while they danced. Those already stirring in the village rushed out to see the Kachinas dancing. Soon the news was whispered around through the whole village that the Kachinas had brought a maiden with them, and some soon recognized Blue Corn Ear Maiden and ran to the house of her parents. The latter refused to believe the news, and four messengers had to be sent to convince them. When they finally went to the Kachinas, the procession had arrived at the dancing plaza in the center of the village. "So you have come," the mother said, and began to cry. She wanted to take her daughter with her then, but the girl said, "Wait a little," and gave her father Spider Woman's instructions. The Kachinas continued their dancing, with the *mana*, the female Kachinas waiting by their side. When finally the father brought the prayer offerings, he gave one *baho* to the leader, the other to his daughter. After the dancing was over, the daughter gave her prayer stick to the leader of the singing. The *nakwakosis* were distributed among the other Kachinas, and after the happy father had thanked them for bringing his child, they returned to their own homes.

Blue Corn Ear Maiden rested at her parents' for a day and a night, but early the next morning she went to grind corn, and as she did, she sang a little song about her adventures. When Yellow Corn Ear Maiden heard her voice, she came rushing out to proclaim how delighted she was at her friend's return. Blue Corn Ear Maiden treated her cordially, just as Spider Woman had told her to. They ground corn together all day, just as they had done before. In the evening they went after water again, to the same spring where they had gotten water before. While they were filling their jugs, Yellow Corn Ear Maiden noticed that her friend was dipping her water with a peculiar little vessel (which Spider Woman had given her) and that the water, which ran into the jug, was very beautiful, glistening with the colors of the rainbow. She said to her friend: "What have you there? Let me see that little cup." Yes," her friend said, "that is a very fine cup, and the water tastes good from it, too." Thereupon she drank from it and handed it to her friend, who also drank. Immediately she fell down and was turned into a bull snake. "There! You will remain on the ground forever," Blue Corn Ear Maiden said. "You tried once to destroy me, but it didn't work. No one will help restore you, though." She laughed, picked up her jug, and returned to the village.

So the bull snake slithered away to begin its lifelong wandering. It was often hungry, but as it couldn't move very fast, it had to capture its prey by luring little rabbits and birds with its powerful intoxicating breath.

Yellow Corn Ear Maiden tried finally to return to her village, where she was killed by her own parents. They, of course, didn't know the snake they had killed was their own daughter. But her soul was liberated to go to the Skeleton House.

Ever since then some dead sorcerers will take the form of bull snakes and leave their graves, still wound in the yucca leaves with which the corpse was tied up when laid away. If such a bull snake is killed, the soul of the sorcerer living in it is set free and can go to the Skeleton House, just as Yellow Corn Ear Maiden did at last.

—*Based on a version collected by Henry Voth in 1905.*

The mana, or female Kachinas, were actually men dressed up like women.

THE MEETING OF THE
WILD ANIMALS

■

[TSIMSHIAN]

A long time ago, when the Tsimshian lived on the upper Skeena River in Prairie Town, they were the cleverest and strongest of all humans. They were good hunters and caught many animals. They went hunting the whole year round, and all the animals feared for their survival.

Grizzly Bear invited all the large animals to his house. "A terrible calamity has come to us with these hunting people, who pursue us even into our dens," he said. "I suggest we ask Him Who Made Us to give us more cold in winter and keep the hunters in their own houses and out of our dens!" All the large animals agreed, and Wolf said, "Let's invite all the small animals—Porcupine, Beaver, Raccoon, Marten, Mink, and even the really small ones such as Mouse and the insects— to join us and increase our strength."

On the following day the large animals assembled on a wide prairie and called together all the small animals, even down to the insects. The multitude sat down, the small animals on one side of the plain, the large animals on the other. Panther came, and Black Bear, Wolf, Elk, Reindeer, and Wolverine.

Then the chief speaker, Grizzly Bear, rose. "Friends," he said to the small animals and the insects, "you know very well how the people hunt us on mountains and hills, even pursuing us into our dens. Therefore, my brothers, we large animals have agreed to ask Him Who Made Us to give our earth cold winters, colder than ever, so that the people who hunt us cannot come to our dens and kill us and you! Large animals, is this so?"

The Panther said, "I fully support this wise counsel," and all the large animals agreed. Grizzly Bear turned to the small animals and said, "We want to know what you think of in this matter." The small animals did not reply at first. After they had been silent for a while, Porcupine rose and said, "Friends, let me say a word or two in response. Your strategy is very good for you, because all of you have plenty of warm fur for the most severe cold. But look at these little insects. They have no fur at all to warm them in winter. Moreover, how can insects and small

animals obtain food if winters are colder? Therefore I say this: don't ask for more cold." Then he sat down.

Grizzly Bear rose again. "We need not pay attention to what Porcupine says," he told the large animals. "You all agree, don't you, that we should ask for the severest cold on earth?" The large animals replied, "Yes, we do. We don't care for Porcupine's reasoning."

"Now, listen once more! I will ask you just one question," Porcupine said. "If it's that cold, the roots of all the wild berries will freeze and die, and all the plants of the prairie will wither away. How will you get food? You large animals always roam the mountains wanting something to eat. When your request brings more winter frost, you will die of starvation in spring or summer. But we will survive, for we live on the bark of trees, the very small animals eat the gum of trees, and the smallest insects find their food in the earth."

After he had spoken, Porcupine put his thumb into his mouth, bit it off, said, "Confound it!" and threw his thumb out of his mouth to show the large animals how bold he was. He sat down again, full of rage. Therefore the hand of the porcupine has only four fingers, no thumb.

The large animals were speechless at Porcupine's wisdom. Finally Grizzly Bear admitted, "It's true what you have said." And the large animals chose Porcupine as their wise man and as the first among the small animals. Together all the animals agreed that the cold in winter should be the way it is now. And they settled on six months for winter and six months for summer.

Then Porcupine spoke again in his wisdom: "In winter we will have ice and snow. In spring we will have showers, and the plants will become green. In summer we will have warmer weather, and all the fishes will go up the rivers. In the fall the leaves will drop, it will rain, and the rivers and brooks will overflow. Then all animals, large and small, and those that creep on the ground, will go into their dens and hide for six months." And after they had all agreed to what Porcupine had proposed, they happily returned to their homes.

That's why wild animals, large and small, take to their dens in winter. Only Porcupine does not hide, but goes about visiting his neighbors. Porcupine also went to the animals who had slighted him at the meeting and struck them dead with the quills of his tail. That's why all the animals are afraid of Porcupine to this day.

—Based on a myth reported by Franz Boas in 1916.

■

A FISH STORY

■

[TEWA]

■ |||||||||||||||||||||||||||||||||||||||||||||||||||||||||||| ■

There occurred in those days a great drought. Rain had not come for many, many days. The crops were dying and the water in the lake was going down and down. Prayers had to be offered to the Great Spirit. This was the duty of the fish people, so they all assembled in the kiva to pray and offer sacrifices to the rain gods.

The custom was to fast and stay in the kiva until the rain came. A woman by the name of Fee-ne-nee was given the duty to feed the fish people, which she did each day at noon. Since the men were fasting, she served them only a small amount of food and a few drops of water.

On the night of the third day, however, one of the men could no longer stand the isolation. When the others went to sleep, he sneaked out of the kiva and ran to a nearby lake. There he drank and drank, swallowing all the water he had been thinking about for three days.

After filling his body with water, he returned to the kiva. He entered slowly and stepped quietly down the stairs so that he would not be heard. Midway between the roof and the floor, however, he burst. Water poured out of his head, eyes, mouth, arms, body, and legs. When this happened, the people who were inside turned into fish, frogs, and all kinds of water animals, and the kiva was filled with water.

The next day at noon, the woman who was in charge of feeding the men went to the kiva. She could not believe what she saw: water was gushing from it straight up into the air, and suspended in the torrent were fish, frogs, eels, snakes, and ducks.

Sadly, with her basket still in her hand, she slowly returned to the village. The first house she visited was that of an untidy old couple. She placed her basket in the center of the room and silently sat by the grinding stone. After making only one stroke of the stone, she too turned into a snake.

Seeing this, the old man and his wife both said, "Something terrible has happened at the kiva." The man ran to find out what was wrong, and at the kiva he saw ducks, beavers, and frogs swimming in the water at the bottom.

The old man knew that this was a bad omen for the people of the village. When he reached home, he told his wife, "One of the men failed us, and all of them turned into ducks, frogs, eels, snakes, and beavers."

"We can no longer live here," his wife replied. "You must let our people know. We must also make preparations to take this snake, our friend Fee-ne-nee, where she belongs."

The old woman prepared a basket filled with blue cornmeal and placed the little snake inside. Her husband took the basket and headed toward the east, where there was a snake burrow. At the home of the snakes, he fed them blue cornmeal, and one by one all kinds of snakes wiggled through the meal. Then he placed Fee-ne-nee among the others and said to her: "I have brought you to live here. You are now a young lady snake, and with the help of the Great Spirit you will live among your own kind. I give you my blessing."

To the other snakes he said, "I have brought you a sister; take her into your arms."

As the other snakes curled around Fee-ne-nee, the man walked away with tears in his eyes.

At home the old couple cried again and told their people that the law required them to move from their home, O-Ke-owin, and seek another place to live. Now you know why we live where we do. The tragedy that occurred at O-Ke-owin forced our people to move to Xun ochute, which is now San Juan.

*—Told at San Juan Pueblo, New Mexico, in the early 1960s
and translated from the Tewa by Alfonso Ortiz.*

THE NEGLECTFUL MOTHER

[COCHITI]

Crow had been sitting on the eggs in her nest for many days, and she got tired of it and flew away. Hawk came by and found nobody on the nest. Hawk said to herself, "The person who owns this nest must no longer care for it. What a shame for those poor little eggs! I will sit on them, and they will be my children." She sat for many days on the eggs, and finally they began to hatch. Still no Crow came. The little ones all hatched out and the mother Hawk flew about getting food for them. They grew bigger and bigger and their wings got strong, and at last it was time for the mother Hawk to take them off the nest.

After all this while, Crow finally remembered her nest. When she came back to it she found the eggs hatched and Hawk taking care of her little ones.

"Hawk!"

"What is it?"

"You must return these little ones you are leading around."

"Why?"

"Because they are mine."

Hawk said, "Yes, you laid the eggs, but you had no pity on the poor things. You went off and left them. I came and sat on the nest and hatched them. When they were hatched, I fed them, and now I lead them about. They are mine, and I won't return them."

"Crow said, "I shall take them back."

"No, you won't! I worked for them, and for many days I fasted, sitting there on the eggs. In all that time you didn't come near them. Why is it now, when I've taken care of them and brought them up, that you want them back?"

Crow said to the little ones, "My children, come with me. I am your mother."

But the little ones said they did not know her. "Hawk is our mother." At last when she couldn't make them come with her, she said, "Very well, I'll take Hawk to court, and we shall see who has the right to these children."

So Mother Crow took Mother Hawk before the king of the birds.

Eagle said to Crow, "Why did you leave your nest?" Crow hung her head and had no answer to that. But she said, "When I came back to my nest, I found my eggs already hatched and Hawk taking charge of the little ones. I have come to ask that Hawk return the children to me."

Eagle said to Mother Hawk, "How did you find this nest of eggs?"

"Many times I went to it and found it empty. No one came for a long time, and at last I had pity upon the poor little eggs. I said to myself, 'The mother who made this nest can no longer care for these eggs. I would be glad to hatch the little ones.' I sat on them and they hatched. Then I went about getting food for them. I worked hard and brought them up, and they have grown."

Mother Crow interrupted mother Hawk and said, "But they're my children. I laid the eggs."

"It's not your turn. We are both asking for justice, and it will be given to us. Wait till I have spoken."

Eagle said to Mother Hawk, "Is that all?"

"Yes, I have worked hard to raise my two little ones. Just when they were grown, Mother Crow came and asked to have them back again, but I won't give them back. It is I who fasted and worked, and they are now mine."

The king of the birds said to Mother Crow, "If you really had pity on your little ones, why did you leave the nest for so many days? And why are you demanding to have them now? Mother Hawk is the mother of the little ones, for she has fasted and hatched them, and flown about searching for their food. Now they are her children."

Mother Crow said to the king of the birds, "King, you should ask the little ones which mother they choose to follow. They know enough to know which one to take."

So the king said to the little ones, "Which mother will you choose?"

Both answered together, "Mother Hawk is our mother. She's all the mother we know."

Crow cried, "No, I'm your only mother!"

The little Crow children said, "In the nest you had no pity on us; you left us. Mother Hawk hatched us, and she is our mother."

So it was finally settled as the little ones had said: they were the children of Mother Hawk, who had had pity on them in the nest and brought them up.

Mother Crow began to weep. The king said to her, "Don't cry. It's your own fault. This is the final decision of the king of the birds." So Mother Crow lost her children.

—*Recorded by Ruth Benedict in 1931.*

THE BEAR AND HIS INDIAN WIFE

[HAIDA]

This story of the Haidas of Queen Charlotte's Island, British Columbia, was told in 1873 by a Haida named Yak Quahu, who heard it related around the evening fires by the old people of his tribe. Yak Quahu began: "Not long ago, as our old people tell us, the bears were a race of beings less perfect than our fathers. They used to talk, walk upright, and use their paws like hands. When they wanted wives, they were accustomed to steal the daughters of our people."

Quiss-an-kweedass and Kind-a-wuss were a youth and maiden in my native village, she the daughter of one of our chiefs, he the son of one of the common people. Since both were about the same age and had been playmates from youth, their fondness in later years ripened into a love so strong that they seemed to live for each other. But while they loved each other, they knew that they could never live as husband and wife, because both were of one crest, the Raven. By the social laws of the Haidas a mother gives her name and crest to her children, whether Raven, Eagle, Frog, Beaver, or Bear. A man is at liberty to take a wife from any other crest except the one to which he himself belongs.

While the youth and maiden continued to love each other, time passed unnoticed. Life to them seemed a pleasing dream—from which they were awakened when both sets of parents reminded them that the time had come for each to marry someone else. Seeing that these admonitions passed unheeded, their parents resolved to separate them. The lovers were confined in their homes, but they contrived to slip away and meet outside the village. They escaped to the woods, resolved to live on the meanest fare in the mountain forests rather than return to be separated.

In a lonely glen under a shady spruce by a mountain stream, they built a hut, to which they always returned at night. While wandering in search of food they were careful lest they should meet any of their relations.

Thus they lived until the lengthening nights and stormy days reminded them of winter. Quiss-an-kweedass resolved to revisit his home, and to make the journey alone. Kind-a-wuss preferred to remain in the solitude of the forest rather than face her angry relations. He promised, however, to return before nightfall of the fourth day.

When he reached home, his parents welcomed him and asked about Kind-a-wuss and her whereabouts since they had departed. He told them all, and when they heard how they lived, and how she had become his wife, their wrath was great. They told him that he would never go back, and they decided to keep him prisoner until she also returned.

When Quiss-an-kweedass could not get away, he urged his people to let him go and get Kind-a-wuss, for she would never return alone. They were unmoved by his appeal. After a considerable time, he managed to escape. He hastened to his mountain home, hoping to meet Kind-a-wuss, yet fearing that something might be wrong.

When he arrived at the place where they had parted, he found by the footprints on the soft earth that she had started to return to their hut. Drawing near it, he listened but heard no sound and saw no trace of her. When he went inside, he was horror-stricken to find that she had not been there since he left. Where was she? Had she lost her way? Hoping to find some clue, he searched the hut, looked up and down the stream, went through the timber up to the mountains, calling her by name as he went along: "Kind-a-wuss, Kind-a-wuss, where are you? Kind-a-wuss, come to me; I am your own Quiss-an-kweedass. Do you hear me, Kind-a-wuss?" To these appeals the mountain echoes answered, Kind-a-wuss.

After searching for days, feeling sorrowful and angry, he turned homeward, grieving for the dear one whom he had lost, and angry with his parents, whom he blamed for his misfortune. Once there, he told the villagers of his trouble and claimed their assistance. Many responded, among them the two fathers, one anxious for his daughter's safety, the other disturbed because he had detained his son.

Early on the morning of the third day after Quiss-an-kweedass arrived, he led a party out for a final search to try and find her, dead or alive. But after ten days, during which they discovered nothing except a place where traces of a struggle were visible, they abandoned the effort.

As weeks gave place to months and months to years, Kind-a-wuss seemed to have been forgotten. She was seldom mentioned, or was referred to only as the girl who was lost and never found. Yet her lover never forgot; he believed her still alive and did all in his power to find her. Having failed so often, he thought he would visit a medicine man, or *skaga*, who was clairvoyant.

The *skaga* asked Quiss-an-kweedass if he had anything that the maiden had worn. He gave a part of her clothing to the *skaga*, who took it in his hand and said: "I see a young woman lying on the ground; she seems to be asleep. It is Kind-a-wuss. There is something in the bushes, coming toward her. It is a large bear. He takes hold of her; she tries to get away but cannot. He takes her with him, a long way off. I see a lake. They reach it and stop at a large cedar tree. She lives in the tree with the bear. I see two children, boys, that she has had by the bear. If you go to the lake and find the tree, you will discover them all there."

Quiss-an-kweedass lost no time in getting together a second party led by the *skaga*, who soon found the lake and then the tree. There they halted to consider what it was best to do.

It was agreed that Quiss-an-kweedass should call her by name before venturing up a sort of stepladder which leaned against the tree. After he called her several times, she looked out and said, "Where do you come from? And who are you?" "I am Quiss-an-kweedass," said he. "I have sought long years for you. Now that I have found you, I mean to take you home. Will you go?" "I cannot go with you until my husband, the chief of the bears, returns." After a little conversation, she consented to come down among them; and when they had her in their power, they hastily carried her off home.

Her parents were glad to have their lost child, and Quiss-an-kweedass

was overjoyed to recover his loved one. Although she was at home and kindly welcomed, she was worried for her two sons and wished to return for them. This her friends would not allow, though they offered to go and fetch them. She replied that their father would not let them go. "But," said she, "there is a way you might get them." She explained that the bear had made up a song for her, and if they would go to the tree and sing it, the bear chief would give them whatever they wished.

After learning the song, a party went to the tree and began to sing. As soon as the bear heard the song he came down, thinking that Kind-a-wuss had returned. When he saw that she was not there, he was upset and refused to let the children go. When the party threatened to take them by force, however, he agreed to send them to their mother.

Kind-a-wuss told the following story of how she had fallen into the power of the bear. After she had parted from Quiss-an-kweedass and turned back toward the hut, she had not gone far before she felt tired and sick at heart for her lover. Deciding to rest a little, she lay down in a dry, shady place and fell asleep.

There the bear found her, took her and carried her to his home near the lake. As the entrance to his house was high above the ground, he had a sort of stepladder whereby he could get easily up and down. He sent some of his tribe to gather soft moss to make her a bed.

She used to wonder why no one came to look for her; and when the bear saw her downhearted, he would do all in his power to cheer her up. As the years passed and none of her relations nor her lover came near her, she began to feel at home in the bear's tree house. By the time the search party arrived, she had given up all hope of being found. The bear tried to make her comfortable and please her. He composed a song which to this day is known among the children of the Haidas as the Song of the Bears. I have heard it sung many times. In 1888 an old acquaintance gave me the words:

> I have taken a fair maid from her Haida friends as my wife. I hope her relatives won't come and carry her away from me. I will be kind to her. I will give her berries from the hill and roots from the ground. I will do all I can to please her. For her I made this song, and for her I sing it.

This is the Song of the Bears, and whoever can sing it has their lasting friendship. Many people learned it from Kind-a-wuss, who never went again to live with the bear. Out of consideration for her, as well as for the hardships that the lovers had suffered, they were allowed to live as man and wife.

As for the two sons, Soo-gaot and Cun-what, they showed different dispositions as they grew up. Soo-gaot stayed with his mother's people, while the other returned to his father and lived and died among the bears. Soo-gaot, marrying a girl belonging to his parental tribe, reared a family from whom many of his people claim to be descended. The direct descendant of Soo-gaot is a pretty girl, the offspring of a Haida mother and Kanaku father, who inherits all the family belongings, the savings of many generations. The small brook which flowed by the mountain home of Quiss-an-kweedass and Kind-a-wuss grew to be a large stream, up which large quantities of salmon run in season. That stream is in the family to this day, and out of it they catch their food.

—Based on Yak Quahu's story recorded in 1873 and published by James Deans in the 1880s.

■

 ## WAKIASH AND THE FIRST TOTEM POLE

■

[KWAKIUTL]

The totem poles of the Northwest Coast tribes were actually family crests rather than religious icons, denoting the owner's legendary descent from an animal such as the bear, raven, wolf, salmon, or killer whale. Coming into a village, a stranger would first look for a house with the totem pole of his own clan animal. Its owner was sure to receive him as a friend and offer him food and shelter. Totem poles "also preserved ancient customs by making sure that in every region within visiting distance of others the old stories were repeated, and the old beliefs about the spirits, the origins of fire and other myths, were basically the same despite linguistic differences between main tribal groups." *

Wakiash was a chief named after the river Wakiash because he was open-handed and flowing with gifts, even as the river flowed with fish.

* Cottie Burland, *North American Indian Mythology*, Paul Hamlyn, London, 1965, p. 31.

It happened once that the whole tribe was having a dance. Wakiash had never created a dance of his own, and he was unhappy because all the other chiefs had fine dances. So he thought: "I will go up into the mountains to fast, and perhaps a dance will come to me."

Wakiash made himself ready and went to the mountains, where he stayed, fasting and bathing, for four days. Early in the morning of the fourth day, he grew so weary that he lay upon his back and fell asleep. Then he felt something on his breast and woke to see a little green frog.

"Lie still," the frog said, "because you are on the back of a raven who is going to fly you and me around the world. Then you can see what you want and take it." The raven began to beat its wings, and they flew for four days, during which Wakiash saw many things. When they were on their way back, he spotted a house with a beautiful totem pole in front and heard the sound of singing inside the house. Thinking that these were fine things, he wished he could take them home.

The frog, who knew his thoughts, told the raven to stop. As the bird coasted to the ground, the frog advised the chief to hide behind the door of the house.

"Stay there until they begin to dance," the frog said. "Then leap out into the room."

The people tried to begin a dance but could do nothing—neither dance nor sing. One of them said, "Something's the matter; there must be something near us that makes us feel like this." And the chief said, "Let one of us who can run faster than the flames of the fire rush around the house and find what it is." So the little mouse said that she would go, for she could creep anywhere, even into a box, and if anyone were hiding she would find him. The mouse had taken off her mouse-skin clothes and was presently appearing in the form of a woman. Indeed, all the people in the house were animals who looked like humans because they had taken off their animal-skin clothes to dance.

When the mouse ran out, Wakiash caught her and said, "Ha, my friend, I have a gift for you." And he gave her a piece of mountain-goat's fat. The mouse was so pleased with Wakiash that she began talking to him. "What do you want?" she asked eventually. Wakiash said that he wanted the totem pole, the house, and the dances and songs that belonged to them. The mouse said, "Stay here; wait till I come again."

Wakiash stayed, and the mouse went in and told the dancers, "I've been everywhere to see if there's a man around, but I couldn't find anybody." And the chief, who looked like a man but was really a beaver, said, "Let's try again to dance." They tried three times but couldn't do anything, and each time they sent the mouse to search. But each time the mouse only chatted with Wakiash and returned to report that no one was there. The third time she was sent out, she said to him, "Get ready, and when they begin to dance, leap into the room."

When the mouse told the animals again that no one was there, they began to dance. Then Wakiash sprang in, and at once they all dropped their heads in shame, because a man had seen them looking like men, whereas they were really animals.

The dancers stood silent until at last the mouse said: "Let's not waste time; let's ask our friend what he wants."

So they all lifted up their heads, and the chief asked the man what he wanted. Wakiash thought that he would like to have the dance, because he had never had one of his own. Also, he thought, he would like to have the house and the totem pole that he had seen outside. Though the man did not speak, the mouse divined his thoughts and told the dancers. And the chief said, "Let our friend sit down. We'll show him how we dance, and he can pick out whatever dance he wants."

So they began to dance, and when they had ended, the chief asked Wakiash what kind of dance he would like. The dancers had been using all sorts of masks. Most of all Wakiash wanted the Echo mask and the mask of the Little Man who goes about the house talking, talking, and trying to quarrel with others. Wakiash only formed his wishes in his mind; the mouse told them to the chief. So the animals taught Wakiash all their dances, and the chief told him that he might take as many dances and masks as he wished, as well as the house and the totem pole.

The beaver-chief promised Wakiash that these things would all go with him when he returned home, and that he could use them all in one dance. The chief also gave him for his own the name of the totem pole, Kalakuyuwish, meaning sky pole, because the pole was so tall.

So the chief took the house and folded it up like a little bundle. He put it into the headdress of one of the dancers and gave it to Wakiash, saying, "When you reach home, throw down this bundle. The house will become as it was when you first saw it, and then you can begin to give a dance."

Wakiash went back to the raven, and the raven flew away with him toward the mountain from which they had set out. Before they arrived, Wakiash fell asleep, and when he awoke, the raven and the frog were gone and he was alone.

It was night by the time Wakiash arrived home. He threw down the bundle that was in the headdress, and there was the house with its totem pole! The whale painted on the house was blowing, the animals carved on the totem pole were making their noises, and all the masks inside the house were talking and crying aloud.

At once Wakiash's people woke up and came out to see what was happening, and Wakiash found that instead of four days, he had been away for four years. They all went into the new house, and Wakiash began to make a dance. He taught the people the songs, and they sang while Wakiash danced. Then the Echo came, and whoever made a noise, the Echo made the same by changing the mouthpieces of its mask. When they had finished dancing, the house was gone; it went back to the animals. And all the chiefs were ashamed because Wakiash now had the best dance.

Then Wakiash made a house and masks and a totem pole out of wood, and when the totem pole was finished, the people composed a song for it. This pole was the first the tribe had ever had. The animals had named it Kalakuyuwish, "the pole that holds up the sky," and they said that it made a creaking noise because the sky was so heavy. And Wakiash took for his own the name of the totem pole, Kalakuyuwish.

—Based on a version reported by Natalie Curtis in
The Indian's Book, *1907.*

PART NINE

SOMETHING
WHISTLING IN
THE NIGHT

GHOSTS AND
THE SPIRIT WORLD

Ghost stories and tales of the dead are essential parts of almost every people's folklore, and American Indians are no exception. The ghosts here, however, are not necessarily always evil or threatening; the dead don't automatically become ghosts, either, so all haunting visions are not necessarily spirits of the departed. Among some tribes there are only vague ideas of the existence of an afterlife. Death was the end, and that was that. At the other extreme of the cultural spectrum were the burial-mound builders like the Natchez, who practiced an elaborate death cult with pyramids for the dead. The ruler was buried with treasures of copper, mica, shell, and pearls, as well as a host of women and retainers, dispatched to serve him in the next world.

In between are the cultures that envision the souls of the dead living in the spirit land in much the same way that they lived on earth—the men hunting buffalo, gathering crops, or fishing; the women tending the home or tipi. The Mandans believed that people had four souls, and the sage and meadowlark souls merged to form the spirit that went on to another world. The third soul remained in its old lodge, and the fourth appeared from time to time simply to frighten people.

In variations on the classical Orpheus theme, the tales here recount several voyages made by the living into the land of the departed, from either curiosity or devotion to a dead relative. While the Greek hero follows his beloved to a world underground, his Indian counterpart may find himself traveling to the bottom of a lake, across the Milky Way, or over mountains and plains similar to those inhabited by the living, although the road is usually strewn with traps for the cowardly or careless.

Exchanges between the dead and the living are common—men or women suddenly find out that they have married a ghost, a discovery that puts an interesting twist in romance. The lives of the dead and the living are not generally compatible over the long run, it would seem; each must return to his or her own kind eventually, so that order may be reestablished.

Relations with the departed continue, however, through ritual. Among many tribes a warrior must purify himself, fast, and abstain from sex in order to propitiate the ghost of an enemy he has killed. When a Sioux died, his *wanagi*, his ghost or soul, left the body but stayed near for four days. "You'd better please this spirit," Lame Deer said, "or it might make trouble."

With every meal, you leave a morsel aside for the spirits. When I drink some *mni-sha*, wine, or some *suta*, hard liquor, I always spill a little bit for an old wino friend, saying, "Here, *kola*, is something for you to enjoy." A good man could take his horse along to the Happy Hunting Grounds. That's why a great chief's or fighter's best horse was sometimes killed after his death, and the horse's head and tail were tied to the funeral scaffold. We didn't believe in burying people in the earth. No, the body of our dead were put on scaffolds or in trees, where the birds, the wind, and the rain could take care of them. The soul went on to the spirit land through the sky, and on the trail sat Owl-Woman, Hihan-Kaha, who would not let them pass unless they had the right signs on their foreheads, or chins, or wrists. When a child died, sometimes the father could not stand parting from it. Then he took some hair from the body and put it into a bundle which he placed in a special tipi. There he kept the child's soul. Soul keeping was hard. It might go on for a year, and during this time the father could not touch his wife, his gun, his weapons; he could not go out and hunt. At the end, the soul was released with a great giveaway feast.

Among the Navajo and some other Southwestern tribes, the dwelling in which a person had died was abandoned or destroyed, and his corpse, the token of lifelessness, greatly feared. People not related to the departed would offer to bury or cover the body as a gesture of good will. They believed that ghosts come out only after dark, and their appearance often betokens the imminent death of a close relative. In some tribes the name of a dead person was never mentioned again.

Some ghosts are harmlessly funny, prompting (or getting caught in) a string of comic episodes among the living. They have also been known

to play tricks on people, making a man's mouth crooked or bringing illness. Parents invoke them as bogeymen to scare children—"If you don't behave, Siyoko will take you away," a Sioux mother might threaten. Other ghosts may bless a person in his dreams, or warn of approaching dangers.

A whistling sound behind a tipi usually announces the arrival of a ghostly messenger. Ghosts are generally dark and indistinct in shape; they nourish themselves only on the smell, not the substance, of food. However, they have also been known to appear in the guise of coyotes, mice, and sparks of fire. The Crow believe that certain ghosts haunt graves, hoot like owls, and manifest themselves as whirlwinds.

Among the Tewa Pueblos, the newly dead soul wanders about in the world of the living, in the company of his ancestors, for four days, during which time the village remains generally uneasy. Relatives fear that the soul will become lonely and return to take one of them with him. The house itself must not be left unoccupied at any time during these four days, in order to keep the soul from reoccupying it. The soul is eventually released when the head elder utters a short prayer and reveals the purpose of the symbolic acts the relatives have performed.

> *We have muddied the water for you (the smoke)*
> *We have cast shadows between us (the charcoal)*
> *We have made deep gullies between us (the lines)*
> *Do not, therefore, reach for even a hair on our heads*
> *Rather, help us attain that which we are always seeking*
> *Long life, that our children may grow*
> *Abundant game, the raising of crops*
> *And in all the works of man*
> *Ask for these things for all, and do no more*
> *And now you must go, for you are now free.*

When Incarnacion Peña, the last sacred clown of San Ildefonso Pueblo, had been dead four days, one of his friends remarked, "He is already up there in the mountains, making rain for us."

TWO GHOSTLY LOVERS

[BRULE SIOUX]

Long ago there lived a young, good-looking man whom no woman could resist. He was an elk charmer—a man who had elk medicine, which carries love power. When this man played the *siyotanka*, the flute, it produced a magic sound. At night a girl hearing it would just get up and go to him, forsaking her father and mother, her own lover or husband. Maybe her mind told her to stay, but her heart was already beating faster and her feet were running.

Yet the young man, the elk charmer himself, was a lover with a stone heart. He wanted only to conquer women, the way a warrior conquers an enemy. After they came to him once, he had no more use for them. So in spite of his wonderful powers, he did not act as a young man should and was not well liked.

One day when the elk charmer went out to hunt buffalo, he did not return to the village. His parents waited for him day after day, but he never came back. At last they went to a special kind of medicine man who has "finding stones" that give him the power to locate lost things and lost people.

After this holy man had used his finding stones, he told the parents: "I have sad news for you. Your son is dead, and not from sickness or an accident. He was killed. He is lying out there on the prairie."

The medicine man described the spot where they would find the body, it was as he had said. Out on the prairie their son was lying dead, stabbed through the heart. Whether he had been killed by an enemy warrior, or a wronged husband from his own tribe, or even a discarded, thrown-away girl, no one ever knew.

His parents dressed him in his finest war shirt, which he had loved more than all his women, and in dead man's moccasins, whose soles are beaded with spirit-land designs. They put his body up on the funeral scaffold, and then the tribe left that part of the country. For it was a very bad thing, this killing which was probably within the tribe. It was, in fact, the very worst thing that could happen, even though everybody was thinking that the young man had brought it on himself.

One evening many days' ride away, when the people had already forgotten this sad happening and were feasting in their tipis, all the dogs in camp started howling. Then the coyotes in the hills took up their mournful cry. Nobody could discover the reason for all this yowling and yipping. But when it finally stopped, the people could hear the hooting of many owls, speaking of death and ghostly things. The laughter in camp stopped. The fires were put out, and the entry flaps to the tipis were closed.

People tried to sleep, but instead they found themselves listening. They knew a spirit was coming. Finally they heard the unearthly sounds of a ghost flute and a voice they knew very well—the voice of the dead young man with the elk medicine. They heard this voice singing:

> *Weeping I roam.*
> *I thought I was the only one*
> *Who had known many loves,*
> *Many girls, many women,*
> *Too many of them.*
> *Now I am having a hard time.*
> *I am roaming, roaming,*
> *And I have to keep on roaming*
> *As long as the world stands.*

After that night, the people heard the song many times. A lone girl coming home late from a dance, a young woman up before sunrise to get water from the stream, would hear the ghostly song mixed with the sound of the flute. And they would see the shape of a man wrapped in a gray blanket hovering above the ground, for even as a ghost this young man would not leave the girls alone.

Well, it all happened long ago, but even now the old-timers at Rosebud, Pine Ridge, and Cheyenne River are still singing this ghost song.

Now, there was another young man who also had a cold heart. He too made love to many girls and soon threw them away. He was a brave warrior, though. He was out a few times with a girl who was in love with him, and he said he would marry her. But he didn't really mean it; he was like many other men who make the same promise only to get under a girl's blanket. One day he said: "I have to go away on a horse-stealing raid. I'll be back soon, and then I'll marry you." She told him: "I'll wait for you forever!"

The young warrior went off and never came back; he forgot all about her. The girl, however, waited for a long time.

Well, this young man roamed about for years and had many loves. Then one time when he was out hunting, he saw a fine tipi. It had a sun-and-moon design painted on it. He recognized it immediately: it was the tipi of the girl he had left long ago. "Is she still good-looking and loving?" he wondered. "I'll find out!"

He went inside, and there was the girl, lovelier than ever. She was dressed in a white, richly quilled buckskin dress. She smiled at him. "My lover, have you come back at last?"

After serving him a fine meal, she helped him take off his moccasins and his war shirt. She traced his scars from many fights with her fingers. "My warrior," she said, "lie down here beside me, on this soft, soft buffalo robe." He lay down and made love to her, and it was sweeter than he had ever experienced, sweeter than he could have imagined. Then she said: "Rest and sleep now."

The young man—though not so very young anymore—woke up in the morning and saw the morning sun shining into the tipi. But the tipi was no longer bright and new; it was ragged and rotting. The buffalo robe under which they had slept was almost hairless and full of holes. He lifted the robe and pulled it aside to look at the girl, and instead of a living, beautiful woman, he found a skeleton. A few strands of black hair still adhered to the skull, which seemed to smile at him. The young girl had died there long ago, waiting for him to come back. He had made love to a spirit. He had embraced bones. He had kissed a skull. He had coupled with a skeleton!

As the thought sank in, the warrior cried aloud, jumped up, and began running in great fear, running he knew not where. When he finally came to, he was *witko*, mad. He spoke in strange sounds. His eyes wandered. His thoughts went astray. He was never right in his mind again.

—*Told by Lame Deer at Winner,*
Rosebud Indian Reservation, South Dakota, 1970.
Recorded by Richard Erdoes.

THE MAN WHO WAS
AFRAID OF NOTHING

[BRULE SIOUX]

Now, there were four ghosts sitting together, talking, smoking ghost smoke, having a good time, as far as it's possible for ghosts to have a good time. One of them said: "I've heard of a young man nothing can scare. He's not afraid of us, so they say."

The second ghost said: "I bet I could scare him."

The third ghost said: "We must try to make him shiver and run and hide."

The fourth ghost said: "Let's bet; let's make a wager. Whoever can scare him the most, wins." And they agreed to bet their ghost horses.

So this young man who was never afraid came walking along one night. The moon was shining. Suddenly in his path the first ghost materialized, taking the form of a skeleton. "*Hou*, friend," said the ghost, clicking his teeth together, making a sound like a water drum.

"*Hou*, cousin," said the young man, "you're in my way. Get off the road and let me pass."

"Not until we have played the hoop-and-stick game. If you lose, I'll make you into a skeleton like me."

The young man laughed. He bent the skeleton into a big hoop, tying it with some grass. He took one of the skeleton's leg bones for his game stick and rolled the skeleton along, scoring again and again with the leg bone. "Well, I guess I won this game," said the young man. "How about some shinny ball?"

The young man took the skeleton's skull and used the leg bone to drive it ahead of him like a ball.

"Ouch!" said the skull. "You're hurting me; you're giving me a headache."

"Well, you asked for it. Who proposed this game, you or me? You're a silly fellow." The young man kicked the skull aside and walked on.

Further on he met the second ghost also in the form of a skeleton, who jumped at him and grabbed him with bony hands. "Let's dance, friend," the skeleton said.

"A very good idea, cousin ghost," said the young man. "What shall

we use for a drum and drumstick? I know!" Taking the ghost's thigh-
bone and skull, the young man danced and sang, beating on the skull
with the bone.

"Stop, stop!" cried the skull. "This is no way to dance. You're hurting
me; you're giving me a headache."

"You're lying, ghost," said the young man. "Ghosts can't feel pain."

"I don't know about other ghosts," said the skull, "but me, I'm
hurting."

"For a ghost you're awfully sensitive," said the young man. "Really,
I'm disappointed. There we were, having a good time, and you spoiled
my fun with your whining. Groan somewhere else." The young man
kicked the skull aside and scattered the rest of the bones all over.

"Now see what you've done," complained the ghost, "it will take me
hours to get all my bones together. You're a bad man."

"Stop your whining," said the young man. "It gives you something
to do." Then he went on.

Soon he came upon the third ghost, another skeleton. "This is getting monotonous," said the young man. "Are you the same as before? Did I meet you further back?"

"No," said the ghost. "Those were my cousins. They're soft. I'm tough. Let's wrestle. If I win, I'll make you into a skeleton like me."

"My friend," said the young man, "I don't feel like wrestling with you, I feel like sledding. There's enough snow on the hill for that. I should have buffalo ribs for it, but your rib cage will go."

The young man took the ghost's rib cage and used it as a sled. "This is fun!" he said, whizzing down the hill.

"Stop, stop," cried the ghost's skull. "You're breaking my ribs!"

The young man said: "Friend, you look funny without a rib cage. You've grown so short. Here!" And he threw the ribs into a stream.

"Look what you've done! What can I do without my ribs? I need them."

"Jump in the water and dive for them," said the young man. "You look as if you need a bath. It'll do you good, and your woman will appreciate it."

"What do you mean? I am a woman!" said the ghost, insulted.

"With skeletons I can't tell, you pretty thing," he said, and walked on.

Then he came upon the chief ghost, a skeleton riding a skeleton horse. "I've come to kill you," said the skeleton.

The young man made faces at the ghost. He rolled his eyes; he showed his teeth; he gnashed them; he made weird noises. "I'm a ghost myself, a much more terrible ghost than you are," he said.

The skeleton got scared and tried to turn his ghost horse, but the young man seized it by the bridle. "A horse is just what I want," he said. "I've walked enough. Get off!" He yanked the skeleton from its mount and broke it into pieces. The skeleton was whimpering, but the young man mounted the skeleton horse and rode it into camp. Day was just breaking, and some women who were up early to get water saw him and screamed loudly. They ran away while the whole village was awakened by their shrieking. The people looked out of their tipis and became frightened when they saw him on the ghost horse. As soon as the sun appeared, however, the skeleton vanished. The young man laughed.

The story of his ride on the skeleton horse was told all through the camp. Later he joined a group of men and started to brag about putting the four skeleton ghosts to flight. People shook their heads, saying, "This young man is really brave. Nothing frightens him. He is the bravest man who ever lived."

Just then a tiny spider was crawling up this young man's sleeve. When someone called his attention to it, he cried, "Eeeeech! Get this

bug off me! Please, someone take it off, I can't stand spiders! Eeeeeeech!"
He shivered, he writhed, he carried on. A little girl laughed and took
the spider off him.

—Told by Lame Deer, and recorded by Richard Erdoes.

■

THE LAND OF THE DEAD

■

[SERRANO]

■ ||||||||||||||||||||||||||||||||||||||||||||||||||||||||||||||||||||||||||||||||||| ■

A great hunter brought home a wife. They loved each other and were
very happy. But the man's mother hated the young wife, and one day
when the husband was out hunting, she put a sharp, pointed object in
the wife's seat, and the woman sat down upon it and was killed.

The people immediately brought brush and piled it up. They put her
body on it and burned it, and by the time her husband returned that
night the body was all consumed.

The man went to the burning place and stayed there motionless.
Curls of dust rose and whirled about the charred spot. He watched
them all night and all day. At evening they grew larger, and at last one
larger than all the rest whirled round and round the burned spot. It set
off down the road and he set off after it. When it was quite dark, he
saw that the dust he was following was his wife, but she would not
speak to him.

She was leading him in the direction of the rock past which all dead
people go. If they have lived bad lives, the rock falls on them and
crushes them. When they came to it, she spoke to her husband. "We
are going to the place of dead people," she told him. "I will take you
on my back so that you will not be seen and recognized as one of the
living."

Thus they traveled on until they came to the river that the dead have
to ford. This was very dangerous for the man because he was not dead,
but the woman kept him on her back, and they came through safely.
The woman went directly to her people, to her parents and brothers and

sisters who had died before. They were glad to see her, but they did not like the man, for he was not dead. The woman pleaded for him, however, and they let him stay. Special food always had to be cooked for him, because he could not eat what dead people live on. And in the daytime he could see nothing; it was as if he were alone all day long; only in the night did he see his wife and the other people.

When the dead were going hunting, they took him along and stationed him on the trail the deer would take. Presently he heard them shouting, "The deer, the deer!" and he knew they were shouting to him that the deer were coming in his direction. But he could see nothing. Then he looked again and spotted two little black beetles, which he knocked over. When all the people had come up, they praised him for his hunting.

After that the dead did not complain about his presence, but they did feel sorry for him. "It's not time for him to die yet," they said. "He has a hard time here. The woman ought to go back with him." So they arranged for both of them to return, and they instructed the man and the woman to have nothing to do with each other for three nights after they were back on earth.

Three nights for the dead, however, meant three years for the living. Not aware of this, the husband and wife returned to earth and remained continent for three nights. The following evening they embraced, and when the husband woke on the morning of the fourth day, he was alone.

—From a story reported by Ruth Benedict in 1926.

■

THE DOUBLE-FACED GHOST

■

[CHEYENNE]

■ ▆▆▆▆▆▆▆▆▆▆▆▆▆▆▆▆▆▆▆▆ ■

There was a ghost who was immensely tall, with arms and legs of colossal length. He had two faces, one looking forward and one looking backward, and for this reason he was called the Double-faced Ghost.

He was not too bad—for a ghost, that is. He was so big that he could step over the widest rivers, and over hills too. He was also a mighty hunter, since he could catch any game that came in sight with his wonderfully long arms. But in spite of his talents, Double-Face was not happy because he could not find himself a suitable wife.

One day he came upon a tent standing all by itself in the middle of the prairie. In it lived a man, his wife, and their daughter, who was young and beautiful. Hiding behind a hill, the Double-faced Ghost saw the girl from afar and immediately fell in love with her. He said to himself: "I must have her for my wife! Of course, she might not want me, and her father too might think that she and I are ill-matched. So I'll start by supplying this family with so much good, fat meat that they'll see what a fine husband I'd make."

The ghost went hunting and caught a lot of game with his long arms. Every morning in the darkness before dawn, he brought a great load of meat and left it in front of the tipi. The parents and the girl were delighted and wondered what hunter was giving them all this fine red meat. The father said: "I must find out who is doing us this kindness," but he never caught a glimpse of the Double-faced Ghost. Yet morning after morning there was a new load of meat stacked up before the tipi—more than the three people could eat, even if the dogs also had their fill.

At last the father dug himself a hole behind a clump of bushes, crept into it on a moonlit night, and stayed awake to watch. Before dawn he saw the Double-faced Ghost come, leave his load of meat, and go away. The man went back to his family trembling with fear. He told his wife and daughter to strike the tent and pack up, because it was a terrible monster who had been bringing the meat. The three got away as fast as they could, and the next morning Double-Face found the tent gone. He waited until it was light and then followed their tracks. With his long legs he soon overtook them.

"Wait wait, good people," Double-Face shouted. "I mean you no harm. I have only kind feelings toward you." In a few more strides he came level with the fleeing family. "Stop! stop!" he cried. "Let's sit down and talk!"

What could the three people do? Though very much afraid, they sat down. The ghost towered over them.

"You were kind to leave all that meat," the man said. "But what do you want from us?"

"I am in love with your daughter," said the Double-Faced One. "I want her for a wife."

Naturally the father was not willing to give her to the ghost, and the daughter would not have gone even if her father had asked it. After

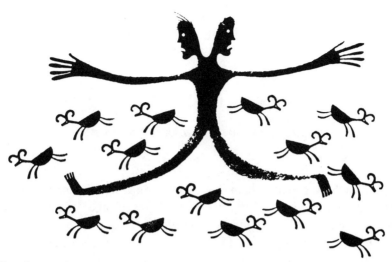

all, what girl wants a husband ten times taller than she, with one face looking forward and one backward? On the other hand, the father did not want to make this giant angry. So he said: "You are indeed kind and handsome, and a mighty hunter too. Who wouldn't want a man like you for his daughter's husband? What daughter wouldn't be happy to have you? Now, I'm sure you know the custom of my people in such matters."

"What custom?" asked the Double-Faced Ghost.

"Well, we always play hide-the-plumpit. If the suitor wins, he gets the girl. If he doesn't, he gives something of value."

"Really?" said the ghost. "I never heard of this custom. It sounds unusual."

"Not at all," said the father. "We've had it since the world began, and we must stick to it or suffer great misfortunes."

"Well, in that case let's play."

"You are a wise and accommodating man," said the father. "As I said, if you win I will give you my daughter, but if you lose you will go on leaving a pile of meat for us in the morning—though maybe only every other day." What the Double-faced Ghost didn't know was that the father was the best hidden-plumpit player in the world.

They played. The father's hands were so quick that the ghost could not follow them and locate the pit. On top of that, the girl and her mother drummed and sang funny songs, which distracted him. So the father won easily. Double-Faced Ghost accepted his loss and went on bringing meat as long as the people lived, even after the daughter married. As I said, he wasn't bad—for a ghost.

—*From a tale reported by Alfred L. Kroeber in 1900.*

A JOURNEY TO THE
SKELETON HOUSE

[HOPI]

Haliksai! In Shongopavi where the people were first living, a curious young man would often sit at the edge of the village looking at the graveyards. He wondered what became of the dead, if they really continued to live somewhere else. He asked his father, who could tell him very little. His father was the village chief, and he said that he would speak to the other chiefs and to his assistants about it. He asked the village criers whether they knew anything that would help his son. "Yes," they said, "Badger Old Man has the medicine that will answer his questions." So they called Badger Old Man, and when he arrived, they said, "this young man is thinking about the dead—whether they live anywhere. You know about it, and you have medicine that can show him." "Very well," he said, "I'll go and get my medicine."

So he went to his house, looked over his medicines, and finally found the right one. "This is it," he said, and took it to the village chief. "Very well," he said. "Tomorrow put a white kilt on your son and then blacken his chin with *tóho*, with black shale, and tie a small eagle feather to his forehead. These are the very preparations used for the dead." The next morning they dressed the young man in this way, and Badger Old Man spread a white *ówa* on the floor and told the young man to lie on it. He gave the young man some medicine to eat and also placed medicine in his ears and on his heart. Then he wrapped him in a robe, whereupon the young man, after moving a little, "died." "This is the medicine," Badger Old Man said. "If he hears this, he will go far away but he will also come back again. He wanted to see something and find out something, and with this medicine he will do just that."

After the young man had fallen asleep, he saw a path leading westward. It was the road to the skeleton house. This path he followed, and after a while he met a woman sitting by the roadside. "What have you come for?" she asked the young man. "I have come," he replied, "to find out about your life here." "Yes," the other one said, "I didn't follow the straight road; I didn't listen, and I now have to wait here. After a certain number of days I can go on a little, then I can go on again, but it will be a long time before I shall get to skeleton house." She pointed to an enclosure of sticks, which was all the house and protection she had.

From here the path led westward through large cactus and agave plants so full that they sometimes hid the way. He finally arrived at the rim of a steep bluff, where a chief was sitting. He was a Kwaniita, and had a white line around his right eye and a big horn for a headdress. He also asked the young man why he had come, and the latter told him. "Very well," the chief said. "Away over there is the house that you are looking for." But a great deal of smoke in the distance hid the house from the young man's view. The chief spread the young man's kilt on the ground, placed the young man on it, then lifted it up. Holding it over the precipice, the chief threw it forward, whereupon the kilt carried the young man slowly down like a giant bird.

When he had arrived on the ground below the bluff, he put on his kilt again and proceeded. In the distance he saw a column of smoke rising. After he had proceeded a distance, he came upon Skeleton Woman and asked her what the smoke was. "Some of those who were wicked while they lived in the village were thrown in there," she said. "The bad chiefs send their people over this road, and then they are destroyed; they no longer exist. You must not go there," she added. "Keep on this road and go straight ahead toward skeleton house."

When at last he arrived at skeleton house, he did not see anyone except a few children playing there. "Oh!" they said, "here a skeleton has come," and by the time he went into the village, all the people—or skeletons, rather—living there had heard about him and gathered to stare. "Who are you?" they asked the young man. "I am the village chief's son. I came from Shongopavi."

So they pointed toward the Bear clan, saying, "Those are the people that you want to see. They are your ancestors." A skeleton took him over to the house where his clan lived and showed him the ladder that led up to the house. The rungs of the ladder were made of sunflower stems, and the first rung broke as soon as he stepped on it, though the skeletons went up and down the ladder with no trouble. "I shall have to stay down here," he said; "bring me food and feed me here." So the skeletons brought him some melon, watermelon, and chukuviki.

When they saw him eat, they laughed at him; they are lighter than air because they never eat the food, but only its odor or soul. And that is the reason why the clouds into which the dead are transformed are not heavy and can float in the air. The food itself the skeletons threw out behind the houses, which is where they got his meal. When he had finished, they asked him what he had come for. He said, "I was wondering whether skeletons lived somewhere. I told my father I wanted to go

and find out, and he dressed me up in this way and Badger Old Man gave me some medicine to make it happen." "So that's what you have come for; well, look at us." Then they added: "It's not light here; it's not as light as where you live. We actually live poorly here. You cannot stay with us here yet; your flesh is still strong and 'salty.' You still eat food; we eat only the odor of the food. But when you go back, you must work there for us. Make *nakwakwosis* for us at the Soyal ceremony. These we tie around our foreheads, and they represent dropping rain. We shall work for you here, too. We shall send you rain and crops. You must wrap up in the *owa* women when they die, and tie the big knotted belt around them, because these *owas* are not tightly woven. When the skeletons move along on them through the sky as clouds, the thin rain drops through these *owas*, and the big raindrops fall from the fringes of the big belt. Sometimes you cannot see the clouds distinctly, because they are hidden behind these *nakwakwosis*, just as our faces are hidden behind them."

Looking around, the young man saw some of the skeletons walking around with huge burdens on their backs. These were mealing stones, which they carried by a thin string over the forehead that had cut deeply into the skin. Others carried bundles of cactus on their backs, and as they had no clothes on, the thorns of the cactus hurt them. He was told that some had to submit to such punishments for a certain length of time, then were relieved of them and could live with the others. At another place in the skeleton house he saw the chiefs who had been good here in this world and had made a good road for other people. They had taken their *tiponis*, their protective medicine,* and set them up there, and when the people here in the villages have their ceremonies and smoke during the ceremonies, this smoke goes down into the other world to the *tiponis* or mothers and from there rises up in the form of clouds.

After the young man had seen everything and satisfied his curiosity, he set off to his own village. When he arrived at the steep bluff, he again mounted his kilt and a slight breeze lifted him up. He met the Kwaniita chief, who told him, "Your father and mother are mourning for you now, so you'd better return home." This was the last person he met on his way back.

When he had just about arrived at his house, his body, which was still lying under the covering in the room where he had fallen asleep, began to move, and as they joined once more, it came to life again. They removed the covering, and Badger Old Man wiped his body, washed the paint off his face, and discharmed him. Then he sat up. They fed him and asked what he had found out. He recounted all of his experiences in detail—the woman with the house of brush, the Kwaniita chief and his flight on a kilt, and all about the skeleton house—the skeletons with heavy burdens of cactus and stones, and even the skeletons' food. "I have seen it all myself now, and I shall remember it. We are living in the light here. They are living in the dark there. No one should desire to go there."

Then he told them about the *nakwakwosis* and *bahos*. "If we make prayer offerings for them, they will provide rain and crops and food for us. Thus we shall assist each other." "Very well," they all said. "Very well; so that is the way." And so they returned to their homes wiser than before.

And from that time, the living and the dead began to work together for the benefit of both.

—Based on a tale collected by Henry Voth in 1905.

* The *tiponi* usually consists of an ear of corn to which are attached feathers of different birds and pieces of turquoise and shells.

THE SKELETON WHO FELL
DOWN PIECE BY PIECE

■

[ISLETA PUEBLO]

This story is influenced by Spanish tales. Gold and silver were hardly known to the Pueblos and not considered particularly desirable. In fact there was no money, as the white man knew it, so that tales of buried treasure are European in origin.

■ ▓▓▓▓▓▓▓▓▓▓▓▓▓▓▓▓▓▓▓▓▓▓▓▓▓▓▓▓▓▓▓▓▓▓ ■

There was a boy living with his mother and brothers. They all went out to different places looking for work, and that night the boy found an empty house to sleep in. He was dropping off when he heard a voice from the top of the house cry, "I'm going to fall."

"Well, fall."

An arm came down. "I'm going to fall!" Another arm came down. Soon the whole skeleton stood there. "You're a brave boy! won't you wrestle with me?" it said.

"Wrestle with a bony man like you! Well, all right."

They wrestled together, and the boy threw down the skeleton, who said to him: "You're a brave boy, and I am going to let you have all the riches I have here."

So the skeleton gave the boy a candle to light so that he could go into a little room where the ghost kept his gold and silver. Then the skeleton jumped on the boy's back and said, "You've got to carry me."

"All right, I'll carry you."

When they came to the room, Skeleton blew out the candle. The boy said, "I want to see what your riches are," and he lit the candle again. Just as he turned to look at the money, the dead man blew out the light. The boy got mad and pushed the skeleton down. "If you're going to blow out the light, I'll break your bones."

"No, my friend, leave me alone, for I think you're a brave boy." When the boy relit the candle, he saw a great pile of money. Skeleton said, "I'm going to ask one thing of you, my friend. After you have gathered everything up, assemble all the poor people and give a little money to everybody. The rest will be for you."

And the skeleton left, and the boy did as he asked, and then became a rich man.

—*Based on a tale recorded by Elsie Clews Parsons.*

THE SPIRIT WIFE

■

[ZUNI]

Here a Zuni Orpheus makes a hair-raising journey to accompany
his dead wife, only to learn of the inevitability of death itself.

■ |||||||||||||||||||||||||||||||||||||||||||||||||||||||||||||||||||| ■

A young man was grieving because the beautiful young wife whom he loved was dead. As he sat at the graveside weeping, he decided to follow her to the Land of the Dead. He made many prayer sticks and sprinkled sacred corn pollen. He took a downy eagle plume and colored it with red earth color. He waited until nightfall, when the spirit of his departed wife came out of the grave and sat beside him. She was not sad, but smiling. The spirit-maiden told her husband: "I am just leaving one life for another. Therefore do not weep for me."

"I cannot let you go," said the young man, "I love you so much that I will go with you to the land of the dead."

The spirit-wife tried to dissuade him, but could not overcome his determination. So at last she gave in to his wishes, saying: "If you must follow me, know that I shall be invisible to you as long as the sun shines. You must tie this red eagle plume to my hair. It will be visible in daylight, and if you want to come with me, you must follow the plume."

The young husband tied the red plume to his spirit-wife's hair, and at daybreak, as the sun slowly began to light up the world, bathing the mountaintops in a pale pink light, the spirit-wife started to fade from his view. The lighter it became, the more the form of his wife dissolved and grew transparent, until at last it vanished altogether. But the red plume did not disappear. It waved before the young man, a mere arms-length away, and then, as if rising and falling on a dancer's head, began leading the way out of the village, moving through the streets out into the cornfields, moving through a shallow stream, moving into the foothills of the mountains, leading the young husband ever westward toward the land of the evening.

The red plume moved swiftly, evenly, floating without effort over the roughest trails, and soon the young man had trouble following it. He grew tireder and tireder and finally was totally exhausted as the plume left him farther behind. Then he called out, panting: "Beloved wife, wait for me. I can't run any longer."

The red plume stopped, waiting for him to catch up, and when he did so, hastened on. For many days the young man traveled, following the plume by day, resting during the nights, when his spirit-bride would sometimes appear to him, speaking encouraging words. Most of the time, however, he was merely aware of her presence in some mysterious way. Day by day the trail became rougher and rougher. The days were long, the nights short, and the young man grew wearier and wearier, until at last he had hardly enough strength to set one foot before the other.

One day the trail led to a deep, almost bottomless chasm, and as the husband came to its edge, the red plume began to float away from him into nothingness. He reached out to seize it, but the plume was already beyond his reach, floating straight across the canyon, because spirits can fly through the air.

The young man called across the chasm: "Dear wife of mine, I love you. Wait!"

He tried to descend one side of the canyon, hoping to climb up the opposite side, but the rock walls were sheer, with nothing to hold onto. Soon he found himself on a ledge barely wider than a thumb, from which he could go neither forward nor back. It seemed that he must fall into the abyss and be dashed into pieces. His foot had already begun to slip, when a tiny striped squirrel scooted up the cliff, chattering: "You young fool, do you think you have the wings of a bird or the feet of a spirit? Hold on for just a little while and I'll help you." The little creature reached into its cheek pouch and brought out a little seed, which it moistened with saliva and stuck into a crack in the wall. With his tiny feet the squirrel danced above the crack, singing: "*Tsithl, tsithl, tsithl,* tall stalk, tall stalk, tall stalk, sprout, sprout quickly." Out of the crack sprouted a long, slender stalk, growing quickly in length and breadth, sprouting leaves and tendrils, spanning the chasm so that the young man could cross over without any trouble.

On the other side of the canyon, the young man found the red plume waiting, dancing before him as ever. Again he followed it at a pace so fast that it often seemed that his heart would burst. At last the plume led him to a large, dark, deep lake, and the plume plunged into the water to disappear below the surface. Then the husband knew that the spirit land lay at the bottom of the lake. He was in despair because he could not follow the plume into the deep. In vain did he call for his spirit-wife to come back. The surface of the lake remained undisturbed and unruffled like a sheet of mica. Not even at night did his spirit-wife reappear. The lake, the land of the dead, had swallowed her up. As the sun rose above the mountains, the young man buried his face in his hands and wept.

Then he heard someone gently calling: "Hu-hu-hu," and felt the soft beating of wings on his back and shoulders. He looked up and saw an owl hovering above him. The owl said: "Young man, why are you weeping?"

He pointed to the lake, saying: "My beloved wife is down there in the land of the dead, where I cannot follow her."

"I know, poor man," said the owl. "Follow me to my house in the mountains, where I will tell you what to do. If you follow my advice, all will be well and you will be reunited with the one you love."

The owl led the husband to a cave in the mountains and, as they entered, the young man found himself in a large room full of owl-men and owl-women. The owls greeted him warmly, inviting him to sit down and rest, to eat and drink. Gratefully he took his seat.

The old owl who had brought him took his owl clothing off, hanging it on an antler jutting out from the wall, and revealed himself as a man-like spirit. From a bundle in the wall this mysterious being took a small bag, showing it to the young man, telling him: "I will give this to you, but first I must instruct you in what you must do and must not do."

The young man eagerly stretched out his hand to grasp the medicine bag, but the owl drew back. "Foolish fellow, suffering from the impatience of youth! If you cannot curb your eagerness and your youthful desires, then even this medicine will be of no help to you."

"I promise to be patient," said the husband.

"Well then," said the owl-man," this is sleep medicine. It will make you fall into a deep sleep and transport you to some other place. When you awake, you will walk toward the Morning Star. Following the trail to the middle anthill, you will find your spirit-wife there. As the sun

rises, so she will rise and smile at you, rise in the flesh, a spirit no more, and so you will live happily.

"But remember to be patient; remember to curb your eagerness. Let not your desire to touch and embrace her get the better of you, for if you touch her before bringing her safely home to the village of your birth, she will be lost to you forever."

Having finished this speech, the old owl-man blew some of the medicine on the young husband's face, who instantly fell into a deep sleep. Then all the strange owl-men put on their owl coats and, lifting the sleeper, flew with him to a place at the beginning of the trail to the middle anthill. There they laid him down underneath some trees.

Then the strange owl-beings flew on to the big lake at the bottom of which the land of the dead was located. The old owl-man's magic sleep-medicine, and the feathered prayer sticks which the young man had carved, enabled them to dive down to the bottom of the lake and enter the land of the dead. Once inside, they used the sleep medicine to put to sleep the spirits who are in charge of that strange land beneath the waters. The owl-beings reverently laid their feathered prayer sticks before the altar of that netherworld, took up the beautiful young spirit-wife, and lifted her gently to the surface of the lake. Then, taking her upon their wings, they flew with her to the place where the young husband was sleeping.

When the husband awoke, he saw first the Morning Star, then the middle anthill, and then his wife at his side, still in deep slumber. Then she too awoke and opened her eyes wide, at first not knowing where she was or what had happened to her. When she discovered her lover right by her side, she smiled at him, saying: "Truly, your love for me is strong, stronger than love has ever been, otherwise we would not be here."

They got up and began to walk toward the pueblo of their birth. The young man did not forget the advice the old owl-man had given him, especially the warning to be patient and shun all desire until they had safely arrived at their home. In that way they traveled for four days, and all was well.

On the fourth day they arrived at Thunder Mountain and came to the river that flows by Salt Town. Then the young wife said: "My husband, I am very tired. The journey has been long and the days hot. Let me rest here awhile, let me sleep a while, and then, refreshed, we can walk the last short distance home together." And her husband said: "We will do as you say."

The wife lay down and fell asleep. As her lover was watching over her, gazing at her loveliness, desire so strong that he could not resist it overcame him, and he stretched out his hand and touched her.

She awoke instantly with a start, and, looking at him and at his hand upon her body, began to weep, the tears streaming down her face. At last she said: "You loved me, but you did not love me enough; otherwise you would have waited. Now I shall die again." And before his eyes her form faded and became transparent, and at the place where she had rested a few moments before, there was nothing. On a branch of a tree above him the old owl-man hooted mournfully: "Shame, shame, shame." Then the young man sank down in despair, burying his face in his hands, and ever after his mind wandered as his eyes stared vacantly.

If the young lover had controlled his desire, if he had not longed to embrace his beautiful wife, if he had not touched her, if he had practiced patience and self-denial for only a short time, then death would have been overcome. There would be no journeying to the land below the lake, and no mourning for others lost.

But then, if there were no death, men would crowd each other with more people on this earth than the earth can hold. Then there would be hunger and war, with people fighting over a tiny patch of earth, over an ear of corn, over a scrap of meat. So maybe what happened was for the best.

—Retold from a nineteenth-century version.

■

THE TRANSFORMED GRANDMOTHER

■

[PIMA-PAPAGO]

An old woman lived with her two grandchildren in a lonely place near a high, steep mountain.

One day she told the children that a plant which the Indians use for food grows on the mountains, and that she had made up her mind to gather some of it.

She started toward the mountain nearby, and when she got to the foot of it, she could not see the top. Yet she was determined to climb it. She took her cane in one hand, and, singing her song, began to clamber up.

She grew weary, sat down, and looked up, but the top did not seem any nearer. She began climbing again.

She had to rest many times before she could even see the summit, and it was evening before she arrived there. She had suffered all the way, and her feet were bleeding from rocks and thorns.

At last, however, she stood before the plant itself and began pulling it out of the ground. But she pulled it too hard, and away she rolled down the mountainside, the plant with her.

Great stones and rocks rolled over her before her body reached the bottom. She was killed on the way, but it was said that the bones picked themselves up and started toward home, singing a song.

In the meantime the children had begun to feel anxious for her. As they sat around the little fire they had built, they heard someone singing or talking far away. Nearer and nearer the sound came, and the younger one asked what was making the noise. The older one recognized the voice of her grandmother, but knew from its strangeness that her grandmother was no longer living. She told the younger one that they must go into the house and close the doorway with a "mine," a kind of blanket that is made from a weed woven like a basket.

They went inside and held the mine over the door, so that the woman might not enter. At last she came and ran around the house many times, singing as she ran. The children wondered what they would do if she should break through the door. The girl said she would turn into a blue stone, and her little brother said he would turn into a stick burning at one end. So they dropped the mine they held in their hands, and when the woman entered, there was nobody to be seen—only the blue stone and the burning stick. She stood calling, but no answer came.

—Based on a tale collected by Lucy Howard.

BIG EATER'S WIFE

■

[PEQUOD]

■ |||||||||||||||||||||||||||||||||||||||||||||||||||||||||||||||||||||||| ■

Big Eater ate and ate. He never stopped eating. He had his wigwam and two canoes on an island close to the mainland shore. Big Eater was powerful, but sometimes an evil ghost woman can defeat the most powerful man.

One day Big Eater was looking across the water, and there on the opposite shore he saw a beautiful young woman digging clams. How could he know that she was a ghost-witch? He hailed her across the water: "Beautiful girl, come live with me. Sleep with me!"

"No," she said. "Yes—No. yes. No. Yes, yes, yes! Well, all right."

Big Eater got in one of his two canoes and paddled over. The woman was even more beautiful close up. All right, pretty one, step into the canoe."

"Yes, but first I must get my things." Soon the girl came back with a mortar and pestle and some eggs. She put them in the canoe, and Big Eater paddled her over.

They ate. The beautiful woman said: "Oh my, what great heaps of food you can eat!" "Yes, I'm powerful that way." They went to bed. "Oh my, how often you can do it!" "Yes, I'm powerful that way." "You sure are." So they lived happily for a long time.

But after a while this girl got tired of Big Eater. She thought, "He's fat, he's not young. I want a change; I want to have a young, slim man loving me. I'll leave."

So when Big Eater went out fishing in one of his canoes, the girl made a doll, a large doll, large as a grown woman. She placed the doll in her bed, took her mortar, pestle, and eggs, put them in Big Eater's second canoe, and paddled off.

Big Eater came home early from fishing. Thinking it was his wife he was climbing in with, he got into bed. He touched the doll, and the doll began to scream and shriek. "Wife," he said, "stop this big noise or I'm going to beat you." Then he saw that it was a doll lying in bed with him.

Big Eater jumped up and looked around. The mortar and pestle and eggs were gone. He ran down to the shore, got into the remaining canoe, and paddled furiously after his wife.

Soon he saw her, also paddling hard. But he was stronger than she and pulled closer and closer. He drew up behind her canoe until both almost touched. "Now I'll catch her," he thought.

Then the woman threw her mortar out of the canoe over the stern. At once all the water around him turned into mortars, and Big Eater was stuck. He couldn't paddle until at last he lifted his canoe and carried it over the mortars. By the time he gained clear water again, his wife was a long way off.

Again he paddled furiously. Again he gained on her. Again he almost caught her. Then she threw her pestle out over the stern, and at once the water turned into pestles. Again Big Eater was stuck, trying to paddle through this sea of pestles but unable to. He had to carry his canoe over them, and when he hit open water again, his wife was far distant.

Again Big Eater drove through the water with all his strength. Again he gained on her; again he almost caught her. Then from the stern of her canoe the woman threw the eggs out. At once the water turned into eggs, and once more Big Eater was stuck. The eggs were worse than the mortar and pestle, because Big Eater couldn't carry his canoe over them. Then he hit the eggs, smashing them one by one and cleaving a path through the gooey mess. He hit clear water, and his wife's canoe was only a little dot on the horizon.

Again he paddled mightily. Slowly he gained on her again. It took a long time, but finally he was almost even with her. "This time I'll catch you!" he shouted. "You have nothing left to throw out."

But his wife just laughed. She pulled out a long hair from her head, and at once it was transformed into a lance. She stood up and hurled this magic hair lance at Big Eater. It his him square in the chest, piercing him through and through. Big Eater screamed loudly and fell down dead. That's what can happen to a man if he marries a ghost-witch.

—*Retold from several nineteenth-century sources.*

THE ORIGIN OF THE
HOPI SNAKE DANCE

[TEWA]

Long ago two Summer People society members—a father and his son—lived in one of the Hopi villages. Whenever offerings were made to the supernaturals, the son would always say, "I don't believe that these things are ever taken by the gods. I wonder if there really are any gods." At last he decided, "I'll find out the truth. I'm going to the Lower Place to see if the gods really are there, and if they're all they're supposed to be." Explanations from his father and other religious leaders that the gods do not take the offerings themselves, but only the essence or the core, did no good. He set out on his way.

After he had traveled for several days, the Silent One, a Tewa rain god, appeared to the young man. The Silent One asked: "Where are you going?"

"I am going to the Lower Place to look for the gods."

"Even if you travel until you grow old, you will never get there," the Silent One replied. "The Lower Place is too far for you to reach. Go no further, and do not doubt the existence of the gods." After saying this, the Silent One turned himself into his supernatural form and then back into a man again. The youth was frightened and impressed, but he could not let the rain god deter him. He insisted on continuing his journey.

After the young man had traveled further, the Deer-Kachina-Cloud god appeared, also in human form. Again the youth did not recognize him as a god, and again the god scolded him and urged him to go back. "I have horns," the god said, "and I am the gamekeeper of your people." Whereupon he also transformed himself into his supernatural form and then back to a man. Despite these warnings, the youth insisted on going on. "Snake Village is closer than the Lower Place, and that is as far as you can go," said Deer-Kachina-Cloud. "After visiting Snake Village, you must return to your own people." Reluctantly the young man agreed to this.

When the youth had gone another short distance, Star-Flickering-Glossy Man appeared, dressed in the feathers of many birds. He warned the young man again: "You can go only to Snake Village; no further.

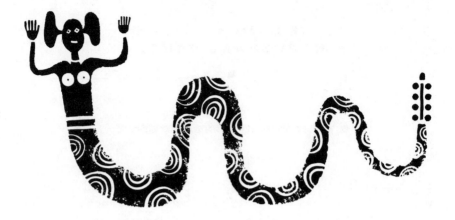

The snakes will try to bite you, because you are a doubter. Use this herb on them. In the middle of the village lives the governor of the snake people, and you should go there right away. The snakes are also spirits who can change themselves into people."

When the youth reached the village, the snakes did indeed try to bite him, but he spat the herb in their direction and they retreated. He reached the snake governor's home unharmed and was received kindly, though the governor also warned him not to proceed further.

The snake governor had two beautiful daughters, who treated the youth so well that he slept with one of them that night. The next day as he prepared to start on his long journey home, the governor offered him his choice of the two daughters to take with him. He chose the one he had spent the night with.

Next the governor told him to make piki, ceremonial bread, in white, yellow, red, and blue, and to scatter it, on his return, before a mountain north of his village. After he had made the piki, he and his wife began their trip in the company of some of the snake people, who went with them for a part of the way.

So great was the distance that the young man's wife had become pregnant and was due to give birth any day by the time they reached the Hopi village. On their way the young man had already scattered the piki before the mountain in this order: white, yellow, red, and blue. Immediately four bands of these colors appeared across the mountains. They were intended to be used by the Hopi people, and so they have been ever since: the red for painting pottery, the yellow and red for painting moccasins, and the blue (or green) for painting their bodies.

When the couple reached the foot of the mesa, the wife said she would remain there until he returned. She told him, however, that no one must touch him and he must touch no one until he came back to her. When he climbed to his village at the top of the mesa, the young man told his people to take him to the kiva, to build a large fire there, and to gather the whole village. As was expected of him, he told his whole story from the time he had set out to the Lower Place. This took the whole of that night.

The following morning as he walked down to the bottom of the mesa to take his wife some food, he met a woman with a water jar coming up. She was a former lover of his, and without warning she ran to him and embraced him. When he reached his wife, she already knew what had happened. Weeping, she said: "You don't care for me, so I shall leave and return to my people. But your child will always remain with you." She gave birth to a baby who, like herself, could change into a snake at will. Then she departed.

That's why the Hopis dance the snake dance today. The dancers are the descendants of the child born to the young man and his snake wife.

—Translated from the Tewa by Alfonso Ortiz.

■

BLUE JAY VISITS GHOST TOWN

■

[CHINOOK]

■ ▏▏▏ ■

One night the ghosts decided to go out and buy a wife. They chose a woman named Io'i, and gave her family dentalia as a dowry. They were married one night, and on the following morning Io'i disappeared.

Now Io'i had a brother named Blue Jay. For a year he waited to hear from her, then said, "I'll go and search for her." He asked all the trees, "Where do people go when they die?" They remained silent. He asked all the birds, but they did not tell him either. Then he asked an old wedge. It said, "Pay me and I'll carry you there." He did, and it took him to the ghosts.

The wedge and Blue Jay arrived near a large town, where they saw no smoke rising from any of the houses except the last one, a great edifice. Blue Jay went into it and found his elder sister, who greeted him fondly.

"Ah, my brother," she said, "where have you come from? Have you died?" "Oh, no," he said, "I am not dead at all. The wedge brought me here on his back." Then he went out and opened the doors to all the other houses. They were full of bones. He noticed a skull and bones lying near his sister, and when he asked her what she was doing with them, she replied: "That's your brother-in-law." "Pshaw! Io'i is lying all the time," he thought. "She says a skull is my brother-in-law!" But when it grew dark people arose from what had been just bones, and the house was suddenly full of activity.

When Blue Jay asked his sister about all the people, she laughed and replied, "Do you think they are people? These are ghosts!" Even hearing this, though, he resumed staying with his sister. She said to him, "Do as they do and go fishing with your dip net." "I think I will," he replied. "Go with that boy," she said, pointing to a figure. "He is one of your brother-in-law's relations. But don't speak to him; keep quiet." These people always spoke in whispers, so that Blue Jay didn't understand them.

And so they started in their canoes. He and his guide caught up with a crowd of people who were going down the river, singing aloud as they paddled. When Blue Jay joined their song, they fell silent. Blue Jay looked back and saw that where the boy had been, there were now only bones in the stern of the canoe. They continued to go down the river, and Blue Jay kept quiet. Then he looked at the stern again, and the boy was sitting there. Blue Jay said in a low voice, "Where is your fish trap?" He spoke slowly, and the boy replied, "It's down the river." They paddled on. Then Blue Jay said in a loud voice, "Where is your trap?" This time he found only a skeleton in the stern. Blue Jay was again silent. He looked back, and the boy was sitting in the canoe. He lowered his voice and said, "Where is your trap?" "Here," replied the boy.

Now they fished with their dip nets. Blue Jay felt something in his net, lifted it, and found only two branches. He turned his net and threw them into the water. When he put his net again into the water, it soon became full of leaves. He threw them back, but some fell into the canoe and the boy gathered them up. Then Blue Jay caught another branch and some more leaves and threw them back; but again a few leaves fell into the canoe, and again the boy gathered them up. As they continued fishing, Blue Jay caught two more branches that he decided to take back to Io'i for making a fire.

They arrived at home and went up to the house. Blue Jay was angry that he had not caught anything, but the boy brought up a mat full of trout, even though Blue Jay had not seen him catch a single one in his net. While the people were roasting them, the boy announced, "He threw most of the catch out of the canoe. Our canoe would have been

full if he had not thrown so much away." His sister said to Blue Jay:
"Why did you throw away what you had caught?" "I threw away nothing
but branches and leaves." "That is our food," she replied. "Did you think
they were branches? The leaves were trout, and the branches were fall
salmon." He said, "Well, I brought you two branches to use for making
a fire." So his sister went down to the beach and found two fall salmon
in the canoe. She carried them up to the house, and Blue Jay said,
"Where did you steal those salmon?" She replied, "That's what you
caught." "Io'i is always lying," Blue Jay said.

The next day Blue Jay went to the beach. There lay the canoes of the
ghosts, now full of holes and covered with moss. He went up to the
house and said to his sister, "How bad your husband's canoes are, Io'i!"
"Oh, be quiet," she said. "They'll become tired of you." "But the canoes
of these people are full of holes!" Exasperated, his sister turned to him
and said, "Are they people? Are they people? Don't you understand?
They are ghosts."

When it grew dark again, Blue Jay and the boy made themselves
ready to go fishing again. This time he teased the boy: as they made
their way down the river, he would shout, and only bones would be
there. When they began fishing, Blue Jay gathered in the branches and
leaves instead of throwing them away. When the ebb tide set in, their
canoe was full. On the way home, he teased all the other ghosts. As soon
as they met one he would shout out loud, and only bones would lie in

the other canoe. They arrived at home, and he presented his sister with armfuls of fall salmon and silver-side salmon.

The next morning Blue Jay went into the town and waited for the dark, when the life came back. That evening he heard someone announce, "Ah, a whale has been found!" His sister gave him a knife and said, "Run! a whale has been found!" Anxious to gather meat, Blue Jay ran to the beach, but when he met one of the people and asked in a loud voice, "Where is the whale?" only a skeleton lay there. He kicked the skull and left it. A few yards away he met some other people, but again he shouted loudly, and again only skeletons lay there. Then he came to a large log with thick bark. A crowd of people were peeling off the bark, and Blue Jay shouted to them so that only skeletons lay there. The bark was full of pitch. He peeled off two pieces and carried them home on his shoulder.

He went home and threw the bark down outside the house. He said to his sister, "I really thought it was a whale. Look here: it's just bark from a fir." His sister said, "It's whale meat, it's whale meat; did you think it's just bark?" His sister went out and pointed to two cuts of whale meat lying on the ground. "It's good whale, and its blubber is very thick." Blue Jay stared down at the bark, astonished to find a dead whale lying there. Then he turned back, and when he saw a person carrying a piece of bark on his back, he shouted and nothing but a skeleton lay there. He grabbed the bark and carried it home, then went back to catch more ghosts. In the course of time he had many meals of whale meat.

The next morning he entered a house and took a child's skull, which he put on a large skeleton. And he took a large skull and put it on that child's skeleton. He mixed up all the people like this, and when it grew dark the child rose to its feet. It wanted to sit up, but it fell down again because its head pulled it down. The old man arose. His head was too light! The next morning Blue Jay replaced the heads and switched around their legs instead. He gave small legs to an old man, and large legs to a child. Sometimes he exchanged a man's and a woman's legs.

In course of time Blue Jay's antics began to make him very unpopular. Io'i's husband said: "Tell him he must go home. He mistreats them, and these people don't like him." Io'i tried to stop her younger brother's pranks, but he would pay no attention. On the next morning he awoke early and found Io'i holding a skull in her arms. He tossed it away and asked, "Why do you hold that skull, Io'i? "Ah, you have broken your brother-in-law's neck!" When it grew dark, his brother-in-law was gravely sick, but a shaman was able to make him well again.

Finally Blue Jay decided it was time to go home. His sister gave him five buckets full of water and said, "Take care! When you come to burning prairies, save the water until you come to the fourth prairie. Then pour it out." "All right," replied Blue Jay. He started out and reached a prairie. It was hot. Red flowers bloomed on the prairie. He poured water on the prairie, using half of one of his buckets. He passed through a woods and reached another prairie, which was burning at its end. "This is what my sister told me about." He poured the rest of the bucket out on the trail. He took another bucket and poured, and when it was half empty he reached the woods on the other side of the prairie. He came to still another prairie, the third one. One half of it was burning strongly. He took a bucket and emptied it. He took another bucket and emptied half of it. Then he reached the woods on the other side of the prairie.

Now he had only two and a half buckets left. He came to another prairie which was almost totally on fire. He took the half bucket and emptied it. He took one more bucket, and when he arrived at the woods at the far side of the prairie, he had emptied it. Now only one bucket was left. He reached another prairie which was completely ablaze. He eked out the last drop of water. When he had gotten nearly across he had run out of water, so he took off his bearskin blanket and beat the fire. The whole bearskin blanket blazed up. Then his head and his hair caught fire and soon Blue Jay himself was burned to death.

Now when it was just growing dark Blue Jay returned to his sister. "Kukukukukuku, Io'i," he called. Mournfully his sister cried, "Ah, my brother is dead." His trail led to the water on the other side of the river. She launched her canoe to fetch him. Io'i's canoe seemed beautiful to him. She said, "And you told me that my canoe was moss-grown!" "Ah, Io'i is always telling lies. The other ones had holes and were moss-grown, anyway." "You are dead now, Blue Jay, so you see things differently." But still he insisted, "Io'i is always telling lies."

Now she paddled her brother across to the other side. He saw the people. Some sang; some played dice with beaver teeth or with ten disks. The women played hoops. Farther along, Blue Jay heard people singing conjurers' songs and saw them dancing, kumm, kumm, kumm, kumm. He tried to sing and shout, but they all laughed at him.

Blue Jay entered his sister's house and saw that his brother-in-law was a chief, and a handsome one. She said, "And you broke his neck!" "Io'i is always telling lies. Where did these canoes come from? They're pretty." "And you said they were all moss-grown!" "Io'i is always telling lie. The others all had holes. Parts of them were moss-grown." "You are dead now, and you see things differently," said his sister. "Io'i is always telling lies." Blue Jay tried to shout at the people, but they laughed at him. Then he gave it up and became quiet. Later when his sister went to look for him, he was standing near the dancing conjurors. He wanted their powers, but they only laughed at him. He pestered them night after night, and after five nights he came back to his sister's house. She saw him dancing on his head, his legs upward. She turned back and cried. Now he had really died. He had died a second time, made witless by the magicians.

—Based on a tale reported by Franz Boas in 1894.

THE GHOST WIFE

[BRULE SIOUX]

Once there was a man, a fine hunter and good provider, who was very much in love with his handsome wife. They had two beautiful children, with a third on the way.

When his wife was about to give birth, she was in labor for a long time. The baby wouldn't come out, and it hurt so much that the woman cried. The husband fetched an old woman who knew about such things, and she tried birthing medicine and all her other powers. But nothing helped; the child wouldn't come out, and the young wife died.

The husband was crazy with grief. He had loved her so much, and now he didn't know what to do. He ate almost nothing. He cut his little finger off to show how much he missed her. He held all kinds of ceremonies for her.

Sometime after she had died, the man was walking near his tipi one night when he saw a ghost. It was something like a white fog, a mist shaped like a woman. It was his wife, calling him. She said: "I couldn't stand seeing you grieve so much. I took pity on you. It's not at all bad where I am, and I can arrange for you and the children to join me. Then we can walk the Milky Way together and never be separated again."

The man said: "Come into the tipi. Let's talk this over." So the white shape went inside with him. They sat down. The man said: "I'm not quite ready to die yet. And the children are too young to die. Instead of our going with you to that spirit place, can't you arrange it so that you come to life again and stay with us?"

The ghost didn't know, and said she would ask and return in four days with an answer.

Four days later she came back, standing outside the tipi in the moonlight like a white mist. She called her husband and told him: "Well, all right; it's arranged for me to come to life again. Make a curtain of buffalo robes that I can hide behind, and don't look at me or try to touch me for four days. If you do I'll remain dead, so be careful, Husband."

The man followed every instruction. He hung the curtain and didn't look or let the children look behind it. He did everything right. And after four days his wife came out from behind the curtain, young and pretty as before.

The couple and their children lived again as if she had never died. They were happy together.

When years had passed, however, the man fell in love with another woman. He told his wife: "I shall marry a second woman, and she will share the work with you. You'll have someone to talk to when I'm away hunting. Things will be more pleasant."

But things were not so pleasant. The first wife tried to get along with the second one, but the new woman was proud and jealous. And as often happens, the man paid more attention to his new wife, the younger and prettier one.

The new woman did not like having the old one around, either, and she told her: "You're nothing but a ghost; you're not even real. Why do you hang around? Why don't you go back up to the Milky Way where you belong? Go away, ghost!"

The first wife said nothing, but the next morning she was gone, and her husband and children were gone with her. They had vanished without a trace. This time the ghost wife had taken them to the spirit land rather than stay with them down on earth. When the new wife realized what had happened, she was sorry for what she had said, but that didn't bring them back.

—*Told by Leonard Crow Dog in 1968, and recorded by
Richard Erdoes.*

PART TEN

||||||

ONLY
THE ROCKS
AND
MOUNTAINS
LAST FOREVER

||||||

VISIONS OF
THE END

The great Oglala leader Crazy Horse used to shout on his way into battle, "A good day to fight and a good day to die!" Bobtail Horse of the Cheyennes, faced with a mission which would probably cost him his life, remarked casually: "I am not afraid. I have already thrown my life away." Elderly Cheyenne warriors, weary of the misery and boredom of old age, made elaborate preparations to end their lives in battle. Yet accepting death was also an affirmation of life, for Crazy Horse also said he could die willingly because all the things he held dear—the sun, the land, the buffalo—were close by; his willingness to die was part of his way of honoring the human spirit. It was the lot of all people. As Sioux warriors acknowledged, "Only the rocks and mountains last forever; men must die."

Death enters the world in many guises. The Blackfoot creator Old Man introduces it as an inherent component of life when fashioning the first men and women. Coyote, in a Caddo legend, encounters death as a whirlwind, but he too acknowledges its crucial role in life.

Individuals are not the only ones to perish; nations and cultures crumble in mythic images, besieged from without and within. A Cheyenne proverb says, "A nation is not lost so long as its women's hearts are high. But if ever the women's heart should be lost, then the nation dies." Many stories tell of the coming of the white man, with his railroads and armies, and of the disastrous consequences for the Indian. For the Sioux, his arrival meant the end of the buffalo, and with them went an entire way of life.

Men and women die, nations disappear, and even the destruction of the world itself is foretold in apocalyptic images of the end of time. The eradication of the world by flood or fire is a widespread motif across the continent, but it is usually accompanied by tokens of renewal, for the end of this world does not mean the end of everything, but merely the passing of one state and the arrival of the next, just as other worlds were destroyed to make way for the one we live in now.

A Hopi prophecy foretells that when the Blue Star Kachinas dance in the village plazas, then the end will be near. And when a special song is heard during the Wuwuchim ceremony, then the world will be plunged into war. This song was heard before the outbreak of World Wars I and II, and it will be heard again just before the outbreak of World War III. Then everything will be destroyed except the Four Corners area in which the Hopi live. From there a new world will start. The end of this world, in which we are living now, will come when people fly through the sky, trying to reach the stars, when the sun turns black, and when the Hopis travel to the House of Mica.

This particular vision was embraced in a rather dramatic way in recent years when, in the 1970s, a Hopi delegation traveled to New York to address a warning to the United Nations. One Hopi spokesman, when passing through Gary, Indiana, saw the sun hidden by clouds of smoke rising from many smokestacks. The sun he was seeing was black. When he saw the United Nations building for the first time, he knew that he had arrived at the House of Mica and that the old prophecies would be fulfilled. There will be a last warning—earthquakes, eclipses, volcanic eruptions, and if this warning is not heeded, and the people of the world do not take better care of it, this world will be wiped out, and a new one will take its place.

Long before the days of world wars or atomic weapons, however, a Paiute medicine man had another vision of a new world. 1890 witnessed the second major outbreak of the apocalyptic Ghost Dance; in 1870, tribes in California and the far west had taken up the great ceremonial dance for the first time in many years, and now it swept with increased fervor throughout the Plains. While the dancers embued it with a more violent tone in the east, where Indian tribes suffered the most severe stress from the incursions of the whites, the first dancers began with more peaceful intent. The medicine man Wovoka spoke of a fantastic vision of a world cleansed and renewed with green grass and spring rains and returned, whole again, to the Indian people. The dead returned from the North, driving before them great herds of game and buffalo, and all the people in the world thrived without death or illness. There would be great fellowship and brotherhood between all the tribes, and between man and animal.

Unfortunately, this vision was shattered in the cold and bloody snow of Wounded Knee in December, 1890, and little progress seems to have been made towards reaching it again since then. The belief that it will come some day, however, endures, and with it the vitality of Wovoka's image of all the people in the world joining hands and dancing together in a single harmonious circle: a peaceful world for all its creatures.

WOMAN CHOOSES DEATH

[BLACKFOOT]

Old Man decided that something was missing in the world he had made. He thought it would be a good thing to create a woman and a child. He didn't quite know how they should look, but he took some clay and mud and for four days tried out different shapes. At first he didn't like the looks of the beings he formed. On the fourth day, however, he shaped a woman in a pleasing form, round and nice, with everything in front and back, above and below, just right.

"This is good," Old Man said, "this is the kind of woman I like to have in my world." Then he made a little child resembling the woman. "Well," said Old Man, "this is just what I wanted, but they're not alive yet."

Old Man covered them up for four days. On the first day he looked under the cover and saw a faint trembling. On the second day the figures could raise their heads. On the third day they moved their arms and legs. "Soon they will be ready," said Old Man. And on the fourth day he looked underneath the cover and saw his figures crawling around. "They're ready now to walk upon my world," thought Old Man. He took the cover off and told the woman and the child: "Walk upright

like human beings." The woman and the child stood up. They began to walk, and they were perfect.

They followed Old Man down to the river, where he gave them the power of speech. At once the woman asked: "What is that state we are in, walking, moving, breathing, eating?"

"That is life," said Old Man. "Before, you were just lumps of mud. Now, you live."

"When we were lumps of mud, were we alive then?" asked the woman.

"No," said Old Man, "you were not alive."

"What do you call the state we were in then?" asked the woman.

"It is called death," answered Old Man. "When you are not alive, then you are dead."

"Will we be alive always?" asked the woman. "Will we go on living forever, or shall we be dead again at some time?"

Old Man pondered. He said: "I didn't think about that at all. Let's decide it right now. Here's a buffalo chip. If it floats, then people will die and come back to life four days later."

"No," said the woman. "This buffalo chip will dissolve in the water. I'll throw in this stone. If it floats, we'll live forever and there will be no death. If it sinks, then we'll die." The woman didn't know anything yet, because she had been walking on earth for just a few hours. She didn't know about stones and water, so she threw the stone into the river and it sank.

"You made a choice there," said Old Man. "Now nothing can be done about it. Now people will die."

—Retold from several nineteenth-century sources.

COYOTE AND THE ORIGIN OF DEATH

[CADDO]

In the beginning of this world, there was no such thing as death. Every-body continued to live until there were so many people that the earth had no room for any more. The chiefs held a council to determine what to do. One man rose and said he thought it would be a good plan to have the people die and be gone for a little while, and then return.

As soon as he sat down, Coyote jumped up and said he thought people ought to die forever. He pointed out that this little world is not large enough to hold all of the people, and that if the people who died came back to life, there would not be food enough for all.

All the other men objected. They said that they did not want their friends and relatives to die and be gone forever, for then they would grieve and worry and there would be no happiness in the world. Everyone except Coyote decided to have people die and be gone for a little while, and then come back to life again.

The medicine men built a large grass house facing the east. When they had completed it, they called the men of the tribe together and told them that people who died would be restored to life in the midicine house. The chief medicine man explained that they would sing a song calling the spirit of the dead to the grass house. When the spirit came, they would restore it to life. All the people were glad, because they were anxious for the dead to come and live with them again.

When the first man died, the medicine men assembled in the grass house and sang. In about ten days a whirlwind blew from the west and circled about the grass house. Coyote saw it, and as the whirlwind was about to enter the house, he closed the door. The spirit of the whirlwind, finding the door closed, whirled on by. In this way Coyote made death eternal, and from that time on, people grieved over their dead and were unhappy.

Now whenever anyone meets a whirlwind or hears the wind whistle, he says: "Someone is wandering about." Ever since Coyote closed the door, the spirits of the dead have wandered over the earth trying to find some place to go, until at last they discovered the road to the spirit land.

Coyote ran away and never came back, for when he saw what he had done, he was afraid. Ever after that, he has run from one place to another, always looking back first over one shoulder and then over the other to see if anyone is pursuing him. And ever since then he has been starving, for no one will give him anything to eat.

—*From a tale reported by George A. Dorsey in 1905.*

THE FLOOD

[HAIDA]

Behind Frederic Island there was a village with many people in it. A crowd of boys and girls was playing on the beach when they saw a strange woman wearing a fur cape such as they had never seen before. A little boy walked up to her to find out who she was, and the others followed. She was indeed strange. One boy pulled at her garment, which was like a shirt. He pulled it way up and saw her backbone, a funny-looking thing with "Chinese slippers," a plant that grows on the seashore, sticking out of it. This made the children laugh and jeer.

When they heard the children's clamor, the old people told them to stop laughing at the stranger. At that moment the tide was at its low ebb, and the woman sat down at the water's edge. The tide began to rise, and the water touched her feet. She moved up a little and again sat down. The water rose again, and again she moved back. Now she sat down at the edge of the village. But the tide kept rising; never before had it come so high. The villagers grew frightened and awe-struck. Having no canoes, they did not know how to escape, so they took big logs, tied them together into a raft, and placed their children on it. They packed the raft with dried salmon, halibut, and baskets of spring water for drinking.

Meanwhile the stranger kept sitting down, and when the tide came up to her, moving away to higher ground, up the hillside, up the mountain. Many people saved themselves by climbing onto the raft with the children. Others made more rafts, until there were a number afloat. The whole island now was covered by the sea, and the hundreds and hundreds of survivors were drifting about without being able to stop, since they had no anchors.

By and by the people saw peaks sticking out of the ocean. One of the rafts drifted to a piece of land and its survivors stepped off there, while other rafts were beached elsewhere. It was at that time that the tribes became dispersed.

—Based on a tale related by Henry Young in 1947 and reported by Marius Barbeau in 1953.

■

THE SEER WHO WOULD NOT SEE

■

[PIMA]

■ |||||||||||||||||||||||||||||||||||||||||||||||||||||||||||||||||||||||||||||||||||||||||||||||||||| ■

Earth Maker took some clay in his hands, mixed it with his own sweat, and formed it into two figures—a man and a woman. He breathed life into them and they began to walk around. They lived. They had children. They peopled the land. They built villages.

At a time when there were already numbers of people living, Szeukha, Earth Maker's son, dwelled in the valley of the Gila River. Near him lived a famous seer who could foretell the future.

One night while this seer slept, someone came to speak to him, making a great noise at his door. The seer woke up and looked out. Silhouetted against the light of the moon was a big bird standing in the doorway. It was the great eagle, who said, "Wake up! Stir yourself! You're a seer; you're a healer. Don't you know that a great flood is coming?"

"I know nothing about a flood," said the seer, laughing at the eagle. "Go away and let me sleep."

The great eagle came three times more to warn the seer, who ridiculed and scolded him. "Don't bother me, bird of misfortune. We all know what kind of person you are. You roam the villages in the shape of an old woman, and afterwards some girls and children have disappeared and are never seen again. We don't want you around here."

"You'd better believe what I'm telling you," said the great eagle. "This whole valley will be flooded. Everything will be destroyed."

"You're a liar," said the seer.

"And you're a seer who sees nothing," said the great eagle.

The bird flew away, and hardly had he gone when a tremendous thunderclap was heard, the loudest there has ever been. Even children in the womb heard it. It began thundering continuously as great flashes of lightning lit up the sky. When morning came, the sun remained hidden behind dark clouds, and there was only twilight, gray and misty. Then the earth trembled, and there was a great roar of something immense moving. The people saw a sheer green wall advancing toward them, filling the valley from one side to the other. At first they did not know what it was, and then they realized that it was a wall of green water. Destroying everything in its path, it came like a huge beast, a green monster, rushing upon them foaming, hissing, in a cloud of spray. It engulfed the seer's house and carried it away with the seer, who was never seen again. Then the water fell upon the villages, sweeping away homes, people, fields, and trees. The flood swept the valley clean as with a broom. Then it rushed on beyond the valley to wreak havoc elsewhere.

When the next day dawned, there was nothing alive except Szeukha, Earth Maker's son, floating on a lump of pine resin. The waters abated a little, and his strange craft bumped into a mountain above the Salt River. He stepped ashore and lived for a while in a cave on that mountain. The cave is still there, and so are some of the tools and weapons that Earth Maker's son used.

Now, Szeukha was going up to fight the great eagle. He was furious at this bird, who, he thought, had caused the great flood. Szeukha took wood from different kinds of trees and made a ladder. He leaned it against the cliff atop which the great eagle had his home, and the ladder reached into the clouds. Szeukha climbed it, found the great eagle, and fought him. It was a big fight and lasted a long time, for both Szeukha and the great eagle were powerful and had strong magic. But Szeukha was more powerful, his magic more potent, and at last he killed the great eagle.

Looking around, Szeukha saw the corpses and bones of all the people the great eagle had abducted and killed. He brought them all back to life, fed and clothed them, and told them to spread out and repeople the land. Inside great eagle's house he found a woman and her child alive. The eagle had stolen her from a village and taken her for his wife. Szeukha fed and clothed her and the child also, and sent them on their way. The woman was pregnant at the time, and she became the mother and begetter of the Hohokam people, from whom the Pimas are descended.

—Retold from various nineteenth-century sources.

THE ELK SPIRIT OF LOST LAKE

[WASCO]

In the days of our grandfathers, a young warrior named Plain Feather lived near Mount Hood. His guardian spirit was a great elk. The great elk taught Plain Feather so well that he knew the best places to look for every kind of game and became the most skillful hunter in his tribe.

Again and again his guardian spirit said to him, "Never kill more than you can use. Kill only for your present need. Then there will be enough for all."

Plain Feather obeyed him. He killed only for food, only what he needed. Other hunters in his tribe teased him for not shooting for fun, for not using all his arrows when he was out on a hunt. But Plain Feather obeyed the great elk.

Smart Crow, one of the old men of the tribe, planned in his bad heart to make the young hunter disobey his guardian spirit. Smart Crow pretended that he was one of the wise men and that he had had a vision. In the vision, he said, the Great Spirit had told him that the coming winter would be long and cold. There would be much snow.

"Kill as many animals as you can," said Smart Crow to the hunters of the tribe. "We must store meat for the winter."

The hunters, believing him, went to the forest and meadows and killed all the animals they could. Each man tried to be the best hunter in the tribe. At first Plain Feather would not go with them, but Smart

Crow kept saying, "The Great Spirit told me that we will have a hard winter. The Great Spirit told me that we must get our meat now."

Plain Feather thought that Smart Crow was telling the truth. So at last he gave in and went hunting along the stream now called Hood River. First he killed deer and bears. Soon he came upon five bands of elk and killed all but one, which he wounded.

Plain Feather did not know that this was his guardian elk, and when the wounded animal hurried away into the forest, Plain Feather followed. Deeper and deeper into the forest and into the mountains he followed the elk tracks. At last he came to a beautiful little lake. There, lying in the water not far from the shore, was the wounded elk. Plain Feather walked into the lake to pull the animal to the shore, but when he touched it, both hunter and elk sank.

The warrior seemed to fall into a deep sleep, and when he awoke, he was on the bottom of the lake. All around him were the spirits of many elk, deer, and bears. All were in the shape of human beings, and all were moaning. He heard a voice say clearly, "Draw him in." And something drew Plain Feather closer to the wounded elk.

"Draw him in," the voice said again. And again Plain Feather was drawn closer to the great elk. At last he lay beside it.

"Why did you disobey me?" asked the elk. "All around you are the spirits of the animals you have killed. I will no longer be your guardian. You have disobeyed me and slain my friends."

Then the voice which had said, "Draw him in," said, "Cast him out." And the spirits cast the hunter out of the water, onto the shore of the lake.

Weary in body and sick at heart, Plain Feather dragged himself to the village where his tribe lived. Slowly he entered his tepee and sank upon the ground.

"I am sick," he said. "I have been in the dwelling place of the lost spirits. And I have lost my guardian spirit, the great elk. He is in the lake of the lost spirits."

Then he lay back and died. Ever after, the Indians called that lake the Lake of the Lost Spirits. Beneath its calm blue waters are the spirits of thousands of the dead. On its clear surface is the face of Mount Hood, which stands as a monument to the lost spirits.

—Collected by Ella Clark in 1953.

THE DEATH OF HEAD CHIEF
AND YOUNG MULE

[NORTHERN CHEYENNE]

This is a true story that took place in 1890, but it is also a legend among our people. Head Chief was a young man in his twenties. He was proud. He would have liked to be a warrior, but the days when a man could gain honor by counting coup were over. The Cheyennes had been put on reservations, the buffalo were gone. The fine old life was over.

That year the people were starving, and the promised government rations did not arrive. Head Chief said: "There's nothing left but a little coffee and a piece of fry bread. How can we live? I'm going hunting, and maybe I'll find some deer." Some relatives tried to talk him out of it, saying: "There's no game left on the reservation. It has all been hunted out, and if you go outside the reservation, there will be trouble with the white men."

Head Chief said: "All this land from horizon to horizon used to be ours. Since when can white men forbid me to hunt? I go now."

Young Mule, a boy of fourteen, always followed Head Chief around like a puppy dog. Head Chief was teaching him how to be a man, how to behave like a warrior. "Head Chief, let me come hunting with you," Young Mule said.

"*Ipewa*, it is well. You can come." They got on their horses and rode off. Soon they were outside the reservation. They found neither deer nor antelope; what they found was a lone cow. A white rancher's cow.

"It probably belongs to a white man," said Young Mule.

"I don't care who it belongs to," said Head Chief. "They killed all the buffalo on the Plains and shouldn't begrudge us a single cow. We're starving; I must bring meat to my people."

Head Chief shot the cow. After they had butchered it and were loading the meat on their horses, a white man called Boyle rode up. He was the nephew of the rancher whose cow they had butchered. Boyle saw what had happened and started cursing the two Cheyenne. "What's he saying?" asked Head Chief, who could not talk English. "He's calling us lousy dogs," answered Young Mule, who had been to the white man's school.

"Oh, is that what he is saying?" Head Chief's blood was up, and he went for his rifle. Seeing this, the white man stopped cursing. He tried to whip up his horse and get away, but it was too late. Head Chief shot him through the head; he was lying there dead.

"Now what do we do?" asked Young Mule.

"Bury him, I guess. Head Chief put a handkerchief over Boyle's face so it wouldn't get dirty as they buried him.

Then Head Chief and Young Mule rode back to their camp. "They'll hang you for this," the elders said. "No they won't," said Head Chief. "If you don't surrender, we must fight to defend you," the older men said. "It will be the end of the Tistsistas, the end of our people."

"No," said Head Chief, "I don't want anyone to die for me. The days when we could fight them are over."

Boyle was missed; and a search party found the body and what was left of the cow. The white police came to the reservation, saying: "We want the one who did this." Head Chief sent word to them that he and he alone had done it. "Tell them I am the guilty one," he said. The white sheriff sent word that he would come to arrest Head Chief. "I'll be coming for that Indian," said the sheriff. "He'll be tried and hanged for sure. There had better be no resistance, either. A lot of soldiers are stationed here, and if you try to help that boy, you'll be wiped out."

Then Head Chief sent some of the elders and headmen to the sheriff. They told him: "Head Chief is ready to die, but not ready to be hanged. He will die like a man. On the next ration day, he wants you to bring the soldiers and line them all up at the foot of that hill. Then he'll come riding out at them as if counting coup. But he won't be armed, and the soldiers can shoot him as if it was in a battle. This will be a good death. Then there won't be any hard feelings."

"But this isn't the regular way of handling it," said the sheriff.

"Maybe it isn't, but if you try to arrest and hang him, then we don't know whether we'll be able to hold back our young men, especially the Dog soldiers. Then you might have a real battle on your hands. Is doing things regularly worth that?"

The sheriff went back to the white folks and the soldier chief to talk things over. He sent word: "It's all right; we'll do this Head Chief's way."

So the night before ration day, Head Chief put on his finest war shirt. He painted his face for battle. He got a fine sorrel horse. He told his father: "Cheer up! It's what I like. Sing a song for me."

He and the other warriors went up to Squaw Hill and pitched a tent there. They were singing and feasting and telling stories all night. The

Dog soldiers guarded them in case the white men decided to come and try to make an arrest.

Toward morning the elders told all the young men to leave. They didn't want them on that hill for fear the young braves would start to fight. "Go; leave now," they said. "Do it for the people." Very unwillingly, the young men of the warrior societies obeyed. Then the chiefs had criers ride through the camp, telling the women not to call out and not to make high-pitched war cries which could get the young men's blood up. The old ones wanted no accidents which could cause a massacre. They knew that you can't fight the white man. They said: "The people must survive."

Early that morning there were a lot of white people, on horseback and in buggies, come "to see the show." A company of soldiers was lined up in the gulch at the bottom of Squaw Hill with their guns loaded. Then everybody saw Head Chief on his sorrel horse at the top of the hill. While they watched, he put on his grandfather's warbonnet. His people were proud of him. Then suddenly there was a second one with him—the figure of a young boy.

It was Young Mule, riding a mule because he didn't own a horse. He had told people: "I won't have it said that I was not with my friend in his last battle. He let me come along when there was hunting and feasting and good times. I might just as well die with him too." The white men were not interested in Young Mule. They knew he was only fourteen, and they knew he hadn't shot Boyle. They had told the chiefs: "We don't want that kid. We only want the older one, the one who shot Boyle." But here Young Mule was, all the same.

Then those two friends rode down upon the soldiers side by side, singing their death songs. The Long Knives were waiting for them, the foot soldiers flanked by cavalry. These two boys circled around some soldiers, counting coup on them, daring them to shoot. Then the soldiers opened up, but didn't seem to have their hearts in it. The boys made it back to the top of the hill. They might already have been hit; nobody knows.

Then Head Chief turned his horse for a last charge, coming down the hill at a dead run. The boy's mule had been crippled by bullets, so he made his charge on foot, running zig-zag, defying the soldiers to hit him. Now the women could not hold back. They made the brave-heart cry, though they had been told not to. Even hardened warriors wept. One old man said: "Watch and see how a warrior should die."

Head Chief had told the young boy: "I shall be riding through the enemy line. Even if I've been shot dead already, my body will still ride through their line." He did just that. He rode through them, then fell off his horse, for he had been hit many times. He lay there, and one of the officers went over and finished him with a shot in the head. The young boy, Young Mule, was counting coups right and left. He went after the soldiers with a knife. Some say he had a gun hidden on him and was using it, but nobody knows for sure. Finally the soldiers killed him too. Then they marched off, as if ashamed.

They brought the bodies of these two friends to camp and laid them out. The people came to see them then. They said that the boys looked as if they were sleeping, with a little smile on their lips.

During that last charge, a feather from Head Chief's warbonnet had come off and was fluttering in the wind near where he was killed. Somebody grabbed this eagle feather and tied it to a rock, right where the officer had gunned him. Head Chief's blood was still on that rock. The eagle feather was there for a long time until, after many years, it finally rotted away. But the rock will be there forever.

—*Recorded on the Northern Cheyenne Reservation,*
Busby, Montana, 1972, by Richard Erdoes.

THE GHOST DANCE AT
WOUNDED KNEE

■

[BRULE SIOUX]

This is a story about the massacre of Sioux ghost dancers at Wounded Knee in December 1890. Under the false impression that the ghost dance was the signal for a general Indian uprising, the white agent at the Pine Ridge Reservation in South Dakota called in the regular army to suppress the ghost dancers. One band under Chief Big Foot surrendered to the Seventh Cavalry—Custer's old command. Among its men and officers were many who had served under Custer and who were eager to avenge his death. At Wounded Knee Creek eighteen miles northeast of Pine Ridge, the army opened fire with many quick-firing Hotchkiss cannon upon Big Foot's people and killed some two hundred fifty men, women, and children. The mass grave in which they were buried is still there.

In 1973 Indian civil rights activists occupied the site and withstood a siege by U.S. marshals, the F.B.I., and local vigilantes. During this siege, which lasted 73 days, two Indians were killed, one of them a local Sioux buried next to his massacred ancestors.

Dick Fool Bull told this story on many occasions. Each time, he remembered something else connected with it. He was the last flute maker and player at Rosebud. He died in 1976. Some say he was 103; others say he was in his nineties. Nobody knows for sure.

This is a true story; I wish it weren't. When it happened I was a small boy, only about six or seven. To tell the truth, I'm not sure how old I am. I was born before the census takers came in, so there's no record.

When I was a young boy, I liked to stick around my old uncle, because he always had stories to tell. Once he said, "There's something new coming, traveling on the wind. A new dance. A new prayer." He was talking about *Wanagi-wachipi*, the ghost dance. "Short Bull and Kicking Bear traveled far," my uncle told me. "They went to see a holy man of another tribe far in the south, the Piute tribe. They had heard that this holy man could bring dead people to life again, and that he could bring the buffalo back."

My uncle said it was very important, and I must listen closely. Old Unc said:

This holy man let Short Bull and Kicking Bear look into his hat. There they saw their dead relatives walking about. The holy man told them, "I'll give you something to eat that will kill you, but don't be afraid. I'll bring you back to life again." They believed him. They ate something and died, then found themselves walking in a new, beautiful land. They spoke with their parents and grandparents, and with friends that the white soldiers had killed. Their friends were well, and this new world was like the old one, the one the white man had destroyed. It was full of game, full of antelope and buffalo. The grass was green and high, and though long-dead people from other tribes also lived in this new land, there was peace. All the Indian nations formed one tribe and could understand each other. Kicking Bear and Short Bull walked around and saw everything, and they were happy. Then the holy man of the Piutes brought them back to life again.

"You have seen it," he told them, "the new Land I'm bringing. The earth will roll up like a blanket with all that bad white man's stuff, the fences and railroads and mines and telegraph poles; and underneath will be our old-young Indian earth with all our relatives come to life again."

Then the holy man taught them a new dance, a new song, a new prayer. He gave them sacred red paint. He even made the sun die: it was all covered with black and disappeared. Then he brought the sun to life again.

Short Bull and Kicking Bear came back bringing us the good news. Now everywhere we are dancing this new dance to roll up the earth, to bring back the dead. A new world is coming.

This Old Unc told me.

Then I saw it myself: the dancing. People were holding each other by the hand, singing, whirling around, looking at the sun. They had a little spruce tree in the middle of the dance circle. They wore special shirts painted with the sun, the moon, the stars, and magpies. They whirled around; they didn't stop dancing.

Some of the dancers fell down in a swoon, as if they were dead. The medicine men fanned them with sweet-smelling cedar smoke and they came to life again. They told the people, "We were dead. We went to the moon and the morning star. We found our dead fathers and mothers there, and we talked to them." When they woke up, these people held in their hands star rocks, moon rocks, different kinds of rocks from those we have on this earth. They clutched strange meats from star and moon animals. The dance leader told them not to be afraid of white men who forbade them to dance this *wanagi-wachipi*. They told them that the ghost shirts they wore would not let any white man's bullets through. So they danced; I saw it.

The earth never rolled up. The buffalo never came back, and the dead relatives never came to life again. It was the soldier who came; why, nobody knew. The dance was a peaceful one, harming nobody, but I guess the white people thought it was a war dance.

Many people were afraid of what the soldiers would do. We had no guns any more, and hardly had any horses left. We depended on the white man for everything, yet the whites were afraid of us, just as we were afraid of them.

Then when the news spread that Sitting Bull had been killed at Standing Rock for being with the ghost dancers, the people were really scared. Some of the old people said: "Let's go to Pine Ridge and give ourselves up, because the soldiers won't shoot us if we do. Old Red Cloud will protect us. Also, they're handing out rations up there."

So my father and mother and Old Unc got the buggy and their old horse and drove with us children toward Pine Ridge. It was cold and snowing. It wasn't a happy ride; all the grown-ups were worried. Then the soldiers stopped us. They had big fur coats on, bear coats. They were warm and we were freezing, and I remember wishing I had such a coat. They told us to go no further, to stop and make a camp right there. They told the same thing to everybody who came, by foot, or

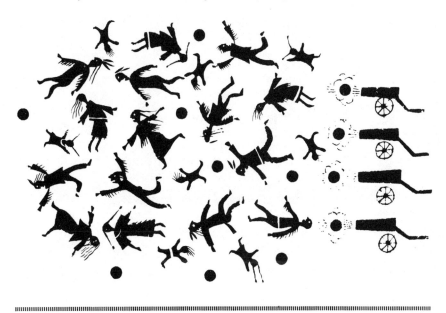

horse, or buggy. So there was a camp, but little to eat and little firewood, and the soldiers made a ring around us and let nobody leave.

Then suddenly there was a strange noise, maybe four, five miles away, like the tearing of a big blanket, the biggest blanket in the world. As soon as he heard it, Old Unc burst into tears. My old ma started to keen as for the dead, and people were running around, weeping, acting crazy.

I asked Old Unc, "Why is everybody crying?"

He said, "They are killing them, they are killing our people over there!"

My father said, "That noise—that's not the ordinary soldier guns. These are the big wagon guns which tear people to bits—into little pieces!" I could not understand it, but everybody was weeping, and I wept too. Then a day later—or was it two? No, I think it was the next day, we passed by there. Old Unc said: "You children might as well see it; look and remember."

There were dead people all over, mostly women and children, in a ravine near a stream called Chankpe-opi Wakpala, Wounded Knee Creek. The people were frozen, lying there in all kinds of postures, their motion frozen too. The soldiers, who were stacking up bodies like firewood, did not like us passing by. They told us to leave there, double-quick or else. Old Unc said: "We'd better do what they say right now, or we'll lie there too."

So we went on toward Pine Ridge, but I had seen. I had seen a dead mother with a dead baby sucking at her breast. The little baby had on a tiny beaded cap with the design of the American flag.

—*From versions told by Dick Fool Bull at Rosebud Indian*
Reservation, South Dakota, 1967 and 1968.
Recorded by Richard Erdoes.

■

THE GNAWING

■

[CHEYENNE]

■ ||||||||||||||||||||||||||||||||||||||||||||||||||||||||||||||||||||||||||| ■

There is a great pole somewhere, a mighty trunk similar to the sacred sun dance pole, only much, much bigger. This pole is what holds up the world. The Great White Grandfather Beaver of the North is gnawing at that pole. He has been gnawing at the bottom of it for ages and ages. More than half of the pole has already been gnawed through. When the Great White Beaver of the North gets angry, he gnaws faster and more furiously. Once he has gnawed all the way through, the pole will topple, and the earth will crash into a bottomless nothing. That will be the end of the people, of everything. The end of all ends. So we are careful not to make the Beaver angry. That's why the Cheyenne never eat his flesh, or even touch a beaver skin. We want the world to last a little longer.

—*Told by Mrs. Medicine Bull in Birney, Montana,*
with the help of an interpreter. Recorded by Richard Erdoes.

THE END OF THE WORLD

[WHITE RIVER SIOUX]

Somewhere at a place where the prairie and the Maka Sicha, the Badlands, meet, there is a hidden cave. Not for a long, long time has anyone been able to find it. Even now, with so many highways, cars, and tourists, no one has discovered this cave.

In it lives a woman so old that her face looks like a shriveled-up walnut. She is dressed in rawhide, the way people used to be before the white man came. She has been sitting there for a thousand years or more, working on a blanket strip for her buffalo robe. She is making the strip out of dyed porcupine quills, the way our ancestors did before white traders brought glass beads to this turtle continent. Resting beside her, licking his paws, watching her all the time is Shunka Sapa, a huge black dog. His eyes never wander from the old woman, whose teeth are worn flat, worn down to little stumps, she has used them to flatten so many porcupine quills.

A few steps from where the old woman sits working on her blanket strip, a huge fire is kept going. She lit this fire a thousand or more years ago and has kept it alive ever since. Over the fire hangs a big earthen pot, the kind some Indian peoples used to make before the white man came with his kettles of iron. Inside the big pot, *wojapi* is boiling and bubbling. *Wojapi* is berry soup, good and sweet and red. That soup has been boiling in the pot for a long time, ever since the fire was lit.

Every now and then the old woman gets up to stir the *wojapi* in the huge earthen pot. She is so old and feeble that it takes her a while to get up and hobble over to the fire. The moment her back is turned, the huge black dog starts pulling the porcupine quills out of her blanket strip. This way she never makes any progress, and her quillwork remains forever unfinished. The Sioux people used to say that if the old woman ever finishes her blanket strip, then at the very moment that she threads the last porcupine quill to complete the design, the world will come to an end.

—*Told by Jenny Leading Cloud at White River,*
South Dakota, 1967, and recorded by Richard Erdoes.

MONTEZUMA AND
THE GREAT FLOOD

[PAPAGO]

Before he made man, the Great Mystery Power made the earth and all things which lived upon it. The Great Mystery came down to earth, where he dug out some clay and formed it into a shape and ascended with it into the sky. Then he dropped it into the hole he had dug. At once out of that hole came the Great Montezuma, leading behind him all the Indian tribes. Last to come out of the hole were the wild, untameable Apaches, running off in all directions as fast as they were created.

The wise Montezuma taught the people all they needed to know: how to make baskets and pottery, how to plant corn with a digging stick, how to make a fire to cook the food. It was a happy time. The sun was much nearer the earth then, so that it was always pleasantly warm. There was no winter and no freezing cold. Men and animals lived as brothers, speaking a common language all could understand, so that a bug or a bird could talk to a human.

But then came the great flood. Long before it engulfed the earth, Montezuma's friend, Coyote, had foretold its coming. "You must make a big dugout canoe," Coyote told Montezuma, who could make anything. "You will need it soon," Coyote said.

Montezuma, following Coyote's advice, built the boat, keeping it ready on top of the high mountain that the whites call Monte Rosa. Coyote also made a strange vessel for himself, gnawing at a tree trunk until it fell down, then hollowing it out with his teeth. Coyote closed up the open end with piñon resin. When the great flood which Coyote had foretold finally swept over the land, Coyote crawled into the tree-trunk vessel he had made, while Montezuma climbed into his big dugout canoe. And so they floated upon the waters while all other living things perished. As the waters subsided, the top of Monte Rosa's peak rose a little above the flood. Both Montezuma and Coyote steered for this spot, the only piece of dry land far and wide. Thus the two friends met, glad to be alive.

Montezuma said to Coyote: "Friend, there must be other dry spots somewhere. You travel fast on four legs. Go west and do some scouting."

Coyote went off and came back tired after four days, saying: "In that direction of the universe I found only water, nothing but water."

Montezuma told him: "Coyote, my friend, rest a while, and then go and see what you can find in the south." Coyote rested and then went southward. Again he came back after four days, saying: "Over there in the south, everything is also covered with water." He went east, and it was the same; water everywhere. Finally Montezuma sent Coyote toward the north, and this time Coyote came back saying: "In the north the waters are receding, and there is much dry land." Montezuma was well pleased to hear this. He told Coyote, "Friend, there in the north we must begin to make a new world."

The Great Mystery Power again was busy peopling the earth with men and animals. After life had been recreated, he put Montezuma in charge of everything. Montezuma divided tribes into nations again, giving them just laws to govern themselves, and once again taught humans how to live. And in these tasks Coyote was Montezuma's faithful helper. Soon the people were increasing together with the animals, and all were happy.

But then Montezuma's power, which the Great Mystery had given him, went to his head. "We don't need a Creator," he said. "I am a Creator myself. My power is equal to the Great Mystery Power. I need nobody to command me; I myself am the Great Commander."

Coyote warned him to be more humble. "You know that there is a power above us greater than yours—the Power of the Universe. Obey its laws."

Montezuma answered: "I don't need your advice. Who are you to try to correct Great Montezuma? Am I not high above you? Am I not your master? Go; I don't need you anymore." Coyote left, shaking his head, wondering.

Now Montezuma called all the tribes together and said, "I am greater than anything that has ever been, greater than anything which exists now, and greater than anything that will ever be. Now, you people shall build me a tall house, floor upon floor upon floor, a house rising into the sky, rising far above this earth into the heavens, where I shall rule as Chief of all the Universe."

The Great Mystery Power descended from the sky to reason with Montezuma, telling him to stop challenging that which cannot be challenged, but Montezuma would not listen. He said: "I am almighty. Let no power stand in my way. I am the Great Rebel. I shall turn this world upside down to my own liking."

Then good changed to evil. Men began to hunt and kill animals. Disregarding the eternal laws by which humans had lived, they began to fight among themselves. The Great Mystery Power tried to warn Montezuma and the people by pushing the sun farther away from the earth and placing it where it is now. Winter, snow, ice, and hail appeared, but no one heeded this warning.

In the meantime Montezuma made the people labor to put up his many-storied house, whose rooms were of coral and jet, turquoise and mother-of-pearl. It rose higher and higher, but just as it began to soar above the clouds far into the sky, the Great Mystery Power made the earth tremble. Montezuma's many-storied house of precious stones collapsed into a heap of rubble.

When that happened, the people discovered that they could no longer understand the language of the animals, and the different tribes, even though they were all human beings, could no longer understand each other. Then Montezuma shook his fists toward the sky and called: "Great Mystery Power, I defy you. I shall fight you. I shall tell the people not to pray or make sacrifices of corn and fruit to the Creator. I, Montezuma, am taking your place!"

The Great Mystery Power sighed, and even wept, because the one he had chosen to lead mankind had rebelled against him. Then the Great Mystery resolved to vanquish those who rose against him. He sent the locust flying far across the eastern waters, to summon a people in an unknown land, people whose faces and bodies were full of hair, who rode astride strange beasts, who were encased in iron, wielding iron weapons, who had magic hollow sticks spitting fire, thunder, and destruction. The Great Mystery Power allowed these bearded, pitiless people to come in ships across the great waters out of the east—permitted them to come to Montezuma's country, taking away Montezuma's power and destroying him utterly.

—Based on a tale reported in 1883.

The Montezuma in this tale is a Southwestern culture hero, not to be confused with the Aztec emperor of the same name. The Aztec name was carried to the Papago by the Spaniards on their northward march, but the Papago turned Montezuma into First Man, creator of humans and animals and maker of the terrible "Great Eagle." The Papago Montezuma died four times, but always returned to life. After he had done his work of teaching the people how to live, or as some say, after the white man's god forced him to retire, he went to his underworld house in the south and returned to earth no more.

THE BUFFALO GO

[KIOWA]

Everything the Kiowas had came from the buffalo. Their tipis were made of buffalo hides; so were their clothes and moccasins. They ate buffalo meat. Their containers were made of hide, bladders, or stomachs. The buffalo were the life of the Kiowas.

Most of all, the buffalo was part of the Kiowa religion. A white buffalo calf must be sacrificed in the sun dance. The priests used parts of the buffalo to make their prayers when they healed people or when they sang to the powers above.

So when the white men wanted to build railroads, or when they wanted to farm and raise cattle, the buffalo still protected the Kiowas. They tore up the railroad tracks and the gardens. They chased the cattle off the ranges. The buffalo loved their people as much as the Kiowas loved them.

There was war between the buffalo and the white men. The white men built forts in the Kiowa country, and the woolly-headed buffalo soldiers [the Tenth Cavalry, made up of Negro troops] shot the buffalo as fast as they could, but the buffalo kept coming on, coming on, even into the post cemetery at Fort Sill. Soldiers were not enough to hold them back.

Then the white men hired hunters to do nothing but kill the buffalo. Up and down the plains those men ranged, shooting sometimes as many as a hundred buffalo a day. Behind them came the skinners with their wagons. They piled the hides and bones into the wagons until they were full, and then took their loads to the new railroad stations that were being built, to be shipped east to the market. Sometimes there would be a pile of bones as high as a man, stretching a mile along the railroad track.

The buffalo saw that their day was over. They could protect their people no longer. Sadly, the last remnant of the great herd gathered in council, and decided what they would do.

The Kiowas were camped on the north side of Mount Scott, those of them who were still free to camp. One young woman got up very early in the morning. The dawn mist was still rising from Medicine Creek, and as she looked across the water, peering through the haze, she saw the last buffalo herd appear like a spirit dream.

Straight to Mount Scott the leader of the herd walked. Behind him came the cows and their calves, and the few young males who had survived. As the woman watched, the face of the mountain opened.

Inside Mount Scott the world was green and fresh, as it had been when she was a small girl. The rivers ran clear, not red. The wild plums were in blossom, chasing the redbuds up the inside slopes. Into this world of beauty the buffalo walked, never to be seen again.

—Told to Alice Marriott by Old Lady Horse (Spear-Woman)
in the 1960s.

THE COMING OF WASICHU

[BRULE SIOUX]

Many generations ago, Iktome the Spider Man, trickster and bringer of bad news, went from village to village and from tribe to tribe. Because he is a messenger, Spider Man can speak any language, so all tribes can understand what he says.

He came running into the first camp, shouting: "There is a new generation coming, a new nation, a new kind of man who is going to run over everything. He is like me, Ikto, a trickster, a liar. He has two long legs with which he will run over you." And Iktome called all the chiefs into council, and the head chief asked: "Ikto, what news do you bring from the east?"

Iktome answered: "There is a new man coming; he is like me, but he has long, long legs and many new things, most of them bad. And he is clever like me. I am going to all the tribes to tell about him." Then Spider Man sang: "I am Iktome, and I roll with the air!"

When he left, three boys followed him to see where he was going. They watched him climb to the top of a hill. There he made his body shrink into a ball, changing himself from a man into a spider. And the boys saw a silvery spider web against the blueness of the sky, and a single strand from it led down to the hill. Iktome climbed into the web and disappeared in the clouds.

The next tribe Iktome visited were the Lakota—the Sioux nation. Two old women gathering firewood saw him standing on a butte near their village. They went home and told the chief: "We saw someone strange standing over there. He was looking at us." The chief called for two of his *wakincuzas*—the pipe owners, the ones-who-decide—and said: "Bring this man to me. Maybe he has a message."

They escorted Ikto, now in human form, into the camp. He stretched out his hand to the west, saying: "I am Iktome. I roll with the air, and I must take my message to seventy camps. This is what I have come to tell you: A sound is coming from the edge of the sea, coming from Pankeshka, the Seashell. It is the voice of Pankeshka Hokshi Unpapi—the Shell nation. One cannot tell where this voice is coming from, but it is someplace in the west. It is telling us that a new man is approaching, the Hu-hanska-ska, the White Spider Man, the Daddy-Longlegs-Man, The Long-White-Bone Man. He is coming across the great waters, coming to steal all the four directions of the world."

"How will we know him? How will we know this man?" asked the chief and the *wakincuzas*.

"Each of his long legs is a leg of knowledge, of *wo-unspe*. This new man is not wise, but he is very clever. He has knowledge in his legs, and greed. Wherever these legs step, they will make a track of lies, and wherever he looks, his looks will be all lies. At this time, *ecohan*, you must try to know and understand this new kind of man, and pass the understanding on from generation to generation. My message is carried by the wind."

Iktome made his body into a small ball with eight legs, and from within the sky again appeared the fine strand of spider web, glistening with dewdrops, and on it Iktome climbed up into the clouds and disappeared.

Ikto next went to the village of the Mahpiya-To, the Blue Cloud people, also known as Arapaho. Again the chiefs and the people assembled to ask what news he was bringing, and he spoke in their own language: "I have brought you a message bundle to open up, and my news is in it. The Iktome-Hu-Hanska-Ska, the White Longlegs, is coming. I flew through the air to bring you the message, but this new kind of man comes walking."

The Arapaho chief asked: "How is it that you fly and he walks?"

"*Wokahta*," said Iktome," he is traveling slowly, going slowly from the west toward the south and east, eating up the nations on his way, devouring the whole earth."

The chief asked: "When is he going to be here?"

"You will know by the star. When you see a double star, one star reflecting the other, then the Hu-Hanska-Ska will be near."

Iktome went away. He passed two women who were looking for wild turnips and using deer horns to dig them out of the prairie. They saw Iktome walking, pointing his arm skyward. All of a sudden he drew himself up into a ball, and at the same time the thread of a spider web from the sky hit the earth, and Iktome climbed up and vanished in the air.

Now, near the village of the Kangi-Wichasha—the Crow people—two old men were gathering herbs for Indian medicine. They saw someone standing behind a tree, then saw him circling the camp. They said to one another: "He is not from our tribe. Let's ask him what he wants."

Ikto spoke in the Crow tongue: "The White Long-legs is coming. Look around you at the things you see—the grass, the trees, the animals. The Iktome Hu-Hanska-Ska will take them all. He will steal the air. He will give you a new, different life. He will give you many new things, but hold onto your old ways; mind what Tunkashila, the Grandfather Spirit, taught you."

The two old men said: "We'd better bring you to our chief." They did so, and the Crow chief asked: "What message have you for us?"

"The White Long-legs is coming! He will eat up the grass, and the trees, and the buffalo. He will bring you a new faith. I am telling you this, I, Ikto, who rolls through the air."

The Crow chief asked: "Why is he coming? We don't want him here. We don't want his new things. We have everything here to make us happy."

"He will come," said Iktome, "whether you want him to or not. He is coming from the east."

"How is it that your name is Ikto?"

"Because I am Iktome, the Spider Man. Remember this tree of the white ash. It is sacred. Remember Iyan, Tunka, the rock. The rocks are forever."

One Crow woman gave Iktome a handful of *wasna*—jerk meat mixed with kidney fat and berries—to take with him on his travels. Iktome thanked her, saying: "You must watch this new man. Whatever he does and says and asks, say *"Hiya"* to him, say "No," say *hiya* to everything. Now I take my message to the west, to Wiyopeyata."

Iktome stood in the center of the tipi circle. All the Crow chiefs were standing around him wearing their warbonnets. Suddenly a great rush

of power was felt by all. Iktome shrank into a ball, and the thread of the spider web which was floating in the sky hit the prairie, causing a trembling and thundering deep inside the earth. And while everybody marveled, Iktome climbed up the thread into the web and was gone.

A man was roaming in a valley. He was seen by a warrior of the Snake People, also known as Shoshone, getting his horses together. The warrior asked the man who he was and why he had come. The stranger said: "I am Ikto. I roll with the air. I come from Wiyohiyanpata, the east, a generation coming with news."

The warrior said: "Stay here. I will bring our chief." The Shoshone chief came, followed by his people. Ikto told him: "A new kind of man is coming, a White Long-legs with many lies and many new things. If you want them, that's up to you."

The chief put two sticks on the ground facing north and south. It was a symbol for saying "No." The Chief told Ikto: "We don't want him. Our generation is good, our nation is good, our land is good. We have no use for this new kind of man."

Ikto told him: "He will come anyhow. I am going to Waziyata, toward the north, to bring my message to the people there."

Ikto climbed a hill, and the Shoshone people saw lightning strike the summit, and they heard the sound of many buffalo in the earth beneath their feet.

Iktome reappeared in the north, walking toward the village of the Palani, or Pawnees, pointing his finger toward their camp, shouting: "A new generation is coming! A new kind of human is coming! He is coming to this world!"

One Palani woman asked him: "Is it a newborn child?"

"No," said Ikto, "this is no little child. It is a man without grand-mothers or grandfathers, a man bringing new sicknesses and worries."

"We don't want him! What shall we do?" the Pawnees asked.

"You yourselves must know what to do. I am going back to my people."

The Pawnees said: "Don't go yet." But Iktome went toward the north with a pine bough in his hand, pointing it in the four directions, up to Grandfather Sky, and down to Grandmother Earth. "Remember, this will be the plant of worship in the center of the earth, and with it you will see and know."

And they all said: *"Ohan, Yes."*

Iktome went back to his own Sioux people. He flew through the air, and the wind carried him into their camp. He told the people: "I am going back into the sea. That new man is coming. He is almost here."

"How will he come?" asked the Sioux chief.

"He is coming in a *wahté*, in a boat. You are the Ikche-Wichasha—the plain, wild, untamed people—but this man will misname you and call you by all kinds of false names. He will try to tame you, try to re-make you after himself. This man will lie. He cannot speak the truth."

"When is he going to come?"

"When the white flowers bloom. Watch the buffalo: when this new man comes, the buffalo will go into a hole in a mountain. Guard the buffalo, because the White Long-legs will take them all. He will bring four things: *wicocuye*—sickness; *wawoya*—hate; *wawiwagele*—preju-dice; *waunshilap-sni*—pitilessness. He will try to give you his new Great Spirit instead of your own, making you exchange your own Wakan Tanka for this new one, so that you will lose the world. But always remember Tunka, the rock. He has no mouth, no eyes, no ears, but he has the power. Hold onto it. And always remember Tunkashila, the Grandfather, the Great Spirit! This new man is coming, coming to live among you. He will lie, and his lie never ends. He is going to make a dark, black hoop around the world."

"Is there no hope?" the people asked.

"Maybe, and maybe not. I don't know. First it will happen as I told you, and with his long legs he will run over you. Maybe a time will come when you can break his dark hoop. Maybe you can change this man and make him better, giving him earth wisdom, making him listen to what the trees and grass tell him. I will now reveal to you his name. You shall know him as *washi-manu*, steal-all, or better by the name of fat-taker, *wasichu*, because he will take the fat of the land. He will eat up everything, at least for a time."

Iktome left, and slowly people forgot about that White Long-legs coming, because for a while things were as they had always been. So they stopped worrying. Then one morning two Sioux women were out gathering chokecherries, and suddenly a black smog covered the place where they were.

And out of this blackness they saw a strange creature emerging. He had on a strange black hat, and boots, and clothes. His skin was pale, his hair was yellow, and his eyes were blue. He had hair growing under his nose and falling down over his lips; his chin was covered with hair; he was hairy all over. When he spoke, it did not sound like human speech. No one could understand him. He was sitting on a large, strange animal as big as a large moose, but it was not a moose. It was an animal no one knew.

This strange creature, this weird man, carried in one hand a cross and in the other a fearful firestick which spat lightning and made a noise like thunder. He took from his black coat something hard, shiny, glittering, and transparent which served him as a water bag. It seemed to contain clear water. He offered it to the women to drink, and when they tried it, the strange water burned their throats and made their heads swim. The man was covered with an evil sickness, and this sickness jumped on the women's skin like many unnumbered pustules and left them dying. Then they realized that the *wasichu* had arrived, that finally he was among them, and that everything would be changed.

—Told by Leonard Crow Dog in New York City, 1972,
and recorded by Richard Erdoes.

REMAKING THE WORLD

[BRULE SIOUX]

There was a world before this world, but the people in it did not know how to behave themselves or how to act human. The creating power was not pleased with that earlier world. He said to himself: "I will make a new world." He had the pipe bag and the chief pipe, which he put on the pipe rack that he had made in the sacred manner. He took four dry buffalo chips, placed three of them under the three sticks, and saved the fourth one to light the pipe.

The Creating Power said to himself: "I will sing three songs, which will bring a heavy rain. Then I'll sing a fourth song and stamp four times on the earth, and the earth will crack wide open. Water will come out of the cracks and cover all the land." When he sang the first song, it started to rain. When he sang the second, it poured. When he sang the third, the rain-swollen rivers overflowed their beds. But when he sang the fourth song and stamped on the earth, it split open in many places like a shattered gourd, and water flowed from the cracks until it covered everything.

The Creating Power floated on the sacred pipe and on his huge pipe bag. He let himself be carried by waves and wind this way and that, drifting for a long time. At last the rain stopped, and by then all the people and animals had drowned. Only Kangi, the crow, survived, though it had no place to rest and was very tired. Flying above the pipe, "Tunka-shila, Grandfather, I must soon rest"; and three times the crow asked him to make a place for it to light.

The Creating Power thought: "It's time to unwrap the pipe and open the pipe bag." The wrapping and the pipe bag contained all manner of animals and birds, from which he selected four animals known for their ability to stay under water for a long time. First he sang a song and took the loon out of the bag. He commanded the loon to dive and bring up a lump of mud. The loon did dive, but it brought up nothing. "I dived and dived but couldn't reach bottom," the loon said. "I almost died. The water is too deep."

The Creating Power sang a second song and took the otter out of the bag. He ordered the otter to dive and bring up some mud. The sleek otter at once dived into the water, using its strong webbed feet to go down, down, down. It was submerged for a long time, but when it finally came to the surface, it brought nothing.

Taking the beaver out of the pipe's wrapping, the Creating Power sang a third song. He commanded the beaver to go down deep below the water and bring some mud. The beaver thrust itself into the water, using its great flat tail to propel itself downward. It stayed under water longer than the others, but when it finally came up again, it too brought nothing.

At last the Creating Power sang the fourth song and took the turtle out of the bag. The turtle is very strong. Among our people it stands for long life and endurance and the power to survive. A turtle heart is great medicine, for it keeps on beating a long time after the turtle is dead. "You must bring the mud," the Creating Power told the turtle. It dove into the water and stayed below so long that the other three animals shouted: "The turtle is dead; it will never come up again!"

All the time, the crow was flying around and begging for a place to light.

After what seemed to be eons, the turtle broke the surface of the water and paddled to the Creating Power. "I got to the bottom!" the turtle cried. "I brought some earth!" And sure enough, its feet and claws—even the space in the cracks on its sides between its upper and lower shell—were filled with mud.

Scooping mud from the turtle's feet and sides, the Creating Power began to sing. He sang all the while that he shaped the mud in his hands and spread it on the water to make a spot of dry land for himself. When he had sung the fourth song, there was enough land for the Creating Power and for the crow.

"Come down and rest," said the Creating Power to the crow, and the bird was glad to.

Then the Creating Power took from his bag two long wing feathers of the eagle. He waved them over his plot of ground and commanded it to spread until it covered everything. Soon all the water was replaced by earth. "Water without earth is not good," thought the Creating Power, "but land without water is not good either." Feeling pity for the land, he wept for the earth and the creatures he would put upon it, and his tears became oceans, streams, and lakes. "That's better," he thought.

Out of his pipe bag the Creating Power took all kinds of animals, birds, plants and scattered them over the land. When he stamped on the earth, they all came alive.

From the earth the Creating Power formed the shapes of men and women. He used red earth and white earth, black earth and yellow earth, and made as many as he thought would do for a start. He stamped on the earth and the shapes came alive, each taking the color of the earth out of which it was made. The Creating Power gave all of them understanding and speech and told them what tribes they belonged to.

The Creating Power said to them: "The first world I made was bad; the creatures on it were bad. So I burned it up. The second world I made was bad too, so I drowned it. This is the third world I have made. Look: I have created a rainbow for you as a sign that there will be no more Great Flood. Whenever you see a rainbow, you will know that it has stopped raining."

The Creating Power continued: "Now, if you have learned how to behave like human beings and how to live in peace with each other and with the other living things—the two-legged, the four-legged, the many-legged, the fliers, the no-legs, the green plants of this universe—then all will be well. But if you make this world bad and ugly, then I will destroy this world too. It's up to you."

The Creating Power gave the people the pipe. "Live by it," he said. He named this land the Turtle Continent because it was there that the turtle came up with the mud out of which the third world was made.

"Someday there might be a fourth world," the Creating Power thought. Then he rested.

—Told by Leonard Crow Dog at Grass Mountain, Rosebud Indian Reservation, 1974. Recorded by Richard Erdoes.

A P P E N D I X

ACOMA

Acoma is, along with the Hopi town of Oraibi, the oldest inhabited settlement in the United States; it was already well established when the Spaniards first saw it in 1540. The ancient pueblo, known as the Sky City, is spectacularly situated like a medieval fortress atop its 600-foot-high rock, halfway between Gallup and Albuquerque in New Mexico. In the midst of the village stands the seventeenth-century Church of San Esteban with its wonderful polychrome altar, one of the great architectural treasures of the Southwest.

ALEUTS

The Aleuts' name derives from the Chukchi word *aliat*, meaning "island" or "islanders." They call themselves Unung'un, the People. The Aleuts are a branch of the Inuit family, with whom they share common ancestors and also vocabulary. They occupy the chain of islands forming the "bridge" between Siberia and Alaska over which man first came to the Western Hemisphere tens of thousands of years ago. The Aleuts fish and hunt in kayaks.

ALGONQUIAN

The Algonquians (or Algonkins), are possibly the largest group of linguistically related tribes in North America, scattered over the whole continent from the Atlantic to the Rocky Mountains. They include the Algonkin of Ottawa proper, the Cheyenne, Arapaho, Ojibway, Sac and Fox, Pottawatomi, Illinois, Miami, Kickapoo, and Shawnee. However, if an Indian legend is said to be of Algonkin origin, it generally means that it comes from an East Coast tribe, such as the Pequod, Mohegan, Delaware, Abnaki, or Micmac.

ALSEA

The Alsea were a small tribe of Yakonan Indians from western Oregon. Once numerous, by 1906 they were reduced to about a dozen individuals who took refuge among the Siletz tribe, which has since disappeared also. Their vestiges have been absorbed by a number of other Oregon tribes.

APACHE

The name Apache comes from the Zuni word *apachu*, meaning "enemy." Their own name for themselves is N'de or Dineh, the People. In the early 1500s, a group of Athapascan-speaking people drifted down from their original home in western Canada into what is now Arizona, New Mexico, and the four-corners area. They were split into smaller tribes and bands, including the Lipan, the Jicarilla (from the Spanish for "little basket," referring to their pitch-lined drinking cups), Chiricahua, Tonto, Mescalero, and White Mountain Apaches.

The Apache were a nomadic people and lived in conical brush shelters (wickiups) to which they often attached a ramada—four upright poles roofed over with branches. They hunted and gathered wild plants; much later they also began to plant corn and squash. They usually dressed in deerskin and wore their hair long and loose, held by a headband. Men also wore long, flapping breechcloths. Their soft, thigh-high moccasins were important in a land of chaparral, thorns, and cacti, since they were primarily runners of incredible stamina rather than riders (though they acquired horses early and were excellent horsemen). Their main weapon was the bow, and it was used long after they had guns.

Apache women wove particularly striking baskets, some made so tightly that a needle could not be inserted between their coils. They carried their babies on cradleboards. Women played an important role in family affairs; they could own property and become medicine women.

The Lipan Apache at first kept peace with the whites, whom they encountered in the sixteenth century. Fierce nomadic raiders, the Lipans roamed west Texas and much of New Mexico east of the Rio Grande, and eventually became the scourge of miners and settlers, particularly in Mexico. Their great chiefs included Cochise and Mangus Colorado, as well as Goyathlay, the One Who Yawns, better known as Geronimo. Apache attacks on whites were not unprovoked, for these tribes had often been victims of treachery, broken agreements, and massacres by white Americans and Mexicans. They were not finally subdued until the 1880s.

The Jicarillas, now numbering 1,500 to 2,000, live on a 750,000-acre reservation high in the mountains of northern New Mexico. The White Mountain Apaches (also called Sierra Blancas or Coyoteros) live in Arizona and New Mexico, including about 6,000 on the 1,600,000-acre Fort Apache Reservation in Arizona.

In 1905, there were only 25 Lipan survivors left, and they were eventually placed on the Mescalero Apache Reservation.

ATHAPASCAN

Athapascan refers to a language group, and it represents the most far-flung of the original North American tongues. Athapascan dialects or related languages are spoken by people in the interior of what is now Alaska, on the western coast of Canada, among some tribes in northern California, and by the Navajo and Apache of New Mexico, Arizona, and Utah.

BLACKFOOT

The Blackfoot people were really three closely allied Algonquian tribes—the Siksikas, or Blackfoot proper; the Bloods; and the Piegans. Siksikas means Black-footed People, and they may at one time have worn black moccasins. The Bloods probably got their name from the vermilion color of their face paint. Piegan means People with Poor or Badly Dressed Robes.

These tribes drifted down from Canada into what is now Montana, driving the Kootenay and Shoshoni before them. They were much feared by early white trappers and fur traders, because they killed all white men who entered their hunting grounds in search of beaver. Though they inhabited the northern edge of the buffalo range, the Blackfoot tribes lived in tipis and hunted bison like other Plains Indians.

The Piegans' main ceremonials were the sun dance and the All Comrades festival held by the warrior societies..

About 7,000 Blackfoot, 2,100 Piegans, and 2,000 Bloods now live on the Blackfoot reservation at Browning, Montana, at the southern edge of Glacier National Park, and some have joined the Piegan Agency in Alberta, Canada.

BLOOD

(See BLACKFOOT)

BRULE SIOUX

The Brules belong to the Oceti Shakowin—the seven council fires of the Lakota or Teton-wan, the seven Western Sioux tribes. Their name comes from the French word brulé—"burned." The Brules are very traditional people, maintaining their old customs and rituals, including the sun dance, flesh offerings, the sweat-lodge ceremony, the vision quest, and the so-called yuwipi ceremonies. Many Brules belong to the Native American Church, which follows the peyote cult. Today they occupy Rosebud, a large reservation in southwestern South Dakota.

CADDO

The Caddo belonged to a confederacy of tribes of the Caddoan language family, whose southern members were the Caddo proper, the Wichita, and the Kichai. Its northern representatives were the Arikara and Pawnees. Mostly sedentary planters, the Caddo, as well as the Wichita, lived in large dome-shaped, thatched grass huts, which were first mentioned by members of Coronado's expedition. Caddoans were once scattered throughout Oklahoma, the Red River area of Arkansas, and northern Texas. About 500 surviving Caddos were eventually settled with the Wichitas in Indian Territory (now Oklahoma).

CHEROKEE

The name Cherokee probably comes from *chiluk-ki*, the Choctaw word meaning Cave People. The Cherokee are one of the so-called Five Civilized Tribes, a term which first occurs in 1876 in reports of the Indian Office; these tribes had their own constitutional governments, modeled on that of the United States, the expenses of which were paid out of their own communal funds. They also farmed after the manner of their white neighbors.

Wealth and fertile land were the Cherokees' undoing. Under the "Indian removal" policy of Andrew Jackson and Van Buren, troops commanded by General Winfield Scott drove the Indians out of their ancestral lands so that white settlers could occupy them. Herded into the so-called Indian Territory west of the Mississippi, one third of those removed perished on the march, remembered by them as the infamous Trail of Tears.

Most Cherokees now live in Oklahoma, though a small number managed to stay behind. Their population has increased to about 7,000 people, living on about 56,600 acres on the Cherokee Reservation in North Carolina.

CHEYENNE

The name Cheyenne derives from the French *chien*, "dog," because of their ritual dog eating. The Cheyenne call themselves Tis-Tsis-Tas, the People. They are an Algonquian Plains tribe that came to the prairies from the Great Lakes region some two to three hundred years ago. They lived in tipis and were buffalo hunters, great horsemen, and brave warriors. They were closely allied with the Western Sioux tribes and fought with them at the Little Bighorn against Custer. Forced after the last battles into a malaria-infested part of the Indian Territory, one group under Dull Knife and Little Wolf made a heroic march back to their old hunting grounds, eventually settling on the Lame Deer Reservation in Montana. Another part of the tribe, the southern Cheyenne, remained in Oklahoma.

CHINOOK

The Chinook lived near the Columbia River in what is now Washington state. They were met and described by Lewis and Clark in 1805, and their trade jargon or lingua franca was widely used throughout the Northwest. Such words as "potlatch" and "hooch" are derived from it.

COCHITI

Cochiti is a Keresan-speaking pueblo situated on the Rio Grande south of Santa Fe, New Mexico. The Cochiti moved to their present reservation from their original home in Frijoles Canyon, now Bandelier National Monument, in New Mexico, and ruins of their old villages can be found on nearby Cochiti Mesa. The population in 1970 was around 500.

Farming, jewelry making, and pottery making are important economic activities. Cochiti is the home of Helen Cordero, the internationally known ceramist, whose pottery group called "Storyteller," a jolly ceramic figure surrounded by clinging children, is prized by collectors and widely imitated.

COOS

The Coos tribe, for whom Coos Bay in Oregon was named, are now almost entirely assimilated into the surrounding culture. They once occupied the Pacific coastal lands of Oregon.

CREE

The Cree Indians, an Algonquian tribe sometimes called Knisteneau, were essentially forest people, though an offshoot, the so-called Plains Cree, were buffalo hunters. They live mostly in Canada, but a few are now sharing reservations with other tribes in North Dakota. They were first encountered by French Jesuits in 1640, lost their people in a smallpox epidemic in 1776, fought many battles with the Sioux, and suffered a great defeat at the hands of the Blackfeet in 1870.

The Cree lived by hunting, fishing, and trapping. Muskrat meat was one of their staples. According to Denig, who lived among them in the 1850s, they made sacrifices to the sun, the Great Master of Life.

CROW

The Crow were a typical Plains tribe of hard-riding buffalo hunters. They split off from the Hidatsa tribe at some time during the second half of the eighteenth century, some say over a quarrel about buffalo meat; others say as a result of rivalry between two chiefs. The Crow later divided into two bands: the River and the Mountain Crows.

Once semisedentary corn planters who lived in earth huts and whose women practiced the art of pottery, the Crow had already reverted to a nomadic hunting people when they were first encountered by whites. This change probably resulted from their acquisition of the horse and the gun, both of which made the nomadic way of life easy and glorious. Like other Indians of the Plains, they lived in tipis; reputedly, theirs were the largest of all tribes. They were fierce fighters and skilled at the universal sport of intertribal horse stealing. The Crows were generally friendly to the whites and furnished scouts for the Indian-fighting army.

The Crows now live on their reservation in Montana, not far from the Custer Battlefield.

DIEGUENOS

(See YUMA)

FLATHEADS

The Flatheads are a Salishan tribe encountered by Lewis and Clark in 1805. Their ancestral home was the Bitterroot Valley in Montana, but they did not resist their removal to their present reservation in Montana, where they were absorbed by the related Salish and Kootenay tribes. Though they lived on the edge of Plains Indian culture, the paintings of Father Nicolas Point, who was in charge of their Catholic mission in the 1840s, show them dressed and hunting buffalo like typical Plains Indians, except that some men wear stovepipe hats bestowed upon them by whites. Contrary to popular belief, the Flatheads did not artificially flatten their foreheads.

HAIDA

The Haida (Xa'ida—the People) live on Queen Charlotte Island off the coast of British Columbia. The first European to visit them was Juan Pérez, who arrived in 1774 in the Spanish corvette *Santiago*, followed in 1786 by the famous French explorer La Pérouse. Contact with Europeans, as usual in most cases, was catastrophic for the Haida, bringing them impoverishment, smallpox epidemics, and venereal diseases.

The Haida were great hunters of whales and sea otters. Canoes were to them, as one visitor remarked, what horses were to the Plains Indians. Their sometimes very large vessels were hollowed out of single huge cedar trunks. The Haida are best known as totem-pole carvers and as the builders of large, decorated wooden houses. Their gifted artists are still turning out splendid masks and other carved objects.

HOPI

Hopi land is an enclave within the much larger Navajo Reservation in Arizona. Their name, Hopitu-shinumu, means Peaceful People, and throughout their history they have lived up to it. They belong to the Uto-Aztecan language family, though the Hopi in the village of Hano, curiously enough, speak Tewa. The founders of Hano were Rio Grande Pueblos fleeing their ancient home under Spanish pressure to seek a refuge among the Peaceful Ones.

The Spaniards made periodic attempts to Christianize the Hopis and fought several battles with them, but eventually left their pueblos alone. They were also the westernmost of the pueblos and therefore hundreds of miles from the center of Spanish power—and intrusion.

The Hopis have been planters of corn since time immemorial, skillfully coaxing their crops to thrive even in desert sands. In the traditional partition of labor, the women made pottery and wove beautiful baskets, while the men did the weaving and hunting.

INUIT

The Inuit are the native inhabitants of Greenland and the North American subarctic regions. The more familiar name Eskimo, meaning "those who eat their food raw," was actually a term used by neighboring Indians. The Inuit are hunters who chased seals, walrus, caribou, and an occasional polar bear. On land they move with the help of dogsleds; on the water they use their kayaks and umiaks, open boats made with wooden frames and skins. While they can still build igloos when and if they have to, today most live in European-style houses with electricity and other modern conveniences. Today the Inuit live all through the Arctic, with major settlements in Alaska, Greenland, and northern Canada, and a few have crossed the Bering Strait and settled in Siberia.

IROQUOIS

The name Iroquois, meaning "real adders," is of Algonquian origin. The Iroquois referred to themselves as We Who Are of the Extended Lodge. They are not a tribal group at all, but an alliance of tribes that dominated the vast area stretching from the Atlantic Coast to Lake Erie, and from Ontario down into North Carolina. According to tradition their league was formed about 1570 by the efforts of Hiawatha, a Mohawk (not to be confused with Longfellow's romantic hero), and his disciple, Dekanawida, a Huron by birth. The original Five Nations confederacy was made up of the Mohawk, Oneida, Onondaga, Cayuga, and Seneca, tribes which before that time had often been at war with each other. In 1715 the Tuscarora joined the league, and from that time the Iroquois have been known as the Six Nations. The league formed a democratic tribal republic with councils of elected delegates. Chiefs were elected from nominations by the tribe's matrons, and acted with the consent and cooperation of the women of child-bearing age.

ISLETA

Isleta is the southernmost pueblo, situated about twelve miles south of Albuquerque. Approximately 2,000 Isletans occupy their reservation of some 211,000 acres. The Franciscans established a monastery at Isleta as early as 1629. In 1681 Spaniards commanded by Governor Otermin destroyed Isleta as a punishment for having taken part in the Great Pueblo Revolt. The village was rebuilt and resettled early in the eighteenth century by Tiwa Indians who had taken sanctuary among the Hopis.

The people of Isleta speak Tiwa, in the Kiowa-Tanoan linguistic family. A government report of the 1890s calls the Isletas industrious farmers who raise cattle and maintain large vineyards; they probably learned to cultivate grapes, a rare activity among Indians, from the Franciscan monks who came from California.

JICARILLA APACHE

(See APACHE)

KALAPUYA

The Kalapuyans were a group of tribes who once occupied the Willamette Valley in northwestern Oregon and practiced a mild form of slavery. Marriage was arranged by purchase. The Kalapuya also flattened the fronts of their heads by "fronto-occipital pressure." In 1824 their population was decimated by epidemics introduced by whites.

KAROK

The Karok (from *karuk*—"upstream") called themselves Arra-Arra, meaning Men or Humans. A tribe of salmon fishers, they lived along the Klamath River between the more numerous Yurok below and the Shasta above them. Due to the absence of redwood in their own area, they made no canoes but bought them from the Yurok. Their culture closely resembled that of their Hupa and Yurok neighbors.

KWAKIUTL

The Kwakiutl are a tribe of Indians which, with the Nootka, belonged to the Wakashan language group. Kwakiutl, according to some linguists, means "beach at the north side of the river," though some tribal elders translate it as "smoke of the rivers." They are located on Vancouver Island and along the coast of British Columbia.

The Kwakiutl used to live in large painted houses decorated with carvings, and their elaborate totem poles and masks are famous. They fished and went to war in huge canoes often painted and decorated with carved prow figures. They gave solemn potlatch feasts, during which a slave was sometimes clubbed to death with an ornamental "slave killer" to show the owner's contempt for property. They waged war for prestige as well as to capture slaves.

The Kwakiutl had secret societies, such as the Cannibal society, whose members were supposed to have power from the Cannibal Spirit of the North and who put on a spectacular—and strictly ceremonial—cannibal (*hamatsa*) dance. Today the Kwakiutl fish with modern boats and equipment; they also work in canneries and the timber industry in British Columbia.

LIPAN APACHE

(See APACHE)

LUMNI

The Lumni are a Salishan tribe of northwestern Washington. Their culture was that of a typical coastal tribe: salmon was their main food, and their ceremonies revolved around salmon and fishing. The women made fine baskets and were renowned for their special dog-hair blankets. The Lumni fought annual cere-monial battles with the Haida for the purpose of capturing slaves. These en-counters are still remembered in the yearly *stommish*, or "warrior," ceremony which includes canoe racing, dancing, and a salmon steak barbecue. Some 700 Lumnis and related Nooksacks now live on the 7,000-acre Reservation with headquarters at Bellingham, Washington.

MAIDU

The Maidu are a northern California tribe, now living above the San Francisco Bay Area. They are known particularly for their exquisite basketry.

MALISEET

The name Maliseet or Malecite comes from the Micmac words *malisit*, "broken talkers," or *mahnesheets*, "slow tongues." An Algonquian family, the Maliseet were part of the loosely knit Abnaki confederation in Nova Scotia, New Brunswick, and Maine. Linguistically they were closely related to the Passamaquoddy. Champlain met them in 1604 and wrote: "When we were seated they began to smoke, as was their custom, before making any discourse. They made us presents of game and venison. All that day and the following night they con-tinued to sing, dance, and feast until day reappeared. They were clothed in beaver skins." By 1904 the Maliseet were reduced to about 800 people in New Brunswick and Quebec provinces, Canada.

METIS

The Métis, who are part French and part Indian, live in Canada. Their name comes from the French *métis*, "mixed." The Ojibway called them *wissakode-winini*, "burned trees" or "half-burned wood man," alluding to their part-light, part-dark complexions. Some Métis have adopted Indian customs and speak a patois made up of native, French, and English words. Some consider themselves white Canadians; others proudly call themselves Métis and stress their Indian ancestry. Their tales show marked European influences.

MICMAC

Micmac comes from *migmak* or *nigmak*, meaning "allies." The Micmac are a large Algonquian tribe of Nova Scotia, Cape Breton Island, Prince Edward Island, and New Brunswick. They were first visited by Cabot in 1497; in fact, the three Indians he took back to England were probably Micmacs. The Micmacs were expert canoeists and fishermen. Fierce and warlike, they sided with the French during the French and Indian Wars.

MIWOK

The Miwok, whose name means Man, were a central California tribe of Penutian stock, living between what is now the modern city of Fresno and the Sierras. They ate nuts, acorns, even grasshoppers; fished; and hunted deer and rabbit. They lived in conical houses made of poles, and their women used communal, many-holed grinding stones to make meal from seeds, nuts, and acorns. Their mystery ceremony was the *kuksu* dance, in which the participants wore feathered headdresses. The Miwok had a rich mythology and, before the gold rush, were a large tribe occupying 100 villages. They are now practically extinct.

MODOC

The Modoc, meaning "southerners," are of Penutian stock and speak a language nearly identical with that of the Klamath tribe. They lived around the lower Klamath Lake in southwestern Oregon and fought hard and long when the government tried to force them onto reservations. Led by Chief Kintpuash, called Captain Jack by whites, they holed up in the Lava Beds, a region of basalt rocks, deep crevasses, and many caves, in the so-called Modoc War of 1872–1873. They defended themselves for months against thousands of soldiers equipped with cannon. After their surrender, the Modoc leaders were hanged, supposedly for killing two members of a U.S. peace mission. Part of the tribe was removed to the Indian Territory in Oklahoma; others were settled on the Klamath Reservation, where a few hundred survive to this day.

MOJAVE

The Mojave (or Mohave) form the most numerous and warlike of the Yuman tribes living on both sides of the Colorado River. Described by early travelers as handsome, athletic, and brave, they cultivated corn, squash, pumpkins, beans, and melons; gathered piñon nuts; and caught fish. They used to paint and tattoo their bodies, and they cremated their dead. They lived in scattered four-sided stick, brush, and mud dwellings and stored their grain in cylindrical flat-roofed structures. At first they welcomed the Spaniards, but later resisted fiercely when the invaders tried to force the white man's way of life upon them. The Mojaves and their cousins, the Chemehuevis, now share the Colorado River Reservation in Arizona, roughly 270,000 acres supporting slightly less than 2,000 people.

MOJAVE-APACHE

(See YAVAPAI)

MULTNOMAH

The Multnomah tribe occupied what is now western Oregon, near Portland, and the few remaining members have been almost entirely assimilated into the white cultures which surround them.

NAVAJO

The Navajo are an Athapascan tribe that drifted down from northwestern Canada into the Southwest around 1300. They call themselves Dineh, the People, as do their linguistic cousins in Canada and Alaska, from whom they are separated by some 1,500 miles. Fierce, skin-clad, nomadic raiders, they terrorized the sedentary corn-planting tribes of the Southwest. The Pueblos called them *apachu*, meaning "enemy-strangers." This led to the mixed Tewa and Spanish "Apaches de Nabahu," which ultimately became "Navajo."

The Navajos adopted many cultural practices from their Pueblo neighbors, such as masked dances (*yebichai*), basketry, and pottery. They became fine silversmiths, learning the craft from the Spaniards, just as they learned weaving from the Pueblos. During the mid-nineteenth century they began making jewelry and weaving rugs; their simple chiefs' blankets have evolved into the well-known Navajo rugs of today.

With a population of over 130,000, the Navajo are the largest tribe in the United States. Their reservation extends over 200 miles of New Mexico and Arizona, from the Gallup area all the way to the Grand Canyon, and contains such natural wonders as Monument Valley and Canyon de Chelly, as well as large coal and oil deposits. Navajos are a comparatively wealthy nation; they farm and raise large herds of sheep, as well as some cattle. The women still wear their traditional costume—velveteen blouses, colorful ankle-length skirts, and silver and turquoise necklaces. Their traditional home is the hogan, a low, dome-shaped structure of mud-covered logs with a smoke hole at the top.

NEZ PERCE

The Nez Percés (French for "pierced noses") got this name from their custom of wearing a piece of dentalium shell through their septum. They belonged to the seminomadic Plateau culture, roaming over the dry, high country of Idaho, eastern Oregon, and eastern Washington. They were known for their trading acumen, their bravery and generosity, their skill in breeding the famous Appaloosa horse, and the fine basketry of their women. They were consistently friendly to the whites. A large tribe of the Shahaptian language family, they lived in large communal houses containing several families. Unjustly driven from their beloved Wallowa Valley, they fought fiercely and skillfully during the Nez Percé War of 1877 under their great leader, Chief Joseph, who won the admiration even of his enemies by his courage and humanity in conducting this war. Today some 1,500 members of the tribe live on the 88,000-acre Nez Percé Reservation with headquarters at Lapwai, Idaho.

OJIBWAY

The Ojibway, or as the whites misname them, the Chippewa, are an Algonquian tribe living today on a number of reservations, mainly in Minnesota. They migrated from the East late in the sixteenth or early in the seventeenth century. They were usually allied with the French, swapping beaver and other pelts for firearms, which they used to drive the Sioux to the West. The Ojibway took part in Pontiac's uprising, and by 1851 white settlers had pushed them beyond the Mississippi. Their most valuable food plant is wild rice. Their culture hero is Manabozho, the Great Rabbit, whose deeds they depict on bark paintings.

OKANOGAN

The Okanogan (or Okinagan) were a small Salishan tribe of seminomadic plateau people who were scattered over the high country of Idaho, western Oregon, and eastern Washington. They were grouped in small, roving bands of hunters, fishermen, and gatherers of cama roots, wild seeds, and berries. Like many Salishans, they were good basket makers. In 1906 there were some 525 Okanogans left in Washington state and a further 825 in British Columbia. Today about 3,000 people, descendants of related tribes, live on the Colville Reservation in Washington, among them the former Okanogans.

ONEIDA

The Oneida—the People of the Rock—are one of the original Five Nations of the Iroquois league. Like other Iroquois, they live in longhouses occupied by several families and owned by women. They traced their descent through the mother. The tribe originally lived near Oneida Lake in New York but, under pressure, sold their ancestral lands and moved to Wisconsin in 1838. Unlike other Iroquois tribes, the Oneida at first stayed neutral and eventually joined the Tuscarora as the only Iroquois nations siding with the Americans against the British in the Revolutionary War. Today roughly 1,800 people reside on the Oneida Reservation in Wisconsin.

OSAGE

The Osage, or Wazhazhe, are Plains Indians of the Siouan language group. Their original villages were situated in Kansas, Missouri, and Illinois. According to their legends, they originated in the sky and descended through four layers of sky until they alighted on seven rocks of different colors near a red oak tree. Later the people received four kinds of corn and four kinds of pumpkin seeds which fell from the left hind legs of four buffalo.

The tribe was divided into *gentes*, which monopolized certain tasks, such as making moccasins, pipes, war standards, or arrowheads. One *gente* furnished heralds (camp criers) to the tribe.

The Osage were eventually removed to Indian Territory in Oklahoma, where they now live.

OTO

The Oto, also called Otoe and Wat'ota, are a Siouan tribe, probably an offshoot of the Winnebago, from whom they are said to have separated at Green Bay, Wisconsin, as they wandered westward in pursuit of buffalo. This group later split further into three closely related tribes—the Oto proper, the Iowa, and the Missouri. Marquette knew of them, and Le Sueur met them in 1700 near Blue Earth River in what is now northwest Minnesota.

They lived in earth lodges, though they used skin tipis when traveling or hunting. They were rudimentary farmers but avid buffalo hunters, and they early adopted Plains Indian culture. In 1882 the last remnants of the tribe left Nebraska, where they had been living along the Platte River, and settled in Oklahoma.

PAPAGO

The Papago—the Bean People—are a Southwestern tribe closely related to the Pima. They are probably descendants of the ancient Hohokam. The Papago are an agricultural people who irrigate by flooding. Though frugal and peaceful, they could be tough when attacked, and they defended themselves stoutly against raiding bands of Apaches. Papago women are renowned for their wonderful baskets woven from yucca fiber. Their traditional houses were round, dome-shaped, and flat-topped, 12 to 20 feet in diameter, and usually had a brush shelter (ramada) attached. They now live on a four-part reservation of almost three million acres in Arizona. Some offshoots of the tribe also live in Sonora, Mexico.

PASSAMAQUODDY

The name Passamaquoddy comes from *peskede makadi*, meaning "plenty of pollock" (a species of herring). They are a tribe of forest hunters and fishermen speaking a coastal Algonquian dialect. They were experts at canoeing, fishing, and trapping and lived in conical wigwams covered with birch bark or woven mats. Several families often shared one dwelling. They belonged to the larger Abnaki confederation, an alliance of Northeast woodlands tribes that also included the Penobscot and Maliseet. Some 600 Passamaquoddy now live on the Pleasant Point and Indian Township Reservations in Washington County, Maine.

PAWNEE

The Pawnees, members of the large Caddoan family, were a federation of tribes living near the Platte River in what is now Nebraska. They were semisedentary, lived in earth lodges, planted corn, and hunted buffalo and other game. Their tribal name comes from *pariki*, meaning "horns," probably because they used to dress their hair in a horn-like coil stiffened with grease. Their own name for themselves was Men of Men. Their chief deity was Tirawa Atius, the Creator, who "threw down from the sky to the human beings everything they needed." Hereditary keepers maintained their sacred bundles, and they had secret societies related to supernatural animal spirits.

The Pawnees, who once numbered 25,000, lost half their population to cholera between 1840 and 1850, owing to contact with westbound settlers taking the Platte River Trail. By the end of the century their numbers had dropped to a few hundred. Though many Pawnees had served the U.S. Army faithfully as scouts during the Indian Plains wars, they shared the fate of many other tribes, being removed in 1876 to Oklahoma, where they settled with the Ponca and Oto.

PENOBSCOT

The name Penobscot means Rockland or It Flows on the Rocks, alluding to a waterfall near their village of Old Town, Maine, a few miles above Bangor. The Penobscot are a once-powerful New England tribe of Algonquian stock. They belong to the Abnaki confederation, which included such tribes as the Malecites and Passamaquoddies. They made canoes, fishnets, shell wampum, carved pipes, and intricate beading and quillwork. They had a reputation for peacefulness and hospitality.

Some 500 Penobscot now live on a reservation comprising 4,500 acres at Indian Island, Old Town, Maine.

PEQUOD

The Pequod, or Destroyers, once a much-dreaded Algonquian people, were originally part of the Mohegan tribe. They occupied a strip of land reaching from what is now New London, Connecticut, into Rhode Island. The Pequods were conquered by English settlers in 1637 during the so-called Pequod War. Spurred on by Puritan preachers who called the Indians "fiends of hell" and "children of Satan," the settlers stormed the Pequod village on the Mystic River in Connecticut, slaughtering and burning to death more than 600 of the inhabitants. Surviving prisoners became slaves of New England colonists; some were even sold to West Indian planters. In 1832 there was a remnant of about 40 mixed-blood Pequods left. In the early 1900s about 12 people remained who considered themselves in some way the descendants of the Pequods and Mohegans. They are now considered completely exterminated.

PIEGAN

(See BLACKFOOT)

PIMA

The Pima, and their closely related neighbors and cousins, the Papago, are thought to be descendants of the ancient Hohokam—Those Who Have Gone Before—prehistoric makers of a vast system of irrigation canals. Members of the Uto-Aztecan language group, the Pima live in southern Arizona near the Gila and Salt rivers. Their earliest contacts with Spaniards occurred in 1589, when they lived in scattered *rancherías* tending their fields of corn, beans, squash, cotton, and tobacco. Like their Hohokam ancestors, they had an advanced system of irrigation. They were consistently peaceful and hospitable to whites.

The typical old-style Pima house was a windowless daub-and-wattle dwelling shaped "like an inverted kettle." Today these dwellings have been replaced everywhere by the typical Southwestern adobe house. The Pima are possibly the best Indian basket makers. Their women weave beautiful baskets of all shapes, designs, and sizes, from huge, man-high storage baskets to miniature horsehair baskets.

Most Pima, together with members of the Maricopa community, now live on the Gila River Reservation in Arizona, with headquarters at Sacaton.

POMO

The Pomo are a large and thriving community in northern California, well known for their beautiful basketwork.

PONCA

The Ponca, a Siouan tribe closely related to the Omaha, Kansa, and Osage, lived in permanent villages of earth lodges. They planted corn, hunted buffalo, and adopted a number of Plains customs, including the annual sun dance, which they called the Great Mystery dance.

After several migrations, the Ponca lived for some time near Lake Andes, South Dakota. There, according to their traditions, they received the gift of the sacred pipes. They finally settled at the mouth of the Niobrara River in Nebraska where, Lewis and Clark reported in 1804, their number had been reduced by smallpox to a mere 200.

For reasons never quite satisfactorily explained, the Ponca land was given to the Sioux in spite of the fact that the Ponca had always been friendly to the whites while the Sioux had fought them. By 1870 their numbers had increased to about 800 but later, due to the enmity of their Sioux neighbors, they were removed to Indian Territory in Oklahoma. Half of them died as the result of their forced removal, malnutrition, and new diseases against which they had no immunity. A few Ponca remained behind in Nebraska seeking a home among related tribes.

SALINAN

The Salinans, a Californian Indian language group, were named for the Salinas River, which flowed through their territory in the Monterey–San Louis Obispo area. Their native name was Hokan. In the late 1700s the Spaniards established two missions among these small tribes. After contact with Europeans, and especially after the gold rush, their numbers declined rapidly. Though they had once been counted in the thousands, by 1906 there were only 20 persons described as Salinans. The tribe is now practically extinct.

SAN JUAN

San Juan, the home of one of the authors of this book, is the largest Tewa-speaking pueblo. Located on the banks of the Rio Grande 25 miles north of Santa Fe, New Mexico, it is a traditional village in which the old culture, language, and ceremonies are still maintained in spite of some intermarriage with whites. Its native name was Oke, but in 1598 the Spanish Governor Onate established his capital at this pueblo and renamed it San Juan de los Caballeros. In 1782 the village was ravaged by epidemics introduced by contact with Spaniards. Today some 700 Tewa Indians occupy about 12,000 acres of San Juan land.

SENECA

The Seneca, meaning Place of the Stone, were one of the tribes making up the Six Nations League of the Iroquois. They were also known as the People of the

Mountain and in the confederacy occupied the place of "keepers of the great black doorway." The great Iroquois religious leader and prophet, Handsome Lake, was a Seneca. He combined traditional Iroquois religion with certain white concepts, teaching his people to build houses like those of white farmers, to work hard, to instruct their children, and to abstain from the white man's intoxicating drinks. The code of Handsome Lake is still kept by many Iroquois people.

The Senecas originally lived west of Lake Erie and along the Allegheny River. Believing that the English would protect them against land-grabbing colonials, they joined the Mohawks under Joseph Brant (Thayendanegea) to fight for the British during the American Revolution.

They now live in various places in the Northeast, including the Allegheny, Cattaraugus, and Tonawanda Reservations in New York State. In the 1950s the Army Corps of Engineers built the Kinzua Dam, which inundated a great part of the Allegeny Seneca Reservation, in spite of a treaty of 1794, signed by George Washington himself, guaranteeing the Indians this land inviolate and in perpetuity.

SERRANO

The Serrano still live in California, though a long history of contact with white missionaries and other settlers has eroded their cultural integrity considerably.

SHASTA

The Shasta were a group of small tribes in northern California near the Klamath River and in the Mount Shasta Valley. They were sedentary and lived in small villages of half-sunken plank houses. Their main food was fish, particularly salmon, which they netted, trapped, and speared. They preserved their fish for winter by drying and smoking it. Acorns, seeds, and roots augmented their diet; hunting played a comparatively small role, and their main weapon was the bow. The intrusion of gold miners and prospectors in 1855–1860 spelled the Shasta's doom, and they have now virtually vanished.

SIA

The Sia, or Zia, are a small Keresan-speaking pueblo in New Mexico.

SIOUX

The Sioux nation is comprised of three divisions, the Lakota or Teton-Wan, the Dakota, and the Nakota. Lakota or Tetons are the seven westernmost trans-Missouri

Sioux tribes; they refer to themselves as Ikche-Wichasha—the Real Natural Human Beings. The Seven Tribes, or Ocheti Shakowin (Seven Campfires), which compose the Lakota are the Hunkpapa, the Oglala, the Minneconjou, the Brules (also known as Sichangu or Burned Thighs), the Ooenunpa or Two Kettles, the Itazipcho or No Bows, and the Sihasapa or Blackfeet, not to be confused with the Algonquian Blackfoot (Siksika) of Montana. The Lakota are the hard-riding, buffalo-hunting Plains Indians par excellence, the Red Knights of the Prairie, the people of Red Cloud, Sitting Bull, and Crazy Horse. Theirs was the nomadic culture of the tipi and the dog—later horse—travois. They worship Wakan Tanka—Tunkashila, the grandfather spirit—pray with the sacred pipe, go on vision quests involving a four-day-and-night fast, and still practice self-torture (piercing) during the sun dance, the most solemn of all Plains rituals.

Originally friendly to the whites, the Lakota fought hard when they were finally forced to defend their ancient hunting grounds. They defeated General Crook at Rosebud, and annihilated Custer on the Little Bighorn. They fought their last battle against overwhelming odds, and in the face of quick-firing cannon, at Wounded Knee in 1890.

SLAVEY

The Slavey Indians (whose name, incidentally, has no connection to the English word "slave") lived inland in British Columbia, and are related culturally and linguistically to the Plains tribes to the south. Their Plateau region culture, as it is termed, represents a transition between the northernmost of the northwest Plains tribes and those of the subarctic. They still make their living as hunters, fishermen, and trappers in this economically marginal geographic area, too far north for much agricultural productivity.

SNOHOMISH

The Snohomish lived in tiny communities scattered across the Olympic Peninsula in what is now western Washington. Only remnants of the original tribes still exist.

SNOQUALMIE

The Snoqualmie or Snoqualmu were a small Salishan tribe of the Pacific Coast. Salmon was their main food, canoeing their form of traveling. The men fished and hunted, the women wove baskets and made mats of cedar bark. They believed they were descended from mythical animals, such as the wolf. By 1854 the Snoqualmies had shrunk to a population of some 200. A handful of Snoqualmies finally went to the Tulalip Reservation in Washington to settle among their Snohomish cousins.

TEWA

The Tewa are a group of Pueblo Indians related by language. Today they live in six villages near the Rio Grande, all north of Santa Fe, namely, Nambe, Pojoaque, Tesuque, San Ildefonso, Santa Clara, and San Juan. According to legend, the Tewa entered this world by ascending from Sipofene, a mythical place beneath a lake. In some Tewa villages it is said that the people climbed up a Douglas fir rising out of the lake, and that the first one up was Poseyemu, the Tewa culture hero, a supernatural being sometimes called the son of the sun, who taught the art of living to the people.

Ancient beliefs and traditions are still strong among the Tewa. Their pueblos are divided into two parts, so-called moities, the summer and the winter people.

TIWA

The Tiwa (in Spanish, Tigua or Tiguex) form a Pueblo language group. Tiwa-speaking villages are the northern Rio Grande pueblos of Taos and Picuris and the more southern villages of Sandia and Isleta in the Albuquerque region. The early Spanish explorers described the Tiwas as cultivating corn, squash, beans, and melons, and as wearing cotton garments and long robes made of feathers. The Spaniards plundered and destroyed several Tiwa pueblos, killing, according to their own chronicler, Castaneda, every male and enslaving the women and children. It was in Taos pueblo that the great Pueblo Revolt of 1680 was planned by Popé, a Tewa spiritual leader from San Juan pueblo. Taos is the northernmost of the pueblos, a natural meeting place for Pueblos and southern Plains Indians. The people of Taos therefore show a number of Plains traits, such as the braided hair worn by the men.

TLINGIT

The Tlingit, the northernmost of the great Northwest Coast tribes, lived in numerous villages from Prince William Sound down to the Alaska Panhandle. Like the Haida, Tsimshian, and Kwakiutl, they occupied large, rectangular, decorated and painted wooden houses; fished in big dugout canoes; held potlatches upon the death and burial of important persons; and made war to capture slaves as well as the booty necessary for giveaways during the potlatch. The sea provided nearly their entire diet. The Tlingit were also great sculptors and carvers of totem poles, masks, ceremonial rattles, bowls, and painted boxes. Their women wove the famous Chilkat blankets and also fine, multicolored baskets. Their dress was highly decorative, often covered with the images of eagles and other animals, the outlines formed of round pieces of pearl shells or buttons acquired from whites. Women wore ornaments in their lower lips, so-called labrets.

The Tlingit were harshly treated and exploited by Russian fur traders. Today some 250 Tlingits live at Craig on Prince of Wales Island in Alaska.

TOLTECS

The Toltecs created a splendid civilization in the Valley of Mexico, their chief cities being Tula and Teotihuacán, the latter the site of the great Pyramid of the Sun thirty miles northeast of present-day Mexico City. The Toltec cities, in which must be included Chichén Itzá, the Mayan site in Yucatán once dominated by the Toltecs, were as much ceremonial centers as they were population centers. Traders and artisans, workers in metal, clay, cotton, obsidian, stone, and feathers, the Toltecs spread the cult of the gentle god Quetzalcoatl, represented by the Plumed Rattlesnake, as well as the practice of the ritual ball game. The Toltecs' empire reached its zenith around A.D. 900 and later declined as a result of foreign and civil wars.

TSIMSHIAN

The Tsimshian, or People of the Skeena River, are a typical Pacific Northwest Coast tribe, culturally related to the Haida and Kwakiutl and, like them, artistic carvers and weavers of Chilkat blankets. Their main food was salmon, halibut, cod, and shellfish, and they also hunted whales. Their original home was on the Skeena River in British Columbia. In 1884 a Church of England clergyman persuaded them to move to Alaska. About a thousand Tsimshian now occupy the Annette Island reserve of 86,500 acres in southeastern Alaska and take an active political and economic role in the state.

UTE

The Utes, who belong to the Uto-Aztecan language family, are a Shoshonean tribe of western Colorado and eastern Utah. They shared many cultural traits with the more northern Plains tribes; they performed the sun dance and lived in tipis. They acquired horses in 1740 and ranged from southern Wyoming down to Taos. The Utes were generally friendly to the whites; their best-known chief, Ouray, made a treaty of peace and friendship with the government. He was a welcome guest, as well as host, among white silver miners.

The Utes now raise cattle for a living. Some 700 southern Utes live on a reservation of 300,000 acres at Ignacio, Colorado. The northern Weminuche Utes consist of some 1,800 people on 560,000 acres on the Ute Mountain Reservation in Colorado. Still another 1,200 Utes live on the million-acre Uintah and Ouray Reservation at Fort Duchesne, Utah.

WASCO

The Wasco (meaning "small bowl of horn") are a Chinookian tribe of sedentary fishing people living along the banks of the Columbia River in Oregon. Their food, such as salmon, sturgeon, and eels, came mainly from the river. They caught salmon in the spring with dip nets or by spearing, and bartered pounded and dried salmon with other tribes. During the cold season they lived in partially underground winter houses with roofs of cedar bark; in summer they moved to lighter dwellings made of fir poles. They maintained ceremonial sweat houses, practiced head flattening, and performed puberty rites for both boys and girls. The Wasco are famous for their beautiful twined baskets. They share the Warm Springs Reservation in Oregon with the northern Paiutes and Warm Springs Indians.

WHITE MOUNTAIN APACHE

(See APACHE)

WINNEBAGO

The Winnebago (from Winipig—People near the Dirty Water), a Midwestern woodlands tribe, belong to the Siouan family. Among their deities and super-naturals, to whom they made offerings, are Earth Maker, Disease Giver, Sun, Moon, Morning Star, Night Spirit, Thunderbird, Turtle, and the Great Rabbit. The tribe is divided into two so-called phratries, the upper or air people, and the lower or earth people.

During the War of Independence and the War of 1812, the Winnebago sided with the British. Between 1829 and 1866, whites forced the Winnebago to give up their land and go to new homes no less than seven times. Some Winnebago joined Black Hawk in his war of 1832. They were removed to the Blue Earth River in Minnesota but were driven from there by white settlers, who were afraid of Indians after the great Sioux uprising. Today some 800 Winnebago live on their own reservation in Thurston County, Nebraska.

WINTU

Wintu refers both to a language group and a tribal community, several of which still occupy what is now northern California, above the Bay Area of San Francisco.

YAKIMA

The Yakima occupy the high mountain country of eastern Washington and live on one of the biggest reservations in the northwest. It is a large and thriving community with a very viable and intact culture.

YAVAPAI

The Yavapai, People of the Sun, also known as Mojave-Apaches, once roamed over a large part of Arizona. A tribe of hunters and gatherers, they are linguistically and culturally related to the Hualapai and Havasupai. Nomads in search of wild crops, their staples were mescal, saguaro fruit, sunflower seeds, piñon nuts, and other wild plants. They also raised corn and hunted deer and rabbit. They lived in caves or primitive brush shelters which could be put up in a short time. Their beliefs were shamanistic. About 700 Yavapais now live on the Camp Verde and Yavapai Reservations in Arizona.

YUMA

The home of the Yuma (from Yah Mayo—Son of the Chief) was situated on both sides of the Colorado River. They were primitive but effective farmers, growing corn, melons, mesquite beans, and pumpkins. Onate visited them in 1604–1605 and reported that they were fine physical specimens. Early Spaniards said of them: "The men are well-formed, the women fat and healthy," and gave the collective name "Diegueños" to a small group of Yuma tribes and *rancherías* near present-day San Diego. Some 60 Yumans now live on the 600-acre Cocopah Reservation in Yuma County, Arizona.

ZUNI

The Zuni were the first Pueblo encountered by the Spanish. Fray Marcos de Niza saw the Zuni village from afar. The light adobe walls glistened like gold in the evening sun, and he reported back to the Spanish viceroy in Mexico City that he had found the fabled Seven Cities of Cibola, whose streets were paved with gold. As a result Don Francisco de Coronado, with a large party of heavily armed adventurers, appeared in 1540 at Hawikuh and, on July 7th of that year, stormed and plundered the pueblo. At the time of their reconquest by the Spaniards in 1692, twelve years after the Pueblo Revolt, the Zuni fled to one of their strongholds on top of a high, inaccessible mesa. Eventually they built one single village on the site of their ancient pueblo of Halona, and have dwelled there ever since.

Today about 5,000 Zuni live on their 40,000-acre reservation some 30 miles south of Gallup, New Mexico.

BIBLIOGRAPHY

Barbeau, Marius. *Haida Myths Illustrated in Argillite Carvings*. National Museum of Canada Bulletin no. 127. Anthropological Series no. 32. Ottawa: The Museum, 1953:52–56 and 184–185.

Barrett, Samuel. *Pomo Myths*. Bulletin of the Public Museum of the City of Milwaukee, vol. 15, p. 373. Milwaukee: The Museum, 1933.

Bell, Robert. "Legends of the Slavey Indians of the Mackenzie River." *Journal of American Folklore* 14 (1901): 26–28.

Benedict, Ruth. "Serrano Tales." *Journal of American Folklore* 39 (1926): 8.

———. *Tales of the Cochiti Indians*. Bureau of American Ethnology Bulletin no. 98. Washington: United States Government Printing Office, 1931; Albuquerque: University of New Mexico Press, 1981.

———. *Zuni Mythology*. Columbia University Contributions to Anthropology, vol. 21. New York: Columbia University Press, 1935.

Boas, Franz. *Chinook Texts*. Bureau of American Ethnology Bulletin no. 20. Washington: United States Government Printing Office, 1894.

———. "Tales of Spanish Provenience from Zuni." *Journal of American Folklore* 35 (1922): 62–98.

———. *Tsimshian Mythology*. Bureau of American Ethnology Annual Report no. 31. Washington: United States Government Printing Office, 1916.

Bright, William. *The Karok Language*. University of California Publications in Linguistics, vol. 13, p. 215. Berkeley: University of California Press, 1957.

Catlin, George. *North American Indians*. London: The Author, 1841, 1856.

Clark, Ella. *Indian Legends from the Northern Rockies*. Norman: University of Oklahoma Press, 1966.

———. *Indian Legends of the Pacific Northwest*. Berkeley: University of California Press, 1953.

Curtis, Edward S. *The North American Indian*. Vol. 13. Cambridge, Massachusetts: The University Press, 1924.

Curtis, Natalie. "Creation Myths of the Cochans (Yuma Indians)." *The Craftsman* 16 (1909): 559–567.

———. *The Indians' Book*. New York: Harper & Bros., 1907; Dover Publications, 1968.

————. "The People of the Totem Poles: Their Art and Legends." *The Craftsman* 16 (1909): 612–621.

Cushing, Frank Hamilton. *Outlines of Zuni Creation Myths.* Bureau of American Ethnology Annual Report no. 13. Washington: United States Government Printing Office, 1896.

————. "A Zuni Folk-tale of the Underworld." *Journal of American Folklore* 5 (1892): 49–56.

————. *Zuni Folk Tales.* New York: G. P. Putnam's Sons, 1901; AMS Press, 1980.

DeAngulo, Jaime, and William Ralganal Benson. "Creation Myths of the Pomo Indian." *Anthropos* 27 (1932): 264.

DeAngulo, Jaime, and L. S. Freeland. "Miwok and Pomo Myths." *Journal of American Folklore* 41 (1928): 236–237.

Deans, James. "The Story of the Bear and His Indian Wife." *Journal of American Folklore* 2 (1889): 255–260.

Dixon, Roland B. *Maidu Myths.* Bulletin of the American Museum of Natural History, vol. 17, p. 95. New York: The Museum, 1904.

————. "Some Coyote Stories from the Maidu Indians." *Journal of American Folklore* 13 (1900): 269–270.

Dorsey, George A. *The Cheyenne.* Field Columbian Museum Publication 99, vol. 9, no. 1. Chicago: The Museum, 1905.

————. *Traditions of the Caddo.* Washington: Carnegie Institute, 1905.

DuBois, Constance Goddard. "The Mythology of the Diegueños." *Journal of American Folklore* 14 (1901): 181–182.

DuBois, Cora, and Dorothy Demetracopoulou. *Wintu Myths.* University of California Publications in American Archaeology and Ethnology, vol. 28, pp. 320–322. Berkeley: University of California Press, 1931.

Fletcher, Alice C., and Francis La Flesche. *The Omaha Tribe.* Bureau of American Ethnology Annual Report no. 27. Washington: United States Government Printing Office, 1911.

Forde, C. Daryll. *Folk-lore.* Vol. 41. London: William Glaisher for the Folk-lore Society, 1930.

Frachtenberg, Leo J. "Shasta and Athapascan Myths from Oregon." *Journal of American Folklore* 28 (1915): 224–228.

————. "Traditions of the Coos Indians of Oregon." *Journal of American Folklore* 22 (1909): 27–28.

Gifford, Edward W. *Californian Indian Nights Entertainments.* Glendale, California: Arthur H. Clark, 1930.

————. "Coast Yuki Myths." *Journal of American Folklore* 50 (1937): 170.

————. "Western Yavapai Myths." *Journal of American Folklore* 46 (1933): 402–403.

Goddard, Pliny Earle. *Jicarilla Apache Texts.* American Museum of Natural History Papers, vol. 8. New York: The Museum, 1911.

Golder, Frank Alfred. "Eskimo and Aleut Stories from Alaska." *Journal of American Folklore* 22 (1909): 10–24.

Goodwin, Grenville. *Myths and Tales of the White Mountain Apache.* Memoirs of the American Folklore Society, vol. 33. New York: J. J. Augustin, 1939.

Grinnell, George Bird. "Cheyenne Obstacle Myths." *Journal of American Folklore* 16 (1903): 108–115.

————. *Pawnee Hero Stories and Folk-Tales.* New York: Forest and Stream Publications, 1889; Lincoln: University of Nebraska Press, 1961.

Harrington, John P. *Karuk Indian Myths.* Bureau of American Ethnology Bulletin no. 107, pp. 12–13. Washington: United States Government Printing Office, 1932.

Jacobs, Melville. *Kalapuya Texts.* University of Washington Publications in Anthropology, vol. 11, pp. 173–178. Seattle: University of Washington Press, 1945.

Judson, Katharine Berry. *Myths and Legends of the Pacific Northwest.* Chicago: A. C. McClurg, 1910.

Kelly, Isabel T. "Northern Paiute Tales." *Journal of American Folklore* 51 (1938): 372–375.

Kroeber, Alfred L. "Cheyenne Tales." *Journal of American Folklore* 13 (1900): 161–190.

————. "Wishosk Myths." *Journal of American Folklore* 18 (1905): 85–107.

————. *Yurok Narratives.* University of California Publications in American Archaeology and Ethnology, vol. 35, no. 9. Berkeley: University of California Press, 1943.

Kroeber, Alfred L., ed. *Walapai Ethnography.* American Anthropological Association Memoir, vol. 42, pp. 16–24. Menasha, Wisconsin: The Association, 1935.

Leland, Charles Godfrey. *Algonquin Legends of New England; or, Myths and Folklore of the Micmac, Passamaquoddy, and Penobscot Tribes.* Boston: Houghton Mifflin, 1884.

Lopez, Barry. *Giving Birth to Thunder, Sleeping with His Daughter.* New York: Avon Books, 1977.

Lummis, Charles Fletcher. *The Man Who Married the Moon and Other Pueblo Indian Folk-Stories.* New York: The Century Company, 1894.

Marriott, Alice, and Carol K. Rachlin. *American Indian Mythology.* New York: T. Y. Crowell, 1968.

Mason, John Alden. *The Language of the Salinan Indians.* University of California Publications in American Archaeology and Ethnology, vol. 14, p. 109. Berkeley: University of California Press, 1918.

Matthews, Washington. *Navaho Legends.* Memoirs of the American Folklore Society, vol. 5, pp. 68–71. Boston: Houghton Mifflin, 1897.

McClintock, Walter. *The Old North Trail: Life, Legends, and Religion of the Blackfeet Indians.* Pittsburgh, 1910; Lincoln: University of Nebraska Press, 1968.

McDermott, Louisa. "Coyote Kills the Giant." *Journal of American Folklore* 14 (1901): 240–241.

Mooney, James. "The Jicarilla Genesis." *American Anthropologist* 11 (1898): 197–200.

————. *Myths of the Cherokee.* Bureau of American Ethnology Annual Report no. 19. Washington: United States Government Printing Office, 1902.

Neff, Mary L. "Pima and Papago Legends." *Journal of American Folklore* 25 (1912): 59–60.

Nicolar, Joseph. *The Life and Traditions of the Red Man.* Bangor, Maine: C. H. Glass, 1893.

Parsons, Elsie Clews. *The Pueblo of Isleta.* Albuquerque: University of New Mexico Press.

————. *Taos Tales.* Memoirs of the American Folklore Society, vol. 34. New York: J. J. Augustin, 1940.

Pradt, George H. "Shakok and Miochin: Origin of Summer and Winter." *Journal of American Folklore* 15 (1902): 88–90.

Russell, Frank. "Athabascan Myths." *Journal of American Folklore* 13 (1900): 11–18.

————.*The Pima Indians.* Bureau of American Ethnology Annual Report no. 26. Washington: United States Government Printing Office, 1908.

Sapir, Edward. *Yana Texts.* University of California Publications in American Archaeology and Ethnology, vol. 9, pp. 38–93. Berkeley: University of California Press, 1910.

Sapir, Edward, ed. *Wishram Texts: Together with Wasco Tales and Myths.* Collected by J. Curtin. Leyden: E. J. Brill, 1909; American Ethnological Society Publications, vol. 2, 1909, pp. 257–259.

Swanton, John R. *Haida Texts and Myths.* Bureau of American Ethnology Bulletin no. 29. Washington: United States Government Printing Office, 1905.

Talayesva, Don C. *Sun Chief: The Autobiography of a Hopi Indian.* New Haven: Yale University Press for the Institute of Human Relations, 1942.

Voth, Henry. *The Traditions of the Hopi.* Field Columbian Museum Publications in Anthropology, vol. 8. Chicago: The Museum, 1905.

Wood, Charles, Erskine Scott. *A Book of Tales: Being Some Myths of the North American Indians.* New York: Vanguard Press, 1929.

INDEX OF TALES

Adventures of Great Rabbit, 347
Always-Living-at-the-Coast, 362
Apache Chief Punishes His Wife, 291
Arrow Boy, 29

Bear and His Indian Wife, The, 419
Big Eater's Wife, 453
Blood Clot, 8
Blue Jay Visits Ghost Town, 457
Bluebird and Coyote, The, 346
Brave Woman Counts Coup, 258
Buffalo Go, The, 490
Butterflies, 407

Chase of the Severed Head, 230
Cheyenne Blanket, A, 251
Chief Roman Nose Loses His Medicine, 256
Children of the Sun, 119
Coming of Thunder, The, 216
Coming of Wasichu, The, 491
Contest for Wives, A, 326
Corn Mother, 11
Coyote and the Mallard Ducks, 318
Coyote and the Origin of Death, 470
Coyote and the Two Frog Women, 384
Coyote and Wasichu, 342
Coyote Dances with a Star, 385
Coyote Fights a Lump of Pitch, 359
Coyote Gets Rich Off the White Men, 369
Coyote, Iktome, and the Rock, 337
Coyote Kills the Giant, 223
Coyote Places the Stars, 171
Coyote Steals Sun's Tobacco, 377
Coyote Steals the Sun and Moon, 140
Coyote Takes Water from the Frog People, 355
Coyote's Rabbit Chase, 368
Coyote's Strawberry, 314
Creation of First Man and First Woman, 39
Creation of the Animal People, 14
Creation of the Yakima World, 117

Daughter of the Sun, 152
Death of Head Chief and Young Mule, The, 477
Deer Hunter and White Corn Maiden, 173
Dogs Hold an Election, The, 403
Doing a Trick with Eyeballs, 379
Double-Faced Ghost, The, 439

Earth Dragon, The, 107
Earth Making, 105
Elk Spirit of Lost Lake, The, 475
Emerging into the Upper World, 97
End of the World, The, 485

Faithful Wife and the Woman Warrior, The, 315
Fight for a Wife, The, 281
First Ship, The, 229
Fish Story, A, 415
Flood, The, 472
Flying Head, The, 227
Foolish Girls, The, 158

Ghost Dance at Wounded Knee, The, 481
Ghost Wife, The, 462
Girl Who Married Rattlesnake, The, 397
Glooscap and the Baby, 25
Glooscap Fights the Water Monster, 181
Glooscap Grants Three Wishes, 365
Gnawing, The, 484
Good Twin and the Evil Twin, The, 77
Grandmother Spider Steals the Sun, 154
Great Medicine Dance, The, 33
Great Medicine Makes a Beautiful Country, 111
Great Race, The, 390
Greedy Father, The, 320
Gust of Wind, A, 150

Hiawatha the Unifier, 193
Hopi Boy and the Sun, The, 145

How Beaver Stole Fire from the Pines, 343
How Coyote Got His Cunning, 382
How Grandfather Peyote Came to the
    Indian People, 65
How Men and Women Got Together, 41
How Mosquitoes Came to Be, 192
How the Crow Came to Be Black, 395
How the People Got Arrowheads, 356
How the Sioux Came to Be, 93
How to Scare a Bear, 375
Husband's Promise, The, 295

Iktome and the Ignorant Girl, 358
Iktome Has a Bad Dream, 381
Iktome Sleeps with His Wife by Mistake,
    372
Industrious Daughter Who Would Not
    Marry, The, 308

Jicarilla Genesis, The, 83
Journey to the Skeleton House, A, 442

Keeping Warmth in a Bag, 143
Kulshan and His Two Wives, 321

Land of the Dead, The, 438
Legend of Devil's Tower, A, 225
Legend of Multnomah Falls, A, 306
Legend of the Flute, The, 275
Life and Death of Sweet Medicine, The,
    199
Little Brother Snares the Sun, 164
Little-Man-with-Hair-All-Over, 185
Little Mouse Counting Coup, 247

Man Who Married the Moon, The, 298
Man Who Was Afraid of Nothing, The,
    435
Meeting of the Wild Animals, The, 413
Men and Women Try Living Apart, 324
Montezuma and the Great Flood, 487
Moon Rapes His Sister Sun, 161

Neglectful Mother, The, 417

Old Man Coyote Makes the World, 87
Old Woman of the Spring, The, 26
Origin of Curing Ceremonies, The, 37
Origin of the Gnawing Beaver, 392
Origin of the Hopi Snake Dance, The, 455
Orphan Boy and the Elk Dog, The, 53
Owl Husband, The, 399

People Brought in a Basket, 109
Playing a Trick on the Moon, 168
Powerful Boy, The, 20
Pushing Up the Sky, 95

Quillwork Girl and Her Seven Star
    Brothers, The, 205

Rabbit Boy, 5
Raven, The, 344
Remaking the World, 496
Revenge of Blue Corn Ear Maiden, The,
    409
Rolling Head, 209

Sacred Weed, The, 62
Salt Woman Is Refused Food, 61
Scabby One Lights the Sky, The, 166
Seer Who Would Not See, The, 473
Siege of Courthouse Rock, The, 254
Serpent of the Sea, The, 327
Skeleton Who Fell Down Piece by Piece,
    The, 446
Snake Brothers, The, 404
Son of Light Kills the Monster, 211
Spirit Wife, The, 447
Spotted Eagle and Black Crow, 260
Stolen Wife, The, 285
Stone Boy, 15
Story of the Creation, The, 156
Sun Creation, 129
Sun Teaches Veeho a Lesson, 162

Tale of Elder Brother, A, 122
Tatanka Iyotake's Dancing Horse, 267
Teaching the Mudheads How to Copulate,
    279
Teeth in the Wrong Places, 283
Theft of Light, The, 169
Three-Legged Rabbit Fights the Sun, 139
Tolowim Woman and Butterfly Man, 290
Transformed Grandmother, The, 451
Turkey Makes the Corn and Coyote
    Plants It, 352
Two Bullets and Two Arrows, 248
Two Ghostly Lovers, 432

Uncegilia's Seventh Spot, 237

Vision Quest, The, 69
Voice, the Flood, and the Turtle, The, 120

Wakiash and the First Totem Pole, 423
Wakinyan Tanka, the Great Thunderbird,
    218
Walks-All-Over-the-Sky, 136
Warrior Maiden, The, 252
Well-Baked Man, The, 46
What's This? My Balls for Your Dinner?,
    339
When Grizzlies Walked Upright, 85
Where the Girl Saved Her Brother, 264
White Buffalo Woman, The, 47
White Dawn of the Hopi, The, 115
Why Mole Lives Underground, 305
Why the Owl Has Big Eyes, 398
Woman Chooses Death, 469
Woman Who Married a Merman, The,
    312

ABOUT THE AUTHORS

RICHARD ERDOES, artist, photographer, and writer, was born in Frankfurt, Germany, and educated in Vienna, Paris, and Berlin. He has lived in this country for forty-five years, and for the last ten has divided his time between New York City and Santa Fe, New Mexico. His many books include *Lame Deer, Seeker of Visions*; *Saloons of the West*; *The Rain Dance People*; *The Sun Dance People*; and *The Sound of Flutes*. In addition to recording and editing many of the tales in this book, Richard Erdoes also created the illustrations that appear throughout, basing them on ancient images found in Indian art across the continent.

ALFONSO ORTIZ was born at San Juan, a Tewa Pueblo in New Mexico, and is one of this country's leading experts on Indian folklore and anthropology. He received his B.A. from the University of New Mexico and holds an M.A. and Ph.D. in anthropology from the University of Chicago. He is the author of *The Tewa World* and was the contributing editor of the two Southwest volumes of the Smithsonian's *Handbook of the North American Indian*. In 1982 he received a MacArthur Fellowship. Alfonso Ortiz lives in Santa Fe and teaches at the University of New Mexico in Albuquerque.